Oscar Wilde's Elegant Republic

Oscar Wilde's Elegant Republic:

Transformation, Dislocation and Fantasy in fin-de-siècle Paris

By

David Charles Rose

Oscar Wilde's Elegant Republic: Transformation,
Dislocation and Fantasy in fin-de-siècle Paris

By David Charles Rose

This book first published 2015

Cambridge Scholars Publishing

Lady Stephenson Library, Newcastle upon Tyne, NE6 2PA, UK

British Library Cataloguing in Publication Data
A catalogue record for this book is available from the British Library

ISBN (10): 1-4438-8360-3
ISBN (13): 978-1-4438-8360-3

TABLE OF CONTENTS

ACKNOWLEDGMENTS

It is customary to conclude an acknowledgments chapter with some such phase as 'last but not least, my wife'. Here I depart from custom: I salute my wife Danielle first and foremost for her encouragement, support and dedication to my project.

The gestation of this book has been a long one, and it would not have come to term without the encouragement and advice of many friends and colleagues, too numerous and varied to list, but it is proper that I should single out Jane Desmarais, Emily Eells, Regenia Gagnier, Michael Patrick Gillespie, Merlin Holland, the late Mary C. King, W.J. Mc Cormack, John McRae, Maureen E. Mulvihill, John O'Beirne Ranelagh, Philip E. Smith II, Margaret Stetz, Florina Tufescu, Emmanuel Vernadakis and Linda Zatlin, who have kept me committed to the task in hand and to the standards desirable in a scholarly endeavour,

I would also like to thank Daniel Ridley, commissioning editor at Cambridge Scholars Publishing for his enthusiasm, and his colleagues Carol Koulikourdi, Sam Baker, Courtney Blades, Sophie Edminson, Amanda Millar and Anthony Wright for their courtesy, patience and help. The book could not have been written without access to the London Library, the National Library of Ireland and the libraries of Goldsmiths College, University of London; Trinity College, Dublin; the National College of Art and Design, Dublin; the Victoria and Albert Museum; The Royal Academy (London), and Exeter University, so thanks are also due to the librarians there.

Much of my material has also been gathered from museums and galleries, and the thoughts evoked by the paintings, prints and sculptures were greatly stimulated by the conversation of companions, notably the late Benjamin Arnold, Holly Barton, Patrick Bridgewater, Richard Butt, Tine Englebert, Glynne Evans, Valerie Fehlbaum, Amanda Finlay, Margaret de Fonblanque, Brian Lalor, Mathilde Mazau, the late Julian Robinson, Franca Baumann Rodriguez, Eva Thienpont, Tanya Touwen. I must also acknowledge my indebtedness to my colleagues of the Association Internationale des Critiques d'Art.

The book is dedicated to the memory of my parents and to that of Cornelia Touwen-Kroesbergen and Yvette Guérin.

PREFACE

'I hate to seem inquisitive, but would you kindly tell me who I am?'
— *The Importance of being Earnest.*

'I am much indebted to you, sir. Perhaps you will add to your favours by
letting me know where I am.'
— Arthur Conan Doyle: *Uncle Bernac.*

'**BETWEEN** me and life there is a mist of words always.' So wrote Oscar Wilde to Arthur Conan Doyle,[1] and penetrating some of that mist is the present endeavour. What lay behind the mist, behind the words? Is it possible to reach an essential Oscar? Representations of the personality of Wilde, of the existential Wilde, are now innumerable. Much emphasis has been given to it in anecdotal biographies, stage and film representations, and collections of epigrams and aphorisms. Frank Harris, in an unusually sensitive passage, gave the humanist view: 'The hate of his judges was so diabolic that they have given him to the pity of mankind forever; they it is who have made him eternally interesting to humanity, a tragic figure of imperishable renown'.[2] Perhaps the best insight we have is that of Max Beerbohm when he wrote that 'Wilde's personality was in great measure a conscious and elaborate piece of work, and outshone other personalities by reason of the finer skill that had gone into the making of it';[3] and something of this is suggested by Masao Miyoshi's study of the divided self – 'Of all the writers of the nineties, it is surely in Wilde that the art of the self is at its most deliberate, its most artificial'.[4] The note of artifice is one that fosters an interplay between the real and the constructed, between fact and fiction, where all boundaries blur.

'I treated Art as the supreme Reality and life as a mere mode of fiction.' This famous avowal was written by Oscar Wilde in *De Profundis*. But if Art is real, life in the conjunction is ideal. This philosophical point, tension between the real and the ideal, so frequently obscured by the vernacular meanings of real and ideal, is returned to again and again in Wilde, and one must accord it a central place in finding his self. When he put (in his own estimation) his talent into his work but his genius into his life, was he putting his genius into a mere mode of fiction, himself after all holding optimistically the Prismatic view that the meaning of fiction is that the good end happily, and the bad unhappily? Or was his really the alternative meaning, that this occurs only in fiction? Although Art was the supreme reality, Wilde had no taste at all for realism in art: 'Yesterday it was Realism that charmed one. One gained from it that *nouveau frisson* which was its aim to produce. One analysed it, and wearied of it,' says Gilbert in *The Critic as Artist*.[5] The gothic or paranormal elements of *Dorian Gray* change it from what might have been a naturalistic novel in the manner, say, of Moore or Gissing.[6] For many Victorians, Wilde's specialised dislike of realism was itself perverse, for the conventional attack made upon it was one that explicitly or implicitly defended romanticism – 'the *nec plus ultra* of all art' said Rider Haggard[7] – and Wilde's romanticism was far more perfumed than his realism: or rather, he used what the Victorians found unpleasant in realism and either impregnated romantic situations with it or else undermined it in new and disturbing ways. In the early plays, and in *Salome*, realism is subordinate to language, and in the comedies, epigrammatic inversion forces realism into retreat until in *The Importance of Being Earnest* it is vanquished altogether. Praising Dostoievsky, Wilde wrote 'we feel, not that fiction has been trammelled by fact, but that fact itself has become ideal and imaginative'.[8]

It is this alchemy that Wilde tried to achieve in his life, through all his various phases, as he believed John Keats to have achieved it in his.[9] Understanding of this quest was for long restricted either by insufficient knowledge of the period, from the props of which Wilde constructed his personæ, or by the undeveloped critical methods of days gone by: these drawbacks have not always been overcome even now. How undeveloped may be judged from the critical agenda set by Robert Ross when he first regretted that there had been an inability to 'separate the man and the artist' and then praised the reception given to *De Profundis* in 1905: 'English critics have shown themselves ready to estimate the writer, whether favourably or unfavourably, without emphasising their *natural* prejudice against his later career.'[10] George Orwell commented that 'Wilde is a difficult writer to judge, because it is very hard to disentangle his artistic achievement from the events of his life'.[11] This is to miss the point: such statements fly in the face of the Wildean project of career as the outward expression of inner life – a project in which one critic has seen 'not only a resemblance but a clear analogy between the Sufi idea of the art of the personality and Wilde's'.[12] This is worth emphasising, for it forms the core of much Wildean criticism. For example, in his essay on Yeats, Sir Maurice Bowra wrote that 'Even in *The Ballad of Reading Gaol*, Wilde failed to free himself of his literary associations and mixed the real poetry of a grim experience with the false verbiage of his earlier work'.[13] I suggest that this should be expressed 'Even in *The Ballad of Reading Gaol*, Wilde was able to suffuse the real poetry of a grim experience with the highly stylised language of his earlier work'.

In reaching an understanding of the personality of Oscar Wilde, it therefore becomes desirable to distinguish personality as a term from its associative cognates: the personality of Wilde from Wilde as 'a personality', Wilde's persona (or personæ) from his self. This is a *social* approach, one I find more rewarding than those other dictates of personality exploration, the psychological one of interaction between the conscious and unconscious, the post-structuralist one of self and sexuality.[14] Wilde himself licenses this, when through his mouthpiece Lord Henry Wotton he suggests that it is more rewarding to be oneself than to know oneself. The distinctions can be made thus: Wilde as a personality is the Wilde constructed by others;[15] the personality of Wilde is the Wilde constructed by himself for the consumption of others; the persona of Wilde is what those others received or thought they received; the self of Wilde was the integration of the man and his art that made the rest possible. 'The egoistic note is, of course, and always has been to me, the primal and ultimate note of modern art,' wrote Wilde, adding in what was clearly self-approval 'but to be an Egoist one must have an Ego'.[16] Looming over all was his admission that he operated within a social framework: 'Having lost position, I find my personality of no avail.'[17]

The anecdotal approach to Wilde has been superseded by what one may broadly characterise as the sociological approach, the attempts at construction of Wilde's sexual identity or identities, and the decodification of male homosexual representation.[18] Michéal Mac Liammoír, who saw deeply into Wilde and took on much of a Wildean manner, regarded him as a many-layered entity: 'at once artist and fop, jester and sage, philosopher and foolhardy adventurer [...] a magician, a dreamer, a poet. Above all he was a born teller of tales'.[19] André Maurois (married to the daughter of Gaston Arman de Caillavet) took this a little further: for him Wilde 'a été un grand poète au sens le plus complet du mot, c'est-à-dire un créateur de mythes',[20] one of which was, obviously, himself. There is something of Odysseus here: 'Oscar, the wily man' Robert Graves called him in recognition of this, and Oscar indeed had his period as No Man – 'We no longer talk of Mr Oscar Wilde,' said Mahaffy.

Oscar Wilde himself understood that he was a self-made man, indeed, as a whole succession of self-made men, a series of constructions (or as we now say for some reason, constructs). But to be a construct is also to be an artifice, as noted by Margot Asquith, no mean artifice herself – 'I have no face, only two profiles,' she once said.[21] 'There was *no* Oscar Wilde,' she decided. 'He was not a human being [...] because his best life lay in his mind, and his mind was non-conducting clay in which more artificial than real roses flourished'.[22] Richard Ellmann has called such construction 'the process by which Oscar Wilde became Oscar Wilde'.[23] It is a process that still continues, and the present work is itself a part of that process, both survey and analysis, a recovery of props from which, as I have said, Wilde constructed himself. As such, it is intended as the first of a trilogy; the other volumes having as provisional titles *City of Light, City of Darkness: Cultures of Paris in the Age of Oscar Wilde* and *Paris as a Work of Fiction.*

Nevertheless, to paraphrase a well-known phrase of Karl Marx, if men make history but are not completely free as to the way they make it, so Wilde was not completely autonomous in the way that he made himself. Three of the props from which Wilde was formed were the cities of Dublin, London and Paris, where Wilde, the archetypal man of urbanity, negotiated different identities for himself. For Richard Ellmann, Wilde could be defined, with Yeats, Joyce and Beckett, as one of his 'four Dubliners'.[24] Of London, more pertinently, Wolf von Eckardt and his colleagues have written that it was 'the city that made Oscar Wilde Oscar Wilde'.[25]

Be that as it may, my concern is Paris, the City of Light, but also of the crepuscular and the nocturnal, of conflict between the artist and the system that sustained him, the unique city for the working out of all these themes. Realism, as it had evolved in France, was a reaction against romanticism, a change from seeking liberty in art to seeking sincerity. The route to this was through documentation, which is why Marx admired Balzac. By 1870, the school of Realism had given ground to Naturalism, with its pessimistic depiction of society as invariably squalid and vicious, Flaubert succeeded by Zola. This was the catalyst by which Æstheticism turned into Decadence instead of developing as a Morrisian arts and crafts movement. Can one imagine William Morris having a live tortoise set with jewels? Arts and crafts in England retained much that had been present in Romanticism; in France the reaction against Naturalism took various forms, Symbolism, Naturism, fantaisism. The Decadent hero is the Romantic hero gone wrong, and Wilde was inevitably the moth – the Melmoth if one proceeds by way of free association or semantic happenstance – drawn to the lights of Paris.

To understand Wilde's place in Paris, and that of Paris in Wilde, calls, not for an annalistic approach that simply records meetings and conversations and quotations, but for an analytical understanding of how Paris functioned. This is not always easy to determine after a century and more has passed: names, dates, places are confused, historians contradict one another. Much is inevitably left speculative, fruit (one may hope) for future plucking, for even in 1896, Thomas March in his attempt to give a day-by-day history of the Commune of 1871, wrote 'of the very many instances I have met with in the course of this work, where even a simple question of fact appears to be beyond the range of absolute denial or affirmation.'[26] One seeks to be authoritative, not definitive, for, inevitably, in the fulfilling of an agenda, a new agenda is adumbrated; and in seeking to correct what W.J. Mc Cormack has defined as the 'transmission of ignorance',[27] there remains the possibility of the creation of new errors. My task, therefore, has been more to explore ambiguities than to establish orthodoxies, or even orthographies.

Jacques Barzun has written

> The process of historical verification is conducted on many planes, and its technique is not fixed. It relies on attention to detail, on common sense, reasoning, on a developed feel for history and chronology, and familiarity with human behaviour, and with ever enlarging stores of information.

This, therefore, is a work of recuperation approached prosopographically, and I have adopted as method 'thickened narrative', where analysis, interrogation of sources and critical commentary are integrated with recovered histories; and broader interpretative flights (the 'over-view') and minute attention to detail alternate and are complementary; the theory growing out of the history, rather than the history deconstructed to support or conform to the theory. Methodologically, this oscillation also allows a certain identification between the telling and the tale. In the course of this, many existing narratives are challenged or corrected. This reading of these recovered histories, their integration, and the revisionism implicit, indicate that mine is chiefly an empirical enquiry, but one that recognises that that empiricism is not enough: one cannot ignore the dilemmas of historicism. The recovered histories, together with the *hypothèse* of the dominance and ubiquitousness of transformation and fantasy as the ruling spirit of time and place, move the work beyond an anthology of anecdote, and form what I offer as an original contribution to the scholarship of the Wilde period.

In some small way, this work must also be informed by the question posed over forty years ago by Theodore Zeldin, namely that of the significance of the special, the peculiar place in French self-consciousness of the intellectual, and of the life intellectual,[28] as my citations from Wilde (above) compel. It may also answer to Isobel Armstrong's call for a 'biography of networks', rather than of individuals: here certainly, will be found networks of fellowship and friendship, if not of kinship, the intellectual interdependences of Armstrong's phrase, the 'filiations de l'esprit [s'associées] l'histoire simple de la socialité et des réseaux de rencontre' of Marylène Delphis-Delbourg.[29] Although Armstrong's further distinction between networks and coteries is not always easy to sustain, it is an approach that sits more readily within the traditions of French historiography than in England. While avoiding determinism, I have also tried to provide some ideas of *mentalité*, of that dynamic which Hippolyte Taine called 'le moment', in context a happier usage than *zeitgeist*. This should demonstrate that when pursuing Wilde among the Parisians we enter a world different from that which has hitherto been composed by his biographers, a world in some ways larger and in others smaller, more tightly-knit, more complex, more tapestried, an intricate skein of propinquities, associations, affinities and referents.

> Cette ville est une source infinie de représentations, une forêt de signes, un intense réseau de correspondances [...] Correspondances entre le Paris réel et le Paris représenté, Paris matériel et Paris comme Idée [...] Paris de l'ombre et Paris de la lumière, Paris du jour et Paris de la nuit, Paris de l'opulence et Paris de la misère [...] Paris masculin et Paris féminin, Paris des vivants et Paris des morts.[30]

What follows, therefore, is an attempt, largely through contemporary sources, to reconstruct the Parisian social and cultural milieu in which Wilde was explorer, participant, hero, and ultimately victim, and to chart his wanderings there.

Notes

[1] Sir Arthur Conan Doyle: *Memories and Adventures*. London: Hodder & Stoughton n.d. [1924] p.80.

[2] Frank Harris: *Oscar Wilde*. New edition, London: Robinson Publishing 1992 p.322. Hereafter cited as Harris.

[3] Max Beerbohm: *Mainly on the Air*. London: Heinemann. New enlarged edition 1957 p.75.

[4] Masao Miyoshi: *The Divided Self, A Perspective on the Literature of the Victorians*. New York: New York University Press 1969 p.290. This particular sentence comes in Part III: 'The Art of the Self' Chapter VI: 'Masks in the Mirror', in which §.3 is an extended discussion of Wilde. This has not yet found its way into any Wilde bibliography, as far as I have discovered.

[5] This was perceptive enough, even if it was the day after the fair. The schools of Naturalism and Realism were reaching exhaustion by the end of the 1880s, giving place to the Symbolism and Æstheticism of the 'yellow nineties'.

[6] *New Grub Street* appeared in the same month as *The Picture of Dorian Gray*, April 1891. Gissing only read Dorian Gray in the summer of 1893. Pierre Coustillos (ed.): *London & the Life of Literature in late Victorian England, The Diary of George Gissing, Novelist*. Hassocks: The Harvester Press 1978. Diary entry for Sunday 23rd July 1893.

[7] Peter Berresford Ellis: *H. Rider Haggard, A Voice from the Infinite*. London: Routledge & Kegan Paul 1978 p.122.

[8] Reviewing *Insult and Injury* in the *Pall Mall Gazette*, 2nd May 1887, reprinted in John Wyse Jackson (ed.): *Aristotle at Afternoon Tea: the Rare Oscar Wilde*. London: Fourth Estate 1991 p.90 (hereafter cited as Wyse Jackson).

[9] Reviewing William Rossetti's *Life of John Keats* in *the Pall Mall Gazette* (27th September 1887), Wilde wrote 'Mr Rossetti commits the great mistake of separating the man from the artist.' Wyse Jackson p.101.

[10] Robert Ross to Max Meyerfeld, Prefatory Dedication to *De Profundis*. London: Methuen 1908 (thirteenth impression) pp.x, xii. My italics.

[11] George Orwell: 'Lady Windermere's Fan, A Commentary'. W.J. West (ed.): *Orwell, The War Broadcasts*. London: Duckworth / BBC 1985 p.168.

[12] Frantisek Deak: *Symbolist Theater, The Formation of an Avant-garde*. Baltimore: Johns Hopkins University Press 1993 p.260. Hereafter cited as Deak. Wilde gave a copy of Hafiz 'the divinest of poets' to Bosie. Oscar Wilde to Lord Alfred Douglas 5th/6th November 1894. Rupert Hart-Davis (ed.): *The Letters of Oscar Wilde*. London: Hart-Davis 1962 p.377, hereafter cited as Hart-Davis 1962; Merlin Holland & Rupert Hart-Davis: *The Complete Letters of Oscar Wilde*. London: Fourth Estate 2000 p.621, hereafter cited as Holland & Hart-Davis.

[13] C.M. Bowra: *The Heritage of Symbolism*. London: Macmillan 1963 p.182. Hereafter cited as Bowra.

[14] The psychological approach adopted by Melissa Knox can hardly be superseded, or even, given the controversy that it roused, emulated. Melissa Knox: *Oscar Wilde, A Long and Lovely Suicide*. New Haven & London: Yale University Press

1994; hereafter cited as Knox. There is much in Knox of *post hoc, ergo propter hoc*, and much circular argument, but she also has flashes of insight that illuminate. Her remark (p.98), part of a larger discussion concerning Jack-Ernest-Algy-Oscar that 'identity is unstable: easily assumed, carelessly discarded', is one that particularly appeals to me.

[15] Wilde himself was not always content with this, writing to George Curzon that he *feared* that Edward Stanhope to whom he was applying for a post, shared the public perception of what Wilde was like. My italics. Holland & Hart-Davis p.264.

[16] Oscar Wilde to Lord Alfred Douglas, perhaps 2nd June 1897. Hart-Davis 1962 p.590; Holland & Hart-Davis p.874. Wilde liked this conceit, saying of Gide that he was an Egoist without an Ego. Curiously, the point had been made earlier by Gide's cousin Albert Démarest, who 'did not quite see what interest I had in life beyond myself; that that was the mark of an egoist, and he had a strong suspicion that that was what I was'. André Gide: *Si le grain ne meurt*. Translated by Dorothy Bussy as *If It Die...An Autobiography*. 1935. New York: Vintage Books 2001 p.67. We need further analysis of how the terms were understood at the time. Meredith's *The Egoist* was published in 1879.

[17] I have not found the origin of this, and quote from John Sparrow: 'Oscar Wilde after fifty years' in *Independent Essays*. London: Faber & Faber 1963 p.123.

[18] This has travelled a long way from the naïf remark of Joyce Bentley on Robbie Ross when first meeting Wilde: 'He was also homosexual. As yet, Oscar was not'. Joyce Bentley: *The Importance of being Constance*. London: Robert Hale 1983 p.173. Hereafter cited as Bentley 1883.

[19] Micheál Mac Liammóir: 'An Introduction to the Author' in *The Happy Prince and Other Stories*. Harmondsworth: Puffin Books 1962 p.7. My italics. Wilde was Mac Liammóir's 'hero [...] Lunching with Mac Liammóir gives one an idea of what Oscar Wilde must have been like'. Ulick O'Connor: T*he Ulick O'Connor Diaries 1970-1981*. London: John Murray, new edition 2003 pp.21-2. Hereafter cited as O'Connor.

[20] André Maurois: 'De Ruskin à Wilde', in *Études anglaises*. Paris: Bernard Grasset 1927.

[21] Quoted with the photograph of Margot Asquith at the Cecil Beaton Exhibition, National Portrait Gallery, spring 2004.

[22] Margot Oxford [Asquith]: *More Memories*. London: Cassell & Co 1933 p.120. Hereafter cited as M.Oxford.

[23] Richard Ellmann: *Four Dubliners*. London: Hamish Hamilton 1987; New York: George Braziller 1988 p.1. See also Vyvyan Holland: Introduction to *The Portrait of Mr W.H.* London: Methuen 1958 p.xiv.

[24] Richard Ellmann: *Four Dubliners*. Yet, paradoxically, the chapter on Wilde is 'Oscar Wilde at Oxford', and one may think that the common characteristic of the four was the amount of their lives spent away from Dublin.

[25] Wolf von Eckardt, Sander L. Gilman & J. Edward Chamberlin: *Oscar Wilde's London: A Scrapbook of Vices & Virtues 1880-1900*. New York Anchor Press / Doubleday 1987 p.ix. Despite the eminence of the three authors, this is a very

superficial survey of London life, highly dependent on lavish illustrations for effect, and written in a journalistic style that soon palls. The impact of Wilde upon what Dixon Scott called the 'peculiarly priggish and self-assertive world of the intellectual London of the eighties' is too well explored to recall here, save for the purpose of pointing up the counter-attraction of Paris. Dixon Scott: 'The Innocence of Bernard Shaw'. *The Bookman* 1913, reprinted in Dixon Scott: *Men of Letters.* London: Hodder & Stoughton 1916 p.2, Hereafter cited as Scott. This essay (pp.1-47) also reminds one of the very different accommodation made by Shaw from the one made by Wilde in the attempt of each Dubliner to find his way.

[26] Thomas March: *The History of the Paris Commune of 1871.* London: Swan Sonnenschein & Co 1896 p.143n. Hereafter cited as March.

[27] W.J. Mc Cormack: *Yeats's Politics since 1943, Approaches and Reproaches.* The Yearbook of English Studies volume 35 2005 p.138. My thanks to Professor Mc Cormack for sending me an off-print of this.

[28] Theodore Zeldin: *France 1848-1945* volume I: Ambition, Love and Politics. Oxford: The Clarendon Press 1973 pp.1-3.

[29] Isobel Armstrong: Unpublished lecture at the University of Exeter, 29th November 2004; Marylène Delbourg-Delphis: *Masculin Singulier, le dandysme et son histoire.* Paris: Hachette 1985 p.71. Hereafter cited as Delbourg-Delphis.

[30] Jean-Pierre Arthur Bernard: *Le gout de Paris.* Paris : Mercure de France 2004 p.11.

CHAPTER ONE

PARIS SIGHTED

'Was it really possible that only this morning, those quiet English fields
had been dozing round one, those sleepy villagers spreading their slow
words out, in expressing an absence of idea, over the space of time in
which a Parisian conveyed a pocket philosophy?'
– Mona Caird.[1]

'In London, twenty or thirty years ago are old times; in Paris, ten years or
five.'
– Thomas Hardy.[2]

'One's time is occupied differently in Paris … Time is differently
disposed of there.'
– The Duke of Marlborough, giving evidence in Campbell v. Campbell
1886.[3]

'It has come to me to think that Paris and May are one.'
– George Moore.[4]

THIS is a tale of two cities, and both of them are Paris. It is also the tale
of two men, and both of them are Oscar Wilde. Or, rather, one of them is
Oscar Wilde, and the other is his shadowy alter ego, Sebastian Melmoth.
Each of these, city and man, operated on a physical and a metaphysical
level. These are not opposites, or if they are, they are not polar opposites,
forever fixed, forever divided, but binary opposites, in orbit about each
other, constantly presenting different and reflecting facets to each other.
Their interaction and their intersecting with other layers and levels of fact
and fantasy, is an exploration to be undertaken both on foot and in the
mind: wandering and wondering. First, there is the Paris of survey maps,
its twenty arrondissements contained within what remained of twenty-five
miles of enclosing walls – 'les fortifs', dating from the reign of Louis
Philippe with their fifteen forts and six detached redoubts – or bounded by
the periphery boulevards that replaced the sixteen miles of the old octroi
wall, and by the railway known as the 'petite ceinture'.[5] Here the Parisians
(774,000 of them in 1831; 1,053,000 in 1846; 1,825,000 in 1866;

2,500,000 in 1890[6]) lived in close proximity, walking, dining, drinking, quarrelling, entertaining themselves and even each other. Beyond lay Arcadia: 'Now we are really in the country,' exclaims Maupassant's M. Dufour when his day-tripping family reach Neuilly from their *quincaillerie* in Montmartre.[7] 'The air of the country, it is exquisite, sublime,' exclaims J.F. MacDonald's M. Durand, who with great *empressement* has moved his family for August to Marie-le-Bois, even by slow train only thirty-five minutes from the Gare St Lazare.[8] Similarly, Maupassant's Chavelin and Lesable move to Bezons: 'the mere word "Country" seemed to have a mystical significance'.[9]

The physical Paris was intersected by the 'grands boulevards'[10] of Baron Haussmann[11] and his successors, while the rebuilding of the quays to give a river frontage integrated the Seine with the city, the twenty-nine bridges promoting the flow and reflow of traffic and pedestrians. The city was opening up to light and air, or 'to light, air and infantry', Philip Guedalla's identification of the interplay of strategies of control.[12] This effect at least of light and air was also achieved by the increase of parks and gardens under the direction of Adolphe Alphand.[13] The parc Montsouris, the second largest in Paris, was laid out by him between 1865 and 1878, an alteration from Paris formalism to the English style; his park of the Butte Chaumont was a deliberate piece of social engineering, an alteration from slum to parkland, just as in 1877 the Butte des Moulins was removed to make way for the extension of the avenue de l'Opéra.[14] The 'wildernesses' of the Bois de Vincennes and the Bois de Boulogne were similarly tamed in this period, 'transformed into ornamental parks'.[15]

These were not the first such endeavours at altering the relationship between the real and the ideal. A century earlier, the father of King Louis Philippe, that duke of Orléans known as 'Philippe Égalité' until he lost his head, had employed the landscapist Carmontelle to lay out the parc Monceau in the English fashion, saying 'I want a land of illusions. Only illusions can amuse one.' Edgar Allan Poe in 'The Mystery of Marie Rogêt' (1842) transposed New York into a Paris that was neither the same size nor the same shape as the French capital, and a century later André de Fouquières compared Paris to 'une carte de muette', a map where no feature is given a name, presumably not even to La Muette.[16] Thomas Hardy noted a slippage in chronological time between London and Paris as a literary conceit, but here one recalls that France did not adopt Greenwich Mean Time (plus an hour) until 1911, and on French maps the prime meridian ran through Paris not Greenwich, despite the latter having been established for international use by the Washington Conference in October

1884.[17] Wilde made an aphoristic link between time and space, between the perceived and the imagined, when he said 'In Paris one can lose one's time most delightfully; but one can never lose one's way.'[18] The symbolic attack on the Greenwich Observatory in February 1894, so discussed in the literature on Conrad's *The Secret Agent*, takes on a particular significance in this context, for the would-be destroyer of the Observatory, Martial Bourdin, was from Paris. In the present work, therefore, spatial/temporal relationships are mutable and the Paris of geography cohabits with Paris imagined, a metaParis, where illusions, echoes, reflections and bizarre coincidences predominate, and where time's slippage could also be time's fusion, as noted by Dumas when, writing of courtesans, he remarks 'news of their death, when they die young, reaches all their lovers at the same instant'.[19] Carolyn Steedman has made of this a cultural conceit: 'A new kind of time came into being in the 'nineties, a form of time that was born both of recastings and rewritings of the historical past, and also of a long nineteenth century development, of an interior space or place within human beings'.[20] This internal / external nexus combined with a loosening definition of time embraces an important approach to the period.

'Subjected to the rigid classification of place name and geography,' Arthur Trottenberg has perceptively remarked, 'the rich sensory world shrivels in meaning'.[21] That is why Paris tangible and Paris intangible are themes that run through this work: the Paris of Haussmann and the Paris of Huysmans. Even the term 'belle époque' is one set loose from time. Edmund Wilson saw a thematic unity that lasted from 1870 to 1930; Charles Rearick dates the beginning of the belle époque to the 14th July 1880; but Raymond Rudorff shifts it forward ten years and Dominique Lejeune a further six.[22] Serge Pacaud precisely dates it from the 1st May 1889 to the outbreak of war in 1914.[23] Jean-Jacques Leveque is not quite as precise, preferring 1890-1914; Michel Winock suggests 1900-1914.[24] Jean-Paul Crespelle prefers the term 'grande époque' but also applies it to what we would call the Edwardian age.[25] Malcolm Bradbury sites it in 'the Third Empire, in these changeable years at the close of the nineteenth century and start of the twentieth'.[26] The Third *Empire*? Whether historical inaccuracy or social critique, this revealing phrase fully encapsulates the idea of the mutability of time and place. For these were changeable years indeed: although the celebration of the centenary of the French Revolution brought about no return to the revolutionary calendar, the introduction of the twenty-four hour clock for railway trains (the Notation Nouvelle) proved just as confusing, especially when it was expressed in such terms as half-past fifteen or a quarter to twenty.[27]

Within this scheme of signification, the identification of places become elusive. Renoir's 'Place Clichy' of 1880 may in fact be the place Pigalle.[28] In 1904 Clive Bell stayed in a pension 'in a street which I can no longer find, though it is said to exist.'[29] Carl van Vechten once went to the Bal Musette, perhaps in the rue Jessaint, although he could never find it again,[30] possibly because 'bal musette' was a type of fairly low dance hall, or a bar with a dance floor, rather than the name of any particular one.[31] 'There is not much stability in such French names, I fancy,' wrote George du Maurier,[32] whose own were George Louis Palmella Busson du Maurier – of which du Maurier had been assumed slightly fraudulently by his grandfather. This aspect of Paris as limbo spills over into fiction: in Zola's *Le Rêve*, Hubert searches for Madame Foucart at the end of the rue des Deux-Ecus, and finds no such name in the directory, and that the end of the rue des Deux-Ecus has been pulled down.[33] Du Maurier himself caught this note: 'He and I would explore the so changed Bois de Boulogne for the little "Mare aux Biches" [...] but we never managed to find it: perhaps it had evaporated'.[34]

As for Paris as heaven: it was certainly that for many at many times and Robert Louis Stevenson was not alone in drawing attention to the wordplay made possible by Paris making up so much of Paradise.[35] In 1887 the ruins of the Théâtre Latin, destroyed in 1870, were rebuilt by Gustave Eiffel as the Paradis Latin[36] for the forthcoming Exposition Universelle; the shop 'Le Paradis des Dames' anticipated the 'Bonheur des Dames' (1883) of Zola's novel, and was there not a toyshop called Le Paradis des Enfants?[37] 'As I stood within the shadow of the Louvre I was murmuring that Paris was another name for Paradise,' wrote the Dubliner Chris Healy, who moved to the 'city of my dreams' in July 1896.[38] One cannot, however, neglect the notion of this Paradise as an artificial one, its Elysian fields a commodified space, nor can one exclude Paris as hell: Verlaine once 'spoke as if Hell is a city much like Paris'.[39] On the boulevard de Clichy the cabarets Ciel and Enfer were side by side, Zola anticipates Marcel Proust in his identification of Paris-Sodom and Paris-Gomorrah, the avenue Denfert-Rochereau was once the rue d'Enfer, and the gates intended for the new museum of decorative arts were Rodin's Gates of Hell.[40] It was always a place in which to spend a season.

～～～～～

Victor Hugo expressed the sense of liberation from rigid classification of geography in his *Appeal to the Germans* of 1870 as, fortunately, not many could:

> Burn our buildings, they are only our bones; their smoke will take shape, become huge and alive, and rise up into the sky; and there will be seen for ever on the horizon of the nations, above us, above you, above all things, above all people, asserting our glory, asserting your shame, this great phantom composed of darkness and light: Paris![41]

James Laver in his study of Huysmans made this distinction: 'There is a poetry of cities which has nothing to do with the things that receive three stars in the guide books: a personality behind the public personality [...] Paris reveals its secret only to pedestrians, with time on their hands. Huysmans was an indefatigable pedestrian [...]'[42] Exploration of the French capital as poetry is a satisfying pastime in metaParis.

It is little wonder that for Émile Zola, 'all-devouring'[43] Paris became its own personification, taking on 'an other-worldly aura of impenetrable mystery [in] shifting, manifold aspects'.[44] The Paris of the imagination thus defines itself both in the imagination of the Parisians and of those who found in Paris the site of their dreams and fantasies; where, repelled, the observer was fascinated by his repulsion; where, fascinated, the observer was repelled by his fascination; where the acts of creation and recreation became acts of re-creation, or of desecration. Thus Arthur Symons was drawn again and again to 'that city of perdition which is Paris',[45] where, as the American painter Will Low noted among his associates, 'project and purpose outweighed action and accomplishment'.[46] These layers of Paris combine in Eugen Weber's later careful phrase 'In the enchantment of the Third Republic, words were equated with acts' and in E.V. Lucas's contemporary apostrophe 'A little apartment overlooking the parc Monceau – there is *tangible heaven*, if you like!'[47] Into this Wilde, as representative of 'a nation of brilliant failures' who 'are the greatest talkers since the Greeks' (his own phrases) could slip observed; although the French taste for intellectual speculation differs from the Irish taste for heaping upon one another conversational flights of fancy.

> Paris is an intellectual Brighton. There the wind blows through your thoughts as at Brighton it blows through your clothes.

> There you may talk at random. Think aloud, and amid the *sans-gêne* of the French mind, have the glorious sensation of the open sea and the mountain top, of a broad unending landscape in which facts fade into a horizon of mystery and conjecture roams amid a freedom that knows no bourn.[48]

Paris in these readings becomes a place ungrounded, more ungrounded indeed than any of the balloons in which the photographer Nadar ascended to photograph his panoramas of the city. Paris as a phantom haunts the imagination. In his own photographic evocation of the city, Arthur Trottenberg takes images, phantoms composed of light and darkness, by the street photographer Eugène Atget and illustrates them with phrases taken from Marcel Proust: 'Hence the Paris considered here is not carefully defined in terms of its metropolitan borders. It is rather a fusion of time and place that must sometimes touch on areas important enough to be included in the Proustian dimension of Paris'.[49] Yet the Proustian dimension was but one of many, interlaced, layered, like a game of three-dimensional chess, superimposed upon the Proust quadrilateral, from the parc Monceau to the place de la Concorde, to Auteuil, to the Bois de Boulogne. Baudelaire had noted that for the stroller, 'the street becomes a dwelling [...] news-stands [the] libraries and the terraces of his cafés are the balconies from which he looks down', and the lingering presence of Baudelaire is central to an understanding of *fin-de-siècle* Paris.

Because Baudelaire died in 1867 he is in these pages very largely *l'auteur absent*, but the appreciation of him by Leon Chai explores with telling economy what my own work expands upon, and forms a benchmark in the remeasuring of Wilde:[50]

> I attempt to show how all the elements of a nascent æstheticism can be found in the work of Baudelaire. Here consciousness dissolves the external world into impressionistic motifs, producing an initial chaos. Beneath the chaos, however, a formative impulse progressively manifests itself in the arrangement of the motifs. Impression passes over into emotion, which in turn is embodied in symbolism.[51]

It is, however, necessary to factor in as a complement to this an awareness of the physicality of Paris, the sound of the *frou-frou* as well as the sight of the *chiffonnier*, the smell of the asphalt as well as the taste of the madeleine.

~~~~~~~~

Round the boulevards paced the Parisians, mapping their city, bringing actors and diplomats, poets and scientists, princes and librarians, artists and jockeys, courtesans and duchesses into conjunctions where influences can be suggested, affinities discerned, proximities charted. When, for example, Maupassant in *Bel-Ami* calls his newspaper proprietor M. Walter,[52] or Gide published his *Cahiers d'André Walter*, they must have done so in the knowledge that Judith Gautier wrote under the name Judith Walter; and when Zola in *Germinal* named one of the pit-horses 'Trompette', he would have been doing it knowing (as a sufficiency of his readers would have known) that 'La Trompette' was the ensemble for which Saint-Saëns had written his 1880 Septet in E Flat. Such coinciding knits together the metaphysical as much as the boulevards knitted the physical Paris, although one must be careful about overstressing this: for example, Gide first met Proust in 1891, but the two men did not meet again until 1916. This, however, also forms part of metaParis, the visible shadow of the person invisible round the corner.

Théodore Duret[53] is quoted as saying that in Édouard Manet the sentiments and customs of Parisians were personified.[54] Assuming that 'customs' is a translation of the rather more resonant 'mœurs', this (apart from giving a centrality to Manet) licences an interplay of place, time, persons, names, shapes, mentality. The proverb 'Il n'y a qu'un Paris' will answer less and less satisfactorily. Paris is established not so much as a state of being as a state of seeming, and John Augustus O'Shea, looking back on 1889 only from 1892, understood Paris not to have, but to be, its own spirit of place: 'It was mine to pass that summer in Paris, and to me now it is as a dream. Very hot and very crowded the gay city was; as wicked, delightful, luxurious and expensive as during the zenith of the Second Empire'.[55] For Félicien Rops, 'Paris vous agriffe par mille côtés et l'on ne sait jamais quitter cette ville diablée'.[56] Sisley Huddleston, Paris correspondent of *The Times*, thought that 'Paris, better than them all, bewitches those who have once fallen under its spell – and what visitor or resident does not succumb to that spell?'[57] The Paris to which Oscar Wilde came, first as explorer, then as would-be conqueror, and finally as exile, was one where the existing cultural forms, whether in theatre, literature, music or the visual arts were challenged by the new movements that bubbled up through the crust, became harbingers of the modern movement.[58] Modernism, modernity, though nourished by a ferment of German, Austrian, Belgian, Scandinavian, Italian and American origins, could not have assumed the form it did without the influence of Paris. The French themselves, like Maupassant's provincial Maître Saval in 'A Night Out', or the anonymous heroine of 'Une aventure parisienne' were perfectly alive to this:

> As soon as he set foot in the rue d'Amsterdam, he felt blissfully happy [...] 'The air of Paris is quite different from any other. There's something about it which thrills and excites and intoxicates you, and in some strange way makes you want to dance and do all sorts of other silly things. As soon as I get out of the train, it's just as if I had drunk a bottle of champagne. What a time one could have here, surrounded by artists! How happy those lucky people must be, the great men who have made a name in a city like Paris! What a wonderful life they have!' And he indulged in dreams.[59]

> She thought constantly about Paris and avidly read all the society pages in
> the papers [...] She was fascinated by what these reports merely hinted at.
> The cleverly phrased allusions half-lifted a veil beyond which could be
> glimpsed devastatingly attractive horizons promising a whole new world of
> wicked pleasure.[60]

Here Saval materialises both aspects of Paris: it is the rue *d'Amsterdam*, a
name which suggests not France but a different country altogether; and, on
levels as much symbolic as geographical and cultural, it leads straight
from the Gare St Lazare to the place Clichy.

This cultural restlessness both emerged from and helped enlarge other
social changes: the loss of influence (if not the self-confidence) of the
aristocracy, the enrichment of the bourgeoisie to the point where it
dominated the Third Republic, the social and political emancipation of the
working class. Although no coherent feminist movement can be readily
discerned, in all the cultural forms women were in the vanguard: Sarah
Bernhardt and Réjane, Berthe Morisot and Louise Abbéma, Louise Michel
and Séverine, Yvette Guilbert and Jane Avril, Marguerite Eymery
('Rachilde') and Colette all have their claims upon our attention.[61] Paris
was thus the appropriate site of Wilde's first metamorphosis, enabling him
to proclaim after his residence there in 1883 that the Oscar of the first
period was dead. It was therefore also the appropriate site of Wilde's last
metamorphosis, for 'Paris killed him'.[62] Abroad is an Other country; we
order things differently there.

> 'Where has he been living all these years?'
> 'In that rookery of pomp and vanity, Paris, I believe.'
> 'Yes, Paris must be a taking place. Grand shop-windows, trumpets, and
> drums.'[63]

Although we will not be treating much of drums, we shall return again and
again to the grand shop-windows, and to the strumpets.

~~~~~~

The city itself was in a state of continual transformation, so much so that
its metaphysical formation seemed often to usurp its physical state. Ralph
Nevill reckoned that 'Of all the great European cities, Paris changes her
aspect the most'.[64] There is a subtext here, the feminisation of the city,
reinforced by the suggestion of the 'feminine' characteristic of maquillage.
Although Paris was not a *tabula rasa*, the Siege and Commune of 1870-
1871 created an inelegant sufficiency of destruction for a new Paris to be

erected. 'Dirty, draggled, starved, broken-hearted and mad with despair,'
was how Lord Dunraven found it in January 1871, staying at the Hôtel
Chatham where furniture and pianos, comfort and culture, were being
burned for fuel.[65] Towards the end of the Commune another British visitor
'walked […] along the boulevard des Italiens […] We got as far as the rue
Montmartre; but there we were stopped […] because there was an
unbroken barricade in front. So back we came […] listening to the
screeching of rifles, the grating jar of mitrailleuses, and the crackling of
our own steps. Could that be Paris? We were, in reality, in the boulevard
des Italiens'.[66] But even the reality of the boulevard des Italiens was
subverted when old people still called it the boulevard de Gand, young
fashionables called it the Boul' des It, and in general it could be referred to
simply as 'the boulevard',[67] a name possibly more commonly used than
that given it by the Goncourts, to wit, 'the clitoris of Paris'.[68] There was
another answer to Callwell's question, however, but one that is no less
subversive of reality. 'Paris is no longer Paris,' wrote Jules Claretie in a
confused passage in February 1871. 'All Paris is at Bordeaux […] This city
is at once exotic and Parisian, a boulevard des Italiens at San Francisco'.[69]
This idea of a mobile Paris strangely echoes a guide book of 1868:

> Trouville is the boulevard des Italiens of the Norman beaches. If the
> *flâneur* of the city pavement, dozing on a divan in the Café Richelieu while
> digesting his succulent dinner, were suddenly transported by the rug of the
> One Thousand and One Nights to the Casino in Trouville, he would not
> believe he had left Paris when he awakened there.[70]

This reinforces Robert Lethbridge's characterisation of the boulevard des
Italiens as the epitome of 'Parisian social values in the second half of the
nineteenth century', and finding it virtually inevitable that *Bel-Ami* should
begin there, an alignment of 'urban geography' and 'fictional destiny'.[71]
The boulevard des Italiens will be referred to in this sense again in this
work.

The great department store 'Au Bonheur des Dames' in Zola's novel of
that name, although set in the Second Empire, is also a metaphor for the
Paris of the period in which it was written,[72] a place of continual
rebuilding and renewal, filled with frantic energy. No sooner had the new
boulevards been more or less completed, work began (1st November
1898[73]) on Ligne 1 of the Métro. The children of light were resistant to
being driven down into the dark, although visits to the Catacombs
provided a frisson for those who like that particular form of Orphism. The
proponents of an underground system were opposed by those who

advocated an aerial one, though Deligny, one of a commission sent to London in 1876, reported that underground was the only possible choice, 'even though the flâneurs who stroll between the Madeleine and the rue Montmartre will not use it.'[74] The alluring entrances by Henri Guimard, the white tiles and abundant lighting of the platforms, were designed to counteract this resistance, and the fear of epidemics, flooding from the Seine, and of course drafts; while the concerns of the Academicians that the works might disturb their labours on their Dictionary caused a loop to avoid the Institut, the pen in Paris being mightier than the spade. Curiously this dislocation is hardly referred to in the paintings or literature of the time: under ground was sub text.[75]

In 1886 a party of soldiers from the English Staff College visited Paris to look at 'the ground where some of the unsuccessful sorties had taken place which were attempted during the great siege; but owing to the numbers of buildings which had sprung up in the interval, the progress of the different combats was not always easy to follow satisfactorily'.[76] The Parisians, in fact, had other forms of progress to follow satisfactorily. Paris, in Walter Benjamin's now tired phrase the capital of the nineteenth century,[77] was where the cultural development of much of the twentieth century was enwombed. This was recognised even by the British. That Lord Dufferin should have called Paris 'the Mecca, the Holy City of the arts, the sciences, the graces and the inventive energies that create civilization'[78] is not perhaps surprising, given that he was Ambassador at the time, but that he should have done so in an address to the British Chamber of Commerce[79] in Paris suggests an appeal to a solidarity of cultural interest between speaker and audience that one can only hope was reciprocated. Dufferin's predecessor had been even more laudatory: 'In all that relates to the grace and enjoyment of social life, Paris seems to me a much more civilised capital than London.'[80]

It is thus not surprising that the phrases that shape much of our cultural discussion are nineteenth century French. 'Art for art's sake' ('l'art pour l'art') and 'the well-made play' ('la pièce bien faite') are by Victor Cousin[81] and Eugène Scribe respectively. 'Naturalism' first occurs[82] in the preface to the second edition of Zola's *Thérèse Raquin* and 'Symbolism' was first used by Jean Moréas[83] in *Le Figaro* on 18th September 1886. That aspect of Naturalism, the literary work that was 'a slice of life', owes the sobriquet ('tranche de vie') to Guy de Maupassant,[84] although Marvin Carlson suggests that 'a slice of life' and indeed 'fourth wall' first occur in Jean Julien's review *Art et Critique* at this time.[85] It is 'unlikely that "avant garde" occurred much before 1890 in French or other languages'.[86] We call the interior monologue 'monologue intérieur' because its originator was Edouard Dujardin;[87] 'vers libre' was an innovation variously claimed by Gustave Kahn,[88] Marie Krysinska, Jean Moréas and Jules Laforgue – the term itself by the Franco-American Francis Vielé-Griffin, as 'le vers est libre', the opening words of his *Joies*.[89] 'On a polémiqué sur le fait de savoir qui était "l'inventeur" du vers libre,' remarks de Paysac.[90] The fashionable photograph size known as 'carte de visite' was expressed in French because it was invented by André Disdéri.[91] 'Operetta' was first applied to Jules Bovery's *Madame Mascarille* in 1866, although it is not clear whether this or 'opérette' was the word used.[92] Even 'demi-monde' is from the play of that name (1855) by Alexandre Dumas *fils*[93]: a half world in half light. *Fin-de-siècle* itself occurs as the title of a novel by A. Claveaux in 1889; a play called *Paris, fin-de-siècle* caught the attention of Ada Leverson – Wilde's friend 'Sphinx' – and she persuaded her husband to buy the translation rights.[94] Other phrases slipped between French and English. 'Grand revue' in Paris became known as 'Music-Hall', while 'Art Nouveau', a term familiar to all English speakers, by one of those inversions that will be found a characteristic of the period, was not perhaps quite so familiar in its country of origin: '[...] ce qu'on a appelé en France le Modern Style, en Angleterre l'Art Nouveau, et, dans les pays germaniques, le Jugendstil'.[95] Introducing his translation of Huysmans' *À Rebours*, P.G. Lloyd asserts that it 'contains the essence of the current ideas of the time':[96] it is significant that the book is usually referred to by its French title.

Nor is it surprising that 'restaurant' and 'café' may be read as French cultural terms, and the social relationships engendered by Parisian congregation are both significant in themselves, and explain much of the attraction of Paris for the more gregarious of the English visitors. Francis Parkman,[97] the Bostonian historian of French Canada, was forcibly struck by the contrast between the eating houses of London and Paris:

> The one being a quiet dingy establishment where each guest is put into a box, and supplied with porter, beef, potatoes and plum pudding. Red faced old gentlemen of three hundredweight mix their 'brandy go' and read *The Times*. In Paris the tables are set in elegant galleries and saloons and among the trees and flowers in a garden [...] The waiters spring from table to table as noiselessly as shadows, prompt at the slightest sign; a lady, elegantly attired, sits in an arbor to preside over the whole. Dine at these places – then go to a London 'dining room' – swill porter and devour roast beef![98]

A key word here is 'dingy': that Paris was better lit indoors as well as out is a frequent comment of contemporaries. It was not merely a question of larger windows, more daylight, though it is to be remembered that the introduction of plate glass ('grand shop windows') made novel our familiar view of ourselves reflected, and allowed the passer-by to see the world within, the customer the world without: indeed, an even more intimate relationship is suggested by the French phrase for window-shopping, *lèche-vitrine*, licking the window. Although the sobriquet 'city of light' ('ville lumière') dated to its mediæval reputation for learning, Paris led in its artificial lighting: so much so that by the end of the nineteenth century the man known as 'le roi de lumière' was not Bergson or Sorel but Pataud, the Secretary of the Union of Electricians. The Café des Boulevards in the boulevard Poissonnière had had gas lighting installed by a Scottish engineer[99] as early as the 1830s; the rue de Rivoli, two miles long, was famous for its 'cordon de lumière', the long flickering ribbon of flame from the gas lamps in every arch of its arcade. The 'brilliantly lit' shop windows of the rue de la Paix and the rue de Rivoli were especially recalled by Ralph Nevill as attracting visitors' attention in the 1880s when his Parisian memories began.[100] The change from gas to electricity intensified the light, but reduced the phantasmal effect of the flickering. Zola caught the latter in describing Les Halles: 'All along the pavement the only things that were truly awake were the lanterns dancing at the end of invisible arms, spanning in leaps and bounds the presence of sleep that lingered there, in the outlines of bodies and the shapes of vegetables, awaiting the coming of day'.[101] Zola also saw very clearly how artificial light moved between the planes of the physical and the metaphysical, when he sends Pierre Froment one afternoon into the house in the avenue Hoche[102] of the princesse de Harn:

> What surprised Pierre was that every window shutter of the mansion was closed, every chink stopped up so that daylight might not enter, and that every room flared with electric lamps, an illumination of supernatural intensity. [...] And to Pierre, who felt both blinded and stifled, it seemed as if he were entering one of those luxurious, unearthly Dens of the Flesh such as the pleasure world of Paris conjures from dreamland.[103]

The supernatural, conjuring ... but Zola was not the only one who drew upon the magical properties in scientific achievement. Gabriela Zapolska, viewing Paris at dusk from the second stage of the Eiffel Tower in 1889, wrote that she was the

> witness of a truly fabulous vision. For, at this moment, Paris began to light up as though under the effect of a magic wand. It became an ocean of light,

a tidal wave of fire and blue light [...] electricity competing with gas [...] in an orgy of light [...] the buildings resembling palaces in fairyland.[104]

Henry James, too, saw the actual and metaphorical application of Parisian light as ambiguous, a lambent stretching of the imagination: 'In the light of Paris, one sees what things resemble. That's what the light of Paris seems always to show. It's the fault of the light of Paris – dear old light!'[105] 'What things resemble', not what things are.

For Guy de Maupassant, gas light served to establish French life in the new age of predatory journalism, predatory journalists, where the ordinary people, the passers-by, become two-dimensional, colourless:

> The words *La Vie française* were blazoned over the door like a challenge, spelt out in huge fiery letters by gas flares. The passers-by, moving abruptly into the brightness cast by these three dazzling words, would suddenly be bathed in light, as visible, clear, and distinct as if it were the middle of the day, before quickly passing back into the shadows.[106]

Whether better lighting produced more illumination is another matter, but one should also note that, whereas it is well-known that the Statue of Liberty by Bartholdi was presented to the United States by the French, the statue's real title offers far more significance: Liberty lighting up the world.[107] There was a double symbolism here, for Paris had ten times more gas lamps even than New York, and was already experimenting with electricity. The Exhibition of 1878 saw a number of electric apparatuses on show, including the Joblochskoff (or Yablochkov) light which the London theatre manager John Hollingshead tried unsuccessfully to obtain for the Gaiety Theatre. The Comédie Française had electric lighting installed in 1887, and in 1889 at the time of the Exposition Universelle, public buildings and monuments were lit for the first time by electricity. The annual Salon had been lit by electricity as early as 1880. Mary Waddington, when French ambassadress in London, noted that 'One of the things that strikes me here – the rooms are so much less well lighted than in Paris'.[108] Mrs Burton Harrison recorded that 'We were asked to a soirée to be given by an English lady in the Avenue de l'Impératrice. Her cards read: "Tea at eight. Electricity at nine. Music at ten."'[109] This was just before the Franco-Prussian War, but as late as 1882, the wealthy M. Walter in Maupassant's *Bel-Ami* is inviting people to view his latest-bought painting 'by electric light', while Mme Verdurin inspires excitement by installing electricity probably even later.[110] Lord Frederic Hamilton remembered the impression made on him at the age of seven of the 'fairy city [...] literally blazing with light'.[111] Thirty years later, when the young Seymour Leslie was taken to Paris, the impression of light and air became an abiding memory. 'Paris was such a contrast to London even to a child. It was so clean and brightly lit.'[112]

Émile Trébet thought that light was the agent through which the architect (and he was one himself) came to know form, and it is no wonder that the Impressionists were fascinated by natural light, but it should not be forgotten that the Paris of Manet and Pissarro was also the Paris of Boldini and Béraud which was also the Paris of Théophile Steinlen[113] and Jean-Louis Forain:[114] light shading away into darkness. A junction of the metaphysical and the physical serves as a reminder that the prosperity of Paris was ultimately determined by 'the shaping and fitting of metal parts [...] Paris, even the city proper, did not stand on the margins of the Second Industrial Revolution, but rather was a participant in it'.[115] Participating in a Revolution, that too is to indulge in qualitative change.

~~~~~~~

'Paris,' reflected Mr Gladstone when staying at the Hôtel Bristol in 1892, 'is greater than anything in Paris',[116] but Paris was also greater than France. This view of Paris as an organism was captured by Hugh Shelley in his introduction to *Le ventre de Paris*: 'What is still exciting to the modern reader [...] is the very just claim by F.W.J. Hemmings for the body of the author's work: "Zola was the first writer to show a society in which the aggregate was greater than the separate unit".'[117] Shelley's introduction of the term *body* has multiple meanings and reminds us that *le ventre* contains more than the stomach.

The search for Paris in its essence, its personification and its re-construction as metaphor is realised in an exchange between Arsène Houssaye[118] and Théophile Gautier:[119]

> [HOUSSAYE:] Between two glasses of champagne, I throw out this prophecy: We are in the year 2000. Because of the fantastic rapidity of our move into the age of electricity, the twentieth century has been a period of unexcelled progress [...] Paris was yesterday and will be for a thousand years the host of all that lives, the central home of all the arts [...] Paris remains the centre of creation.

> [GAUTIER:] Gentlemen, what remains of Golconda, of Babylon, of Athens, of Carthage, of Thebes with its hundred gates, of Rome with its hundred ruins? Six grains of dust. Paris will be the seventh.[120]

This was an elegant republic, a republic of letters, of fraternity, of a certain qualified liberty. It was also a third republic, rather low in a rating when to come third, to travel third class or take a third class degree offered but a slight claim to quality. That said, the elegant republic supposes a category that recognises universalism; and the intrapolation of the universal into the particular, to the small streets and café *terrasses*, allows a minute scrutiny as well as a theoretical exposition. This is not arguing banally from the general to the particular, but establishing the shifting relationships between the local (topos) and the global (cosmos), contending components of Parisian cosmopolitanism. Whether the cosmopolis makes the deracinated cosmopolite, or the cosmopolite makes the dislocated cosmopolis, is a question to which more than one answer may emerge, 'between two glasses of champagne', the drink, effervescent but soon flat, that more than any other typifies the era.[121] For Zola at his most despairing, this posed the essential question of decadence, 'Was it then a necessary thing, that decomposition of the great cities that have governed the world?'[122]

This may also work towards a position where one is reducing the capacity for agency by the individual, by seeing the individual as subservient to the demands of a personified and gendered City. This cannot be argued to any final conclusion: but the point can be pursued through a number of case studies in which the argument is adumbrated. Part at least of this is to construct an idea of identity without agency, the essential mode of metaParis, where the shadows fall on the wall of the cave. It is easy to see how such a Paris formed for Wilde, as for so many other visitors, the necessary 'other' site, the city where, in Michael Hamburger's perceptive phrase 'the truth of poetry became inseparable from what Oscar Wilde called "the truth of masks"',[123] and where the idea of an uniform identity is mocked. This has a long reach. For example, Madame van der Velde wrote of the Austrian Graf von Beust 'At all times, in various phases of Count Beust's career, Paris had for him a powerful attraction and an abiding charm; he spent there all the time he could spare from his duties'. This so worked on him that Mary Waddington seems to have thought of him as a Frenchman, for she refers to him, though writing in English, as the Comte de Beust.[124] The German Ambassador found something unsettling about Beust. 'It seemed to me that he talked of himself as of a third person, a bad character, quite outside and apart from himself. His mocking laugh, as we spoke, made a very repellent impression upon me.'[125] Attraction and repulsion: these will become the familiar poles of Paris and metaParis.

There were, after all, so many tastes to be indulged, whether as in the case of Walter Palmer, it was for new biscuits,[126] or for more outré concerns. It seems that all we know of Olive Schreiner's activities when she made a clandestine visit to Paris in March 1889 is a visit to the Morgue.[127] Undoubtedly there was a confluence between the Morgue and theatre, the former being one of the three ultimate destinations designated by Henri Murger for the Bohemian.[128] Henry Irving, who used to visit Paris with Joe Comyns Carr, 'had a morbid passion for visiting the Morgue and declared it was the most entertaining place in Paris'.[129] Edward Gordon Craig linked it with seeing Bernhardt when in Paris in 1890 at the age of eighteen. George du Maurier recalled it 'with the charmed eyes of Memory' as a place of 'weird fascination', but the young Winston Churchill was disappointed only to find three bodies.[130] Evelyn Wrench also saw only three. 'Lying on small carts or trucks, they looked very ghastly,' he remembered. 'To shake off my recollections, I dined at the Café Américain and went to see a very Parisian play called *The Princesse de Flirts* at the "Parisiana".'[131]

The actress Mary Anderson[132] (whom Wilde had wanted as his Duchess of Padua), visited the Morgue with Lord Lytton in 1884 and found the corpses 'far more beautiful' than the sculptured figures she had seen in the studio of Rodin,[133] death loitering in arcadia. Robert Sherard adds the Baudelairean thought that 'morbidity was in great demand in Paris in those days',[134] finding its way into popular songs, notably those of Jules Jouy.[135] Chris Healy tells how he made the Montmartre cemetery 'one of my favourite haunts',[136] a revealing choice of words. Wilde himself, however, thought it a dignifying place.

> I remember going to the Morgue after seeing a brilliant function – all colour and music – at Notre Dame. A woman of the lowest class was on one of the slabs. She was having her day. All Paris might look at her gravely. She was no longer despised.[137]

The Morgue, that disrobing room between the home and the grave, with 'its little jet of water playing on each corpse on its slab',[138] may have been an extreme example of the maxim that it is better to travel than to arrive, but it symbolises Paris as a place of withdrawal.

When Edmund Gosse's uncles 'were obliged to fly from their creditors',[139] it was to Paris and oblivion; in his turn, Whitaker Wright fled to Paris from his creditors, but was brought back to trial and suicide. Paris was the refuge of Abington Baird when he was warned off the Turf in April 1882; no doubt this wealthy thug made himself as unpleasant there as elsewhere.

The better to abscond with his wife's *dot*, Maupassant's M. Lebrument first proposes a visit to Paris, where he abandons her.[140] Charles Hawtrey once knew a London clubman (whom he calls 'Green Park') who, having been suspected of cheating at cards 'disappeared from London and England thereafter and I have only seen him once or twice in Paris, and there in not very respectable company'.[141] In *Les Diaboliques*, Barbey d'Aurevilly's Spanish Duchess of Sierra Leone, determined to revenge herself on her husband for killing her lover, goes to Paris to become a five-franc harlot; conversely, Alice Howard, a flower-girl at a London music-hall, arrived in Paris in 1873 and became the mistress of the painter Lewis Hawkins in a complicated erotic relationship that involved George Moore. Ten years later it could be declared 'with feelings of mingled pride and confusion that she [is] the handsomest whore in Paris', with an address in the avenue d'Iéna.[142] This fate was escaped by Violet Hunt 'when in the eighties I was sent to Paris, on the advice of a good friend of my mother, Mr Crackanthorpe, to avoid the possibility of being dragged ever so slightly into a divorce case, a prime disaster for an unmarried girl in those Victorian days'.[143] Just such a disaster befell Lady Aylesford, who stayed in the Hôtel Rivoli with Lord Blandford as Mrs Spencer: her husband 'Sporting Joe' Aylesford divorced her in 1878. Six years later, Lady Colin Campbell, staying at the Hôtel Windsor, was closely watched by an English 'inquiry agent' called Alfred Davis, who worked in Paris obtaining evidence for divorce proceedings. The brothers Aubrey and Herbert Boyd also seem to have been thus employed, though the latter worked as a solicitor's clerk in Paris, and the former described himself as an accountant.[144]

Among the less innocent, the cook who killed Mrs Riel[145] (the Park Lane Murder 1871) was captured in Paris. When the anarchist Ossipon in Conrad's *Secret Agent* learns that Mrs Verloc has killed her husband, it is to Paris to which he automatically thinks she should flee. When pursued by Lord Durham for criminal libel in his paper *The Bat*, Jimmy Davis ('Owen Hall') slipped away to France till the affair blew over; Eustace Grenville-Murray fled there from the consequence of his court action with Lord Carrington, and died there in 1881 after publishing a number of satirical sketches on Parisian life in the *Pall Mall Gazette*.[146] Lillie Langtry hid herself in Paris to have her daughter by Prince Louis of Battenberg.[147] In 1903, in his room at the Hôtel Regina, General Sir Hector MacDonald[148] shot himself rather than face charges of homosexual conduct.

Although death in Paris provides the final illustration, even Paris as a site of honeymoon could lend itself to more than one state of alteration. (But when John and Ada Galsworthy were there on honeymoon in April 1895, they had omitted the usual precaution of marrying first.) Wilde may have embarrassed Robert Sherard by talking of the delights vouchsafed him by Constance in the Hôtel Wagram, but Baroness Marie von Wallersee, who married Count George Larisch in October 1877, found things otherwise: 'I spent my honeymoon in Paris and like many another wedding trip it was not a happy experience [...] My husband was haunted by the fear of developing signs of his father's madness'. She had already been warned by Count Nicholas Esterhazy: '"Baroness, I cannot wish you happiness. I have no respect for a girl who sells herself to a monkey"'.[149]

Amongst these *fantaisistes*, Wilde re-inventing himself as Sebastian Melmoth was only absorbing a culture wherein Théophile Dondey could re-invent himself as Philothée O'Neddy; where the real name of Camille Mauclair[150] should turn out to be Severin Faust and Auguste Wisteaux took the stage name Mévisto[151]; where the magazine *La Pléiade* should be founded by a man called Pilate but who preferred to known as Louis-Pilate de Brinn'Gaubast[152]; where in the magazine *L'Hirondelle* a journalist wrote under the by-line of either Frou-Frou[153] or Flou-Flou, his real name unknown unless it really was Nuctémeron d'Apollonius[154] (although I feel that this is quite unlikely) – and where Octave Mirbeau could name himself Sébastien[155] and a student at the École des Beaux Arts called Lehoux was once nicknamed Mummoth.[156] Even Maupassant hid his aristocratic origins for a while under the name Joseph Prunier, which 'has a very lower middle-class ring, with a hint of absurdity about it.'[157] It seems inevitable in this world of transformations that A.J.A. Symons' chapter on Oscar Wilde in Paris, one of the few to be completed for his projected biography of Wilde, has been lost; and almost superfluous to add that the name Symons was an assumed one, his original one being a matter of conjecture.[158]

In Paris it was not only the Parisians who changed their names. The shifts in the names of the people assimilate them to the shifts in names of the streets in defining the city as a place of metamorphosis and uncertainty. When the name of the rue du 2 décembre was changed to rue du 4 septembre, Hippolyte de Villemessant, founder of *Le Figaro*, suggested that it should be permanently called the rue de la prochaine Révolution.

If Manet personified the customs and sentiments of the Parisians, Jean Béraud[159] turned them into anecdote: 'la bourgeoisie et son libertinage discret, la sortie bruyante des lycées, les étalages gourmands des pâtisseries, la mode, les courses [...] Bref, tout ce qui fait la vie parisienne de cette époque!'[160] Patrick Offenstadt extravagantly claims that in Béraud the *belle époque* had its 'chroniqueur spirituel': this is to take a view that sees that epoch as one restricted to 'le Tout-Paris', as well as to confuse the material with the spiritual, but Béraud's work is certainly iconographic for any superficial view of Marcel Proust's. 'Je suis bien certain,' reflected André de Fouquières, 'que Jean Béraud mérite la gratitude de ceux qui sont perpetuellement en quête du temps perdu.'[161] This was not Manet's world, for Manet, while ambitious for success and honours, never sought to placate his academic critics; while Béraud, by adopting bourgeois realism, *l'art pompier*, disarmed them, gaining the entrée into upper class society and a gold medal at the Paris Exhibition of 1889. Nor was this the world of bourgeois interiors depicted by Vuillard or Bonnard or Vallotton, where the trappings of bourgeois style suggest an emptiness of interior life amongst a clutter of furniture and knicknacks, in Bertrand Lorquin's phrase 'un air irrespirable, une angoisse sourde'.[162]

John Milner, in his study of the period, captures the Romantic view of Paris but colours it with symbolic meaning:

> A studio in Paris, in the capital of art, was the ambition and achievement of thousands. The geography of art in Paris is full of such rooms, their gaunt rooms sipping the steady north light. Within the studio, be he Bonnard or Bonnat,[163] the painter steps back from his canvas, and considers its colours and forms, intuition prompting the adjustment of a red or a green. The light illuminates canvas and painter and is captured in both. The looking and the making go hand in hand. A painter looks at a canvas. A model poses or waits. In the corner paintings are stacked against the wall. Outside is the bustle of the street, and the milling public boulevard. One is stillness, creativity and isolation; the other is activity, business and competition. Paris proffered both in abundance. From Montmartre to Montparnasse there were artists at work, painting, carving and looking. As the commitment to painting experience grew and spread, Paris itself increasingly provided not only the artists' dwellings and means of support but also their subject [...] In the simple act of looking lay inexhaustible potential [...] In the simple act of applying paint to canvas, or modelling clay with the fingers, lay a cultural process generating an elaborate structure of both patronage and refusal of patronage, of tuition and its rejection, of success and failure, of recognition and obscurity.[164]

> Long after nightfall, when the streets were empty, you could hear the sounds of music from studios where some lonely musician was still working, and you knew that in hundreds, perhaps thousands of rooms or

studios, the artists would be at work hammering out the turn of phrase or trying to get the correct rhythm of a line in drawing. The whole of Paris seemed to be intent on some of these things.[165]

One can add that if all this seems a little high-flown, no better emblem of Paris as a site of both patronage and refusal of patronage, of tuition and its rejection, of success and failure, of recognition and obscurity, can be found than the occasion in December 1882 when a criminal calling himself Martin Dupont, of whom all that is known is that his name was neither Martin nor Dupont, was arrested for trying to steal empty bottles.[166]

But who, after all, were the Parisians? 'There are no Parisians,' said the man Stevenson met in Origny Sainte-Benoîte. 'It is you and I and everybody who are Parisians'.[167] The population increase of Paris was more because of immigration from the rest of France than because of the birthrate. Paris was becoming a twentieth-century city in that only the XXth arrondissement was without a significant non-Parisian population. When Charles Maurras first came to Paris in 1885, he was struck (or so he was to say) by the number of shop names containing the 'foreign' – indeed, 'Jewish' – letters K, W and Z. 'Were the French still at home in France?' he asked himself.[168] Maurice Barrès gave an answer in *Les Déracinés* of 1897, in which seven friends from Lorraine move to Paris to make their careers, but are disorientated by the experiences and find only spiritual anomie.

～～～～～

Paris provides a spectrum of cultural expression that pivots on the double decade 1881–1900, giving the point to Mary-Anne Stevens' remark that 'the avant garde was caught up in the rising tide of religiosity in the 1890s [...] It was a period in which the achievements of the previous decade were modified and sustained to provide an inheritance for the twentieth century.'[169] The age was both *fin-de-siècle* and *limen*, its protagonists Janus-faced. One may take as emblematic of this the dates of Victor Hugo (1808-1885), Jules-Amadée Barbey d'Aurevilly (1808-1889), Nadar (1820-1910), Charles de Freycinet (1828-1923), Juliette Adam (1836-1936), Théodore Duret (1838-1927), Giovanni Boldini (1842-1931), Jean Dampt (1854-1945), Raymond Poincaré (1860-1934), Paul Claudel (1868-1955), Charles Maurras (1868-1952), Caroline Otero (1868-1965), André Gide (1869-1951), Tony Selmersheim (1871-1971), Mistinguett (1875-1956), and Cléo de Mérode (1875-1965). Where these overlap, this work explores.

In 1897, almost at mid-point between the birth of Hugo and the death of Selmersheim, Gide published *Les Nourritures Terrestres*.[170] While this 'caused only a faint ripple in the sea of words'[171] of *fin-de-siècle* literature, yet the ripple reached as far as Dieppe, where the exiled Oscar Wilde bought a copy, and Dublin, when the young Enid Starkie found a copy in a second-hand bookshop. The long result was that she spent three years at the Sorbonne between 1921 and 1924, living an impoverished existence that reads as if from a Latin Quarter novel. Here she met René Ghil[172], André-Ferdinand Hérold[173] and Francis Vielé-Griffin; saw Lugné-Poë[174] act; wrote a thesis on Émile Verhaeren.[175]   Later she projected books on Renée Vivien,[176] Charles Cros[177] and Jules Laforgue; and negotiated an honorary doctorate at Oxford for Gide, who in Oxford in June 1947 made pilgrimage to Oscar Wilde's rooms in Magdalen. We shall become familiar with all these names before this tale is over. The confluence is just sufficient to provide a *différance* that will be worked out in the course of this book, as will be Wilde's accommodation within it. My title is taken from a remark of Wilde's that in politics he espoused an elegant republicanism.[178]

In Paris the 'canker of Romanticism'[179] that still lingered in London had been given its fatal wound as long before as 1845 with the failure of Victor Hugo's *Les Burgraves*. The collapse of the revolution of 1848 into the reactionary Empire of Napoléon III was its death blow: in the sense that new art must always oppose the established, it was the turn of Realism, subject of a manifesto by Champfleury in 1857.[180] A painting in the National Gallery of Ireland by Thomas Couture,[181] whose studio was in Montmartre, neatly shows how Realism appeared to the Romantic or neo-Greek view. A young artist is drawing a pig's head in rather squalid surroundings (there is an empty bottle at his side), while indifferent to the stone or marble head from a classical statue on which he is sitting. This is dated 1865. According to Marvin Carlson the move from Romanticism to Realism was already showing itself in literature in Scribe and Halévy's *La Juive* of 1835, under the influence of Fanny Elssler.[182] The 'école de bon sens' took a new look at the social questions that interested the bourgeoisie, while realism of another kind was demonstrated in Ferdinand Lalou's *Pilules du Diable* (of 1839 at the Cirque Olympique but revived at the Châtelet in 1874), with a train that exploded.

From about 1865 (one may take the death of Ingres in 1867 and the publication of *Thérèse Raquin* in 1868 as waymarks), Realism shaded into Naturalism, to give way in its turn to Symbolism and Impressionism[183] in the mid-1890s, and as with the movements, so between light and shade with Paris itself.

> Round them the grey immensity of Paris, with its deep chasms and rolling billows of roofs, stretched away to the bluish horizon; the whole of the Right Bank lay in the shadow cast by a great ragged sheet of coppery cloud, from the gold fringed edge of which a broad ray of sunlight came down and lit up the myriad windows of the Left bank, striking from them cascades of sparks and making this part of the city stand out bright against a sky washed very clean and clear by the storm.[184]

Wilde distinguished Romanticism and Realism in the preface to *The Picture of Dorian Gray*: 'The nineteenth century dislike of Realism is the rage of Caliban seeing his own face in a glass; the nineteenth century dislike of Romanticism is the rage of Caliban not seeing his own face in a glass'. Symbolism, as we shall see, marked the greatest integration yet of painting, poetry and music: it took Marcel Proust to incorporate sensory perceptions.

~~~~~~~

If Paris is thus a place of illusion, deception and concealment, it lends itself peculiarly to the study of Wilde's shifting identities, as Irishman, Englishman and Frenchman; as Protestant and Catholic; as successful man of letters and as broken exile; as heterosexual and homosexual. The reconstruction of Oscar Wilde's Paris should have been undertaken long ago, perhaps by Philippe Jullian, who was well-placed for the task.[185] Unfortunately his chapter on Wilde in the French capital is full of inaccuracies, and this is also true for Jacques de Langlade and Herbert Lottmann. Nor is this approach the concern of the leading French Wilde scholar, Pascal Aquien; or the more old-fashioned work of Xavier Darcos, neither of whose biographies are available in English.[186] Richard Ellmann restricted himself to a narrative tracing of Wilde's connection with the literary men,[187] so much remains to be done.

Jullian is, however, a source for the account of Wilde's rudeness to Marcel Proust's parents in Paris in April 1894: this is not recorded by Painter. What Painter does recount is that Proust met Wilde at dinner with madame Aubernon de Nerville,[188] and that the impression he made was not good, for his hostess thought him a cross between the Apollo Belvedere and Albert Wolff[189], whom the prejudiced Drumont called a 'creature of no religion, no country and no sex', but to which Painter adds 'a fat, fluting, rouged caricature of Wilde the pervert'.

Possibly there is a little of Wilde in Charlus; and there is, more probably, something of the dangerous, beautiful Lord Alfred Douglas in Charlie Morel.[190]

Whether Proust read anything by Wilde is debatable: Painter implies that he did not.[191] Of course, Proust was not the man to forgo the study of Wilde the man, and when at a dinner party given by the Alphonse Daudets he had the opportunity to meet Wilde's friends the Palmers he

> overwhelmed Mother with questions about his personal habits and personal opinions, and was particularly anxious to know whether Oscar Wilde's courage failed him in the great legal battle with the traditional philistines. He had the idea that Oscar Wilde was fighting all that was stupid and that the codes that condemned him were as much an anachronism as the law for burning witches [...] But he was consoled and smiled delightfully when Mother described to him the courage with which Oscar Wilde faced his accusers.

> 'What harm did he do them? He gave them beauty, wit and a renaissance of the stage, and an intimacy with the culture of Athens – and yet they wanted to kill him. They put old mildewed codes before the beauties which he gave them.'[192]

Alphonse Daudet[193] died in 1897, so this dinner party took place while Wilde was in prison.

~~~~~~~

Wilde skated on thin ice in this world and his activities became of concern to his friends. As early as 28th January 1895 Gide told his mother that Wilde and Douglas were facing ostracism in Paris as well as London, and Paul Valéry also told Madame Gide of Wilde's approximation to 'a Roman emperor of extreme decadence.'[194] Gide, indeed, writes of' 'a persistent rumour' that Wilde had 'strange habits' and that 'already out of prudence numbers of his old friends were deserting him'.[195] This seems to date to Paris, 1894. This concern increased after 1897 when Wilde returned to Paris. 'I hear that Oscar is under surveillance by the French police,' wrote Max Beerbohm. 'I am afraid he may be playing the fool.'[196]

The operative word is 'playing', for it fits the atmosphere of Paris where so much was play. Gertrude Atherton, for example, found Jules Massenet[197] 'a charming creature, volatile, effervescent, as playful as a child',[198] which also suggests this. Play, masquerade, make-believe, transformation: one strikes it again and again as the supreme trait, the dominant metaphor. 'One of the weaknesses of the French,' wrote Atherton's friend Richard Whiteing, 'is a taste for make-believe wickedness, and they play at being naughty as others play at being good.'[199] Wilde, or rather Sebastian Melmoth, slips readily into this. 'For some part of his life Oscar Wilde masqueraded in defiance of Society, and then later on Society made him masquerade in defiance of himself.'[200] 'If a man has a mind to make a fool or vagabond of himself,' wrote Francis Parkman,

> he can do it admirably in Paris; whereof I have seen many instances. If a man has a mind to amuse himself then there is no place like it on earth; diversions of every character, form and degree are waiting for him at every step; let him taste them – then get into the diligence and ride away, or stay, and go to the devil.[201]

For their part, the police were careful spectators rather than players, and the surveillance of Wilde is perfectly possible. Indeed, for what it is worth, which is not much, in 1906 Sherard asserted that 'the fact should be put on record that he was at all times under the close supervision of the police'.[202] In 1928 he elaborated upon this.

> Let me repeat here from my *Life of Wilde* that during the whole time he lived in Paris after his release he was under strict police supervision: Henri Bauër[203] had told me that the Minister of the Interior had informed him that Wilde was being carefully watched by the police, and that on the least provocation he would be arrested, punished and expelled the territory of the Republic, and he asked me to convey this warning to Oscar Wilde.[204]

Sherard's further comment, however, seems to have been inspired by his lifelong desire to absolve Wilde of any behaviour unsuitable to a Victorian drawing-rooM. He approached Chiappe, then Prefect of Police, whom he says had known Wilde as a café companion, and that a search of the Paris police records revealed no trace of Wilde. 'M. Chiappe spoke to me very nicely about Wilde with absolutely nothing in his tone or manner to show that he had conceived at the time or harboured since any unfavourable opinion whatever about the man [...] He had never noticed anything reprehensible in his conduct or conversation.' Sherard further cites another police official who assures him that 'You may deny the truth *in toto* the stories you say have been published about his conduct in Paris during the last years of his life.'[205] This does suggest that Wilde's conduct was under scrutiny, even if it involved no transgression of the law. The scrutiny might even have been by Huysmans, from 1892 sous chef de 4e bureau, Sureté Générale, Ministry of the Interior.[206] That the scrutiny was not always accurate, however, is suggested by the police report of 7th April 1884 that Zola (under surveillance since September 1873) had left Paris: they were a month late.[207]

'There is one part of Paris police work which is exceedingly well done,' says one British Military Attaché with approval, 'and that is the watching and registration of the stranger'.[208] His predecessor had been surprised to be warned by his German and Italian colleagues that he should expect to be shadowed by the police; at one time the Italian (Alessandro Panizzardi) was followed everywhere. W.S. Haine has written that 'police typically kept cafés under close surveillance, especially in working class districts.[209] Regular meetings of large groups, even if non-political like the Hydropathes, were either watched or penetrated; secret agents even attended the annual celebrations that were held to commemorate Henri Murger.[210]

Under its lights, Paris was a well-policed city,[211] though the Préfet de Police was hardly a less impermanent official than any Minister of the Interior.[212] Unlike London or Washington, Paris also had a military governor[213]: during the building strike of 1898 troops were brought in during the night of 8th October and Parisians woke to find them patrolling the streets. The only successful riot was the one that occurred when the travellers at the Gare St Lazare, exasperated beyond endurance by the service, smashed up everything that was breakable.[214] À propos the 1892 cab drivers strike, the United States Minister noted that 'In America this would have been accompanied by disorder, drunkenness and violence, assaults on people and destruction of property [...] but here, although it was impossible to get a carriage for love or money, the police kept everything quiet'.[215] Of the security precautions for the visit of the Tsar with their crackdown on the Russian community, John MacDonald wrote 'the state of panic and siege still haunts me after the interval of eighteen long years',[216] but the police also dealt in minutiæ – an ordinance of 1st May 1881 attempted to ban elaborate ladies' hats from theatres by making it an offence to obstruct the view of those sitting behind, though it turned out to be easier just to ban the women – and in morals. A *commissaire* could enter a private residence to substantiate an adultery – but only before seven o'clock in the evening in winter, nine o'clock in summer. It is difficult to find rationalism behind this extraordinary mixture of public and private moral policing, but Maupassant used it to good effect.[217]

In the fashionable areas the police ensured the undisturbed enjoyment of the boulevardiers, and in the working class quarters ensured that authority was to be remembered. Officers of the Brigade des Réunions attended public meetings in plain clothes – as the préfet de police Louis Andrieux once said 'Remember that each time three of you come together, I will be among you'.[218] The police also exercised some control over the prostitutes, although here as in all cities the relationship was ambiguous. At the low dance hall in the boulevard de Clichy, the Reine Blanche, Maupassant's middle class visitors are reassured by the presence of 'a solemn, motionless, military policeman [...] "There's a constable who looks a reliable type".'[219] The cosmopolitan Felix Moscheles, towards the end of the century thought the policing of the quais in the name of morality more strict, or at any rate more obtrusive, than in his own Bohemian days when he had been a student at the atelier Gleyre in the 1850s.[220] This hardly finds its way into the iconography, although 'La sécurité des rues' by Steinlen (1884), showing a fierce policeman, is an exception, while 'The Arrest' by Jules Lambeaux (1882) shows a pedlar on a street corner being arrested by a policeman and a soldier carrying a rifle.[221] Presumably the police crack-down on gambling hells such as the Arts libéraux in the rue Vivienne in 1884 was the result of political pressure rather than local initiative.

The care with which this was exercised is revealed by Louis Lépine,[222] Prefect of Police from 1893 to 1897 and again from 1899 to 1913, who described his rôle in his memoirs:

> Un préfet de police qu'on ne voit pas, dont on ne connaît pas la physionomie par les caricatures des journaux, qu'on n'a pas coudoyé dans les rues, avec lequel on n'a pas échangé quelques propos, ce préfet-là peut avoir toutes les qualités du monde; pour le Parisien, il lui en manquera toujours une: ce n'est pas son homme.[223]

Lépine 'gave orders to his officers that Verlaine was never to be arrested, no matter what he did', and this casts an interesting light not only on Lépine and on the position of Verlaine, but suggest that the *flic* on the beat would always recognise Verlaine when he saw him. This was a rare dispensation in a state where the maintenance of order, and the ordering of social relationships, was the reality behind the frivolity.

Patricia Mainardi has suggested[224] that the Republic, in its concern for order and moral order, discontinued a process of liberalisation that characterised the last period of the Empire, yet it remained secularist as part of the legacy of 1789, part of being Republican, despite the 'religious fervour, bordering on hysteria'[225] when MacMahon was President. This took the form of a cult for the Sacred Heart, culminating in the building of the Basilica on Montmartre, architecture then as ever in the service of social aims. François Loyer has observed of the 1880s that 'at first glance, the new use of architectural ornament, which greatly changed the way the city looked, might seem rather ambiguous. In fact, there were two contradictory approaches: one was a very dry, severe interpretation of the Haussmann style: the other, an exuberant eclecticism whose raison d'être was above all to oppose the other approach [...] After 1880 [...] there was a burst of creative energy that totally contradicted the rationalists' standardised brand of historicism'.[226] This dialectic between control and freedom, between the moral order and decadence, between reason and emotion, between the bourgeois and the Bohemian, is repeated many times in many forms, as this work explores. In doing so, it rejects the argument advanced by Ian Small – insofar as it relates to Paris and therefore *pro tanto* to England – that 'generally speaking, nineteenth-century French culture is seen as determining the underlying patterns of artistic radicalism.'[227]

The task of policing the moral order took many forms, and policing in a more general sense was carried out not only through censorship of books and plays, but also through the regulation of the religious orders (many of which were teaching orders) and state control of education, as well as by various societies of busybodies, such as the Société Protectrice de l'Enfance, which existed not so much to protect children as to regulate the employment of wet-nurses, the point being that in the moral society, women nursed their own children. All this aroused the satire of Octave Mirbeau, whose M. de Tarves works for the League Against Secular Education, the League for the Suppression of Obscene Publications, the Society for the Promotion of Religious Literature, the Association of Catholic Wet-Nurses for the Feeding of Working-Class Children (Ligue contre l'enseignement laïque, Ligue contre les publications obscènes, Société des bibliothèques amusantes et chrétiennes, Association des biberons congréganistes pour l' allaitement des enfants d' ouvriers). He wants his maid Célestine to become a member of the Society of the Servants of Jesus – and then gives her salacious magazines to read, *Le fin de siècle, Le rigolo, Les petites femmes de Paris*.[228]

Perhaps the strangest manifestation of all this was the motto of the Société Protectrice des Animaux: 'For the moralisation of the labouring classes, for social progress, for international union'. Somehow, the animals have slipped from view.

This desire to control touched hands with censorship both in news management (there was an opaque relationship between the Government and Havas) and also where it reached into the arts, setting up a further source of tension, as Miriam Levin has explained.

> While the language of art education was flexible, allowing individuals a great deal of leeway in interpretation, it required the presence of an external authority to institute and monitor its use. This fact raises the question of whether the Republicans' programme to create independent and self-motivated individuals caught them in a paradoxical situation that contradicted their aim.[229]

In the official view, 'art for art's sake' and art as simple play were rejected as self-indulgent, anti-social, and therefore morally suspect pleasures to be discouraged wherever possible, or else harmlessly canalised. This, in Levin's view, amounted to 'the management of human sensibilities'.

> The Republicans attributed to art the power to transform a multitude of individual psychic realities into socio-economic realities.
>
> Yet this synthetic environment perpetuated an illusion of a middle class composed of independent and self-motivated individuals [...] There was an element of deception introduced by Republicans. In part it was self-deception arising from their own feelings about art and their belief that it had helped them achieve their position as leaders of the middle class.[230]

The rather straight-laced Richard Harding Davis ('a robust flower of American muscular Christianity', according to Will Rothenstein, who handles him satirically[231]) worried about a contagion of acculturation in that attraction of make-believe, saying disapprovingly that 'the American Colony is not wicked, but it would like to be thought so, which is much worse'.[232] ('I do not say you are it, but you look it, which is just as bad,' Queensberry had said to Wilde.) Another serious Bostonian, Francis Parkman, 'finding that complete idleness now seemed necessary, and *preferring Paris to any other place for such a life*, went abroad for the winter, establishing himself at 21 boulevard St Michel'.[233]

Make-believe wickedness was also identified by Edmund Gosse in his 1912 essay 'The Hôtel de Rambouillet'.

> If this age dotes on the dirtiness of tramps, it is because every one of us is obliged to be occupied and clean; and if the apache is the object of our poetry, it is because, in our extremely settled, confident and comfortable lives, we miss the excitement of being in personal danger [...] If London or Paris were to burn, even if only for a fortnight, literature and art would

hurry back to the study of princesses and the language of the Golden Age.[234]

Apart from offering a glimpse into Gosse's secret imaginings (and one should remember that Marcel Schwob thought him 'charming but pedantic'[235]), this passage firmly locates Paris as the place other to respectability (the reference to apaches is the signifier here). This was of some concern to the English, especially when it became necessary to find families in which their children could be boarded to learn French or music, like Angela and Edith Barnes, daughters of the Vicar of Heavitree in Devonshire. They and their sister Irene (who became the actress Irene Vanbrugh) boarded with a music teacher, Signor Marcolini and his English wife in the boulevard Haussmann, before removing to Passy, where 'Mme Clerc, a hard-working, jolly Frenchwoman, whose husband had a clerical job with the railways, ran her small flat, eking out their small income by taking in English girls who studied'.[236] This was in 1897/8.

Gosse's essay also affords us a wry glance at the difference between Gosse's imaginings should Paris burn, and those of Victor Hugo, cited earlier in this chapter. Paris at once becomes a site where the master narratives of modernism – sex, time, space, identity – are on the loose.

CHAPTER TWO

PARIS MUTUELS

'Paris is always within reach if anything new turns up.'
– Lord Derby to Lord Lyons.[237]

'Ask a quite ordinary Frenchman to come and dine with you in London,
and see what a genial and charming person he can be. Then go and call on
him when you find yourself in Paris – and you will soon learn to leave
quite ordinary Frenchmen alone, on their own side of the Channel.'
– George du Maurier.[238]

'And how, my dearest Dombey, did you find that delightfullest of cities?'
'It was cold,' returned Dombey.
'Gay as ever,' said Mrs Skewton, 'of course.'
'Not particularly. I thought it dull,' said Mr Dombey.
– Charles Dickens: *Dombey & Son*.[239]

MUCH of the London-Paris axis can be linked to the railway timetable,
first published in 1882. The preferred route was Newhaven-Dieppe and the
Gare St Lazare[240], rather than the more expensive Dover-Calais and the
Gare du Nord, which perhaps explains why Robbie Ross investigated
Dieppe as a place of exile for Wilde. The 9.00 a.M. train from Charing
Cross allowed one to arrive in Paris at 4.45. The fashionable Club Train
left Charing Cross at 3.00 p.m.[241] and it was possible to leave Paris at 3.45
p.m., change at Amiens into the Basle Express, and arrive at Dover in time
for boat and train connections that would leave one in London twenty
minutes before midnight. In August 1886 Oliver Wendell Holmes went to
Paris viâ Folkestone-Boulogne: 'leaving London at twenty minutes before
ten in the forenoon, we arrived in Paris at six in the afternoon'.[242] The
standard fare was £3/-/-. A Channel Tunnel was even then discussed, and
work begun, and the sea route would have been superseded long before the
Eurostar, had the idea of M. Baudin, Minister for Public Works in 1900,
been adopted. With a certain lack of hold on reality, but falling in with the
belief in electricity, he suggested slinging electric cables under the Straits
of Dover, from which cable cars would be suspended.[243]

Oscar Wilde was neither the first nor the most frequent London visitor to seek a place in Parisian intellectual society. While it is clear that Paris had always exerted a pull for the English, this quickened after 1870,[244] so that Wilde's impact is to be assessed against that of his contemporaries. Rudyard Kipling, who was later to claim 'a life-long love for France', first visited Paris in 1878, with his father, Lockwood Kipling. Lockwood, who was working on the Indian Pavilion at the Exhibition, turned Rudyard loose in the city: 'It was an education itself. [Lockwood] also saw to it that I should learn French at least for my own amusement [...] French as an accomplishment was not well-seen at English schools in my time, and knowledge of it connoted leanings towards immorality'[245] – or as Lady Bracknell said, 'French songs I cannot possibly allow. People always seem to think that they are improper'. A visit to the Salon brought Kipling before the picture by Pascal Dagnan-Bouveret[246] of Des Grieux kneeling in front of the body of Manon Lescaut and this, viâ the abbé Prévost, resurfaced later, for *The Light that Failed* was a sort of inverted, metagrobolized phantasmagoria on *Manon*.[247] He was also to fall under the influence of the novels of 'Gyp', the right-wing novelist who is less well known as Sybille Gabrielle Marie Antoinette de Riquetti de Mirabeau, comtesse de Martel et de Janville.[248] Kipling, of course, came to understand the parts played by the transformative, the exchanging of identities: Morrowby Jukes, Lieutenant Golightly, Holden, Strickland, Kim, The Friendly Brook, Dick Heldar, Fleete, Mowgli, Hurree Babu, Friars Pardon, Peachey Carnehan and Daniel Dravot, Lispeth, Colonel Creighton, Puck, Dayspring Mishandled, 'The Worm', the bank fraud ... The list is almost endless.

His 1878 visit induced Kipling to adapt Wordsworth to Tennyson, relocating Paris as other site in very radical fashion:

> I hold it truth with him who sung
> Unpublished melodies,
> Who wakes in Paris, being young
> O'summer, wakes in Paradise.[249]

In late May 1890, Kipling again was in Paris for four days, visiting Flo Garrard and possibly meeting Charles Furse.[250] It is the more remarkable how little attention has been paid by Kipling's biographers to his visits to France, or to his popularity there with such writers as Robert d'Humières or Marcel Schwob, who persuaded Colette to read him: by 1904, Remy de Gourmont was noting 'Maintenant Kipling est à la mode et Wells est en

train de conquérir la popularité'.[251] Andrew Lycett adds that Paris was
Carrie Kipling's favourite city.[252]

Robert Louis Stevenson was also in Paris in 1879, assisting Fleeming
Jenkin at his work on the Exhibition. Stevenson was very much at home
in France. His stepson Lloyd Osbourne said that 'France had a profound
influence on Stevenson; mentally he was half a Frenchman; in taste, habits
and prepossessions he was almost totally French. Not only did he speak
French admirably and read it like his mother tongue, but he loved both
country and people and was really more at home in France than anywhere
else.'[253] This is a useful yardstick against which to measure Wilde,
although it is no easier to arrive at a view of Stevenson's French than it is
of Wilde's. 'Bob [R.A.M. Stevenson, Louis' cousin] spoke French
somewhat hesitantly, choosing his words with care, but with excellent
knowledge of the idiom; Louis' French was not unlike his cousin's.'[254]
(Of the third musketeer in this group, Will Low, it was said that his French
was the joke of Montparnasse.[255]) Their taste in literature was similar, for
Stevenson read Zola, Balzac, Baudelaire, Daudet, and de Musset, and
wrote on Victor Hugo as early as 1874;[256] although Wilde travelling with a
donkey in the Cevennes is about as likely as Wilde canoeing from
Antwerp to Grez.[257]

The exhibition of 1878 also gives us a rare glimpse of Lawrence Alma-
Tadema in Paris, for he won a gold medal there. (We also get an even rarer
glimpse of his wife,[258] one of the only two women invited to exhibit and
winner of a silver medal.) This imperfectly anglicised Dutch painter must
have been much at ease with painters like Gérôme and that 'fossilised old
bourgeois painter' William Bouguereau,[259] staying when in Paris with the
art dealers Pilgeram and Lefevre in the rue de Lancry, a street which, not
far from the Gare de l'Est, one can hardly suppose to have been *bon ton*.
He was also a friend of Paderewski,[260] giving the American actress Mary
Anderson a letter of introduction to him when she was in Paris with her
husband J.M. (Tony) de Novarro on their wedding tour in 1889 (they were
staying with de Novarro's 'Aunt Kate at her attractive apartment in the
Champs Elysées'[261]).

Alma-Tadema's 'Expectations' was shown at the Salon of 1889, and
attracted the favourable attention of Robert de la Sizeranne. Here further
research into Alma-Tadema may be justified.

~~~~~~~

By the 'eighties, the English had become more and more familiar with France in general and Paris in particular: when Wilde removed himself there in 1882 and again in 1891, he was part of a movement, not setting a trend. Paris in April was as much part of the social round for what later came to be known as the international set as was Scotland in August or the Riviera in February. Moreover, French influence was as manifest in London as American influence was a hundred years later, from plays and fashions to novels and servants. Wilde gives Dorian Gray a French manservant, Gladys Lady Windermere a French chef. Lady Bracknell extols the virtues of a good French lady's maid; Lady Windermere's maid Rosalie is presumably French – Rosalie is Hélène Grandjean's maid in Zola's *Un Page d'amour*.

The friendship of Wilde's lover John Gray with Ricketts and Shannon led to Gray's introduction to Félix Fénéon, and this in turn eventually led to enthusiasm for the work of the Goncourts, to meetings with Verlaine and Mallarmé. With an essay on the Goncourts Gray became yet another 'literary mediator between France and England'[262]. He first visited Paris in mid-July 1890 (staying at the Hôtel Continental, which must have strained his pocket) and found Fénéon through inquiry at Vanier's bookshop[263] on the quai St Michel; hence the introduction to Gray that Fénéon gave Lucien Pissarro. Gray told that Fénéon that he was 'the last of a little band of artists, painters and men letters in London which, like yourself, cares about nothing except art', and despite Gray's 'amateur command of French and of the new French poetry',[264] Fénéon generously took him at his own estimation, introducing him to Francis Vielé-Griffin, who had started the review *Entretiens politiques et littéraires* that May with Henri de Régnier[265] and Paul Adam.[266] Vielé-Griffin commissioned an article on Rossetti; but Gray was far more interested in writing on the French poets for English consumption than on English poets for the French. More dramatic in its consequences, of course, was the effect of Ricketts and Shannon bringing Gray to the attention of Oscar Wilde.

John Singer Sargent[267] was another bridge. The process of exchange can be indicated by the example of the London visit in 1885 of prince Edmond de Polignac, comte Robert de Montesquiou and the fashionable doctor (and man of fashion) Samuel Pozzi.[268] Sargent introduced them to Henry James; James introduced them to Whistler. Wilde had met Sargent at dinner, where Paul Bourget was also present, as early as April 1883.[269] The painter was an admirer of Leconte de Lisle, the leader and best known of the Parnassians, and a close friend of Monet and Helleu; like Bourget he used the Café d'Orsay,[270] overlooking the rue du Bac: Wilde and Robert

Sherard would meet both men there in 1883. Although he moved to London in 1885, Sargent was one of the subscribers to the fund to present Manet's 'Olympia' to the Louvre in 1889 along with Durand-Ruel, Huysmans, Antonin Proust,[271] Toulouse-Lautrec, Helleu, Rodin, Boldini and others.[272] His painting 'Claude Monet painting at the edge of a wood' dates to 1887.[273] Rothenstein also notes Sargent's close friendship with Émile Verhaeren and the Laurence Harrisons, which may help explain Kenneth Mc Conkey's rather obscure comment that Sargent 'sought to derange his visual language.'[274]

There were also links between Sargent and the musical world. When in 1883 he moved his studio from the rue de Notre-Dame-des-Champs to 41 boulevard Berthier, it was to a house owned by Paul Poirson, a friend of Gounod and Massenet. Massenet's opera *Berengère et Anatole*, first performed at the Cercle de l'union artistique in February 1876 and last performed at the Renaissance for the benefit for the régisseur P. Callais on 15th October 1876, had a libretto by Henri Meilhac and Paul Poirson; Gounod set the poem 'Nuit Silencieuse' by Paul Poirson and Louis Gallet to music. Sargent himself was an advocate for Gabriel Fauré, his 'greatest friend' according to Jacques-Émile Blanche.[275] Sargent's portrait of Fauré dates to 1898 when the composer was in London. Madame Paul Poirson, also painted by Sargent, was before her marriage Seymourina Cuthbert, an illegitimate daughter of Richard Lord Hertford, and so presumptive half-sister to Sir Richard Wallace – the Poirson daughter was named Richardine.

Sargent also provided another link between London (or, at any rate London society) and Paris when he exhibited his portrait of Lord Ribblesdale in the Salon. Ribblesdale himself viewed it, attracting admiring glances and references to 'ce grand diable d'un milord anglais'. Ribblesdale, or Thomas Lister as he was then, had spent a good deal of his childhood and youth in France, and studied art with a historical painter called Comte. He and his wife Charty (Charlotte Tennant) continued to spend a good deal of time there – Charty took an apartment in October 1896, and brought her sister Margot Asquith to stay in May 1898 when the latter was grieving for Gladstone.[276] Ribblesdale's brother Regy Lister spent many years in Paris, first in 1886 when he was working for his Foreign Office examinations, then in the British Embassy from 1889, and he became a friend of the prince and princesse de Sagan[277] and of the comtesse de Pourtalès.[278] (These Listers were not related to the medical scientist Sir Joseph Lister, who visited Paris in 1892 to present an address from the Royal Society to Louis Pasteur.)

The Listers knew Paris because their parents had moved there in order to curtail their expenditure,[279] and this experience was also the introduction to the city for the family of the young Charles Rivers Wilson,[280] who became as a result the close friend of comte Joseph de Montbron and comte Julien de Rochechouart. The baron de Moidrey became his brother-in-law. 'I was as much at home in Paris as in London,' he was later to say.[281]

Sargent had studied under Carolus-Duran (whose portrait he exhibited in the Salon of 1879) and one of his contemporaries was R.A.M. Stevenson, whom Sargent also painted. Will Low, referring to himself and the two Stevensons as the Three Musketeers, reckoned that Bob Stevenson 'in all the qualities of dominating wit [...] outshone us all'.[282] As a critic R.A.M. Stevenson was not universally beloved: 'Read with some pleasure of R.A.M. Stevenson's death. Though toothless, and belated, he had lived on the works of others. He was insincere and pettifogging to the last, and against all Art in its higher and creative manifestations,' wrote Charles Ricketts in 1900.[283] Nevertheless, he was one of the nodes of the London-Paris axis; Yeats admired his conversation and thought his charm superior to Wilde's;[284] and he was one of the supporters of Wilde's application to join the Savile Club.

Other British students with Carolus-Duran at this time were Henry Detmold, Arthur Hesletine, Henry Enfield, Hamilton Minchin, and Middleton Jameson,[285] the brother of Dr L.S. Jameson of the Jameson Raid. Bob Stevenson was also one of the group of painters and writers that formed a colony at Grez-sur-Loing, based at the Hôtel Chevillon. This drew Fanny Osbourne, another American in Paris and studying with her daughter Belle at the women's atelier of the Académie Julian[286] in the impasse des Panoramas, and led to her meeting Robert Louis Stevenson, her future husband, who spent several weeks at Grez in the summer of 1875, in the autumn of 1876 and again in July 1878.

The Académie Julian, begun in 1868 by Rodolphe Julian[287] in the rue du Dragon in the former dancing academy of Markouski became the leading establishment for foreign art students in that city of art students, offering an alternative both to the official École des Beaux-Arts and to the private arrangements at studios. When George Moore arrived in 1873 it was still very small, Julian himself living on the premises. There were four American students, three English (including Arthur Temple Clay, later Sir Arthur), one Chilean and the rest French.[288] Julian's owed much of its success to its admission of lady students ('crowded to suffocation with ladies from every quarter of the globe, Swedes, Russians, and four or five

Americans' – two of these being 'Yankee old maids'[289]). Women could also study the male nude at Julian's, the social effect of which was to set in train another alteration. Julian himself thought that 'sometimes his female students are as clever as the young men',[290] and indeed he married one of them, Amélie Beaury-Saurel, who took over the Académie Julian after her husband's death in 1907. Henrietta Rae studied there, and there came Kipling's beloved Florence Garrard and her friend Mabel Price, transformed into Maisie and the strangely nameless red-headed girl in *The Light that Failed.*[291]

A.S. Hartrick, following to Paris Harrington Mann,[292] Frank Emanuel[293] and George Gascoyne 'joined up with a number of other English students from the Royal Academy Schools and elsewhere in the Académie Julian' where he reckoned there were about four hundred students 'gathered from every country and nationality in the civilised world'.[294] Most names are lost, were perhaps lost within days of their leaving; others can be recovered from divers sources. English art students alone formed 'a vast migration' to Paris, as Anita Gruetzner has written, adding significantly 'To understand what lured students to Paris in the 1880s, we should look to Paris itself.'[295]

Although the École did not admit women until 1897, other art schools did – such as 'Amitrano's', where Somerset Maugham's Philip Carey studies.

> Philip went to buy drawing materials; and next morning at the stroke of nine, trying to seem self-assured, he presented himself at the school. He had been anxious about the reception he would have as a *nouveau*, for he had read a good deal of the rough joking to which a newcomer was exposed at some of the studios; but Mrs. Otter had reassured him.

> 'Oh, there's nothing like that here,' she said. 'You see, about half our students are ladies, and they set a tone to the place.'[296]

Harold Burke was a pupil of both Émile Vernet-Lecomte and Gérôme; William Henry Bartlett was at both the Académie Julian (under Bouguereau) and the École des Beaux Arts (under Gérôme) in the mid '70s. Also at both, in about 1880, was Alfred East, later R.A., influenced by Corot and other French landscape artists. Hartrick, himself of Scots, Irish and Welsh descent and later to illustrate Thomas Hardy's *A Changed Man*, studied first under Gustave Boulanger and Jules Lefebvre and then under Fernand Cormon: he was sufficiently unconventional to marry his step-sister, the artist Lily Blatherwick. Shirley Fox was then the youngest student that Julian had admitted, being hardly more than a boy – indeed, he had a spell at school, the Collège Chaptal, before returning to Julian's. Fox had been taken to Paris by his parents (his father worked for *Galignani's Messenger*, becoming editor and then editor of the European edition of the *New York Herald*), and was more Parisian than most English students, for all that when his parents returned for a time to England, he lived in the Hôtel de Londres et New York.[297] Later he took a studio in the rue Jouffroy and lived in Paris until the end of the 1880s, continuing to visit as long as his parents lived there, as they did till 1904. Shirley Fox's reminiscences[298] are a primary source for the Académie Julian, well supported by John Cameron's illustrations; he nevertheless felt impelled to reassure his readers that 'although at one period I lived almost entirely with French people, and spoke and thought in their language as readily as any native, I still retained beneath the surface an absolutely British mind.'[299] Fox is too minor a character to warrant exploration of the interplay of surface and *la vie intérieure* in his life or work, but the tension suggested is one that informs study of the expatriates in reaction to their Parisian occasions, and in that light it is worth recounting how Fox occasionally hoaxed his acquaintances by disguising himself as a girl, a piece of cross-dressing that neatly epitomises the gender ambiguity of his first name and the trans-species suggestion of his last.

Around 1890, the English painters Hugh Bellingham-Smith (a former pupil of Legros at the Slade, and in Paris studying under J-P. Benjamin-Constant), Harold Harvey, Robert Polhill Bevan and the Scot Joseph Crawhall[300] were also at the Académie Julian, the latter staying in the same pension as A.S. Hartrick (the painter John Macallan Swan stayed there too), and another Scot, Francis Cadell,[301] was a contemporary at the Académie Julian of Paul Henry, as was the Spaniard Manuel Ortiz de Zarate.[302] Eric Forbes-Robertson went to the Académie Julian in 1885 and stayed in Paris until 1900, becoming a friend of Sérusier and Jarry, and being painted by Gauguin. This brother of Norman Forbes and Johnston Forbes-Robertson, and once addressed by Wilde as his 'affectionate friend', met Wilde by chance in Paris in late spring 1899 and kept in touch.[303] Harold Knight was there, studying under Benjamin-Constant and Jean-Paul Laurens,[304] but returned to England when his money ran out. Among Hartrick's contemporaries were Gibbon, who had once managed a Manchester cotton mill, the future cartoonist Leonard Raven-Hill ('an impish figure'), and a man called Jacquet who was 'half French, half Mexican and wholly American'.[305] Before the century ended, Henri Pierre Roché was a student there, and more than fifty years later was able to draw upon his memories for his novel *Jules et Jim*, if not always quite accurately, as when he calls the Bal des Quatz' Arts the Quat-z'Arts.[306]

The attraction of Julian's in pulling British and American art students to Paris cannot be under-emphasised. For many it was an introduction to the Paris art world that was rarely relinquished, even if at the time they had little to do with the wider world, or their experience was indifferent – Harold Knight only stayed nine months, for example. Philip Wilson Steer, at Julian's in 1882 and learning little under Bouguereau, 'worked industriously, going little outside the daily round of hotel and atelier'[307] – the hotel being first the Beau Séjour in the boulevard Poissonnière, then the Britannique[308] in the avenue Victoria, where the future illustrator G.R. Halkett was also staying. Steer's contemporaries included James Charles, James Elder Christie, T.B. Kennington, W.J. Laidley (an ex-barrister who later became the mainstay of the New English Art Club), a doctor Wells and the son of Tom Taylor of *Punch*. Steer then studied (with Edward Stott[309] and Arthur Rendall) under Cabanel at the École des Beaux Arts, until the compulsory French exam, intended to reduce the number of foreign students, drove him away. 'What happened to Steer in Paris?' asks his biographer. 'It is tempting to suppose that he was open to every avant-garde influence available in the years 1882-1884, but the immediate results of his stay indicate no such thing.'[310] Indeed, he had never even heard of Manet until going to the retrospective at Durand-Ruel in January 1884. Steer, although influenced by Cazin, in fact was not 'bitten' by Paris, only returning once, in 1907, according to MacColl, but according to Laughton possibly in 1885, 1887, 1889, and 1891, though definitely not between 1894 and 1907; he also visited Boulogne during the 1880s. In 1910 he was dismissive of the London exhibition 'Manet and the Post-Impressionists'. His presence in Orpen's 'Homage to Manet' of 1909, however representative it might have been of the New English Art Club, may not have been altogether justified, although it does add to the ambivalent ambience created by Orpen's incorporation into the picture of Manet's portrait of Eva Gonzalez, who is herself shown painting, so that her work becomes a painting within a painting within a painting, a layering increased when 'Homage to Manet' is reproduced, and when it is the subject of the onlooker's gaze.[311]

As Steer, so with William Nicholson and James Pryde at the beginning of the 1890s: their time at the Académie Julian seems to have left them untouched, though Nicholson did acquire a housekeeper/model/mistress called Marie Laquelle and was to exhibit a portrait of Sarah Bernhardt in 1897.[312] Other students at the Académie Julian passed on to greater obscurity, such as Albert Wilkinson and Sidney Hebblewhite, acquaintances of Chris Healy's, or Harold Harvey, taught by Benjamin-Constant and J.-P. Laurens, and perhaps we shall never know where some of them studied, or the lives they lived. Obscurity awaits its historian, and presumably will continue to do so, though one may be able to learn more of Sidney Storr, for instance, who was Walter Sickert's friend and collaborator, or Arthur Hacker,[313] studying with Bonnat in 1880-1, or William Fortescue, or Frank Wright Bourdillon, in 1883-1884, which were also the years in which Fred Jackson was at the École des Beaux Arts under Lefebvre and Boulanger. Ralph Todd spent time in Paris, and is now, like so many here named, associated chiefly with Newlyn. With Lefebvre can also be associated the name of William Gerard Barry[314] from Co Cork, who studied with him and with Boulanger, and then with Carolus-Duran. His 'Retour de la pêche aux crevettes' was exhibited in the Salon of 1886.

One can also list Arthur Douglas Peppercorn, at the École des Beaux Arts under Gérôme in 1870, whose name deserves greater recognition; John Noble Barlow who studied under Benjamin-Constant; Samuel John 'Lamorna' Birch, who spent 1895 to 1896 studying at the Académie Colarossi in the rue de la Grande Chaumière; Albert Chevallier Tayler at J.-P. Laurens' atelier in 1881-2 and possibly also at Carolus-Duran's. William John Wainwright was also at Laurens' in 1881, as was Henry Hack Tuke from 1881 to 1883. To this last, who stayed with J.-E. Blanche in Passy, a certain reputation clings, as it does possibly to Thomas Gotch and his wife Caroline. Both studied with Laurens in 1881-2; Caroline (then Caroline Yates) had previously been at the Académie Julian in 1881. Of Gotch it has been judiciously written that 'unfortunately the subject matter which Gotch chose has made him best known among admirers of pictures of young girls, but he was once one of the most respected artists in Britain.'[315] From 1884, before emigrating to the United States, Dawson Dawson-Watson studied and painted in Paris and Giverny, where with Thomas Meteyard, John Leslie Breck and the poet Richard Hovey (author of *Songs from Vagabondia*) he produced the journal *Le Courrier Innocent*: his 'Giverny' of 1888 and his 'Giverny looking west' of 1892 are now both in the Musée de l'Art américain in Giverny. More involved in the French art world was Wilfred De Glehn, whose French *particule* disguised the fact that he had been born von Glehn at Sydenham, in south London. De Glehn was in Paris from 1880 to 1886, studied at the École des Beaux Arts under Moreau, and showed in the Salon and with Durand–Ruel in 1891. He became Associetaire of the Société des Artistes Français in 1895.

Art schools, studios, students: here was a benign spiral of upward growth. This was seen both by Julian, who made a success of it, and by Whistler, who did not. The Atelier Rollins was founded in the early 1880s

specifically to cater to enhanced demand, beginning as a small studio in
Montparnasse, with afternoon classes which attracted the more serious
students from the École des Beaux Arts, where only morning classes were
held. This enterprise soon needed larger premises, in the rue Campagne-
Première[316], where Aimé Morot and Antonin Mercié were engaged as
professors of painting and sculpture. Outgrowing this, Rollins moved to
the rue Notre-Dame-des-Champs. 'Students of all ages and nationalities
flocked to the place, those from England and America being in the
majority.'[317] These included the future Academicians F.W. Pomeroy and
George Frampton. There was enough overspill for Rollins to induce
Benjamin-Constant to open an associated atelier in the impasse Hélène,
which again attracted a cosmopolitan crowd, Belgian, Swiss, Spanish,
Italian, American and English, and with a great number of Scots. M.
Rollins is not, however, to be traced under that name: he was actually an
Englishman, an ex-actor called Rawlins. His success led to other financial
ventures which brought him down. His studios closed and he vanishes
from history.

To Grez too came Theodore Robinson, the Californian Hiram Bloomer
and another American, a sculptor called Ernest Pasdessus who seems to
have risen no higher, as well as the Scots Walter (later Sir Walter) and
William Simpson and Bob and Louis Stevenson.[318] Fanny Stevenson in
her introduction to *An Inland Voyage* said of Walter that 'His leniency
towards the faults of others very nearly touched the borders of cynicism', a
remark that neatly suggests the relationships of this band of Bohemians.
Fanny Stevenson (Osbourne as she was then) is described by her
biographer in terms that suggest her adaptability, certainly, but perhaps her
mutability as well, for she 'would always pass for a foreigner, even at
home. From the plains of Indiana to the Pacific Islands, from San
Francisco to Grez-sur-Loing, from Edinburgh to Sidney, she was always
from somewhere else'.[319]

A.S. Hartrick also 'endeavoured to keep up with what was going on in the
art world in Paris by going over for an occasional week, usually when the
Salons were open'[320] throughout the 1890s. His usual companion was the
London Irishman Edmund Sullivan,[321] the illustrator who worked on the
Daily Graphic and the *Pall Mall Magazine*, and who Hartrick thought the
'naturally most gifted of the younger black-and-white artists of my time,
not excepting Beardsley'.[322]

The study of architecture drew few English to Paris, differing from the
Americans. Richard Phené Spiers was the only leading architect of the day

to train in Paris at the École des Beaux Arts, though certain English architects went to look: Norman Shaw and Ernest Newton went to examine French apartment blocks, for instance, with their commission for Albert Hall Mansions in mind, and Shaw became an admirer of the railway stations. Shaw and W.H. Lascelles designed a house for the 1878 Expo, in the Queen Anne style but using concrete bricks, looking backwards and forwards simultaneously.

~~~~~

Another intermediary between London and Paris was the journalist and writer of comic plays Joe Comyns Carr, Carr 'with his lion head, his flowing beard, his fine diction and choice of words'.[323] It comes as something of a surprise to find him described as 'one of the most remarkable personalities involved in the dissemination of English art in France'.[324] As the London correspondent of the illustrated journal L'Art, he was frequently in Paris on business: 'M. Gauchez, the proprietor of L'Art, gave us wonderful dinners at the old Maison Dorée, as well as at quaint little out-of-the-way eating-houses, now long since disappeared, but which produced some of the best meals I have ever tasted'.[325] The Carrs, and Alice Comyns Carr's sister Alma, who was married to the Paris-based painter Laurence Harrison,[326] also dined with Whistler in Paris towards the end of the painter's life, and it was Whistler, fluctuating between London and Paris, who was the greatest bridge (if this Irish bull may be permitted). Among younger people, the wealthy amateur painter Arthur Studd[327] would invite Paris acquaintances back to Hyde Park Gardens. These comings and goings need to be calibrated with those of H.B. Farnie, the Scottish writer of libretti. 'Many are credited to him but most of his work was in collaboration or taken outright from the French. He would run over to Paris, do the rounds, choose his fancy, and write the libretto on the way home,' says Barry Duncan, but Richard Trauber is both more and less enthusiastic about the man he calls a 'literary hack without any noticeable talent for witty dialogue and even less for rhyming ability', saying that he was 'almost single-handedly responsible for the initial success of the opéra-bouffe in England.'[328] His greatest triumphs were Offenbach's Madame Favart, when his libretto served for that of Chivot and Duru when it ran for five hundred and two performances at the Strand Theatre from April 1879 and its successor, Audran's Olivette, which ran for four hundred and sixty six. Madame Favart was even praised by Bernard Shaw for its 'grace, gaiety and intelligence'.

It was art criticism that first took Edmund Gosse to Paris, when he went with the sculptor Hamo Thornycroft to review the Salon of 1881 for the *Fortnightly Review*, returning for the same purpose in 1882 and 1885. It was the theatre that chiefly claimed their attention, however, on what appears to be a somewhat unvaried menu of lunchtime sole vin blanc, at least on that first visit. 'In Paris, whenever he was there, he went night after night. He was disgusted at *Sardou* in 1881, delighted with Molière in 1882.'[329] He also found 'Coppel's new piece at the Odéon in verse and very stately and declamatory [...] Victor Hugo's *Lucrezia Borgia* was wonderful.'[330] In 1885 it was Corneille at the Comédie Française, and the circus. France became for Gosse 'the country which was to mean more to him than any other', although his spoken French was rather literary and academic, doubtless derived from his reading *Le Figaro* and the *Journal des Débats*, and he himself referred to it as shallow.[331] In February 1904 his French connection was saluted by a dinner organized by the Société des Conférences at Durand's when some fifty guests met to honour him.

John Barlas, the anarchist poet who wrote under the ambiguous name Evelyn Douglas, and was befriended by Wilde, also reviewed the Paris Salon from time to time and occasionally met Wilde in Paris.[332] D.S. MacColl went to cover the Salons for *The Spectator* in May 1893; four years later he married Andrée Zabé, the daughter of a doctor in the avenue de Neuilly, whose own mother was 'Bébé' (Adèle), sister of Apollonie Sabatier. At about that time Chris Healy saw 'walk through the Louvre, dictating criticisms of the pictures and statuary to a shorthand writer'.[333] Israel Zangwill also took a studio in the avenue de Maine at this time, writing there his *Dreamers of the Ghetto*.[334] Somewhere in all this is Willie Heath, a beautiful young Englishman whose mix of 'spirituality, mystery and sexual ambiguity' attracted Marcel Proust. This Mr W.H., said to resemble Leonardo's portrait of John the Baptist, died in October 1893 at the age of twenty-two.[335]

From 1892, Sir Charles Dilke spent a month in Paris at each Christmas time. This coincided with Wilde's being in Paris in December in 1897, 1898 and 1899. Wilde had dined with Dilke in 1881, and Sir Rupert Hart-Davis gives an anecdote recounted by W.H. Chesson of Wilde saying in 1898 'I've only one fault to find with Dilke; he knows too much about everything. It is hard to have a good story interrupted by a fact. I admit accuracy up to a certain point, but Dilke's accuracy is almost a vice'.[336] This was an unerring description of Dilke's conversation and suggests recent encounter, the fallen politician and the fallen playwright each out-talking the other, but there is no evidence of any meeting that I have so far unearthed.

The francophilia of Dilke, John Morley and other English Liberals softened some of the asperities of French anglophobia. Gladstone seems to have been generally admired and his death in May, 1898 was marked by sympathetic articles in the press. Dilke's Liberal colleague, the very different Sir Henry Campbell-Bannerman, was also a frequent visitor to Paris, usually at Whitsun between 1886 and 1892, and after his annual visit to Marienbad. His biographer[337] also records visits in May 1885, December 1889, March 1895, from the 6th to the 13th October 1899, and in April 1900, as well as subsequently: Henry Brackenbury first met him in Paris in 1881.[338] Campbell-Bannerman was Chief Secretary for Ireland in 1885, when the activities of the Paris Fenians would have been known to him. As Secretary of State for War under Rosebery he was far removed from any connection with the Wilde case, and although Wilde was in Paris during Campbell-Bannerman's 1899 visit we do not know if either noticed the other. Spender is silent on how 'C.B.' spent his time in Paris, doubtless because it was too everyday rather than too scandalous, only mentioning a dinner at Foyot's because it was followed by a heart attack – this in 1907 – but Bannerman was a cosmopolitan and some interesting juxtapositions may yet be discovered, either political or social.

Another British M.P., so far unidentified, neglected his Parliamentary duties in pursuit of Nina Melcy, an actress at the Gymnase: there is more to be discovered here in this form of exchange. Captain Cecil Norton M.P. (later Lord Rathcreedan) on a visit to Paris met at his hotel 'a charming lady, a widow, with whom I became great friends, and whom I frequently visited afterwards whenever I could get a few days leave to cross the Channel.' One may doubt the platonic nature of this, as Norton believed in 'A Frenchwoman for a mistress, but an Englishwoman for a wife'.[339] Yet, however obscure at times, such Anglo-French interchange is better documented than in the financial sphere. Lord Redesdale (then Bertram Mitford), for example, in the 1870s was often in Paris as a director of a French railway company, but this is accorded one line in his volumes of memoirs, and he does not even say which company.[340]

~~~~~~~

That Wilde, abandoning the Italy that had first attracted him, should find his way to the city of light is not surprising. Wilde's Europe did not take in either the Vienna of the Secession;[341] or Brussels, almost as much the

home of avant-garde theatre and art as Paris, and with considerable
connection between the two,[342] not least the telephone link opened on 1st
February 1887. It does appear, however, that Wilde at one time considered
Brussels as a place of exile,[343] and another alternative Wilde can be
constructed from that possibility, building on the suggestion of Jean Paul
Bouillon that Brussels was 'neutral ground, half way between English
æstheticism and French rationalism'.[344] One may also view Brussels as
Paris's own 'Paris'. According to the anonymous author of *The Pretty
Women of Paris* 'the capital of Belgium is the recognised centre for the
publication of all the erotic works of the French language',[345] a statement
which, if scarcely verifiable, at least gives an aperçu into contemporary
ideas. There was certainly a dubious publishing house there called
Kistemaeckers, whose volume of stories by Maupassant probably helped
fasten the reputation of indecency upon him, and Huysmans' prostitute
novel *Marthe: l'Histoire d'une Fille* was also published in Brussels by
Callewaert. But just as English fugitives went to Paris, so it was to
Brussels that General Boulanger retreated when his movement collapsed,
and to Brussels to escape her creditors went the blowsy old courtesan
madame Foucault (and how one relishes that naming) in Arnold Bennett's
The Old Wives' Tale.

Given the economic and social domination of Wallonie, it is not surprising
that Brussels fed Paris with cultural figures. Stefan Zweig, writing about
his friend Émile Verhaeren, calls Belgium 'the land of excessive
vitality'.[346] Verhaeren, Émile Wauters, Alfred Stevens, César Franck,
Pierre Louÿs, Jane Hading, Maurice Maeterlinck, Felicien Rops and Theo
van Rysselberghe (Rijsselberghe) are representative figures among the
Belgian artists in different disciplines who settled in the French capital;
and one should perhaps add the ballet dancer Marie van Goethen, who
modelled for Degas.[347] Sometimes Brussels reflected Paris back on itself,
as when Séverine discovered there Henry Bernstein's play *Le Marché* and
recommended it to André Antoine.[348] Octave Mirbeau's article on
Maeterlinck in *Le Figaro* 22nd August 1890 was only the second critical
assessment of the author whom Wilde discerned as caught between his
ancestral Flemish and the need to write in French. Stevenson's view that
Belgium was 'tentatively French, truly German, and somehow falling
between the two,'[349] though odd, at least suggests a cultural troilism.
Mary-Anne Stevens stresses the importance of Les XX, 'located at the
crossroads between the Arts and Crafts Movement and the non-naturalist
decorative tradition of France, it became the cradle of Art Nouveau and a
leading forum for the decorative arts.'[350] The Théâtre de la Monnaie
hosted and sometimes premièred many of the plays and operas that went

on to have Paris productions, its greatest days being between 1875 and 1889.[351] Melba's first success was here, in *Rigoletto* in October 1887. It is difficult to escape the conclusion that anyone seriously interested in new trends would have visited Brussels in that period, even though the journey took six hours from Paris, especially as the annual exhibitions arranged by Maus were accompanied by lectures by Villiers de l'Isle Adam, Mallarmé, Verlaine, Catulle Mendès[352] and others. Not only did Wilde pay no such visits, but in addition it was Vincent O'Sullivan's view that 'the modern German playwriters and novelists were not even names to him'[353] – yet his father had studied German 'so thoroughly that afterwards the whole of German literature was open to him'[354]. Indeed, as Anita Roittinger has pointed out,[355] Wilde hardly ever comments on the work or achievements of others. This cannot be overlooked in determining Wilde's place in *fin-de-siècle* culture, as well as his status as a critic.

Interchange between Paris and Brussels was frequent. The Brussels group associated with Octave Maus, 'Les Vingt' or 'Les XX' brought together Symbolists and Impressionists of different categories. This began in October 1883 and dissolved ten years later when Maus inspired another group called 'La Libre Esthétique' (1894-1914). Maus invited twenty guest artists to the annual salon of Les Vingt: these included Rodin and Whistler in 1884; Whistler, Monet, Renoir, Redon and Monticelli in 1886; Morisot, Pissarro and Seurat in 1887; Whistler, Caillebotte, Toulouse-Lautrec and Signac in 1888, Henri-Edmond Cross,[356] Gauguin, Monet, Pissarro and Seurat in 1889; Cézanne, Redon, Renoir, Signac, Sisley, Toulouse-Lautrec and van Gogh in 1890; Gauguin, Pissarro, Seurat and van Gogh in 1891; Mary Cassatt, Maurice Denis,[357] Lautrec and Seurat in 1892. The 1889 Salon also showed work by the Paris-based German painter Max Klinger as well as by Philip Wilson Steer and William Stott 'of Oldham', 'a Wordsworth of the brush […] in keen sympathy with the school of Cazin, Lhermitte and Bastien-Lepage' and, according to Kenneth McConkey, 'a hero figure'.[358]

Maus used Téodor de Wyzewa, whose 'prodigious intellect [...] filled us with amazement',[359] as a 'talent scout'. Although he was a lover of Jane Avril's and a friend of Renoir, a leading Wagnerite and author of *Le Mouvement Socialiste en Europe,*[360] he has been described by Pierre Coustillas as an 'influential critic of the conservative school, today utterly forgotten'.[361] His obscurity runs to his name. Although Téodor is the spelling usually given, Jose Shercliff calls him Théodore de Wyczéwa, which makes him appear both less and more Polish at once.[362] Mary-Anne

Stevens calls him Téodor de Wyzéwa.[363] His biographer, who possibly dissents from the idea that Wyzewa is utterly forgotten, prefers Théodor.[364]

Georges Lemmen[365] put into the Salon his collection of works illustrated by Walter Crane, presumably including Wilde's *Happy Prince*, which had been published in 1888 and reprinted in 1889. Lemmen accompanied this by an article on Crane in *L'Art moderne*, the journal of Les Vingt. Both through Crane, and through his treasured possession of a painting by Monticelli, there were for Wilde paths to Les Vingt that he did not tread. Had he done so, he would have found one more common interest: James Ensor was a founder member of Les Vingt, and his cartoon 'Dangerous Cooks' shows Octave Maus with Ensor's head on a salver.

CHAPTER THREE

ANGLOMANIA, FRANCOPHILIA AND ANGLOPHOBIA

'Que l'humeur de Paris est changeable!'
– Louis Lépine.[366]

'Was it at all possible for instance to like Paris enough without liking it too much?'
– Henry James.[367]

'The Englishmen who love France are always the worst.'
'The worst?'
'Each man kills the things he loves, you know.'
– Nancy Mitford.[368]

IF Wilde was not the only Irishman familiar with Paris, he was not the only Englishman either. '*Anglomanie* is very fashionable over there now, I hear. I can't think why,' says Dorian Gray. This perhaps is tongue-in-cheek, for Langlade writes that it was this very anglomania that had made Wilde 'l'arbitre des élégances et le héros des cenacles parisiens'.[369] Wilde understood the connection between anglomania and elegance. In *An Ideal Husband*, the French attaché, the Vicomte de Nanjac, is described as 'known for his neckties and his Anglomania.'[370] This was tacitly acknowledged by Langlade when he wrote of Wilde's little-known visit to Paris in April 1892 that it was 'surtout pour s'insurger contre l'anglomanie récente.' The 'English gentleman' is often surprisingly well treated, as in Maupassant's story 'La naufrage'. Here an Englishman is trapped with his two daughters and the French narrator on a wrecked fishing boat on New Year's Eve, and in imminent danger of drowning. He glances at his watch from time to time.

> Suddenly he said to me with magnificent gravity over the heads of his daughters: 'A happy New Year to you, Sir!'
>
> It was midnight. I held out my hand and he shook it; presently he said something in English and his daughters immediately broke into 'God Save the Queen' […]

My first reaction was a desire to laugh, but almost at once the singing
evoked in me a strange but powerful emotion.

There was something sinister and at the same time inspiring in this song of
people condemned to death by shipwreck, a sort of prayer and something
even finer like the sublime cry of the gladiators: 'Hail, Cæsar, those about
to die salute thee!'[371]

Maupassant's Englishmen in 'The Duel' are more absurd, but also display
sang froid to a remarkable degree in unusual circumstances, the
implication being that the French expect that the English abroad expect all
manner of strange effects from Johnny Foreigner.[372]

As a social import, 'le dandy', one of the most significant terms, was by
this time well established, having replaced 'le fashionable' as a descriptor.
Raymond Rudorff has related anglomania specifically to fashion,[373] a
reversal of the usual perception of fashion-induced francophilia. Dorian
Gray was imperceptive in failing to understand the popularity of
anglomania: Nanjac was closer. Marylène Delphis-Delbourg names
Barclay of the avenue de l'Opéra as making his fortune out of tailoring in
the English fashion, although he was really a Frenchman called
Champcenetz,[374] and one must also notice the success in Paris of the
English couturier, Redfern, whose Paris house opened in the rue de Rivoli
in 1881. Among the classes in which *anglomanie* prevailed, that is to say
in the aristocracy and the *haute bourgeoisie*, it was possible to admire
England as the motherland of that dandyism to which they aspired, the
England, as Delphis-Delbourg insists, of Brummell, Byron and Oscar
Wilde.

Un unité de ton en quelque sorte traverse le dandysme anglais, qui sera
rompue, et encore n'est-ce que partiellement, avec Oscar Wilde, à la fin du
siècle, et qui reprendra, augmentée de la tradition wildienne, avec Harold
Acton ou les Sitwell au début de ce siècle.[375]

Brummell, forgotten in the England of the fin-de-siècle, was a live point of
reference in France, thanks to Barbey d'Aurevilly, though in the process
he became less an historical figure and more 'une légende à l'usage des
historiens et des hommes de lettres'.[376] Eustace Grenville-Murray observed
that '*grand-genre* insists that a young Frenchman of status shall be clad as
if he haunted Pall Mall'.[377] It may be that Edouard Dujarrin's dandyism
owed something to his Anglophilia, though waistcoats patterned with
Wagnerian motifs, a monocle and a gardenia in his buttonhole might not
have been quite the thing in Pall Mall, but others too owed more to a

fantasy of Englishness. Juliette Caze, the Catalan prostitute of the rue de Naples, liked to dress in 'the English style – stick-up collars, tailor-made jackets and a man's scarf and pin' and the rather more 'up-market' Hortense Daubinesco also dressed 'like an Englishwoman, and sports elegant patent-leather boots with flat heels'.[378] Paul Léautaud described the dress that his friend Yvonne was wearing in 1896 as 'ugly. Not too ugly, however, with its rather English, half-proper, half-wanton look about it'.[379] In 1904 Chris Healy noted that 'the aristocratic dandy may insist on wearing English boots and English linen'.[380] Léon Bouglé, the director of a bicycle company 'for business purposes adopted the name Spoke and dressed like an Englishman'.[381] Huysmans' duc des Esseintes set out for London in what he conceived to be English attire, a suit of 'mottled check in mouse grey and lava grey, a pair of laced ankle-boots, a little bowler hat, and a flax-blue Inverness cape';[382] there was also a fashion for broad velvet collars and stocks which were believed to be worn by the English.[383] This was furthered by Sargent, whose portraits of W. Graham Robertson and the Marquess of Dalhousie are clearly attempts at portraying the dandy rather than the man.[384]

'In their admiration of everything English in club life,' wrote Richard Whiteing, 'the French have gradually come to tolerate the wearing of the hat indoors. The Jockey does more: it is almost a mark of fashion there not to uncover on entering the club'.[385] This was all very upper class – when aristocrats sent their sons to Oxford or Cambridge, they returned 'with a slight English accent that was regarded as a mark of the highest breeding'[386] – but it caused a certain emulation.

> Curiously enough, while to an Englishman an English accent in French is unpleasant, to a Frenchman it is agreeable and distinguished, so much so that French dandies imitate it.[387]

One can also relate this to Captain Bordure in Jarry's *Ubu Roi*, who in the original production spoke with an exaggerated English accent, 'a parody of a milord'.[388] Bernard Shaw, whose French connections were admittedly slight, picked up on this, when his Lieutenant Duvallet speaks better English than the Englishman Knox, 'having learned it on both sides of the Atlantic.'[389] The meal of *gigot à l'anglaise* cooked by de Hermies in *Là-Bas*[390] is however, probably the limit to which any French author was prepared to go in incorporating anglomania into a text, and probably did not go so far as incorporating mint sauce into the meal.

It would be useful to examine the dating of hotels that included 'Angleterre' in their names at this period.[391] Perhaps one might also see significance in the cigars 'Londres extra' (2fr.10 for six, and clearly esteemed[392]). It was at about this time that 'barmaid', 'le five o'clock', 'le high-life' (or 'hig lif'), 'le week-end', 'le sport' ('le football'[393]) and, subsequently, 'le smoking', crept into French usage or misusage. Marylène Delphis-Delbourg prints an advertisement for the Café Riche of 1900 which advertises its 'déjeuners, five o'clock teas, diners, soupers' and its 'orchestre very select'; she also adds 'keepsake' for 'morceaux choisis' and 'spleen' for 'ennui' to a lexicon in which Langlade's contribution is 'roastbeef', 'meeting', 'lunch', 'square' and 'record'.[394] 'The Anglo-Saxon women have their afternoon tea-parties,' noted the German music teacher Mathilde Marchesi, 'the Anglo-Saxon men have their tennis, their polo, and their football'.[395] 'Je vois, mon vieux, que tu es devenu *sportsman*,' said a gilded youth to another, who had broken out into 'the brightest of neckties, and a tie-pin with a hunting crop, a stirrup iron, a fox's head etc., to which [he] replied "Oh, non! Mais je pense acheter un cheval".'[396]

This did not passed unobserved or unamused by the English themselves. Leonard Merrick's 'editor of the *Le Demi-Mot*' alludes to the way "Our readers demand fiction generously decorated with colloquial English – we cannot *foot it* or drink *veesky soda* too much in our feuilletons to please them nowadays";[397] whereupon the poet Tricotin decides he will write a series of stories about an English lord with the doubly unlikely name of Bill Walker – doubly unlikely, for this is the name of a rough in Shaw's *Major Barbara*.[398]

Whisky and soda, of recent popularity in England (for no Scot would have put soda in his national drink), seems to have come to represent English chic (or 'pschutt', to use the contemporary word[399]) quite quickly in France, although ideas of it seem to have changed in the crossing – Merrick's heroes drink it through straws 'in accordance with the national belief that all foreign beverages are imbibed through straws'.[400] What the soda might have been can only be conjectured: in England Schweppes had been making soda water since 1851 and Apollinaris had been popular ('Scotch and Polly') since the London subsidiary of this German company was set up in 1873, but in Paris soda-water 'except in rather doubtful siphons',[401] could be found only in resorts that specialised in goods for English visitors. The German origin of Apollinaris was obscured and it was marketed as part of Parisian 'naughtiness', the whole association of sparkling water, champagne and France becoming ever more inseparable.

Did the French who could drink Vichy water for their stomach's sake also drink Tonic Water, first made by Schweppes in the 1870s? After all, there was now English plumbing: one may mention the introduction of what Marcel Proust called 'the small private rooms which we have baptised with an English name', that is to say water closet, but even in French one called it *une anglaise*.[402]

Anglomania was certainly a change from the usual feelings about *la perfide Albion*, but seems to have coexisted with it in a state of disunion. 'We have things quite as bad as this in Paris,' was Sarah Bernhardt's way of being polite about English art.[403] 'Notre manie de vouloir aimés pour nous mêmes par les étrangers,' thought Joseph Reinach, 'est à la fois touchante et ridicule' ;[404] and some notion of English uprightness maintained itself along with the perfidy. William Waddington was once caricatured as a coachman of a brougham, sitting up straight and imperturbable, with the caption 'John Cocher Anglais n'a jamais versé, ni accroché'.[405] Yet there were many occasions of Franco-British discord. After all, England had a free hand in Egypt because the French disengaged themselves from joint action in 1881 over the Arabi Pasha insurrection. (The opposite policy, engagement in Tunisia, isolated them from Italy: faced with two evils, they contrived to choose both.)

Thomas Barclay thought anglophobia 'a sort of inflammable ingredient in the French brain.'[406] In his character 'Mr Hartford', Barbey d'Aurevilly merged a number of French anglophobic stereotypes, for Hartford 'was reputed to possess all those Pharisaic and Protestant qualities which English people sum up under the smug word "respectable"'.[407] Did this echo in Wilde's mind when he gave the family name of Harford to his far from respectable peer Lord Illingworth? Less literary was the anglophobia of Juliette Adam, which was grounded in the belief that Britain and Germany wanted to partition Europe between them (it is curious that Wilde wanted her to write for *Woman's World*), but usually anglophobia was occasioned by more substantial (though in the longer term, just as evanescent) events: the acquisition of the Khedive of Egypt's Suez Canal shares by the British government in 1875, the renegotiations in 1877 of the Cobden Treaty of 1860, the Anglo-Turkish Convention of 1878 which was supposed to threaten French interests in the Levant, the strains over Madagascar and Tonkin in the 1880s and tension in the New Hebrides in the early 'nineties, the Bangkok crisis of July 1893, the Anglo-Congolese agreement of May 1894, the Jameson Raid of December 1895, the Niger boundary dispute of 1897, argument over Newfoundland fisheries, and above all the Fashoda crisis in 1898. This manifested itself in the *culte* for

Joan of Arc, which aligned anglophobia and right-wing Catholicism:[408] it
was for his 'Saint Joan Listening to Voices' that Bastien-Lepage first came
into prominence; Antoine Bourdelle's 'Jeanne d'Arc en prière' dates to
1886; Jules Barbier's *Jeanne d'Arc*, with Sarah Bernhardt, opened at the
Porte St-Martin in January 1890.   One notes, too, Ernest Chausson's
Jeanne d'Arc, for women's voices, choir and orchestra, and Gounod's
Messe à Jeanne d'Arc. In 1884 there was founded a newspaper simply
called *L'Anti-anglais*, although it did not survive long. Lord Newton, who
was at the British Embassy in the mid 1880s under Lord Lyons, titles
Chapter XVI of his biography of his old chief simply 'Anglophobia 1883-
1885', writing in his own autobiography that

> The one unsatisfactory feature of my stay at the Paris Embassy was the
> continually increasing growth of Anglophobia, and I cannot recall a single
> French Government which could be described as friendly between 1881
> and 1886.[409]

Anita Roittinger, indeed, has come to the conclusion that 'in reality, the
sympathy shown to Wilde was not so much pro-Wilde as anti-English',[410]
but Wilde, the son of Speranza, took no notice of this when in Paris in
1883, nor advantage of the anti-British feeling over Fashoda (largely
confined to the *pays politique*), or during the Boer War, although this was
widespread among the public at large and in the Press in particular. Paul
de Cassagnac in *L'Autorité*, Lucien Millevoye in *La Patrie* and Juliette
Adam in *La Nouvelle Revue* all indulged in 'wild extravagances'[411] of
anglophobia.   This was never returned in quite the same way, although
there were those who presented hostile views of the French to English
readers. Here history played its part. Thomas March, writing in 1896 and
uniformly hostile to the Commune, also denounced the excesses of the
Versaillais in no measured terms. Firmly of the opinion that had the
Prussians behaved as the Versaillais behaved they would have met with
universal condemnation as barbarians, his conclusion was that, for the
atrocities committed by both Communards and Versaillais, 'the real
barbarians were the French themselves'.[412] This view of the inherent
instability of the French character, presented with all apparent balance and
impartiality, is an important aperçu in the history of Anglo-French representation.

Harry de Windt was in Paris when Kruger arrived: 'English residents had
anything but a pleasant time of it during the South African campaign'.[413]
Jerome K. Jerome found that 'In Paris, the English were hooted in the
streets and hunted out of cafés. I got through by talking with a strong

American accent.'[414] Cartoons and caricatures satirising the English, and even Queen Victoria, were rife, and the Prince of Wales avoided the opening of the Exhibition of 1900. There was a 'scurrilous publication' specifically addressing anglophobia called *V'là les Anglishes*.[415] Colonel Henry Mapleson, who lived in Paris, wrote that 'The proprietors of the French newspapers are coining money by constantly attacking England, and their increased circulation is proof positive that the majority here endorse the action of the Press. Whenever there is a report of a Boer victory, the habitués of the Boulevard cafés are mad with delight and any English looking people, who happen to be in these places, are accosted with the most insulting epithets'.[416] This anti-British feeling was sufficiently regarded by the German Ambassador, Prince Radolin, to report on it to Berlin. For all that, the Prince of Wales was able to slip into Paris and dine at the British Embassy in the winter of 1899; at Christmas 1900 the London surgeon Sir Alfred Cooper visited Paris where his daughter Stephanie was at school, and his sister-in-law Anne Marchioness of Townsend lived, and stayed in a hotel in the rue de Rivoli with rooms overlooking the Tuileries Gardens, without incident; and Anstey Guthrie, in Paris for the Expo in late September 1900 with Alexander Wedderburn, recalled that 'In spite of our nationality we never during our three days in Paris met with the slightest discourtesy'.[417] Wilde, too, seems to have been accepted without demur. Parisians were therefore curiously selective about whom they abused – or perhaps Guthrie and Wedderburn talked broad Scots?

The desire of each nation to admire another is one mundane answer to Gray's point about Anglomania, and England was useful when Germany could not be admired (later Russomania took over[418]). The work of the British ambassadors may well have helped: Lord Newton says of Lord Lyons that 'even the French, perhaps the most suspicious people in the world, used to put complete trust in his assurances'.[419] The popularity of the Prince of Wales is another answer: even the police regarded him as 'très sympathique [...] le type du gentilhomme anglais'. If the Prince's behaviour informed this definition, another answer must be that, while the British saw Paris as a place where all was permitted, Britain was gaining a reputation for decadence. In 1895, the conservative critic Arsène Alexandre attacked Bing's Maison de l'Art Nouveau,[420] saying that 'it all smacks of the vicious Englishman, the Jewess addicted to morphine, or the Belgian spiv, or a good mixture of these three poisons'.[421] Jean-François Raffaëlli 'was seriously concerned that the rage for Liberty silk would result in an increase in homosexuality'.[422] This 'rage' began in 1889 when Liberty showed aesthetic gowns at the Exposition Universelle; in the following year Liberty opened the 'Maison Liberty' at 38 avenue de l'Opéra. Liberty silks met art nouveau in the workshops of the couturier Doucet, who 'perhaps best understood how to translate the fluid lines of art nouveau into garments that were as eloquent as the decorative forms of the day'.[423] Max Nordau, who thought he could recognise decadence when he saw it, refers to the 'peculiarly anæmic and almost chlorotic' Liberty colours, adding dismissively and erroneously that Liberty was 'an American tradesman'.[424]

More curiously, 'towards 1880 the more fashionable cocottes, such as Laure Hayman[425] and Liane de Pougy, began to adopt a slight accent and copied the Princess of Wales' appearance, even to her fringe'.[426] Jane Avril adopted 'an anglomania that almost amounted to idolatry'[427] and had a season at the Palace Theatre in London in 1897.[428]

While some writers (Bourget or Schwob, for example) were anglophile, Anglomania was also expressed by an interest taken in Symbolist circles in English pantomime, and in a vogue for English, or supposedly English, comedians at the café-concerts. Even Sarah Bernhardt admired Marie Lloyd, Arthur Roberts and Little Tich, who appeared on stage in Paris. A number of these artistes were of ambiguous origins or personæ. Marie Lloyd's real name was Matilda Wood; Little Tich's Harry Relph.[429] Albert Chevalier, an Englishman of French descent who adopted a stage persona called Armand Thibault, began as a straight actor with the Bancroft company; Cissie Loftus, much admired by Max Beerbohm, is the Cecy Loftus of Toulouse-Lautrec's 1894 lithograph.

The most successful of them was Harry Fragson, under contract at the Parisiana in April 1897, and described as 'a genius' by Lord Winterton who saw him at this time.[430] The journalist Sidney Dark calls Fragson an 'Anglo-Frenchman or 'Franco-Englishman', an ambiguity which earns him his place in the masquerade of Paris, especially as he was born on three different dates in three different places, from Whitechapel to Antwerp. His original name seems to have been Léon Pot[431] or even Vincent Potts, and he sang in French with an English accent and in English with a French one. Dark, before recounting a remarkably unfunny story about Fragson, remarks that he was 'as funny "off" as "on"'.[432] Fragson married the French dancer Alice Delysia[433] but took up with another dancer, a madame Christiné, incurring the jealousy of his old father, which perhaps was funny. His father then shot him dead, which was not funny at all.[434]

Marie Lloyd appeared in Paris in 1893, one biographer commenting that 'any association with the city was good for her image, adding yet another suggestion of raunchiness',[435] that is to say, salaciousness. Here is one more example of how expectations of Paris could be nourished by Paris to be re-served in London. The reception of Yvette Guilbert in London is part of this reflective process. Lloyd, so essentially a Londoner, perhaps did not see this as clearly as Little Tich, who learned to swear in French and eventually acquired a flat in Paris.

Anglomania could have its drawbacks. Theodore Child refers slightingly to the 'pseudo-English' cuisine at Weber's and Lucas; it is significant that Wilde dined frequently at the former, which also became popular with Marcel Proust and his friends Lucien Daudet, Debussy (in the process of changing from the bohemian Achille to the respectable Claude), Jean-Paul de Toulet, and Louis de la Salle at the end of the century, but for all its popularity with Proust, he still gave Françoise the line 'It's not a real restaurant, it's only a flashy big café'.[436] Colonel Newnham-Davis says of it, rather disparagingly, that the cookery was 'semi-British', which gave it the nickname of 'His Lordship's Larder', but it became 'entirely French'.[437] Discovery of the inventory of the English-owned grocery shop in the boulevard Saint-Michel, where in 1900 Baroness Orczy and her English husband bought 'various delicacies for our picnic lunches'[438], may increase our understanding of this.

Anglomania is perhaps more explicable amongst those who made money out of the English. Even during the bitter and snowy weather of Easter 1888, the British Ambassador noted that Paris was 'swarming' with English even before the 'Season'.[439] One of these was the Duke of Marlborough, an ex-Lord Lieutenant of Ireland who was also Prince of Mindelheim in Suabia and a Prince of the Holy Roman Empire, which no longer existed. The Duke may have been an eclectic example of the visitor with a cloud of fantasy hanging about him, but the growth of tourism naturally ensured a reflexive process of supply and demand, the commodity supplied being the Paris of the visitors' own imaginings – when indeed the tourists were emancipated from the notion perpetuated by the guide books that 'Paris seems to consist of the Boulevards, the sewers, the Arc de l'Étoile and the tomb of Napoleon',[440] or when 'they all asked the same questions, made the same exclamations, went out on the same excursions, returned with the same judgments, and exhibited the same assurance that foreigners were really very peculiar people'.[441] Chris Healy doubted 'whether many English people see Paris',[442] but this indicates that

he too was inventing a Paris invisible to all visitors save those like
himself.

> To match the moon's white rays lighting the solemn magnificence of Notre
> Dame, the long line of buildings from the Sainte Chapelle and the
> Conciergerie to the Institute, which represent the materialised soul of the
> city of Louis XI, Francis I, Henry IV and Louis XIV; to stand on the Pont
> Neuf at three in the morning, when the red lamps throw their sickly glare
> on the Seine's restless waters, and see the sunlight wrestling with darkness
> for possession of the sky; to walk along the silent boulevards whilst the
> city is sleeping; to watch gay crowds which pour along the streets on a
> June day; to see the dainty work-girls walking to their work-rooms with the
> coquettish grace which is the exclusive possession of the Parisienne; to see
> the artist, writer, professional man, gathered at the café tables during the
> 'green hour', when the absinthe stimulates conversation to a series of
> epigrams, which sweepingly criticise all things human and Divine, from
> the latest creed to the newest cult; to tread the streets of the Latin Quarter
> […] to enter a little café in a back street and find it thrilling with the arts,
> wit, and passion of painters and poets still unknown […] that is to see and
> know Paris.[443]

The Pont Neuf was also regarded by du Maurier as the mystic cross roads
of Paris:

> There one stood, *spellbound* in indecision, like the ass of Buridan between
> two sacks of oats; for on either side, north or south of the Pont-Neuf, were
> to be found *enchanting* slums […] like *haunting* illustrations by Gustave
> Doré.[444]

Although no historical study of tourism as such in Paris has been
undertaken (and it would be instructive to analyse the postcard and
guidebook industries[445]), this does indicate the enthronement of leisure at
its most developed: in 1889 in his book *Les Plaisirs et les curiosités de
Paris*, Camille Debons hailed the city as 'the very capital of the *Kingdom
of Pleasures*'.[446] This point has been assessed by Enid Starkie:

> By the end of the nineteenth century, Paris was considered the centre of
> civilisation, and the place where happiness and fulfilment could most
> readily be found. France was beginning to have, in literature, art and
> music, a snob value, and cultivated people began to pride themselves on
> their understanding of French ideals. It may still have been a sophisticated,
> an adult taste – like caviare – but those who needed to be considered
> civilised and cultivated were obliged to make a parade of love and
> admiration for France. She was still seen as immoral and loose-living; but
> then too strict a sense of morality was considered a sign of philistinism.[447]

In this analysis, 'Paris' was playing a part in constructing not merely the socio-cultural identity of its own inhabitants, but also of those from overseas. Harold Kurtz precisely dates the World Fair of 1867 as the launch of the *fin-de-siècle* conception of 'gay Paree'. 'Many of the foreign guests, crowned and otherwise, regarded Paris as a kind of gas-lit Venusberg in which distinction between classes and even between sexes became increasingly blurred while the pursuit of pleasure offered stimulating vistas of temptations without limit'.[448]

Ralph Nevill regretted that the smart restaurants started to cater for tourists by arranging themselves 'to give the impression of what wealthy foreign clients think a Parisian restaurant ought to be like.'[449] Chris Healy refers to an English newspaper which offered him in the late 1890s two guineas a column for a weekly article on 'interesting murders' to a maximum of a column and a half, or on 'a truly French divorce case', in which case he might extend himself over two columns. 'I preferred to roam about Paris and be in touch with the men of the moment', was Healy's response,[450] indicating his understanding of where Paris was to be found. The creation of Paris as 'Paris' was to be seen more on the Colonnes Morris than at the Concerts Colonne.

The British Ambassador was perhaps able to identify his fellow-countrymen by signs that Francis Parkman or Henry James also noticed. Parkman compared the English with his fellow Americans, these being

> slight, rather pale and thin men, not like the beef-fed, ruddy Englishmen; speaking low to the waiters instead of roaring in the imperative tone of John Bull. There was not a shadow of that boisterous and haughty confidence of manner that you see among Englishmen.[451]

Henry James wrote of the British tourist that 'You recognize him farther off than you do an American; he makes a more vivid spot in the picture. He is always and everywhere the same – carrying with him, in his costume and physiognomy, that indefinable expression of not considering anything out of England worth making, physically or morally, a toilet for. The unanimity with which Englishmen abroad dress is indeed surprising.' Happy days, when Americans could fault the English for the way they dressed abroad! Peter de Polnay quotes an anonymous boulevardier of the boulevard de la Madeleine who noted the extraordinary number of English ('he imagined himself in London on his way to Buckingham Palace') with yellow jackets, bandy legs and faces reflecting their spleen.[452] 'The English tourists dressed in flannel shirts and hunting caps and knickerbockers, exactly as though they were penetrating the mountains of

Afghanistan or the deserts of Syria,' said Richard Harding Davis.[453] Although Jean Méral came to the conclusion that the English in Paris brought out the latent anglophobia of Americans,[454] it was the cosmopolitan Dorothy Menpes who noticed that at the Louvre the English tourists were 'all preternaturally serious and dressed in outlandish clothes such as one never seems to come across in England'. 'At one time,' adds the Irish Chris Healy, 'England was supposed to have a monopoly of the badly dressed idiots who went to France on a cheap trip and covered their own nation with ridicule during their short stay.'[455]

Even so, one may not be able to justify totally Sheldon Novick's view that the Americans on the boulevards were 'distinguished not so much by their clothes as by their loose-jointed manner and their open, almost childlike faces'.[456] Either way, such was their number (1894 to 1899 were boom years) that the Douanier Rousseau referred to all tourists simply as 'les Américains',[457] another transformation that the English would have found 'Shokin''.

In May 1890 Wilde's Balliol friend J.E.C. Bodley settled in France with letters of introduction to Léon Gambetta and Thiers[458] from Sir Charles Dilke (whose private secretary he had been), and in the next seven years hardly spent a week a year out of the country. 'He commenced to live among the French more closely than any Englishman had lived before [...] His eighteenth century manners and his perfect French opened a way where no Englishman and few Frenchmen ever trod.'[459] The result was Bodley's book on France.[460]

John Lane went to Paris in pursuit of French poets to publish with the Bodley Head, and when he contributed to *The Yellow Book* he caught the French vogue for dissimulating identity by doing so under the name 'Jean de France'.[461] Will Rothenstein went with him to the Louvre in September 1893, only to tell him that he had no taste in art. Richard Le Gallienne, whose quasi-French name was of his own contriving,[462] was introduced to Paris by the *Yellow Book*'s editor Henry Harland, arriving on the 14th or 15th October 1894, and staying to the 22nd.[463] The result was the poem 'Paris Day by Day', published in *Robert Louis Stevenson: An Elegy, and Other Poems Mainly Personal*,[464] in which Paris is invoked as 'Half Angel, Half Grisette'. Le Gallienne spent a night in Paris between Davos and London in 1896, and in 1900 spent three more days there (12th to 15th

March), his biographer noting that 'Paris enchanted him and he suddenly felt more at home there than in any city of the world.'

It was to Paris that Le Gallienne was eventually to return in the 1920s, with his third wife Irma, and to streets haunted by the past; this is when he wrote his book *The Romantic '90s*. His second wife, Julie, had moved there when she fled their household in 1904, settling with their daughter Eva at 60 rue de Vaugirard; in December 1905, she was joined by Richard's sister Sissie, who had also left her husband, the actor James Welch. A joint household was set up at 5 rue du Regard; after Sissie's departure in November 1906, Julie moved to 1 rue de Fleurus, where viâ a small hat shop she struggled out of poverty into the successful proprietorship of a boutique with the Sardoudly name 'Madame Fédora'. Richard's and Irma's Paris, true to form, intersected this. They lived at 29 quai de Bourbon in 1927; at 89 rue de Vaugirard in 1928; in the rue de Fleurus in 1929 and in Julie's former house, 60 rue de Vaugirard in 1931. Nor did they neglect Wilde's Paris, visiting the Hôtel d'Alsace[465] and viewing Wilde's old rooms. As a result a table that had once been in Wilde's suite became the desk on which Le Gallienne composed the musings that were published as *From a Paris Scrapbook* in 1938.

Rather less interested in such things were those Englishmen who spent some months of the year in Paris from economy or for obscurer reasons: Lord George Loftus, for example, or the brothers General Herbert and General William Slade. Of these perhaps Captain Howard Vyse, nicknamed 'Punch', and once in the Life Guards, stands for the rest. He 'never mastered the French language, though he lived for years in Paris'.[466]

If Vyse and his like[467] resisted acculturation, what were the characteristics of those Englishmen who did not resist? One such was the Hon[ble] Alan Herbert,[468] a son of the 3rd Earl of Carnarvon, who ran the Hertford British Hospital financed by Sir Richard Wallace. Herbert, a bachelor, had moved to Paris after graduating from Christ Church, Oxford, and read medicine there, something sufficiently unusual to warrant more comment in the sources than he seems to have earned. He is presumably that 'Allen Herbert' who attended the American sculptor Augustus Saint-Gaudens, who lived off and on Paris.[469]

The description of him by his cousin Esmé Howard suggests a certain insular prejudice, but also reveals transformation and ambiguity once more:

There never was a kinder man than Alan Herbert. He was essentially English in his thoughts and feelings, but his long hair and rather unkempt beard, his seedy frock coat with the rosette of the Legion of Honour in his buttonhole, and even his manner of speech – when speaking English, not French – would have made anybody who did not know him believe that at first sight he was a Frenchman. His habits of life had become completely French.[470]

~~~~~~

One at the heart of Anglophone official Paris was Mary Waddington. She had been Mary King, daughter of Charles King, President of Columbia University, whose widowed mother had moved to Paris in 1871. In 1874 she married William Waddington, born in Paris in 1826 of an English father and a Scottish mother, and educated at Rugby (where he had been a schoolfellow of Francis Adams, in the British Embassy in Paris in the late 1870s) and Trinity College, Cambridge, before entering French politics. This was to surmount considerable disadvantages, not least that of being a Protestant[471] whose social circle was largely Orléanist. He became Minister for Public Instruction under Thiers in 1873 and under Dufaure in 1876, then Minister for Foreign Affairs (December 1877), Prime Minister for a month in 1879 and Ambassador in London (1884-1894). His brother Richard served for a time in the British Army and married an Englishwoman; his sister Marie married Charles de Bunsen and so was aunt of Maurice de Bunsen, attaché at the British Embassy in 1886-1890 (as a widow, Marie moved in with the Waddingtons in 1887). His enemies said (predictably) that the bilingual Waddington spoke French with an English accent and English with a French one; and his friends were just as wounding: 'It was difficult to remember when talking to M. Waddington that he was not an Englishman [...] He was to all intents and purposes socially an Englishman'.[472] 'It was a luxury,' said Lord Salisbury, 'to have a French Minister who worked in principles intelligible to the English mind',[473] although the Liberal Foreign Secretary Lord Granville was not so sure. When Waddington's embassy to London was proposed, he told the British Ambassador in Paris, Lord Lyons, 'I am not particularly anxious to have Waddington [...] He would be burning to distinguish himself and very *agissant*'.[474]

When Waddington left London he became a Director of the Suez Canal Company and had to face cries of 'Vendu aux Anglais' when the French shareholders disliked any decisions in which he was involved.[475] Lord Lyons' own view was that Waddington 'had the greatest of all recommendations, that you could believe him, and feel sure of him'.[476] The rather ponderous Lyons clearly found most French politicians mercurial.

CHAPTER FOUR

AMIS & FAUX AMIS IN A CULTURE
OF EASY DUPLICITY

'Je est un autre.'
-- Arthur Rimbaud.

'Mais alors, vous êtes en perpétuelle transformation.'
-- The comtesse de Montesquiou to the Isola brothers.[477]

'To know Paris, the culture of easy duplicity.'
– Colm Tóibín.[478]

THERE was, clearly, a different engagement, a different kind of engagement, between the arts from Montmartre to Montparnasse and those from St John's Wood to Chelsea, even if all these salons and cénacles and circles and groups must occasionally sound like mutual admiration societies – Vuillard's biographer, for example, has written of 'the camaraderie and support that the Nabi association offered'.[479] French intellectual life was lived in a series of interlocking relationships, giving access, and perhaps exclusive access, to 'those direct, deep references of which Paris was invariably so full'.[480] In the 1870s Flaubert, Alphonse Daudet, Zola, Edmond de Goncourt and Turgenev ('when he was free from gout'[481]) dined monthly either at Flaubert's in the rue Murillo, or at the Café Riche, or at Brébant's, or 'sometimes at the Adolphe et Pelé, behind the Opéra; sometimes in the square of the Opéra-Comique; then at Voisin's'.[482] These were 'diners des auteurs sifflés', writers whose plays had been booed. They thought of themselves as 'Les Cinq',[483] giving a certain coherence to occasions that began at seven o'clock and lasted until two o'clock in the morning. 'Flaubert must have his Normandy butter and stewed Rouen ducks; Edmond de Goncourt, exotic and refined, demanded preserved ginger; Zola, sea-urchins and cockles; while Tourgénieff enjoyed his caviare'.[484] It cannot have been entirely innocently that Flaubert introduces into his *Hérodias* the glutton Aulus Vitellius, whose 'faculty for guzzling marked him out as a remarkable being sprung from a superior race'.[485] Maupassant, who occasionally attended the larger

Sunday receptions at Flaubert's[486] and dedicated *La maison Tellier* to Turgenev in 'homage with deep affection and great admiration', must have thought of these gatherings when describing the monthly dinners of the five friends in his story 'Les tombales': these too went on till two in the morning.[487] In a private room 'Les Cinq' exchanged arguments about style and anecdotes about women, 'telling one another stories which Zola feared would have a disastrous effect on the waiters' morals'. This rather Wildean reflection also provides a view of the representation of five other men, Lord Darlington, Lord Windermere, Lord Augustus Lorton, Mr Graham and Mr Dumby in Act III of *Lady Windermere's Fan*.

The irony would not have been lost on Zola's friends that it was another group of five, all once regarded as Zola's disciples, who wrote a manifesto against Zola following the publication of *La Terre*: Paul Bonnetain, Rosny, Paul Margueritte, Lucien Descaves and Gustave Guiche. Anatole France compared this with the treatment meted out to Noah: 'Five of his spiritual sons have, while he slept, committed against him the sin of Ham', adding 'M. Fernand Xau, imitating Shem's piety, has stretched his mantle over the old man'.[488]

Mallarmé contributed a catalogue preface to the 1896 exhibition of Berthe Morisot, who was an 'intimate friend'[489] and by way of being Manet's sister-in-law. To her Thursday 'at homes' in the rue Weber came Mallarmé, Villiers de l'Isle Adam, Henri de Régnier, Monet, Mary Cassatt, the 'socially timid'[490] Fantin-Latour, Théodore Duret, Emmanuel Chabrier, Jules Jouy, Téodor de Wyzewa, Camille Mauclair, Zacharie Astruc, Pierre Puvis de Chavannes, Degas, Whistler, Renoir, Manet.[491] Chabrier was a friend of Renoir's, a buyer of Monet, Cézanne, Sisley. A portrait of Chabrier attributed to Manet is in the Winthrop Collection, Harvard University. Manet's 'Bar aux Folies Bergère'[492] hung above his piano and Manet died in his arms. After his death his collection was sold at the Hôtel Drouot, 23rd March 1896. The sale was managed by Durand-Ruel. He knew (independently of meeting them at the receptions of others) Mallarmé, Zola, Alphonse Daudet, Jean Moréas, Jean Richepin (who wrote the libretto for Chabrier's *La Sulamite*), and Villiers de l'Isle Adam – 'but it was above all with Verlaine that Chabrier was most closely associated'.[493] This produced the two pieces *Fisch-ton-kan* and *Vaucochard et fils 1er*, although these were not performed until 1941. His opera *L'Étoile* was produced at the Théâtre des Bouffes Parisiens in November 1877, the music a satire on that of Donizetti, 'and Chabrier became famous overnight'.[494] *L'Étoile* contains characters called Tapioca, Hérisson de Porc Epic, and King Ouf, thus prefiguring *Ubu Roi*.[495] It is thought that Chabrier and Verlaine met *chez* the marquise de Ricard, mother of Xavier de Ricard, a leading Parnassian poet, or else *chez* Nina de Villard. (Verlaine managed doubly to metamorphose Chabrier by describing him as 'chirpy as a finch and melodious as a nightingale'.[496]) When Chabrier died, Henri de Régnier and Francis Vielé-Griffin wrote threnodies for him.[497]

On Saturdays the 'La Plume' group, of whom de Régnier was one, met in an underground room at the Soleil d'Or in the place St-Michel, with Verlaine in attendance; other members of this group were Moréas, Marie Krysinska and Pierre Louÿs, while Jules Renard encountered Aurélien Scholl, Deschamps and Marcel Schwob there one evening in March 1892. Verlaine was also there that night, 'a dismal Socrates and a soiled Diogenes'.[498] Sisley Huddleston lists the names of Villiers de l'Isle Adam, Laurent Tailhade, Toulouse-Lautrec and Georges d'Esparbès as habitués of the Soleil d'Or.[499] The group round Anatole Baju's magazines *Le Scapin*, and *Le Scapin-revue* also met there. It was a 'rather murky' place according to Jean Émile Bayard, who adds Charles Cros, Toulouse-Lautrec, Alfred Vallette and Edouard Ratté.[500] The Soleil d'Or later changed its name to the more ambiguous Café du Départ,[501] and is now the Café de Départ-St Michel. We catch an echo in the café Robert Service called L'Escargot d'Or:

O Tavern of the Golden Snail!
Ten *sous* have I, so I'll regale;
Ten *sous* your amber brew to sip
(Eight for the *bock* and two the tip),
And so I'll sit the evening long,
And smoke my pipe and watch the throng,
The giddy crowd that drains and drinks,
I'll watch it quiet as a sphinx;
And who among them all shall buy
For ten poor *sous* such joy as I?
As I who, snugly tucked away,
Look on it all as on a play,
A frolic scene of love and fun,
To please an audience of One.

O Tavern of the Golden Snail!
You've stuff indeed for many a tale.
All eyes, all ears, I nothing miss:
Two lovers lean to clasp and kiss;
The merry students sing and shout,
The nimble *garçons* dart about;

Lo! here come Mimi and Musette
With: "S'il vous plait, une cigarette?"
Marcel and Rudolf, Shaunard too,
Behold the old rapscallion crew,
With flowing tie and shaggy head . . .
Who says Bohemia is dead?
Oh shades of Murger! prank and clown,
And I will watch and write it down.

O Tavern of the Golden Snail!
What crackling throats have gulped your ale!
What sons of Fame from far and near
Have glowed and mellowed in your cheer!
Within this corner where I sit
Banville and Coppée clashed their wit;
And hither too, to dream and drain,
And drown despair, came poor Verlaine.
Here Wilde would talk and Synge would muse,
Maybe like me with just ten *sous*.
Ah! one is lucky, is one not?
With ghosts so rare to drain a pot!
So may your custom never fail,
O Tavern of the Golden Snail! [502]

~~~~~~

When Pierre Louÿs moved to the rue Grétry in January 1894, he inaugurated Wednesday afternoon receptions, where one might find Gustave Kahn 'who takes the French language as a violin and lets the bow of emotion run at wild will upon it',[503] Henri Albert, Francis Vielé-Griffin, Robert de Bonnières, Pierre Quillard, the Natansons, Heredia, Henri de Régnier, Valéry and Debussy, who once projected setting Louÿs' *Aphrodite* to music as he did with the *Chansons de Bilitis* (which Louÿs had dedicated to Gide). 'Among my friends you are certainly the one I have loved most,' Debussy told Louÿs.[504] Louÿs and Gide had been friends since school: Louÿs decorated the cover of Gide's *Le Traité de Narcisse*.[505] Henri Bataille was another of this set, and provided a portrait of Louÿs for the latter's *Têtes et pensées*.[506] Dr Filleau, the collector of Impressionists, was 'at home' on Tuesdays, while from 1884 Robert Caze held Friday gatherings at which would appear Paul Adam, Paul Alexis, Vielé-Griffin, Moréas, de Régnier, Gustave Kahn and Charles Morice.

Pauline Viardot, who has been called 'one of the greatest and most influential singers in operatic history',[507] had been an early promoter of

Berlioz, Gounod (it was rumoured they were lovers[508]), Fauré and Massenet, and sang the title rôle of the latter's *Marie Magdeleine* in 1873. 'No singer on the French stage has ever equalled Pauline Viardot.'[509] Francis Grierson, who was in love with Viardot in his early days in Paris, wrote with a certain *arrière pensée*, was 'one of the four most wonderful women living in the period from 1840 to the end of the century'.

The others were Letizia Bonaparte-Ratazzi, Princess Helene (or Helena) Racowitza and George Sand,[510] all women of multiple identity, but Racowitza (Helene von Dönniges, 'the Red Countess') having perhaps the strangest life – she was the mistress of Ferdinand Lassalle until Prince Racowitz killed him a duel and married her. She later moved to Saint Petersburg and became involved with the revolutionary Count Serge von Schwitzch. She then moved briefly to Paris where she modelled for Carpeaux' 'Genius of Dancing' on the Palais Garnier, which changed sex in the course of its execution. She was joined by Schwitzch, and they went to live in New York. After publishing her autobiography in German in 1910,[511] she died by her own hand in the following year. She is the Clotilde of George Meredith's *The Tragic Comedians* (1880), 'a short novel which might almost be termed a free translation or a transcript',[512] where Lassalle is Alvan and Racowitz is Marko. Grierson's description of her suggests a certain unease with personality: 'Her presence gave the illusion of a room full of witty and cultured women; and though her conversation disclosed a mind of the highest intelligence, there was nothing of the masculine to be noticed in her looks or her manner.'[513]

~~~~~~~~

Gauguin admired Degas and Degas befriended Gauguin; more surprisingly he was also a friend of the Italian society portrait painter Giovanni Boldini, who had settled in Paris in 1871. Frantisek Deak suggests that Émile Bernard was a probable link between Gauguin and the Wagnerite circle of Téodor de Wyzewa.[514] Pissarro told his son of Alfred Sisley 'Je suis d'avis c'est un maître égal aux plus grands'[515] and Sisley's work was admired by Coquelin *cadet*, who was introduced to Vuillard by Lugné-Poë.[516] Zola, Duret, Fantin-Latour, Alfred Stevens, Monet and Antonin Proust were the pall-bearers at the funeral of Manet on 3rd May 1883, of whom Fantin, Stevens and of course Manet himself had attended the funeral of Baudelaire. At Sisley's funeral on 1st February 1899, the eulogy was pronounced by Cazin in the presence of Renoir, Monet and Adolphe Tavernier. Zola was the intimate friend and former school-fellow of Cézanne and the author of a catalogue preface for Manet, a friendship Zola acknowledged by dedicating *Madeleine Férat* to him; while Rothenstein records that for Edmond de Goncourt, Zola 'expressed unbounded admiration [and] was delighted to hear his friend Hennique praised'.[517] Zola's own pall-bearers included Halévy, Georges Charpentier, Abel Hermant, the publisher Eugène Fasquelle, Théodore Duret, Octave Mirbeau and Fernand Bruneau. When Gustave Caillebotte died, Camille Pissarro wrote to Lucien Pissarro 'He is one we can really mourn. He was good and generous and a painter of talent to boot'.[518] Nadar took the deathbed photograph of Victor Hugo 'whom he had loved and venerated'.[519] André Antoine and Sarah Bernhardt enjoyed a good, if surprising, relationship. Burty dedicated his *Maîtres et petits maîtres*[520] to Bracquemond. Gyp de Martel once considered engaging Verlaine as a tutor to her children, perhaps on the recommendation of Barrès. Émile Bernard was introduced to Odilon Redon by Claude-Émile Schuffenecker, resulting in 'a firm friendship based on the younger artist's profound admiration for the older painter'.[521] Bernard, who severed most of his friendships when he went to Egypt for a number of years, nevertheless remained an admirer of Anquetin. Schuffenecker became a friend of Gauguin, who stayed with him on three occasions, sculpting a bust of madame Schuffenecker and painting 'little Schuff' in his studio during the third visit in 1889.[522]

'John Swan thought Dagnan-Bouveret the greatest living painter, while Dagnan held Swan in high regard'.[523] Chéret collaborated with Bracquemond and Alexandre Charpentier. Fénéon was an enthusiastic propagandist for a number of writers and painters, notably Seurat. On one occasion he wrote to Signac that 'the opinion of people whose opinion might interest you [...] was absolutely unanimous' in praise, and he went on to name Paul Adam, Vielé-Griffin, Adolphe Retté, Henri de Régnier.[524] J.-F. Raffaëlli wrote to Huysmans of *À Rebours* 'Your book has made me literally ill and I hasten to tell you that you have achieved something remarkable which will earn you the greatest literary esteem.'[525] Anatole France also admired Huysmans and said of Richepin's *Le Chansons des Gueux* 'this wonderful book is unique.'[526] Albert Mockel produced a little book on Verhaeren for which Vielé-Griffin produced a biographical note.[527] Paul Adam, the author (under the name 'Jacques Plowert') of the *Petit Glossaire pour servir à l'intelligence des auteurs décadents et symbolistes*, ranked Jules Laforgue with Moses, Æschylus, Virgil, Dante, Rabelais, Shakespeare, Goethe and Flaubert:[528] it is a pity that Laforgue did not live long enough to improve upon this promising beginning.

Among the composers, Fauré's settings greatly extended the appeal and renown of the poets in whom he was interested: Victor Hugo, Théophile Gautier, Albert Samain, Leconte de Lisle, Villiers de l'Isle Adam, Jean Richepin, Catulle Mendès, above all Verlaine, at whose funeral he played the organ. Debussy set Maurice Bouchor, Verlaine, Théophile Gautier, Mallarmé, Baudelaire, Leconte de Lisle, Banville, Paul Bourget.[529] Poems by Verlaine and Gautier were also set to music by César Franck; poems by Baudelaire, Victor Hugo, Maurice Rollinat, Catulle Mendès and Edmond Rostand by Chabrier (who also taught music to Villiers de l'Isle Adam); poems by Verlaine by Reynaldo Hahn; poems by Fargue by Satie; poems by Tristan Klingsor by Ravel (and dedicated to the wife of Debussy). Henri Duparc also set poems by a number of contemporaries during his brief career; poems by Montesquiou were set to music by Léon Delafosse, that 'thin, vain, ambitious, blond young man, with icy blue eyes and diaphanously pale, supernaturally beautiful features'[530] who made his début as a pianist at the Salle Erard in April 1894. Fauré op.32 was *Promothée*,[531] with a libretto by André-Ferdinand Hérold and Jean Lorrain. It is, however, perhaps fortunate that the plan by 'some wild drunken companion'[532] of Verlaine to set to music Renan's *Life of Jesus* was ridiculed by Renan himself – doubtless it violated his dictum that 'la vérité est dans les nuances'.

~~~~~~~

It must not be inferred that all these groups consistently exhibited amity and fraternity, or even when they did that it was sincere. There were as many dislikes and hostilities as there were the affinities and support already noted: in the *huis clos*, Hell is other people. Some of these were literary or artistic rivalries sometimes misanthropic; sometimes just sexual – it did not endear Jules Lemaître to Anatole France that a lady had thrown him over for the former. This is not only not surprising according to ordinary social behaviour; not even not surprising because within the human condition both hostility and affinity co-exist, but also not surprising within the whole pattern of alterity and mutation, of conflict and order, that made Paris. This was a society that lived at the breaking point of nervous tension.

The examples are multiform and revealing. Albert Dubeux for example, writing in Julia Bartet's lifetime, suggests that one reason why the reputation of Sarah Bernhardt outshone that of Bartet – and in particular the performances of each as Maria de Neubourg in Hugo's *Ruy Blas* – was that Bartet was belittled by 'la presse juive' in both Paris and London.[533]

In 1895, in terms which Zola might have used, the painter Gérôme told the *Journal des Artistes* 'We are in a century of decadence and imbecility. And I'm not speaking only of the world of art, it's all of society that is stinking'.[534] Gérôme led the opposition to the acquisition by the State of the Caillebotte bequest of Impressionists. Ambroise Thomas threatened to resign if Fauré were appointed to the Conservatoire; Massenet actually did so. 'I am staying in town to speak ill of *Pelléas*,' said Saint-Saëns, who had a sort of vendetta against Debussy, and as well as regarding Massenet as 'sugar and water'.[535] Debussy 'never missed the chance to say an unkind word about [Charpentier's] *Louise*'.[536] Marie Belloc believed that the glacial outward manner of Dumas *fils* contained 'a strong streak of violence',[537] for all that he seemed according to another acquaintance to exist in a state of perpetual childhood,[538] and Albert Dubeux thought that he attracted and repelled at the same time, 'la bouche amère sous la moustache avantageux; la voix métallique semble faite pour la sarcasme'[539]. When personality traits were turned outward, there was little kindly feeling. 'The courteous Manet and the caustic Degas took little pleasure in each other's society'[540] and frequently sneered at each other. Renoir disliked Pissarro and quarrelled with Cézanne. Manet thought little of Renoir as a painter (although Berthe Morisot thought him Monet's only rival[541]) and less of Bohemians such as Champfleury and Duranty whose manners and linen left much to be desired.[542] Degas and Morisot demanded the exclusion of Seurat from one of the Indépendant exhibitions[543]. Toulouse-Lautrec insulted Carabin in public.[544] Manet refused to exhibit with Cézanne, and Whistler 'much'[545] disliked him. Cézanne loathed Gauguin, and never spoke again to Zola, his friend of thirty years, after reading *L'Œuvre*. Antoine Guillemet, who had introduced Zola to Manet,[546] resented what he thought was his portrayal as Fagerolles in the same work, although J.-F. Raffaëlli would also seem to match. Zola said that it was Henri Gervex whom he had in mind.[547] As a result, Gervex vanished under the weight of Fagerolles, 'captif de l'ombre de Fagerolles'. 'Y a-t-il eu un mystère Gervex,' ask the editors of the sole work devoted to him, 'un complot contre sa mémoire qui explique ce silence?'[548]

The novel also led to a coolness between Zola and Pissarro who 'felt that [it] was a betrayal of Zola's comradeship with the artists who had constituted the Café Guerbois group in the 1860s'.[549] Zola himself quarrelled with Arthur Ranc and vigorously attacked Victor Hugo. Huysmans 'with that benevolent malice so characteristic of him', once said of Zola's famous researches that they consisted of going for a drive in a carriage with madame Zola.[550] André Antoine noted that 'Mendès is really a strange chap. We regarded each other coldly for some years, because for some reason he had persuaded himself that I disliked poets and he went round saying so. He wasn't much put out, therefore, by the collapse of the Théâtre Libre'.[551] Verlaine, according to Yeats, thought Maeterlinck 'a bit of a mountebank'.[552] There was a feud between the comtesse de Martel and the comte d'Haussonville, a member of the Académie Française and a close adviser of the comte de Paris;[553] Jean Lorrain quarrelled publicly with Séverine, who published an open letter to 'ma bonne Lorrain'.

One must not underestimate the general antipathy to the works of the Impressionists, at least until the 1880s. At the sale of works by Monet, Sisley, Renoir and Berthe Morisot at the Hôtel Drouot salerooms in 1875, there had been a demonstration against the artists by the students of the École des Beaux Arts, among them George Moore and Lewis Welden Hawkins, the 'Marshall' of George Moore's *Confessions of a Young Man*, and, in part, the Lewis Seymour of Moore's *A Modern Lover*.

Raffaëlli attracted the 'vehement dislike'[554] of Caillebotte, and Gauguin refused to exhibit with the Impressionists in 1882 because of his dislike for Raffaëlli, who was a friend of Degas and Pissarro. Subsequently Gauguin quarrelled with Signac and Émile Bernard, in the latter case irrevocably, causing Bernard to fall out with Albert Aurier because of the latter's admiration for Gauguin. Gauguin also resented any suggestion that he owed anything to Anquetin. Pissarro defended Seurat against criticism by Degas, but thought the work of Gauguin's friend Schuffenecker 'amateurish and lacking in character',[555] a widely-held opinion made the more interesting by the recent suggestions that a number of works credited to van Gogh are in fact by Schuffenecker, who taught drawing from 1889 to 1914 at the Lycée Michelet. Whistler thought nothing of Cézanne; Cézanne dismissed the work of van Gogh.[556] Caillebotte told Pissarro that Degas' protégé Lepic 'had no talent at all'.[557] Degas dismissed Bastien-Lepage as 'the Bouguereau of the modern movement', was jealous of Lautrec, and 'greatly disliked' Rodin.[558] Stevens 'had a particular dislike' for the work of Carrière.[559] Ironically, Durand-Ruel lived to denounce the work of Cézanne, Gauguin and Matisse at the autumn Salon 1900: 'I was much amused to hear him use the same arguments against them as other dealers had used forty years before against the Impressionists', wrote Antony Ludovici, an Englishman of Italian background who in 1875 married a Parisian called Marie Cals.[560]

Among the literary men, Huysmans referred to Léon Bloy as 'this literary louse'.[561] Verlaine and Leconte de Lisle 'despised each other'.[562] René Ghil launched a violent polemic against Théodor de Wyzewa. Henry Bauër held 'une rancune tenace' for André Antoine; it took the death of Henri Becque to reconcile them.[563] There was also an estrangement between Antoine and Lugné-Poë.[564] Jacques-Émile Blanche became estranged from both Marcel Proust and the comte de Montesquiou. 'Burty! Don't mention Burty to me!' Manet once exclaimed.[565] Edouard Lalo was 'among the few people for whom Léon Daudet had a good word,' recalled Marie Belloc, while Ernest Renan was the only man of whom she ever heard Anatole France speak well – yet France was, in the opinion of Chris Healy, 'a cultured, kindly gentleman'.[566] Felicien Rops took strongly against François Coppée: his etching 'Tombe numéro 2' shows a tank of semen labelled 'produit de la patrice de M. François Coppée, guaranti pur'. One may guess that the satire lay in the 'garanti pur'.[567] Ferdinand Brunetière and Albert Delpit severed a ten year friendship over the former's bitter and vindictive opposition to the erection of a statue to Baudelaire, and Robert Sherard described Brunetière as 'made up of equal proportions of spite and envy',[568] a view to set beside that of Maurice Baring that Brunetière was 'the last of the great critics of the period',[569] although the two positions are not necessarily in conflict. Professor at the École normale supérieur from 1886 and editor of the *Revue des Deux Mondes* from 1893, Brunetière was 'a man of extraordinary force of character. [He] resisted the idea that literature was merely an entertainment or pastime. He asserted that it was the crown and apex of a virile education […] its aim […] the maintenance and progress of morality'.[570] In this he would clearly have had no time for Wildean æstheticism, and indeed opposed Anatole France and Jules Lemaître for their lack of concern with ethics.

The founding manifesto of Symbolism by Jean Moréas was attacked by other Symbolists as 'erroneous and incomplete'.[571] thought himself surrounded by enemies; Becque and Dumas *fils* loathed each other.[572] Sardou 'had a sharp malicious tongue',[573] as befitting a man who in old age came to resemble Voltaire. Huysmans, whom 'one could recognise by his hatred of Rosny',[574] also disliked Edmond de Goncourt and detested Alphonse Daudet; Goncourt grew increasingly misanthropic. It is ironic that Goncourt should refer to Leconte de Lisle's 'rancorous, cannibal malice'.[575] 'M. de Goncourt talked freely to me of his fellow writers. Of them all, he cared only for Daudet. As to the others he sometimes spoke of them with contempt, and always with malice,' wrote Marie Belloc, who thought him the only snobbish Frenchman she had ever met.[576] Goncourt,

Marie Belloc also recalled 'was not liked and he did nothing to make himself liked, by most of his contemporaries'.[577] This was a sad conclusion to the friendship of 'les Cinq', the jovial little dining circle of Daudet, Goncourt, Flaubert, Turgenev and Zola, which had never quite recovered after Flaubert's death in 1880, had been reduced by that of Turgenev, and had finally collapsed under the weight of the jealousy of Daudet and Goncourt for the success of Zola.

Jules Renard gave a telling example of Goncourt's snobbery, quoting him as saying 'Maupassant isn't a great writer, not what *we* would call an artist'.[578] Goncourt wrote in his diary that Maupassant had 'an undeniable but second rate talent',[579] a verdict repeated by Richard Whiteing but transmuted into Anglo-Saxon disapproval. Maupassant, he thought, was 'a second and more objectionable Flaubert, a writer of power, but absolutely unreadable according to what the French are pleased to call our Puritan rules'.[580] One night at Daudet's in March 1889, the guests were Goncourt, Rosny, Carrière, M. et Mme Toudouze and Georges Rodenbach and his wife: 'How they worked over that poor Zola,' recorded Jules Renard.[581] Marie Belloc, who called on Zola whenever she visited Paris, found him 'a singularly friendless man'[582] disliked by all his fellows apart from Daudet. Goncourt, Huysmans and even Daudet (despite his 'inexhaustible kindness of heart'[583]) all refused to make a congratulatory speech at the dinner for Zola that marked the publication of *Le docteur Pascal* and the completion the Rougon-Macquart cycle,[584] and the speech was made by Catulle Mendès. Turgenev told George Moore that he disliked Zola's vulgar realism; Zola himself regarded Turgenev 'more in the light of an obliging business connection than as a man of letters'.[585] Popular writers like Jules Verne only seem to have escaped calumny by not intersecting with Parisian literary circles, although the photographer Nadar appears as 'Ardan' in Verne's *De la terre à la lune*. Daudet, having written a long article on Turgenev full of kindly feeling which was published in the *Century Magazine* of New York, was correcting it again in proof for his book when

> a book of *Souvenirs* is brought to me, in which Tourgénieff from the other side of the grave criticises me without mercy. As an author, I am beneath all criticism; as a man, I am the lowest of my kind. My friends were all aware of it and told fine stories about me. What friends did Tourgénieff allude to, and could they remain my friends if they held such an opinion of me? And himself, that excellent Slave [i.e. Slav], who obliged him to assume so cordial a manner with me? I can see him in my house, at my table, affectionate, kissing my children. I have in my possession many

exquisite warm-hearted letters from him. And what lay behind that kindly smile? Good heavens! How strange life is.[586]

Despite this revelation of duplicity, Daudet re-published his article, an act that was either honourable or itself with duplicit *arrière pensée* in the light of the above. Not that Daudet was always charitable in his own judgments. 'What poor, absurd creatures,' he once said of the Symbolists.[587] It is little wonder that Marcel Schwob once reflected that kindness is the rarest thing in the world, to which Jules Renard added the mordant reflection that 'To write about a friend is to break with him'.[588] Even in the social salon, it was possible to discern artifice and mixed intentions behind the courtesies.

> The straining after effect, the desire to outshine others, the angry silences frequent in Paris literary salons used to depress me [...] Even Barrès, who certainly had a soul and who strove towards greatness all his life, who, moreover, attained something like literary perfection in several of his books, was too restless under his apparent confidence and too near ill-nature in his brilliant sarcasms.[589]

Of his brief visit to London, Manet wrote to Zola 'There is none of that ridiculous sort of jealousy that exists with us; they are nearly all gentlemen'.[590] Nevertheless, apart from the Wilde/Whistler feud, something of Parisian confrontation spilled over: Walter Crane did not have much time for Degas, for example, and Moore 'couldn't abide'[591] Sickert.

~~~~~~

The vogue for Wagner resulted in attempts to compose in the Wagnerian manner, most derivatively in *Sigurd* by Reyer[592], which had its Paris première on 12th June 1885. Mendès' enthusiasm for Wagner was such that he wrote the libretto for Chabrier's pseudo-Wagnerian opera *Gwendoline*, a 'second-rate text' according to Chabrier's biographer.[593] The influence of 'the incorrigible Mendès' on Chabrier, thought Poulenc, was 'pernicious', making the composer 'alas! a lifelong slave'; the libretto of *Gwendoline* was 'balderdash'.[594] Edward Lockspeiser, noting a plan for co-operation on a version of *Le Cid*, thought that 'there is something grotesque about Debussy's association with this picturesque character'; and Marcel Dietschy refers to Debussy 'tricking' himself in associating with Mendès.[595] The composer Gabriel Pierné, a pupil of César Franck and of Massenet, was pulled into Mendès' orbit, writing music for *Le Collier des saphires* (1891), *Les joyeuses commères de Paris* (1892) and *Le Docteur Blanc* (1893). Poulenc wrote of Mendès 'I have never been fully able to understand this question of Mendès. One has only to read the libretto of Messager's *Isoline* to realise what kind of writer he was. One day in Colette's presence I expressed astonishment at the prestige this mountebank enjoyed in 1880s. With marvellous peasant logic, Colette replied "What do you expect, he was a Zeus, smelling of patchouli!"'[596] George Moore has left an extended description of Mendès, 'his fragile face illuminated with the idealism of a depraved woman'.

> He takes you by the arm, by the hand, he leans towards you, his words are caresses, his fervour is delightful, and to hear him is as sweet as drinking a perfumed yellow wine. All he says is false [...] An exquisite artist; physically and spiritually he is art [...] He never wrote an ugly line, but he never wrote a line that some of his brilliant contemporaries might not have written. He has produced good works of all kinds, 'et voilà tout'. Every generation, every country has its Catulle Mendès. Robert Buchanan is ours, only in the adaptation Scotch gruel has been substituted for perfumed yellow wine.[597]

This subtly-expressed dislike was apparently reciprocated, Heinrich Felbermann writing 'I shall never forget with what amazement Catulle Mendès asked me one day if it could be true that Moore had actually written a book which had made some stir, as he did not think him capable of expressing two ideas coherently'.[598] Mendès, to whom Debussy came to feel 'a profound antipathy',[599] is also described in the biography of Massenet in unattractive terms: 'His Silenus-like figure, globular eye, flabby cheek and greedy mouth were a familiar presence in the boulevard cafés, where he trumpeted his judgments in a voice hoarsened by champagne.'[600] One may imagine Mendès and Wilde, also somewhat Silenus-like, outside cafés on opposite sides of a street, each with his claque. It should be possible to establish just such a scenario: Mendès, 'that prince of *causeurs*',[601] favoured the Café Napolitain at no.1, boulevard des Capucines, for instance, and Wilde, 'this Fabergé in words',[602] used the Grand Café at no.14. We have one account of a meeting between the two:

> 'Wilde had further remarked,' said Mendès, as we sat together in the low-ceilinged Vapori restaurant inhaling cigarette smoke and indolently watching the opaline rings it made, 'that paradoxes, though only half truths, were the best we could get, as there were no absolute truths'. Mendès had then said: 'There should be a paradoxist to act as your balance on the moral side'; to which Wilde replied 'Yes, but Christ was the only one there has ever been; our familiarity with the New Testament blinds us to the enormity of its paradoxes. What could be more enormous than 'Blessed are the Poor?'[603]

Debussy's music, like the composer himself, was firmly embedded in the art and literature of the day. His 'Girl with the Flaxen Hair' (1881) was inspired by a poem of Leconte de Lisle's, and his 'Drowned Cathedral' (1909-10) owes much to Monet's pictures of Rouen Cathedral.[604] Debussy, interested in the interplay of light and shadow that he explored in his Nocturne compositions, was close to the ideas of the Impressionists, although he did not like the term being applied to himself. Are we looking once more here at the blurring of the lines, the effects of shimmering, reflets sur l'eau? The first section of 'La Mer' of 1903 was inspired by a story of Camille Mauclair's. Whether written then or later, many of Debussy's compositions reflect the æsthetic concerns of the period: 'You would do me a great favour by calling me a pupil of Monet,' he told a friend.[605] In his personal tastes, too, Debussy was an æsthete. Nevertheless, 'the greatest influence on Debussy was Nature itself'.[606] He admired the landscapes of Frits Thaulow, and Thaulow's own remark 'naturalism was a religion and we were its fanatical adherents'[607] seems the apposite link.

Did Wilde know Debussy? There is one occasion, not mentioned by Ellmann, when Wilde was invited to a dinner party given by Georges Louis,[608] the brother of Pierre Louÿs. The other guests were Debussy, Valéry, Heredia, Blanche, Antoine de Rochefoucauld, the marquis de Montebello[609] (sometime ambassador in St Petersburg), Captain Walewski (grandson of Napoléon I) and Léon Bourgeois,[610] who as Minister of Education in 1891 had refused to overturn the decision of the Board of Censors to ban La Fille Elisa. This gathering would place Wilde in very exalted company – if it happened. Lockspeiser dates it to February 1893, and Roger Nichols also says that Wilde met Debussy in February 1893[611] (perhaps just following Lockspeiser) but an examination of Holland and Hart-Davis shows that Wilde was in Devonshire all that month. Lockspeiser also says that Louÿs was at this dinner, but Nichols dates Debussy's first meeting with Louÿs, who became one of his closest friends, to May 1893. It seems insubstantial enough to disbelieve (Dietschy, in his very social biography of Debussy, makes no mention of Wilde; Wilde, in his letters, no mention of Debussy). Wilde's strictures on Massenet ('endless false alarms of a real melody, and incessant posing of themes that are not resolved into any development'[612]) hardly argue any affinity between Wilde and Debussy, though Debussy later found himself caught up in Wildean echoes, faint but pursuing, when he wrote the score for d'Annunzio's The Martyrdom of Saint Sebastian, with Ida Rubinstein, who played Salomé in St Petersburg,[613] and again when in 1911 he wrote

Kama for his 'girl anglaise', Maud Allen, whose own version of Salomé was to have such scandalous consequences.

~~~~~~

Seven days before he died, Cézanne gave his final judgment on the artists of his day: 'All my compatriots are arseholes beside me'.[614]

CHAPTER FIVE

CONVERSE

'Princess, for such and such as we
No song hath such a glad refrain; –
Never again to part from thee!
I am in Paris once again.'
– Richard Le Gallienne.

'I am in Paris! What boundless delight!'
– Marie Bashkirtseff.[615]

'Paris is a city that pleases me greatly.
While in London one hides everything, in Paris one reveals everything.'
– Oscar Wilde.[616]

OSCAR Wilde first visited Paris in August 1867, when he was twelve years old, taken there with his fourteen-year old brother by their mother 'to visit an exhibition', says Speranza's biographer,[617] but surely to visit the Exposition Universelle of that year, even though Lady Wilde thought exhibitions 'vulgar'. (Oscar's illegitimate half-brother, Henry Wilson , had been educated in Paris many years earlier.[618]) The expedition seems to have been more conceived in the spirit of taking children to Disneyland than from any higher motives, although three weeks is a long time to spend in Paris under an August sun with two boys in tow. Lady Wilde at least appreciated the city and found Dublin provincial on her return. She did not go back to Paris, however, until October 1875, and then it was in order to get away from Sir William's valetudinarianism. This worked well enough – she remarked upon the 'fine, pure clean air' as being restorative – but she thought Paris had declined in *ton* since the end of the Empire. (There was not much of the Republican about Speranza.) 'All the glory of fashion is gone,' she told her friend Rosalie Olivecrona. 'I have not seen a well-dressed woman in Paris. There is no one to lead society.'[619]

Lady Wilde's idea of being a well-dressed woman herself would hardly have detained a Paris couturier for longer than it took him to smile, but it is curious that it was fashion and the social round, rather than art, politics or literature that Speranza wished to report upon to her Swedish friend.

> The foreigner usually has a quite false idea of Paris. He looks on it as a city of pleasure strongly underlaid with vice, inhabited by a population which is never serious and rarely goes to bed. Nothing hurts the true Parisian more than this conception of his beloved city, for it is full of hard workers, clever craftsmen and serious thinkers.[620]

'You Englishmen,' Ernest Renan told H.A.L. Fisher in 1889, 'think of Paris as a great fair, a place of frivolity and amusement. I tell you it is nothing of the sort. It is the hardest working place in the world'. Of course, in 1889 Paris *was* a great fair – it is said that twenty-five million visitors visited the Exposition Universelle of that year – but perhaps Renan was working too hard to notice; nor does one associate frivolity with the high-minded Fisher, the future historian and Cabinet Minister. Even Henry James, recording that 'there are moments when I grow rather weary of M. Sarcey',[621] ascribed this to the fact that the critic had 'in an eminent degree both the virtues and the defects which attach to the great French characteristic – the habit of taking terribly *au sérieux* anything you may set about doing'.[622] The ability to distinguish serious Paris from 'gay Paree' marked out those who claimed to know Paris from the inside from those who saw it only as a site of projected fantasy, usually lubricious.[623] Filson Young's 'John Lauder' was one of the former, and he puts the point: '"Dear, charming people! And they call them frivolous – the most serious people in the world".'[624] Spencer Hughes also noted that

> There is a rather general impression in this country that Paris is altogether given over to gaiety, or at any rate to lounging, sauntering and idleness, but in reality the residents, when taken apart from visitors, are a remarkably strenuous, hard-working and business-like people.[625]

This bears directly on 'Paris' as a negotiated concept – and on the reception of Wilde.

That scholars came to Paris to work rarely shows through in the accounts of Paris life. There was not much frivolity when in 1879 Francis Parkman spent the spring and summer arranging the copying of more than ten thousand pages from the Archives de Marine. Perhaps it is necessary to hunt for such people in the Paris summer, when austere duty was the only mistress that kept them there. 'There is little to do or see,' wrote Henry James in 1876, 'and therefore little to write about. There is in fact only one thing to do, and that is, get out of Paris.'[626] Henry Adams, looking for secret documents on the Louisiana Purchase, arrived in Paris in September 1879, but it took until November before he could start work and he retired to Spain for the interval. Three years later, Richard Jebb preferred October for collating a manuscript in the Bibliothèque Nationale, which allowed him to see Sarah Bernhardt twice in the same play at the Comédie Française. This was within a couple of minutes' walk of where he and his wife were staying: 'in a little street off the rue de Rivoli, in a small French hotel, well-known to English people, *but* very quiet and altogether French in its ways.'[627] Jebb should have felt at home in Paris, for he was a somewhat dandified figure: W.H. Thompson, Master of Jebb's Cambridge college, said of him 'The time he can spare from the neglect of his duties, he devotes to the adornment of his person'. Wilde called him, to his face, 'not only a perfect scholar but also a brilliant man of letters.'[628]

It was also possible for members of the public to attend the lectures at the Collège de France throughout this period. One finds at the Cours Talbot in the boulevard des Capucines well-attended afternoon lectures by Henri de Pommeraye, Francisque Sarcey, Jules Lemaître, Camille Flammarion and even Laurent Tailhade.[629] Maurice de Bunsen, in Paris to learn French in April 1875, attended lectures there, notably those of St René Tallandier on French literature, and other lectures at the Sorbonne. He also met Renan at Madame Mohl's, and another who met Renan at this time was Henry James, at a dinner given by Auguste Laugel, correspondent of *The Nation*. James had imagined Renan as 'a thin and delicate aristocrat'; the reality 'struck him as hideous […] almost dwarfish and so remarkably corpulent that he had difficulty walking. His head seemed too large for his squat body'.[630] But then, James was no Infanta, and nor was it his birthday.

If James was struck by the difference between the imagined and the real Renan at the time, Herbert Tint has discerned more that was paradoxical in the philosopher. 'Renan remains an enigma to his reader, as long as he assumes that a man of Renan's renown cannot really have been guilty of the basic contradictions apparently contained in his writing. But he was. The contradictions it so elegantly exhibits are of the very essence of the author.'[631] There was much here that might have fascinated Wilde; and Wilde, who once had the temerity to quote Renan to Mr Gladstone, admired Renan's *Life of Christ*; and once claimed to have heard Renan say that he preferred a military despotism to that of the Church[632] – Wilde could easily have found his way, had he so wished, to its author. Wilde shared Renan's distaste for the Naturalist school and its coarseness.[633] Again, one might have supposed that Wilde would have been interested in the lectures of Gustave Larroumet,[634] dramatic critic of *Le Temps*, perpetual secretary of the Institut de France from 1898 to his death in 1902, and intellectual mécène of the actress Cécile Sorel.[635] 'His lectures drew writers, artists and students from all countries to hear his novel and profound ideas about our classics.'[636]

~~~~~~~

In 1889 H.A.L. Fisher, armed with letters of introduction to Renan and to Hippolyte Taine, moved into a 'genteel pension' in the rue St Jacques, kept (it is incumbent to record) by a M. et Mme Casaubon.[637] 'M. Casaubon claimed descent from the Genevan Calvinist and Greek scholar, and was himself secretary in the Mairie of his arrondissement.'[638] From here Fisher 'explored every nook and cranny of the Latin Quarter' before joining William Rothenstein and Arthur Studd in the Hôtel de France et de Lorraine on the corner of the quai Voltaire and the rue de Beaune.[639] Renan and Taine dominated French intellectual life in the 1880s and the generation that was beginning to emerge into the limelight 'owed much of its inspiration' to them, opposing 'youthful energy and idealism to the decrepitude, complacency and cynicism of those in power. It blamed the materialistic complacency for the decline, and advocated government by an élite, animated by spiritual ideals.'[640] To their frequently linked names, Maurice Baring adds a third, Fustel de Coulanges, but he has become largely invisible to posterity. [641]

Clearly, this debate lit with varying degrees of luminosity the way for Barrès, for Péguy,[642] for Laugel, for Maurras. De Vogüé and Bourget acknowledged Taine their master. Yet Taine was essentially a pessimist ('high priest of the cult of misanthropy and pessimism,' Baring calls him[643]), his pessimism linked philosophically to his materialism, but also politically to his work as an historian. 'I went to call on Taine', wrote Morley of a visit to Paris in January 1892. 'It was his wife's day at home. The only other interesting person was Leroy Beaulieu, brother of the economist, and himself the author of the excellent and elaborate book on Russia [...] Taine *as usual* very despondent about France and democracy'.[644] Who, therefore, were the élite to whom government should be entrusted? The old nobility, the Academy, the officer class, the Normaliens, the *philosophes*? Albert de Mun[645] and the Catholic social reformers? Or the class conscious knights of labour? And whence the 'spiritual ideals'? Elusive as a concept, disappointing in its components, and unable to shake the secure bourgeois of the Palais Bourbon, government by an élite seemed far away from the concerns even of a future Minister of Education who became Head of an Oxford college.

When Fisher came to survey the Third Republic in his monumental *History of Europe*, he recalled that the French spent little time discussing parliamentary politics: 'The theatres, the salon, the Académie Française, constitute a pleasanter, more absorbing interest',[646] but Taine was also the philosopher of both Realism and Naturalism[647] and at his house in the rue Cassette Fisher met Leconte de Lisle – and 'the God we were taught to worship was Monet'.[648]

All this, of course, was in the interval between Boulanger and Dreyfus, but if politics did not absorb conversation then, when it did do so it killed conversation. Fisher's insight into the place of the conversationalist in Paris is given a different slant by Mary Waddington, who refers to the divisive nature of politics.

> The political talk [in London] was exactly like what I have heard so often in Paris, only [...] the men talk more quietly [...] and with less gesticulating. Also they don't carry politics into private life as they do with us [...] In France there is a great gulf between parties, even moderates, royalists and republicans, and I was astounded when I first mixed in political life in France to see people in society turn their backs upon some perfectly distinguished, honourable gentlemen because they did not have the same opinion as themselves in politics.[649]

Frederic Harrison, whose son, the landscape painter Bernard Harrison, took over Will Rothenstein's studio in Montmartre, came to know Turgenev, Francisque Sarcey, Edouard Rod[650], Victor Hugo, Jules Ferry and Victor Cherbiliez, as well as P.G. Hamerton.[651] He also recorded his admiration for 'the sympathetic soul of Jules Michelet, the unctuous charm of Ernest Renan, and the indomitable optimism of dear, good, simple Louis Blanc'. Harrison here was showing a good deal of simplicity himself, for there were many who regarded Blanc as the reverse of dear and good, who anathematised Renan, and who would have agreed with Huysmans' more ambiguous view of Michelet:

> Though the garrulous old gossip drivelled endlessly about matters of supreme unimportance and ecstasized in his mild way of trivial anecdotes which he expanded beyond all proportion, and though his sentimentality and chauvinism sometimes discredited his quite plausible conjectures, he was nevertheless the only French historian who had overcome the limitation of time and made another age live anew before our eyes. Hysterical, garrulous manneristic [...] the personages were raised from oblivion [and] became live human beings. What matter then if Michelet was the least trustworthy of historians since he was the most personal and the most evocative?[652]

Harrison also noted that 'one must be young and strong of nerve to enjoy to the full the society and intellect of Paris'.[653] Whether Oscar Browning fulfilled these criteria may be questioned, but when he was in Paris researching the foreign policy of William Pitt in January 1881, he made his number with Albert Sorel and with Taine, recording that the latter 'was particularly kind to me and I met a delightful society at his hospitable table'.[654]

For those of lesser sociability than Browning, Paris provided much free intellectual stimulation in lecture rooms and pulpits. In the autumn of 1896, G.P. Gooch, the future historian, spent two months in Paris, and although Taine and Renan were dead,[655] he sought out the lectures of Émile Gebhardt the mediævalist, Ernest Lavisse on history, Gaston Maspero[656] on Egyptology, Émile Boutroux on philosophy, Émile Faguet on literature, and (at the École Libre des Science Politiques) Albert Sorel. Faguet, nicknamed 'the eunuch' by his students, seems to have been particularly accessible: 'His congested rooms in the rue Monge were open to any young inquirer'.[657] Dramatic critic for the *Soleil*, from 1892 he was literary critic for the *Revue Bleue*; and in 1896 successor of Jules Lemaître on the *Journal des débats*, open-minded enough to be fair to Zola. His three volumes of collected articles should be consulted: *Notes sur le théâtre contemporain, Questions de la théâtre* and *Propos de theatre*.

> Faguet, who was the recognized academic critic of the end of the last century, while he held that posterity would be unable to understand how Zola could ever have been popular, yet recognized him in *Germinal* as the heroic representative of democracy, incomparable in his power of describing crowds, and he realized how marvellous is the conclusion of this book.[658]

A lecture by Jules Lemaître took Gooch to the Comédie Française, and he became a dedicated theatre-goer, a devotee of Bernhardt; while 'the bright memories of *Tartuffe* and *L'Avare, Le Médecin malgré lui, Les Précieuses Ridicules* and *Les Fourberies de Scapin* have never dimmed'. He was later to write two significant essays on Juliette Adam, 'Madame Adam and Gambetta' and 'Madame Adam and the *Revanche*',[659] but if Gooch, who on Sundays would go to 'sample the leading preachers of the day', ever extended his pursuits to Montmartre, he left no recollection of it.[660]

In Paris two years after Gooch, the ruined Wilde found none of this intellectual stimulation, not even the lectures on the Celts and Hellenes by d'Arbois Jubainville at the Collège de France, which John Millington Synge attended. One may hope that the publication in 1899 of a French translation by Arthur Symons of Walter Pater's *Imaginary Portraits*, gave Wilde pause for reflection that was not entirely melancholy.

~~~~~~~

It is impossible not to notice the immense output of the literary men, and not only the literary men.[661] This has not always led to posthumous fame. Gabriel-Jules Delarue's fifty volumes of poetry, written under the name José de Strada, soon became as obscure as their creator, living behind closed shutters in his house in the avenue Henri-Martin. 'Le nom est mort,' wrote André de Fouquières in 1953, 'et bien mort. Et sans doute était mort avant l'homme.'[662] Other names remain alive, even if the works do not. As a representative sample: the duc d'Aumale wrote a history of the princes of Condé in five volumes; Léon Say's book on the national finances was in four, Jean-François Bladé's *Poésies et contes populaires de la Gascogne* in six. Francisque Sarcey, apart from his regular theatre column in *Le Temps* and the *Revue d'art dramatique*, wrote a daily political article for Edmond About's journal *Le XIXᵉ Siècle* and the monthly series 'Comédiens et Comédiennes – La Comédie Française' in the *Librairie des Bibliophiles*, as well as holding a weekly symposium on theatre (Cécile Sorel went to this and as a result was invited to his 'brilliant and amazing dinner parties').[663] His *Quarante Ans de Théâtre* was published in eight volumes.[664] Romain Coolus' *Théâtre complet*[665] was published in ten volumes. Émile Ollivier wrote his memoirs in seventeen volumes. Jules Claretie's *La Vie à Paris* ran to twenty volumes, which perhaps why Marcel Dietschy includes him among the 'second-rate literary and artistic types';[666] Romain Rolland's novel *Jean-Christophe* was published in ten volumes, his *Cahiers* in thirty. The Mercure de France edition of the criticism of Remy de Gourmont is in sixteen volumes, with fifteen devoted to his other works. Gyp de Martel[667] wrote twenty plays and over a hundred novels. Paul Bourget's collected works in the edition published by Plon amount to six volumes of criticism, fourteen volumes of novels, eight volumes of novellas, two volumes of plays, two volumes of travel writing and a volume of poetry. Zola, having completed twenty volumes of the Rougon-Macquart cycle[668] at once began on a new trilogy followed by a tetralogy – this apart from novellas, stories and adaptations. There is an element of surplus here. 'The longer I knew him and the more I read his books,' wrote one English acquaintance of Zola, 'the more convinced I was of his utter lack of imagination.'[669]

~~~~~~~

English literary interest, in the period post-1870, may be dated to Arthur O'Shaughnessy's *Lays of France* and Andrew Lang's *Lays and Lyrics of Old France* of 1872.[670] Interest in French verse forms was neither confined to Wilde, nor stopped with him – in 1887 Gleeson White published an anthology of ballades, rondeaux, virelays, triolets and villanelles. Generally speaking, recent critics have been less interested in Wilde's awareness of or experimentation with these ancient forms than with his interest or place in Symbolism. In this context it is worth considering Enid Starkie's view that Symbolism was 'the least French of all the literary movements of France, and this explains the appeal it had for foreigners of all nationalities, as varied as Stuart Merrill, Vielé-Griffin, Jean Moréas and Verhaeren – not to mention Oscar Wilde and George Moore'. If Wilde's attraction to Symbolism was not because it was quintessentially French but because it was *not* so, we come to a new view of Wilde's acculturation within French intellectual life.

No one has attempted to track Moore in parallel with Wilde and though Moore's own accounts of his own life are fanciful, some facts that stand scrutiny seem to emerge. In particular, his *Confessions of a Young Man*, dedicated to Jacques-Émile Blanche, although it is highly coloured, does represent what Moore wished to have known in its year of publication, 1889.[671] Setting off for Paris with the intention of becoming a painter in 1873, he read the work of François Coppée,[672] Verlaine, Léon Dierx, Mallarmé, Jean Richepin, Villiers de l'Isle Adam, Catulle Mendès and José-Maria de Heredia – he refers to the 'fiery glory'[673] of this last, whose neckties, according to Anatole France[674] 'were as splendid as his sonnets'.[675] When he returned to Ireland, Moore had become 'a magnificent young Montmartrian, with a blonde beard *à la Capoul*, trousers hanging wide over the foot, and a hat so small that my sister had mistaken it for her riding hat.'[676]

Paris was a similarly intoxicating experience for the young Violet Markham in the early 1890s, when she was sent *en pension* to a Madame Jacquinot, 'a typical Frenchwoman, kind but without illusions'.

> Many doors and windows opened in such surroundings for a girl brought up in the country and fresh from school [...] My whole being was flooded with new and intoxicating values concerned with pictures, sculpture, and mediæval art. And then there was music, music of a quality previously unknown to me as performed at the Opéra and at the famous concerts conducted by Lamoureux and Colonne.[677]

But the supreme memory of those days is the Comédie Française [...] I went there week after week till I knew nearly every stone of the building. Theatre-going was illumined for me by Mounet-Sully, the greatest actor I have ever known, whose genius swept me off my feet. But the Maison de Molière did not rely for its appeal on one actor, however famous. The Sociétaires at that date included the Coquelins,[678] Got, de Féraudy, Le Bargy,[679] Albert Lambert, Paul Mounet among the men; Madame Bartet, Mlle Reichenberg, Madame Baretta, Mlle Dudlay among the women [...] I look back with nostalgic happiness on my Paris days and after such an experience it was not easy to settle down to life at Tapton in the neighbourhood of a small country town.[680]

Such sentiments may have been shared by Marie Nordlinger from Manchester, when enrolled at the Académie Julian from December 1897 to August 1898. This cousin of Reynaldo Hahn's became a close friend of Marcel Proust and returned to Paris in 1902 to work for S. Bing as a silversmith, collaborating with Proust in translating Ruskin. To thank her for this, Proust gave her Montesquiou's copy of Whistler's *The Gentle Art of Making Enemies*.

Dorothy Menpes sought out the *jeunes* of 1909 in the cafés and cabarets of the Latin Quarter, and finding only types, not for the last time fell into some confusion about identity.

One always sees the same people – the poet, the singer, the actresses, the dreamy novelist, the vivacious artist, the wicked little music-hall person with black hair and sparkling eyes. If one only knows where to go, there are cabarets in which one can see the real student-life of Paris, the real Bohemians, men who sleep during the day, after writing a few lines, or painting a little picture, just sufficient to gain enough money to spend a night in a cabaret, some underground dirty old hole, which seem neither dirty nor a hole to them, who live in a delightful world of their own [...] Extraordinary looking people these Bohemians are – long-haired, shabby, their faces alive with a deathless hope, a certain dignity and gentleness in their manner, continually rolling and smoking cigarettes.

These are not real students.[681]

J.J. Conway, writing just before the Great War, adds to the picture by suggesting that the glory had departed from student life, but the journalist E.C. Bentley contemporanæously offered a rather more wordly-wise interpretation in *Trent's Last Case*, when Trent, a painter, returns to the Paris of his nonage.

There are still amorous evenings in the boulevard St Michel and attic
suppers in the boulevard Montparnasse, but the Latin Quarter of the olden
time has become a pleasure of memory – a joy departed never to return.[682]

[Trent] was admitted to the momentous confidence of *les jeunes*, and found
them as sure that they had surprised the secrets of art and life as the
departed *jeunes* of ten years before had been [...] But the *jeunes*, he
perceived with regret, were totally different from their forerunners. They
were much more shallow and puerile, much less really clever. The secrets
they wrested from the Universe were not such important and interesting
secrets as had been wrested by the old *jeunes*. This he believed and
deplored until one day he found himself seated at a restaurant next to a too-
well-fed man whom, in spite of the ravages of comfortable living, he
recognised as one of the *jeunes* of his own period. This one had been wont
to describe himself and three or four others as the Hermits of the New
Parnassus. He and his school had talked outside cafés and elsewhere more
than solitaries do as a rule; but, then, rules were what they vowed
themselves to destroy. They proclaimed that verse, in particular, was free.
The Hermit of the New Parnassus was now in the Ministry of the Interior
and already decorated: he expressed to Trent the opinion that what France
needed most was a hand of iron [...] Thus he was brought to make the old
discovery that it was he who had changed [...] and that *les jeunes* were still
the same. Yet he found it hard to say what precisely he had lost that so
greatly mattered; unless indeed it were so simple a thing as his high
spirits[683]

Bentley's reflections are a more pleasant version of a passage in Sherard's
biography of Wilde, whose high spirits after 1898 appeared only
intermittently, and frequently out of a glass.

A number of minor writers of verse, who called themselves the new
Hedonists [...] published little books of unpleasing verses [...] But the
readers of these verses were very few, and the nasty, little poets soon crept
back into their suburban kennels, to take to easier and more remunerative
forms of writing [...] They are middle-aged now, the new Hedonists,
whiskered and paunchy. The thin veneer of artistry has long since peeled
off their faces, and the rank stigmata of the Philistine now stand forth.[684]

Other *jeunes* who underwent a transformation was the Latin Quarter poet
Henri Woestyn, who might well have been a hermit of the new Parnassus,
turning himself into a 'round, industrious little bourgeois'[685], writing
detective stories in the quai de Bologne; and Julien Green's friend Jean
Simonin whose nearest approach to becoming a Parnassien was to become
the proprietor of a small pharmacy near the Gare Montparnasse. This sets
up a whole other mythopœia, well expressed by Robert Service:

O days of glamor, glory, truth,
To you to-night I raise my glass;
O freehold of immortal youth,
Bohemia, the lost, alas!
O laughing lads who led the romp,
Respectable you've grown, I'm told;
Your heads you bow to power and pomp,
You've learned to know the worth of gold.
O merry maids who shared our cheer,
Your eyes are dim, your locks are gray;
And as you scrub I sadly fear
Your daughters speed the dance to-day.
O windmill land and crescent moon!
O Columbine and Pierrette!
To you my old guitar I tune
Ere I forget, ere I forget.[686]

One may, however, take Marcel Boulestin as a more representative figure. Reading of the Symbolists and Décadents in the *Mercure de France*[687] in his native Poitiers, Paris beckoned. 'I always chose a time when was produced some opera or some play of the kind which even Bordeaux could not procure,' he wrote. This led him to the plays of Ibsen, Hauptmann and Björnson (that is to say, to the Théâtre de l'Œuvre) and 'to hear Antoine,[688] Edouard de Max,[689] Lugné-Poë, Suzanne Desprez,[690] Réjane and Jeanne Granier', this last apparently being as versatile in bed as she was on stage.[691] The Exposition Universelle of 1900 was especially notable: 'I did everything everybody did; saw the realistic dramas of Sada Yacco [...] the dances of Loïe Fuller, Oscar Wilde, aged and tired, having drinks at the Grand Café[692], Sarah in *L'Aiglon*'. Could he also have encountered Isadora Duncan, who went 'night after night' to see Sada Yacco, in the company of Charles Hallé who spent the summer of 1900 in Paris?[693] Falling in with the spirit of place, Boulestin became, not a writer, but one of the many 'nègres' (ghost writers) employed by Willy, the husband of Colette. He also translated Beerbohm's *The Happy Hypocrite*, published by the Mercure de France as *L'Hypocrite Sanctifié* in 1905. This was used a few years later as a libretto with music by Armande de Polignac (the nom-de-plume of the comtesse de Chabannes La Palice); but Boulestin failed to persuade Shaw to let Lugné-Poë produce his translation of *Mrs Warren's Profession*. It was no wonder that on a visit to London (where he was in May 1925 to establish a famous restaurant) that he contrasted the English capital's 'solid luxury as opposed to the façade of Paris'. Boulestin himself offers us something of a façade. He worked for a time as secretary to Cosmo Gordon Lennox, was befriended by Robbie Ross and Reggie

Turner[694] and tried to enlist the support of Lord Alfred Douglas in a project of translating more English plays for the French theatre (Douglas referred him to Lady Gregory). One wonders if the 'aged and tired' Oscar Wilde returned Boulestin's gaze,[695] or indeed, whether Wilde ever caught the eye of the handsome young Brazilian Alberto Santos-Dumont, conspicuous for his dandified dress and the $3^1/2$ h.p. Peugeot motor car he had bought in 1892.

Boulestin's enthusiasm for Paris may have been that of a young gay man from the country, but it was not significantly different from that of the dress designer Paul Poiret, who grew up in the rue des Halles, and was stage struck from an early age. In the 1930s he dwelt on his youthful visits to the Gymnase, the Vaudeville and the Comédie Française – on Mounet-Sully in *Œdipus Rex*, Edmond Got in *L'Ami Fritz*, de Feraudy in *Le Fils de Giboyer*, Bartet in *Antigone*, Réjane in *Ma Cousine*, Granier in *Les Amants*, Bernhardt in *Gismonda*.[696]

Paul Léautaud was less concerned with the successive waves of the *jeunes* than with the breakwater formed by the old: 'the seniors are always there, and even the ancestors, M. Catulle Mendès, for instance'.[697] 'J'ai maintes fois rencontré Mendès, naturellement; comment un Parisien aurait-il pu ne pas le rencontrer?' says André de Fouquières.[698] It is possible to identify where the Hermits of the New Parnassus, and their progenitors, all gathered: Coppée, Valade, Verlaine and Albert Mérat were to be found in the Café Fleurus, 'a delightful little café'[699] in the rue de Fleurus overlooking the nearby Luxembourg Gardens, but the Vachette, the Procope, the François Premier, these also fit the bill. So does the Café d'Harcourt on the corner of place de la Sorbonne and the Boul' Mich', run by two men called Alexandre and François, a favourite of Verlaine's and a sort of headquarters for Pierre Louÿs and Jean de Tinan – the latter saying of the former 'il naquit sans doute à Harcourt' and nicknaming him Petro Ludovico Harcourtensis.[700]

As in so many cafés, habitués of the Harcourt such as de Tinan used it to write letters, and presumably it also acted as a poste restante, a useful rôle when it was so often necessary to cover one's tracks from landlords and tradesmen, from other women's husbands and one's own wife. Arthur Lynch and J.M. Synge once took refuge there from the police during a pro-Greek demonstration at the time of the Graeco-Turkish War. Tinan's poem 'Sonnet Romantique pour une qui portait le même nom' was written there on 30th January 1896, but who bore the same name as whom has not yet been elucidated to my knowledge.

> I went sometimes with Oscar Wilde to the Café d'Harcourt, in the corner
> of which Moréas reigned over a cénacle of noisy poets [...] The Rat Mort
> and the Café de la Place Blanche were temples of silence and order
> compared to the Café d'Harcourt [...] The atmosphere was stifling, and
> thick with tobacco smoke, with the strong perfumes of the grisettes and the
> fumes of alcohol, and the noise deafening [...] At times there would glide
> in among the crowd a sinister figure, often with flowers – stolen, of course
> – which he would place in front of some favoured poet. This was the
> notorious Bibi-la-Purée. I didn't at the time take men like Moréas very
> seriously; indeed, I was surprised to discover, many years later, that
> Moréas was a man of some distinction.[701]

It fell, however, to Picasso, not Rothenstein, to paint Bibi (in 1901).

Rothenstein was more perceptive than Sherard, who in his best *puffiste*
vein wrote that the Greek 'by many is considered the first poet in
France'.[702] Arthur Symons thought little of Moréas[703] and his escape from
the Alexandrine into the line of twenty syllables, comparing him to 'the
little littérateurs who are founding new revues every other week in Paris.
These people have nothing to say, but they are resolved to say something,
and to say it in the newest mode'.[704] (Moréas died reciting Ronsard.)
Symons of course was not merely a commentator on the Symbolists but
active in the literary movements of the 'nineties. Enid Starkie regarded
him as 'more responsible than any other writer for the propagation of
French influence in England'[705] in the 1890s, a large claim. Lord Ronald
Gower, who met him in Rome early in 1897, called him 'one of the chiefs
of a rather morbid school of English decadent writers, a follower and
admirer of Huysmans, *but* a very agreeable companion'.[706] Symons was
the first English translator of Zola's *L'Assommoir*; his *From Toulouse-
Lautrec to Rodin, with Some Personal Recollections*,[707] provides a useful if
frequently overheated guide to the decadents. His mixture of advocacy of,
and fascinated repulsion for, his subjects was caught by George Moore in
his description of him as 'a man of somewhat yellowish temperament,
whom a wicked fairy had cast for a parson.'[708]

The cénacle of the Café Harcourt, says Rothenstein, included Stuart
Merrill, Raymond de Tailhade [*sic*, for de la – Rothenstein was not the
only writer to confound this name with that of Laurent Tailhade[709]] 'and
other poets of the École Romane'.[710] E.V. Lucas reckoned the Harcourt
'the haunt of young bloods [...] I know them not; I merely rejoice in their
existence, admire their long hair and high spirits and happy indigence, and
wish that I could join them among Jullien's [*sic*] models or in the
disreputable cabaret of le Père Lunette'[711] – but by 1912 the Harcourt had

apparently become rather tame.[712] Perhaps the Père Lunette, in the rue des
Anglais (place Maubert), had also improved by the time Lucas was
writing, for Richard Harding Davis (admittedly inclined to New England
priggishness) had characterised it as 'a resort of the lowest class of women
and men [...] The place dreary and the pictures indecent and stupid'.[713]
Sherard adds that the Père Lunette was a two-room café with obscene
frescoes in the inner room, but locates it in the rue Maubert.[714]

This affords one construction of Paris decadence, but, given that in the
classification of Adolphe Baju, very few poets are listed as decadent,[715]
one has to have a sense of the elusiveness of the term (Wilde he lists as a
Neo-Decadent or *Neo-Symbolist*). Baju himself, as founder of the literary
review *Le Décadent* (1886-1889),[716] to which Jean Lorrain,[717] Jules
Renard, Laurent Tailhade, Georges Rodenbach, Maurice du Plessys and
Verlaine all contributed, earned the right to be a guide, though as an editor
Baju was more enthusiastic than successful – *Le Décadent* and its
successor *Le Décadent-revue* were as transient as its predecessors, the two
versions of *Le Scapin*, *Le Scapin* and *Le Scapin-revue* (December 1885 to
December 1886), printed and published by himself in his sixth floor
apartment 'avec la zèle d'un catéchumène'.[718] Pierre Dufay writes
mysteriously that 'on trouver sur l'homme et sur sa gazette des curieux
détails dans le tome 1er de *La Mêlée symboliste* de M. Ernest Raynaud
(p.63-100)'.[719]

Were all æsthetes decadent?   Were all decadents æsthetes?   These
questions multiply. Were all dandies homosexual? Marylène Delphis-
Delbourg answers this one: 'tout homosexuel n'est pas dandy mais la
plupart des dandys de la fin-de-siècle sont des homosexuels notoires.'[720]
There was nothing very 'greenery-yallery' about the homosexual Verlaine,
for example. There is a clear necessity to distinguish between stylistic and
moral decadence. Chris Healy decided that Forain, Steinlen and Rops
were all decadent, but the decadence of Rops was obviously different from
that of Forain and Steinlen. 'With the exception of a few men like Puvis de
Chavannes and Dagnan-Bouveret,' says Healy, 'French painters have
sacrificed sentiment to technique'. But if the privileging of technique over
sentiment is one form of decadence, surely the privileging of sentiment
over technique is another. Among sculptors, Healy exempted Rodin and
Falguière from decadence, but no one would now yoke these two together
for any serious analysis: it was after all Falguière's bust of Balzac that the
commissioning committee, the Société des Gens de Lettres, then presided
over by Zola (1891-1893), preferred to Rodin's. One may also compare
Falguière's bust of Victor Hugo with those by Rodin.[721] Similarly, Healy's

view that all French literature was decadent 'despite the delicate irony of Anatole France, the magnificent strength of Jean Richepin, and the romantic grace of Rostand'[722] depends upon a view of decadence that it would be hard to sustain from a longer perspective, although one might agree with Healy about the 'gilt-edge eroticism' of Pierre Louÿs.[723] (The charge of decadence against Rodin was expressly made by Nordau, who regarded him as having been 'raised to the dignity of a test for decadent ways of feeling [...] an article of faith among the degenerates [...] the 'Gates of Hell' an illustration of hystero-epilepsy and feminine sadism [...] a subsoil of corrupted sensuality in the artist's soul.'[724])

Again, what of Fernand Gregh? If a decadent at all, it was only for his nonage, and the journal that he edited (the 'vaguely symbolist'[725] *Le Banquet*, which lived from March 1892 to March 1893) was a forum for literary young men about town rather than decadents of the Jean Lorrain sort: Gaston de Caillavet, the marquis Robert de Flers,[726] Léon Blum, Jacques Bizet, Louis de la Salle, Gabriel Trarieux[727], Henri Ribaud, Henri Barbusse, Robert Dreyfus, Marcel Proust. These met above Roquette's bookshop in the passage Choiseul.[728] A number of them were homosexual, and Bizet was a depressive who killed himself in 1922. De Caillavet and de Flers were neighbours in the boulevard de Courcelles,[729] and collaborated on pieces for the stage. Gregh contributed to *Le Banquet* under various noms-de-plume, and to this extent he was certainly attached to the prevailing mode of confused and diverse identities. By the end of the century he was rejecting the literary movements of the day, especially Symbolism, and advocating (like Moréas) a return to early forms, and the *Banquet* group were absorbed into the *Revue Blanche*.[730]

Eustace Grenville-Murray satirises the poetry of the early 1880s in his versifier 'M. Poupette', whose saccharine narrative poem 'La Giroflée: An Idyll of City Life' destines him for the Académie Française. This is described at length, and its romantic and anodyne sentiments are surely *décadent* from any more rigorous poetic values. Grenville-Murray, however, makes his point by insisting on the wholesomeness of this drivel. The hero is a young poet whose 'name is Peter, for such names as Oscar and Fernand, in which poets of Alfred de Musset's insalubrious school revelled, must now be discarded: we live in regenerating times when manly heroes must have strong simple names'.[731] This clearly distinguishes decadent form from decadent content.

'The word décadent,' wrote Robert Sherard in 1893, carefully accenting its foreignness for an English readership, 'suggests a dismal, greenish, pimply youth with shabby clothes and frowzy hair.' [732] Nothing of the æsthete there, clearly, let alone the dandy. He then hastens to acquit Stuart Merrill, Adolphe Retté[733], Vielé-Griffin and Maeterlinck of this dreadful charge: 'a finer set of young men one could not wish to see'. This is an important mediation by Sherard, for whom the ideal poet was the chevalier sans peur et (plus importamment) sans reproche – and it is a waymark on his road to his lifelong posthumous defence of Wilde. As for youth, George Moore had just turned twenty-one when he arrived in Paris, Maurice Denis was only twenty in 1890, Misia Godebska was twenty-one when she married Thadée Natanson. Camille Mauclair declared in the *Mercure de France* that youth should be used 'in order to live violently and passionately through our works'.[734] As in England, where Edgar Jepson 'saw the minds of five of my most brilliant friends drown in whisky. It always came in the end to whisky', there was also a Totentanz, 'vie courte, vie fievreuse' in the phrase of Henri Perruchot.[735] Will Low comments on the number of his Parisian friends who died untimely – Gaston La Fenestre and Arthur Cocks the chief of them – Arthur Cocks, who died singing a song by Henri Murger. 'As the gem is to the imitation, so was my friend Cocks to the pseudo-Bohemian,' wrote Low.[736] Villiers de l'Isle Adam, André Gill, Georges Bottini, Alfred Hennequin[737], Guy de Maupassant all died mad – and one symptom of Maupassant's madness was frantic physical activity, dashing round and round his room. One might die of humours other than the *mal de siècle*, of course: Louis Thuillier, Pasteur's assistant, was carried off at the age of thirty-seven by cholera. 'Thirty-five is a very attractive age,' wrote Wilde, 'London society is full of women of the very highest birth who have, of their own free choice, remained thirty-five for years' but Louis Germain died at twenty-three; Lautréamont, Jean de Tinan and Marie Bashkirtseff (a patient of Charcot's) died at twenty-four or twenty-five; the neoclassical poet Jules Tellier succumbed to typhus at twenty-six; Laforgue, the painter Henri Evenepoel[738] and the critic Albert Aurier[739] at twenty-seven, the poet Emmanuel Signoret at twenty-eight. Tinan's hopeless passion for Édith Durand had already induced a nervous breakdown, and his mistress Stephanette, or Phanette, died even before he did. Jules Lambeaux and Seurat were only thirty-two when they died in 1890 and 1891; Bizet, Blanche d'Antigny and Albert Glatigny were thirty-four. Bastien-Lepage died at thirty-six; Toulouse-Lautrec at thirty-seven; de Nittis and Schwob were thirty-eight at their deaths in 1884 and 1905. Charles Buet[740] was thirty-nine. André Gill was forty-five. Charles Cros lived, like Wilde, to be forty-six, but died, according to Verlaine 'dans la plus honorable mais plus déplorable pauvreté'[741] – and for Verlaine to identify this – Verlaine who at one time was drinking wine at sixteen sous (eighty centimes, or a little over a shilling) the litre[742] – the poverty must indeed have been abysmal.

~~~~~~

There was a frenetic energy about much of life in the city, perhaps suggested by the life of the streets, perhaps suggested by youth (of which Wilde was so praising: 'Twenty-three! It is a kind of genius to be twenty-three' he said 'with a dramatic sigh', on learning that this was Richard Le Gallienne's age[743]). This was striking enough to attract the attention of a variety of commentators. Somerset Maugham noted the first when he wrote 'There is in the streets of the poorer quarters of Paris a thronging vitality which excites the blood and prepares the soul for the unexpected'.[744] Harold Nicolson, looking at it from the point of view of an English diplomatic historian, wrote that 'During that restless *fin-de-siècle*, there was a state of nervous exasperation with which we in England failed to sympathise and which we totally failed to understand.'[745] Here, Nicolson implies, the spirit of Paris, that literary concept, spilled over to affect Anglo-French political relations.

Clive Bell decided that the characteristic that best defined his friend J.W. Morrice, who spent most of his working life in Paris, was 'gusto'.[746] Max Nordau reckoned that the uprising of the avant garde artists was one of 'uproar' in what they painted, 'plunder and carnage' in conversation, supported by literary men and journalists 'with fury and wild gesticulation'.[747] Arthur Symons wrote of Verhaeren that his poetry 'more than that of any other modern poet, is made directly out of the complaining voices of the nerves';[748] and Stefan Zweig related this to the spirit of Paris itself, writing that 'Verhaeren creates the poem of the great city in the dionysiac sense; the hymn to our time, to Europe; creates ecstasy, renewed again and again, in life'.[749]

Maurice Donnay, too, caught this tone:

> And in 1890 there were in ideas and morals, an ease and freedom which we found very new. We breathed the air not of liberty but of liberties and that air at first seemed very light. At the Moulin Rouge the *quadrille naturaliste* was danced, a symbol of *La Vie Parisienne*. Soon the expression *Fin de Siècle* flew from mouth to mouth. We went out of Boulangism into Pantheism. We spoke of the black horse of the brave General, the black corset of Mme Marnier, the black gloves of Yvette Guilbert, women wore black stockings, we sang the refrains of the Chat Noir and saw *La Vie en Rose*.[750]

This energy also had a perverse side, to follow Zola's description of Guillaume de Viargue. Although the natural son of the comte de Viargue by a bourgeoise, this 'tall, thin young man of aristocratic air' is degenerate: 'His whole countenance revealed the brainy but weakened tail end of a vigorous line'. Thus Zola as early as 1868,[751] prefiguring his grappling with heredity and strength and weakness of character in the Rougon-Macquart sequence, but thirty years later he had not mined out the theme when he came to describe Hyacinthe Duvillard, fourth generation of a family that while it had gained in wealth, declined in vigour.   In Hyacinthe, the family's push and go has become degenerate, and he is described in a passage which allows him to be usefully be compared with Dorian Gray.

> A wretched scholar, regarding every profession with the same contempt, he had decided to do nothing. [...] He took some little interest in poetry and music, and lived in an extraordinary circle of artists, low women, madmen and bandits; boasting himself of all sorts of crimes and vices, professing the very worst philosophical and social ideas, invariably going to extremes – becoming in turn a Collectivist, an Individualist, an Anarchist, a Pessimist, a Symbolist, and what not besides.[752]

A certain febrile, neurasthenic quality was therefore part of the ambience of decadence in France, just as in England decadence was characterised by languor – and how languid the work produced in contemporary London is by comparison by that of Paris! Edmund Gosse thought the French élan more genuine and spontanæous: 'The English verse of the 'nineties is wistful; it seems to confess to a lack of high animal spirits'[753]. This spilt into a wider perception. Charles Rearick quotes an English *Pleasure Guide to Paris*, which refers to the 'delightful experience of being suddenly transported from the dull commonplace surroundings of a silent and monotonous life in England or elsewhere to the exuberant joy of a gay city which laughs, sings, dances and shouts, eats and drinks from dawn to dusk'.[754] Robert Louis Stevenson noticed that 'the very pace of the vehicles is so brisk'[755] while Booker T. Washington thought that 'Frenchmen might be ahead of black Americans in thoroughness because of the intense competition of their lives'[756] – although this was not the usual perception of American visitors, and may have more to do with Washington's wishing to urge his own people to greater endeavour.

This exuberance did not always commend itself to English observers. Thomas March, writing in 1896, describes the crowd scenes of 5th September 1870 and 28th March 1871 in terms of opprobrium that are cast in the language of national stereotyping:

In their mad frenzy, men would embrace one another, or commence to dance; then, as insane people do, would suddenly relapse into a state of perfect quietude and self-control, making a singular contrast to the effervescence of the previous moment [...] the unchecked and unheeded babbling and gesticulating mass of people.

The Hôtel de Ville was crowded with Guards, who smoked, drank and ate with the utmost freedom and licence within the halls and corridors of the stately edifice.

[The Churches] were taken possession of by an irreverent populace [...] Clubs were formed within them, and were frequented largely by women, who were often addressed from the pulpit by members of their own sex [...] The people generally went to these churches in their ordinary attire and with perhaps less than their ordinary decency – they ate, drank, smoked, spat, shouted, laughed and vulgarly discussed events.[757]

March consistently reports an hysteric quality in those whom he describes, Charles Lullier for example, 'a man of energy and ambition; his intellect was, however, too highly strung: it lacked solidity, and occasionally bordered on madness'.[758]

The frenzy is also captured in Willette's Montmartrois painting *Parce Domine* of 1885, which adorned the Chat Noir. Speaking of the cabarets and cafés-concerts, Steven Moore Whiting says 'the giddy atmosphere at such establishments virtually leaps off the page of any contemporary lithograph, whether by Jules Chéret or Toulouse-Lautrec'.[759] After all 'even Henry James, the austere and melancholy James' was induced to stroll down the boulevard St Michel with Bobinette and the Queen of Golconda on either arm'.[760]

Paul Fort at the time wrote that 'every night the [Café] Voltaire bubbled like a crater',[761] a phrase echoed by Marie-Sophie André and Christophe Beaufils in their description of Gérard Encausse's Sunday morning occult gatherings, 'une chaudron en ébullition'.[762] They accept this as 'ridicule mais pardonnable chez de trop jeunes gens'[763], but another, contemporary, writer related it to a national condition: 'The fatal war [of 1870] was an attack of nerves. The Jew-baiting is another [...] The awful "affaire" is a third'.[764] The abbé Dimnet also related it to the national condition, but made it the subject of censure: 'There is a sort of dreary gaiety in life and literature and on the stage – the admixture of pessimism, of excitement often artificially created, of frankness constantly exaggerated to cynicism and of unmanliness complacently displayed which modern slang calls *veulerie*'.[765]

This of course was written from the standpoint of a believer in Throne and Altar, and is exceptional in its *weltschmerz*. Nevertheless, Dimnet was correct is identifying pessimism as one of the strands of the times: one thinks of Zola's Vagnosc, who once 'dreamed of literature, but his association with certain poets had left him with a feeling of universal despair'.[766] Yet usually the excitement was regarded as benign, positive, creative. Writing in *Le Figaro*, Henry Fouquier thought that

> In this Paris of ours, there is not a blind alley in the poorest quarter, where behind a half-closed door, or window, one may not discover the mysterious gleam of the lamp of some midnight student, intoxicated by Idealism, mad with the fervour of creation.[767]

Even the constant tearing down and rebuilding, although at one level a sign of benign economic development, still fits into this pattern of nervous activity, satirised by Zola in the futile construction of the groynes in *Joie de Vivre*. Miriam Levin, I think unconsciously, picks up on this when discussing the layouts of the Expositions Universelles, saying that they were 'like huge electrical circuit boards in which the productive energies of the Republic coursed along interconnecting paths'.[768]

Arthur Symons links Verlaine and Toulouse-Lautrec ('both faces devoured by visions, feverish and somnolent') with the Ukrainian pianist Vladimir de Pachmann as three examples of abnormal men driven by demonic energy, the last in terms that suggest Dorian Gray's own musical soirées.

> Vladimir de Pachmann – who has in him Russian and Turkish and French blood – is absolutely abnormal and inhuman, and so he evokes, with this ghostly magic of his, the innermost life of music. He has the head of a monk who has had commerce with the Devil, and it is whispered that he has sold his soul to the diabolical instrument which, since buying it, can speak with a human voice. The playing of Pachmann has in it something fantastically inhuman, like fiery ice, and it is for this reason that it remains a thing uncapturable, a thing whose secret he himself could never reveal. It is like the secret of the rhythm of Lautrec's pictures, it is like the secret of the rhythm of Verlaine.[769]

This febrile intensity was a contagion, the bacillus of decadence – and a gynophobic response to the New Woman, for one is never far from Beardsley's Salomé embracing the severed head of the Baptist, or Vallotton's Orpheus being mutilated by the Mænads. Émile Verhaeren was, in the words of Stefan Zweig, 'seized by a limitless thirst for the intoxication of life, as though with one leap he would make good the last years of his loneliness, of his illness, and of his crisis'. Symons also

perceived this in Léon Cladel, 'who had a touch of tenebrous genius […]
He was too highly-strung, too morbid, too nervous […] whose work is
epic […] as in the tumult of his coloured and clotted speech, which
tortures the French language.'[770] In the reverse case of Nina de Villard, the
pursuit of sensation turned into an hysterical condition and she died in an
asylum in July 1884. The *élan français* could easily revert to the *furia
francese*.

CHAPTER SIX

THE THEATRE OF PARIS

'"You gave us a very nice write-up in your last review," Fontan said to
Fauchery. "But why did you describe actors as vain?"'
                                                    – Émile Zola.[771]

'French painters take themselves seriously enough, but oh! The awful
importance of French actors!'
                                                    – H. Vivian.[772]

IF Paris was the cultural capital of Europe, what was the cultural capital of
Paris? The view of our day is that the great medium of expression in fin-
de-siècle Paris was visual art, but, with due acknowledgment to Albert
Wolff, whose *Le capitale de l'art* was published in 1885, and to Catherine
van Casselaer, for whom Paris in the 1890s was 'the undisputed capital' of
something she calls 'world lesbianism',[773] for those at the time this was
matched if not outweighed by the stage. Theatre was all absorbing, and of
great importance in forming the cultural ambience of Paris, using cultural
in all of its many senses. An examination of the theatre of Paris reveals its
fascination for visitors from England or America, who were as likely to
make for the Théâtre Français as for the Salon; and were discriminating in
their judgment, as well as affording a case history within the prevailing
intellectual climate. Theatre should have been a magnet for Wilde, author
of the most successful play of modern times (*The Importance of being
Earnest*), inspirer of one of the most performed operas (*Salomé*) and actor
supreme in the play that was his own life.

At the end of the 1870s, James Welldon (subsequently Headmaster of
Harrow and Bishop of Calcutta) went to Paris to learn French, and found
the Théâtre Français: 'I wonder how often I have seen Sarah Bernhardt
play Doña Sol,' he reflected, recalling Delaunay,[774] Got, Mounet-Sully and
Reichenberg, and adding that he went to the theatre two or three times a
week. He varied this by going to hear sermons, notably those of the
Protestant pastor Bersier. Welldon makes no further reference to the
Français, but says 'The stage, and particularly the French stage, has always
possessed a certain fascination for me', so perhaps this unlikely personage

may be sought again amongst the English visitors.[775] Admiration for Reichenberg, Got, Mounet-Sully and Delaunay was shared by Frederick Pollock, a devotee of the Comédie Française, who describes Delaunay as 'an exquisite *jeune premier* long after he was middle-aged off the boards'.[776]

Max Beerbohm thought French acting superior to English.[777] Esmé Howard, in Paris to learn French from the Protestant clergyman Edmond Stopfer, remembered that he 'learned quite as much French from going frequently to the theatre as from my grammatical studies',[778] his favourites being the Français, the Porte St-Martin, the Odéon, and 'the Palais Royal, with one or two extraordinarily funny actors whose names I now forget'.[779]

Thomas Coolidge, who thought much had declined in Paris between his visits of 1865 and 1881, made an exception for the theatres (and for some cafés), although the only play he mentions seeing then was Sardou's *Divorçons* at the Palais Royal.[780] Henry James, who was to explore theatre in *The Tragic Muse*, as Goncourt explored it in *La Faustin*, was dismissive of the Odéon ('never seemed to me in any degree a rival of the Comédie Française, although it is a smaller copy of that establishment'[781]). Maupassant too found the Odéon pretentious, as we may assume from his referring to its staging of a French verse adaptation of Don Quixote by a writer whom he calls Cabanon-Lebas, a clearly absurd project by someone with a somewhat ridiculous name.[782] James' view was that the only two theatres which did come anywhere near the Comédie Française ('an institution which – if such language be not hyperbole – I passionately admire'[783]) were the Gymnase and the Port-Royal – and both were defective.

> The Gymnase, since the death of Mademoiselle Desclées, has been under a heavy cloud; but occasionally, when a moment's sunshine rests upon it, there is a savour of excellence in the performance.

> The Port Royal has always been in its way very perfect; but its way admits of great imperfection. The actresses are classically bad, though usually pretty, and the actors are much addicted to taking liberties.[784]

This is perhaps an over-jaundiced view. As Raymond Recouly remarks 'In Paris the theatre is nearly always to the fore',[785] but theatre was far more than merely a form of entertainment.

> The second half of the nineteenth century is characterised by a great passion for theatre both as an art form and as a style of life. Rôle-playing,

the transformation of oneself as well as of one's environment by treating it
as a stage set, proliferations of public and private performances, all point to
a kind of theatremania, or theatocracy, as Nietzsche referred to the hold of
theatre over art and life.[786]

'One must not underrate the influence of the stage on the formation of
French character,' wrote Grenville-Murray. 'It is an influence which, in
Paris at least, has well-nigh superseded all others.'[787] This is both theatre
in Paris and Paris as theatre: not for nothing did E.V. Lucas characterise
the cafés as 'the open-air theatres of the Boulevards'.[788] 'The crossroads
of Paris were not its streets but its cafés,' writes W.S. Haine[789] in a well-
considered phrase, for was it not the crossroads where the strolling players
set up their stages? And does not the crossroads offer a choice of ways
forward? Dr Deak's comment may also be an echo of a remark of
Alexandre Benois of his stay in Paris between 1896 and 1899: 'We saw
countless operas and plays, but our theatre-going acquired the character of
a mania in 1897 when we were joined by Kostia Somov [...] mostly to the
Opéra-Comique, the Opéra, less frequently to the Comédie Française, and
the Odéon.'[790] John Henderson adds 'The literary reviews of the period
abound in theatrical articles and discussions on dramatic realism. These
articles often serve as a prelude to projects for founding new theatres, and
are an essential part of the ferment which eventually led to the
transformation of the French theatre.'[791] Here the significant word is
ferment. The dissentient voice is that of Bernard Shaw, who thought that
theatre in Paris was so backward as to make 'the intelligent Englishman
imagine himself back in the Dublin or Edinburgh of the eighteenth
century'[792] – although this too would have involved some casting of spells,
including one of selectivity – Shaw reviewed none of the Zola adaptations,
nor any of Antoine's plays, either in Paris or London. Indeed, Shaw seems
to have had a deliberate disengagement from things Parisian: even his Mrs
Warren, owning two brothels in Brussels, one in Ostend, one in Vienna
and two in Budapest, has no Paris interests. He did review Rostand's *La
Princesse lointaine* at Daly's Theatre, on the 22nd June 1895. Would he
have been conscious of the affinities between the opening scene of *Pelléas
et Mélisande* and *Cæsar and Cleopatra*? He reviewed the former in his
article on the visit to London of the Théâtre de l'Œuvre with productions
of Ibsen's *Solness le Constructeur* (*The Masterbuilder*) and *Rosmersholm*,
and Maeterlinck's *L'Intruse* and *Pelléas et Mélisande*, 25th-30th March
1895.[793]

Shaw's view of Paris theatre was largely shared by Pinero, who could
write to Augustin Daly in 1891 that 'There is nothing very interesting on

here theatrically'. Given that the two plays that he did see were Blavet and Carré's *Mon Oncle Barbasson* at the Gymnase and Meilhac's *Monsieur l'Abbé* at the Palais Royal ('the eternal mother-in-law play and not a good edition of her'), one cannot think that he had taken much trouble to inform himself. In Paris in April 1887, he was only able to record that he had not seen *Françillon* (though he had bought the book).[794] In 1893 he was telling William Archer that he had seen *Gigolette*[795] at the Ambigu, 'a tearing melodrama of the old Porte St-Martin pattern with one very fine, and equally objectionable, scene stuck in the middle of it' and 'that terrible' *Madame Sans-Gêne* piece at the Vaudeville. The only other play that he noticed was *La Duchesse de Montélimar*[796], at the Gymnase, only to comment that 'it is scarcely a success [...] and what you tell me will deter me from seeking La Duchesse de Montélimar's acquaintance'.[797] In 1896 his occasions took him while staying at the Hôtel Chatham to *Les Viveurs*[798] by Henri Lavedan at the Vaudeville and *Les Amants* by Maurice Donnay at the Renaissance: 'My dear Réjane gave you some moments of her best [...] Two delightful nights [...] even the frank indecency of many of the incidents of these plays is preferable to the Clapham-and-Brixton morality of our home made article'.[799] Unqualified praise was reserved for *Cyrano de Bergerac* in 1898, 'a beautiful, a fine thing'.[800]

Truly, when they were not looking for an imaginary Paris, the English even when they were Irish or Anglo-Portuguese could go to Paris taking England with them.

~~~~~~~

Although theatre has always presumed illusion – the stage at which disbelief hangs fire – Paris theatre at the time was creating new forms. Transformation scenes, known as *féerie*, were a specific and elaborate feature, at its height under the Empire, but surviving in the burlesque and even spreading into operetta, with Edmond Audran's *Les Pommes d'or* of 1883 being described as an 'opérette-féerie'.[801] One may associate with this the 'panorama' which replaced the Théâtre Marigny between 1883 and 1893, graphic representation of scenes from the history of Paris, illusion in many senses. Paradoxically, this had its counterpart in the realist drama with its attempt to suggest that what was taking place on stage was reality. It was in order to further realism that house lights were turned down, and this too has been seen as an enhancement of illusion:

> The darkening of the house is a significant gesture in the creation of
> illusionist theatre, establishing once and for all the claims of the stage over
> the auditorium as the centre of attention.[802]

This was an attack on the values of the Boulevard theatre, which had been
given an impetus by the replacing of the theatres demolished in
Haussmanisation or, like the Théâtre de la Ville, the Lyrique and the Porte
St-Martin,[803] destroyed in the Commune. The new houses not only
increased the quantity but had also, in the vogue for semi-circular
auditoria, increased the ability of audiences not only to view the stage but
also themselves. No longer did actors make speeches directly to the
audience: the French had invented the fourth wall, a phrase first used by
Jean Jullian in *Le Théâtre vivant* in 1892. This wall, transparent for the
audience, opaque for the cast, itself is more than illusory – for what were
the other three walls but flats, and painted drops? The iconographic
response to this is interesting. Constantin Guys' 'La Loge' shows two
buxom women who are clearly on display: their dresses are transparent
enough to show their nipples.[804] In his 'At the Opera' (1885), Georges
Clairin's woman is ambiguous: on display (she is overdressed and over-
rouged) but also on the look-out, her direct gaze at the spectator
suggesting her own command of the situation at least for the time being.
In Renoir's 'La Loge'[805] of 1874, the gentleman with the opera glasses is
clearly gazing at a box on the other side of the theatre, while his female
companion is looking at nothing very much; Mary Cassatt's 'In the
Loge'[806] of 1879, repossesses the gaze for her woman, but similarly may
be directing it at the audience and not the stage. Eva Gonzalez' 'Une loge
aux Italiens'[807] of 1874 is more anecdotal. The woman holds her opera
glasses away from her, a wistful expression on her face, while her
companion seems more interested in the rose in her hair. Equally, in
Madeleine Lemaire's 'Une loge à l'Opéra' (c. 1884), the three women
shown are hardly more than the sum of their elaborate gowns, and the
woman with the opera glasses seems to be pointing them at one of her
companions. In Toulouse-Lautrec's 'La Loge', the opera glasses are laid
down, and the two spectators, unusually both women, are looking
meaningfully at each other,[808] but in his 'La loge au Mascaron doré', the
woman has become an incident in the story of the box, itself characterised
by its mask, its disguise.[809] It is, of course, the opera glasses, which negate
realism, that unify the paintings. With the audience as spectacle, the
'fourth wall' was porous, but Susan Griffin quotes one contemporary critic
who referring to Blanche d'Antigny on stage, spun together the dominant
traits of the form: 'Under the electric lights and the trained opera glasses,
she represented the apotheosis of matter'.[810] This is also the contemporary

ambience for the audience for *Salomé* in general and the Dance of the Seven Veils in particular.

Even life became less absorbing than its mimic representation, according to the wife of the Belgian Minister in London:

> No play enacted off the boards of a theatre will ever have for Parisians the vital interest of a dramatic performance. The theatre is their great pre-occupation, the master passion of their lives.[811]

If there is a sense here of the audience being part of the performance, then it too was entering upon the double life that those on stage were obliged to lead. *Ma Double Vie*, Bernhardt called her memoirs, but of course this doubling was also one of mirrored effects: Bernhardt led several lives on stage, and several off-stage as well. She was even born in three different places, rue de l'École de Médecine 3, rue Michodière 22 and rue St-Honoré 265. When she is called by one biographer 'a modern yet mythical being', this seems to go beyond the conventional description of such people as 'legendary'.[812] Conversely Bartet, thought her biographer, led but a single life:

> La plupart des acteurs illustres ont deux personnalités: celle du théâtre et celle qu'ils retrouvent, le rideau tombé. Avec Madame Bartet – et peut-être touchons-nous ici au secret de sa perfection – rien de pareil: chez elle, l'artiste et la femme ne font qu'une.[813]

This all implies that within the context of time and place, more was involved than the simple and banal view that actors have one personality for the stage and another off it. By suggesting that even at home, Bartet's identity was bound up with her artistry, we have a view not of simplicity but of complexity: Paris as theatre has become theatre as the Parisian. This may make Bartet in this sense a more representative figure than Bernhardt, as well as explaining why Bernhardt's reputation has so much eclipsed that of Bartet,[814] for it is the woman distinct from the artist that has attracted the lavish biographical attention.[815]

Maurice Baring wrote that the enthusiasm of French theatre audiences was only matched by the English at boxing and football matches.[816] Reliance on spectacle played a part in this: one American critic noted that in January 1880 seven out of the twenty-three most important theatres were staging operas, while at three others the plays included songs.[817] This was not quite reflected in the taste for grand opera, if one can make assumptions from the number of seats in the Palais Garnier[818] – two thousand one hundred compared to Covent Garden's two thousand five hundred.[819]

In 1893 Émile Goudeau stated that the success of the Chat Noir could be explained in the single word theatre – the appeal of the Chat Noir was that it involved proprietors, performers, staff and clientèle in a theatrical experience. F.W.J. Hemmings has seen the accelerated growth of the cafés-concerts in this period as posing a threat to theatres, rivalling them in number by 1894, with audiences for theatre already damaged by the recession of the following the Panama collapse, so that a six franc excursion by a couple to a caf'conc' became preferable to a thirty franc excursion to a theatre. Unfortunately, Hemmings does not clearly define where theatres ended and cafés-concerts began. He notes that in 1875 there were a hundred and fifty of the latter in Paris, while twenty theatres closed between 1885 and 1889; he also numbers the theatres at only twenty-three in 1882.[820] On his own showing, therefore, theatres were numerically much inferior; but this measurement argues too rigid a division between the two as representing theatre in the abstract. Hemmings himself suggests that the success of the cafés-concerts had the unintended effect of both driving up their prices and causing them to become more like theatres.[821] For the theatre-goer there was simply a spectrum, and Arthur Meyer or the Grand Duke Vladimir or the Prince of Wales might be found in the place Pigalle or the place de l'Opéra on consecutive nights. Into this climate was introduced the Théâtrophone: telephones in public places from which one could dial a theatre and listen to the play.

That theatre had elements of the unreal is a sense greater than is ordinarily understood, is well illustrated by *La Dame aux Camélias*. This, the greatest dramatic success of the century, is a case history of the themes of this book *en petit*. Its transformation as *La Traviata* was only the last in a series, for the play had of course originated in the novel (1848), being reworked by Dumas *fils* for the stage the following year. It was first performed in February 1852 with Eugénie Doche in the title rôle. In the novel, Dumas wrote of his heroine 'I have seen Marguerite many times in the theatre. I never saw her once paying the slightest attention to what was happening on stage'.[822] Marguerite Gautier was based on Marie Duplessis, Armand Duval on Dumas himself. The implication of Armand and Marguerite went beyond that of Dumas with Marie, however, for when Aimée Desclées played Marguerite, Dumas had an affaire with her (and a daughter, Jeannine): was Aimée Marguerite or Marie or Aimée for Dumas? This forms ancestry for Dorian Gray's infatuation with Sybil

Vane, down to Dumas' exclamation on the death of Desclées: 'Elle nous a emu, et elle en est morte. Voilà toute son histoire!'[823] Even the name of the piece blends fact and fiction, for Dumas misspelled camellias out of ignorance and left it unchanged out of stubbornness, while the first American stage version, in 1856, was renamed *Camille*, as was the heroine, who became an innocent seduced and abandoned; and in *La Traviata*, Marguerite was renamed Violetta. In one of Sarah Bernhardt's revivals of the play Armand Duval was played by Camille Dumeny. Into all this one may introduce the echo of Jeanne Duval, Baudelaire's mistress. Aubrey Beardsley's 'Dame aux Camélias' appeared in the third Yellow Book, October 1894.

Desclées had also shone in the rôle of Frou-Frou, but at least in one view, her performance was ephemeral: 'I wish I knew for certain whether we saw Aimée Desclées in her most famous part,' wrote Walter Leaf of his visit to Paris in June 1871. 'But I have no record. If I did not see her then, I never saw her.'[824] As David Coward has remarked 'Marguerite has had many faces.'[825]

~~~~~~

On their Paris honeymoon in March 1884 Stanford and Bessie White went to the theatre every night. Their fellow-American Brander Matthews spent most of his summers in Paris, becoming a friend of Coquelin *aîné* to whom he dedicated his book on the theatres of Paris, in which he noted that the theatres of New York were far more comfortable.[826] Coquelin was a great friend of J.M. de Novarro, the husband of Mary Anderson, and Novarro 'seldom visited Paris without visiting Coquelin'[827] – usually in his dressing room at the theatre. Even before her marriage, Anderson was an admirer of the Comédie Française, on her very first visit to Paris in 1878 going there on her first evening to see *Hernani* and being invited backstage by Sarah Bernhardt. But, although she also met Adelaide Ristori, she decided that 'our stay in Paris should have been rich in improvement [...] but I doubt if much was gained in actual experience'.[828] This rather equivocal view was frequently found among the more staid American visitors, and may provide an insight into her rejection of *The Duchess of Padua*. Anderson makes no comment on her appearance, somewhat altered, in either Mrs Humphrey Ward's 1884 novel *Miss Bretherton* or Henry James's *The Tragic Muse*.

If one section of the English cultural community came to Paris for the Salon, another certainly came for the theatre, although Bernard Shaw thought the English theatre critic in Paris a false quantity, for his 'Trotter' is described as 'thoroughly English: never happy except when he's in Paris, and speaks French so unnecessarily well that everybody there spots him for an Englishman the moment he opens his mouth.'[829]

Rothenstein, who seems to have known everybody, remembered the Cambridge don J.W. Clark 'coming to Paris with Arthur Shipley'[830] on purpose to see a performance of one of Victor Hugo's plays – I think it was *Le Roi s'amuse* – at the Théâtre Français. He appeared to have been present at every representation of Victor Hugo's plays for almost half a century'.[831] Similarly John F. MacDonald contributed a series of articles over several years to the *Fortnightly Review* under the heading 'French Life and the French Stage', aware of the entangling of the two.

Clark wrote on French theatre for *The Academy* and the *Saturday Review*, and visited Paris on this and other quests in 1852, 1853, 1867, 1868, 1873, 1878 (visiting the Expo), 1893, 1894, 1895, 1897 (with Lionel Cust, later keeper of the King's Pictures, and doing 'a round of theatres'[832]), 1901, 1902, 1906, 1907 and 1909, sometimes more than once in those years, and perhaps in more years than those, usually staying at the Hôtel St Romain, in the rue St Roch.[833] The visit in March 1893, when they dined with Arthur Studd and Will Rothenstein, was particularly remembered by Shipley for being asked by Jacques Reubell to dine to meet the Whistlers, and for a visit to Charles Yriarte, the critic who wrote for the *Revue des Deux Mondes*. Shipley returned home on the 21st but Clark stayed on till the end of the month 'visiting innumerable theatres',[834] Shipley being replaced as a companion to Clark by Stanley Leathes. Of the Paris theatre world, Clark's biographer only refers to a friendship with Louis Delaunay of the Comédie Française, cemented during the company's London season in 1879, and the articles in *The Academy* and the *Saturday Review* await excavation, seemingly unknown to the histories of French theatre which I have consulted. (Conversely, J.T. Grein wrote on London theatre for the *Revue d'art dramatique*.) Delaunay was significantly described by Prince Volkonsky as 'The most elegant figure I have ever seen on stage: he was Duke from his head to his heels. I don't know what was more elegant, – his appearance or his speech.'[835]

This confounding of stage and stalls, of promenoir and boulevard, of dressing room and drawing-room, was one sort of interface between illusion and reality. Or rather between two different forms of illusion. The boulevard du Temple had become known as the boulevard du Crime, not because of its dangers in the street but because of the melodramas in its many theatres: and this phrase lingered even after Haussmann had pulled down the theatres in 1862.[836] Another sort of confusion that the theatre typically conjured forth was the possibility of the play itself reflecting the multiplicity of identities of players and audience alike: after all, *loge* is both the actors' dressing-room and the private box. The story of *Miss Fanfare* here is symptomatic. This was written by Louis Ganderax, literary editor of the *Revue de Paris*, a man known for the innumerable corrections he would make to the manuscripts submitted to him. Ganderax (this seems to have been his real name) submitted *Miss Fanfare* to Dumas *fils*, who offered (doubtless with a certain *arrière pensée*) to rewrite it. In some indignation, Ganderax persuaded the Gymnase to take it as it stood, but seventeen performances exhausted the interest in it from that day to – as far as one can ascertain – this. That was in 1881. Dumas then went ahead with re-writing it in any case, a neat act of appropriation, and it was produced as *Françillon* at the Comédie Française in 1887 with Julia Bartet, and many times thereafter, including a production with Bernhardt in London in 1888. This perhaps would be unexceptionable, were it not for the fact that *Françillon* was then itself re-written by anyone who cared to, and it appeared on stage as *Franlichon*, *Franctrognon*, *Farçillon* and perhaps best of all *Franc-Chignon*, translatable as real false hair. *Françillon* also made another appearance: in James Pryde's cartoon of Oscar Wilde in Shakespearian pose,[837] he is leaning on a pile of copies of *Odette*, *La Supplication d'une femme*, and *Françillon*. *Françillon* played again in London at the Duke of York's Theatre in 1897, evoking the comment from Shaw that Mrs Brown Potter 'congenitally incapable of impersonation [...] coached herself into a capital imitation of a real French actress playing the part'.[838]

Confusion of actor and audience was heightened by the new class divisions among theatre goers. Harold Hobson argues that the prevailing conservatism disliked working class patronage of the theatre, which encouraged a democratic spirit. Paradoxically, the naturalist or realist stage did not appeal to working class audiences, but to the bourgeoisie: 'the social standing of audiences rose as the social standing of characters in plays fell.'[839] This served to present social views to the bourgeois, who could absorb, rather than to the workers whose class consciousness might have been raised by them. It was certainly safer to arouse the conscience of the rich than the anger of the poor: the artist as crisis in yet another form.

Sometime in the early 1890s, Rachilde wrote in the journal *Théâtre d'Art*
that one day 'on lancera le mot de Cambronne, la plus haute expression de
l'art naturaliste, et nous autons la paix'.[840] This was prescient. *Ubu Roi*
was produced, with the support of Rachilde, only ten months after Lugné-
Poë had first produced *Salomé*. (Rachilde also gave Lugné-Poë her play
L'Arraignée de Cristal, which the Théâtre de l'Œuvre played in
Amsterdam and Copenhagen as well as in Paris.[841]) Alfred Jarry had
become Lugné-Poë's assistant the year before, and in 1898 sent Wilde a
complete collection of his works. Wilde, however, was rather disdainful:

> He is a most extraordinary young man, very corrupt, and his writings have
> sometimes the obscenity of Rabelais, sometimes the wit of Molière [...]
> The point of the play [*Ubu Roi*] was that everybody said 'Merde' to each
> other, all through the five acts, apparently for no reason. The play was so
> hooted that Jarry became famous, and the *Mercure de France* has
> published *Ubu Roi* in an edition de luxe. Jarry is now the rising light of the
> Quartier Latin.[842]

This was upon after seeing the marionette version at the Théâtre des
Pantins, which he attended with Robert d'Humières,[843] not of course the
original, which had taken place in 1896. *Ubu Roi* itself took on other
forms: when the Menus-Plaisirs re-opened as the Théâtre Antoine in
September 1897, it had been with a play by Georges Courteline called
Boubouroche.

Jarry, who may have had an affaire with the bisexual Léon-Paul Fargue,
was certainly one of the more picturesque examples of the artist and his art
becoming indistinguishable. From the time in 1894 when a portrait of him
by Douanier Rousseau was mislabelled 'Madame Jarry' to his adoption of,
or merging into, the rôle of Ubu even off the stage, Jarry was the
personification of ambivalence. Elizabeth Wilson strongly implies that
Jarry put Wilde into the person of Ubu.[844] Did Wilde know that Jarry
called his apartment the 'Chasublerie'?

Although Lugné-Poë visited Wilde in Dieppe in June 1897, only once
again in a long career did he direct a play by him, *A Florentine Tragedy* in
1907.[845] The Théâtre de l'Œuvre was the principal producer of Ibsen –
Rosmersholm, An Enemy of the People (6th October and 10th November
1893 respectively, with programmes designed by Vuillard[846]); *The Master
Builder* (3rd April 1894); *Brand* (22nd June 1895, programme designed by
Maurice Denis); *Peer Gynt* (November 1896); *Little Eyolf* (8th May 1895,
programme by Rops); *Pillars of Society* (23rd June 1896, programme by
Vuillard); *John Gabriel Borkman* (1897, programme by Edvard Munch);

The Comedy of Love (23rd June 1897, programme by Ernest La Jeunesse); *Rosmersholm* and *The Master Builder* (revived respectively 22nd January and 25th June 1898); *An Enemy of the People* revived (18th February 1899 with a poster by Steinlen[847]). Ibsen productions were frequently preceded by a lecture, or *causerie*, Mauclair, Schwob and Tailhade being favoured. This all attached Ibsen firmly to the Symbolist movement, a very different appropriation from that of London, where he became a sort of honorary Fabian, but one needs to remember that both *A Doll's House* and *Borkman* were first performed in Paris in the drawing-room of madame Aubernon de Nerville. Plays by Maeterlinck, Hauptmann (*Lonely Lives* as *Ames Solitaires*, 13th December 1893, programme by Vuillard, suppressed by the police but reprieved by the Minister; *La Cloche engloutie,* 5th March 1897, programme by Paul Ranson) and Strindberg (*The Father*, 13th December 1894, programme designed by Vallotton;[848] *The Creditors*, 21st June 1894, programme by Vuillard) were also produced by the Théâtre de l'Œuvre. This last was praised by Achille Segards in *La Plume*, by Romain Coolus in the *Revue blanche* and by Camille Mauclair in the *Revue encyclopédique*, but disliked by Jules Lemaître in his review for the *Journal des Débats*.[849] Rodin and Gauguin were in the audience. In January 1895 Lugné-Poë also produced *Le Chariot de Terre-Cuite*, an adaptation by Victor Berrucand of a classical Hindu play, with the set designed by Toulouse-Lautrec, followed in December by *The Ring of Çakountala*, in an adaptation by A.-F. Hérold.[850] There was little here that would have attracted Wilde; much to attract Yeats.

The production of *Peer Gynt* brought Bernard Shaw on a rare visit to Paris, reviewing for *The Saturday Review* and enthusiastic for the production, in which Lugné-Poë played Mr Cotton the travelling Englishman, Suzanne Auclair[851] was Solveig, Gina Barbieri (who played Herodias in *Salomé*) was Aase and an actor called Deval was Peer Gynt. Lugné-Poë himself played the Pastor in *The Father* and Stockman in the 1899 *Enemy of the People*. These plays were the new canon, with Ibsen pre-eminent. Moreover, it had a wide appeal – what else would an audience which included Sardou, Puvis de Chavannes and the Curies have had in common? – and Lugné-Poë cast his net wide, for example engaging Jane Avril to dance Anitra's dance[852] in *Peer Gynt* at the Nouveau Théâtre[853], and Edouard de Max (with whom he had studied at the Conservatoire) as Ulrich Brendel in *Rosmersholm*.[854]

Despite Princess Metschcheskaia withdrawing her financial support for Lugné-Poë's production of *Pelléas et Mélisande*, her own play *Tamara* was performed at the Pleyel-Wolff concert hall in March 1892, by Les

Escholiers, an amateur group of which Lugné-Poë was the leading light, originally formed by him and his classmates at the Lycée Condorcet in November 1886. 'We cannot judge the merits of the play, as it was not published,' says John Henderson somewhat *de haut en bas*, 'but her main contribution to the avant-garde was apparently financial'[855]. The princess also instigated the Théâtre de la Rive Gauche, which opened in February 1894, directed by Paul Larochelle. Larochelle, however, then joined Antoine in the Théâtre Libre.

It was not all success. *Ghosts* was the first of Ibsen's plays to be produced in Paris (by Antoine as *Les Revenants*, 29th and 30th May 1890[856]), and George Moore, Arthur Symons and Henri Céard were in the audience. Antoine was Osvald, Mdlle Barny was Mrs Alving (who, with a nod towards Eleanor Marx, Moore calls Mrs Avling[857]), and the production even attracted the British Ambassador, who was, indeed 'greatly interested in all Ibsen's plays'.[858] Much of its impact was through its being a faithful translation, not an adaptation, but even that status carries within it in its own contradictions: whether one accepts either of the phrases 'traditore, tradutore' or 'if beautiful, unfaithful', 'a faithful translation' only argues a change in presentation, not essence.

Ghosts had been published the previous year, with a preface by Édouard Rod. It had already been performed in Germany, in Saxe-Meiningen with Ibsen's assistance, in December 1886, when free tickets were given to government workers and the entire police force was placed on alert in case of disturbances. Hans von Bülow called it 'a play for seamstresses', which suggests no very great capacity for fluttering dovecots, and admittedly the Saxe-Meiningen police force numbered only six men. Antoine went to Brussels to see the Meininger Theater in August 1888, which was the nearest the company came to Paris. Ibsen himself was little in Paris, though Munch painted his 'Ibsen au Grand Café' in, it is supposed, 1898.[859] Wilde could easily have seen him there.

In December 1891, the less controversial *Hedda Gabler* was booed off the stage when it was given a matinée performance at the Vaudeville, Marthe Brandès as Hedda saying that she was out of sympathy with the character.[860] Lugné-Poë admitted that this was a major setback for Ibsenism but *Ghosts* itself was hardly a play to appeal to the greater audience for boulevard theatre, even if there was no other reason than that Osvald Alving had contracted his syphilis in Paris. After Antoine's two performances, *Ghosts* was not staged again in that city until 1908. Such interest as Wilde had in Ibsen[861] does not seem to have caused him to attend any of the productions of the Théâtre de l'Œuvre (or gone to the production of *A Doll's House* at the Théâtre de Vaudeville with Réjane in 1894) but given Lugné-Poë's view of symbolist acting, this is perhaps not surprising.

> A fixed style was adopted: the actors behaved as if drugged, their movements sluggish, their voices hollow and querulous in turn. The whole production was made as unnaturalistic as possible, and Lugné-Poë himself, whether he was playing Rosmer, Solness or Brand, always wore the same long black overcoat and waistcoat buttoning up to the chin, a costume which the young symbolists paid him the compliment of adopting as the unofficial uniform of their movement.[862]

Lugné-Poë in so doing was setting himself against the received way of playing Ibsen, for example rejecting Herman Bang's interpretation of psychological realism in *Rosmersholm* despite the assistance that he received from Bang in staging the play (Lugné-Poë produced Bang's own play, *The Brothers*, in June 1894). It is significant that the French found it useful to consult Scandinavians when it came to Ibsen. When 'Les Escholiers' put on *The Lady from the Sea* at the Théâtre Moderne[863] in 1891, they were helped by Jens Petersen, a Danish art critic and occasional actor, and when Lugné-Poë in January 1894 staged Bjørnson's *Beyond Human Power* (as *Au-delà des forces humaines*), it was directed by Bang and had sets by Frits Thaulow; Toulouse-Lautrec drew Lugné-Poë and Berthe Bady in their rôles. Bang also organised support from the Norwegian community, despite his own financial and health problems.

As Herod, Lugné-Poë presumably wore a different costume from the one he wore in Ibsen, but little is known about his production of *Salomé*, and according to the standard authority on the play 'it is by now impossible to reconstruct the performance with any accuracy'.[864] It did not, however, only run for one night, playing on 10th and 11th February 1896 and again in October. Jules Renard saw the play, and recorded 'C'est impressionnant, mais il faudrait supprimer encore, çà et là, quelques têtes d'Iokanan. Il y en a trop, il y en a trop ! Et que de cris inutilement répétés, et que de richesses en toc!'[865]

The Théâtre de l'Œuvre's later nods towards Oscar Wilde were in February 1935, with a production of a three act play *Les Trois Procès d'Oscar Wilde* by Edmond Rostand's son Maurice, which ran for several months[866]; and in 1983, a play called *L'Extravagant Mister Wilde, ou 'le diable n'existe pas'*, written and directed by Raymond Gérôme, who also played Wilde.

The Théâtre de l'Œuvre under Lugné-Poë was not much concerned with works by British authors. Although *Measure for Measure* was produced in December 1898, the only other exceptions were a production of Maeterlinck's *Annabella* (an adaptation of Ford's *'Tis Pity She's A Whore*[867]) in November 1894 and Otway's *Venice Preserv'd* in November 1895, and eventually *The Playboy of the Western World* (*Le baladin du monde occidentale*, 1913); but the weakness of French plays – *Ubu Roi* apart – is also notable. When *La Belle au Bois dormant* by Henri Bataille and Robert d'Humières was given in May 1894,[868] the anarchist designer Francis Jourdain recalled that 'our orthodoxy could not justify such derogation, such concession to capitalism, to the Institute and to the Boulevard. We booed the Money Fairies, the Academy and "Tout Paris", their clothes embroidered with real gold and the counterfeit they tried to pass on to us. We booed Bataille, Lugné-Poë and in the bargain that bore Burne-Jones, who inspired the sets; he is also a fake, fake artist, fake great man for real snobs'.[869] Jourdain would have agreed with Daudet's definition of *le tout Paris* as 'that infinitesimal number of Parisians, whose existence begins and ends with the Gymnase and the Opera, Notre Dame de Lorette, and the Bourse, and who fancy they alone exist!'[870] (Romain Rolland confirms this view: '[...] cette petite ville de province qu'est le Tout-Paris des théâtres et des boulevards'.[871]) Nevertheless, there was that much was undiscriminating in Jourdain's diatribe. The orthodoxy of Bataille and Lugné-Poë (whatever about Burne-Jones) is not readily discernible. For Bataille, indeed, drama's task was to recast and interpret human experience as it lies between 'the external world of everyday life and the inner world of thought, feeling and emotion',[872] a tense dualism in interstitial space between the quotidian and the hermetic, well suited to Symbolist beliefs.

Symbolist taste was reflected in Rachilde's *L'Arraignée et le Cristal*[873] and Bjørnson's *Beyond Human Power* produced by the Théâtre de l'Œuvre in February 1894.[874] Bataille's play *Ton Sang* was produced by the Théâtre de l'Œuvre in 1897[875] but none of his shadow plays were taken up by Lugné-Poë although shadow plays, together with pantomime (both commedia dell' arte and English panto), had originally been projected. Perhaps, like Harold Hobson, Lugné-Poë thought Bataille meretricious: of Bataille's *Manon Colibri* Hobson writes 'very clever, very well contrived, very brilliant. But it glitters with greasepaint instead of shining with life.'[876] This of course is peculiarly what the spirit of the time required. The pantomime *Pierrot Assassin de sa Femme* by Paul Margueritte was produced at the Théâtre Libre,[877] and Massenet's *Cendrillon*, which opened at the Opéra-Comique on the 24th May 1899, can also be seen as a response to this.[878] Maupassant, who hated the theatre, was attracted to the circus, pantomime, *féerie* and puppets.[879] The Folies Bergère interested itself in pantomime, the most successful production being one by Catulle Mendès performed by a mime artist called Severin.[880] Mime itself was not neglected, and the Cercle Funambulesque, founded in 1888 by Eugène and Félix Larcher, was 'devoted to every style of mime and it soon attracted much attention',[881] holding performances at the Théâtre d'Application, a theatre for young professional actors, whose education at the Conservatoire was largely theoretical.[882]

The style of the Théâtre de l'Œuvre links together all the contemporary fascination with puppets, masks and mirrored images, a rejection of Realism that offered no return road to Romanticism. Marionettes and masks were central to the intellectual explorations of the period, and therefore are central to the identification of Paris as a place of transformation and shape-shifting. Puppet theory, says Frantisek Deak, 'may have directly influenced symbolist productions and the symbolist theories of acting', and he cites Marcel Guichteau's phrase 'the primitive power of the magical gesture [*geste incantatoire*]' to affirm the connexion between Nabism and the hieratic (this is a word that recurs frequently in descriptions of both the Nabis and the Théâtre de l'Œuvre). This was clearly of significance to Lugné-Poë. Dr Deak also refers to the lecture by Maurice Bouchor at the Théâtre d'Application on 2nd February 1890 when he urged that the classics should be performed by puppets[883] in May 1888 Bouchor had himself staged puppet plays (*Tobie* and *Noël*) at the Petit Théâtre de la Galerie Vivienne, an arcade of shops off the rue Vivienne. Anatole France expressed a 'preference for puppets over live actors because of their simplicity, their ability to express universal situations through limited gestures, and their lack of personality'.[884] In adopting 'the geste incantatoire', actors were therefore aspiring to the condition of puppets. This particular transformation – actor into puppet, puppet into actor – developed not so much in theatre as in opera and ballet, where a long list may include *The Nutcracker*, *I Pagliacci*, *L'Enfant et les Sortilèges*, *Petrouchka* and Pierné's *Marche des petits soldats de plomb* as exploring the puppet/doll/toy relationship.[885] Nor should one omit reference to the magic glasses that Berselius gives to Hoffmann, through which the doll Olympia becomes a live woman: no bad metaphor in an age when opera glasses were used to scrutinise women and turn them into dolls, extending this to the artificial woman of Madame B's 1899 novel *La Femme endormie*.[886] In the visual arts this opened the way to the 'Demoiselles d'Avignon', but far earlier, in the work of Cézanne, as F. Novotny has pointed out, 'the human figure often has a puppet-like rigidity, while the countenances show an emptiness of expression bordering almost on the mask.[887] Even more compelling is the mask-like face of Susanna in Vallotton's 1893 'Suzanne et les vieillards'.[888]

Bonnard made the puppets for the second production of *Ubu Roi*, at the Théâtre des Pantins in 1898; in 1900 he illustrated Verlaine's *Parallèlement* for an edition published by Ambroise Vollard. Ranson, Vuillard, K.-X. Roussel and Alfonse Hérold also did the designs for another marionette play, a version of *Paphnutius* by Hroswitha, directed by Hérold's brother André-Ferdinand. Henri Signoret's Le Petit Théâtre des Marionettes 'had much to do with the development of the symbolist theory of drama',[889] but puppetry was important in Paris theatre even beyond Symbolist circles – Judith Gautier made marionettes, compared to Tanagra figures by Pierre Louÿs, for a version of *The Valkyries*.[890] One can align Pierre Louÿs' novel *La Femme et Le Pantin*[891] with this interest, and perhaps even Edmond Audran's 1896 operetta *La Poupée*. Puppets were added to the repertoire in the Chat Noir at the suggestion of Charles de Sivry, and were developed by Henri Rivière to accompany a song by Jules Jouy. Brander Matthews found some ten marionette theatres, five of them opposite the Palais de l'Industrie in the Champs Elysées, and noted the distinction between the *jeux de castollets* or glove puppets (guignols, after an original Guignol established in Lyons after the Restoration) and the *jeux de triangle*, the marionettes suspended from wire. Of the latter, 'the typical French play in which they appear is the "Temptation of St Anthony", full of peculiar spectacular sensations'; while the best of the glove puppet theatres was the Vrai Guignol, run by a M. Anatole, 'a most ingenious and inventive spirit'.[892] *Spirit*, one notes, not man: Brander Matthews has caught the prevailing cadence. The marionettes of the Petit Théâtre des Marionettes were about thirty inches high and actors manipulated them by levers while other spoke the lines. Another marionette theatre was that of Paul Ranson, for which the puppets were made by Georges Lacombe, sculptor of the bust of Sérusier on the latter's tomb. A more specifically politicised use of marionettes was in Gyp de Martel's Boulangist *Tout à l'Égout* of 1889, with its representations of Drumont, Rochefort and Floquet. The British Ambassador went to see a puppet version of *The Tempest* in December 1888, and this was probably the version, a translation by Maurice Bouchor, that Oscar Wilde saw at the end of 1891.[893]

Wilde's attraction to marionettes, set out extensively in a letter to the *Daily Telegraph* of 19th February 1892 seems, however, to have died away before 1895 and in any case perhaps was at best never more than the occasion for either an easy joke about marionettes being more alive than live actors, or else an uneasy rhyme: 'In ['The Harlot's House'] Oscar Wilde overcame his objection to the use of words ending in 'ette' for which he professed a real artistic horror'.[894]

Such transformation was carried as far as fantasy could take it by the waxworks at the Musée Grévin. This had been inspired in 1881 by Arthur Meyer of *Le Gaulois* as a three-dimensional record of the celebrities of the day and he engaged the sculptor and caricature artist Alfred Grévin to execute them. It opened on the 5th June 1882. Gabriel Thomas, the financier behind the Eiffel Tower operating company and the Théâtre de Champs-Elysées, took it over, adding historical scenes to those of current events, a theatre on the first floor decorated by Antoine Bourdelle[895] and Jules Chéret, and most appropriately of all the 'Palais des Mirages' with its 'Dances of Light', created for the Universal Exhibition of 1900 and presented to the Museum in 1906. Nevertheless, the possibilities for literary conceits afforded by the Grévin – the waxworks mistaken for humans, the humans mistaken for waxworks – do not seem to have found their way into the Parisian imagination.[896]

~~~~~~~~

The Théâtre de l'Œuvre, which with the Théâtre Libre, Yeats wished to emulate in Dublin,[897] began when Lugné-Poë broke away from Antoine, with whom he had become increasingly unhappy, but his new venture also grew out of Paul Fort's Théâtre Mixte, which became the Théâtre d'Art. This had been founded by Fort and Princess Metschcheskaia in 1890, with Jules Méry as Secretary General, when Fort was eighteen, expressly to perform Symbolist drama; it closed on 7th December 1891 at the end of a production of Maeterlinck's *Les Aveugles*.[898] (The Mixte had been founded when Fort was still at the Lycée Louis-le-Grand.)

Latour and Clavel suggest that Camille Mauclair was an influential collaborator with Paul Fort, and instance as part of their engagement with Symbolism (Mallarmé) and opposition to Naturalism (Antoine), productions of *The Cenci* (Shelley), *Faust* (Marlowe) and *Les Flaireurs* (van Lerberghe[899]). With this Latour and Clavel include Fort and Mauclair's enthusiasm for Bonnard, Redon and Maurice Denis, adding 'ils ont pour conseillers artistiques André Gide, Pierre Louÿs et Oscar Wilde.'[900]

Antoine was not the first to try experimental theatre, which had been a characteristic of the matinée movement of the 1870s, when Hilarion Ballande was director from 1874 at the Théâtre Déjazet[901] (which he claimed to be the Troisième Théâtre Français) and Talien at the Cluny after 1879; but he was certainly the most influential. A number of 'little theatres' sprang from the Antoine / Lugné-Poë initiatives such as the Théâtre de l'Avenir Dramatique (1891), the Théâtre de l'Art Sociale (1893), the Théâtre des Lettres (1894) and perhaps the Théâtre Maguera ('Le Théâtre Maguera eut une existence éphémère'[902]) but this influence was widespread. Marvin Carlson says that 'no theatre was so receptive to the young dramatists discovered by Antoine'[903] as the Théâtre Vaudeville. Victor Koning, married to (and then divorced from) the actress Jane Hading and director of the Gymnase to 1892, was the first of the boulevard directors to acknowledge the work of the Théâtre Libre, reviving *La Chance de Françoise* by Georges Porto-Riche in 1889. This was the play that made his reputation: two years later his *L'Amoureuse* was produced at the Comédie Française, 'perhaps the first modern comedy in the repertoire of the French National Theatre'.[904]

The first production of the Théâtre d'Art was *Pierrot et la lune* by Marc Legrand and *Le Florentin* by Sœur de Chanmêlé (25th June 1890 at the Salle Duprez). Among those at the opening night were Saint-Saëns, Remy de Gourmont, Maurice Denis, Jules Renard, Charles Morice, Maurice Barrès. This bill was followed by Fort's own *La Petite Bête* and Louis Germain's *François Villon* on the 5th and 12th October 1890 at the Théâtre Beaumarchais. Louis Germain had joined Paul Fort and mounted this one production with him. They then split up, Germain dying shortly afterwards at the age of twenty-two.

Almost as ephemeral as Germain were other 'little theatres' like the Théâtre Idéaliste or the Théâtre Féministe, one of the few manifestations of the New Woman in its English stage sense in Paris. There were also Jean Rouché's Théâtre des Arts, a name clearly mimicking that of the Théâtre d'Art (but not to be confused with the actual Théâtre des Arts, which after a time as the Théâtre des Menus-Plaisirs became the Théâtre Antoine), and the Théâtre des Poètes, founded by Charles Léger, which produced but two plays of substance, *L'Empereur* by Charles Grandmougin and *Kèmener* by the Breton writer Eugène le Mouël. Fort himself produced Shelley's *The Cenci* in 1891, presumably in Princess Metschcheskaia's translation, and Rachilde's *La Voix de sang*. Like Lugné-Poë after him, Fort brought in as set designers Émile Bernard, Maurice Denis, Bonnard, Ibels, Vuillard and Sérusier, the last of whom designed the set for a quasi-religious melodrama by Pierre Quillard called *La Fille aux mains coupées* (played in a double bill with Rachilde's *Madame la Mort*), a stylised play the description of which suggests the play-within-a-play in Chekhov's *The Seagull*. The influence of Fort's successor André Antoine, and his Théâtre Libre, was greater than that of the Théâtre d'Art itself. Yeats may have wished to emulate it, but it was George Moore who went to some effort to publicise it in England.

The Théâtre Libre had been founded by Antoine in 1887 to promote Naturalism on the stage and its closure in 1896 marked the end of the Naturalist movement in the theatre, just as Zola's last novel in the Rougon-Macquart sequence, *Le docteur Pascal* of 1893, marked the exhaustion of Naturalism in the French novel. After all, the Naturalism that demanded real meat to hang on stage in a butcher's scene was no nearer to responding to what was à la mode than was the detailed depiction of a horse in a painting by Morot. The new vogue was for Symbolism in which Antoine had no interest. Although John Henderson thinks that by June 1894 the Théâtre Libre was 'played out', he still regards it as 'the most successful and most important group in the first avant garde'.[905] Somehow Antoine's endeavours caught the popular imagination: a sometime bookseller's apprentice,[906] a worker in a gas company who finances his first production from his savings and persuades his colleagues to support him is the epitome of the artistic Bohemian hero. 'A favourite and typical anecdote tells how Antoine tramped the streets delivering invitations by hand because he could not afford postage.'[907] This paid off remarkably well. On the 20th May 1887 the first audience included Edouard Lockroy, on his last day as Minister for the Arts, his brother-in-law George Hugo, Alphonse Daudet, Puvis de Chavannes, Jean Richepin, Coquelin *cadet*, 'à côté plus au moins gros bonnets de la presse, Sarcey, Vitu, Blavet, La Pommeraye […] et tant d'autres, rapins, photographes, journalistes, monologuistes, poètes décadents, les ratés, les parvenus ou les parvenants, avec ou sans mesdames les épouses, tous ceux, enfin, qui ont la prétention d'être dans le train, comme on dit'.[908] The play was *La Nuit bergamesque* by Émile Bergerat, the brother-in-law of Judith Gautier, so oddly described as a 'solid bourgeois' with 'the eyes of a dreamer and a fighter' who would sign himself Caliban.[909]

The theatre's first home was in a hall in the passage d'Elysée de Beaux-arts off the place Pigalle, belonging to a dramatic society called the Cercle Gaulois, so tiny that the lane served as the foyer. In 1888 it moved to the Menus Plaisirs, with offices in the rue Blanche: Théâtre Libre was the name of the company, never that of the venue. Success followed. In

George Moore's words 'Paris literary and artistic was in the stalls […] a triumph […] deep and pronounced […] The theatre is packed from floor to ceiling at every performance'.[910] On 11th October 1887, Antoine produced *Sœur Philomène*, adapted from Goncourt's novel by Jules Bidal and Arthur Byl. Goncourt went with Gustave Geffroy and Lucien Descaves and encountered Zola and Raffaëlli there: 'A strange theatre. Lost among streets which look like streets in provincial suburbs where one expects to find a brothel, a middle-class house, and in that house a stage trodden by actors reeking more strongly of garlic than any Vaugirard omnibus. A strange audience too, not at all like that to be found at the big theatres.'[911] Zola's presence was later explained to Goncourt's satisfaction: 'Young Descaves confided to me that Zola spends every evening at the Théâtre Libre, that he has taken two subscriptions, that he pays the most extravagant compliments to Antoine […] in fact that with the aid of his disciple Céard he is trying to get hold of the theatre for himself.'[912] Antoine himself did not care for Busnach's stage adaptations of Zola – *Pot Bouille* he described as 'a platitude in five acts'[913] – and when he staged Zola's *Jacques Damour*[914] it was in a version by Léon Hennique, who supported the Théâtre Libre.

Given the dominance of Augier, Dumas and Sardou, Antoine's success was remarkable, and he was able to move into the theatre in the boulevard de Strasbourg that still bears his name. The opening play was *Les Bouchers*, by Ferdinand Icres, 20th October 1888. Those who wrote for, or who had plays staged by, the Théâtre Libre included Hauptmann (*L'Assomption de Hannele Mattern*,[915] a translation by Raymond Bouthor (known as Jean Thorel) of *Hanneles Himmelfahrt*), François de Curel, Hennique, Catulle Mendès, Émile Bergerat, Rodolphe Darzens, Jean Jullien, editor of *Art et Critique* whose play about avaricious peasants, *Le Maître* (1890) demonstrated the hold Zola had on this generation, and Oscar Méténier, whose *La Casserole*[916] was 'a sordid tale of intrigue and jealousy in a world of prostitutes and criminals'.[917] This was set in a bar in the dangerous district of La Roquette (made hardly more attractive by the public executions in the place de la Roquette[918]), and was based on the Château Rouge. The bouncer in the play is known as 'le terreur de la Maube', and the actor Pinsard, playing the patron, imitated Père Trolier[919] of the Château Rouge. The place Maubert, at the east end of the boulevard St Germain and behind the Musée de Cluny, was clearly one of the places that gave the Left Bank a sinister reputation – E.V. Lucas refers to the 'network of very old, squalid and interesting streets' between the Cluny and the Seine.[920]. Méténier also, with Paul Alexis, adapted the Goncourts' novel of circus life *Les Frères Zemganno* for the Théâtre Libre (February

1890). The Théâtre Libre also staged the only play written by Maurice Barrès, *La Journée Parlementaire*, in February 1894; two months later[921] it staged its last play, *Le Missionnaire* by Marcel Luguet. But Antoine could sometimes take the social concerns of theatre more lightly, for example playing opposite Judic in Jules Lemaître's *L'Age Difficile*.

Harold Hobson has observed that there is more needed to define naturalism than merely taking romanticism or melodrama and moving it down the social scale: real naturalism 'is the reproduction of the audible and visible surfaces, not of exceptional misfortunes, but of quite ordinary life'.[922] This may be better seen in art in the tradition that runs through Raffaëlli,[923] not usually seen as one of the Naturalist school, for as Hobson points out, there were no theatrical equivalents of Willette or Steinlen. This is to demand a very high standard, instead offering the antagonism between Romain Rolland, who wanted a theatre of jollity for the proletariat, and Antoine, who wanted to present great plays with a social message. In any case, those who depicted scenes of misery in the end fell away from their own sensibilities, Steinlen retreating into his world of cats, Willette into a sort of resigned sentimentality inherited from Gavarni, Raffaëlli himself into bourgeois art.

One response to naturalism may be dubbed unnaturalism, the vogue for plays set as unlikely representations of exotic places, India (*Le grand Mogol, Nana Sahib*), China, Japan (*Madame Chrysanthème*), the Middle East. This was explored in operetta, which has hardly received its due in discussion of *fin-de-siècle* theatre, as well as on the legitimate stage. Much can made of *La reine Indigo* at the Théâtre de la Renaissance in 1875. This piece by Johann Strauss II had opened in Vienna in 1871 as *Indigo und die vierzig Raübner*; in Paris (with the appropriately-named Zulma Bouffar in the lead rôle of Fantasca) it underwent a series of changes, Ali Baba becoming Babazouck, Zaire and Florinda becoming Banana and Piastrella, and Romadour the High Priest turned into the Chief of the White Eunuchs. This, with the necessary adjustments, can be aligned with *Ubu Roi* and other strange plays.

Arthur Symons left a description of a poster Toulouse-Lautrec produced for Antoine, 'Au Théâtre Libre: Antoine dans l'Inquiétude', which suggest that Symons saw the play as well as the poster; he certainly knew the man, 'vivid, impressionable, reflective'.[924] In any case, it is a compelling evocation.

Au Théâtre Libre: Antoine dans l'Inquiètude is magnificent; he has a beaked nose and huge wary eyes, his coat up to his shoulders, hand in pocket – intensely living; an ardently designed woman holds up a lighted lamp not far from his face. The whole thing gives one a sudden shudder, a sense of suspense, at this tragically dramatic moment of the play, when certainly a crime is going to be committed. Here in the narrow room where the very air breathes murder and all hangs on the suspense of the next moment, these two figures surge out of the void: and as it were, with some far-thoughted reflection of the blindness of Fate, and of death's ignobility.[925]

Antoine himself went on to become director of the Odéon (raising it from the dead, thought Arnold Bennett[926]) from 1906 to 1914 and lived until 1943. One student who spent a year (1903) with Antoine was Elli Tompuri, who in 1905 acted Salomé in the Finnish National Theatre in Helsinki, and again in 1919 with her newly founded Free Stage theatre.[927] Wilde himself told Frank Harris in 1898 that Antoine was doing 'great work';[928] one wonders what he had in mind, for the plays of a Méténier or an Auguste Linert were not such as to appeal to Wilde, unless we can postulate a very different Wilde beginning to emerge out of his twilight; nor did Antoine ever produce a play by Wilde or refer to Wilde in his memoirs.[929] (Linert's play *Conte de Noël*, staged by Antoine at Christmas 1890, is characterised as 'revolting' even by the professionally detached John Henderson.[930]) But by 1898 Antoine had removed himself from the position of standard-bearer to the vanguard: directing Jules Lemaître's *L'age difficile* at the Gymnase in 1895, 'je retrouverais les méthodes de l'ancien théâtre que j'avais tant combattues.'[931] He rejected Mourey's lesbian play *Lawn-tennis*, and he also drew back from Théodore de Chirac, founder in the autumn of 1891 of the (perhaps rival) Théâtre Réaliste. *La Plume* wrote 'It is no part of a critic's job to have anything to do with the work of M. de Chirac, but rather a job for a scavenger of cess-pools [...] We shall not mention the Théâtre Réaliste again.'[932] Chirac was sentenced to fifteen months imprisonment for outrage to public morals, and Antoine thought this 'not a bit more than he deserves'.[933]

These scabrous plays co-existed with the mystery plays at Rodolphe Salis' Chat Noir and at the Petit Théâtre de la Galerie Vivienne. These were not a late return to mediævalism, for all Salis' enthusiasm for Louis XIII. Something more subtle was at work:

The disarming sincerity of the plays of Fragerolles and of Bouchor[934] are reflected in the numerous enthusiastic remarks by various critics, who saw in these modern Mystery plays a fresh and original approach to the theatre, owing nothing to contemporary art forms and offering escape from over familiar themes [...] The period also more ambitious attempts to further the notion of religious or mystical drama [...] dominated by Grandmougin, Haraucourt, Dujardin and Péladan.[935]

Haraucourt's *La Passion* was successful enough when a part of it was recited by Sarah Bernhardt at the Cirque d'Hiver on Good Friday 1890 for full performances to be given at the Théâtre d'Application. This was at Easter 1891 and 1892. Reginald Lister, who wrote at length about it to his mother, thought it 'the Bible publicised as tenth-rate Racine.'[936]

Dujardin's *La Légende d'Antonia* was a trilogy about a courtesan fallen and redeemed. This symbolist drama, with sets by Maurice Denis, was produced in three parts: *Antonia, une tragédie moderne*, on the 20th April 1891 at the Théâtre d'Application; *Le Chevalier du Passé* on the 17th June 1892 at the Théâtre Moderne and *La fin d'Antonia* on the 14th June 1893 at the Vaudeville: Gide saw the first and third parts. This ambitious work seems to have taken Dujardin's talent to beyond its limit.

There were other ways that Realism came to theatre. The old Paris Opera house in the rue Le Peletier was destroyed by fire in 1873. On the 14th May 1887 a fire at the Opéra-Comique,[937] caused eighty-four certain and perhaps a hundred deaths (or hundreds of deaths, according to Hemmings[938]). Carvalho, the director since 1877, was tried for negligence (the fire doors were locked) but acquitted and remained in post until his death ten years later, the Opéra-Comique being transferred to the place du Châtelet until the reconstruction by Louis Bernier was ready, in 1899.[939] Fire too signalled the end of the age of the operas of the mid-century when the Palais Garnier warehouse was destroyed with thirty sets. Only eleven operas of the old repertoire were ever to be revived. And on the 8th March 1900, the Théâtre Français was also destroyed by fire.[940]

~~~~~~

If Paris as theatre was typified by Antoine's use of real street people as extras, on the one hand, and by the painting of supernumeries on the flats to mimic the hurly-burly of the boulevards on the other, then a craze for new illusions added a third conceit. Silhouette or shadow plays, known curiously as 'ombres chinoises', were popular at the Chat Noir, many created by the illustrator Henri Rivière, and were a significant by-product of Symbolism, as Jules Lemaître pointed out at the time.[941] These became extremely successful, with Friday the most fashionable night. Rivière made innovative use of colour and glass transparencies, and his technique was not only itself a play with illusion, but favoured the illusory: hence his production of mystery plays in this somewhat unlikely setting, *La Tentation de Saint Antoine* perhaps the most famous. *Sainte Geneviève de Paris*, with music by Léopold Dauphin,[942] achieved a certain acclaim, and *L'Éléphant* by Henry Somm[943] was also a success, and was staged at other venues. In 1894 August Strindberg thought of adapting his play *The Keys of Heaven* for performance *en silhouette* at the Chat Noir, although this did not in the end happen. One can add Maurice Donnay's *Phryne* (14th January 1891) and *Ailleurs* (11th November 1891), designed by Rivière with music composed and played by de Sivry.[944] Donnay thought that Rivière brought the art of the shadow play to a degree never surpassed. There was further scope for illusion when André Antoine engaged Rivière to recreate the Temple of Dionysus at Athens for his Greek season at the Odéon in September 1896. It is to be regretted that Wilde's prose poems did not come to Rivière's attention.

Ralph Nevill quotes an unnamed 'typical Boulevardier' as saying of the shadow theatre that 'to spend an evening in its picturesque setting [...] was to live for two hours in the world of magic and dreams'.[945] Arnold Bennett, seeing the shadow play *La marche à l'étoile* at the Cabaret du Conservatoire (*ancienne* abbaye de la Butte) in the boulevard Rochechouart, thought it 'the most artistic show we had seen in Paris'.[946] Marie Belloc was excited enough by *ombremanie* to exaggerate its impact: 'The whole of artistic Europe was beginning to be stirred and excited'[947]. She ascribed the origin of shadow plays to Caran d'Ache, and certainly his play *L'Épopée* at the Chat Noir with its four thousand silhouettes performing thirty scenes, was the acme of the genre. Even though the Chat Noir was then 'out of bounds for the kind of Frenchwomen with whom I was acquainted', this restraint broke down under the appeal of *L'Épopée*. The Prince of Wales, says Belloc, went to Paris specially to see it, as did 'every one of the younger German and Scandinavian princes'.[948] Even if this is untrue as stated, it demonstrates the impact. Caran d'Ache produced two more such plays, a vision of Paris called, significantly, *Bois de Boulogne*; and another called *Les Steppes*. Jacques Bizet and Robert Dreyfus, helped by Jacques-Émile Blanche and Forain, produced a shadow play called *Les lauriers sont coupées*, a satire on literary figures of the day, which ran for three nights in March 1897.[949] In 1892 the Théâtre des Ombres Lyriques du Lyon d'Or and in 1898 the Boîte à Musique became specifically dedicated to shadow plays: theatres of shadow in the city of light.

Paris was also being offered other theatres of silhouettes. In the city where Daguerre had once frozen life into stillness, it is not surprising that anything that now had to do with the moving image and its metaphysical properties was a fascination to Parisians. In 1886 Louis Le Prince began experimenting with animation, although his own became problematic, for he disappeared without trace on 16th September 1890 while on a train from Dijon to Paris, he, his papers and his luggage vanishing (like Basil Hallward) for ever. In 1888 Étienne-Jules Marey combined the technology of the Gatling gun and the camera to produce multiple images.[950] The Isola brothers patented a projector that they called the Isolatograph, appropriate to illusionists, and were soon showing spectacles in their theatre.[951] In 1896 Jules Terme patented a reversible camera[952] and in the same year Auguste Baron patented his first devices for adding sound to film, and spent his entire fortune of two hundred thousand francs over the next few years while coping with failing eyesight. In 1899 he became blind while experimenting with 3-D, dying a forgotten man thirty-nine years later. Rather younger was Alice Guy, who was working as a secretary for Léon Gaumont when she made her first film, *La Fée aux Choux*, in 1896 and so became 'the mother of cinema': unfortunately, nearly all her children have perished.

Gaumont established his company in 1895, the brothers Émile and Charles Pathé established theirs in 1896. Originally restaurateurs, the Pathés had exchanged the larding needle for the phonograph needle in 1894. They also invented the Pathéphone, a primitive juke box listened to through headphones. Celluloid film was also invented at this time, by Georges Balagny of the rue Salneuve, while Jules Richard invented a small successful stereoscope (bringing a double image into a three-dimensional one) which he called the Verascope. That the pioneers of cinema had backgrounds in engineering, science or manufacturing is hardly surprising; but the necessary factor was the connection of these activities with matters of illusion, reflection, insubstantiality. Gaumont was an optical craftsman, Louis Lumière invented visual reading processes, Pathé at one time dealt in counterfeit Edison phonographic cylinders. This gives point to Robert Abel's view that 'perhaps the most successful genre for French exhibitors during this early period was what they themselves called "transformation views" or "transformation scenes".'[953] That these were called *féeries* in French, further grounds the whole enterprise in the magic realms.

The interplay between film and Paris life is explicit. Once the Lumière showings at the Grand Café[954] were fairly established, queues stretched as far as the rue Caumartin, a quarter of a mile away and the Lumières, remembered to this day for foreseeing the end of the fad of cinema,[955] undertook further screenings at the Théâtre Saint-Denis. Passers-by would look in and 'come back quickly with a few friends they'd managed to find on the boulevard'.[956] Leonard Merrick's Bohemian composer Pitou is reduced to playing the piano at the Bioscope in Montmartre.[957] The silhouette artist Trewey[958] became the Lumières' demonstrator in London. The department store Dufayel showed films from early on, bringing this entertainment into the great Parisian experience of shopping. Georges Meliès, a conjuror who at one time ran the Théâtre Robert-Houdin, became 'the father of trick photography'.

> After building a camera based on an English projector, Meliès began filming unstaged street scenes and moments of passing daily life. One day, the story goes, he was filming at the Place de l'Opéra and his camera jammed as a bus was passing. After some tinkering, he was able to resume filming, but by this time the bus had gone and a hearse was passing in front of his lens. When Meliès screened the film, he discovered something unexpected: a moving bus seemed to transform itself instantly into a hearse. The anecdote may be apocryphal, but it at least illustrates Meliès' recognition of the magical powers of mise-en-scène. He would devote most of his efforts to cinematic conjuring.[959]

That the father of trick photography should also have produced a documentary on the Dreyfus case[960] was fitting enough in that affair of forgery and fraud. His trademark 'Star-Film' can be interpreted not in the sense of 'film stars' but in terms of distant points of light illuminating the darkness.

How to transform static images into motion pictures was also known from the photographic work in California of Eadweard Muybridge,[961] for it had become of interest to Professor Jules Marey of the Collège de France, whose subject was the physiology of animal movement. Marey invited Muybridge to Paris in the autumn of 1881 where his work of photographing movement engaged not only the animal scientists and photographers like Nadar, but also the horse painters, at least one of whom, Aimé Morot, had come to the conclusion, finally established by Muybridge, that galloping horses did not ever have all four legs extended.[962] Some two hundred guests came to a soirée at Meissonier's to hear Muybridge lecture, among them Detaille, Cabanel, Bonnat and Gérôme. The ground was prepared by Muybridge's patron Leland Stanford, sometime Governor of California, who visited Paris in 1879. The Stanfords returned to Paris in October 1881 and accompanied Muybridge.[963] Leland's portrait by Meissonier and that of his wife by

Bonnat,[964] now in the Stanford University Museum, date to this visit. The art of the future was thus grounded among the conservative artists, whose art was already of the past.

The Exposition Universelle of 1900, intended not only to celebrate past and present achievements but also to light the way to the future, boosted film by providing a vast audience that poured into Paris. It did so, however, by using the existing language of entertainment and the metalanguages of illusion. There was the Phono-Cinéma-Théâtre of Paul Decauville, which showed brief scenes featuring Sarah Bernhardt, Réjane, Coquelin *cadet* and Cléo de Mérode, but there was also the 'Panorama au Tour du Monde' which allowed the novel experience of being in Paris while looking at the world. As for the Cinéorama of Raoul Grimoin-Sanson, with its 360° auditorium, it 'posed so many technical problems that it never opened'.[965] This interaction of film and society also occurs in a particularly poignant instance, for it was a flash fire of film that caused the tragedy of the Bazaar de la Charité in 1897. Even here the fantastic intrudes. The fire was started within the projector by the overheating of its lamp: the lamp was manufactured under the name *Securitas*. Each of the moving image experiments or inventors seems to have had something of this sort of erratic aspect. The inventor of the Securitas, Molteni, who was known as 'projection incarnate', also manufactured and distributed 'Robertson's fantascope' and photographic plates with the brand name Wheel of Life,[966] as if it were all a branch of the occult sciences. Melies, regarded by the leading film historian of early French cinema as a 'representative figure of the period'[967], liked to show himself in the guise of the devil, and a number of his films featured satanic motifs. In this, thinks Richard Abel, Melies' films signify a tension between order and disorder, but within the context of fin-de-siècle Parisian society, this is not merely not out of the way, but must be seen as a contribution to the prevailing climate. The photograph, its signification a fixed system, gives place to the film and its floating signifiers, as the primary form of record.

Cinema, categorised by the authorities for licensing purposes as 'spectacle de curiosité', was nourished in the theatres and music-halls it was to replace. The Eldorado, the Olympia, the Casino de Paris and the Folies Bergère all showed short films. By 1914, the Cirque d'Hiver, the Hippodrome, and the Parisiana had become cinemas; the Ba-ta-Clan, the Cigale, the Gaîté-Rochechouart (once painted by Seurat[968]), the Vaudeville followed after the war.

~~~~~~~

Studies of Paris theatre, from the Comédie Française to the caf''conc', unfortunately pay little attention to circus, even when it was itself the subject of theatre, such as Louis Ganne's *Les Saltimbanques* (Théâtre de la Gaîté, December 1899), doubtlessly overlooked because it was an operetta. Yet the iconographic record is bountiful enough, as painted by Degas and Renoir, Toulouse-Lautrec, Forain and Seurat, even if not all the paintings identify the circus concerned.[969] Here artifice and illusion also predominated, Paris as Paradise as Parade as Parody.[970] Hughes Le Roux[971] published a book called *Acrobats and Mountebanks* in 1890, with voyeuristic illustrations by Jules Garnier added for the English edition, another example of how France was mediated for English expectations.[972] Fact and fiction coincided when Goncourt's novel of circus life *Les Frères Zemganno* was staged at the Théâtre Libre. Wilde called this novel 'the apotheosis of the acrobat', which may or may not indicate praise – indeed, may or may not indicate that he had read it.[973] Perhaps the view was shared with Stevenson that, with the circus gymnast 'there is little or no tincture of the artist in his composition; his soul is small and pedestrian'.[974] Be that as it may, there were four permanent circuses in Paris during this period, the Cirque d'Hiver, the Cirque d'Été, the Nouveau Cirque and the Hippodrome. These were not 'big top' circuses, but substantial buildings. At the Nouveau Cirque[975] in the rue St Honoré, for example, the arena could be artificially flooded with water, into which a certain Auguste, as a bogus member of the audience, regularly fell. The clowns John and William Price appeared at the Cirque d'Hiver, where John was painted by Renoir.[976] Nor must one overlook the Cirque Fernando, named after the proprietor Fernando Wartenberg, and subject of Renoir's 'Au Cirque Fernando' of 1875/6. Toulouse-Lautrec also used the Cirque Fernando for subjects,[977] and Boldini was there often in 1877. Richard Brettel finds something of the demi-monde here, when commenting on Renoir's picture of Francesca and Angelica Wartenberg ('Two Little Circus Girls').[978] The Wartenberg sisters were using their real names, but circus even more than theatre encouraged the use of fanciful *noms-de-ruse*, such as that of the versatile Rita del Erido of the Nouveau Cirque, who out of the ring was not Spanish but a German called Margaretha Liebmann who wrote waltzes, played the flute and painted on porcelain.

> Rita del Erido caracoled on horseback between the supper tables, wearing a divided skirt of white lace flounces, a white hat on her black hair with white ostrich feathers frothing round the relentless beauty of her face.[979]

Forain's 'The Tightrope Walker' of 1880 has been seen as 'a metaphor for the moral ambiguities of Parisian nightlife,'[980] and this brings the iconography of popular entertainment into the domain of the more general ambivalent readings characteristic of the day. Seurat's well-known picture of equestrian acrobats, 'Cirque' of 1880/1,[981] for example, affords some of the puzzling aspects associated with 'The Bar at the Folies Bergère', as it appears to be a scene within a scene, contained by the foregrounded clown opening a curtain, in what is perhaps the artist's position; while the relationship of the acrobats, horse and ringmaster convey a fluidity of movement that has little connection between them, but much contrast with the static audience. This audience contains what appears to be the same male spectator twice, once with, once without a beard.

Circus combined fantasy and pageantry with political significance, both literally (the Cirque Fernando was used for political rallies[982]) and metaphorically. Old Mr Gladstone, visiting the Hippodrome in September 1889, tried to puzzle this out:

> The performance was arrested as God Save the Queen was played. The cycling wonderful, said to be English. The Russian spectacle most interesting, received with an enthusiasm I thought full of meaning.[983]

Circus also provided one of the strangest of contemporary transformation scenes when in 1880 a M. Molier created an amateur show, the Cirque Molier (itself a seeming pun on the maison de Molière). Here young members of the upper classes, 'forgetting that their ancestors had fought at Rocroi and Fontenoy', turned themselves into acrobats and clowns and strong men. The performances were private, but packed, *horizontales* mixing with the upright. The demand to attend grew so much that Molier agreed to two public performances, one limited entirely to an audience drawn from the demi-monde, the other from members of society. A third public performance was ensured when the duchesse d'Uzès engaged the whole company for a charity performance.[984]

If there seems a strong element of parody in this, it should also be remembered that parody was a form much used at the lighter end of the theatrical spectrum, notably in operetta, where opera was frequently burlesqued: Gounod's *Faust* and *Roméo et Juliette* and Berlioz' *Les Troyens à Carthage* becoming, for example, in the hands of Florimond Hervé, *Le Petit Faust*, *Roméo et Mariette* and *Les Troyens en Champagne*. Hervé played Jupiter in Offenbach's revival of *Orphée aux Enfers* in 1878, signifying that Paris could laugh once more at Glück.

It may be surprising to learn that Ludovic Halévy, who had been Offenbach's librettist (notably for *La Belle Hélène*, *La Vie Parisienne*, and *La Grande Duchesse de Gérolstein*) and had moved on after Offenbach's death in 1880 to write rather light-hearted novels, was an admirer of Zola's *L'Assommoir* and provided the novelist with source material for *Nana*, notably about the Théâtre de Variétés and Anna Judic, who appears in *Nana* as Rose Mignon – her lightness of morals implicit in this earns her a place in *The Pretty Women of Paris*.[985] Curiously, Julian Field refers to an actress at the Variétés called Rose Mignon, the *chère amie* of an American gambler called Deutsch, known as the Baccarat King,[986] who 'won and lost two millions in about the shortest time on record' at the Washington Club;[987] perhaps she took her name from *Nana*, or, more likely, from the opera *Mignon* by Ambroise Thomas,[988] commemorated on his statue in the parc Monceau. (The name derives from *Wilhelm Meister*, 'rewritten and represented across every artistic form'.[989]) The Grand Duke Vladimir was enamoured of a young actress called B̲ignon, 'who had hair the colour of moonlight';[990] while Barbara Wilson gives the name of the mistress of the comte de Montemar as baroness de Bignon.[991] One can also add in Rose Michon, the heroine of Offenbach's *La jolie parfumeuse*, played by Louise Théo at the Théâtre de la Renaissance in November 1873 and by Kate Santley at the Alhambra in May 1874. The interaction between stage and life here has a tragic aspect, for when *Nana* was produced at the Ambigu, the title rôle was taken by an actress called Léontine Massin 'but she died in a lunatic asylum soon afterwards'.[992] As for Ambroise Thomas – 'There are three sorts of music,' said Chabrier, 'good music, bad music and the music of Ambroise Thomas.'[993]

J.E.C. Bodley thought that Halévy 'had an aspect of gentle melancholy and a manner of polite reserve. But in intimate intercourse he was the most entertaining of companions and the most entrancing of causeurs.'[994] Halévy numbered among his friends baron Alphonse de Rothschild and the prince de Wagram. His sons were at this time at the outset of their own distinguished careers as critics and historians; in 1895 Wilfrid Blunt found one of them to be 'a most interesting young man of the serious student kind one reads of in French novels but so seldom meets, an abler man, I should say, even than his father'.[995] In 1889 Lord Lytton, staying in Dieppe, saw Jane Hading act at the Halévys 'very badly'.[996] Ludovic and Daniel Halévy, Albert Boulanger-Cavé, Jacques-Émile Blanche, Walter Sickert and Henri Gervex are the subject of the painting 'Six Friends at Dieppe' of 1885 by Degas;[997] Halévy and Boulanger-Cavé, 'a noted backstage dandy',[998] were painted by Degas backstage at the Opéra.[999] If the longevity of Halévy's success seems surprising in the age of Jarry, it should be remembered that just as for most Parisians *the* artists were Bougereau and Cabanel,[1000] so for most Parisians, the playwrights of the 'nineties were Lemaître, Rostand, and Hervieu.[1001] Of these, the one reference that Wilde makes to Rostand in his letters suggests that the two were unacquainted; and though he certainly was anxious to know what Lemaître made of *Salomé*; he does not refer to Hervieu.[1002]

Jane Hading is worth closer attention in this Vanity Fair. She had begun in operetta (Audran's *Le Grand Mogol* of 1877 then Lecocq's *La Jolie Persane* in 1879), but was eclipsed by Jeanne Granier. Gervex painted her portrait in 1888 and Roll in 1890. Jane Hading was not her name, but an æstheticisation of Jeannette Hadingue – though whether even that was her name is argued, as James Harding says that her real name was Jeanne-Alfrédine Tréfouret.[1003] De Fouquières, who calls her Jeanne Hading, remembered her with a certain reserve. After her divorce from Victor Koning, she continued 'sa vie tumultueuse, aimée des princes, emplissant Paris de ses éclats, *car infiniment spirituelle*, elle était hardie en ses propos et n'avait point perdu – avec une pointe d'accent marseillais – une certaine vulgarité naturelle', although how a Belgian came by a marseillais accent is not explained, except that accents seem as undetermined as everything else – it was said of Napoléon III that he spoke all languages with a German accent except German. De Fouquières mentions a Japanese prince followed by a Russian prince who kept her, and that she returned to Belgium in obscure circumstances, the princely gifts sold at the Hôtel Drouot.[1004]

Hading should be counted among those actresses who, overshadowed by Bernhardt, have fallen out of the limelight, notably Brohan, Reichenberg and Judic.

> Il n'y a pas longtemps que j'ai vue, aux Folies-Bergères, une jeune femme d'une figure adorable, qui chante, et dit surtout le couplet, avec un art, inférieur peut-être à celui de Theresa, mais enveloppant au possible. Elle s'appelle Judic.[1005]

Anna Judic, Judic 'with the bewitching smile', Judic 'malicious and pernicious', Judic 'even more monotonous that that everlasting chrysanthemum Sarah Bernhardt',[1006] whom Marie Belloc preferred to Sarah Bernhardt.[1007]

Judic was her married name (after a fashion – her husband's real name was Israël). Conservatoire trained, she moved from comedy to café-concert to operetta, becoming the heroine of Hervé's *Mam'zelle Nitouche* at the Théâtre des Variétés in 1883. Not surprisingly this is concerned with double lives: Nitouche (*anglice*, bread-and-butter miss) is a convent girl with a secret passion for theatre; the organist is a secret composer of operettas. At one point both disguise themselves as dragoons. *Mam'zelle Nitouche*, with its libretto partly written by Meilhac, was a great success; of its author, Richard Traubner has written that his 'life story [...] is as fanciful the genre he helped create'.[1008] In 1886 Richard Whiteing noted that Judic, who 'used to live in a quiet way in the rue de Boulogne, until she had rounded off her colossal fortune,[1009] is now lodged like a queen in the rue Nouvelle [...] It looks sixteenth century [...]';[1010] but by 1900 he was commenting that 'Judic, that once beautiful and incomparable creature, is fallen from her high estate'.[1011] Here too was a decadence.

CHAPTER SEVEN

CAFÉ AU FAIT

'"Now, where shall we go?" asked Lauder. "Café de Paris, Durand's,
Paillard's? All excellent and gay."
'"Let's go to a quiet place,' said Richard. 'I'm a little bit tired of the
gilded world. Let's go where we won't see any cocottes.'
'"Let me see, then. Voisin's – no, we'll go to Noel Peters', and dine in
peace and quiet."'
– Filson Young.[1012]

'There is a subtle influence in supper.'
– Oscar Wilde: 'The Critic as Artist.'

'YOU'LL dine your man in Paris tomorrow,' Sir Frank Lockwood said to
Sir Edward Clarke while waiting for the verdict of the jury at Wilde's
second trial.[1013] Although Lockwood probably meant nothing more than to
indicate his belief that Wilde would be acquitted, his assumptions are
significant: that even acquitted, Wilde would leave England; that it would
be to Paris that he would go; and that a convivial meal would be among
his first occasions. These associations indicate how inextricable were the
notions of Paris, sexual licence, celebration, and dinner, that strange
symbiosis between licentiousness and literature, a point also made by
Henry James when he wrote of 'the Parisian place, the feverish hour, the
putting before her of a hundred francs' worth of food and drink'.[1014]

When first George Moore and then Oscar Wilde sought to insert
themselves into Parisian society, they were not moving amongst
friendships new minted, and it is much to the credit of Moore that his
social skills, which were otherwise unremarkable, afforded him so easy an
entrée. Referring to the Human Comedy, Moore wrote 'I have walked
many years in its streets and mused many years on its terraces'.[1015] These
lines could only have been written with Paris in mind, terraces to be read
as the *terrasses* of the cafés, not the terraces of Irish (or English) country
houses. The first café of this period to be the gathering place of Bohemia
was the Café Guerbois in the rue des Batignolles, haunt of Manet, Zola,

Paul Guigou, Bazille, Degas, Duranty, Burty, Renoir, Pissarro, Monet, Sisley, Cézanne, Bracquemond, Zacharie Astruc, Nadar, Duret, Paul Alexis, Armand Silvestre,[1016] Carjat, Constantin Guys, Guillaumin, Marcel Desboutin and Alfred Stevens.[1017] The supersession of the Guerbois by the Nouvelle-Athènes, which opened in 1870, is a significant waymark in the supersession of Batignolles by Montmartre: the Guerbois set seems to have migrated there en bloc. George Moore may have impressed these men less than he was impressed by them – according to Heinrich Felbermann, who employed Moore on *The Examiner*, Villiers de l'Isle Adam 'said that he did not believe that his head was so shaped as to hold the particle of a single idea'[1018] – but Paul Alexis became Moore's friend, correspondent and at times fugleman; while in March 1886 Duret took Moore to the dinner at which the eighth Impressionist exhibition was planned by Pissarro, Monet, Mallarmé, Huysmans and Burty. Moore repaid the compliment by returning to Paris and reviewing the exhibition in *The Bat* (11th May 1886), the undistinguished journal edited by James Davis.

The group of friends was known as the 'Batignollais' and recognised Manet as their principal, at any rate for much of the time. Fantin-Latour's 'Un atelier aux Batignolles' (1870) shows Zacharie Astruc, Zola, Edmond Maître, Otto Schölderer, Renoir, Bazille and Monet standing round Manet at his easel.[1019] One of the Batignollais is surely the subject of Manet's 'Le Bon Bock' of 1873. Manet at this time also associated with the Parnassian poets, whom later critics have either not used kindly – Stefan Zweig, for example, says that Émile Verhaeren was a Parnassian until 'socialism fell like a red drop into the morbid paleness of his poetic work'[1020] – or else not used at all: who now reads the *Ame Brûlante* of the baronne Baye? Some of these associations went back even beyond the Guerbois, for example to the soirées of Commandant Lejosne, where at the end of the 1850s Manet met Barbey d'Aurevilly, Nadar, Bracquemond and Baudelaire.[1021] One outcome was Manet's 'La Musique aux Tuileries',[1022] peopled, as well as by Manet himself, by Gautier, Baudelaire, Baron Taylor,[1023] Aurélien Scholl, Champfleury, Fantin-Latour and Astruc. This last 'carried about with him ten thousand manuscript verses, which he liked reading to anyone who cared for well-turned alexandrines'.[1024] He cannot have been overly occupied.

Manet never moved further from Batignolles than the 'Europe' district. At first he lived in the rue Saint-Louis, then in the rue de l'Hôtel de Ville – these are now to be sought as the rue Nollet and the rue des Batignolles. Later he had a studio at 81 rue Guyot on the western side of Batignolles;

this too has gone, being the site of the intersection of the avenue de Villiers and the rue Fortuny. Only his last studio at 77 rue d'Amstersdam and his later homes, at 34 boulevard des Batignolles and the rue de Saint-Pétersbourg (49 and later 39) still exist – the latter, after a spell as the rue de Leningrad, is the rue de Saint-Pétersbourg once more, while the former might have had the distinction of being the subject of the last, unfinished, painting by Marie Bashkirtseff.

The Guerbois was the first café to achieve such a position since the vanished Café Momus in the rue Saint-Germain-l'Auxerrois, twenty years earlier – vanished, but of course immortalised by Henri Murger: *Vie de Bohème* and reappearing every time Act II of *La Bohème* is created on stage, where it is clear enough that Momus is the god of laughter. The Café Guerbois has also vanished, leaving some confusion even where it once was, Raymond Cogniat suggesting either at number 9 or number 11, grande rue des Batignolles [1025] – in fact, the street became the avenue de Clichy in 1868, and number eleven was renumbered nine, while the Guerbois was subsequently renamed the Brasserie Müller (allowing for confusion with the restaurant Müller in the rue Pasquier). The Brasserie Müller has also vanished, gone since 1957, its site now occupied by a nondescript modern block.

Those who wished to find the artists therefore could easily do so. Salons and studios apart, the café or bar was the prevailing social site. A plaque on the Auberge de la Bonne Franquette,[1026] for example, now commemorates its rôle as a meeting place for Pissarro, Degas, Sisley, Toulouse-Lautrec, Cézanne, Monet, Renoir and Zola between 1850 and 1900. It was in the latter year that Renoir became a Chevalier of the Légion d'Honneur, the private person receiving public recognition. As will become clear, the café was the public equivalent of the salon, but incorporated a private space within the public space, usually in the social sense, but sometimes physically so.

Some, however, saw the public space as eroding the private one, Huysmans writing that 'there was now no place where one could meet a few artists privately, intimately, and discuss ideas at ease'.[1027] Maupassant, who once favoured the Café de la Rochefoucauld, seems to have acquired a distaste for all 'public houses of call' for just this reason.[1028] The artists, far more than the writers, were on view, en plein air, and at vernissages, as well as in salon or café.

> The daily and weekly rituals surrounding the café reveal that social
> perception and purpose may be generated as much through the collective
> experience of public assembly as through the intentions of private
> individuals [...] Café sociability provides a privileged space within which
> to view the [habitués'] myriad identities [...] as customers, friends, lovers,
> relatives, strangers and enemies [...] Cafés were the primary circuit for
> Parisian social networks.[1029]

Clearly, one would be seen at a café, and this implies that one wanted to
be seen, unless a *cabinet particulier* was at one's service (there was one
reserved at the Café Anglais exclusively for the Prince of Wales whenever
he was in Paris). When Sir Charles Rivers Wilson of the Egyptian
Ministry of Finance with his colleagues Larking and Dicey, met Nubar
Pasha[1030] at the Café de la Paix[1031] for what would come to be called a
'power breakfast', this combination of private and public came
together.[1032] That they were subsequently joined by Campbell Clarke, Paris
correspondent of the *Daily Telegraph*, enforces this modern note. But if
this was being private in public, so one could also be public in private:
Cécile Sorel tells of the writer Abel Hermant[1033] habitually 'alone at his
small table, smiling over his cakes at some mental *gourmandise*, oblivious
of all at else' at Larue's, the fashionable restaurant in the place de la
Madeleine,[1034] the favourite of the actress Réjane. Similarly Laurent
Tailhade once hid from a woman he calls Yeu-Yeu ('plus sèche et plus
ridicule que jamais') in the most obscure corner that he could find in the
Café de la Paix,[1035] which would not have been obscure at all. The ultimate
elision between the private and public moment in a café was the
assassination of Jean Jaurès at the Café de Croissant in the rue de
Montmartre on 31st July 1914.

There was no hard and fast distinction between the cafés of the artists and
those of the writers. For these too a café could also be an elegant republic,
an academy, the talk instructive: 'Café conversations and rituals helped
shape modern republicanism, socialism, Bohemianism, anarchism and
syndicalism'.[1036]   In the aftermath of the attempted palace coup by
MacMahon in May 1877, two thousand two hundred cafés were closed to
prevent them becoming focuses of sedition. The academy was thus also a
forum, but not always conducive to high endeavour. 'I didn't care for the
poets' cafés,' Rothenstein eventually remembered. 'They were too
crowded and too noisy [...] I was too keen on my work to waste many
nights with these wild poets.'[1037] Nevertheless, 'Besides the Latin Quarter
poets, I used to meet Mallarmé, Rodenbach, Henri de Régnier, André

Gide, Camille Mauclair, Montesquiou, Remy de Gourmont, and, most frequently, Edouard Dujardin'.[1038]

The Nouvelle-Athènes, remarks Joanna Richardson, 'brought some unlikely characters together'.[1039] There came 'Pissarro, dreamy and vague; Manet, loud, declamatory, and eager for medals and decorations; Degas, sharp, deep, more profound, scornfully sarcastic; Duranty, clear-headed, dry, full of repressed disappointment',[1040] as well as the Dutch composer Louis Benedictus, introduced by Villiers de l'Isle-Adam. One also finds the names of Daumier, Théodore Rousseau and Daubigny.[1041] It was here that Duranty introduced Raffaëlli to Degas, Zandomeneghi and Forain, and where, introduced by the decayed dramatist Bernard Lopez (despite his Spanish name, of English parentage), Moore met Manet (whose sketch 'George Moore au café' of April 1879 captures the moment, Moore all collar and cuffs), Degas, and Pissarro as well as Villiers de L'Isle Adam, Mendès, Paul Alexis, Léon Dierx, the art critic Duranty, and Jean de Cabanes, or Cabaner, as he preferred to be called, a hollow-chested man with a goat-like beard,[1042] who was there every night, doubtless a striking contrast to Lopez, there every Monday, short, fat and bald 'his chin descending step by step into a voluminous bosom, a sort of human guinea pig'.[1043] Here Moore learned to 'æstheticise', a form of enjoyment,' says his principal biographer, 'for which there is no common English word. One did not just talk about art; one speculated. One invented the idea of works of art that did not yet exist; one sought for a description of all existing works of art that showed their limits, and proved that the existent was not everything: there were other worlds to make. In æstheticising, paradox and aphorism were the preferred elements of composition.'[1044]

Zola stayed away,[1045] and this may have been as well. In a letter to Jacques-Émile Blanche, Moore, high on his academic horse, said of La Terre 'I have read Zola's new book; I shall never read another by him – he does not address the scholarly instincts in readers and if a man does not do that I fail to see on what ground he claims my attention and consideration'.[1046] Moore did not always manage to convey this air of lofty detachment.

> As is well known, he strongly disliked all contemporary writers {…} Indeed, as a rule he hated them more than he hated their books, which is saying a great deal […] And of all the French writers for whom he had a hatred, he loathed Zola more than all the others.[1047]

Signac, Seurat and Gauguin also went to the Nouvelle-Athènes, the latter introduced by Pissarro, and the photographer Nadar, 'a particular friend'

of Manet.[1048] This was a society in which Gauguin could recall that he was
the grandson of the socialist poet Flora Tristan, reflected in the remark of
Gauguin's biographer that, in the early 1890s, Gauguin 'now led a
thoroughly Parisian life *and got himself talked about*'.[1049] Forain's picture
'Intérieur de la Nouvelle-Athènes'(1876) is a graphic depiction in his
acidulated manner, satirising the lack of warmth within the café, and
revealing the equal lack within himself – André de Fouquières described
him as 'un homme sec, nerveux, au visage pâle et à l'expression triste. Il
avait le regard froid et aigu, un mélange de mélancholie et d'insolence
dans la physionomie.'[1050]

The café created its own literature not only as a resort of writers, but as the
place where journalists went for copy and, therefore, the resort of those
who wished to provide copy. In the Bodega on the corner of the rue
Castiglione and at Austin's in the rue d'Amsterdam,[1051] Huysmans,
notebook in hand, brought Naturalism to the service of æstheticism as he
did fieldwork for *À Rebours*, 'the first signal of literary Symbolism'.[1052]
This was not only in Bohemia: the Café de la Légion d'Honneur at 262
boulevard St Germain, for example, was frequented by army officers[1053]
who wished to air their views on the 'affaire Dreyfus' and by journalists
who wished to repeat them. The officers, to paraphrase Karl Kraus, no
doubt then believed what they read in the newspapers.

It has been estimated that Paris contained an enormous number of cafés at
this time – some twenty-seven thousand according to Theodore Reff and
Charles Rearick, but forty-two thousand according to W.S. Haine, 11.25
per 1,000 of population, compared with London's 1:1,000 and New
York's 3.5.[1054] Moreover, the number open at any one time does not reveal
the even larger turn-over. 'Between 1881 and 1912 an astonishing 145,972
establishments opened [...] In 1885 one in every three bankrupt business
was a café.'[1055] What this does demonstrate is the social institutionalisation
of conviviality: although the literature of the period is full of waiters who
aspire to own their own premises and then retire, to run a café, let alone to
run one successfully, required social as well as business savoir faire –
although, to be sure, both personal observation and the literary sources
also suggest that while the patron was being convivial, Mémé kept an eye
on the cash: this arrangement survives. Henry Lucy noted of the café
proprietor 'Père' Camie that 'as far as I observed, he never did a stroke of
work. The mainstay of the establishment was Madame.'[1056] Of Thirion's,
Nathaniel Newnham-Davis wrote, 'just inside, Madame, plump and

smiling, sits at her desk'.[1057] W.J. Locke captured an extreme example of the type in his madame Gougasse[1058]; Octave Mirbeau's Célestine when married runs a thriving bar 'À l'Armée Française' in Cherbourg, and 'in charge of the till, sat enthroned behind the bar'.[1059] The Select Bar at St-Cloud was kept by two sisters. At Lavenue's, the inner room was presided over by 'the perennial Mademoiselle Fanny', who might also have been Mademoiselle Rosalie.[1060]

Few waiters can have succeeded in setting up on their own, out of a working population of some sixty thousand restaurant employés and a further twelve thousand café workers,[1061] yet the idea was a powerful one. Célestine's husband Joseph is clearly going to make his fortune, for it was not only at the upper end of the scale that men (like César Ritz) grew rich. The brothers Coudon, who ran the Café Frontin in the boulevard Poissonière, sold up in 1877 with profits of a quarter million francs. Henri Pineau, a waiter in a restaurant near the Opéra where he could observe how gentlemen comported themselves, went to unusual extremes, for he saved fifty pounds and turned himself into M. le comte Henri de Tourville and embarked upon a life of crime.[1062] The typical Parisian waiter was thought of as loquacious and worldly-wise, and was so parodied in Gide's *Prométhée mal enchaîné* of 1898.[1063] 'Most Paris waiters look like great men,' noted Sisley Huddleston, adding cynically 'the great man seldom does.'[1064] The Bouillon Duval chain of cheap eating places (there were sixty of them in Paris by 1890), participated in this desire to be dignified with 'sober and respectable-looking façades painted dark red and lettered simply "Établissement Duval".'[1065]

The multitude of cafés both encouraged and nurtured the formation of groupuscules, whether political or cultural. 'Literary men,' reflected the art critic and editor Gualtieri di San Lazzaro, 'lived in cafés like champion exhibits of the human race, but painters lived in cafés as though cafés were academies.'[1066] The Nouvelle-Athènes was certainly one of these. 'I did not go to either Oxford or Cambridge,' wrote George Moore, 'but I went to the Nouvelle-Athènes'; spending 'many instructive years there', and describing himself as having been defined by this experience: 'I am an objectivist, reared among the Parnassians, an exile from the Nouvelle-Athènes'.[1067] Even the information that the Nouvelle-Athènes was visited by Cézanne 'so seldom that most of the younger habitués knew of him only by hearsay'[1068] has a flavour of the college common room about it; and, apart from casual meetings, the habitués' use of a backroom indeed gave the gatherings something of the nature of an Oxford Senior Common Room, something of the nature of a club.

The Nouvelle-Athènes was not the only haunt of its habitués: on Wednesdays in the 1870s Sisley, Renoir, Monet[1069], Pissarro and Guillaumin gathered in the restaurant of Eugène Murer[1070] in the boulevard Voltaire, and the naturalist group of writers – Huysmans, Céard, Alexis, Hennique, Maupassant – favoured the Café Joseph in the rue Condorcet as an alternative to the Nouvelles-Athènes.[1071] In her Paris novel of 1910, Katherine Cecil Thurston wrote that 'the true note of this Bohemianism is not so much spontaneous friendship as a spontaneous capacity for the interchange of thought – that instant opening of mind to mind, when place becomes of slight, and time becomes of no importance.'[1072]

As in the London Club, one could be both visible and unseen, part of life yet isolated from it, time and space confused. Maupassant's Monsieur Parent

> got into the habit of spending his day in the café, where the jostling throng of drinkers surrounds you with a crowd you know by sight but never speak to [...] He lived in the café. The first thing in the morning he went there so as not to be alone, to have someone to look at […] Soon, too indolent to move, he took his meals there […] From four to six he strolled about the boulevards, and after that he came back to the place reserved for him at the café and called for his absinthe.[1073]

The stroll was 'his usual walk from the Madeleine to the rue Drouot', hardly two hours' worth even sauntering. Parent seems transformed into a snail, a creature without a spine, as his wife had always supposed him to be. This became his life: 'year followed year in unbroken monotony; but the time did not seem long, because nothing ever happened. He did not notice the passing of time [...] and only the big mirror behind his head, which was getting balder very day, reflected the ravages of time'.[1074] Nevertheless, Parent sees out five proprietors, a small flux round the centre of his stillness.

The café and the salon may be seen as the analogue of the London club, with the occasional difference of the presence of women[1075] in the one, and the continued difference of the absence of much literature in the other; but for all we learn of the cafés, of the 'cercles', those deliberate imitations of London clubs: we learn hardly anything: something of le Jockey;[1076] a little of the Cercle de Mirlitons, perhaps;[1077] nothing of the Cercle National des Armées de Terre et de Mer; next to nothing of the Mortigny, or the Épatant, for all that Thomas Barclay called it 'the chic social and literary club of Paris' and Pierre Andrieu describes it as 'le cercle le plus chic de Paris'.[1078] This can be compared with the prolific literature on the Carlton

Club, White's, Brooks's, the Savile, the 'Rag', the Garrick. It is also the case that in crossing the channel, the club underwent a sea change. One would not write of a Pall Mall club that, like the Cercle St Simon in the rue St Simon, it had 'the finest reading room in Paris'[1079] or like the Cercle de la Presse, above Klein's in the boulevard des Capucines, it had a gaming room that was 'the finest room of the kind in Europe'[1080]. Nor did French clubs aspire to the English ideal, that the atmosphere should be that of a ducal mansion when the duke is lying dead upstairs (a description applied in particular to Brooks's). 'The French,' wrote Sir Horace Rumbold, 'seem to me not really to understand club life [...] Their clubs are pleasant salons, scarcely homes like ours',[1081] yet these did represent attempts to realise the anglophilia of many upper class Frenchmen, notably the more sporting ones. The names 'le Jockey Club', 'le Hunting'[1082] and 'le Sporting'[1083] (of which the duc de Fitz-James, descendant of James II, was president) make this clear, as does that strange coinage 'le clubman'. The British Club began in the Grand Hôtel, moved to the boulevard des Capucines, then to the rue de l'Arcade, and finally to the boulevard Malesherbes.[1084] There is something English too about Richard Whiteing's description of the Cercle de l'Union as 'a little tainted with the dullness almost inseparable from studied dignity', but nothing English in the description of the La Marmite as 'a liberal club with anticlerical leanings'.[1085]   As for their being homes: the duc de la Rochefoucauld, separated from his wife, lived above Le Nouveau Cercle; had this been London, he would have lived in it.

That cafés should be the congregating sites of particular groups is significant without being surprising. The Café de la Régence, the address of which is given alternatively in the rue de Rivoli (161) and the rue St Honoré, had been the principal rendez-vous of chess players since the eighteenth century, although the original café had been destroyed in 1852, and its interim incarnation had been in the rue de Richelieu. Fox, the editor of *Galignani's Messenger* and then of the European edition of the *New York Herald*, was one who played chess in the Régence. Chess was also played at the Café Turc,[1086] the Grand Café and the Café de la Paix, and the Cercle des Echecs above the Café de la Rotonde.[1087]   Billiards were played at the Grand Café and at the Café Mangin in the passage des Panoramas. The Régence was also favoured by the Scandinavian community, who could read the *Morgenbladet* there; paradoxically the Café de Suède attracted a theatrical clientèle. The Coq d'Or in the rue St Marc was the chief resort of newspapermen, but the staff of the Paris office of the London *Morning Post* gathered at the Café Napolitain, boulevard des Capucines, where Feydeau, Courteline and their circle were to be found in the 1890s: Feydeau, with his untouched glass of wine; La Jeunesse, with his beringed fingers, dominating the hubbub with his 'high-pitched, eunuch's voice'; the priest-like Jean de Bannefroi; the inevitable Catulle Mendès.[1088] 'Le 27' was a soldiers' café at 27 place Maubert, a square also favoured by anarchist cafés. American art students initially preferred Picot's, on the corner of the rue Jacob and the rue de Seine,[1089] then Thirion's, which 'looks like a cheap photographer's studio', in the boulevard St Germain.[1090] The Café de Mulhouse and the Café de l'Europe were patronised by commercial travellers and tradesmen.[1091] The Clarisse[1092] in the rue Jacob was favoured by the anarcho-literary set and by painters from Alsace, the Soufflot in the boul' Mich' by army cadets and medical students. The Drapeau, rue Galande, was favoured by the *ramasseurs de mégots*, the scavengers of cigar and cigarette butts: it cannot have been favoured by many others. Conversely, at the Café Weber or Larue might be found Proust, the duc de Guiche, Prince Léon ('Loche') Radziwill, Louis marquis d'Albuféra, Gabriel de la Rochefoucauld, George de Lauris (all of whom Proust 'adorait pour leur aristocratisme'[1093] quite as much as Wilde might have done). In 1899, Colette's Gaston Lachaille dined at Larue with de Dion, Feydeau 'and one of the Barthou'.[1094] The Café Frontin was a Radical gathering place in the 1870s; the headquarters of the 1878 International Congress of Workers committee was the café of Charles Braun in the rue de la Bastille. Out of the meetings between Jules Guesde and the socialist students who gathered at the Café Soufflier in the Latin Quarter, there came the paper *L'Égalité*. The royalist organisation L'Œillet Blanc met in an inner room in the Chatham Bar. Nor is it out of the way that the Comité de l'Action Française was founded late in 1898 by a small group of nationalists that met regularly at the Café Flore in the boulevard Saint-Germain.[1095] Eustace Grenville-Murray's notion that 'the café is a middle-class and Bohemian institution, frequented mainly by tradespeople, Bourse men, professional subalterns, second-rate artists, and journalists' has something in it, even if his conclusion that 'a Frenchman who lives above these spheres [...] never visits it, save under compulsion' is more of an attempt to assume authority than to observe practice.[1096] Charles Brookfield, frequently in Paris in the years 1873-1875 and going much to the theatre, liked the Palais Royal, for its 'unrivalled company of comedians – Geffroy, L'Héritier, Gil Prez, Hyacinth, Brasseur, Lassouche [...] I used to watch these old men over their *mazagrans* at the Cent Milles Colonnes or one of the cheap restaurants in the place du Palais Royal'.[1097] Old-fashioned English visitors favoured the Café d'Orléans, 'where,' says

Ralph Nevill in a phrase that suggests a sexualisation of the transactions, 'a fair dinner could be procured'.[1098]

This dedication to social exchange in Paris may help to explain the failure of the telephone. On 18th May 1891 the link between London and Paris was inaugurated with an exchange of messages between the Prince of Wales and President Carnot, yet despite this illustrious advertisement, by 1900 there were but 30,000 telephones in the whole of France compared to the 20,000 telephones not merely in New York but in *four* hotels in New York – and this despite the invention of a telephone apparatus by the electrician Mildé.[1099] Conversation in France did not involve the disembodiment of the voice,[1100] but the café meeting did not exhaust the social intercourse for which the Parisians seemed to have a frenzy at this time.

> A few lines from someone dazed, who no longer reads, who no longer sleeps, nor eats, nor thinks, – but runs around, in cafés or in salons, shaking hands and smiling at people. Heredia, Régnier, Merrill, the æsthete Oscar Wilde [...].[1101]

Gide did not, however, say that he had no time to drink. It was not coffee or milk shakes that one consumed in the cafés or at the zinc counters of the dram shops. 'In no other French and few foreign cities did drink become the consummate art form throughout the class hierarchy that it did in Paris,' notes W.S. Haine. 'The history of drinking in Paris is as much about social aspirations as it about social degradation.'[1102] Obviously Zola's *L'Assommoir* provides all the colour one requires for the degradation, but Will Low recalled that five of his most talented contemporaries destroyed themselves through drink. In *L'Assommoir*, Zola charts the distinctions between the drinking of beer and the drinking of cognac; in the 1880s, absinthe moved from Bohemia into the working class[1103]. The consumption of spirits, especially absinthe, tripled between 1860 and 1890; even among the employés of the Prefecture of Police, drunkenness was a problem.[1104] In 1900, the consumption of absinthe was 130,000 hectolitres, that of all other alcoholic drinks combined being 82,000 hectolitres.[1105] This worked as an agent of transformation in more senses than one. On entering upon employment 'the new worker had to buy a round of drinks for his comrades and thereby won the right to be called "Mon vieux"',[1106] a companionable notion but also one that required from the *bleu* a change in his self-identification from being a new recruit to being 'the old one'. At the other extreme of conviviality, Robert Louis Stevenson recalled a Beaujolais Fleury so excellent at 2 fr. 50 that the patron raised the price to three francs, then to six, and then withdrew it from sale to drink himself. Drink was therefore both symbol and commodity, cultural expression and regulator of behaviour. Was it not said that whenever a detachment of soldiers passed the vineyard of Clos Vougeot, they presented arms? But to drink absinthe was not always to enter into a world of the convivial: Béraud's 'Les buveurs d'absinthe', Bertrand's 'La buveuse d'absinthe'[1107] and Raffaëlli's 'Le buveur d'absinthe'[1108] show people so solitary as to defy sodality.

~~~~~~~

In 1878 Zola lunched at the Café Anglais with one of its habituées of the previous decade, gathering material for *Nana*, and short scenes are set there in both *Nana*[1109] and *Pot-Bouille.*[1110] The Café Anglais, founded in 1822 at 13 boulevard des Italiens, corner of the rue Marivaux,[1111] which had reached its greatest prominence under the Second Empire, was, according to Baedeker, a 'restaurant of the highest class', although one would hardly suppose so from some of the stories of its twenty-two *cabinets particuliers,*[1112] (the comte de Muffat takes Nana to one as he does not wish to dine in public with her) and indeed it was said, not least by M. Burdel the lessee, that its history had never been written because it never could be written 'without telling tales anent great men which should not be put into print'.[1113] Marie Bashkirtseff who 'dined and breakfasted there' on the 10th January 1879, said it was 'the best restaurant'.[1114] The civil servant Lantin in Maupassant's story 'The Jewels' celebrates his fortune by dining there, and du Maurier's Taffy Wynne takes his wife there to 'a nice little room on the *entresol* overlooking the boulevard [for] a nice little supper; salmi of something very good, mayonnaise of lobster, and one or two things better still – and Chambertin of the best'.[1115] It was Adolphe Dugleré[1116] of the Grand Seize (chef for the private room reserved for royalty), former chef of James de Rothschild, whom Rossini dubbed 'the Mozart of French cooking'.[1117]

Cafés were, however, subject to alteration. Dorothy Menpes noted that

> The dainty white-and-gold café with its red velvet divans where one felt at home always – where the waiters were familiar, yet respectful – where the proprietor was treated more or less as a friend – where the pretty little woman had always a gracious smile of welcome for you – that type of café, once so general, is almost extinct now. One comes across it but rarely, and never on the boulevards.[1118]

This seems more to be a lament for the 'English tea-rooms' than for anywhere where her artist husband, the one-time friend of Whistler,[1119] might have visited. Be that as it may, the commodification of 'Montmartre' as a product for tourists had its transformative effect on the cafés there. By 1909, the Menpes' found that

> on the whole Montmartre is more or less a fallacy. Those cafés which are known as 'literary' and 'artistic' are mostly got up to amuse the tourist and the stranger, and are counted among the shows of Paris. One must not think when one visits these strange and extravagant places that one is seeing anything characteristic of Paris and Bohemia.[1120]

An iconography of these cafés must include, among lesser known works, Caillebotte's 'Au café',[1121] Renoir's 'Le Café' of 1876/7,[1122] Gervex' 'Scène de Café' of 1877,[1123] Seurat's 'Au Concert Européen' and 'Café-Concert' of 1887/8,[1124] William Metcalf's 'Au Café' of 1888,[1125] Vuillard's 'Au Café-Concert' (c.1898),[1126] Vallotton's 'Le Bistrot' of 1898,[1127] Béraud's 'La lettre' and 'Les buveurs d'absinthe', and the unknown painter of the Café de l'Écrivisse, avenue Trudaine.[1128] Lautrec's 'Aux Ambassadeurs: Gens Chics' of 1893'[1129] shows a fashionably-dressed Charles Conder with a woman at a small table, but 'M. Boileau au café'[1130] portrays a grosser figure. Van Gogh's restaurant interior of 1887 has been identified as 'Chez Bataille' and is unusual in showing an empty dining-room, while Raffaëlli's 'Bohèmes au café' is unusual in showing the patrons (one of whom may be Hennique) sitting outside.[1131] The lesser known Richard Miller painted the enigmatic 'Café de Nuit' (c.1906),[1132] which shows a woman seated outside at a table, another woman behind her. A woman also passes on the arm of a man, and there are two more women in the background. The social reading is that the women are courtesans, but they are shown in control of their situation, and the relationship between their crowded private space on the left and the open public space of empty tables on the right, suggests that we, like the painter, are observing, and perhaps observed, but not participating.

~~~~~~

When Robert Sherard brought Wilde, Mallarmé and Moréas together at the Café Riche, one wonders who paid. The Café Riche, on the corner of the boulevard des Italiens (number 16) and the rue Le Peletier, was expensive, and Sherard was not usually in any great financial surplus, while Moréas depended on subsidies from the armaments king Basil Zaharoff.[1133] Perhaps they used the room reserved for journalists and artists where the prices were less than half, but no such expedient was open to him when he invited Wilde to meet Coquelin *cadet* at the even more expensive Paillard's; as Coquelin 'was not greatly impressed'[1134] this was love's labour's lost for Sherard. If this was the Coquelin (and not his elder brother) whom the United States Minister Coolidge found 'conceited beyond measure',[1135] his failure to be impressed by Wilde is hardly surprising, but Wilde was interested in Coquelin *aîné*, and it is suggested wanted to involve him in *Salomé*.[1136] Paillard's, with its ceiling painted by Besnard, was also popular with a clientèle as diverse as Cléo de Mérode, Lina Cavalieri, Mary Garden, Réjane, Henri Meilhac, Arthur Meyer, the cartoonist Sem,[1137] ex-King Milan of Servia, and the English critic A.B. Walkley.[1138] The only other glimpse of Wilde in Paris in 1891 that Sherard offers is his mentioning having met Wilde when the latter was coming out of the Théâtre des Variétés:[1139] it should be possible to discover what was playing.

To dine was to live. These were what became known as the 'banquet years'. From the monthly dinners that the wealthy German-American amateur of painting Gustav Natorp arranged with Rodin, de Nittis, Sargent, Besnard and Frank Baden-Powell[1140] to the testimonial banquet for Puvis de Chavannes attended by six hundred men at the Hôtel Continental, these were as much the measure of the artistic standing of those who attended as they were of those in whose honour they were given (the 1882 'Macedoine' dinner, also at the Hôtel Continental, is a good example of this[1141]).

Official dinners also conferred recognition of social or other success. Those at the Ministry of Public Instruction would furnish interesting guest lists: at her first, Mary Waddington was the only lady present with fifty male guests, and sat between Gérôme and Renan. We have much of the guest list of the banquet held in honour of the Prince of Wales at the Hôtel du Louvre on 3rd May 1878. This was to acknowledge his work in connection with the Exposition Universelle and was hosted by the British exhibitors with the Foreign Secretary, Lord Granville, in the chair.[1142] Less exclusive was the dinner held by the Government on 18th August 1889 for the mayors of France: thirteen thousand, four hundred and fifty-six of them arrived. This was to help publicise the Exposition Universelle and a date was chosen with no political significance as an anniversary, for, as the caustic English writer Thomas March had observed, 'an inoffensive and intrinsically meaningless date [is] the most convenient label for Frenchmen to affix on their kaleidoscopic political events'.[1143] This was successful enough for the Government to repeat the event during the 1900 Expo, on the 20th November,[1144] when twenty thousand, seven hundred and seventy-seven mayors dined in a tent in the Jardins des Tuileries. This elided completely the notion of banqueting as generating private conviviality into an exercise in 'puffisme'.

A dinner at the Restaurant Trappe (rue Saint-Lazare/passage Tivoli, and also referred to as either Trapp or Trop[1145]) on 16th April 1877, was given for de Goncourt, Flaubert and Zola, 'the three masters of our day', by J.-K. Huysmans, Henri Céard, Léon Hennique, Paul Alexis, Octave Mirbeau and Guy de Maupassant.[1146] This is 'often regarded at the foundation of the Naturalist movement'.[1147] Raffaëlli arranged the 'diners de banlieu', with Huysmans, Rodin, Gustave Geffroy, Léon Daudet and Chéret: Rodin's bust of Geffroy dates to 1905.[1148] The centenary dinner of the Théâtre du Palais-Royal was held at Voisin's in 1884. Towards the end of the 1880s the Academician and Scandinavian scholar Xavier Marmier gave a dinner at Vefour's for a hundred bouquinistes.[1149] Goncourt presided over a dinner in Rodin's honour in February 1889. There were three dinners in 1893: for Mallarmé on the 9th February, for Victor Hugo (a memorial) on the 17th June, for Rodin, Mallarmé and Zola on 9th December. In March 1890 thirty-five guests honoured Edmond de Goncourt at Marguery's restaurant (going on for beer at the Café Riche), but five years later, on 1st March 1895, three hundred men attended the Goncourt banquet at the Grand Hôtel. Goncourt and Zola presided over a dinner in June 1896 at the Cubat, the restaurant Pierre Cubat had installed in the Hôtel La Païva, now the Travellers Club, to celebrate the award of the Légion d'Honneur to Charpentier's editor Fasquelle, 'a very likeable and decent chap'.[1150] The Restaurant Drouant[1151] was the scene of Friday banquets whose habitués included Goncourt, Rodin, Monet, Lautrec and Clemenceau; Jacques Saint-Cère (a journalist and political commentator whose real name was Armand-Maurice-Dieudonné Rosenthal) gave Sunday evening dinners in the rue Auber for Jules Lemaître, Marcel Prévost, Fernand Vandérem, Forain, Abel Hermant, Hervieu, Donnay, Capus and others.

One literary dinner, that given to celebrate the publication of L'Œuvre in 1886, had no convivial outcome, if George Moore's account is to be believed.

> A discussion arose as to whether Claude Lantier was or was not a man of talent. Madame Charpentier, by dint of much provocative asseveration, forced Émile Zola to take up the cudgels and defend his hero. Seeing that all were siding with Mme Charpentier, Zola [...] did not hesitate to confirm that he had gifted Claude Lantier with infinitely greater qualities

than nature had bestowed on Edouard Manet. This statement was received
with mute anger by those present, all of whom had been personal friends
and warm admirers of Manet's genius, and cared little to hear any word of
disparagement spoken of their dead friend.[1152]

The point that Zola was making was that no contemporary painter
produced work to rival that of Flaubert, Daudet or Goncourt, but this was
not emollient, especially as, to weaken the implied criticism of Manet,
Zola explicitly ruled out Degas.

The Puvis de Chavannes dinner was held on the 16th January 1895, on
which date Wilde and Lord Alfred Douglas were on their way to Algiers,
arriving on the 17th. Their route was viâ Paris and Marseilles, and they, or
at least Wilde, would have been able if invited to attend the dinner. Roger
Shattuck, in his study of Henri Rousseau, Alfred Jarry, Erik Satie and
Guillaume Apollinaire, refers to the banquet having 'become the supreme
rite',[1153] the epitome of the period, although his book hardly confirms this
view. Nevertheless, dining was clearly an integral part of social exchange,
although obviously dinners both private and semi-public had long been a
feature of Parisian life. The students at Carolus-Duran's atelier held an
annual dinner, for one example; very different was the dinner at the Grand
Hôtel for the nobility of Provence, organised by the prince de Valori, the
marquis de Gallifet, the marquis de Mirabeau, the duc de Gadagne, and the
marquis de Forbins.[1154] The Grand Hôtel was also the scene of the monthly
dinner of the Société d'Économie Politique.

There were also the annual dinners of the Bretons in Paris, the *diner
Celtique* and the monthly *dîners Dentu* at the restaurant Notta in the
boulevard Bonne-Nouvelle. Albert Lemerre held monthly dinners for his
published poets (Parnassians[1155]) at Brébant's, and the dinners of the Four
Seasons, a dining club of landscape painters, also took place there. The
Hippopotame was the dining club of the holders of the Prix de Rome: 'at
one time it was, from motives of economy, at a dirty little trattoria kept by
a gentleman whose particularly lumpish appearance procured him the
sobriquet of "the sea horse".'[1156] The 'Men with Spades' was another
dining club ('dîners de l'Homme à la Bêche'), but whether this implement
referred to their prowess at the trencher rather than the trench I have not
elucidated.

Zola himself presided over dinners at the Café Procope attended by Alexis,
Céard and Huysmans, the so-called 'diners du Bœuf natur'; Paul Bourget
and Cézanne sometimes came. All were admirers, disciples of Zola –

Alexis wrote a book about Zola as early as 1882. There was also a Pen and Pencil Club which met, there, with Walter Crane as honorary president after Whistler had declined the position. Chris Healy was secretary: 'The minutes were supposed to be a representation of what did not take place [...] I had no difficulty in attaining this high standard of veracity.'[1157]

The Procope, which proclaims itself the oldest café in the world, was founded by the Sicilian Procopio dei Coltelli in 1686, at 13 rue de l'Ancienne Comédie (formerly the rue des Fossés-Saint-Germain). It too partook of an atmosphere of metamorphosis. During the Revolution it was known as Zoppi, and a sign with this name is over its second entrance in the cour de Commerce St-André, which connects the boulevard St-Germain with the rue St-André-des-Arts. Here for many years Sainte-Beuve had gone every day to work in a room hired under the assumed name of Delorme in an hotel at the entrance of the cour de Commerce, under the arch that leads into the rue Saint-André-des-Arts. One must assume that he did not adopt the other Delorme name, Marion.

At the end of the nineteenth century the Procope was owned by a certain Théo Bellefonds, a violent anti-Dreyfusard, who put up the shutters one night apparently in a fit of pique, which is perhaps why J.F. MacDonald recorded sometime before 1914 that it was now no more.[1158] It re-opened as a restaurant for the students of the Beaux Arts and the Collège de Médecine. Dorothy Menpes must have visited it on a quiet night to come to her view that 'there is nothing frivolous about the Procope'.[1159] In 1904 Chris Healy thought that it had remained almost unchanged since its first opening up to 'quite recently',[1160] but its current eighteenth century décor dates to 1989.

The 'Réunions Café Procope' were arranged by Gustave Aimard, a writer of Westerns, for the former Hydropathes – Healy names Clement Privé, Jean Lubin and Emile Goudeau as attending. In 1893 the chansonniers Dumestre, Pierre Trimouillet and Xavier Privas founded the Soirées Procope, and these were attended by Verlaine, Moréas, Huysmans, Laurent Tailhade, Alfred Poussin and Anatole France – the nineteenth century habitués whom the Procope chooses to acknowledge to-day on a plaque are Victor Hugo, Gambetta, Verlaine and Anatole France. De Musset, in 'a life only distinguished by a catastrophic affair with George Sand',[1161] had played dominoes there, Cros wrote there, and Gambetta, Tailhade and Richepin were habitués. Verlaine was a familiar figure at the Procope, which replaced the François Premier in his affections, and here he would meet Monsieur Parfait, a law lecturer who would sit between Verlaine and the 'formidable, stupid and vicious'[1162] Bibi-la-Purée, a thing sufficiently eccentric even if Parfait had not also tried to live up to his name at the age of seventy-five by 'his enamelled complexion, monocle and corseted figure'.[1163] In 1895 it hosted a banquet (at two francs a head, organized by F.-A. Cazals and others) to protest against the bust of Murger in the Jardin du Luxembourg. This was in opposition to the official banquet (six francs, organized by Raymond Poincaré) at the Café Voltaire, but itself opposed by a third dinner at the Café de la Bohème (at seventy centimes). In 1897 there were rival dinners to commemorate Verlaine: war to the knife and fork.

One has a sense of how restricted was the Paris within which these proximities took place from the story of Henry James returning after nine months or so to breakfast at the Café Riche: 'The garçon remarked that Monsieur had been away a long time [and] led him to his favourite table.'[1164] The Riche, with its neighbour the Café Hardy, had given rise to the squib 'Il faut être bien riche pour diner au Café Hardy et bien hardi pour diner au Café Riche'.[1165] One may nominate the Café Riche, in the boulevard des Italiens, as the generic Paris locus of Henry James as described by Sheldon Novick, and the occasion as representing how cafés functioned for social exchange. The passage has a particular, if unintended, relevance to Oscar Wilde.

> He is sitting comfortably at a sidewalk table on a broad crowded boulevard. He has just come from the theatre, and there is his usual pink grenadine glacée, with two straws, on the white tablecloth beside him [...] He sits calmly watching the passers-by [...] A young man stops to talk, and then sits down with him. A couple in evening dress stop. Soon there is a circle of young people around him, and they remain until long after midnight, talking.[1166]

Wilde himself once wrote of his work 'I can't describe action. My people sit in chairs and chatter', and that this was 'rather like my own life — all conversation and no action.'[1167]

Literary and artistic dinners[1168] were held monthly at the Café Riche, Gustave Caillebotte being one of the prime movers, and it was used by Fauré, Georges Charpentier, Alphonse Daudet and Edmond de Goncourt; the club, the Cercle de Paris, was housed above it. To this, Robert Lethbridge adds sexual exchange, for the décor of the Café Riche's private room is described by Maupassant as 'draped in red', which Lethbridge regards as 'brothel-like'.[1169] Perhaps this is why Theodore Child in 1886 thought that the Riche had fallen from the first to the third category of restaurants.[1170] We still catch a glimpse of it in 1902, when Debussy wrote to Mary Garden 'from his table'.[1171] Certainly the dinner party of M. and Mme Forestier, madame de Marelle and Georges Duroy that Maupassant sites there is deliberately erotic, with its oysters 'dainty and plump' and trout 'with flesh as pink as a young girl's'. Not surprisingly 'the conversation turned to love'.[1172]

The boulevard des Italiens was also the location of the Café de la Bade (attached to Verdi's favourite hotel, also called La Bade[1173]) and Tortoni's, (according to Eustace Grenville-Murray the only really fashionable establishment[1174]) on the corner of the boulevard des Italiens and the rue Taitbout until it closed in 1894, after making a fortune for a succession of owners. 'The wont of the world of art and letters was to assemble at Tortoni's; everybody was there at five o'clock; and to Tortoni I went the day I arrived in Paris to make known the fact that I was back in Paris again.'[1175] The opening scene of Maupassant's story 'Un lâche' is set there. A characteristic of this restaurant was a private door for regular customers, literally a *limen* between private and public. The habitués were regular enough to be known as 'tortonistes'. Manet lunched there nearly every day (his 'Chez Tortoni' is now in the Isabella Stewart Gardner Museum in Boston) and exhibited both at the gallery opened by Louis Martinet at number 26 and, in April 1880, at the later gallery opened by the publisher Georges Charpentier next door to the offices of *La Vie Moderne* at number 7. De Nittis and Renoir also had one-man shows at this gallery, and exhibitions organised by Edmond Renoir were held in the offices of *La Vie Moderne* itself. After dark, things were different.

For over half a century, from Talleyrand and Musset to Théophile Gautier and Rossini, literature and the arts, diplomacy and finance, had gathered on these four or five hundred yards of pavement, where, towards six o'clock, dressed like queens, gleaming with jet and braid, their hair done in magnificent chignons beneath hugely feathered hats, the prostitutes of the Notre-Dame de Lorette quarter appeared with a rustling of silk and a penetrating scent of musk.[1176]

Along the pavements of the rue Notre-Dame de Lorette two files of women hurried towards the boulevards, their skirts hitched up and their heads bent, keeping close to the shops, but never once glancing at the window displays. This was the frantic descent from the Bréda district which took place nightly when the gas lamps had just been lit. Nana and Satin used to skirt the church and then go down the rue Le Peletier. When they were about a hundred yards from the Café Riche, and had almost reached their parade ground, they would drop the trains of their dresses and start walking with tiny steps and swaying hips,[1177] sweeping the pavements regardless of the dust, and slowing down even further when they crossed the bright patch of light in front of one of the big cafés. Strutting along, laughing loudly, and throwing backward glances at the men who turned to look at them, they were in their element. In the dusk their whitened faces, their rouged lips, and their darkened eyelids, took on the suggestive charm of an Oriental bazaar let out into the open street.[1178]

Filson Young caught the same note for his protagonists Grey and Lauder.

Paris welcomed them with a glow of evening sunshine and a full-blooded tide of life in her broad streets […] They dined at the Café de la Paix […] They loitered over their cigars, and sauntered in the Boulevards until eleven o'clock […] The two men sat outside a café and allowed the crowd to hypnotise them by its endless flowing. Solitary women by the dozen passed across their view; their stereotyped air of invitation – skirt held up with one hand, the other arm swinging, the hat tipped over the face, the head held rigidly straight, the oblique glance of the eyes, the sudden glittering smile, the admirable acceptance of a refusal or rebuff, – interesting though it is for a moment, became nauseating immediately.[1179]

The iconography supports the view that women who sat unescorted by men in cafés were either prostitutes or lesbians, or in some other sense, *déclassées*. One may cite Degas 'Au Café'[1180] and Picasso's 'The Absinthe Drinker'.[1181]

Commerce and conviviality, the social and the sexual, here were blent.

CHAPTER EIGHT

PERVADING PARIS

'Paris or else the desert for me!'
– Marie Bashkirtseff.[1182]

'Was it at all possible for instance to like Paris enough without liking it too
much?'
– Henry James.[1183]

'What people call insincerity is simply a method by which we can multiply
our personalities.'
– Oscar Wilde: 'The Critic as Artist'.

'WHEN Oscar Wilde made his astonishing appearance in Paris two years after Villiers' death, it was to Villiers [de l'Isle Adam] that his wit and eloquence were compared', says Richard Ellmann of Wilde's 1891 visit, but there was nothing really to astonish about it, unless one also takes 'astonishing appearance' in its other sense, as referring to Wilde's physical and sartorial presence.[1184] Certainly he was a more commanding figure than Villiers, and the comparison hardly does Wilde justice. It seems, indeed, to depend entirely on a remark by Henri de Régnier that 'M. Wilde used to tell his stories like Villiers de l'Isle Adam told them',[1185] which hardly praises Wilde, while Jean Joseph-Renaud, who admired Wilde, found in him 'the hoaxing cynicism of Baudelaire and Villiers de l'Isle Adam as it appeared through an English medium', and which failed to impress his audience.[1186] Gide too wrote that when Wilde talked he thought of Villiers and Baudelaire, but Baudelaire had died two years before Gide was born, and it is doubtful if Gide ever heard Villiers. George Moore thought that Villiers 'was often tiresomely talkative about trifles' and that 'part of his genius' lay in his resounding name. 'He chose it, and it has influenced his writings'.[1187] Villiers was also known for his biting wit, which was much dreaded: this was not the Wilde style. Who compared Wilde to Villiers? Gide records that the talk of the Paris tattlers was only that Wilde was the man who smoked gold-tipped cigarettes and walked the streets carrying a sunflower.[1188] In *If it die*, Gide went further:

'To tell the truth Wilde was not taken very seriously [...] People thought him slightly shocking, but rather a joke'.[1189] Gide may not have been completely truthful, but his testimony cannot simply be overlooked as Ellmann and others have overlooked it. Even Sherard noted that though Wilde 'had become a *personnage* [...] the French had little appreciation of his genius. They treated him rather as a fashionable man of the world', and Wilde himself came to recognise and regret this.[1190]

The 'pervading' of Paris is an important concept. Montgomery Hyde even antedated it to Wilde's 1883 visit: 'Wilde had no difficulty in securing an entrée to the literary and artistic society of Paris, which welcomed him with the respect due to a foreign poet.'[1191] Hyde lists those Wilde met in 1883, with a strong implication that he frequented their company: Hugo, Goncourt, Daudet, Bourget, Zola, Rollinat, Degas, Pissarro, de Nittis, Blanche. In 1891, Wilde was in Paris for March and Hyde adds the names of Pierre Louÿs, Retté, Schwob, Merrill, Mendès, Moréas and de Gourmont, a rather lesser group. Wilde himself was to refer to his 'high social position' in Paris.[1192] All this needs careful scrutiny. Maupassant wrote truly 'It is not enough merely to *be* in Paris; you have to become part of it, quickly to know its houses, its people, its ideas, its ways and intimate customs, its banter, its wit.'[1193] Thus expressed, it is the test by which we must judge Wilde's success; and the measure of Wilde's success in this respect is vital to any revisionist view of Wilde. From March to July 1891, Jules Huret published his *L'enquête sur 'l'évolution littéraire'* in *L'Écho de Paris,* essays on Anatole France, Barrès, Goncourt, Huysmans, Leconte de Lisle, Maeterlinck, Maupassant, Mirbeau, Verlaine, René Ghil, Gourmont, Charles Morice, Péladan, Saint-Pol Roux, Zola and Mallarmé, a useful 'control group' for looking at those regarded as the leading or coming men.

French social circles were not easy to penetrate, and the picture Richard Ellmann painted of Paris at Wilde's feet is not supported by examination of the sources that Ellmann used uncritically. Wilde might have been less eager to flatter his way into Parisian literary society by sending inscribed copies of his *Poems* to those whom he wished to meet had he known of Remy de Gourmont's dictum 'One sends one's books to people one profoundly despises'.[1194] Even the Natansons, 'especially the powerful Alexandre, were regarded as interlopers in the tightly structured, traditional French literary élite',[1195] yet Thadée Natanson was the driving force of *La Revue blanche*,[1196] and Alfred[1197] was a theatrical promoter.

Could Wilde really have been regarded in such company as an *homme sérieux*? Certainly Sherard, who was Alphonse Daudet's friend and biographer as well as Wilde's, says that Daudet 'who met him […] both at his own house and at soirées, notably in the house of the famous painter de Nittis, conceived a distrust of him which he was never able to shake off'[1198] on the grounds that Wilde was only a trifler. Sherard adds (and the point is interesting in the construction of French dandyism) that 'there were certain points about his dress which did not please the Parisians […] In those days gentlemen did not wear fur-coats in Paris'.[1199] One can counter this with Jacques de Langlade's view that Wilde 'inaugure la mode des manteaux de fourrure en couleur pour se rendre tous les soirs dans les meilleurs restaurants,'[1200] but there seems no evidence for this. Can the view of Wilde as a *blageur* also account for the lack of contact between Wilde and Maupassant? Wilde was in Paris when Maupassant's play *Musotte* had its successful run at the Théâtre du Gymnase (March 1891), but there is no reason to suppose that he saw it. Maupassant's love of word-play might have appealed to Wilde, had either been prepared to be second fiddle, though Wilde certainly was no admirer of Maupassant's work.

Sherard also suggests that the formal minds of the French intelligentsia were quick to spot that Wilde would try to pass off epigrammatically a lack of discipline in his thinking: 'I believe that this was the reason why in Paris he never enjoyed that admitted mastership which was his in England.'[1201] Sherard suggested that the quality of wit had been so honed in the salons that Wilde's failed to sparkle in the way that it did among the more prosaic English: this gives point to the idea that Wilde was able to succeed in London where he would have passed unregarded in Dublin. 'I have never met an Englishman yet who could distinguish himself in a Parisian salon',[1202] says Sherard, forgetting momentarily the origin of his friend. Indeed, even at a meeting of the Playgoers' Club in February 1892 where Wilde and John Gray were invited by J.T. Grein to explore the theme of 'The Modern Actor', Gray 'used the occasion to make a statement' but Wilde, in the chair, 'contented himself with making debating points'.[1203] André Gide, who combined sensual indulgence with intellectual rigour, was also suspicious of Wilde's contrived and over-polished conversational style;[1204] while his identification of style with subject, the radical position of English æstheticism, in France was already determined by Flaubert's and Maupassant's concern with Naturalism.[1205] Moreover, deep within Naturalism, Realism and Symbolism there lay the French concern with reason, the accessibility of ideas to the intellect; but Wilde, for all his classical training, by following Pater privileged sensation over reason. English pragmatism has always distrusted ideas and the men of the 1890s were no exception: 'intensely anti-intellectual' is Jerusha MacCormack's description of the Rhymers' Club.[1206] Even Kipling, who took English indifference to the arts as a moral imperative and elevated anti-intellectualism into a code of laws, wrote of the English that 'their starvation in their estimates is sometimes too marked'.[1207]

Madame Mohl, the widow of the Orientalist Julius Mohl (originally von Mohl), whose experience stretched back to the early years of the century, was in a good position to review the relative attitudes to conversation in England and France.

> We are scarcely aware now in England how seldom we practise that form of talk which alone can be called good conversation, in which what we really think is brought out, and which flows the quicker from the pleasure of seeing it execute thought in others [...] Conversation is the mingling of mind with mind, and is the most complete exercise of the social faculty.[1208]

There are further indications that Wilde's conversation did not travel well, in complete contrast to the many accounts of Wilde in England not only holding a table enthralled but also encouraging the talk of others.[1209] Here we touch on the difference between the tongue-tied English, the eloquent Irish, and the disputatious French. At the meal at the Café Harcourt with Pierre Louÿs, André Gide and possibly Stuart Merrill, Wilde was the only one who talked.[1210] Gide's description of this is slightly ambivalent, for although he says that they were all content to listen, it is clear that Wilde did not give them much choice. He 'did not converse – he told tales. During the whole meal he hardly stopped.'[1211] The tales, told 'in a slow musical tone, and his very voice was wonderful', may have been captivating, and it is fortunate that Gide wrote down some of them, but as table talk, as the flashing exchange of intellect and wit, it falls short. Gide's further point is not quite as regularly quoted: 'When [Wilde] was no longer the only one to shine, he would shut himself up'.[1212] One can also offer a translation slightly less favourable to Wilde than Stuart Mason's: Gide's 'Wilde ne causait pas: il contait [...] il n'arêta pas de conter [...] Les contes qu'il nous dit interminablement ce soir-là étaient confus et pas de ses meilleurs'[1213] can be rendered 'Wilde did not converse but soliloquised, endlessly telling in a confused manner stories that were not among his best.'

Jules Renard was clearly not charmed by Wilde.

> Oscar Wilde next to me at lunch. He has the oddity of being an
> Englishman. He gives you a cigarette but selects it himself. He does not
> walk round a table, he moves a table out of the way. His face is kneaded
> with tiny red worms, and he has long teeth, containing caves. He is
> enormous and carried an enormous cane.[1214]

'He does not walk round a table, he moves a table out of the way'. This
extraordinary sentence, which biographers have quoted unthinkingly, is
clearly a mistranslation of 'il ne fait pas le tour de la table; il dérange la
table'. This should be read as indicating that Wilde did not encourage
general conversation round the table, but interrupted the flow of
conversation.

One must contrast all this with the dinner party given by Brunetière, where
Edouard Rod, Paul Bourget and Robert Underwood Johnson were among
the guests:

> Here was conversation *par excellence*, the host directing the course of it
> unobtrusively and all the guests instinctively contributing from to time in
> the progress towards definite conclusions [...] Intellectual discourse at its
> best, a combination of wit, grace and deference of manner.[1215]

Both Max Beerbohm and E.F. Benson recorded that Wilde's conversation
tended to the monologue, albeit monologue welcome to his hearers.[1216]
Robert Ross said that on visiting Wilde in prison 'when we asked him to
talk more, he said he had nothing to say and wanted to hear us talk. This
as you know is very unlike Oscar.'[1217] Yeats referred to this as Wilde's
'dominating self-possession' and quotes him as saying 'Who can dominate
a London dinner table can dominate the world', but this was an
imperialism (or 'monarchism', as Yeats calls it, the monarch presumably
being Wilde himself)[1218] that would have not charmed the French. 'Oscar
Wilde, who appeared to me the most wonderful talker the world had ever
seen, achieved in this respect no notable success in Paris'.[1219] Flaubert
once derided Zola for excessive egoism – 'Such bad taste to be always
talking about one's self'[1220] – and this indicates that something more
flexible than the Wilde style was expected. E.F. Benson never makes it
quite clear that he knew Wilde – he certainly knew Douglas – but he says
that Wilde 'monopolised conversation. That monopoly was gladly
accorded him. But he talked too much to be called a wit in the
conversational sense: he resembled floodlighting.'[1221] This perhaps was
too brilliant to illumine. It is certainly true that when Wilde attended on
Victor Hugo, the great man remained peacefully asleep – although to visit
Hugo suggested a certain self-confidence, if we are to judge by the

behaviour of Henri Gervex, who, taken to Hugo's by Albert Mérat, got cold feet and ran away.

A further idea of what constituted good conversation in the English view can be found in the reaction to George Curzon as a talker. Curzon, Wilde's Oxford contemporary, 'remained a brilliant talker, various guests recalled, dominating the party yet knowing how to draw out the best from his companions. In good company he was a surprisingly willing listener. He did not deliver monologues, said Lord Spencer, because he was "interested in the other fellow as well as himself".'[1222] This was not the way of Oscar Wilde, neither in London nor in Paris.

We can come to a view of the nature of French intellectual conversation at this time. 'Frenchmen rarely wish to listen,' wrote (with uncharacteristic feeling) Lord Newton, who served for a time at the British Embassy. 'They desire to talk themselves, and be listened to; to them, as a rule, a foreigner is a foreigner and nothing more, and whether he speaks French well or ill, they seldom notice and rarely care.'[1223] At the dinners at the Café Riche, Caillebotte's 'intelligence and powers of debate were apparently so formidable that his tablemate Renoir felt compelled to purchase an encyclopædia as an aid in getting the upper hand in discussions'.[1224] In any case, Renoir was not a man for sophisticated conversation, or high-falutin' ideas, once declaring 'When I paint, I never believe that I am saving the Republic'.[1225]

Turgenev once remarked upon 'the exclusiveness of the French upper class literary men, such as Flaubert and Daudet, who declined to know lesser authors such as Arsène Houssaye and Alexandre Dumas'.[1226] This has its implication for siting Oscar Wilde, who had some awareness of the Russian, reviewing his 'A Fire at Sea' in *Macmillan's Magazine* in May 1886.[1227] It may be noted that Houssaye was the spelling adopted by Arsène Housset, 'laying claim to an aristocratic lineage that he did not have'.[1228] Although by itself this did not much help Houssaye, 'la belle Arsène', as the actress Rachel called him, 'went from banquet to bal masqué, from salon to soirée, for fifty years or more'.[1229]

Sir Maurice Bowra, viewing Symbolism as 'a mystical form of Æstheticism', noted that 'English Æstheticism was less exacting, less theoretical, less mystical than French [...] their theories not so transcendental, so exacting, so complete' as those of Mallarmé, through whose 'desperate logic' it came to its full realisation.[1230] This may explain why Wilde saw so little of Mallarmé, and did not seek out French academic circles, for all his first class degree in Greats. It was, after all, possible to meet the French intelligentsia if one came sufficiently well recommended, despite the opinion of Delcassé, Foreign Minister at the end of the century, that 'You will never get a Frenchman to understand an Englishman, or an Englishman to understand a Frenchman'.[1231] The Scottish economist Thomas Barclay, after education at the University of Jena and the Collège Jean-Bart at Dunkirk, was offered a job in *The Times* Paris office in May 1876. 'Paris was my Mecca,' he remembered. 'The French intellect, I had been taught, was the motive-power which was driving the machinery of the human mind throughout the world'.[1232]

~~~~~~

Ellmann records Wilde's meetings with Stuart Merrill (who translated Wilde's *The Nightingale and the Rose* into French[1233]), Marcel Schwob and Léon Daudet, and a meeting with Gide at the house of José Maria de Heredia which led to a dinner at the Café d'Harcourt with Wilde, Gide, Louÿs and 'probably' Stuart Merrill,[1234] but it is an exaggeration of Ellmann's that 'Wilde pervaded Paris'.[1235] This is largely because he accepted his sources at face value, such as the statement by J. Joseph-Renaud that 'Paul Bourget, Maurice Barrès, Alphonse Daudet, Stuart Merrill, Paul Verlaine, Alexandre Parodi, Jean Moréas etc. fêtaient M. Oscar Wilde par leurs articles ou leur acceuil. Chaque matin les gazettes célébraient son talent, son élégance, ses 'Mots' ...'[1236] This relates to late 1891 and is clearly over-written: one has only to cross reference with the articles collected by E.H. Mikhail. As for Parodi, Wilde found him tedious – indeed, for someone as conscious as Wilde of the sound of words, for him to say 'I have been praised by Parodi' would have rung rather hollow — but, after all, Parodi was sufficiently punished by having to listen to Wilde recite passages from Carlyle's *French Revolution*.

Wilde does not appear to have visited Paris between his honeymoon in 1884 and his short visit in February/March 1891, the visit which Jonathan Fryer identifies as signalling that he 'was determined to conquer Paris as well as London', although Jacques de Langlade places Wilde at the Hôtel l'Athénée, rue Scribe in August 1890.[1237] It is certainly true that Paris pervaded Wilde. It seems perfectly possible that it was here that he learned of Etienne Arnal's remarks to the audience at the first night of one his plays back in 1834: 'My word, gentlemen, I never thought that you had so much good taste'.

Langlade, a more serious writer than Philippe Jullian, was working in parallel with Ellmann, but his work does not suggest that he was aware of Ellmann's great endeavour, and his bibliography does not list any of Ellmann's earlier work on Wilde. Even more than Ellmann, Langlade insists upon Wilde's Parisian success, stressing his impact on the *mouvements* that made the fin-de-siècle, and upon and their adherents:

> Il est une célébrité du Tout-Paris [...] Depuis quelques années, Wilde est à Paris le grand prêtre d'un période décadente où règnent le factice, l'art élaboré, l'éxcessif, le macabre; on admire l'étrange sauvagerie de la musique de Wagner, le climat étouffant des pièces d'Ibsen, alors que les muses sont bien vivantes, affublées des oripeaux à la mode ou déshabillées par Worth, Paul Poiret ou Jacques Doucet, que l'on nommais les 'petits Botticelli': haschich et éther, redingote à col de velours, gilets de couleur complètent le paysage où le lys et les paons sont de rigueur. Au milieu de ce décor, l'auteur de Salomé promène sa lourde silhouette, son regard amusé et ses mœurs scandaleuses.[1238]

This is very clearly a synoptic view and must not be taken as a researched conclusion (there was no Paris conjunction between Wilde, Ibsen and Wagner, for example): it is also very much the pre-Ellmann view of Wilde, concentrating on the genius put into the life, rather than the talent put into the art, a phrase which Langlade quotes several times. Unfortunately, in a work of over three hundred pages Langlade draws on remarkably few sources. Chief among these are the Hart-Davis *Letters*, irritatingly cited as R.H. Davies — he is cavalier with names, Anne Clark Amor, Constance Wilde's biographer, being referred to as Mary Clark Amor, for example while Kenneth Rose appears as R. Kenneth, H. Montgomery Hyde is merely M. Hyde, Violet Wyndham is confused with Horace Wyndham and so forth. Robert Merle, in his introduction, wrote that Langlade had written just such a biography as he liked: bustling with characters and stuffed with facts. It seems churlish to point out that many of these characters did not exist (an actress called Patrick Campbell being notable (p.111)); and that many of the facts are wrong, but there it is. The odd error may be overlooked, or ascribed to the printer, but a work as slipshod as this suggests that Langlade was not up to his subject, suggests no very convincing deployment of either knowledge of time and place or the demands of scholarly disciplines,[1239] even though they can afford a good deal of amusement. A good example is when Langlade in a would-be learned footnote (p.139) informs the reader that, when Whistler advised Wilde to return his extravagant clothes 'borrowed from Kossuth and Mr Mantolini' to Nathan, a well-known theatrical costumier from that day to this, he was referring to Nathaniel Rothschild! And 'Mantolini', twice spelled thus, is an error for Mantalini. This is venial enough, but what is one to make of the confusion between Arthur Symons and John Addington Symonds (p.161), whom Langlade thought were the same person? This is not forgivable from a professor of comparative literature at the University of Paris, with some claim to be a Wilde scholar (his edition of Wilde's *Œuvres Complètes* was published by Stock in 1977, who also published his edition of *The Ballad of Reading Gaol*, and other editions followed, published by Les Belles Lettres or Complexe). Nor was Langlade's carelessness confined to the names of English writers: his reference to Charles Brookfield's rôle as Mason rather than Phipps in *An Ideal Husband* is also typical (p.212). To list these faults goes beyond literary one-upmanship, therefore, and other specialists may add to the total.

For all that, even Langlade records that Wilde's work was 'à peu près ignorée en France' except among those of the circles of Mallarmé and Moréas, and that his reputation in the 1890s in Paris was made in the little magazines that dabbled in decadence. These, says Langlade, give a true panorama of the 'image wildienne', and it is a pity that he hardly follows this up, being content to quote an article from the *Écho de Paris* by Gaston Routier,[1240] who gives a rather fanciful account of a meeting with Wilde at Stratford-upon-Avon, and another by Stuart Merrill in *La Plume*.[1241] Otherwise, he prefers Mikhail's anthology to reference of its original source material.

Mythopœia, however, is another form of transformation, transformation a process within mythopœia. When, during that late 1891 visit, Stuart Merrill and Henri de Régnier introduced Wilde to Jacques Daurelle in a Left Bank café, Merrill assured Daurelle that at Oxford Wilde 'used to dress in short breeches, with a velvet doublet and lace sleeves'. This was one of 'a group of charming anecdotes about Wilde' that Merrill was collecting 'which can't help make him more interesting to us'.[1242] Wilde seems to have made no comment on this. Gide, too, within ten years was ready to cry up Wilde, writing that at the time of this first meeting in 1891, that his books astonished and enchanted, that his plays were going to make the running in London ('allaient faire courir Londres'), that he was rich, loaded with fortune and honours.[1243] It is certainly true that Wilde and Gide met frequently in November and December that year, in rather mixed company: at one time or another with Henri de Régnier, Marcel Schwob, Aristide Bruant, and Princess Ouroussoff; and it is certainly true that 1891 had been a remarkable year for publishing: *The Soul of Man under Socialism, The Picture of Dorian Gray, Intentions, Lord Arthur Savile's Crime and Other Stories,* and *A House of Pomegranates.* But much as these may have been *succès d'estime ou de scandale*, they brought neither wealth nor honours, and the one play of Wilde's that was staged that year was *The Duchess of Padua*, produced in New York as *Guido Ferranti*. *A House of Pomegranates* was not a success at all, and as late as 1903 or 1904, bookshops were still disposing of remaindered copies. The first, tiny, French edition did not appear until 1902.[1244] Gide here misattributes the causes of Wilde's Paris success.

Nor was meeting Léon Daudet any great sign of social and literary acclaim, for Daudet was at this time a twenty-three year old medical student, and hardly up to Wilde's weight in any sense except dandyism, although Wilde might have been favourably impressed by his youthful appearance. In any case, the note of sympathy was lacking, as Daudet later recorded.[1245] The dandyism and the youthful appearance struck Paul Henry even seven years later when Daudet was taking art lessons: although, to be sure, Henry is probably confusing him with his brother Lucien, who studied at the Académie Julian and was gay.

> One morning in the studio I found myself standing beside a very elegant young man, very good-looking in an effeminate way [...] This boy was dressed in the height of fashion and his carefully creased trousers were very noticeable in such company. He never sat down while working, because it would spoil the effect of the crease.[1246]

It was however, Alphonse Daudet, and neither Léon nor Lucien, who was the man to meet at this time. The Irish painter Henry Jones Thaddeus, who met him in April 1882 (as he also met Goncourt), recalled that 'to the many young authors who sought his advice he assumed the form of a demi-god'[1247]: but then, Wilde had come to Paris to conquer, not to be conquered.

Stuart Merrill, the American poet who had been brought up in Paris, was for a time the manager at the Théâtre de L'Œuvre,[1248] and Wilde consulted him over the French of *Salomé*. Will Rothenstein thought him 'a charming fellow, intelligent, but, I fancy, rather idle and easy-going [...] He was not very productive'.[1249] Robert Sherard praised him in just the terms that makes his praise of Wilde so suspect, those of a man devoid of judgment: 'One of the most charming poets [...] a young American of some fortune who has lived many years in France, and who has published a volume of poems which are considered masterpieces in the world of letters'.[1250]

Merrill was at least a point of entry for many who wished to know the Paris literary world (although George Moore thought 'it is impossible to talk of Stuart Merrill for more than half an hour'[1251]), introducing Edgar Saltus[1252] to Verlaine and Leconte de Lisle, for example; he was also a close friend of Rudmose-Brown, the Professor of French at Wilde's old college, Trinity. It was at Merrill's house that Henri Mazel[1253] met Wilde, but although Mazel wrote 'I can recall him clearly', clearly he could not – for one of his recollections was of Wilde wearing a monocle. Moreover he dates this to 1892, when evidence for Wilde's being in Paris is sketchy. Apart from his weekend in November with the bookmaker's runner Fred Atkins, whom he would hardly have been showing to his literary acquaintance, there is only the record by Jules Renard of having sat next to him a restaurant in April.[1254] Although it is possible that Mazel encountered Wilde in April 1893, when the latter was in Paris on a 'quick trip'[1255] with Sidney Mavor, as he also claimed to have seen Wilde on the terrace of the Café de la Paix in 1901,[1256] Thomas Hardy's principle in Chapter XXIX of *Far From the Madding Crowd* of the clock that strikes thirteen may be cited.

Merrill, who held Friday evening 'at homes' in the rue de Seine, published in French, and his only English work was a volume of translations from Banville, Huysmans, Baudelaire, Mallarmé and others, with the very nineties-ish title *Pastels in Prose* (1890), with an introduction by W.D. Howells. Saltus wrote two of his books, *Mary Magdalene* and *Imperial Purple* in Paris (for which he retained 'a painful nostalgia'[1257]), and became a close friend of Wilde's (Merrill dropped Wilde later). Saltus' memoir of Wilde, *Oscar Wilde: An Idler's Impressions*,[1258] was thought by Van Wyck Brooks to be one of the best of his works.[1259] Saltus' half-brother, Francis Saltus of New York, was a protégé of Théophile Gautier and is described by James Huneker's biographer as a 'dissipated Bohemian poet [who] spoke thirteen and wrote twenty languages, played the piano, was an expert on Donizetti and coined more witty epigrams than any man Huneker ever heard except Oscar Wilde'.[1260] (Huneker himself was 'a virtuoso of language', capable of 'astonishing conversational pyrotechnics',[1261] which is why it fails to surprise that he edited a volume of Bernard Shaw's dramatic criticism.)

Wilde was keen to be read in France, of course, authorising a translation by Jean Cantel of his critical essays, but this did not appear until 1914, when it was published by L'Édition Moderne in Paris under the title *Opinions de Littérature et de l'Art*. It must always be remembered that contemporary translations of Wilde into French were few, dating from

'The Birthday of the Infanta', which had appeared translated by Stuart Merrill as *L'anniversaire de naissance de la petite princesse* in *Paris Illustré* on 20th March 1889. In late December 1891 Marcel Schwob published his version of 'The Selfish Giant' in *L'Écho de Paris*; but Wilde's hopes at this time for a French translation by Paul Delair of *Lady Windermere's Fan* were in vain, and the play was first staged at the Théâtre des Arts in a translation by Albert Savine only in 1909. *Salomé* was published on 22nd February 1893 (Librairie de l'Art Indépendant). In February 1892 Sherard had written that 'a run is expected on the translation of *The Picture of Dorian Gray* which is being undertaken by a leading man of letters of this city',[1262] but it was not until October 1895 that Savine published *Le Portrait de Dorian Gray*, by which time Wilde was in gaol. The translators were Eugène Tardieu and Georges Maurevert, but one is not pleased by the information that Savine was also the founder of the publishing house La Bibliothèque Antisémitique.[1263] *Dorian Gray's* reception in France was muted enough at the time: it has taken a much later commentator to note how Dorian Gray fits into the convention of 'l'homme vaincu par le temps' formed in France by Balzac's comte de Saint-Forbin, Maxime de la Traille, and Lucien de Rubempré.[1264] The publication of *La Ballade de la Geôle de Reading*, in May 1898 in the *Mercure de France*, followed by its publication in book form the following November, unfortunately made little or no difference to Wilde's collapsed state. Jean Lorrain used his review more as an attack on the English for their aggression in the Transvaal and for their hypocrisy in sentencing Wilde for a practice prevalent among them, than as indicating that Wilde himself might regain an honoured place in French circles.

The fact is that Wilde not only did not further his reputation through French translations, but contrived, in different ways and for different reasons, to dissolve the friendships that he made: Schwob, Richepin, Lorrain, Merrill, Louÿs – none of these were *bons bourgeois* to recoil at Wilde, yet all fell away from him. Perhaps it was no more than a preference for careers of their own (to adopt Joseph Chamberlain's alleged reason for not marrying Beatrice Potter). Ironically, the early association has prevailed over the later alienation, giving Wilde a *posthumous* place as a French man of letters by accord of the critics. Jean-Paul Goujon, for example, is happy to include Wilde with Verlaine, Mallarmé, Leconte de Lisle and Heredia when listing Pierre Louÿs' literary circle, yet the translations of Wilde by Jean Joseph-Renaud and Hugues Rebell[1265] only came in 1905 and, posthumously, in 1906. These were, respectively, *Intentions* and *Pen, Pencil and Poison* as 'La Plume, le crayon, le poison'. The latter was published by Charles Carrington (whose real name was

Paul Ferdinando), a Londoner who was a sort of Paris equivalent of Leonard Smithers, selling erotica from a shop in the rue due Faubourg Montmartre and rue de Châteaudun); Rebell (whose real name was Georges Grassal de Choffat) was a minor poet, pornographer and historical novelist, and a partisan of Wilde's. The later reputation of Wilde in Europe cannot be gainsaid, far outshining his reputation in Britain or Ireland, but that does not licence an acceptance of the idea that his reputation dates to Wilde's own Paris period; nor can one really follow some of the more overblown claims even about the posthumous standing of Wilde, such as Douglas's in 1928.

> That Wilde was a Heresiarch and a most powerful and convincing one, does not alter the fact that he was a man of enormous genius, and that his influence on the whole of literary Europe has been more profound than that of any other English writer except Shakespeare [...] I am alluding to the place which he actually occupies in European literature.[1266]

One of the chief witnesses to Wilde's social success in Paris was Will Rothenstein: 'Oscar Wilde was one of the lions of the season in Paris; he was invited everywhere. The newspapers were full of his doings and sayings; Madame Adam took him up, and asked numbers of people to meet him'.[1267] Rothenstein is usually fairly reliable, but he is not sufficiently supported by the sources to allow one to take this at face value. Even Sherard came to think that Wilde's social successes in Paris 'were less than at the time I imagined',[1268] Constant repetition of Wilde's success has added a spurious validity to the argument. In his 1982 study of Wilde, for example, Robert Keith Miller wrote of 1883 'He quickly established himself in French literary circles, numbering among his acquaintances Victor Hugo, Émile Zola, Paul Verlaine, and André Gide. Among artists he was friendly with Edgar Degas, Camille Pissarro and Henri de Toulouse-Lautrec.'[1269] Ellmann places an idea in Wilde's mind and then takes it for reality: 'Wilde knew that his effect on the French had been extraordinary and unprecedented'; Langlade at the same time was writing that 'le Tout-Paris' was talking of Wilde.[1270] Jerusha McCormack goes even further in referring to Wilde's 'triumphal progress through the Parisian *salons* in November and December 1891'.[1271] In Simon Callow's little study of Wilde this has become 'To say that before his fall Oscar Wilde knew [...] everyone of importance in literary and social circles in both London and Paris is simply to state the truth'.[1272] This is to elide, and greatly magnify, Wilde's 1883 and 1891 socialising. Mark Hichens is alone in supposing that even before 1891 Wilde had formed a close friendship with Anatole France; nor will I be substantiating Mireille

Dottin-Orsini's view that in Paris Wilde was 'adulé et fêté'.[1273] Even Lord
Alfred Douglas's cautious judgment, that in 1883 Wilde 'had a minor
success among French men of letters, including Edmond de Goncourt and
Victor Hugo',[1274] while preferable to Callow, goes further than the
evidence.

During Wilde's Paris visits in 1891 (February and March, then October to
December), Sherard saw Wilde 'frequently' and noted that the Irishman
had 'now begun to be counted among European celebrities. In December
he was much fêted in the best houses, and leading littérateurs and artists
crowded to his hotel.'[1275] Again, one must ask, Who? When? Why?
Sherard claims the credit for himself (and gives none to Marcel Schwob):
'I was able to do something towards imposing him on the attention of
Paris [...] I contributed a long article about him to Le Gaulois [...] It was
printed on the first page and made him the topic of the day in Paris.'[1276]
This is less than impressive: a passage full of weasel words, of which
'impose' is the most curious, and 'topic of t he day' most revealing. Was
Sherard ashamed of this ludicrous piece, only published after the editor
had asked him if Wilde was a man of any real importance? A year later he
refers to its having been written, not by himself but only by 'an English
friend' of Wilde's.[1277] It is also necessary to remember that Sherard
submitted the text of the article to Wilde beforehand,[1278] and it may have
been Wilde rather than Sherard who inserted the references to Lady
Wilde's salon as 'one of the most famous in London' and to himself as
having 'directed the æsthetic movement' from Magdalen. More to the
point, the article appeared on 17th December 1891, on the very day Wilde
returned to England,[1279] so it played no part in popularising Wilde in Paris
(one also notes that the publication of 'The Selfish Giant' in L'Écho de
Paris, translated by Schwob, did not appear until the 27th). Doubtless
Wilde was gratified that the piece appeared in Le Gaulois, this being a
Royalist and conservative paper, edited by the 'socially ambitious, clever
and opportunist journalist'[1280] Arthur Meyer with leading articles by Jules
Simon – something which itself gives us a view of Wilde's 'radicalism';
and it was to Maurice Sisley of Le Gaulois that Wilde asserted that he
would transfer himself to Paris after the banning of Salomé in London.
'There is but Paris, d'you see, and Paris is France': revealing an ignorance
not only of Paris the multiform but of the French maxim that insists that
Paris is not France.[1281]

Why did Wilde want this puffisme by Sherard? Was this a friendly gesture
towards the admiring Sherard, allowing him to bask in the reflected glory
to the burnishing of which he was contributing? Sherard did in fact have

his abrupt side – it is startling to read in his 'Notes from Paris' of 23rd February 1892 'I am afraid from what I have heard from the very best sources that, as a writer at least, we may speak of de Maupassant in the past' or in those of 1st March 1893 that 'Taine is not expected to live much longer'[1282] — but Wilde he always overpraised.

There had already been pieces on Wilde in *Le Figaro* and *L'Écho de Paris*, fulsome enough to have pleased his mother[1283]: had he inspired these as well? Another article appeared in *Le Figaro* on the 2nd December which gave a very Parisian view of things the other side of the Channel, stating that it was in order to obey Wilde's orders that the London boutiques had opened to sell 'æsthetic' stuffs.[1284] The *Echo* article, an interview by Daurelle, appeared on the 6th, and contained many of Wilde's phrases and philosophies — that nature imitates art, that the London fogs were invented by Turner — grown stale with repetition. To be sure, if one believes Maupassant, the publication of an interview was no proof that the interview had taken place. His journalist Saint-Potin ("'Is Saint-Potin your real name?" "No, my name's Thomas'") simply recycles old interviews and charges a mythical cab-fare up to his paper.[1285]

The *Écho* returned to Wilde on the 19th December, but calling him 'une des plus grandes personnalités de la literature anglaise contemporaine' at that date, would hardly be supported to-day even by his idolaters. Wilde might have been less pleased with all this had he known that only a few years before, the official English view was that 'the *Gaulois* is hardly looked upon as a serious paper here',[1286] and while *Le Figaro* is described by Shirley Fox as 'really the only great morning paper in France' and commendation by it was worth having (although its editor, François Magnard, was mixed up in Bonapartist plotting while admiring the Bourbon pretender Don Carlos[1287]), *L'Écho* was only a gossip sheet. Wilde was indeed now famous for being famous, but one need not take this superficial and ephemeral status for other than what it was.

Sherard also relies heavily on an eulogy of Wilde published by de Régnier in *Figures et Caractères*, in which Wilde is referred to as 'an English poet and wit', who visited Paris every year in the spring and sometimes in the winter as well. This is unsustainable, and suggests that when de Régnier goes on to say that Wilde 'passed from a luncheon with M. Barrès to a dinner with M. Moréas', we need only take it that '*a* luncheon and '*a* dinner' may have been accurate.[1288] De Régnier may have had a confused or combined, memory of the dinner for Moréas on 31st January 1891, over which Mallarmé presided, when Barrès took as a guest, not Wilde but

Gide, and the lunch given by Moréas at the Côte d'Or in December 1891, where the guests included Merrill, Lorrain, Schwob, Retté, and (surprisingly) Maurras, and at which Wilde was a disgruntled guest who left early.[1289] De Régnier also includes reference to a dinner party of 'the highest Parisian society' at which Wilde outshone the crystal glasses and 'the gold-tipped cigarette went out and lighted itself [sic] incessantly in the lips of the story teller'. Over dinner! I think not.

Michael de Cossart also suggests an extravagant rôle for Wilde in Paris.

> Wilde had been a frequent visitor to Paris in years past and Paris had loved him [...] Sarah Bernhardt and the duchesse de Richelieu [the subsequent Princess Alice of Monaco] took him to their hearts. Lady de Grey and the tenaciously Pre-Raphaelite baronne Deslandes fawned over him. Jacques-Émile Blanche and Marcel Schwob imitated his dress and manners. When he appeared in Paris in the spring of 1894 with the beautiful Lord Alfred Douglas, he had caused a sensation [...] Winnaretta [de Polignac] associated with him in public and entertained him and Lord Alfred in her house.[1290]

There are a number of difficulties about this, exacerbated by de Cossart's not sourcing his material. While Wilde certainly knew Alice of Monaco (he had tea with her on the 4th November 1891, and de Régnier met him at dinner there in 1893), she was Constance's friend[1291] rather than his.[1292] Wilde was in Paris at the end of May / beginning of June 1894, and was joined there by Bosie, who had been in Egypt. The description of this by William Freeman ('He lingered a week there alone with Wilde'[1293]) hardly gives one confidence in de Cossart's version. Rupert Croft-Cooke is even more elliptical, using only Wilde's account in *De Profundis*.[1294] This account contains much demonstrable fiction, but, that aside, makes no suggestion that the visit was in any sense a social triumph. The baronne Deslandes said that she saw Wilde six times and would avoid a seventh.[1295] I do not know why Lady de Grey is included in this list of Wilde's *Parisian* admirers though Nellie Melba first met Wilde at her house (it is very difficult to think of this aristocrat 'fawning' over anybody[1296]), and I doubt whether Schwob would still have been imitating Wilde by 1894, as he had been extricating himself from Wilde's acquaintance for some time, as Pierre Louÿs had done.[1297] It is largely agreed that the friendship had been weakened by Louÿs' cavalier response to Wilde's dedication to him of *Salomé* and that he was alienated by Wilde's neglect of Constance, culminating in an argument on 25th May 1893. This is precisely dated by H.P. Clive, and took place when Louÿs visited Wilde in London. Jonathan Fryer, while following this in general, says that the quarrel took place in

Paris that May, though there seems no other evidence that supports the suggestion that Wilde was in that city. Louÿs never saw Wilde again.[1298] After dedicating his story *Pays bleu* to the Irishman, Schwob had 'quickly became disillusioned with Wilde'[1299] and it was also from this period that Wilde and Sherard gradually became alienated. Sherard is not specific about the reasons for this, but he had married a woman called Marthe Lipska in 1887 and this may have had something to do with it – he hints as much. The following year Marie Belloc moved in with them as a paying guest, and remembered that 'Bob' and 'his beautiful young wife were most kind to me'.[1300] Unfortunately the usually prolix Belloc says nothing more and none of this appears in Sherard's autobiographical writing, although in 1926 Sherard wrote that in 1895 'I was writhing under the whip of fate at the downfall and destruction of a greatly loved friend'.[1301]

There is no reason to doubt that the princesse de Polignac entertained Wilde, although there is no other account of this known to me, and given the fact that Wilde dearly loved a title, it is surprising that we do not find him augmenting the acquaintance; but the assumption that she did so also gives us another perspective on Wilde in Paris after his release from prison. Clearly the princess did not hasten to Wilde's side (she was no Ada Leverson), nor did she help him financially, however covertly. Clearly, too, he could not be received in her salon. Although Wilde's Paris and Proust's did not overlap, and the homosexual prince de Polignac was of the latter, Paris was not big enough to contain both without chance encounter, so the fact that the above reference is Cossart's only one to Wilde in the Polignac story creates further doubts about Cossart's accuracy. One of the few substantial references to Wilde as a social success in Paris therefore turns out to be flawed, problematic, elusive. This makes it clear that when Robert Sherard wrote of Wilde in 1891 'He loves Society, and Society runs after him',[1302] he was not referring to the *très snob* salons. Since the princess was one of the few upper class hostesses to welcome foreigners (she was of course American herself), any suggestion that Wilde might not have been one of these is a significant undermining of his position. The other hostesses who did cultivate foreigners included Anna de Noailles, the duchesse de Clermont-Tonnerre, the duchesse Gabriel de la Rochefoucauld, the princesse Murat[1303] and the comtesse Greffulhe.[1304] It would be necessary for his 'high social position' in 'highest Parisian society' to locate Wilde within the orbit of at least one these to reverse that undermining: to learn that he was one of the forty guests whom a Madame Gabrielli received at dinner on Sunday evenings[1305] does not quite establish this.

~~~~~~

Kerry Powell very tentatively draws attention to the possibility of Wilde's having seen Maurice Barrès' *Une Journée Parlementaire* in February 1894: 'If he was in the audience [he] must have been stunned by the likeness of this play to [*An Ideal Husband*] – if he had finished it by then'.[1306] I am not sure that a point that depends upon two conditions and an assumption has a great deal of strength, especially as it is predicated on Wilde's having been attracted to the play because Barrès was an 'old friend', which I do not think is sustainable.[1307] Jacques-Émile Blanche mentions a 'resplendent banquet' for Wilde that Barrès arranged at Voisin's, with Anatole France in the chair and a speech by Dujardin. This is assigned to April 1887[1308] but one would need some confirmation of this from another source, since for something so striking, it is strangely unchronicled unless indeed it be the dinner on the 15th December 1891 which in Robert Sherard's contemporary account becomes 'M. Maurice Barrès […] invited some friends to a dinner at Voisin's, in honour of the English [*sic*] poet, Oscar Wilde'.[1309] Langlade lists the guests as Blanche, Lorrain, Schwob and François Chevassu.[1310] This does not have quite the same bravura as 'a resplendent banquet', especially as the only François Chevassu known to cultural history was not born until 1929. Moreover, Wilde does not appear to have been in Paris in April 1887.

Barrès was, says Alan Sheridan, 'the most influential French novelist of the day,'[1311] but Douglas Ainslie called him 'so coldly sinister' as to suggest St Just,[1312] while Cécile Sorrel says of him that 'Grave and tormented, with long aristocratic hands and mild, distant eyes, he looked like a man of the seventeenth century'.[1313] It would have been an odd friendship between him and the esurient Wilde. As for *Une Journée Parlementaire*, one might do better to look at *J'attends Ernest*, produced at the Théâtre des Variétés in October 1890.

Another associate of Barrès was the deputy for the first Paris arrondissement, the millionaire Edmond Archdeacon, who was of Irish descent, and should be traceable in the circle of Maud Gonne. Barrès succeeded to his seat in the Assembly.[1314] He was a financial backer of both the Ligue des Patriotes and its successor, the Ligue de la Patrie française, and his house at 15 avenue des Champs Elysées, the former Hôtel Morny, was known as La Niche de Fidèle. Archdeacon is an unusual name, more so if spelled Archdéacon, and given his ear for such things, if Wilde heard of him at all, it might have surfaced in Archdeacon Daubeny in *A Woman of No Importance*, granted that Daubigny was also a name he came across in Paris as that of a well-known painter, Charles-François Daubigny[1315] – there is a reference to him in *The Decay of Lying*.

It was not as a 'a man of the seventeenth century' that Oscar Wilde himself struck Cécile Sorel, although her account of their two meetings is so highly coloured that it has not found its way into any Wilde biography. This account may be cited not because it is true (it may even have been true) or even because Sorel wished it to be thought of as true, but because it fits perfectly into the fantasies of the day, not least in the lines that Sorel puts into Wilde's mouth:

> You are the image of the woman whom I have brought to life in my books. You had become myth which I could no longer approach. I met you in my nights of creation. You will never know what you have given me. You alone could have saved me. For me you were all the goddesses, all the beings, all the sexes and all the souls [...]
>
> It seems to me that I am looking at the most beautiful page of my work.[1316]

This to the actress, once known as 'Bouboule', whose début in de Massa's *L'Épatant* had suggested that she had neither the voice nor the talent for future success, and whose reputation by 1900 rested on no more than parts at the Vaudeville and the Gymnase in such plays as Jules Barbier's *Struensée*,[1317] Abel Hermant's *Les Transatlantiques* and Henri Lavedan's *Les Viveurs*, but within twenty years would earn the avowal that 'one might almost say that Sorel was Paris'.[1318] It is pertinent to quote the rest of this description. 'She was a curious combination of lavish generosity and good bourgeois thrift [...] She was the most cultured, most intelligent woman one could hope to meet in a generation, yet she could argue and haggle with a tradesman and what is more, get the better of him over the matter of a few francs'. Her real name was not Cécile Sorel but Céline-Emilie Seurre. Here indeed was Paris.

~~~~~~~

It should also be emphasised that such success as Wilde enjoyed was a private success, among a few people. It is not comparing like with like, but it is worth noting that when the Russian Admiral Avellan visited Paris in October 1893, his squadron being at Toulon, he received nineteen thousand letters asking for his photograph. The visit 'provoked scenes of delirious joy which nobody who lived in Paris at the time will ever forget [...] Englishmen hardly ventured to show themselves while the delirium lasted, which it did for seven days'.[1319] More perhaps to the point, Edmund

Gosse noted of Henry James that he 'talked with increasing ease, but always with a punctiliousness hesitance, about Paris, where he seemed, to my dazzlement, to know an even larger number of persons of distinction than he did in London'.[1320] Will Rothenstein remembered that Henry James was 'persona grata among French writers, as well as among his own compatriots' and ties this in with his being 'elaborately correct and precise'.[1321] James had been educated in Paris in the late 1850s, principally at the Institution Fezandié, where the pupils were largely from Anglophone families who wished to learn French. When he returned to America he immersed himself in Balzac and Prosper Merimée and translated de Musset's *Lorenzaccio*; in 1873, he was to succeed Arsène Houssaye as the writer of the weekly letter from Paris for the New York *Tribune*.

This sounds far more the way to gain the respect of the Parisian intelligentsia than Wilde's mixture of over-blown flattery and egotism. As Rothenstein put it, 'There was certainly something florid, almost vulgar in his appearance; and his manners were emphasised'.[1322] Rothenstein gives an example of Wilde sacrificing manners for humour, when Coquelin sent Rothenstein tickets to bring Wilde to *The Taming of the Shrew* at the Comédie Française.[1323] There was a curtain raiser about a dinner party, and Wilde affected to believe that this was the cast of the *Shrew* having their dinner on stage: Coquelin was not amused. Rothenstein's comment that Wilde '*appeared* to have read all the books, and to have known all the people'[1324] also shows Wilde as less than endearing.

If Jacques-Émile Blanche's account of the 'resplendent' banquet given by Maurice Barrès for Wilde needs to be confirmed from another source, the same must be said for the 'banquet' given for him in Paris by his Oxford friend J.E.C. Bodley 'to meet some of the critics of France',[1325] which implies Wilde's début: 'It was an important step in Wilde's life,' says Bodley's biographer, 'and led eventually to the writing of *Salomé* in French'.[1326] Be that as it may, Bodley himself failed to refrain from some well-meant post-prandial advice.

> Taking Oscar into the Bois de Boulogne after lunch, Bodley remonstrated in the most friendly way with his old friend. He felt that the criticisms and enmities which Dorian Gray had recently produced must be met or avoided in future. But Oscar swept all remonstrance aside in his most fantastic manner, insisting that Dorian Gray was written with a fine moral motive and had been completely misunderstood. He had received letters of pleasure and approbation from the Bishop of London and the Archbishop of Canterbury! After this there was nothing more to be said.[1327]

Equally elusive is what Sherard calls 'the public dinner given to Wilde by Edouard Ducoté after his release from prison'.[1328] This is not mentioned by either Langlade or Philippe Jullian, nor is Ducoté mentioned at all in these or any other biographical sources for Wilde.[1329] Léon Pierre Quint does refer to a dinner given by Gide and Ducoté and a few friends to which Wilde was invited,[1330] but all other sources (including his own) agree that Gide avoided Wilde in Paris after 1897. Wilde was invited to dine with Ducoté in June 1898, but this is not a date which can be held to indicate social success.

What is to be said is that the descriptions of Wilde that Ellmann quotes by these lunch-met authors are not flattering. Wilde also apparently resented the tributes paid by Raymond de la Tailhède (one of the post-Symbolist École romane group of poets) and Maurice du Plessys (another of the group) to Jean Moréas, even though de Tailhède had been one of those to whom Wilde had sent an inscribed copy of *The Picture of Dorian Gray*.[1331]

Indeed, it is to be argued that those who cry up Wilde's success in 1891, are in fact confirming that his 1883 visit had *failed* to establish him as a figure in the Parisian coteries. Theodore Child, the Paris correspondent of the New York *World* and contributor to various American magazines, had written 'Mr Wilde is, of course, utterly unknown to the French'.[1332] Obviously, for in the previous years Wilde had published very little (hence his expedient of distributing signed copies of his poems with flattering inscriptions). These, says Sherard, were well-received and opened doors, but given Sherard's highly tendentious account, Anita Roittinger's reading in her study of Wilde strikes the truer note.

> By the simple device of dedicating his poetry to all and sundry, Wilde had managed to associate himself with virtually everyone that possessed name and distinction in France. But many of his enforced meetings with French notables went somewhat awry, and he often left behind almost the opposite impression from the one he wanted to create [...] His peculiar behaviour and conversation caused only shaking of heads, demonstrative of lack of understanding.[1333]

Sherard goes on to say that Wilde was given dinner by 'some English and American artists and journalists'[1334], which is anodyne enough, but his subsequent statement has to be regarded more circumspectly. Wilde, he says, 'was frequently in the exclusive society which numbered Edmond de Goncourt among its ornaments; he frequented the leading painters of the impressionist school; and he was welcomed at the house of Sarah Bernhardt where he met many of the most distinguished people of

Paris'.[1335]   None of this is capable of overmuch substantiation, yet it is
from this that so much of the view stems of Wilde as a success in Paris;
hence Gide's phrase that 'In Paris his name passed from mouth to mouth
as soon as he arrived', which is an obvious inexactitude, and Rothenstein's
remark that the French took Wilde 'more seriously as a writer than I
expected'.[1336]   These are the best ur-sources – and they must be handled
with circumspection.   Rothenstein goes on to refer to 'the ignorance of
French writers and painters of all but their own art and literature';[1337]
which may well have led to their taking Wilde (at least before his
successes on the stage) at his own valuation.

Sherard, who believed in occupying outposts only in order to abandon
them, pulled back from his position of giving a high-flown account of
Wilde, and then tried to soften the effect by further exaggeration.   He
describes an occasion at Goncourt's on the 21st April 1883.[1338]

> Oscar Wilde in the presence of a large number of highly cultured people
> was heard to remark that that the only Englishman who till then had read
> Balzac was Swinburne. Such as statement as that would appear [...]
> nothing more than [...] *une blague*, and Oscar Wilde would create the
> impression of being *un blagueur*. Now no worse impression can be created
> in literary Paris than this.[1339]   The Parisians have a certain reverence for the
> things of literature and art; they desire these things to be treated with the
> respect that is accorded to religion by others; and to be paradoxical and
> *outré* about them is to forfeit the attention of those whose good opinion it
> is worthwhile to cultivate. It is to be feared that Oscar Wilde was never
> really understood in Paris [...]

> It is only since his death, since the publication of Jean Joseph-Renaud's
> masterly translation of *Intentions*[1340] and the writings which have appeared
> as *De Profundis* that the Parisian men of letters are beginning to see that
> they had totally misunderstood the brilliant young man who made such
> efforts to amuse them.[1341]

The desire of Wilde to know Edmond de Goncourt when he disliked the
sort of work he wrote may be attributed to that 'exclusive society', since
Zola had for Wilde no such redeeming appeal. The reference to the
presence of 'a large number of highly cultured people' is a typical
Sherardism: was he there himself? Sherard's comment rather ranks with
his remarks on Wilde's *Duchess of Padua*, a failure whenever it has been
staged (and that not often): 'that great play [...] which some of his
admirers rank with the Elizabethan masterpieces'[1342]. In the same way,
Sherard says that the description of Wilde by Joseph-Renaud in his
introduction to *Intentions* was 'described by a great English novelist, who

is at the same time our sternest literary critic, as masterly'.[1343] Who was
this? Andrew Lang? Austin Dobson?[1344] It is mere cant, yet Sherard began
the dissemination of views on Wilde that are rarely traced back to him in
any critical fashion, so that an absurdity such as 'as an artist, and as an
intellect, there were not more than three men in the Paris literary world of
that day who were [Wilde's] equals'[1345] becomes subsumed into some
general remarks about Wilde's success. 'Only last year,' Sherard goes on
about *The Duchess*, 'negotiations were being made between a young and
beautiful actress, who was anxious to mount the play, and a lady who
owns the American acting rights.'[1346] The keyword is 'beautiful': the
excellence of the play is validated by the beauty of the actress who wants
to stage it; just as Sherard validates Joseph-Renaud's praise of Wilde by
pointing out that he was 'one of the finest athletes in France'.[1347] This
occasionally reaches a sort of sublime idiocy: '"I can remember him,"
writes a lady of refinement and culture from a Midland town, "as though I
had seen him yesterday […] though I was only a girl then […] this
wonderful youth".'[1348] One can only regret that 'Lady of Refinement and
Culture from a Midland Town' has not joined Person from Porlock as an
exemplar.

The charge of *blagueur* is an interesting one, for the *blague* had its place
in contemporary French effects, a sibling of *fumisme*. Chris Healy noted
that 'In France, the man who has arrived is always accessible to the man
who is struggling',[1349] presumably with reference to his own experience,
but the implication is that the struggler is serious in his work. Felix
Moscheles offers a definition of *blageur* that would not be offensive as
applied to Wilde, whom he knew. A *blagueur*, he says, was one who
'could chaff unmercifully, talk tall, make a fool imagine himself wise, and
a wise man feel foolish,' adding 'It takes a double-distilled Frenchman to
make a full-grown *blagueur*'.[1350] Ernest La Jeunesse wrapped up the
qualities of being Parisian and *blageur* with Wilde's other identities:
'Wilde in exile always remained English. Irishman by birth, an Italian in
his inclinations, Greek in culture and Parisian in his passion for paradox
and *blague*'.[1351] Of Wilde's biographers, I think Barbara Belford is the
only one to take up the point, and her conclusion is that 'Wilde's passion
for *blague*, or humbug, never abated'.[1352] One should remember that when
Sarah Bernhardt quarrelled with the Comédie Française in 1880, in the
eyes of Coquelin her great fault was that 'elle n'est pas sérieuse',[1353] and
when Marcère succeeded Ricard as Minister of the Interior in 1876, this
was 'although Baude characterised him as a *farceur* who is always
changing sides'[1354]. 'Impressing Paris,' Merlin Holland has noted, 'was
considerably more difficult than London or New York'.[1355] *Farceur*,

blagueur, cabotin, grandin, olibrius: these were all epithets to be avoided. Wilde's association with Gabriel de Lautrec would not have helped him to be taken seriously. Gide is clear: 'Wilde montrait une masque de parade, fait pour étonner, amuser ou pour exaspérer parfois. Il n'écoutait jamais.'[1356] This was not to endear. I think it was this austerity of the French intelligentsia that Henry James had in mind when he expressed himself rather forcibly: 'Chinese, Chinese, Chinese! They are finished, besotted mandarins, and Paris is their celestial Empire!'[1357] Or, as the light comedy actress Marie Tempest put it, 'The French loathe stupidity as much as the British exalt it'.[1358]

Princess Radziwill wrote a perceptive description of Wilde in this period, capturing both his popularity and (perhaps with hindsight) why he was regarded with some suspicion by the serious.

> In those bygone days about which I am writing, Oscar Wilde was still at the zenith of his fame, and no one suspected that this idol of the public was destined to end his says in shame and disgrace. He was always a desired and much sought after guest at dinner, and hostesses were eager to secure his presence at their entertainments. But in spite of this unreal popularity, because it was nothing but that, there was something most eerie in the man and his ways. A keen observer could not help wondering if, sooner or later, something would become known which would be to his detriment, and which would do away with the poetical halo hovering around his head. He had an agreeable manner, but such a conviction of his own importance and genius that it sometimes bordered on the ridiculous. At times it seemed as if for him there existed but one man on earth, and his name was Oscar Wilde. He did not admit superiority, refused to bow down before any talent, and subordinated everything to a love for what he called the beautiful. Women toadied to him, but I doubt if one had ever loved him, because there was nothing to love in him, nothing to be attracted in him nothing to make one think it would be possible to play any part in his selfish existence. He said he worshipped beauty, as he did in Nature and people, but it was marred by his overweening estimate of his intellectual achievements or physical charms.[1359]

Robert Sherard adds to his account of Wilde's failing to impress the intellectual set: 'A large number of Parisians, listening to Wilde's brilliant talk and failing to observe the humour which overhung his remarks simply set him down as a charlatan who was trying to deceive them, and resented the attempt.'[1360] This is supported by Vincent O'Sullivan, a friendly witness, who recorded that certain French opinion dismissed Wilde as being 'at his best a boulevardier like that Milord Arsouille who was a by-word in Paris'.[1361]

This milord is not to be found in Debrett. 'Arsouille', variously translated as 'blackguard' or 'ruffian', was a name fastened upon Lord Henry Seymour[1362] many years before. Although Seymour always denied that his was the roistering behaviour that occasioned the nickname, it might just as well have been for he 'led the way in every kind of personal eccentricity [...] the last of the English milords of the old school'.[1363] 'Milord Arsouille' in fact was not a lord at all but, according to Donald Mallet, a certain Charles Le Battet. Despite his name, Le Battet was actually more English than Lord Henry, for the latter was not really a Seymour at all, being the illegitimate son of either General Junot or the comte de Montfond by the Italian Maria, or 'Mie-Mie', Lady Hertford, whose husband, the third Marquess,[1364] allowed the boy to carry the family name and title. Le Battet was also illegitimate, his father 'an English chemist of very limited means who had persuaded a Breton friend to give his name'[1365] – if indeed it was his name, for Peter de Polnay calls him Charles de la Battut.[1366] Later there was a belief in Paris that this person, however named, was in fact Seymour in disguise. Ralph Nevill simply says that 'Milord Arsouille' was not Battut but Seymour's nickname, and goes on to tell numerous unseemly anecdotes about him. Although all this dates to the reign of Louis Philippe ('Arsouille' died in about 1835), the name was perpetuated in a song sung by Mistinguett at the Scala in 1912, where he is 'a caricature of an eccentric English nobleman, complete with floral brocade waistcoat and gold-headed cane [...] drawn from life [...] a decadent, outrageous lovable blackguard I once knew, a man of feeling after my own heart'.[1367] Marylène Delbourg-Delphis excavated Seymour as 'l'un des plus éclatants fashionables de Paris [...] taillé en Hercule, propriétaire de plus que trente chevaux et réputé pour ses farces cruelles', but without reference to Arsouille, whom she identifies as 'Charles La Battut'.[1368] George du Maurier invented a Café Larsouille in the rue Flamberge-au-Vent,[1369] but the most recent incarnation of 'Milord Arsouille', so far as I know, has been as the name of the Paris nightclub in the 1950s, associated with Boris Vian and Lucien Ginsburg – that is to say, Serge Gainsbourg, certainly a successor to Bruant, Xanrof and the others.

~~~~~~

The chief reason, therefore, why Wilde's Paris needs to be recreated is that doing so must influence our understanding of both Wilde's creativity and his social position. The presence of so many of the French intelligentsia at different salons makes it necessary to have some idea of cliques and factions, for Wilde's cultivating acquaintance with Parisians suggests his own affinities, on the one hand, and his standing, on the other.

Wilde was interested in making a good impression with those who did dominate, notably Mallarmé, Verlaine, Victor Hugo and Zola. In April 1893 the Dutch critic Willem Byvanck (Bijvanck) visited Paris and Marcel Schwob 'arranged for him to meet those whom he regarded as the significant figures of the epoch, including Rodin, Monet and Carrière, as well as Verlaine, Richepin, Barrès, Rosny and Moréas'.[1370] Rosny was actually either one person or two people, the brothers Joseph-Henri Rosny and Séraphin-Justin Rosny, who published under the joint name of the elder, although their real name was not Rosny at all but Boëx-Borel – the Irmine Boëx who had an amatory adventure with Jean de Tinan in the spring of 1896 was Joseph-Henri's daughter. George Moore wrote of Rosny that he 'is a really a decadent, a litter of ancient elements in a state of decomposition'.[1371] This forms another control group in assessing Schwob's involvement as Wilde's chief guide to the city in 1891. Although Edmund Gosse, eulogising Schwob, called him 'perhaps the most learned man of his generation', Wilde would surely have preferred the company of his other guide, the 'seraphically beautiful' Theodore Child.[1372]

~~~~~~~

How fluent was Wilde's French? According to Frank Harris, it was 'quite good' after his stay in Paris in 1883,[1373] but how good it became is difficult to assess (Harris's own French seems to have been excellent). Pater lent Wilde a copy of *Trois Contes* in 1877,[1374] presumably in the Charpentier edition published on the 24th April that year, suggesting a familiarity superior to what might be expected from instruction at Portora Royal School. Sherard decided that his French was one of the things for which he could overpraise Wilde.

> His visits to France seem to have laid the foundations of that great knowledge of the French language which he displayed in the writing of *Salomé*. As to the writing and language of this play, the best French critics are unanimous in expressing their wonder that any foreigner could have acquired such a mastery of the French language, its beauties and intricacies.[1375]

Douglas allows both points of view: 'In French he talked as well as in English; to my own English ear his French used to seem rather laboured and his accent too marked, but I am assured by Frenchmen who heard him talk that such was not the effect produced on them.'[1376] Clearly, this turns on whether one is referring to 1883, 1891 or 1900. The point is of some significance in determining the relationship of Wilde with the French intellectuals by whom he so very much wished to be accepted. It is difficult to imagine 'the best French critics', whoever they might be, agreeing unanimously upon anything, leave alone a foreigner's mastery of French, and other testimony is not quite so ecstatic. Gide says that Wilde 'knew French almost perfectly, but pretended, now and then, to hesitate a little for a word to which he wanted to call attention'; this smacks of the specious, especially when linked to Gide's less quoted remark that Wilde retained 'a slight English or Irish accent'.[1377] The American Mary Waddington, after living for forty years in France, reflected that 'There is so much repartee and sous-entendu in all French conversation that even foreigners who know the language well find it sometimes difficult to follow everything'.[1378] After all, to speak another language fluently is not necessarily to speak it well; and to speak it well is not necessarily to speak it without one's own accent.

Leaving aside Harold Nicolson's reference to Wilde's 'Chelsea French, of which he was so proud' in talking to Verlaine (for Nicolson never heard Wilde) and Chris Healy's remark (not necessarily with reference to Wilde) that 'Irishmen, as a rule, speak French with a brogue', Joseph-Renaud refers to Wilde's 'accent anglais', while Will Rothenstein remembered 'A rather Ollendorfian French with a strong English accent' ('but Ollendorf,' remarks du Maurier, 'does not cater for the Quartier Latin').[1379] In his autobiography the Nicaraguan poet and diplomat Ruben Dario, who met Wilde in 1898, recorded that he spoke French 'avec un net accent d'outre-Manche'.[1380] Gustave Le Rouge, writing much later, in 1928, says that Wilde 'expressed himself in French without trace of an accent and with a purity and correctness that were disconcerting', but Gedeon Spilett in 1897 wrote that Wilde 'expresses himself with ease in a modern, highly-coloured French to which his slight British accent adds a certain charm of its own' and this is more convincing: it coheres with Stuart Merrill's view that Wilde 'wrote French as he spoke it, that is to say with an air of whimsicality'.[1381] Max Beerbohm told Reginald Turner that 'it seems [Wilde] speaks French with a shocking accent, which is rather a disillusionment, and that when he visits the *Décadents* he has to repeat once or twice everything he says to them, and sometimes even has to write down for them.'[1382]

As for the letters that Wilde wrote in French, Langlade points out that faults in the originals were not reproduced 'dans l'édition de R.H. Davies' [*sic*].[1383]

Wilde praised the French translation of *Macbeth* by Richepin in literal prose, which a contemporary critic has described as 'woefully inadequate'.[1384] Aubrey Beardsley's cartoon of Wilde writing *Salomé* with the aid of French dictionaries and phrase-books is probably accurate enough – given the exotic words, far from everyday speech, that Wilde introduces. As for Wilde's speaking French to Verlaine, the latter spoke good English,[1385] which, he told Francis Grierson, 'is made for sentiment and poetry'.[1386] It is perfectly possible that the conversation was in English: at best, would not those of his French listeners who understood English wish to hear the 'lord of language' in his own domain? And would he not have wanted to oblige?

When one puts side by side Wilde's letter to Mallarmé in French of 25th February 1891 and Richard Ellmann's literal English translation, one sees how English Wilde's French actually was.[1387] Sherard's final comment that 'French was so familiar to him that, as he used to say, "He often thought in French",'[1388] demonstrates only that Wilde shared the self-deception common to most English speakers who pride themselves upon their French. The biographer of Pierre Louÿs states roundly that 'that although often credited with an excellent command of the French language, [Wilde] could be guilty of the crassest of howlers'.[1389] In any case, Wilde would have needed to speak a different French to Mallarmé or to Gourmont from that he would have had to use on the street, although it is difficult to imagine the lofty phrase-maker of *Intentions* expressing himself in *verlan* or *louchébem*.[1390] In any case, thought Romain Rolland, 'remarkable as Wilde's knowledge of French may have been, it is quite impossible to regard him as a French poet'.[1391]

It is well-known that Wilde consulted Adolphe Retté, Pierre Louÿs, Stuart Merrill and Marcel Schwob on points of French usage when writing *Salomé*.[1392] It was probably Schwob who at the time of *Salomé* was the most significant of Wilde's helpers in literary reputation (Jarry dedicated *Ubu Roi* to him), although Louÿs' reputation has perhaps survived the best. The Rosenbach manuscript *Salomé* shows that Louÿs made many suggestions, not all of which Wilde followed;[1393] and the intervention of these 'script doctors' did not prevent Rolland (a writer of far greater significance than any of them) from referring to the pretentious effeteness of its style when working on a libretto for Strauss. Rolland also marked 'mal français' on the text that Strauss sent him; Strauss replied that this was word for word from Wilde's original.[1394]

The dedication of the play to Louÿs perhaps indicates that Wilde was recognising a considerable indebtedness[1395] (although in turn Wilde thought that Louÿs should have been more grateful for the dedication), and Wilde introduced him to Sarah Bernhardt during the rehearsals in London; but it is also true that he was always more fond of Louÿs than Louÿs was of him. Although Louÿs dedicated *Astarte* to Wilde, he was but one dedicatee among many; while his literary judgment was perhaps questionable, at least when he called Dumas *fils* the master of Tolstoy and of Ibsen.

Schwob, who was Catulle Mendès' secretary when both worked on the *Écho de Paris*, was a friend and disciple of Mallarmé; and it was Schwob who had published the first French translation of a work by Wilde, *The Selfish Giant* in *L'Echo de Paris* on 27th December 1891. (He had already translated work by Robert Louis Stevenson.) This was not necessarily to his advantage, for according to Vincent O'Sullivan 'Wilde was not at all pleased if one praised his fairy tales at the expense of the rest of his work'.[1396] Francis Vielé-Griffin was also said to have had a hand in revising Wilde's French for *Salomé*.[1397] This is not substantiated either in Ellmann, who only mentions a criticism of Vielé-Griffin by Mendès, or Hart-Davis, who does not record any mention of Vielé-Griffin at all. Vielé-Griffin had left Paris for the Touraine in 1888, and although he entertained friends such as Henri de Régnier, Gérard d'Houville, Paul Adam, André Gide, Whistler, Émile Verhaeren, and Alphonse and Léon Daudet, no substantive connection with Wilde has been established.

~~~~~~~~~

Those who make so much of Wilde's indebtedness to Huysmans' *À Rebours* (read on his honeymoon, just after its publication[1398]) have been slow to inquire why he seems so little concerned with Huysmans' *L'Art Moderne* of 1883, perhaps because Huysmans praises the work of Degas, Manet, Gauguin, Pissarro, and Cézanne, painters in whom for the most part Wilde had little interest. Moreover, according to the Huysmans scholar G.A. Cevasco, it seems that Wilde never met Huysmans, which is surprising, and Christopher Lloyd, in his well-tempered study of Huysmans, only makes two passing references to Wilde, although as Dr Lloyd refers to the 'hundreds, even thousands, of critical essays and articles' on Huysmans, a pertinacious researcher might discover more.[1399] (Equally surprising is that 'We can be almost certain that Huysmans never met' Montesquiou.[1400]) There is no need here to go more into *À Rebours*;

suffice to note that Wilde read Huysmans' *En Route* in 1897 shortly before
leaving prison and found it

> most over-rated. It is sheer journalism. It never makes one hear a note of
> the music it describes. The subject is delightful, but the style is of course
> worthless, slipshod, flaccid. It is worse French than [Georges] Ohnet's.
> Ohnet tries to be commonplace and succeeds. Huysmans tries not to be and
> is.[1401]

If Wilde read Huysmans' *La Cathédrale*, published in February 1898 and
translated as *The Cathedral* by Clara Bell, we certainly do not know of it,
and later, surprisingly, Wilde was to tell Chris Healy that he had never
read any of Huysmans' work 'but he must be a great artist, because he has
selected a monastery as his retreat. It is delightful to see God through
stained glass windows'.[1402] If Healy has not made this up, it sounds as if
Wilde was allowing himself to be Boswellised for posterity. 'I see no one
here, but a young Irishman called Healy, a poet', Wilde told Robert Ross
in February 1898.[1403]

Georges Ohnet, a cousin of Jacques-Émile Blanche, was a popular novelist
who adapted his a number of his works as plays that were produced at the
Théâtre Gymnase – *Serge Panine* in 1882 and *Le Maître des Forges* in
1883 were great successes, much derided by the critics. The latter play,
'widely regarded as the most powerful social drama of the post-Augier
generation'[1404] was notable for Jane Hading's Claire de Beaulieu. This was
adapted by A.W. Pinero as *The Ironmaster*, and produced on 17th April
1884 at the St James's Theatre in London. Ohnet's novel, *The Rival
Actresses*, set in the early 1880s, though hardly distinguished, contains
what reads like his own theatrical credo.[1405] Wilde's views here expressed
are more trenchant than illuminating about his own critical stance.

Wilde would have been gratified to learn that Octave Mirbeau, a partisan
of César Franck, Paul Cézanne and Maurice Maeterlinck, found *Dorian
Gray* 'très supérieur'[1406] to Huysmans' books; he himself found Mirbeau's
Le Jardin des Supplices with its '*sadique* joy in pain' a wonderful but
horrible book to read.[1407] Mirbeau was ready to speak up for Wilde after
his imprisonment[1408] but during the trial he attacked the Decadents twice in
Le Journal,[1409] specifically targeting homosexuals. His defence of Wilde
did not stop him portraying Wilde and Lord Alfred Douglas unflatteringly
as Sir Harry Kimberly and Lucien Sartorys in his 1900 novel *Le Journal
d'une Femme de Chambre*,[1410] where Kimberly tells a long anecdote at a
dinner party about his friends the poet John Giotto Farfadetti and the
painter Frederic Ossian Pinggleton, who seem to be based on some idea of

Ricketts and Shannon[1411]. According to Sherard, 'Mirbeau personally detested Wilde',[1412] a feeling not reciprocated.

> Mirbeau rarely made a mistake in picking out what he believed to be the best and the most likely to endure [...] Mirbeau was a man ahead of his time and many of his judgments have been vindicated by posterity.[1413]

As the founder in March 1886, of a group called 'les bons Cosaques'[1414] which included Maupassant, Rodin, Paul Helleu, Paul Hervieu,[1415] Paul Bourget, Jean Richepin, Félicien Rops, and the composer Vincent d'Indy,[1416] and as a collector of work by Cézanne, Sisley Monet, Pissarro and van Gogh, Mirbeau might have been a more interesting cicerone for Wilde than Marcel Schwob was to be. After all, Wilde, like van Gogh, had once been concerned with sunflowers. Although with Alfred Capus, Paul Hervieu and Etienne Grosclaude Mirbeau founded in 1883 a satirical weekly called *Les Grimaces* that was both monarchist and antisemitic, he leaned towards anarchism, and his wife Alice Regnault[1417] was suspected of throwing vitriol at 'Gyp' de Martel. Mirbeau was also an occasional member of another group which called themselves 'les Mousquetaires': Lucien Guitry, Jules Renard,[1418] Alfred Capus, and Tristan Bernard. Alphonse Allais, journalist and practical joker,[1419] was another occasional member. It is curious to read that in 1973 William Logue could describe Mirbeau as 'forgotten to-day'.[1420]

Tristan Bernard had an equivocal rôle in Paris. Known as Paul Bernard before he adopted Tristan in 1893, Bernard wrote a number of comedies and light satires (including the well-known *L'anglais tel qu'on le parle* of 1899). His *Le Fardeau de la Liberté* was produced by the Théâtre de l'Œuvre. He was Parisian[1421] and Jewish, which, to follow a dictum of the duchesse de Clermont-Tonnerre, made him doubly Parisian. The bearded man in the bowler hat in Lautrec's 'The Lady Clown Cha-u-Kao'[1422] has been identified as Bernard. He was also editor of the *Journal des vélocipédistes* and owned two vélodromes, one called the Buffalo. In December 1913 Sarah Bernhardt played Jeanne Doré in Bernard's play of that name, her last appearance in a full length drama, which she also successfully filmed. In 1928 the princesse de Polignac, who had once been painted by Carolus-Duran as The Happy Prince, attended a fancy dress ball dressed as Tristan Bernard. Appropriately, Paris now has a theatre named after him.

~~~~~~~~

'Sincerity did not rule in all parts of the Paris Universal Exhibition,' noted Max Nordau, 'but a quickening of freedom was breathed in the great palace of art.'[1423] It is not quite plain what Nordau meant by this, and one wonders if he was referring to breathing out or breathing in: after all 'the amiable, modest, polite, delicately humorous, and even tolerant and considerate'[1424] Nordau believed that an advanced sense of smell was the sign of a degenerate. Here one might reflect on the scent of Paris, which Lord Frederic Hamilton defined as 'a peculiar smell which a discriminating nose would analyze as one-half wood smoke, one-quarter roasting coffee and one-quarter drains', while Georges Ohnet recorded 'the odour of absinthe and beer, spilt on the marble tops of the tables, mingling with the acrid smell of cigar smoke'.[1425] As one would expect, it was Zola who gave full rein to this sensory experience when he describes the cheeses of madame Lecœur's *fromagier*.[1426]

The 1900 Expo became one of the greatest showcases for art of all time, as was demonstrated at its daughter shows at the Grand Palais, the Royal Academy and the Montclair Museum, New Jersey[1427] a hundred years later, but at the time, even an educated mind could find it elusive.

> Adams haunted it, aching to absorb knowledge and failing to find it [...] Adams had looked at most of the accumulation of art in the storehouses called Art Museums; yet he did not know how to look at the art exhibits of 1900.[1428]

Among the Rodins shown was 'The Kiss', but Rodin decided to set up his own exhibition as Courbet had done before him. By 1900, Rodin's reputation was unshakeable, his fame as the century turned as secure in England as it was in France. This was largely thanks, not to Wilde of course, but to W.E. Henley and Robert Louis Stevenson. He had been promoted by Henley for years in England (Rodin's bust of Henley dates to the poet's 1886 visit to Paris), and for his part, Rodin had 'warmly praised' *The Suicide Club* and *Treasure Island*,[1429] the latter published in French in 1886 by J. Hetzel et Cie of the rue Jacob. (Rodin's English was uncertain; even twenty years later he used Gerald Kelly and John Tweed as interpreters when he was in London.[1430]

Rodin was not a Symbolist, although he was a friend and admirer of Mallarmé. Paul Claudel's sister, the sculptor Camille Claudel, bore him two children; he knew Zola and Verlaine, Moréas and Stuart Merrill. Success also brought Rodin to the Sunday afternoon open house of the realist novelist Léon Cladel at Sèvres, 'one of the crossroads of literary and artistic Paris',[1431] where a circle met that included Mallarmé, de

Régnier, Maurice Rollinat[1432], Clovis Hugues[1433], Bracquemond[1434] and the Belgians Verhaeren, Theo van Rysselberghe, Claude Lemonnier and Georges Rodenbach.[1435]

We do have some remarks of Wilde's on Rodin, but these are restricted to the portrait busts of Balzac and Daudet; one could wish to have had Wilde's views on 'Le Cri'[1436] as one would to have them on Tchaikowski's 6th Symphony. These might have provided an interesting revision of his view that 'everything matters in art except the subject'.[1437] Ellmann, unwittingly, is slightly misleading (or misled) in his account of the meeting between Wilde and Rodin, for he refers to Wilde visiting Rodin's 'studio' when 'the great man himself showed Wilde his "dreams in marble", *The Gates of Hell.*'[1438] This was in fact the Rodin Pavilion on the corner of the avenue Montaigne and the Cours la Reine.[1439] A hundred and sixty-five works by Rodin were on view, as Rodin was himself – D.S. MacColl called in May, for example and 'spent a very interesting afternoon'.[1440] Wilde was also present at a dinner for Rodin in June, when Adolphe Retté found 'something humble and contrite'[1441] about him: yet another mask, perhaps.

Wilde's response was to describe 'all the old works of art' as 'quite wonderful' (presumably the exhibition 'Art 1800-1889') and Rodin 'as by far the greatest poet in France [who] has completely outshone Victor Hugo'.[1442] This is a back-handed compliment, Victor Hugo even then being regarded as an extinct volcano.[1443] Rodin for his part told Jean Lorrain 'I don't attract quantity but I do get quality. Yesterday, for instance, Countess Potocka came to see me and the poet Oscar Wilde.'[1444] So few people indeed visited the Pavilion that Gabriel Mourey described it as 'a refuge of silence and pure beauty'.[1445] What was the 'quality', exactly? The Countess was Emmanuela (or perhaps Hélène[1446]), known as 'La Sirène', the Italian wife of the Count Nicholas Potocki of whom it was said that his stables in the avenue Friedland were one of the sights of Paris[1447], and she kept a stable of her own, for Jean Béraud's 1887 painting 'Le salon de la comtesse Potocka'[1448] shows the military painter Edouard Detaille,[1449] Gervex, Gustav Schlumberger the Byzantinist, Professor Caro and Xavier Charnes. She herself is shown with Gervex, Schlumberger, Albert and Marie Kann, Georges Legrand, General Caro, Adrien de Montebello and Dubois de l'Etang[1450] in a group photograph[1451] of 'The Macchabees', the name given to her group, this having no reference to Jewish Zealots or Händel, but a word signifying corpses. Other members of this set were Maupassant, the painter Cazin, the comte de Fels and one or other of the Vogüés; as well as the painter Béraud, Tissot's successor as the recorder of the vapid social anecdote, whose work she admired.[1452] This admiration was returned. A second painting by Béraud of a soirée at the hôtel Caillebotte is mentioned by André de Fouquières as showing Potocka, 'Mme Cahen d'Anvers au bras du comte Chouvaloff, le comte de Béarn, les dames Baignières, la comtesse Rose d'Alvaray [sic, for d'Avaray]'.[1453] 'Comme nous étions gais et que de farces nous fîmes', remembered Gervex.[1454] She and her husband separated in 1887. Although Jacques-Émile Blanche was her lover (they first met in 1882) she was 'known to be a furious disciple of Sappho';[1455] later she bred greyhounds. Her sister, Marie-Gaetana Pignatelli, described as 'Princess of Cerchiara, Princess of the Papal Empire, Patrician of Rome and Grandee of Spain' sang at a 'low music-hall' in Paris 'in order to shame her aristocratic relations': another corpse.[1456] While this enables us to catch an echo of Barbey d'Aurevilly's duchess of Sierra Leone, it also provides a context for Wilde's Mrs Erlynne: 'I will make my name so infamous that it will mar every moment of her life [...] There is no depth of degradation I will not sink to, no pit of shame I will not enter.'

One cannot quite view Rodin as a *farceur*, and it is therefore not impossible to regard his remark as sardonic, especially as expressed to Lorrain who regarded Wilde with no little hostility – Douglas erred in saying that Lorrain kept up a friendship with Wilde after 1897.[1457]

Neither Rodin's nor Wilde's remark suggests any great acquaintance between the two, and if it is true that Rodin was not only a coarse feeder but stank as well,[1458] Wilde may be allowed his aversion. But Wilde's taste in *chinoiserie* figurines does not engage with Rodin's bronzes:

> Under the rose-tree's dancing shade
> There stands a little ivory girl
> Pulling the leaves of pink and pearl
> With pale green nails of polished jade.[1459]

Wilde's numerous references to Tanagra figurines suggest the impression that these ancient Greek discoveries had made on him; one cannot imagine any engagement between Wilde and the ceramics made by Gauguin. It is true that Richard Buckle, looking at Wilde's praise of the Chicago water-works – 'the rise and fall of the steel rods, the symmetrical motion of the great wheels' – decided that this 'foreshadowed Soviet Constructivism and even a late ballet produced by Diaghilev',[1460] but this strikes me as far-fetched ('foreshadowed' can mean anything): it is to Kipling that we must look for contemporary celebration of machinery.

Rodin, of course, did not produce work that resembled Tanagra statuettes, but one who broke into Rodin's refuge of silence and bringing her own pure beauty was Isadora Duncan, who 'stood in awe before the work of the great master', seeing in it 'the conception of the ideal of life'.[1461] Duncan tracked Rodin to his studio. 'My pilgrimage resembled that of Psyche seeking the God Pan in his grotto, only that I was not asking the way to Eros, but to Apollo'.[1462] It is compelling to place Wilde, old, jaded, played out at forty-five, moving from bar to café to bar, in apposition to Duncan, moving from the Louvre to the Musée Cluny, to the Musée Carnavalet, to Notre Dame, and from the library in the Palais Garnier to the Bibliothèque Nationale, revelling in the first flush of excitement and enthusiasm.

> We used to [...] walk for miles all over Paris, and spend hours in the Louvre [...] Day after day we returned to the Louvre [...] and I have since met people who saw us there – me in my white dress and Liberty hat, and Raymond in his large black hat, open collar and flowing tie [...] There was not a monument before which we did not stand in adoration, our young American souls uplifted before this culture which we had striven so far to find.[1463]

Wilde on Rodin's Balzac was in fact far more appreciative than one would have expected from this admirer of Corot, Clouet and Clodion, judiciously balancing it between the real ('is') and the ideal ('should be'). 'Rodin's statue of Balzac is superb – just what a *romancier* is, or should be. The leonine head of a fallen angel, with a dressing gown. The head is gorgeous, the dressing gown an entirely unshaped cone of white plaster. People howl with rage over it.'[1464] The statue had been commissioned as a memorial to Balzac, and then rejected by the committee.[1465]

Wilde also approved of D.S. MacColl's notice of 'Balzac' that appeared in *The Saturday Review*,[1466] but for all that, consciousness of Rodin's work seems to have been remarkably weak in Wilde. Robert Sherard had seen the rough model seven years earlier with its 'monkish dressing gown', and wrote a short note about it.[1467] Although Léon Dierx and Jean Lorrain attacked the 'Balzac', it was defended by Antonin Proust, Georges Rodenbach, Anatole France, Léon Daudet, Jules Renard, Octave Mirbeau, Forain, Félix Vallotton, Mallarmé, Valéry, Henri Becque. Subscriptions to purchase the work ranged from the five hundred francs given by Lucien Guitry to the five francs that the wretchedly poor Alfred Sisley gave. The Natansons raised eight hundred francs through the *Revue blanche*. In all thirty thousand francs were contributed, only to be declined by Rodin. The dispute over the Balzac statue had become enmeshed with that over Dreyfus, and the pro-Balzac group were very largely pro-Dreyfus (Léon

Daudet and Forain the notable exceptions) while Rodin and Camille Claudel were not, and the sculptor did not wish to be beholden to Dreyfusards.[1468] 'Anti-Semitism became a fashion which suited certain jealousies remarkably well' thought the duchesse de Clermont-Tonnerre.[1469] It also suited certain snobberies, especially when these over-rode a scrupulous regard for logic. J.E.C. Bodley's son recalled of his father 'The only people he disliked with a real hatred were solicitors and Jews', yet Bodley himself could say 'I am so little affected by anti-Semitism that I stay with the French Rothschilds. I am one of the few faithful friends of Reinach'.[1470]

There is none of this to be learned from Wilde, who repeated his view of the Balzac in virtually identical words to Reggie Turner, humorously adding 'I have suggested that the statue to Alphonse Daudet should consist merely of a dressing gown, without any head at all'.[1471] Is it possible to take this remark a little further? Wilde may well have known, through Sherard if through no other channel, that Daudet had not been well-disposed towards him (Daudet, in London at the time of Wilde's trials, had told Sherard that he thought justice had been done);[1472] and he may certainly have known Daudet's reputation as 'an amazingly brilliant and varied talker'.[1473] On both these counts, Daudet's severed head might have been a conceit to be tolerated. And further still? An empty dressing gown might well have been Wilde's comment on Daudet as a writer, and he did not live to see the white marble statue of Daudet by Saint-Marceaux erected in the Jardin des Champs Elysées in 1902.

Although Wilde was appreciative, he was also brief. Wilde had been, after all, an admirer of Balzac, publishing 'Balzac in English' in *The Pall Mall Gazette*,[1474] and himself adopting a Balzacian gown ('a white dressing gown fashioned after the monkish cowl Balzac used to wear') when working during his Paris stay in 1883.[1475] A more developed view of Rodin's interpretation might have been expected. One might also have expected Wilde to notice the portrait 'Mrs Noel Guinness and her Daughter Margaret' by his fellow-countryman Walter Osborne, which won a Bronze Medal. A Gold Medal was won by Klimt, but Wilde and the world of the Sezession never touched, any more than he noticed the seven-room pavilion devoted to Art Nouveau that was erected by S. Bing[1476] and reviewed in *The Studio* by Gabriel Mourey.[1477]

It was at the Exposition Universelle that it was for many years supposed that Wilde had recorded a few lines of *The Ballad of Reading Gaol*, and that this was the only recording he ever made.[1478] Unfortunately, the recording is now regarded as a forgery, joining a small and interesting collection of Wildean apocrypha and pseudepigrapha from Paris where so much was illusory,[1479] not least at the Exposition Universelle. In one booth, for example, visitors were offered a cruise to Constantinople, with the effect that a number of the spectators were seasick;[1480] a simulated Trans-Siberian Railway was also constructed, though shorter than the original. Once more, Wilde's presence in Paris turns out after all to be an absence, perhaps precipitated by the Scotland Yard Inspector from Chelsea on duty outside the British Pavilion. This pavilion was itself a piece of make-believe, being a full scale replica of Kingston House, Bradford-on-Avon. One may also add that it was not ready in time for the opening of the Exhibition.

As Wilde missed the chance of recording his voice, so he failed to show any interest in the industrial machinery, despite his fascination with the Chicago water works long years before. Zola, with his eagerness to absorb the details of contemporary life, did find his way to the machinery halls, as did Henry Adams, guided there by the aviation pioneer Samuel Langley. Wilde, so signally represented as 'the first Modern Man',[1481] seems not have to noticed aviation, though the experiments of Alberto Santos-Dumont, whose fourth dirigible made a number of ascents during August and September from the Expo, were the talk of Paris; thirteen years earlier, a Captain Jovis, founder-president of the Union aéronautique de France, had designed a dirigible which he called The Horla. Perhaps Wilde recalled his Remarkable Rocket.

The Aeroclub de France had been founded in 1898 by comte Albert de Dion[1482] (president), prince Roland Bonaparte, Gustav Eiffel, M. de Fouvielle, comte Henri de la Vaulx and the comte de la Valette. De Dion was the lover of Marguerite Moreno, the actress wife of Marcel Schwob, and supported their household on the Île St Louis; Moreno was also at one time the mistress of Catulle Mendès. (Ellmann, who mis-spells her Marguérite, curiously describes her as Mendès' wife and implies that she was Schwob's mistress, perhaps having misunderstood Catherine van Casselaer's cryptic remark that Moreno was 'versatile enough to cope with any eventuality'.[1483]) In 1891 Schwob published a novel called Le Cœur Double. Gerald Kelly only got as far as drawing Moreno's hands, but his picture 'Monelle', the painting of a heroine of a story by Schwob, was exhibited in 1904 at the Guildhall Irish Exhibition.[1484] The Île St Louis was also the home of the poetically-inclined Thérèse de Carpentras, the Hôtel de Lauzun at 17 quai d'Anjou, which projects into the Seine like the prow of a ship. Anatole Dunoyer, with whom Marie Belloc stayed in 1886 also lived on the Île St Louis.

The name of de Dion (with that of his engineer Georges Bouton[1485]) is now better recalled as that of their motor car, another modern invention the significance of which Wilde, for all his occasional resemblance to Mr Toad, did not appreciate. The earliest De Dion-Bouton was made in 1894, but Bouton's engines were first used to power tricycles that pulled governess carts, the four wheel 'voiturette' appearing in 1899. Wilfrid Blunt, who was staying at Groisbois with the Wagrams, motored up to Paris in September 1900 with Berthe Wagram in her new automobile to go the Expo. 'It is certainly an exhilarating experience, quite new to me', he wrote. Blunt was lucky, for the de Dion-Bouton was notoriously unreliable. 'These awful little de Dion-Boutons' was the memory of the Duchess of Sermoneta, whose father-in-law owned 'two or three'.[1486] Another English motorist to be seen in the French capital was the Hon[ble] John Scott-Montagu, who drove his Daimler in the Paris-Ostend-Paris race in 1899. The equation between personal time, distance and speed was altering for ever.

~~~~~~~~

In fact the most popular attractions of the Exposition Universelle were not the harbingers of future flights, but flights into fantasy yet again, whether the 'rue de Caire',[1487] the reconstruction of an Oriental bazaar more thoroughly Oriental than anything to be found in Egypt; the reconstructed mediæval Paris streets; the similar German reconstruction of what appeared to be the set of the Meistersingers; or, above all, the Swiss village in the avenue Suffren, simple, tranquil, rural,[1488] which Paris was not. The Tunisian Pavilion might have attracted Wilde, as it did Gide, and there Jacques-Émile Blanche painted him in the Moorish Café with Henri Ghéon, Charles Chanvin, Eugène Rouart (a son of the collector Henri Rouart) and the poet Athman Ben Salah.[1489] This was what informed the description by Paul Greenhalgh when he described the Expo site as 'a magical city that sprang up, like a mirage, for a few months in 1900'.[1490] When Wilde wandered down the rue de Caire to be served drinks by the 'slim brown Egyptian, rather like a handsome bamboo walking-stick' at the Café d'Egypte, would he have recalled the factual Egypt of his father's book, or the fantasy Egypt that he conjured up in *The Happy Prince*?[1491]

Winston Churchill, visiting the Expo with his cousins Ivor Guest and the Duke of Marlborough, was not impressed, and compared it to a large scale village fair.

CHAPTER NINE

WALKING WITH AN AIR

'After dinner we went to the cafés of the Latin Quarter, and afterwards we
walked about Paris.'
– Robert Sherard.[1492]

'If you want to understand the real Paris, study her streets and
boulevards.'
– Dorothy Menpes.[1493]

'As I walked along the Bois de Boulogne...'
– 'The Man who Broke the Bank at Monte Carlo.'[1494]

ALTHOUGH Wilde was not much given to walking, an understanding of
life on the boulevards as well as in the cafés and salons is necessary to
understand the construction of his social as much as his sexual identity in
Paris. Even if the Haussmann boulevards were an assertion of public
control of the social, their appropriation by the *flâneur* represented a re-
inclusion of them into the private sphere, while the life on the streets of
marginal people – *chiffonniers*, beggars, flower and vegetable sellers,[1495]
artists, street entertainers, prostitutes – brought into proximity the idler of
every cut, and elided the distinction between public and private pleasure.
That many of the street entertainers were in one way or another illusionists
can be seen as an assertion of this relationship in a specifically Parisian
mode: the street juggler whose pitch was by the western entrance of the
Institut de France, for example, or the street conjuror whose pitch was
between the Pont des Arts and the pont des Saint-Pères (now the pont du
Carrousel),[1496] or the itinerant trimmer of poodles. The sellers too
specialised in illusions. Georges Ohnet describes the 'the orange women,
with suntanned faces and heads swathed with handkerchiefs of printed
cotton, stooping over their narrow, flat baskets', selling 'fine Valencia'
oranges, that may not have been fine, and may not have been from
Valencia.[1497] Lord Frederic Hamilton remembered the 'marchands de
coco', apparently selling cocoa to drink out of silver goblets 'or, at all
events, goblets that looked like silver', the cocoa in fact 'a most mawkish

beverage compounded principally of liquorice and water'.[1498] Equally ephemeral was the sale of caged birds in order that they could be set free.

André de Fouquières, justifying having cast his memories of his contemporaries in the form of a stroll through Paris, described himself as 'only a loiterer, who, without trying to conquer or hide his nonchalance, parades his memories under the silent façades of a Paris district.'[1499] 'Parades' is important, for this is Paris *as* parade. Christopher Hibbert, writing of Edward VII, implicitly links the promenade and the dandy: 'As Prince of Wales he had loved to go for walks in the Bois de Boulogne and down the Champs Elysées, to stroll along the boulevards, looking into the shop windows in the rue de la Paix, buying shirts at Charvet's, jewellery at Cartier's, handkerchiefs at Chaperon's and hats at Genot's.'[1500] Edward's taste in hats was of course idiosyncratic, and it was generally held that the English silk hat was of finer quality than the French. One may also add that if the Prince bought scent or soap at Houbigant's[1501] (19 rue du Faubourg Saint-Honoré) which would be likely enough as Houbigant was parfumier to Queen Victoria, he was buying from the family firm of the Nabi painter Paul Sérusier. This promenade would also have taken in the florists Debac (63 boulevard Malesherbes) or Lachaume, 'which all the world patronised',[1502] and where Proust bought his *cattleya* buttonhole.

Paris of the boulevards was personified by princesse Mathilde Bonaparte, her path intersecting that of the Prince of Wales, even if they did not encounter each other, and that of Charles Swann, an encounter that took place in fiction[1503]:

> Nearly every day she drove towards la Madeleine, and got out of her carriage at the boulevard des Capucines; and [...] accompanied by her lady-in-waiting or by someone else she had invited on the expedition, she would walk delightedly, briskly, along the *asphalte adoré.*[1504]

'Nonchalance', 'loving to walk', 'walking delightedly,': these are the characteristics of the dandy-*flâneur*, for life on the boulevards had meanings beyond those of simple topography. The first was understood by Prince Chlodwig von Hohenlohe-Schillingsfürst when on the day after he arrived in Paris as German Ambassador, he noted in his diary 'In the afternoon walked on the Boulevards'.[1505] This promenading also gives the meaning to the duchesse de Clermont-Tonnerre's description of Alexandre de Gabriac as 'that Parisian so well-known to Parisians'.[1506] It is what Jules Laforgue meant when he asked the absent Gustave Kahn 'Aren't you homesick for the boulevards?'[1507] André Gide was introduced by his father to what became a favourite pastime, walking the streets of Paris, as his biographer says, 'for the sheer pleasure of it'.[1508] Laurent Tailhade described his own homesickness for the society of Bagnères-les-Bains as 'soif comme un Parisien de l'asphalte des boulevards.'[1509] It was what the Australian Florence Morrison, studying music under Ivan Caryll[1510] at the Conservatoire, remembered nearly sixty years later as the 'fascinating and favourite walk'[1511] along the Champs-Elysée. This could be elevated into an almost mystical communion, even for Sigmund Freud in 1885:

> Paris had been for many years the goal of my longings, and the bliss with which I first set foot on its pavements I took as a guarantee that I should attain the fulfilment of other wishes also.[1512]

James Laver noted that '*Flâner*, the favourite verb of the *Siècle du Boulevard*' implicates the *flâneur* with the fashionable promenades.[1513] The *flâneur* has been elevated from his streets into the critical lexicon, but other terms remain to serve the strollers, notably *Paris-piéton*, which does not carry the freight of dandyism. Wilde himself, at least in the mood that writing *De Profundis* provoked, associated the *flâneur* with unworthy aims:

> I let myself be lured into long spells of senseless and sensual ease. I amused myself with being a *flâneur*, a dandy, a man of fashion. I surrounded myself with the smaller natures and the meaner minds. I became the spendthrift of my own genius, and to waste an eternal youth gave me a curious joy. Tired of being on the heights, I deliberately went to the depths in the search for new sensation.

This must be read as a repudiation of the *flâneur* as a status which one could recall with pleasure, as well as an acknowledgment that the *flâneur* could seek the depths without forfeiting that status. To be 'on the streets' has its full range of meanings here. There was in any case a confluence between the boulevard and the boulevardier: 'The rue de Rivoli is a symbol; a new street, long, wide, cold, frequented by men as well-dressed, as cold as the street itself.'[1514] When Maupassant's Duroy decides to improve his name to du Roy, the change from private persona to public takes place in the street. 'It seemed to him that he had just acquired a new importance. He walked along more jauntily, his head held higher, his moustache bolder, the way a gentleman should walk.'[1515] Here one thinks of Coupeau, Zola's parodic boulevardier with the boulevardier's buttonhole of a red carnation now become his nose, at the age of forty 'bent and doddery, and old as the streets themselves'.[1516] This theorising of space and its denizens informs our understanding of the visual representation of open-air Paris, in the work of Caillebotte for example where 'one might argue that the street is a principal organising space, even where the subject is ostensibly different'.[1517] Indeed, Caillebotte, so much the painter of central Paris, by his favoured device of depicting streetscapes seen from windows or balconies, opens up the possibility of a Paris that stretches beyond the limitations imposed by the street-level gaze, to who knows what distant kingdoms?[1518] Thus, while still providing a pictorial record, even anecdotal painting carries more than the anecdote, not least for the fact that, as François Loyer has pointed out,[1519] the multiplication of balconies was a characteristic of Paris architecture that only dated to the 1870s: the views were up to date ones.

The boulevard could also be as much a forum of debate, or self-debate, as the café. In February 1896, Jean de Tinan and Henri Albert[1520] pondered over the editorial board of *La Centaure*

> tout le long du classique trajet
> De la rue Caulaincourt
> Au d'Harcourt.[1521]

The boulevards were not the only avenues to Paris, however. Other strollers explored different concepts of the city. According to Lord Ribblesdale's daughter Barbara (born at Fontainebleau in October 1894), Ribblesdale 'spoke French without any English accent, idiomatically and appreciatively. He liked and understood the finesse of the language. His was the kind of personality greatly admired in France'.[1522] Elsewhere she calls Ribblesdale 'a character of romance', who spoke 'pure and idiomatic French'.[1523] Nevertheless, 'I do not think that modern France won his allegiance [...] He enjoyed the world of small busy French streets, all the *petit commerce*, women *en cheveux*, in black shawls doing their marketing among the big orange pumpkins and the barrows laden with snowy cream-cheese.'[1524] These were the 'sinuous little streets which thread the neighbourhood of the Faubourg Saint-Honoré, filled with excited voices, hurrying footsteps and street vendors'.[1525] Clearly this milord was a 'ruiste' rather than a boulevardier, for all his familiarity with the Hôtel Westminster (also favoured by Henry James) in the rue de la Paix. It was a world he shared with Huysmans, who was also fond of the back streets in a very restricted circuit round St-Sulpice. James Laver, noting this, draws the necessary conclusions:

> There are many people who say, and think, that they adore Paris, but by Paris they mean the bright lights, the smart cafés, the theatres and the boulevards. What they love is the city of pleasure, the cosmopolitan rendez-vous. The true lover of Paris is very different. On him the

unfashionable quarters, the back streets exercise a perpetual fascination. For there are other boulevards beside the boulevard des Italiens, other squares beside the place de la Madeleine; by-streets and forgotten corners, alleys and cul-de-sacs, dilapidated doorways and peeling façades, houses in abandoned *quartiers* where once the famous lived. What mere tourist explores the rue d'Alésia, enters the backyard of the rue du Paradis, or is brought to a halt, pensive, in the impasse Floriment?[1526]

Similarly, the Liberal journalist and M.P. Spencer Hughes, whose first trip abroad was to Paris in 1889 ('I have formed the opinion that no city is seen to advantage in exhibition time, and that exhibitions themselves are nearly all alike') on subsequent visits 'learned to love Paris, and have found continual delight in exploring her famous thoroughfares and her quaint back streets and byways'. Hughes managed to obtain a picture of Paris unusual for a foreign visitor, by borrowing a flat above the printing firm in the rue du Bac with the services of a valet who, Hughes thought, had quite possibly never been out of the city. On another occasion he stayed at the Buffet Hotel at the Gare du Nord, and experienced a city again different from that of the Hôtel Westminster. His recollection of dining suggests a certain naïvety, but also the ability of Paris to disguise itself, for he strayed into the Bœuf à la Mode in the rue de Valois and into Prunier's, each time thinking them to be modest and simple establishments. Undeceived, he discovered that the former was much patronised by English High Court judges.[1527] Their verdicts at least on the food could be relied upon.

Another who recognised that the promenade was the necessary way of understanding the essence of Paris was Arnold Bennett: 'Walking from the Trocadéro to the Bois de Boulogne, and so to the Arc de Triomphe and down the Champs-Elysées, I search for the formula which should express Paris – in vain'.[1528] Little wonder that Violet Hunt recalled him as 'my old friend of the Paris boulevards'.[1529] Three days later, Bennett tried again, walking the entire length of the Champs-Elysées between ten and eleven o'clock at night, but there found only Paris in its metaphysical aspect.

> The immense thoroughfare had a depressing, deserted appearance. In the side alleys under the trees a light mist hung low, and through this the forms of empty chairs were made spectrally visible by the gas-lamps. Down the road at intervals passed cyclists with Chinese lanterns, swiftly overtaking the few fiacres. Occasionally the light of a flying lantern lit up the face of a girl pedalling hardily in her neat knickerbockers over the perfect surface of the gloomy thoroughfare.

In the rue de Rivoli and the rue de la Paix all was obscure, save for a few bright squares of illumination, marking shops which vended obscenities for the convenience of travelling Englishmen.[1530]

Bennett's observation that young women were still up and about at eleven o'clock was acute, even if perhaps inspired rather more by the knickerbockers than by sociology (and perhaps that he concealed his own identity under the noms-de-plumes 'Barbara' and even 'Cécile'). Women despite the risks did move around Paris. Marie Belloc, for example, hardly out of her teens and a passionate theatre goer, used to walk home to her hotel at midnight, something unthinkable in London.

Bennett, despite the fitful lantern gleams, found the spirit of place elusive. 'I left Paris. None of my deepest impressions about it seems to have been set down at all,' he recorded after a week's conscientious journal keeping in the autumn of 1897.[1531] It is a long way from the bookshop of Charles Péguy to Riceyman Steps, and perhaps his time would have been better spent had he known that to promenade was not enough. It was also necessary for the stroller to remain still. Dorothy Menpes realised this: 'Sitting there, hour after hour, and watching the people as they pass, one begins to understand the real Paris, the Paris of the Parisians.'[1532]

'Obscenities for travelling English men' were presumably contraceptives ('French letters' / 'capots anglais'), but it was both part of the reputation of Paris for the English, and a construct of the English by the French, that they should also be provided with obscene literature. This is difficult to quantify: undoubtedly the Palais Royal had fallen from favour, and Will Low's growing censoriousness is directed to this, but Thomas Coolidge also lamented its fall from grace and E.V. Lucas noted a decline (or perhaps just a police crack-down). Like the grisette, it becomes part of vanishing Paris, but the date of its disappearance is disputed.

Books of a character that in my boyhood enjoyed only a restricted circulation in select schools, not 'impudently French' but *printed in English* for the probable uses of some other nationality than that of native Parisians, now openly proclaim their impudicity in the shop windows along the rue de Rivoli where decency reigned thirty years ago.[1533]

When I was here forty to fifty years ago it was the liveliest part of Paris, filled with brilliantly lighted cafés and crowds of fashionable people, and surrounded by beautiful shops. It is now completely deserted.[1534]

When I first knew Paris [1889] the Palais Royal was filled with cheap restaurants and shops to allure the excursionist and the connoisseur of those books which an inspired catalogue once described as very curious and disgusting. It is now practically deserted.[1535]

For all that, in 1903 Duncan Grant bought a book in the Palais Royal called *How We Lost Our Virginities*. The 'very curious and disgusting' aspect of Paris can be followed by those with 180 euros to spare in Jean Pierre Dutel's *Bibliographie des œuvres érotiques publiés clandestinement en français entre 1880 et 1920*.[1536]

This significance of searching for the spirit of Paris by wandering is also indicated by Zola in *L'Assommoir*, when the Coupeau wedding party set out for the Louvre: from the rue Saint-Denis across the boulevard Bonne-Nouvelle where 'the line of couples stood out like a string of garish splashes of colour', into the rue de Cléry to the rue du Mail and the place des Victoires; on to the rue Croix-des-Petits Champs and so to the Louvre. En route, this parody of the progress of the dandy-boulevardier is made explicit, when loungers and guttersnipes laugh at the men's hats 'ancient hats carefully preserved, their lustre deadened by dark cupboards, their shapes replete with comedy, tall, bell-shaped or pointed, with extraordinary brims, curled or flat, too wide or two narrow'. In the Louvre itself this journey becomes odyssean as the uncomprehending party wanders at random or else lost from gallery to gallery, unable even to find their way out until a *deus ex machina* in the form of an attendant leads them to safety. The party has moved from the reality of the streets to the dreamscape of the arts and back again, climbing the Colonne Vendôme in order to recover their mastery of the city's topography.[1537] The boulevardier-gastronome is also parodied when Coupeau and Auguste Lantier go from café to café eating tripe, oysters, fried rabbit, kidneys, calf's head.[1538]

Zola does this again in *L'Œuvre* when Claude Lantier and his friends are walking across the city. This is a stroll that takes them from the boulevard des Invalides to the quai d'Orsay to the Pont de la Concorde; on to the rue Tronchet (where Lord Alfred Douglas was later to live) and the place du Havre; up the rue d'Amsterdam to the boulevard des Batignolles, where, at the corner of the rue Darcet, is 'their' café, the Café Baudequin, based upon the Café Guerbois, predecessor of the Nouvelle-Athènes. They then return to the rue d'Enfer 'down the rue de Clichy, along the rue de la Chaussée d'Antin into the rue de Richelieu, crossed the Seine by the Pont des Arts, and reached the Luxembourg by the rue de Seine'.[1539] This walk is then twice parodied, once as comedy and once as tragedy. The first is in the conversation of two gentleman 'one fat, one thin, both wearing decorations [...] talking very earnestly' at the Salon: '"Well, I followed them" the fat one was saying, "down the rue-Saint-Honoré, along the rue Saint-Roch and the rue de la Chaussée d'Antin, then up the rue Lafayette".'[1540] Walking along the rue Saint-Roch would have taken the man, and the contemporary reader who follows him, past the Hôtel Saint-Romain, where Robert Louis Stevenson stayed in April 1881, Beardsley in February-March 1896 and Hilaire Belloc in the summer of 1900, and past the Café Saint-Roch, 'a little café in which the shop assistants from the Ladies' Paradise usually congregated, and where they brawled and drank, and played cards in the pipe smoke' and where Zola's Baugé has an apartment.[1541] The rue Lafayette is the site of the Coq-Faisan, 'a popular middle-class restaurant' in *Bel-Ami*. Duroy goes here to dine before setting off to entrap his wife, not quite a springe to catch a woodcock.[1542] The use of the name, indeed, may be one of Maupassant's more involved pieces of word play, for the rue Lafayette was home[1543] to the Italian cocotte Dinelli, the name carrying suggestions of dîner and *dinde*. The Faisan Doré was actually in the rue des Martyrs: Maupassant lunched there with Céard and the poet Tancrède Martel sometime in 1880.

The second reprise is when Christine Lantier follows Claude when he contemplates throwing himself into the Seine: 'When he left the rue Lepic he turned down the rue Blanche, then went along the rue de la Chaussée d'Antin and the rue Quatre Septembre till he came to the rue Richelieu.'[1544] This is very like the definition of Manet's Paris as bounded by the Porte St-Denis, la Madeleine, the rue de Richelieu, the rue de la Chaussée d'Antin and the boulevard des Italiens,[1545] the very Paris that the Irish politicians John Dillon and Andrew Kettle made the area of a Sunday morning stroll in 1881. Francis Rombeau and Henri Bernard, on their way to the Café Riche in Ohnet's *Lise Fleuron* 'went down the rue de Richelieu, which was full of busy wayfarers, and blocked with carriages and omnibuses. It was the hour in Paris when everyone in Paris is going to dine. In the streets near the Boulevards the traffic was quadrupled. The cafés overflowed with customers'.[1546] It is also the Paris of the stroll of de Maupassant's 'M. Parent', 'along the boulevard de la Madeleine, and past the Paris Opera in the boulevard des Capucines and the fashionable cafés in the boulevard des Italiens'[1547] and the Paris that Zola himself explored on foot while writing *Paris* in 1897/8 and with his children in 1899 and 1900, but without, it seems, encountering Wilde – or even being seen by Paul Léautaud, for whom 'a walk in Paris [was something] which I have always been crazy about doing':[1548]

> How often have I made that journey by the rues Saint-Jacques, Gay-
> Lussac, Monsieur-le-Prince, de l'Ancienne Comédie, and Mazarine, the
> Pont des Arts, the avenue de l'Opéra, and the Chaussée d'Antin.[1549]

A similar stroll is undertaken by Richard Grey and John Lauder in *The
Sands of Pleasure*: 'They walked into the boulevard des Italiens until they
came to the rue Lafitte, that curious fissure in the mass of Paris [...] They
walked on through streets of shuttered business houses, into the region of
small dwellings, shops, and studios, arriving at last, rather hot and weary,
at the rue Blanche.'[1550] Shirley Fox struck a variant: 'I used to jog off on
the outside of a Filles-du-Calvaire omnibus, and getting down in the rue St
Honoré just by the Magasins du Louvre, walk across the square courtyard
of the Palais du Louvre and the Pont des Arts, which landed me exactly
opposite the Institut de France'.[1551]

The foreigner, the *flâneur*, and most of all the would-be Bohemian, all
strolled through imagined Paris: who could resist setting out like Armand
Duval from the rue de Provence, walking down the rue Mont Blanc,
crossing the Boulevard, and following the rue Louis-le-Grand, the rue de
Port-Mahon and the rue d'Antin, and then to look up at a window that one
might think was Marguerite's?[1552] This spatial relationship, eliding private
and public, ground and upper floors, pavement and roadway, movement
and the frozen moment, and productive of fantasising, is also understood
by Maupassant's monsieur Vestey:

> I do my outings in a bus. After a leisurely lunch in the wine-merchant's
> shop on the ground floor, I make out my route with a map of Paris and a
> time-table of the bus routes that give the connections. Then I climb up on
> to the top, open my sunshade and off we go. The things I see! [...] I visit
> different quarters. It's as good as a journey round the world; the inhabitants
> of one street aren't a bit like those of another. Nobody knows Paris as well
> as I do. And there's nothing so entertaining as the first-floor windows.
> The things you see in those rooms, as you pass, you'd never guess. You
> can imagine the domestic rows from the face of a man who has raised his
> voice [...] You return the glad eye of the girls in dress-shops, just for fun,
> because you don't have time to get off [...] It's as good as a play, the
> simple genuine drama of real life, as you see it from behind a pair of
> trotting horses.[1553]

Play, drama: Maupassant insists on this. As Joseph de Bardon says 'You
know I often roam about Paris like collectors who are always searching the
shop-windows. What I look for is incidents, people, everything that passes
by, everything that happens.'[1554] So too Monsieur Parent takes rooms on
the mezzanine of the Hôtel Continental 'so he could watch the passers-

by'.[1555] Perhaps it is no wonder that Maupassant disliked the Eiffel Tower, where the spectator remained static, detached, unobserved; those viewed foreshortened, diminutive.

~~~~~~~

For Harold Nicolson, in Paris to read for the diplomatic service, the Pont des Arts came to have a specifically Wildean significance. He had met a former school fellow whom he refers to as J.D. Marstock:

> I had shown him the hotel where Wilde had died, and we emerged on the Quay at a moment when every window in Paris and Montmartre was flaming back at a low red sun. We leant over the parapet and looked at the purple river swirling below. The hum of life reached us in the hot air; behind was us the Quartier Latin, in front those myriad flaming windows. I showed him the two sphinxes at the end of the bridge and told him how Wilde in those last shabby years would tell how that sphinx there on the right was the only person who returned his smile.[1556]

The description is very Zola-esque: 'the myriad windows of the Left Bank' is a phrase from *L'Assommoir*.[1557] Zola's own reference to the rue Blanche would have rung familiarly in many of his readers' ears. Edouard Dujardin and Téodor de Wyzewa shared a house at number 79, and in the same street the English watercolourist William Wyld[1558] lived for many years. Could Oscar, the son of Sir William Wilde, the brother of William Wilde, not have noted the name? Wyld had certain characteristics that might have appealed to Wilde, apart from his name: Alice Diehl, meeting him in 1861, thought that 'even then he seemed to me to be elderly',[1559] while P.G. Hamerton found him still at work in 1887 'an octogenarian with the health and faculties of a man of fifty'.[1560] Wyld's son-in-law, Howard Tripp, was a dealer with a gallery in the rue St Georges,[1561] showing among others Corot, Constant Troyon[1562] and Daubigny.

So fundamental to the idea of the Parisian spirit was the concept of wandering that it created in fictional form its own antithesis. When des Esseintes sets out for London and decides that has gone far enough when he has reached the rue d'Amsterdam, the strolling *flâneur* merges with the languid æsthete. Here, to arrive is not merely *not* better than to travel hopefully – to arrive it is not necessary to travel at all. Colette's Chéri takes this to its conclusion when he goes into exile from Paris by remaining in Paris. His reflection 'Curious how people can go on doing the same thing day after day. I could almost believe I had never left

Paris'[1563] bears out his doting mother's description of him as 'fantasy incarnate'.[1564]

The significant recorder of the outdoors, at least in 1880s (in the 1890s prosperity and the Légion d'Honneur awarded in 1889 softened his outlook and blunted his work) was J.-F. Raffaëlli. 'He scrupulously recorded the inhabitants of the industrial zones along the Seine: vagabonds, absinthe drinkers, petits industriels, workers, petits bourgeois and, in particular, rag-pickers. Departing from the traditional picturesque image of this marginal member of society […] he regarded the rag-picker as a symbol of alienated individualism in modern industrial society'.[1565] This was to express in paint what Zola was expressing in words; but it is also to say that even the *chiffonnier* was not just a *chiffonnier*, but part of a Barthesian world of signification.[1566] The introduction of the neat metal containers for refuse decreed by M. Poubelle was an extension of the moral order to the anarchic one of discarding refuse into the street for the *chiffonniers*. Maupassant understood this:

> Down [the street] an army of sweepers was sweeping. They swept the pavements and the cobblestones, driving all the litter and filth into the stream of the gutter. With the same regular movement, like reapers in the field, they swept up all in a wide semi-circle ahead. And as she ran through street after street, still they came to meet her, moving like puppets on a string, with the same mechanical, mowing movement, she felt as though something inside her, too, had been swept away.[1567]

The public and private spheres are again being renegotiated, Maupassant's woman being assumed into the process of cleansing, and the subclass of *chiffonniers* suitably æstheticised. Shirley Fox captures the ambiguity between social realism, æstheticisation and the transgressive when he calls the *chiffonniers* picturesque birds of the night, even though 'some of them were wrinkled and withered old men and women who looked more like animated mummies than human beings'.[1568]

One should also consider how the work of a Steinlen, of an Edgar Chahine, or of a Francisque Poulbot, whose drawings of Parisian ragamuffins made him famous[1569], functioned between social denunciation and æsthetic taming. Paintings such as Guillaumin's 'Charcoal Thieves on the Quai d'Orsay'[1570], or Bonnard's 'The Barrel Organ Grinder' of 1895, or Anquetin's 'Street, Five O'Clock in the Morning'[1571], not merely chart activities on the street, but place the artist as *flâneur*. Raffaëlli's 'Blacksmiths Drinking'[1572] goes further, as it was intended as an illustration for *L'Assommoir*. Such works, supplementing the anecdotal reminiscence, are crucial for those who wish to pervade Paris. The narrator/ navigator, invited to respond to whatever comes within view, does so through the alteration of his own perspective, so that shifting topographical stance is matched by a shifting in the sense of locality, together with an alteration in social observation, as no one knew better than Proust. Further, the narrator/navigator, when himself viewed, is seen by different observers in different guises: this is the donning and doffing of a stylistic mask. Here is an extrapolation from the novel of the picaresque into the concept of the *flâneur*, the two converging in Joyce's *Ulysses*, set in Dublin but completed and published in Paris. This is also a masculine privilege within the feminine city, and is to be used as a critique of such paintings as Pissarro's 'Boulevard Montmartre on a Winter Morning'[1573] (painted from a window in the Grand Hôtel de Russie), where the viewer is offered a standpoint that seems to have him hanging in space, or Caillebotte's paintings where the viewer is invited to share the point of view of a character looking from a window, balcony or bridge. Henry James saw this as evoking mystery and magic: 'It was in the long watch from the balcony, in the summer night, of the wide late life of Paris'.[1574]

It is therefore the street, not domesticity, that defines the Parisian, and it is flux that defines the street, constant ebb and flow, as David Harvey suggests, 'between the railway stations, between centre and periphery, between left and right banks, into and out of central markets, to and from places of recreation, between industry and commerce'[1575] – and one fittingly may add of the latter, between the Crédit Mobilier and the Compagnie Immobilière.

'The Grands Boulevards might be called the showrooms of Paris; it is here that one sees the Parisians', wrote E.V. Lucas. It was an unintended effect of the work of Haussmann that the new boulevards should nurture the growth of the café *terrasse*, and the emergence of the clientèle out of the interior on to the pavement. When Pierre Louÿs was in Cairo in January 1898 he wrote to Henri Albert suggesting that when Albert next found himself at the Restaurant Julien, he should ask for all things necessary for writing ('tout ce qu'il faut pour écrire') and send him an off the cuff ('petit impromptu') letter in twelve columns concerning the passers-by, notably Alexandre Hopp of *Le Journal* or Ernest La Jeunesse.[1576]

Henry James saw this *va-et-vient* in terms Odyssean.

> The Boulevards are a long chain of cafés, each one with its little promontory of chairs and tables projecting into the sea of asphalt. The

promontories are doubtless not exactly the islands of the blessed, peopled though some of them may be with sirens.[1577]

The importance of this liminal space has been tellingly recognised by Jean Méral, writing of the way the Great War altered the Paris of literature: 'It is as if the spirit of Parisian gaiety, directly affected by the spectacle of the city huddled round its blue lights, has moved indoors and set up quarters in dark, enclosed spaces'.[1578]

When the purpose was so clearly both to see and to be seen, it is not surprising that the scrutiny of the boulevardier was as much part of his *batterie* as his cane, although this was not always appreciated by those from more reticent societies. 'Staring – more than staring, a cool cynical appraisement – is one of the privileges a Boulevardier most prizes,' Lucas noted. 'I have heard it said that he carries staring to a fine art; but it is not an art at all, and it is certainly not fine; it is just a coarse and disgusting liberty'. Lucas added resignedly 'If one is going to be annoyed by Paris, one had better stay at home.'[1579]

The critical gaze after all is appropriate to the showroom, especially when there were goods on view: namely, the prostitutes, women with a street life that gained them such measure of independence that they enjoyed (or endured). The claiming of the street by non-prostitute women – women shopping, women on the way to or from work – weakened the street as a place of male dominance, contributing to the instability of rôles and to the feminine gendering of the city, salesgirls, as noted by Zola, forming 'a vague class floating between the working and middle classes',[1580] drawn from the first and aspiring to the second, a new genteel bourgeoisie in the making.[1581]

One might find much on the boulevards, but some of it, clearly was what one brought oneself, for meaning is imported as well as discerned. Of the kiosks, those characteristic pieces of Parisian street furniture,[1582] Oscar Wilde wrote that they were 'institutions I think we should at once introduce in London [...] a delightful object, and, when illuminated at night from within, as lovely as a fantastic Chinese lantern, especially when the transparent advertisements are from the clever pencil of M. Chéret'[1583] though it is not entirely clear whether Wilde was referring to the kiosks of the newspaper sellers, or the Colonnes Morris. Later he wrote to Will Rothenstein 'I wish you were working for a Paris newspaper, that I could see your work making *kiosques* lovely'.[1584] Richard Whiteing, on the other hand, only saw the kiosk as 'gorged to overflowing with flying sheets and flying fancies from every part of the planet, from every corner of the human mind, even the foulest […] a hurly-burly of imaginative suggestion'.[1585] Truly, to the pure all things are impure — and not the least of them the dreadful verse of Wilde's

> Sometimes about the gaudy kiosk
>   The mimic soldiers strut and stride
>   Sometimes the blue-eyed brigands hide
> In the bleak tangles of the bosk.

There is little to choose between the imagery that Chéret employed for posters for department stores, the Palais Garnier, or the Elysée-Montmartre,[1586] and we even find a poster for *La Terre* by him (1889).[1587] Chéret's subjugation of his subjects into his style equivalenced them, but one sees this as formulaic commercialism, not as post-modernist collapsing of high and low art. Chéret, the unlikely friend of Monet, Degas, Seurat, Bracquemond, Besnard, Roll, Rodin, Steinlen, Willette, Caran d'Ache, Rivière, became a Chevalier of the Légion d'Honneur in 1890, sign of his acceptability to the Establishment.[1588] When Wilde referred to Chéret's 'clever pencil', he produced praise faint enough, but probably not intended as damnation. For the radically challenging Lautrec, the creator of the modern poster,[1589] he had no word at all.

It may be rather a pity that Wilde left no specific reflection on the Colonnes Morris,[1590] though, to be sure, he may have been better acquainted with the third feature of the Paris streets, the *vespasiennes* (or *tasses* in gay argot). His reference to newspapers is a reminder that one could buy the anglophone publications – *Galignani's Messenger*, the *Morning News*, the *American Register* – chiefly at kiosks, especially at those between the Grand Café and the Opéra, notably at number 12 (Madame Dupeyron) on the corner of the rue Scribe, and at another one opposite the Café de la Paix. The activity of buying a newspaper was therefore also an aspect of sauntering, while the position of the kiosks in proximity to cafés once more brings those oases into the picture.

I do not think that W.S. Haine's view can be sustained, that Haussmann had changed the boulevards from a social space to a traffic management project, 'the Champs Elysées merely a route to the Bois de Boulogne'. The function of the Boulevard was seen clearly at the time, implicitly in the novels, explicitly by contemporary observers. The Haussmann vista was always carefully closed, with either a new building or else an existing building given a new context. There was an end in view: there was no vanishing point. For the Parisian 't'es dans la rue, va t'es chez toi', and if, to take Aldo Rossi's phrase, buildings are the furniture of cities, then this re-ordering of the buildings that was effected by haussmannisation meant indeed that the boulevard was the living room. Richard Whiteing, an authority on Paris, writing either as himself or under the nom-de-plume 'Alb', puts the point that 'To the Frenchman it [the boulevard] is more than a place of transit; it is almost a place of sojourn. So the Parisian common man has his share of the Champs Elysées, of the boulevards [...] He comes down to them, so to speak [...] It is a place made for the waking hours [...] The Boulevard is the source or the distributive centre of all the flitting fancies of France.'[1591] This is the background to Xanrof's 'La rue':[1592]

1	2
What we sing to-day	Sadness or joy we find
In the street.	In the street.
Our muse is the noise	Good and bad beside
Of the street.	In the street.

Marie Belloc Lowndes described the Anglo-Irishman Lewis Wingfield, then resident in Paris and writing dramatic criticism for *The Globe* (one regrets to record under the name of Whyte Tighe) as 'a noted English boulevardier',[1593] clearly thinking she was according him sufficient description, just as in London one would have said 'well-known man-about-town'. This persisted: J.-P. Goujon describes Pierre Louÿs' friend Paul Robert as 'peintre et boulevardier'.[1594] Lysiane Bernhardt, granddaughter of the actress, describes one such man about his occasions, in this case her father: 'For the rest of the afternoon Maurice strolled about the streets, bought some ties at Charvet's and a new walking stick, sent some flowers to an actress at the Odéon and had a drink at Tortoni's'.[1595] Hence one may paraphrase Baudelaire: the street was the living-room of the *flâneur*, its features his furniture, its shops his wardrobe.[1596]

As for traffic management, there was a clash once more between order and individualism, between the demands of managing the public space and the claims of the private space. Edward VII's chauffeur is authoritative here:

> Parisian traffic, *of course*, is not regulated as is the traffic of London. A certain disregard of order and convenience prevails, and, if it occurs to a driver to stop in the middle of the road, he does so.[1597]

It was for the uncommon man, however, for whom the Champs Elysées was the social lounge. There was General Robineau 'the elegant sportsman who, in his tall hat and jacket, toured the Champs Elysées, whenever the weather was pleasant, on his bicycle'.[1598] There was Macchetta d'Allegri (or Alligri[1599]), later Monte Carlo correspondent of the *New York Herald*, who 'would take two hours to dress; he spent at least an hour ironing and cleaning his clothes and brushing his boots and then he sauntered forth and paraded up and down the Champs Elysées'.[1600] The Ambassadeurs, the Café de l'Horloge, the Alcazar d'Été, these all beckoned these wanderers. It is easy to see why J.E.C. Bodley suggested that in Paris 'it is so easy to imagine that a day of sauntering had been fruitful in good work'[1601] – and why the prolific Dumas *fils* preferred to do his walking in the country.[1602] At the other end of the social scene, the 'Vachalcades' of 14th March 1896 and 20th June 1897 were a carnivalesque (or *fumiste*) occupation of the streets: Io Saturnalia! as the Romans would have said. Degas remarked of Manet. 'Il est très parisien, il comprend la plaisanterie',[1603] once again identifying Manet as a personification of the city, and identifying the city with its humour.

It is hard to see how within this map it was possible to avoid even the people one wished to avoid: one evening a group of Dreyfusards found themselves sharing the Café Weber, with a group of anti-Dreyfusards. 'I saw Stuart in the street the other day. He looked fat and married,' said Wilde caustically of Stuart Merrill, who had dropped him.[1604] After the drowning of Hubert Crackanthorpe in November 1895, the newspapers carried a statement that 'for the last two months of his life he was living in Paris, during which period he had never left it for a single day, and the circumstances of every day of his life there are said to be perfectly well known to his family'.[1605] It is unfortunate that we do not have these circumstances; though not, of course more unfortunate than Crackanthorpe's tragic end.

> Paris is not a late city; it is a city with a few late streets [...] The number of all-night cafés is very small, so small that by frequenting them with any diligence one may soon come to know by sight most of the late fringe of this city, both amateurs and professionals.[1606]

'Who does not know Aurélien Scholl?' wrote Daudet.

> However little you may have frequented the Boulevards of Paris, or visited their neighbourhood during the last thirty years, you must have remembered in front of Tortoni's, under the lime trees of Baden, or in the

parks of Monte Carlo, this pre-eminently Parisian and Boulevardier figure.[1607]

Daudet might have added what Chris Healy[1608] calls the Café de la Paris, a conflation of the Café de Paris and the Café de la Paix, where he encountered Scholl. 'You have only to sit for an hour every evening under the "de la" [on the awning of the Café de la Paix] and you will find that you will know by sight half the faces of the men who pass you,' wrote Richard Harding Davis, adding rather censoriously that anyone 'need only walk the boulevards for a week and he will be recognised as a boulevardier. It is a cheap notoriety.'[1609] It was the very notoriety to which Wilde had once declined to be averse. What, after all, was a boulevardier? Ralph Nevill thought him 'a distinct Parisian type who practically disappeared with the fall of the Second Empire'.[1610] Felix Moscheles noted his resurgence after the Siege of Paris and the Commune, defining him as 'the typical Parisian who must have his daily stroll along the boulevards; he must stop somewhere where he can sip something and see somebody else sipping and strolling. He must watch his opportunity of saying something polite to somebody, and at a given hour, he must call for absinthe and concentrate his thoughts on the importance of an approaching meal.'[1611] This could be a picture drawn directly from Wilde.

'When do these people work?' asked a puzzled Thomas Edison in 1889.

> 'What do they work at? I have not seen a cartload of goods in the street since I came to Paris. People here seem to have established an elaborate system of loafing. These engineers who come to see me, fashionably dressed, with walking sticks in their hands, when do they do their work? I can't understand it at all.'[1612]

Edison had clearly seen but failed to observe: after all thirty thousand men were engaged as coachmen, cab drivers and delivery men. He was also presumably ignorant of the fact that traditionally many people worked on Sundays and took the next day off, preferring 'Saint-Lundi' 'because it required fewer ceremonies and bourgeois pretensions'.[1613] Dorothy Menpes noted the interaction between work and leisure, and the nexus with the boulevard, that catalyst which changed without changing:

> Enjoyment for the Parisians – as much for the mason, the carpenter, and the small shopkeeper, as for the bourgeois, the Bohemian and the boulevardier – begins at four o'clock in the afternoon. Then the carpenter lays aside his plane, the tailor his scissors, the artist his brush, and the politician his pen. At that hour one and all prepare for recreation.'[1614]

As well they might, for 'until the 1890s most industries or crafts had days of eleven or twelve hours',[1615] reducing to ten hours as normal by the century's end. The assimilation by Dorothy Menpes of the different categories of worker one with another is a significant aperçu of how the outsider brought a distinctly æstheticised perspective to bear, even when taking notes in the age of Sidney Webb.

Whiteing sited the promenade of the boulevardier from the rue Royale to 'just beyond'[1616] the boulevard des Italiens (that is, taking in the boulevard de la Madeleine and the boulevard des Capucines), which conforms with the other accounts quoted; and he also mentions the group of 'broken down gentlemen' which congregated at the junction of the avenue du Bois de Boulogne and the place de l'Étoile. 'They take their seats there on fine afternoons, to watch the long procession of carriages and live again in the memories of their former splendour'.[1617] Maupassant saw this turn with twilight into a lust procession:

> They took an open cab, and drove down the Champs-Elysée, then the avenue du Bois de Boulogne. The night was completely still, one of those scorching nights when the air of the overheated city feels, as it enters your lungs, like a blast from an oven. A huge number of amorous couples were being driven under the trees in an army of cabs. These cabs moved along one behind the other, never ending […] A vast river of lovers was flowing towards the Bois […] The warm darkness seemed full of kisses. A feeling of love hovering overhead, of ever present animal desire, thickened the air, making it seem more stifling. All these couples, intoxicated by the same thought, by the same passion, created a febrile aura around them. All these carriages, heavy with love […] gave off, as they passed by, a kind of sensual aroma, at once subtle and unsettling.[1618]

Arthur Symons understood the Grands Boulevards to be a literary conceit: 'They live on the pages of Balzac, of Flaubert, of Cladel, of Mendès; they live in the creations of Gavarni and Constantin Guys.'[1619] One may take 1900 as the highpoint of the boulevardier, for in the digging of the new Métro a future under the streets was being engendered,[1620] and the autonomous and visible walker, selecting his routes, became the regulated and subterranæan passenger. Ligne 1 was opened on the 19th July 1900, with ten three-carriage trains; Ligne 2 (Étoile to Trocadéro) followed on the 2nd October, extended to Port Dauphine on the 13th December. Each carriage could take fifty passengers. This was not simply a new method of transport, but a new and disorienting method of finding one's way about a once familiar territory. 'How often had he asserted that one could not cross the road by the Metropolitan without having to change twice,' reflected

Leonard Merrick's Tricotin.[1621] Orfée could indeed now descend aux enfers. Further relocation was effected when in 1907 the station rue St Denis became Réaumur-Sébastopol, and after 1914 when the stations Berlin and Allemagne became Liège and Jaurès.

One could no more walk these routes without being conscious of them as literary conceit, than one can walk down Eccles Street and be unconscious of Leopold Bloom or Baker Street and be unconscious of Sherlock Holmes. Just as Villiers de l'Isle Adam celebrated the boulevard des Italiens in *Les Demoiselles de Bienfilâtre* in 1883, so after the publication of *L'Œuvre* in 1885 it was impossible to follow the routes described there without knowing one was engaging with the footfalls of Claude Lantier and his friends, nor could one again cross the rue du Bac after the publication of *Le Débâcle* in 1892 without being aware that that was where Jean Macquart bayonetted his adoptive brother Maurice Levasseur.[1622] Zola himself was conscious that he was map making, for he made a diagram to show the locations mentioned in *L'Assommoir*.[1623] Moreover, the promenade of Lantier and the others is given heightened significance as the occasion of one of Zola's flights where the timed becomes the timeless, where Paris itself becomes Paris herself.

> It was four o'clock, and the day was just beginning to wane in a golden haze of glorious sunshine. To right and left, towards the Madeleine and the Corps Législatif, the lines of buildings stretched far into the distance, their rooftops cutting clean against the sky. Between them the Tuileries Gardens piled up wave upon wave of round-topped chestnut trees, while between the two green borders the Champs-Elysées climbed up and up, as far as the eye could see, up to the gigantic gateway of the Arc de Triomphe, which opened on to infinity.[1624]

This understanding of Paris was specifically followed by Henry James, when Lambert Strether arrives and wanders about looking for somewhere to write letters home:

> Strether […] set himself to walk again. […] This restlessness became therefore his temporary law; he knew he should recognise as soon as see it the best place of all for settling down with his chief correspondent. He had for the next hour an accidental air of looking for it in the windows of shops: he came down the rue de la Paix in the sun, and passing the Tuileries and the river, indulged more than once – as if on finding himself determined – in a sudden pause before the bookstalls of the opposite quay. In the garden of the Tuileries he had lingered, on two or three spots to look; it was as if the wonderful Paris spring had stayed him as he roamed. The prompt Paris morning struck its cheerful notes – in a soft breeze and a

sprinkled smell, in the light flit, over the garden-floor, of bareheaded girls
[…], in the type of ancient thrifty persons basking betimes where terrace
walls were warm, in the blue-frocked officialism of humble rakers and
scrapers, in the deep references of a straight-pacing priest or the sharp ones
of a white-gaitered, red-legged soldier. He watched little brisk figures,
figures whose movement was as the tick of a great Paris clock, take their
smooth diagonal from point to point; the air had a taste of something
mixed with art, something that presented nature as a white-capped master-
chef. The palace was gone; Strether remembered the palace; and when he
gazed into the irremediable void of its site the historic sense in him might
have been freely at play – the play under which in Paris indeed it so often
winces like a touched nerve. He filled out spaces with dim symbols of
scenes; he caught the gleam of white statues […]. But his drift was […] to
the other side, and it floated him unspent up the rue de Seine and as far as
the Luxembourg.[1625]

'The palace was gone,' burned in the Commune, and its going provoked
some thoughts by Wilde. Passing the ruins with Sherard, he remarked
'there is not one blackened stone that is not to me a chapter in the Bible of
Democracy'. Although this has been read as praise of democracy, the
opposite view seems more compelling: that Democracy unleashed burns
down the House Beautiful and its art treasures. It is difficult not to relate
this to Baudelaire's line 'Mon cœur est un palais flétrie par la cohue'.[1626]
Both men believed in aristocracy, and Wilde had already had something of
the same thought in *Theoretikos*. 'And the rude people rage with ignorant
cries / Against an heritage of centuries.'

The streets were not the social space solely of the *flâneurs*, however.
These had to share it with those for whom it was their working and
sometimes their sleeping space as well, not to be forgotten in too dandiacal
a view of the city. Zola provides a route for Pierre and Guillaume
Froment – the rue des Martyrs, the rue du Faubourg Montmartre, the
grands boulevards, the boulevard Poissonnière, the boulevard Bonne
Nouvelle, the boulevard St-Denis, the place de la République, the
boulevard Voltaire, the rue de la Roquette, – a sort of *anti-flâne* through
'want and grief-stricken districts […] Vague spectral forms slink by and
then are lost to view in the depths of the night.'[1627]

Dorothy Menpes noted with some disdain 'Women with babies tramp the
streets and look pitiably at you; but they do this for fifteen years or more.
They always have babies, and nearly always different ones'. Over fifteen
years, although the women might have been the same, even in Paris one
might be forgiven for taking it as natural that the babies were different

ones: that Mrs Menpes wanted to make it a point about transformation
again demonstrates the hold, if hold be the right word, that Paris exercised
as Circean enchanter over the minds of visitors. Infant mortality in Paris
was amongst the highest in France. Parisians were also said to be
significantly smaller than people from the provinces.

~~~~~~~

The boulevardier and the *flâneur* overlapped with the dandy: cane, gloves,
silk hat, buttonhole, the tie that according to the *Art de Toilette* of 1830
could be tied in any one of seventy-two different ways. Wilde understood
this well: 'I amused myself with being a *flâneur*, a dandy, a man of
fashion'.[1628] But the dandy also overlapped with the snob, and here the
interior and outside worlds met, for one must not exclude the element of
snobbery among all these high-minded people. Adolphe Dennery's
success at the Châtelet with *Les Deux Orphelins* and his adaptations of
Jules Verne prompted him to become d'Ennery, although this particular
distinction was more the sign of a snob than of a man of honour, the
pursuit of the quasi-aristocratic *particule* much facilitated if one's name
already began with d, but added even by such courtesans as Marie Antigny
when she became Blanche d'Antigny. Gabrielle Caire, who began by
adopting Gabrielle des Lys as a stage name, became Gaby Deslys when
she decided that the *particule* made her name too much like a courtesan's.
Edmond de Goncourt was a snob of a magnitude that in England would
have covered him in ridicule: his disgust when Bruant sang in the drawing-
room of the Charpentiers indicates how much he preferred slices of life to
remain between the covers of his books.[1629]

Of Paul Bourget, Douglas Ainslie wrote 'I have known him, on more than
one occasion, interrupt a literary conversation in order to exchange
platitudes with some anodyne Countess'.[1630] Austen Chamberlain, meeting
Bourget in 1886, thought him a 'writer of clever but detestable novels and
disappointing in conversation. He was, I think, then and later a good deal
of a poseur'.[1631] Perhaps Chamberlain was put off by Bourget's English,
which was 'rather comic and not entirely fluent'.[1632] Yet Bourget enjoyed
the support of the Faubourg: 'it is doubtful whether, without its protection,
he would have become as popular as he is with a certain section of French
Society – its most elegant section let me hasten to add.'[1633] His highly
developed social sense outstripped his sensibility. When Téodor de
Wyzewa tried to enlist the help of Bourget for Laforgue, dying in poverty
of tuberculosis, Bourget sent four bottles of claret.

Snobbery also seems to have touched Gabriel Fauré when in the early 'nineties he was taken up by the princesse de Polignac and the comtesse Greffulhe, and came under the influence of Robert de Montesquiou. The princesse had first encountered Fauré at the château of her mother, the duchesse de Camposelice, at Blossville, near Trouville in 1880. The composer was 'almost automatically drawn into the duchesse's circle,'[1634] and his 'Cinq Mélodies de Venise' were written after a stay at the Palazzo Polignac. Fauré's biographer suggests that 'a historical sociology of his melodies would show that, until around 1914, his vocal works were cultivated in the atmosphere of the artistic, cultivated salons of the upper bourgeoisie'. This is to express in the language of Roland Barthes what Debussy put more pithily: 'Fauré is the mouthpiece of a group of snobs and imbeciles.'[1635]

Chapter Ten

Masquerade

'If you want to be singers, don't be satisfied with the songs Paris sings.'
– Cécile Sorel.[1636]

Part 1: Masks and Veils

'In so vulgar an age as this we all need masks.'
— Oscar Wilde.[1637]

IF the previous chapters established the liminal spaces of Paris, the flow between Left Bank and Right, between *terrasse* and pavement, this chapter explores the theme of fantasy as a dominant ambience for those who inhabited this space, suggesting that the very notion of the *limen*, neither in nor out, is the appropriate site for those whose personalities were themselves neither here nor there. This is Paris as Parade, where masks could be donned and doffed, or even become the face of the wearer. For Wilde the mask changed from a prop that aided the multiplication of identities in the manner of the Venetian carnival to a disguise that *protected* the wearer from the crudity of the 'real world'.

Paris as an attractive place for refuge has been noted. Exiles could be other than what they were, or perhaps, simply themselves. This is illustrated by the Flight of the Gays after Wilde's arrest: France for them was where they could mask themselves, or retain their masks. Described in graphic fashion in many sources, the most pertinent (and hyperbolic) is that of Robert Sherard, which clearly shows fact becoming a literary conceit, carnivalesque in its imagery.

> It was indeed a horrible time, to be remembered by me not without a shudder for all my days. A wave of terror swept over the Channel, and the city of Calais witnessed a strange invasion. From the arcana of London a thousand guilty consciences, startled into action by the threat of imminent requitals. Every outgoing steamer numbered among its passengers such nightmare faces as in quiet times one cannot fancy to exist outside the

regions of disordered dreams […] As soon as it was known in Paris that [Wilde] had been released on bail, the nightmare faces which had become familiar on the boulevards were seen to peep and peer.[1638]

It was an *huis clos* to which they came. The Irish painter Paul Henry, who immersed himself in the cafés of the Latin Quarter and Montparnasse, noted that 'in the art circles in which I moved there was very little hint of an outside world. In fact for a great many of us the Bal Bullier or the Moulin Rouge might not have existed.'[1639] Yet the Quartier Latin itself was not above the suspicions of the more cautious, or more timid. 'I have been told by daring tourists that there are good hostelries on the other side of the Seine. I cannot speak from experience' wrote the journalist Arthur À Beckett.[1640] Sherard had a horror of the Latin Quarter.[1641] John Milner in *The Studios of Paris* remarks of Whistler and Carolus-Duran, with studios in the rue Notre Dame des Champs, that it was an extraordinary achievement persuade possible buyers to visit them there – although I think this is an exaggeration. D.S. MacColl went with Joseph Pennell to visit Whistler in Paris in May 1893 and 'spent many happy hours' there with the Beardsleys before going to Dieppe where Charles Conder was staying.[1642] Even Dorothy Menpes recorded that 'You have only to cross one of the bridges leading from the Rive Droite to the Rive Gauche to notice the difference. You leave behind you all that is blasé, all that is bourgeois, all that is joyless and sick and dispirited among a people to whom boredom is unknown'.[1643]

~~~~~~~

Bridge-crossing or cross-bridging: to Paris one also took one's own 'Paris', just as Frances Spalding suggests that Roger Fry took Cambridge there with him.[1644] Stevenson's 'Loudon Dodd' says 'I did not see the facts, I brought them with me ready-made'.[1645] Francisque Sarcey, a covert Anglophile, complained 'Your countrymen come over here, stare at the prints on the boulevards, see a play or revue, more or less obscure, and then conclude that we are past praying for.'[1646] Shirley Fox, whose fluent French made him useful as a guide, acquired

> a general knowledge of Paris that can rarely have been vouchsafed to one so young. Even the less reputable resorts such as the Folies Bergère, the Bal Bullier, and the then existing Skating Rink in the rue Blanche were to me quite familiar ground, and the gay ladies of the time who frequented these resorts used to make much of me and do all in their power to acquire my good will, knowing full well that, whenever I appeared, it was usually

with a little crowd of *Anglais* in my wake [...] So it was not surprising that
I was at this time very popular at places of entertainment of this class.

These were strange experiences for a boy of my age.[1647]

Even when the purpose was innocent, Paris served as masquerade as well
as mask, provided a cloak even on the occasions when there was no
dagger. At Mi-Carême, masquerade became institutionalised as carnival:
'Triumphal cars and people with noses and fancy dresses,' Martin Lister
wrote to his mother in 1883[1648] – although by the end of the century
Aurélien Scholl[1649] noticed that false noses were getting hard to find.[1650]
Carnival is by definition transformative, transgressive of order and morals:
how far its acceptance was a canalisation of this, placing riot in a
controlled setting, can be argued.

Disguise was further aided by the holding of masked balls – four times a
year in the rue Condorcet by Lucien Guitry's father-in-law, René Pont-
Jest; every Tuesday at the disreputable cabaret Elysée-Montmartre;[1651]
every week during winter at the Eden, for example. If these were, in Roger
Shattuck's phrase, the banquet years, they were also the years of the ball.
The American Louis Sullivan, who was studying architecture under
Vaudrenne at the École des Beaux Arts, attended a masked ball one
Thanksgiving and told his brother that the costumes were 'as grotesque
and outlandish as possible'.[1652] The group calling themselves the
Incohérents also held an annual fancy dress ball under the direction of
Jules Lévy; the comtesse de Beausacq gave a fancy dress ball for Pierre
Loti,[1653] although both hostess and honoured guest spent much of their
time in fancy dress anyway. Even Juliette Adam gave a fancy dress ball,
at which Judith Gautier appeared as Cleopatra, wearing a stuffed
guineafowl on her head, in the company of Pierre Loti dressed as a
Pharoah. At the 1889 annual ball given by *Le Courrier Français*,
Toulouse-Lautrec dressed as a choir boy, and carried a wolf's head on a
pole, rather more resonant than Gide's costume as a pastrycook a few
years before at the annual fancy dress party of the Gymnase Pascaud. The
masked balls at the Opéra, painted by Gervex,[1654] Manet[1655] and Toulouse-
Lautrec,[1656] became 'rather squalid'[1657] and were denounced by Léon Taxil
in 1891 as 'nothing else to-day but great festivals of pederasty'. The
Concours de Masques au Bal de l'Opéra was held on the 13th February
1897 with a jury including Toulouse-Lautrec, Willy, Willette,[1658] Jules
Renard,[1659] Arsène Alexandre, Tristan Bernard[1660] and Georges
Courteline[1661] 'who happened to be alive'[1662] (although given his status as a
fumiste, a practical joker, one might not be too sure).

For the more conservative, a whiff of scandal hung over the masked ball, for when in May 1893 madame de Ferronays wished to give one for charity, so many ladies declined that the occasion was a failure. Henry James went to the 1876 Opéra ball in ordinary evening clothes, and he declined an invitation to a costume ball at the Viardots when he understood that those in evening dress would be handed a kitchen boy's white hat and apron. Clement Scott saw it as realism out-realised. He writes

> Real private boxes, real curtains, hangings and real people in the *loges*, real trees and flowers, the floor of the mimic opera literally crammed with dancers and dominos, merriment and masks, pierrots and pierrettes, polichinelles, clowns and pantaloons, shepherdesses and *débardeurs*, ballets girls, monks, pilgrims and comic dogs.[1663]

Taking this as an accurate capturing of one of these balls (the emphasis on 'real' is a curious touch), many clues can be unpacked that suggest the dislocated: the snobbery implicit in leaving 'débardeurs' in French, the juxtaposition of ballet girls and monks. The 'floor of the mimic opera' reminds us that this was a play within a play, a double distancing. What was real? The spectator was continually faced with this puzzle. Meanings here are quite easily read: flights from reality into the grotesque suggest an unease with surface appearance completely different from that expressed in the English taste for pageants, and correspond with other Parisian characteristics, the sliding from light to dark, the omnipresence of mirrors, and even the establishment of Paris as a realm where the couturier was the magician-king.

The marquis de Briencourt had an affaire with a masked lady whose name he never knew; and according to Isidore de Lara, someone whom de Lara only identifies as the Prince de S [Sagan?], along with a Greek composer called Samora and de Lara himself, were entertained at dinner in a very grand house by three ladies who remained masked.[1664] In 1886, Henri Gervex exhibited a painting called 'La Femme au Masque' (her sole garment). This was the model Marie Renard, but the baron de Gast alleged that it was his sister in order to try to deprive her of an inheritance as a woman of dissolute morals. It was with no great originality therefore that Marcel Schwob in 1892 published a slender novel called *Le Roi au Masque d'Or* (described by Robert Sherard as 'the book of the day'[1665]) or that Emilienne d'Alençon published a volume of poems in 1915 under the title *Sous La Masque*.

Given the epigrammatic as well as the symbolic dimension of the relationship of mask to face, there was much here to intrigue Wilde.[1666] Had he not once told Olive Schreiner that he lived in the West End because 'nothing in life interests me except the mask'?[1667] Wilde's own involvement with fancy dress was a complex one. As an Oxford undergraduate he had gone to Mrs George Morrell's ball as Prince Rupert, recalling that Oxford was Royalist during the Civil War: a curious choice for anyone other than a Jacobite. It also seems the case that part of the attraction of becoming a freemason for Wilde was the curious dressing-up it involved, although this can hardly have been the motivation of his father. Moreover, at a masked ball given by the Alma-Tademas in 1881, Wilde was the only person not to wear a mask: 'The Tademas think this most conceited of him and beg that everyone will tease him as much as possible,' noted Edmund Gosse.[1668]

People donned new guises even without resorting to fancy dress, of course. When W.E. Henley[1669] went to Paris in August 1886, he stayed at the Hôtel Jacob in the rue Jacob, lunching with Rodin, Robert Louis Stevenson – who wished to write on Rodin – and the American painter Will Low at Lapérouse (a favourite with the Stevensons), where an excellent Château Pauillac could be had for two francs a bottle. This was their first meeting for eight years and Will Low wrote of it 'Everything conspired that evening to wipe away the eight intervening years and their many changeful events that had elapsed since we bade one another adieu in the parc Monceau. Henley [...] was this evening, and during the rest of his stay in Paris, blithe as a great over-grown schoolboy on holiday'.[1670]

The same note is struck by Caroline Jebb of drives to St Cloud or St Germain with her husband: 'On all such occasions his delight was as fresh as a boy's'.[1671] It is therefore not altogether surprising that one writer on Parnell came to the conclusion about his visit to Paris to see Victor Hugo that 'although a serious-minded expedition, it was also something of a jaunt to partake of the French salon atmosphere in La Belle Époque'.[1672] This view of Paris finds echoes at many levels.

> I have a distinct and charming recollection of a little 'escapade' to Paris and a stay of a fortnight in that brilliant city in May 1879. The present Dowager Duchess of Hamilton, then Marchioness of Hamilton, was my companion and we had the jolliest time imaginable.[1673]

After a three day Whitsuntide jaunt (the word again seems to be the *mot juste*) by F.C. Burnand, Linley Sambourne, Arthur À Beckett, Anstey Guthrie, Harry Furniss, E.K. Milliken and George du Maurier in May

1889, *Punch* brought out a supplement 'Mr Punch in Paris', which may be worth excavating: 'Poor Kiki, what fun he was at times like this,' recalled Burnand, making one's blood run cold. 'I never remember having seen him so boyish, so "Trilbyish", as on the occasion of our memorable trip to Paris.'[1674] 'Kiki' was of course du Maurier, not the French model 'Kiki de Montparnasse' who is the 'Violon d'Ingres' in Man Ray's photograph,[1675] (there is a model called Kiki Toulette in Leonard Merrick's story 'The Banquets of Kiki'.[1676]), nor Princess Alice of Monaco's monkey nor the duchesse d'Uzès' chihuahua, both called Kiki. 'Kiki' is argot for 'gullet', which is perhaps why the du Mauriers actually spelled it Kicky or Kycke.[1677]

Du Maurier and Guthrie (who as F. Anstey wrote *Vice Versa* [1678] and *Baboo Bannerjee B.A.*, the latter of which has fallen into deserved neglect while the former has not) shared a room at the hotel attached to Durand's Restaurant. Du Maurier reverted to true Parisian type by cutting a formal dinner at the Ambassadeurs and taking Guthrie 'on a long walk through the streets of Paris, which provided "local colour" but no food'.[1679] Unfortunately, Guthrie does not refer to this in his autobiography, although his remark that whenever Linley Sambourne was in Paris he took a morning walk down the Champs Elysées may relate to it.[1680]

This was in fact the third *Punch* expedition. In May 1886, Burnand, Furniss and du Maurier stayed at the Grand Hôtel for three days, du Maurier finding Burnand rather conventional in this setting.[1681] 'There is probably no place in all Paris that is less Parisian' than the Grand Hôtel's courtyard, thought Richard Harding Davis,[1682] but when Mrs Potter Palmer stayed there in June 1891 with a suite on the first floor overlooking the corner of the avenue de l'Opéra and the boulevard des Capucines,[1683] those with her thought that 'it was but the work of a moment to step out into the June day and be right over the gayest corner of the gayest street in Paris, with its multitudes of little tables, and its beautifully dressed promenaders.'[1684] Lord Acton had no substantial interest in Paris, and when he wanted books on French local history he engaged Paris booksellers to find them, but he was staying at the Grand Hôtel in November 1893.[1685]

Du Maurier himself describes the Grand Hôtel in this period in *Trilby*, comparing it to the days of the Empire

> little is changed in the aspect of the place: the same cosmopolite company, with more of the American element, perhaps; the same arrivals and

departures in railway omnibuses, cabs, hired carriages; and, airing his
calves on the marble steps, stood just such another colossal and beautiful
old man in black cloth coat and knee-breeches and silk stockings as of
yore, with probably the very same pinchbeck chain [...] and also the same
fine weather. It is always fine weather in the courtyard of the Grand
Hôtel.[1686]

The second *Punch* expedition was to the Expo of 1887: Henry Lucy (who
wrote Parliamentary sketches under the name 'Toby'); Furniss; W.H.
Bradbury; William Agnew; Burnand; À Beckett; John Tenniel; Milliken;
and du Maurier. A group photograph showing a good deal of
attitudinising, survives.[1687] There were doubtless other such visits, and we
know of one in 1895.

The *Punch* men could have found in their Paris much that was familiar,
including the pastimes of the overgrown schoolboy, for practical joking
was in Bohemia one of weapons used against bourgeois society,
translating the rhetoric of a Coupeau – 'Politics is nothin' but a big
joke'[1688] – into satirical but non-political opposition. René Berthelot, for
example, once managed to pass off on Fernand Gregh a spurious
'Entretiens avec Schopenhauer', which Gregh published in *Le Banquet*.
Alphonse Allais (known as 'Alfy') and his colleagues elevated this
'fumisme' into a cultural expression that broke out of the cabarets, thus
differing from the satire of pre-Nazi Berlin or 1960s London.[1689]
Essentially anarchic, and definitely evoking *l'esprit montmartrois*, it
helped undermine not only respectability but also authenticity.[1690] When
fumistes like Gabriel de Lautrec threw water out of carriages in the Bois de
Boulogne so that the fish could have somewhere to sit, the first stirrings of
Dada may be discerned, and of Theatre of the Absurd. With Gus Bofa[1691]
and Roland Dorgelès, then a young journalist in pursuit of sensation,
Lautrec founded *La Petite Semaine*, 'the only daily weekly [*quotidien
hebdomadaire*] magazine in the world'. Lautrec's cousin Henri exhibited
a painting under the name Tolau-Segroeg called 'The Batignolles Three
and a Half Years before Jesus Christ' at the Exposition des Arts
Incohérents in 1886; Tolau-Segroeg was described as a Hungarian from
Montmartre, who lived in the rue Yblas under the third lamp post on the
left, a pupil of 'Pubis de Cheval'. This was the *esprit* which created the
Club de La Clay-Pipe, which had three presidents (Satie, George Auriol
and Georges Delaw) but no members; the *esprit* which caused Laurent
Tailhade, Ernest Raynaud and Maurice du Plessys to write and publish
poems by 'Mitrophane Crapoussin'. Neither name seems necessarily more
unlikely than that of Onésime Pouydebat, author of *De L'Inspectorat Des*

Eaux Minérales; and the articles by General Boulanger in *La Revue Décadent* are by Raynaud. Here names, nations, places, time and even the elements enter a vortex of unmeaning.

One may discern this as an outgrowth of the practical joking, and of the ragging that took place as initiation of the *nouveaux* in the art schools, described by du Maurier, Robert Louis Stevenson, Shirley Fox and others. *Fumisme* reached its high point, however, when a picture of a sunset over the Adriatic[1692] by Boronali was accepted for exhibition in the 1910 Salon des Indépendants, and the painter's name found its way into dictionaries of artists. Boronali was Aliboron, or Lolo, the donkey belonging to Frédé Gérard at the Lapin Agile, and the painting had been produced by tying a paintbrush to his tail (*aliborno* means jackass). The idea was that of Dorgelès (whose real name was Roland Lecavelé) and arranged by five Montmartrois *fumistes*.[1693] This perhaps was the last moment when the Lapin Agile adhered to the old Hydropathes' *esprit montmartrois*, rather than its subsequent, tourism-driven version.

Another expression of *fumisme* was when Paul Masson (a friend of Willy and Colette, and known as Lemice-Ternieux, but 'unknown to-day'[1694]) sent a questionnaire to the luminaries of the day asking for the 'phrases, interjections ou onomatopées' they used during 'les heures d'extase', 'heures' presumably intended satirically. But it was Allais who first painted 'The Anæmic Girl having Her First Communion in a Snowstorm', an all white canvas, 'Negroes Fighting in a Cave at Night', an all black canvas, and 'Apoplectic Cardinals Harvesting Tomatoes on the Shore of the Red Sea', an all red one, their titles perhaps guying Degas' 'Peasant Girls Bathing In The Sea At Dusk', and it was Allais who reinvented Carjat, Léon Valade and Henri Dierx as Orgeat, Limonade and Bière. Something fictive about Allais is discerned by the Frèches, who call him 'a character straight out of a novel by the Goncourts'; but for Jane Avril, he had the manner of an English foreman.[1695]

In the person of Gabriel de Lautrec, *fumisme* combined the world of the Bohemian with that of the dandy. There was something sardonic even in his assuming this rôle: he should have liked to have been a painter, but the name was already taken. He arrived in Paris from Béziers in 1889, 'svelte et élégant, portant monocle – il est vicomte – et fumant le cigare.'[1696] Smoking seems to have been a dandy's appurtenance – Maurice Agulhon says of Aristide Briand[1697] that he was 'a brilliant forty year-old bachelor, somewhat Bohemian and indolent, with a casual hairstyle, cigarette in hand',[1698] and this may help explain Wilde's chain smoking when he could

afford gold-tipped cigarettes. (The other signs of the dandy, and indeed of
any gentleman, were the buttonhole and of course the cane, 'obligatory
symbolic attribute of the man of leisure taking a walk',[1699] with both Wilde
and Whistler setting especial store by theirs.) As for monocles, Marie
Bashkirtseff observed acutely that 'A Frenchman always seems to me to
be dissecting things with a long instrument held delicately between his
fingers and a magnifying glass in his eye'.[1700]

Lautrec made the acquaintance of Alphonse Allais at the Chat Noir, but it
was his *Poèmes en prose* of 1898 that opened the literary doors to him.
Prose poems? Oscar Wilde had once made something of this genre.
Holding court at Passy, Lautrec received Wilde, Jean Lorrain, Willy, Jean
de Tinan, Alfred Jarry and Paul Verlaine; and he watched at the deathbed
of this last, whom he had first met at a café in the rue Soufflot[1701]
(presumably the Taverne du Panthéon).   Lautrec also had an almost
serious side, for at the suggestion of Marcel Schwob (another café
acquaintance) he translated Mark Twain into French, and with Henry-D.
Davray, Arthur Ransome's book on Wilde.[1702]

Part 2: The Dancer and the Dance

ANDRÉ Gill wrote

> Il semble que Paris en rut,   Et qu'on entend, reins cassés,
> Apres les avoir polluées,   Un bastringue de trépassés,
> Rejette au lieu de leur début   Dans le Moulin de la Galette.
> Les ombres des prostituées.   Chahuter, parmi la tempête,

The 'chahut' was a development of the cancan, although not so inhibited:
'roughly speaking, the *cancan* died with the Bal Mabille, the *chahut* was
born with the Jardin de Paris'.[1703] Its striking representation by Seurat
(1889-1890) is described as 'not a direct representation of reality, but a
sample of Seurat's ideas about art'.[1704] The Bal Mabille in the avenue
Montaigne,[1705] which closed in 1876, had been the original haunt of
Valentin le Désossé, together with dancers remembered only as 'le Dinde',
'la Toquée', and 'le Bébé'. It was expensive for men, cheap for women –
that is, it attracted poor women and well-to-do men, the constituents of a
'pick-up' place. Cocottes who were regulars included Rose Pompon and
'la Reine Pomaré' who makes an appearance, anachronistically old and
ruined in *Nana*. And where was the cancan born? Synonymous with the
Paris of the period though it was, the answer, it appears, is in London in

1861, invented by Charles Morton for the music hall, though Ralph Nevill says that it 'achieved immense popularity in the thirties', first introduced to Parisian balls by Charles La Battut, 'Milord Arsouille'. 'Up to this time it was unknown outside low suburban dancing-places.'[1706] The *danseuse* Rigolboche is credited with its Parisian form by Brewer's Dictionary, but this seems a confusion between the cancan and the chahut.[1707] The cancan was known, even in France, as the French Cancan (pronounced 'frawnsh'), and this is the title that Jean Renoir gave to his 1954 film about the Moulin Rouge. The film ends with a bacchanalian dance, not at all the high-kicking but disciplined dancing in line that usually represents the cancan, with the dancers showing knickers rather than pantalettes.

> Tandis que les britanniques sont particulièrement *schoking* par cette pratique à la limite de l'indécence, à Paris la popularité du Cancan ne cesse de grandir. Ses formes se dessinent petit à petit: une danse ritualisée, exclusivement féminine où tout est dans l'art de faire le grand écart et de soulever ses dentelles.[1708]

The public dance halls represented the conspicuous side of ecstatic dance, which in formal and private settings had begun with the polka, introduced in March 1844 by a dancing master in the rue Vivienne known as 'Le Grand Cellarius'.[1709] This was followed by the mazurka, the redowa and the schottisch. Paris dancing, a carnivalesque concept, is very much part of the construction of Paris the gay city, a popular diversion linked to the masked and fancy dress balls. Given the very high number of non-native Parisians, dances from places of origin were both socially cohesive yet unsettling to conformity. In the cabarets there was of course the convention that the prostitutes were dancing partners, and at some point the *thé dansant* allowed the mirror image, a distorted image perhaps, of the gigolo as dancing partner. Here more illusion was fostered.

Public dance halls, which were very numerous, catered to all classes (though not at the same time). Even the rag-pickers had their own dance hall, the Bal du Vieux-Chêne in the rue Mouffetard. Clearly, etiquette differed from the rough and ready to the over refined, and confirmed the demarcation between the folk dances of the countryside, which could be danced on grass or on beaten earth floors, and of the city, with wooden floors; between dances where management, participants and audience were all the one, and where musicians were hired, profits made, behaviour regulated. It was a combination of Dionysiac freedom and controlled and commodified formality.[1710]   At the Bal des Grands Pavillons in the rue de Ménilmontant, for example, 'a man who wished

to dance with a girl first presented her with a rose, which he sent by a
waitress. If the recipient were willing, she pinned the flower to her
bodice'.[1711] Some dance halls, like the Salle Giffard, also in the rue de
Ménilmontant, were used for clandestine political meetings; while
dances could reveal the fault lines in the social order even within classes.
At the Domestic Servants' Ball held at the Salle Wagram in 1898, 'it was
remarked that the younger, more coquettish chambermaids clearly
enjoyed dancing the waltz or the quadrille, while the heavier, more
gauche-looking cooks looked on enormously'.[1712]

Charles Rearick suggests that in the 1880s the dance halls were in decline
under pressure from the cabarets or cafés concerts, which implies that this
leisure activity was becoming more intimate and conceivably more
private, enjoyed in smaller groups. Margrethe McLeod, or Mata Hari,
arriving in Paris in 1903 with her 'eastern' dances performed for private
clients, took full advantage of this trend, and like Maud Allan helped form
our notion of the *pas seul* danced by Salomé. This was matched by the
way that the 'couple dance', with body contact, was being advanced by the
tango (1895),[1713] and in the new century by the cakewalk (1903), the
maxixe (1904)[1714] and the foxtrot (1912), beginning that *défi américain* to
which no end is in sight: 'In 1900 – and indeed for many years afterwards
– nobody in Paris knew how to dance,' is the astonishing remark of one
American, adding 'at least none of the society people could dance as we
Americans understood dancing.'[1715] This meant the boston and the one-
step.

The decline in 'bals publics' must be chiefly related to Paris, as Michael
Marrus has noted that in 1900 there were still hundreds of them in France
in general,[1716] '*bals du quartier* where we danced with simple-minded
damsels who thought *choucroute garnie* a generous supper and a bottle of
vin cacheté as setting the seal of all that was most distinguished upon the
host'.[1717] The Coupeau wedding party in *L'Assommoir* dines at the
'Moulin d'Argent', where the company join in 'Le Marchand de
moutarde', 'a quadrille with a lot of hand-clapping in the country-dancing
style' played by a cornet and two fiddles.[1718] Maupassant with some
distaste described an informal dance at the *guingette* 'Le Grillon' in 'La
femme de Paul'.

> Couples faced each other and capered about madly, kicking their legs as
> high as their partners' noses. The women, who appeared to have double-
> jointed legs and hips, leapt about in a frou-frou of lifted skirts, flashing
> their knickers and kicking their legs up over their heads with amazing

agility [...] The males cavorted and turned cartwheels, posturing meanwhile in hideous parody.[1719]

Names like Bal Tabarin, Bal Mabille, Bal Bullier reflect their origins in the public dance hall; while Renoir's 'Bal à Bougival' refers to the week-end exodus beyond the suburbs by the *banlieusards* in pursuit of pleasurable public dancing.[1720] Trilby and her British friends go to Meudon for the dancing at 'la loge du garde champêtre' where transformation again takes place:

> Trilby on this occasion came out in a new character, en demoiselle [...] To look at [...] she might have been the daughter of an English Dean – until she undertook to teach the Laird some favourite cancan steps. And then the Laird himself [became] no longer like the son of a worthy, God-fearing, Sabbath-keeping Scotch solicitor.[1721]

> The roughest of these entertainments, the *bals des barriers*,[1722] took place beyond city limits, 'where the criminal classes enjoyed their brief leisure.[1723]

The provision of chorus lines of dancers at the cabarets further divided participants from spectators, and, eccentrics like Valentin le Désossé aside, dancing became part of the commercial régime, with women dancing-partners for hire. 'Dancing could no longer be a visible sign of class and good breeding,' writes one of its few historians for this period. 'In dance, as in many aspects of life, there were obvious signs of an aristocratic society in ruins'.[1724] More than that: Zola created a connection between dancing, hysteria and madness when he made the comte de Viarge dance when he becomes mad at the end of *Madeleine Férat*, and the working class Coupeau performs a sort of parodic dance when in the throes of delirium tremens in *L'Assommoir*.

~~~~~~~

Into this mêlée was inserted one of the most remarkable of the Paris Americans, Loïe Fuller, called by Rodin 'the lovely modern Tanagra' and by Arthur Symons 'the flaming firefly'.[1725] Mallarmé wrote that she was not a woman, but a sign. Fuller, who had moved into the Grand Hôtel in late October 1892, made her début at the Folies Bergères on the 5th of November of that year, and took Paris by storm. Although she was something of a frump herself, 'men's as well as women's clothes were affected, and boulevardiers were wearing Loïe Fuller hats, scarves and ties'.[1726] Fuller was back at the Folies Bergères on the 20th October 1893 and appeared there until the summer of 1894 (Wilde was in Paris in April and May of that year). After staying at the Grand Hôtel, she moved to a cottage of the avenue Henri-Martin in Passy. After a performance at the École des Beaux Arts on the 23rd March 1895, she had been pelted with violets and her horse removed from the shafts of her cab in that most typical of all pre-1914 gestures of audience adulation, having her carriage pulled by a cheering crowd.

Fuller inspired an article that W.E. Henley published in London ('Considérations sur l'Art du ballet et la Loïe Fuller') by Mallarmé himself;[1727] she was imitated by Émilienne d'Alençon and Caroline Otero; she was asked to dance at the American Legation; she was admired by Camille Mauclair and Jules Clarétie; she was drawn by Whistler; she was taken up by Roger Marx. 'One is tempted,' wrote this last, 'to imagine that she found her inspiration and her model on ancient Greece, since she so much reminds one of a Tanagra figure'.[1728] Did any of this strike a chord with Wilde? It would afford a reading of the mysterious stage instruction 'Salomé dances the dance of the seven veils' that does not include removing the veils. 'La Loïe' seems to be an interesting yardstick against which to measure Oscar's impact: on Paris, on fashion, on Mallarmé, on painters and sculptors. 'It was said at the time that she may well have been portrayed by more distinguished artists than any other woman in modern history.'[1729] Her swirling draperies became part of the imagery of art nouveau: she was admired by Émile Gallé, Lalique and Tiffany, and transformed into lamps by Raoul Larche.[1730] The Pathé trick film *Métamorphose du papillon* of 1904 seems[1731] to feature her. Yeats recalled

> When Loïe Fuller's Chinese dancers enwound
> A shining web, a floating ribbon of cloth,
> It seemed that a floating dragon of air
> Had fallen among the dancers, had whirled them round
> Or hurried them off on its own furious pace.

It was not always success, however. Her *Salomé* (with music by Pierné[1732]) at the Comédie Parisienne from 4th March to 27th April 1895 had earned a rebuke from Jean Lorrain. Her performance, he wrote was 'luminous without grace, with gestures of an English boxer and the physique of Mr Oscar Wilde. [...] A Salomé for Yankee drunkards'.[1733] Yet even this seems to indicate the amount of illusion that Fuller could create, for Wilde was a six-footer and Fuller was short and dumpy, as shown in the photograph of her taken at about this time by Samuel Beckett.[1734] Again, the note of transformation is struck: 'so plain offstage [...] onstage [...] transfiguration'.[1735]

By then she was well enough known to have her wax figure placed in the Musée Grévin;[1736] of this her biographers say that it gave 'an effect so lifelike and realistic as to be quite startling'.[1737] This seems the appropriate Parisian metamorphosis for somebody whose stage success depended upon illusion produced with light, smoke and mirrors, who so subsumed herself in her art that it was said that 'it was not Loïe Fuller as a person who was the art nouveau dream, but rather the vision she created'.[1738] Certainly her use of light is symbolic of Impressionism; her use of dance, an impression of Symbolism. One interviewer 'expected to meet not a woman but some kind of mythological creature'.[1739] Even so, Fuller's theatre in the rue de Paris on the Expo site (near the place de l'Alma), which opened on the 25th June 1900, was a financial failure.

Part 3: 'C'est "shokin'" ça?'

THE power of masquerade was not simply that it was transformative, but that it was also frequently transgressive. Lurking in twilight zones, it evoked the reaction of shock, experienced as either *frisson* or disgust. Nevertheless, one needs to be cautious: those who were easily shocked might find shocking, or affect to find shocking, (or affect not to find shocking), performances that would now appear very anodyne indeed. The first striptease in Paris was 'Le Coucher d'Yvette' at the Divan Fayanon[1740] in the rue des Martyrs on the 13th March 1894, a sort of 'what the butler saw', hardly arousing to anyone more sophisticated than a lubricious schoolboy.[1741] Toulouse-Lautrec's 'Monsieur Prudhomme' was possibly one of these.[1742] It is significant for the identification of English hypocrisy in French eyes that whereas the comtesse de Loynes could move from street-walker to salonnière, when the Foreign Minister, the supple Charles de Freycinet, proposed as Ambassador in London a man 'married to a lady whose antecedents were not considered to be satisfactory', the Foreign Office indicated that he would not be *persona grata*.[1743] Jules Renard made a link between two versions of hypocrisy: 'In this Oscar Wilde affair, if there is something more comical than the indignation of all England, it is the show of being shocked on the part of certain Frenchmen with whom we are all acquainted.'[1744]

Mademoiselle Tusini of the Eldorado sang a song called 'Les Allumettes du Général' which was said not to be suitable for mixed company, but this was an age less robust, more innocent, when for example Leonard Jerome could naïvely address his wife as Mrs Clit.

> On the one hand, I am allowed a most convenient liberty of action on the ground the plea *c'est une jeune fille anglaise*; on the other, I am supposed, if true to my nationality, to be always in an attitude of shocked prudery. They are, however, pathetically off the track as to what really shocks English susceptibilities. '*C'est "shokin'"* *ça*?' they inquire anxiously of something wholly inoffensive, but the next minute without a qualm will say what makes you feel as if six thousand years of civilisation had been suddenly blown away.[1745]

This exchange ran deep in the hermetic construction of national identities on both sides of the Channel: 'I know no immoral plays,' said Dumas *fils*, 'I know only ill-made plays',[1746] a phrase which doubtless read all very well in Paris, but rather less so when Oscar Wilde used it in the witness box in answer to Edward Carson.   Writing as well into the twentieth century as 1913, Francis Gribble prefers not to use the phrase 'a kick on the backside', writing instead 'what the French call *un coup de pied quelque part*'.[1747]   C'est shokin', ça? Marie Belloc, to protect the morals of her visitors ('it was in no way suitable for survival in a respectable English home'[1748]) tore each page of Pierre Louÿs' *Aphrodite* into little pieces and burned them one by one – although she was inquisitive enough to read them first. This is not the only controversial part played by *Aphrodite*. When Wilde was arrested, it was widely reported that this was 'with a yellow book under his arm'. The public took this to be a reference to The Yellow Book, and the windows of the publisher, John Lane, were accordingly broken by the decent people. 'Actually,' Montgomery Hyde tells us, 'the book which Oscar Wilde was carrying was [...] *Aphrodite*, which happened to have a yellow cover'.[1749] 'Actually' in this context is an interesting usage: Wilde was arrested at the Cadogan Hotel in London on the 5th April 1895; *Aphrodite*, written at Judith Gautier's retreat at Saint-Enogat on the outskirts of Dinard and dedicated to Albert Besnard, was first printed on 20th March 1896 and placed for sale in the bookshops in Paris on the 28th.   Given the circumstances of the birth of the mythical Aphrodite, the involvement of the book with her name with Wilde may be poetic, but it is not justice. Twenty years after Wilde's arrest, Richard Le Gallienne added another ingredient to all this, writing that 'when Oscar Wilde went arrogantly to his trial in a lordly carriage and pair, he appeared on the witness stand with a copy of The Yellow Book under his arm'.[1750] David Pierce joins the circle: refuting the idea that it was The Yellow Book, he says that Wilde went into court carrying a copy of *Aphrodite*.[1751]

Marie Belloc also records a dinner party – herself, the Ranee of Sarawak, Princess Alice of Monaco, Lady Helmsley and Sir Frank Swettenham – where 'the talk was rather free, much of it in French'.[1752] This sounds like the decent obscenity of a learned language, but one may judge that it fell well short of 'that modern *esprit gaulois* which would make the good Rabelais turn uneasily in his grave and blush there like a Benedictine Sister'.[1753] Maupassant ambivalently refers to 'the natural taste of Parisian audiences for faintly bawdy entertainment, for rather smutty elegance, for what is pseudo-pretty and pseudo-graceful, like café-concert singers and songs from operettas'.[1754]

If the English thought the French immoral, the French were certainly aware of the Puritanism of the English, and Brander Matthews left an account of the Théâtre du Palais Royal that neatly joins the two:

> The daughter cannot take her mother to the little theatre in the Palais Royal; nor do you ever see there young ladies not married, either *de jure* or *de facto*. Innocent English families, ignorant of the freedom of speech existing there, frequently quit the theatre before the close of performance, horrified. More than once have French authors, at a loss to raise a laugh, placed among the audience as party of actors caricaturing the English, who at a certain point blushingly rise and leave the house, murmuring 'Shoking! shoking!'[1755]

Elaine Aston has argued for the responsibility of Sarah Bernhardt in contributing to this in the overt sexuality she brought in particular to her Lady Macbeth (well-captured in the 1892 portrait of Bernhardt in the rôle by Franz von Lenbach[1756]) and Cleopatra.

> A Victorian public could happily deceive itself into thinking that it went to the theatre out of the purest of motives; to see a great artist in an adaptation of a classic text. In reality it went with the craving of a sexually repressed society to see an actress who, with all her charms, subverted the Victorian ideology of passive femininity, of the sexless female. It was virtually impossible for an English actress to achieve the same image with impunity because it was Sarah's 'Frenchness' or her Parisian aura which distanced sufficiently in the eyes of the puritan from the notion of chaste and virginal womanhood.[1757]

It has to be remembered that 'there was not yet any question of thighs', that even at the Folies Bergère, which had been founded in 1869, breasts (Colette's) were not bared before 1907, and that it was not until 1925 that Josephine Baker appeared at the Théâtre de Champs-Elysées 'vêtue s'une simple ceinture de bananes'.[1758] (I am inclined to be sceptical about

Brander Matthews' report of Mdlle Delval at the Porte St-Martin 'robed only in her innocence and a halo of electric light'.[1759]) The corps de ballet danced to the music of Messager as shepherdess and swain rather than strip-tease. Douglas Dawson, arranging an evening for the Prince of Wales, thought that a box at the Folies Bergère could suitably follow dinner at the Jockey Club.[1760] Affect to find shocking: when in October 1897 Arnold Bennett visited the Folies to see Loïe Fuller and Cinquevalli, it was 'with the expressed intention of studying the audience'.[1761] Mario Borsa, writing in 1908, noted that the Moulin Rouge or the Folies Bergère were more décolleté than the London music halls, but the latter were more vulgar.[1762]

Maurice Delsol, in his *Paris-Cythère* of 1896, referred to 'the old English ladies and the young misses [...] who sit always in the front row in order better to ascertain the immorality of the French dances'.[1763] This is further explored in the episode 'A Café chantant' in Constance Maud's novelette *An English Girl in Paris*: 'I saw Edith Rogers' programme erected between her face and hands more than once: but a fatal fascination to see what the shameless one was doing invariably drew the barricade down before long'.[1764] But even Phil May's 'Arry is shown blushing behind his hand at the Moulin Rouge.

> The café concerts are among the most popular of Parisian amusements [...] They are, I believe, quite the most demoralising of Parisian entertainments. I have never been able to understand a word of what the performers were saying, but I am told that the songs are so vulgar and so indelicate that it is incomprehensible why they are tolerated.[1765]

Affect to find shocking: of places like the Chat Noir or the Rat Mort, Ernest Vizetelly wrote that 'it must be admitted that whilst they are frequented by certain classes of Frenchmen, they owe much of their success in a pecuniary sense to the patronage of foreigners. Among the latter, Englishmen are particularly conspicuous.'[1766]

Du Maurier understood this well enough. His hero Taffy Wynne is persuaded to take his wife to the 'Mouches d'Espagne' in the boulevard Poissonnière to hear Madame Cantharidi, as being funny without being vulgar. La Cantharidi

> in private life is 'quite the lady', but on the stage – well, go and see her, and you will understand how she comes to be the idol of the Parisian public [...] She amused them all through the Empire; during the *année*

terrible she was their only stay and comfort, and has been their chief
delight ever since and is now [...]

Mrs Taffy is a poor French scholar. One must know French very well
indeed (and many other things besides) to seize the subtle points of
Madame Cantharidi's play (and by-play!) […] So heartily does she laugh
that a good Parisian bourgeois turns round and remarks to his wife 'V'là
une jolie p'tite Anglaise qui n'est pas bégueule, au moins! Et l'gros bœuf
avec les yeux bleus en boules de loto – c'est son mari, sans doute! Il n'a
pas l'air trop content par exemple, celui-là!'

The fact is that the good Taffy (who knows French very well indeed) is
quite scandalised […]

In identifying the 'good Parisian bourgeois', du Maurier here is as
observant as Maupassant, whose successful journalist Forestier looks
down on the café-concert: 'The café concert may amuse my pharmacist
and his wife, but not me'.[1767] The Wynnes leave after the first act: the
accompanying illustration shows the French audience (male and female)
laughing immoderately, Mrs Wynn smiling pleasantly ('to the pure,' said
Wilde, 'all things are obscure') and Taffy indeed staring furiously.[1768]
Affect to find shocking: Dorothy Menpes as Mrs Grundy did manage to
bring herself to name some of the offending women, and managed too to
get their names slightly wrong: 'Mimi patte-en-l'air', 'Sauterelle',
'Mouch-d'Or' – as well as one not mentioned in other sources, 'Zizi',
Dorothy Menpes surely innocent of its argot meaning of a penis.

Maupassant's story 'The Mask' opens in the Elysée-Montmartre where the
regular clientèle is described as coming

from the four corners of Paris, people of all classes, who like their
pleasures vulgar and noisy, stimulated by alcohol and not quite respectable
[…] Clerks, pimps, and girls of every grade, from cotton frocks to silks and
satins, girls with money, no longer young, and covered with diamonds,
sixteen-year-olds without a penny, only in search of a good time, wanting
to pick up a man and have money to throw about. Men in full evening
dress, on the lookout for something young, not quite virginal perhaps but
still attractive, were prowling rounded the heated throng, like hounds on
the scent.[1769]

'It is significant,' says Philippe Jullian, that 'a party to celebrate the
success of *L'Assommoir* should have been held at the Elysée-
Montmartre',[1770] and indeed the Elysée-Montmartre is referred to in Zola's
novel, set on the eastern periphery of Montmartre, in the deliberately
unedifying simile of the blacksmith's hammer dancing off the anvil 'like a

dancing-girl at the Elysée-Montmartre showing her knickers'.[1771] It was at the *Assommoir* party that George Moore met Zola for the first, and Turgenev for the first and last, time'.[1772]

There were plenty of knickers to be shown: those of Georgette la Vaudrouille, Nini (or Nana) la Sauterelle, Brise du Soir and La Torpille among them. The Elysée-Montmartre became steadily nastier: 'Here, nightly, now gathered the perverts, the pimps, and birds of prey', in such numbers that the management were forced to engage a sort of bouncer, known as 'Père Pudeur' to keep order. (His real name was Courtelet du Roche,[1773] a photographer by day, and he also seems to have been known as 'Pierre le Pudeur'.[1774]) Thirty years after the Elysée-Montmartre closed, Ralph Nevill (a frequent customer, perhaps because few English went there) wrote that he 'well remembers the unrestrained gaiety which pervaded the place'.[1775] Those ejected presumably went on to resorts like the Bal des Gravilliers 'above all frequented by malefactors, pimps and girls of low standing'.[1776] All this led to 'a tawdry kind of satanism' as a commercial lure to provincials, 'a mixture of piety, viciousness, cultural refinement and superstition', which Jullian sees as personified in the form of Max Jacob, Jean Lorrain's successor in the new century as the epitome of the decadent, ether-drinking homosexual.1777 Not unnaturally, it was to the advantage of many to turn Paris itself – Paris herself – into a commodity.

Augustus Saint-Gaudens described a sketch that he found in questionable taste at another café concert: an actor dressed as a new born baby gazes about him, exclaims 'O quel sale monde!' and stabs himself declaring 'Je rentre dans le Néant' – 'That's pessimism with a vengeance,' is Saint-Gaudens' laconic comment[1778] – but this play on words – néant is 'nothingness' – also refers to a rival house, the Cave du Néant, described by Alexandre Benois as 'the lowest'[1779] of the cabarets. While the primary meaning of *néant* is nothingness, its relation with 'being' a Sartreian trope, one can also read it as linking the suffix that signifies the present participle ('-ant', '-ing') with the past participle of *naître*, né, born. Thus the Cave du Néant has a multiple decadent connotation, coupling the newborn and therefore innocent *idea* with the degraded *object*, a reification of the finding of the 'nouveau' when one has plunged into the depths, the Cave or cellar, flinging Baudelaire in the face of Mallarmé. Filson Young, naming this place the Cabaret des Néants, calls it 'that sordid little place so well-known to travelling Americans and to the natives of Montmartre, but comparatively little known to Englishmen and ordinary Parisians', but the description that follows is of the Cabaret de Morts, with its 'entertainment like some nasty sport of vicious and overgrown children'.[1780]

Even Zola found the Bal Robert, in the impasse du Cadran, 'very disgusting',[1781] which did not stop him from combining it with the Chat Noir and turning it into the 'Chamber of Horrors', in the boulevard Rochechouart. 'It was a suffocating place, narrow, irregular, with all sorts of twists, turns and secluded nooks [...] There was no luxury no artistic feature, no cleanliness even. Globeless gas burners flared freely, heating a dense mist compounded of tobacco smoke and human breath.'[1782] Here the singer 'Legras' shocks and scandalises an audience there to be shocked and scandalised, like the aristocrats and bankers in Zola's account or, in real life, Gyp de Martel, in search of material but also realising her own taste for low company and, perhaps, driven by her problematic sexuality.[1783]

This slumming – *s'encanailler* – was widespread. We read of Frederick Delius indulging 'a decided pleasure for low life, and it is hard to resist the impression that he had been digging into *Les Mystères de Paris* as much for enlightenment as for amusement. Dressed in his oldest and shabbiest clothes he frequented all sorts of dubious quarters'.[1784] The Lapin Agile is described even by the scrupulously non-judgmental John Milner as 'enjoying very mixed company'; it had formerly been called the Cabaret des Assassins, run by a dancer called Adèle, the partner of Jules Jouy.[1785] He sold it to the chansonnier Aristide Bruant[1786] in 1903 and it was run for Bruant by Frédéric Gérard ('Frédé'), proprietor of an estaminet called Zut in the place de Ravignan,[1787] who subsequently acquired it. The Lapin Agile derived its name from its sign (là, peint à Gill), the drawing of a rabbit by André Gill, whose real name was de Guines (hence Pierre Mac-Orlan's insistence on calling it the Lapin à Gill and Elliot Paul's 'the Lapin à Gil [not *Agile*]'[1788]), and it is also possible to scry a covert reference to Maeterlinck's *Tintagiles*. The association between Gill and this *estaminet* follows neatly on his having illustrated the 1878 edition of *L'Assommoir*.

Ralph Nevill refers to the Boule Noir, on the corner of the boulevard Rochechouart and of the rue des Martyrs, popular with the *lorettes* in the 1860s, which 'fell on very evil days and at its demolition in 1885 there were no regrets'.[1789] In 1879 Augustin Daly went to a masked ball at Frascati's[1790] 'and saw the can-can on its native floor. A beastlier exhibition cannot be shown anywhere. Argyle Rooms in London was a sort of paradise to that place'.[1791] The rue des Martyrs was also home to

L'Âne Rouge, described by Richard Whiteing as the Chat Noir and Rat Mort 'in palingenesia';[1792] it was run by Rodolphe Salis' younger brother Gabriel and closed in 1898. George Moore sought out the Château Rouge, where on Sherard's visit 'thieves and the saddest daughters of joy listened to the obscene songs of a frightful old noseless hag',[1793] as well as the Rat Mort, the Elysée-Montmartre and the Bal Bullier.

There was often something of the innocent about English visits to such wicked places, and about the English assumption of wickedness. This was the view of Edmund Gosse, who thought that the poets of the 1890s were self-consciously trying to shock the country rectory or scandalise the manse. 'The passage of a maiden aunt would have snatched any one of them from the absinthe which in reality he so much disliked and would have re-installed him at the tea-table', Gosse wrote. Apart from its tribute to the dragon aunt, this perhaps is self-serving, for one remembers Gosse's prim withdrawal from The Crown when entertaining Verlaine became a little too uninhibited – but then, even the *mondain* Harry de Windt, meeting Verlaine in Montmartre, wished he hadn't. According to Marcel Boulestin, visiting London, the English Bohemian was a Bohemian on a domestic scale, in general being

> a charming companion, sensible and intelligent, hardly different from several other charming young men I had met, but he took pleasure in dressing badly and thought it his duty to despise well-tied ties, patent-leather shoes and correct hats [...] but none of them would dream of cheating his landlady like the primitive and rather dreadful Parisians of Murger. And the poorer specimens would suddenly drop their Bohemianism at 12.45 (and 11.30 on Sunday) to catch the last Tube back to Earl's Court or West Kensington.[1794]

Nor did *la vie de bohème* play a part in English student life, not even among art students. It was Morris's invigorating of Pre-Raphaelitism by socialism that 'took', ignored in the *Punch* view of æstheticism though this was. 'Instead of velvet jackets and a slap-dash joviality, young artists took to *saeva indignatio* and sandals.'[1795] At the dinner given for Rodin by the International Society of Painters, Sculptors and Engravers, Prince Troubetskoi said that he had come over to London 'expecting to find myself in a company of artists: I find myself in a company of gentlemen'.[1796] This was presumably intended as a compliment; it was certainly – and idiotically – taken as one. It was the difference between the Bal des Quatz'Arts and Boat Race Night or absinthe in a crystal glass and beer in a pewter tankard, between the champagne of the imagining and the 'great cups of steaming cocoa'[1797] served by Ricketts and Shannon.

The *Englishness* of the English 'Bodley Headsmen' is stressed by the publisher's historians.

> They were minor figures all and (except Wilde) proud to see themselves as such […] The lesser talents of the day turned every which way for escape – some looked across the Channel, involving second hand *nostalgie de la boue*, worshippers with absinthe as their so daringly sacrilegious communion wine, opium their incense, and the ludicrous tinsel of the music-halls their temples, stocked with accommodating vestals. These were proudly known as the Decadents, but in fact all the minor writers who made a mark of sorts in the world of, say, Kipling and Hardy and Henley were decadent. They lacked essential energy at best, substituting bluster. They were a symptom of a sick civilisation: not least those who […] conjured up an ideal Britain, all meadowsweet and roses and lush green pastures, into which the ghost of the great Pan, not to mention Cuchullain and the leprechaun, had been wistfully translated.[1798]

In the first issue of *The Savoy* (January 1896) Symons announced 'We are not Realists, or Romanticists, or Decadents'. Verlaine died on the eighth of that month, Wilde had been in Reading Gaol since the previous November and Symons' words resound like the blowing of the Last Post. 'Heartiness' did not need the fall of Wilde to triumph: the Brasenose of Walter Pater was already being succeeded by the brass neck of Rudyard Kipling, and shortly Stenbock would be superseded by Belloc, Sir Percy Blakeney by Sir Richard Hannay. 'There was little or no Bohemianism among the Slade students,' Rothenstein recalled, 'at least among those I consorted with. I cannot remember going to a restaurant, café or music hall during this first year in London'.[1799] At the Royal Academy Schools 'eccentricity of costume, for which art students were accused of having a weakness, was taboo in our set', although one student (unfortunately unnamed) wore 'the brown velveteen short jacket, black flowing bow-tie, waistcoat cut low and tight-fitting lavender-coloured trousers of fantasy.'[1800] It was little wonder that Paris both appealed and appalled.

When Isabella Stewart Gardner wanted a look at Bohemian Paris, Whistler asked Will Rothenstein to be her cicerone. This must have been in December 1891. Rothenstein took her to hear Yvette Guilbert, Xanrof and Aristide Bruant, and to Conder's studio. It was somewhat daring, for when Rothenstein first encountered Guilbert, his impression had been that although she was 'of virginal aspect, slender, pale, without rouge […] her songs were not virginal'.[1801] American reaction to her was not uniquely favourable. Robert Underwood Johnson and his wife listened to her in a café chantant in the Champs Elysées: 'Her voice fairly rang with pathos and feeling, and sounded like the wail of a mother for a child. We were much moved by it' – until its meaning became clearer.[1802] The United States Minister to Paris came to a more succinct view: 'I went to hear Yvette Guilbert, a celebrated singer and a *canaille* of the worst description.'[1803] Subsequently he was surprised to find her engaged to sing after dinner at a certain count's:

> Although I suppose she attempted to produce her more refined songs, they were vile beyond belief. She is quite ugly, but has the power of giving an air of indescribable vulgarity to any song. The French did not seem shocked in the least, and there were very respectable and excellent people there.[1804]

CHAPTER ELEVEN

THE ARTIST AS CRISIS

Part 1: Vision

'Was it for this that I fought, for this decomposition of light? Was I mad?'
– Émile Zola.[1805]

'Vive la Révolution! Vive Manet!'
– Henri de Toulouse-Lautrec.[1806]

'The artist becomes his own imitator.'
– Max Nordau.[1807]

THE opening years of the Third Republic, uncertain in their forms of political and economic transition, ensured a cultural and social instability, where contradiction and transgression could pass as a normal expression of the times. The loosening of political restraints that began with the overthrow of the Second Empire required in the arts the overthrow of the professors in the schools of art. As one historian has written, 'The grand old Academy masters, laden with years and honours, who alone had the power to judge whether an artist deserved a silver medal or mere praise, now became grotesque "officials", bereft of all prestige [...] After the decisive turning point of 1863 [the Salon des Refusés], the École failed to produce a single French artist.'[1808] The Salon des Refusés was of course an officially sanctioned exhibition, instigated by Napoléon himself. Thirty-six years after the Salon des Refusés, Paul Signac, writing in *La Revue blanche*, could still refer to the École's 'dismal influence'.[1809] The professors – at least those of the École des Beaux Arts – may have been bereft of prestige, but they still wielded considerable power, manifested in the rejection of the Caillebotte bequest to the nation of his Impressionist collection in 1894,[1810] creating a debate which in fact furthered the work of the painters concerned. This was a lengthy battle. Max Nordau saw it as one of revolt: 'In the last years of the Empire and the first of the Republic, great things occurred on the sacred hill of Montmartre, on the summit of which the Church of the Sacred Heart had not yet supplanted the Muses and Graces. A group of painters, diminishing in numbers, yet brave as lions, and pugnacious, arose in defence and attack against the official art of the Académie, the École des Beaux Arts and the Salon.'[1811] The undercurrents were, however, imperfectly realised by those experiencing them. 'Although we students did not realise it,' wrote A.S. Hartrick of his days at the Académie Julian, 'this was a time of change. The Impressionist Movement was coming into fashion and the Academicians of the salons were being cast down from their pedestals.'[1812] Part of that dethronement may be seen in the art itself: the application of paint by the Impressionists Monet, Sisley and Pissarro; by the Divisionists Seurat and Signac; and eventually by the Cloisonnists and the Cubists, involved a disintegration of the planes and perspectives of academicism. More, it required a switch from privileging the appearance of the thing painted to the experience and pre-occupation of the artist, representing a crisis of art both for the bourgeois who wished to own an artwork, and for the painter who wished to provide one.

The Académie Julian itself contributed to this process by offering a form of mass art instruction to hundreds of students who would never become successful, very possibly never again taking up brush or chisel once their Paris fling had ended. Art was part of the magnetic attraction of Paris and part of the belief in its ability to effect magic transformations. Zola lured there from Aix-en-Provence was never slow to create characters who followed his path – not Claude Lantier, merely, but for example Payan, first encountered as 'a stone-cutter just arrived from the South, whom his native town wanted to turn into an artist',[1813] or Jean Baudu, who is found a job in Paris as an apprentice ivory carver.[1814]

In her essay 'Liberal Democracy through Art Education',[1815] Miriam Levin discusses the system of art education introduced by the State into the school curriculum. She suggests that the teaching that 'perfection and balance in a product and in life consisted of the precision and balance attained among the various elements, not in the erasure of distinctions.' This offers a paradigm for society as a whole, one that was in tune with French liberal thinking back through de Tocqueville to Montesquieu. It required optimism as the prevailing *mentalité*, whereas Naturalism was essentially pessimistic;[1816] and the tension between, on the one hand, the art favoured by the State and its organs and the *art pompier* favoured by the bourgeoisie, exemplified as the notion of republican virtue residing in order and tranquillity, that is to say the moral republic, and, on the other hand, the oppositional art and rejectionist lifestyles of those who practised it – what I am calling the artist as crisis – is the counterpart in this area of the other tensions and conflicts that create the distinction between Paris and metaParis. At another level, this was a clash between the bourgeois republic, which was born middle-aged, and the 'joyeuse enfance'[1817] of its counter-culture. If nineteenth century Paris indeed was, as Richard Schiff has it, 'the chief testing ground for modernity and the central location of modernity's art',[1818] it was also, contemporanæously, where pre-modernity fought and sometimes won a series of rear guard actions. It was in the heavily symbolic year of 1889 that an artist was given the Grand Cross of the Légion d'Honneur for the first time; that the artist was Meissonier illustrates this point.

The École was still under the influence of the Académie des Beaux Arts, one of the five constituent academies of the Institut.[1819] Fourteen of the forty 'Immortals' were painters,[1820] and the leading academicians of this period are generally held to have been Bonnat, Meissonier, Benjamin-Constant, Detaille, Alexandre Cabanel and Cormon. The École, once characterised by Ingres as 'a place of perdition', still put enormous emphasis on drawing (painting had only been taught after the 1863 reforms), and women were still not admitted (when they were admitted in 1896, there were protests).[1821] Most important of all was the control over the Prix de Rome, awarded for history or historical landscape painting and carrying a four or five year residency at the Villa Medici. The elaborate selection process for this tended to discount individuality of style, while the requirement to produce a smooth, finely worked surface militated against experimentation in technique. It is little wonder that the Salon Nouveau of 1880, the Salon des Indépendants and the various women's salons were created to offer a different path to official approbation from that from the École. Given the prevalence of jokes about Academicians in London – jokes that were elderly even when Wilde made them – it is useful to discover that they did not order these matters better in France.

For all that, the Beaux-Arts remained the choice for those seeking official validation of their hopes, however illusory or ephemeral, that in Paris they would become artists. Thus, in Maupassant's 'A Night Out' the young Montmartre painter Romantin, for all his Bohemianism, has won a gold medal at the Salon and says that he has invited to the celebration at his studio in the boulevard de Clichy Bonnat, Guillemet,[1822] Gervex, Béraud, Ernest Hébert,[1823] Ernest Duez,[1824] Georges Clairin and Jean-Paul Laurens. Antony Ludovici, began at the studio of the classicist Émile Bin, and worked at the Académie Charles in the evening to draw from the nude, then went to the Beaux-Arts as pupil of Cabanel. Here he was a contemporary of Bastien-Lepage, Besnard, and Gervex. He then entered Gérôme's studio with Dagnan-Bouveret. It was to the Beaux-Arts also, where Shirley Fox (October 1882), Edward Stott and James Clark were his contemporaries, that Solomon J. Solomon betook himself in his yearning for a Paris training. 'It was in Paris that he found his true outlet, and Gallic influences remained with him throughout his life. Truly patriotic Englishman as he was the whole air of Paris delighted him.' There was nothing of the Bohemian about Solomon, who lodged with a Jewish family in the place des Vosges, 'then a good-class residential neighbourhood', and studied with Cabanel (a choice more apt than when Steer made it), under whose influence 'he almost became a French Academician'.[1825] This is perhaps why, despite being elected R.A. in 1894 at the age of thirty-four, despite his portraits of Prince Lucien Bonaparte, and Mrs Patrick Campbell as Mrs Tanqueray, even despite his illustrations for books by G.A. Henty, he has passed into oblivion, save only when he is confused with Simeon Solomon. This fate has also overtaken his near contemporary the genre and portrait painter the Hon. John Collier, who studied in Munich as well as Paris. And who to-day regards Axilette, another contemporary of Solomon's, who won the Prix de Rome, or André Castaigne, who turned novelist as well as black-and-white artist?

The École was also bound up with the official Salon. The last true official Salon, in the sense that the Government formally sponsored it, was that of 1880; thereafter it was held under the auspices of the Société des Artistes français ('the Old Salon'), from which the Société des Indépendents split in 1884.[1826] The Government intended sponsoring a triennial 'exposition nationale' for conventional work, but that of 1883 was the only one held. After 1890, the Salons were those either of the Société des Artistes français (the Champs de Mars) or of the Société national des Beaux Arts, which also split from the first. (Georges Rouault, otherwise invisible at this period, showed with the Artistes français from 1895 to 1901.) There was also the Société Internationale de Peinture et de Sculpture, which held an exhibition at Georges Petit's in August 1900: Whistler was the only non-Continental exhibitor.[1827] Moreover, these divisions are directly analogous to the ideological divisions of the workers' organisations, and sometimes included the same disputants. One may note that the old Communard Jules Dalou, sculptor of the statue of Blanqui in Père Lachaise, was one of the dissidents.

Such splits were replicated in other areas of cultural activity. Herman Lebovics, looking at the intellectual milieu of *fin-de-siècle* Paris, discusses the division between the group of sociologists round the review *Réforme Sociale* and that round the review *Science Sociale*, both claiming to be the heirs of Frédéric Le Play, and both opposed to the followers of Émile

Durkheim – 'it was at this moment that Durkheim and the Durkheimians attempted to move with their multifaceted "sociology".' Similarly, the Société d'Anthropologie and the Société d'Ethnographie turned from internal disputation only to oppose each other. 'As we would expect in the case of such passionate commitments [...] a major consequence was intellectual and organizational fragmentation.'[1828]

Whereas the artists of Bohemia represented a counter-culture, the academic painters answered to the need for the republic of moral order, the republic of good taste, to have an *Æsthetpolitik*. Except for the brief period that Proust held office as Minister for Fine Arts with a seat in the Cabinet, the Fine Arts portfolio was part of the Ministry of Public Education, and that qualifying adjective Public signifies not merely the regulatory rôle of the State, but its supervisory one. This was not simply a matter of the regulation of taste, although it was that, and public taste at least at first seemed to respond if one may judge by the failure of Offenbach's post-1871 productions of the previously successful *Les Brigands* and *Les Bavards*. But there was also the alignment of the arts (and architecture) with design and therefore, as Miriam Levin argues,[1829] with industrial prosperity: a specific elision of private and public spheres. The Bohemian artist, unpredictable, uncontrollable, challenged the moral order as represented not simply by the bourgeoisie, by 'le p'tit épicier', but also that of the artisanat that the bourgeoisie was creating in response to what they most feared, a recrudescence of the ochlocracy of the Commune.[1830] In the purely literary sense, as Claud Cockburn observed in his *marxisant* study of W.J. Locke, 'The helpless Bohemian could be brigaded at will as a kind of cultural bank-robber engaged by the author to attack the intellectual strong-rooms of the bourgeoisie'.[1831] The two were linked in the phrase of the publisher Hetzel on Huysmans: 'Il recommence la Commune de Paris dans la langue française'.[1832] But Cockburn's keyword is surely 'helpless', acknowledging that as a threat it was merely a turnip-ghost, another illusion, and as such could be vicariously enjoyed as well. The individualised Bohemian might be a discalced aristocrat, or an anarchist, but never a socialist, his motive artistic self-expression, not social reform. However much the moral order was challenged, the social order was unaffected.

~~~~~~~

Philippe Perott most interestingly suggests that the moral order ramified into the domestic interior, manifesting itself as an 'obsession with covering, enveloping, carpeting, paddings, or burying at any cost a nudity

that seemed, like emptiness, threatening'.[1833] Lord Esher remembered the
house of Sir Richard Wallace and John Scott in the rue Lafitte as having
been 'smothered in clocks',[1834] a curious form of anthropomorphism.
Certainly, something was being held in subjection by the glass dome over
the clock, the cloth on the mantel piece, the cover on the cushion, the anti-
macassar on the cover, rugs over carpets, swags around pictures, doyleys
over tablecloths, shades over lamps, festoons, ribbons, garlands, bows,
tassels, brocade, braid: it was as if disguise, the mask, had leaped from the
animate to the inanimate, and in so doing blurred the distinction between
the two. And what a flurry of materials clothed either the one or the other:
the silks and wools, the cottons and linens, tulle, voile, faille, chenille,
foulard, satin, percale, damask, twill, bombazine, barathea, serge, duck,
nankeen, tarlatan, taffeta, batiste, calico, muslin, velvet, plush ... all part of
the 'giant fairground of display',[1835] all cut and sewn and selvedged and
trimmed and tucked and gored and ruched and basted and hooked and
boned and buttoned and embroidered in an orgy of control, made all the
more tense when confronting also the voluptuous nudity of a picture by
Renoir or Vallotton, or visualising Odette de Crécy.[1836]

As early as 1875 Jules Castagnary[1837] identified two classes of artists, 'an
intolerant and jealous aristocracy composed of members of the Institute,
winners of the Prix de Rome, bemedalled and decorated artists, altogether
1,155 persons' and 'the tumultuous commoners, estimated at four to six
thousand independent workers'.[1838] Bohemianism was a defence against
embourgeoisement, anarchism a reaction to its control. This provided an
effective milieu for Wilde's own thinking, as set out in *The Soul of Man
Under Socialism*, which advocates the liberation of the artist from the
controls of state regulation, bourgeois values and public opinion, also
succinctly expressed when Wilde addressed the Royal General Theatrical
Fund in May 1892: 'I have been accused of lashing vice, but I can assure
you that nothing was further from my intentions [...] It is not for anyone
to censure what anyone else does, and everyone should go his own way, to
whatever place he chooses, in exactly the way he chooses'. This was not
really either a socialist or an English position, but it was a French anarcho-
Bohemian one. 'You are absolutely ungovernable,' Jules Ferry told artists
in 1879 when Minister for Public Instruction with responsibility for the
Arts, and here it becomes useful to record Maurice Agulhon's comment on
Ferry: 'This distinguished bourgeois, somewhat élitist, and in some
respects, rather inflexible, had his good points, or perhaps his aspects of
goodness. [He] adored nature and *even* did some painting.'[1839]
Conservative forces combined in the person of Charles Beulé, Secretary-
General of the Academy and Minister of the Interior under the duc de

Broglie;[1840] a similarly defining moment was the appointment in 1881 of Proust as Minister of Fine Arts *and State Manufactures.* (Zola thought little of the Ministers of Public Instruction with their Fine Arts portfolio, satirising them in the person of Fauverge, whose qualifications are that he once wrote a verse play and had it produced in his native Dijon, but more importantly had good looks, riches, a charming young wife and agreeable parties at his house in the boulevard St-Germain.[1841])

Again to cite Miriam Levin, 'the consistency with which the Republicans developed their art theory offers a striking contrast to the sense of disorder that prevailed within French Society. The rationalistic character of the art theory, intended to reconcile contradictions and incoherencies in French psychic, economic and social existence, was a direct response to this state of affairs.'[1842] This contradiction was embodied in Maupassant, combining exposure of vice and hypocrisy with élitist social views. Ultimately, neither anarchism nor Bohemia despite many mutations could maintain the initiative; and the twentieth century artist did indeed become a 'cultural producer', controlled by a new *apparat* of media fame, awards and the art market.

To define the Bohemian in terms of Marcel Desboutin (or of Douanier Rousseau or of Eugène Atget), is also to define the bourgeois, just as to define the *flâneur* is also to define the *épicier*, and to define the aristocrat is also to define the *nouveau riche.*[1843] These are cultural definitions that owe little to Marx, little to the 'estates', but, whereas the border between the aristocrat and the Bohemian was permeable, that between the aristocrat and the bourgeois was not, nor was the border between the Bohemian and the bourgeois, nor was the border between the Bohemian and the *ouvrier.* Timothy Clark has perhaps gone too far when he states that 'what bourgeois culture lacked was any real sense of its own identity: a sense of what was different in its whole relation to the world'. This is to confer marginal status on an increasingly confident and powerful class. That said, if Clark's definition of identity is valid, it is certainly true that as far as public expression is concerned, the bourgeoisie was not setting the prevailing agenda: 'An identity is made out of modes of feeling, speaking, understanding; finding some things funny, some tragic, others in bad taste, understanding; having your own criteria for pity, forgiveness, disbelief'.[1844]

Having one's own criteria: that is the essential ingredient of individualism, the Joycean Non Serviam. Neither aristo nor proletarian, and aware that bourgeois was a derogatory term in the mouths of both, Bohemia could provide an outlet. If Bohemianism was *pour épater les bourgeois,* the bourgeois were ready to be *épatés*. This ensured their own security, or else allowed them, half disapproving, half admiring, to have the artists do their living for them like Axël's servants ['Vivre? Les serviteurs feront cela pour nous']. The bourgeois who thronged the salons, the audience for the works that the Government bought for the Luxembourg, could partake of the world of taste and manners, of art and artists, in a safe environment, while reading let us say the adventures of Maître Saval,[1845] which would warn them against getting too close. Oscar Wilde, who despised the supreme bourgeois value of respectability, but liked to commit his sins at the Savoy, had to negotiate his own way through these shallows, taking his stand (or rather, his stroll) as a gentleman Bohemian, as a displaced Anglo-Irishman, as a poet whose poetic output had dried up.

Thus for the bourgeois, Bohemia was their 'Paris', a safe, vicarious haven for their fantasies, and a rather more risky one for their sons (and more dangerously an occasional daughter) to sow wild oats before settling down. In Bohemia, the individualist could pursue individualism *à outrance*, yet still be part of a community, or of a congeries of communities. Indeed, Chris Healy distinguished between the American, the English and the French Bohemias, each knowing little of the others.[1846] This afforded them, as Jerrold Siegel puts it, 'the appropriation of marginal life styles by young and not so young bourgeois for the dramatization of ambivalence toward their own social identities and destinies', licensing Bohemia as 'a locus of ambivalence and a means for exploring and testing the boundaries of bourgeois life'.[1847] This assisted Bohemia's commodification and in doing so brought about its own decay. Healy adds 'Despite the glamour which has been thrown over Bohemia, I cannot but think that it is an intellectual Valley of the Shadow of Death.'[1848]

⁓⁓⁓⁓⁓

Des Esseintes, during his conceptual journey to London, let his mind dwell on the pictures of Millais and Watts, but one may also guess that *Anglomanie* did not greatly extend to official British painting. At the 1889 Exposition Universelle, Britain was represented, as far as the arts were concerned, by Alma-Tadema, Wyke Bayliss, Walter Crane, G.J. Jacomb-Hood, John Lavery, Lord Leighton, Millais (the portrait of Gladstone, 'Bubbles' and 'The Last Rose of Summer'), Orchardson, Prinsep, Sickert, Watts, Whistler (the portrait of Lady Archibald Campbell) – and Kate Greenaway. The influence of the Academicians was longer lived in England than in France. Here Wilde offers an apposite definition: 'that curious mixture of bad painting and good intentions that always entitles a man to be called a representative British artist'.[1849] Late Victorian England accepted Poynter and Orchardson and Fildes and Herkomer, but in Paris the dealers were setting a pace of which academic London was only just becoming aware. 'I cannot say exactly when we first heard of certain lively doings in Paris among the artists – sometime about the end of the century, I think,' recalled Henry Tonks, that self-confessed 'hurdy-gurdy with only two tunes' whose name perhaps now represents all that was conservative in English art teaching. [1850] After all, it would have been about twenty years earlier that 'the spirit of unrest was beginning to disturb some of the [Royal] Academy students'.[1851] This certainly did not touch Orchardson, for all his francophilia and his regular visits to the Salon: it was Bouguereau and Meissonier who attracted him, and in turn Bouguereau campaigned for Orchardson to be awarded the Légion d'Honneur.[1852]

It is in assessing Wilde as observer rather than as observed that one comes to an understanding not only of his place in Paris but also of his place within the referents of æsthetics, of sensibility, and of modernism. Before his fall, it is easier to imagine Wilde in Neal's English Tea Room than in the Café Volpini, but he had no need to hunt for Impressionists only in their Paris haunts; for they were in London if he had wanted to see them. Of all his contemporaries, we know that Wilde's favourite artist was Charles Ricketts. Whatever Ricketts' considerable merits as a book and set designer (his *Mikado* drew upon all the vogue for *japonaiserie* of the period[1853]), he looked back into the nineteenth century, not forward into the twentieth, the art of which he frankly detested.[1854] Visiting the Paris Exhibition of 1900, Ricketts recorded that he 'wandered through miles of glaring modern rubbish'.[1855] It was not therefore for any *avant-garde* qualities that Wilde admired him. Some years later, Ricketts came to the support of Robert Ross when the latter attacked the Post-Impressionist exhibition organised by Roger Fry.[1856] Of course Wilde had the precedent of his old master Ruskin, who could, Quentin Bell tells us, 'allude to the muddy darkness of the modern French School, a school in which he could only see one supreme master, Edouard Frère.'[1857] Ruskin was presumably referring to the dark palettes of the Realists. His view of Whistler needs no recapitulation and although Ruskin outlived van Gogh by nearly ten years his æsthetics had long lost their value as a guide to his world.

Even so, it is open to conjecture how far Degas (who regarded Wilde as a mountebank), Cazin and Pissarro would have listened patiently while Wilde talked about pictures, as Sherard suggests,[1858] particularly if he was

rehearsing what he was writing in *The Critic as Artist*. The passage should
be quoted, and deconstructed, at length for it is frequently cited as showing
the development of Wilde's æsthetic by literary critics who may be
attracted by Wilde's view that painting subserves literature, but who seem
to fail to understand its limitations in comprehension of the Impressionist
æsthetic. Even Edouard Roditi appears to rely upon it for his assertion that
Wilde 'in England [...] had been one of the first to sponsor Impressionism
and also to recognize its limitations'.[1859]

I am very fond of the work of many of the Impressionist painters of Paris
and London. Subtlety and distinction have not yet left the school. Some of
their arrangements and harmonies serve to remind one of the unapproachable
beauty of Gautier's immortal Symphonie en Blanc Majeur, that flawless
masterpiece of colour and music which may have suggested the type as
well as the titles of many of their best pictures. *For a class that welcomes
the incompetent with sympathetic eagerness, and that confuses the bizarre
with the beautiful, and vulgarity with truth, they are extremely
accomplished.* They can do etchings that have the brilliancy of epigrams,
pastels that are as fascinating as paradoxes, and as for their portraits,
whatever the commonplace may say against them, no one can deny that
they possess that unique and wonderful charm which belongs to works of
pure fiction.

But even the Impressionists, earnest and industrious as they are, will not
do. I like them. Their white keynote, with its variations in lilac, was an era
in colour. Though the moment does not make the man, the moment
certainly makes the Impressionist, and for the moment in art, and the
'moment's monument,' as Rossetti phrased it, what may not be said? They
are suggestive also. If they have not opened the eyes of the blind, they have
at least given great encouragement to the short-sighted, and while their
leaders may have all the inexperience of old age, their young men are far
too wise to be ever sensible. *Yet they will insist on treating painting as if it
were a mode of autobiography invented for the use of the illiterate, and are
always prating to us on their coarse gritty canvases of their unnecessary
selves and their unnecessary opinions, and spoiling by a vulgar over-
emphasis that fine contempt of nature which is the best and only modest
thing about them.*

*One tires, at the end, of the work of individuals whose individuality is
always noisy, and generally uninteresting.* There is far more to be said in
favour of that newer school at Paris, the Archaicistes, as they call
themselves, who, refusing to leave the artist entirely at the mercy of the
weather, do not find the ideal of art in mere atmospheric effect, but seek
rather for the imaginative beauty of design and the loveliness of fair
colour.[1860]

In other words; their paintings are only valuable because they do not convey their subjects; they are didactic, coarse, short-sighted, vulgar ... At this point one wonders if Wilde knew and resented that Monet's middle name was Oscar, and that early works were signed Oscar Monet!

One also catches something of the vapidity of his criticism in Wilde's comment on E.W. Godwin as 'one of the most artistic spirits in England', and in his praise of the 'portrait of Mr W.H.' which he commissioned from Ricketts, 'an authentic Clouet of the highest authentic value'.[1861] In the same vein we are also told that Hallward 'painted with that marvellous bold touch that had the true refinement and perfect delicacy that in art, at any rate, comes through strength', or when Lord Henry Wotton exclaims of the Hallward portrait of Dorian Gray, 'It is one of the greatest things in modern art', he is acclaiming a painting that has just been authorially described in the words 'It was certainly a wonderful work of art and a wonderful likeness as well'. As for the portrait of Gray's mother, we are almost told authorially that 'the eyes follow you round the room': 'the eyes were wonderful [...] They seemed to follow him wherever he went'. What is to be argued is that Wilde, trapped in the discourse of Hellenic beauty,[1862] could not have comprehended the Impressionist project even if he could respond æsthetically to the surface effects of Impressionist painting, to say nothing of what their successors were attempting. For Jacques de Langlade to refer to him as 'l'apôtre de l'art moderne' is another example of the all too usual fault of knowing about Wilde without understanding him (or, in this case, modern art as well).[1863]   Wilde continually referred to the classical world, whether he was writing about Philosophy personified as a girl treading grapes or rejoicing in a boatboy called Omero. Even in tableware, 'exquisite taste' is manifested and valorised through Dorian Gray's '*antique* gold and silver plate'. To the end, his ideal of beauty was to be found by looking backwards, at a time when the very concept of beauty was being re-assessed and even overthrown. In the year that Wilde died, Dufy turned twenty-three, Mondrian twenty-eight, Matisse thirty-one, Klimt thirty-eight. Cubism, Vorticism and the Futurist Manifesto were only just over the horizon.

It is significant that Robert Sherard, usually so concerned to present Wilde in a good light, was completely dismissive of Wilde's pretensions, although much of the passage, which in general refers to Wilde at Magdalen, is itself highly tendentious.

A rôle was forced upon the young man which he had no natural qualifications to play; it was here that the curtain rose on that tragi-comedy in which his fine intellect was to lend itself to grotesque performances until, just before a period was put to his existence, he really found himself. It was from these reunions [i.e. undergraduate parties] in Magdalen that dated that virtuosity in music and painting and the decorative arts which he was forced to assume by the hazards of life, his own necessities and the folly of his contemporaries. He knew little about music, and little about painting, and in the matter of furniture, tapestries, wallpapers and architecture he was no more of a connoisseur than any man who can assimilate the current modes and chatter of the arbiters.[1864]

T.H.S. Escott, in his contemporary survey, identified the distinguishing cultural characteristic of England as a preference for 'the beauty of colour as superior to the beauty of form' and relates this to the poetry of Swinburne, Morris and Rossetti, the paintings of Burne-Jones, Whistler and Albert Moore, and the novels of William Black, Richard Blackmore and Mrs Ritchie 'skilled, each of them, in the grouping of rich and varied tints, sometimes dazzling, often lulling the senses and causing them to sink into a slumber exquisitely sweet, but troubling themselves comparatively little, if at all, to attain to severity of outline or classical symmetry of proportions'.[1865] The slumber was about to be disturbed.

Quentin Bell continues:

> Once again we see how easy it is to be misled by the judgments of history: we imagine that the visitor to Paris could hardly have avoided seeing the works of Manet, Renoir, Sisley, Pissarro and Monet, whereas the unavoidable painters would indeed have been Meissonier, Bonvin,[1866] Besnard, Cormon and Bonnat. The Impressionists were there but they were not easy to find. Monet does gradually emerge in the 1890s as a recognisable influence on British painting; but the rest are not clearly perceived until very late in the century. It was not simply that they were hard to find, but that the English were not looking for them.[1867]

The Impressionists were not really all that hard to find in Paris – after all, they showed each year in the Salon des Indépendants – but Wilde, despite his visits to Paris and his acquaintance with the advanced literary men, cannot be said to have frequented them. I doubt whether this was because, like Arnold Bennett in 1897, he judged that Monet and Manet had been 'extinguished by several painters of the present generation',[1868] for on his honeymoon he showed his artistic interests by going to a Meissonier exhibition.[1869] Antony Ludovici encountered him at this time and remembered his experience in terms that express both a view of Wilde and of French attitudes.

The year Wilde married I had a picture in the Paris Salon [...] One day I was sitting with madame Garnier [...] when we noticed a crowd collecting in the centre avenue and people standing on chairs to see over those in front of them; and we wondered what the excitement could be. We then saw coming towards us two strange-looking figures – a man in an overcoat almost reaching the ground, and a young woman in a Liberty fabric dress which was then new to Paris. As they approached, I recognised Oscar and his wife, on their wedding tour. The French ladies all laughed and immediately said "Oh, they are English" – "Ces sont des anglais, quelles caricatures!" which they certainly looked amid the fashionably dressed crowd. Fortunately Oscar was much too concerned at what he took to be a triumphal entry to notice me, and so passed on. Had he only heard some of the remarks it might have upset his little vanity. This occurred some years before his reputation was made abroad, but in England at that time he was only known as an eccentric poseur, who walked up the Strand carrying a sunflower or a lily, a strange form of self-advertisement.[1870]

Richard Whiteing gives names of the fashionable artists, some of whom even Quentin Bell ignores: 'Israels, the great Dutch painter, is one of the lights of the salon [...][1871] Jules Breton is highly esteemed, but one has to forget Millet before one can remember *him* [...] Puvis de Chavannes and Henner may be called Idealists for want of a better name [...] Bonnat, Carolus-Duran, Sargent, Cabanel and Chaplin are the greatest portraitists, or at least the portraitists *à la mode*'.[1872] The appearance of Sargent in this list of Salon painters may surprise, but the vogue for his work that characterised the end of the twentieth century should not obscure the feeling in earlier critical assessments that there was something meretricious in his work. Thus Osbert Sitwell, whose father commissioned work by Sargent, said of him that 'by supplying old masters, to which was added the skin-thin glint of the French Impressionists, novel to the English public, [he] precisely supplied the demand [of] the client who [demanded] "Give me the sort of Gainsborough that my grandfather had," – or, more usually, somebody else's grandfather had, and which the grandson had sold, – "but not so old-fashioned" [...] His portraits are usually good period pieces, *de luxe*, and bearing the same relation to the portraits of Gainsborough [...] that the Ritz Hotels [...] bear to the Place Stanislas in Nancy.'[1873] Sitwell here does more than simply indicate the falsity of Sargent's taste and the taste for Sargent. Although he may have undervalued the element of Sargent's own understanding of this, by specifically implicating it with the French Impressionists, *luxe*, the Ritz Hotels and the Place Stanislas, Sitwell allows us to see that the falsity is to be assessed in French terms.

This suggestion of the spurious leads back to Carolus-Duran, under whom Sargent had studied, and whose influence he never repudiated. Marie Bashkirtseff, even while praising him, discerned something false about Carolus, which perhaps Sargent caught at in his own portrait of him.

> What an astounding and charming creature! [...] He thinks himself a Spaniard and a Velasquez [...] There is in his whole manner something so good-natured, so much self-satisfaction, so much ease and pleasure at admiring his own dear self, that no one can object. [...] He is in such deadly earnest about himself [...] The visitors have a formal and admiring air, and Carolus plays the master with a counterfeit air of Fauré in *Don Juan* or *Rigoletto*.[1874]

Sargent she calls 'a counterfeit Velasquez of the counterfeit Carolus'.[1875] There was, however, much that was counterfeit about Bashkirtseff herself. As Parker and Pollock say, the *Journal* represents 'a particular figure of Marie Bashkirtseff [...] This "Marie" was in many ways a figure restructured to confirm all that against which the diary's subject struggled in the writings',[1876] but this does not give full measure to the blend of myths (self-created, created by others) that Bashkirtseff can be seen to have been, and for all the intelligence of their introduction, which is more concerned with sexual politics than social history, the absence of explanatory notes in their edition demeans it. They might have made more of the fact that she never refers to her father's name, and to herself invariably without her patronymic, the usual Russian fashion; or that she adopted the name Marie Russ for professional purposes, the 'Russ' identifying her as an exotic other. But this was not her only playing with identity, as she swung between self-confidence and self-doubt. Visiting the office of Hubertine Auclert's Droits de Femmes in the rue Cail in 1880 in the hope of painting her portrait, Marie Bashkirtseff thought it necessary (or possibly just fun, *fumiste*) to give her name as Pauline Orelle, and further obscured herself by saying that she painted under the name Daria; while her companion, a certain Madame de D—, called herself Alexandrine Norskott, which one may guess was an attempt at Northcott. Bashkirtseff was fond of such disguises, telling the sculptor Falguière that she was American, and writing to Maupassant as 'Miss Hastings' and to the painter George Bertrand as 'Pauline Orell'.[1877] It was as Pauline Orell that she wrote a number of articles for Auclert's *La Citoyenne*.

> And myself? ... What does my name express? *Marie Bashkirtseff* ... I will change it, for it has a certain strange and harrowed effect, though not without promise of brilliancy; it is even a certain style – something proud and stirring, but it is jerky and uneasy.[1878]

~~~~~~

A representative English view of more advanced French art was that of John Morley in 1892. As something of a political philosopher, something of a man of letters, Morley was not the average John Bull philistine, yet when he went to the Luxembourg to see an exhibition of modern French sculpture with his friend Jusserand (then assistant director for Oriental politics at the Ministry of Foreign Affairs), he could only record 'Admirable it is, most of it – and curiously free from the odious quality that stains and splashes the French literature and much of the French painting of the day. Capuy's figure of Joan of Arc is truly admirable'.[1879] Jusserand's view I have not yet ascertained; but as a mediævalist he too might not have been impressed by the contemporary.

Certainly, Meissonier, Bonvin, Bonnat, Cormon and Besnard were at the height of their reputations, and Quentin Bell might have added Bastien-Lepage ('in every country, the most promising youths were frankly imitating his work'[1880]), Gérôme, Gervex, Detaille, Boudin and others. Jean-Louis-Ernest Meissonier was the painter *par excellence* of military and historical subjects which brought him immense wealth. His portrait of Dumas *fils*[1881] was criticised by Nadar the photographer for failing to capture its subject, yet what might Dumas' character have been? Marie Belloc thought that he combined 'a strong streak of violence' with a glacial outward matter[1882]: such tension should be easier to convey in portraiture than in photography. Even at the time Meissonier had his detractors: his works were small, but not so small that history would regard them as even smaller, said Jules Castagnary in 1879.[1883] Nor did his Paris house become, as he had wished, the home of a Foundation, a Museum and a School of Art. When Meissonier died, the army provided artillery for his funeral possession, but 'in a hundred years his reputation has largely vanished [...] In the histories of art he is rarely mentioned'.[1884] George Painter reflects the opinions of the mid twentieth-century when he refers to the work of Meissonier as 'execrable' and to Gounod as 'a Meissonier of music'.[1885] Even the dispassionate Marc Gottlieb firmly fixes Meissonier in the school of painting that had flourished in the *first* half of the nineteenth century, aligning him with Delaroche, Charles Gleyre, Vernet and others. The late nineteenth century painters with whom he might have been compared (Bonheur for horses, Detaille for military scenes) are hardly mentioned, while Aimé Morot, who painted both, is not mentioned at all.[1886] Gottlieb reinforces this by his choice of illustrations, representing Meissonier chiefly by works that are anecdotes set, quite needlessly, in the eighteenth century. The effect is to remove Meissonier completely not merely from the artistic concerns of his own day, but from that day entirely. This too is to demonstrate the artist as crisis.

Delaroche makes an appearance in one of Wilde's remarkably rare references to painters, and it is one that also inculpates Mallarmé. As part of his terminal quarrel with Whistler, Wilde wrote

> By the aid of a biographical dictionary I discovered that there were once two painters called Benjamin West and Paul Delaroche, who recklessly took to lecturing on Art. As of their works nothing at all remains, I conclude that they explained themselves away. Be warned, James; and remain, as I do, incomprehensible; to be great is to be misunderstood.'

There was no need to have recourse to a biographical dictionary. Delaroche's work was popular enough (his 'Princes in the Tower' in the Louvre[1887] and 'The Death of Lady Jane Grey' of 1853 in the National Gallery, London,[1888] demonstrate his facile talent). The first of these would have been known to Wilde as it had been acquired in 1831. It was Delaroche who uttered the celebrated greeting to the work of Daguerre, 'From to-day, painting is dead'.[1889] He had inherited David's studio, and his statue stands with those of Horace Vernet, Delacroix and Ingres on the north-east corner of the Albert Memorial (1876) in Hyde Park.[1890] His 'Vendredi Saint' was shown at the Guildhall Gallery in 1892, where it was much admired by Rider Haggard. According to Andrew Lambirth 'during his lifetime Delaroche enjoyed greater international renown than any of his contemporaries', although it is true that the same authority asserts that 'Delaroche's critical reputation has been at rock bottom since 1860', which allows a certain margin for Wilde.[1891] The atelier of Delaroche was taken over by Charles Gleyre, under whom Whistler, Poynter, Thomas Armstrong and du Maurier (and later Monet) studied or did not study – it is the setting of the art students in du Maurier's *Trilby*. In Wilde's day it was the studio of Jean-Léon Gérôme. The reference to Delaroche may, however, have been one of Wilde's more pawky attempts at humour, like his feigning ignorance of the work of Henry Arthur Jones or Jean Moréas, for he owned a work by Delaroche's pupil Monticelli, who was much admired by Napoléon III, never a good sign, and by Eugénie, which was a worse one.[1892]

Léon-Joseph-Florentin Bonnat was a much honoured portrait painter, known as 'the favourite painter of millionaires',[1893] but called by Sickert 'Rembrandt-and-treacle'.[1894] He received the Grand Cross of the Légion d'Honneur in 1890. Edward VII invited him to Windsor, where his chief enthusiasm was for the portraits by Sir Thomas Lawrence.[1895] His

'Beheading of St Denis', now in the Panthéon, may have been one of the 'tête coupée' paintings known to Wilde, who also seems contrarily to have admired Sir Thomas Lawrence.[1896] Gustave Caillebotte was a pupil of his. His portrait by Degas (1863) is in the Musée Bonnat in Bayonne. For some reason, Quentin Bell spells his name Bonnât, not a mistake made by his father, who remembered him in 1904 as 'not precisely a big-wig but an old painter whose connoisseurship we all admired'.[1897] André de Fouquières is less kind: 'To-day, painting by Bonnat appears to us horribly vacuous, boring, and pompous.'[1898] His portrait of Victor Hugo[1899] (1877) seems adequately to demonstrate this.

Fernand Cormon, nicknamed 'Père la Rotule', was also a portrait painter, rather less conventional than Bonnat, at least in his life if not in his practice, for he also painted scenes from prehistory. A.S. Hartrick describes him as having 'the quick movements of a bird, which he somehow resembled'; and perhaps the bird was a sparrow, for he was reputed to keep three mistresses. This may have been why Toulouse-Lautrec described him as the thinnest man in Paris.[1900] Nor was his name Cormon, for all its resemblance to the French for cormorant, but Fernand-Anne Piestre (1845-1924). To his atelier came van Gogh, Rothenstein, Louis Anquetin, Lautrec, Matisse and Conder. Emile Bernard was expelled in 1886.[1901]

Paul Albert Besnard was a successful mainstream artist, a pupil of Cabanel. The sculptor Charlotte Besnard was his wife. He is perhaps the 'odd man out' in this list. He won the Grand Prix de Rome in 1874 and spent two years in London 1876/7 where he came under the influence of Burne-Jones. His portraits included one of the actress Réjane[1902]; rather more surprisingly the 1880 portrait of Field Marshal Sir Garnet Wolseley in the National Portrait Gallery in London is also by him.[1903] Unlike most French mainstream artists,[1904] he associated with both the Impressionists in general and Les XX (Les Vingt) in particular; he even travelled in Spain with Jules Chéret. There is much to remind one of Besnard in Zola's character 'Bongrand' in L'Œuvre. Roger Marx and Camille Mauclair both wrote monographs on him, and he lived long enough to enjoy a State Funeral.

There is a good account of Cabanel as a teacher in Barbara Weinberg's The Lure of Paris – Nineteenth Century American Painters and their French Teachers.[1905] Weinberg quotes a critic of 1870: 'M. Cabanel is not an artist; he is a saint. He doesn't make art; he makes perfection. He does not deserve criticism; he deserves paradise'. It was Academicians like

Cabanel who thought that the Impressionists also deserved paradise, or perhaps somewhere hotter; and his own work seems to have been warmed by an attenuated romanticism/Pre-Raphaelitism.[1906] His full-length portrait of Napoléon III was hung by Eugénie at Farnborough amongst her Winterhalters. Philip Wilson Steer was a pupil of Cabanel at the École in 1883/5 (and of Bouguereau at Julian's). Bastien-Lepage was also a pupil of Cabanel, which no doubt explains William Feldman's remark that 'the obscurity surrounding Bastien-Lepage is all the more surprising in the light of the esteem in which he was held by his contemporaries'.[1907]

Maurice Agulhon adds another cautionary note when he says that for Parisians *the* Courbet, 'a hundred times more famous' than Gustave, was Admiral Courbet, hero of the Franco-Chinese War of 1885.[1908] At the exhibition organised by Georges Petit 'Portraits and Writers of the Century 1793-1893', Henri Gervex exhibited a portrait of Maupassant, with whom he had toured Italy in 1885, but also portraits of William Busnach, Eugène Paz, Albert Mérat and Léonce Detroyat, none of whom have remained exactly household names. Similarly, the panorama 'Histoire du Siècle', on which both Gervex and Alfred Stevens worked, shows many figures now forgotten. This was displayed in the Jardins des Tuileries from 1889 to 1896.[1909]

Quentin Bell was right to remind us that it was such people who dominated the contemporary scene, but, inheriting the reaction to the English adverse view of the Post-Impressionists formed in 1910 and 1912, gives too narrow a view – Whistler went to the sixth Impressionist show to see work by Degas, Camille Pissarro, Berthe Morisot and Mary Cassatt and took some trouble to keep up with their work throughout the decade. Henry James had no trouble in finding the Impressionist exhibition at Durand-Ruel's in 1876 and thinking it 'decidedly interesting'.[1910] Lady Frances Balfour (who was not English either, but a Scot) also found Impressionists in 1891, even though she came to a different conclusion. 'We have been to the Salon. Certainly the Impressionists are too sickening!'[1911] On the other hand, the unsophisticated Sam Osbourne, primed by his wife who was studying painting, found his way to the Impressionist Exhibition of 1877, and liked what he saw. This clearly has implications for the siting (as well as the sighting) of Wilde.

Part 2: Supervision

'The form of government that suits the artist best is the absence of
government'
– Oscar Wilde.

WILDE famously threatened to move to France after the censorship of
Salomé in England, and this has given rise to some exaggeration of the
difference between what was permissible in each country. When the
Franco-Irish Agnes de Stoeckl commented that 'England often reminded
me of a well-run school', she could have almost said as much for
France.[1912]

Although sodomy had been decriminalised in 1791 and was unknown to
the Code Napoléon, France did have a law of 'outrage to public and
religious morality – 'outrage public à la pudeur', sometimes referred to as
'attentat public â la pudeur' or 'outrage aux mœurs', dating to May 1819,
under the Bourbon reaction of Louis XVIII, and the corruption of minors
remained an offence. Flaubert, in a letter to Goncourt, made merry over
the arrest in a Vespasienne of Eugène Lebègue, comte de Germiny, caught
in flagrante with a jeweller's assistant and in June 1903 'le misérable
disciple d'Oscar Wilde' the baron Jacques d'Adelsward-Fersen was
arrested 'for taking too much interest in schoolboys from the Lycée
Condorcet'.[1913] Wilde and Bosie Douglas trod on thin ice in Paris with
their boulevard pick-ups. Although freedom of the Press was guaranteed
by a law of 1881, and even if the French were less easily outraged than the
English, it is still true that in 1873 a lecture on feminism by Olympe
Audouard was banned and a year later unsold copies of Barbey
d'Aurevilly's *Les Diaboliques* were confiscated and destroyed;[1914] and
although the Catholic Index Librorum Prohibitorum had no legal force in
France, it could still influence public opinion: all three of Zola's *Les Trois
Villes* trilogy, *Lourdes*, *Rome* and *Paris* were put on the Index, and the
hostility of Catholic reviewers thus guaranteed. 'The power of the Roman
Catholic Church,' says Alan Schom, 'ensured that the press reviews were
blistering.'[1915]

In 1874 the song 'C'est dans l'nez qu'ça me chatouille' was banned; in
1874, too, Manet was prosecuted for his caricature of President
MacMahon as Polichinelle. Two years later Jean Richepin was imprisoned
for his *Chansons des Gueux*, and as late as 1885 Louis Desprez was sent to
prison for his *Autour d'un Clocher*, an experience that hastened his
premature death. Paul Adam also spent six months in prison for his

prostitute novel *Chair molle*, while, says Richard Whiteing 'Madame Marc de Montifaud goes to prison for every book she writes'.[1916] Édouard Dujardin spent a month in prison for 'some remarks he made in *Fin-de-siècle*, a journal no more subversive than *Esquire'*.[1917] A prosecution followed the publication in 1889 of *Les Sous-Offs*, an anti-military novel by Lucien Descaves,[1918] but even the 1878 revival of *La grande duchesse de Gérolstein* had been opposed by the Minister of War on the grounds that it ridiculed the army.[1919] In 1900 Laurent Tailhade was sentenced to a year's imprisonment for an article attacking the Tsar Nicholas II.

Censorship in the theatre had existed since 1874. All theatre directors had to submit manuscripts fifteen days before they wished to produce a play to the 'Commission d'examen des ouvrages dramatiques', under the Ministry of Public Instruction and Fine Arts. This did not end until 1906, sixty-three years before the licensing of plays was ended in England, by the rather *fumiste* approach of the Chamber of Deputies abolishing not censorship but the salaries of the censors, causing the staff of the censorship office to resign en bloc.[1920] The very popularity of theatre naturally attracted the concern of the guardians of public morals, and these were not only the self-styled leagues of decency or purity but also the government. Police informers, *mouchards*, attended plays and reported on them.[1921] The rôle of the Minister for Fine Arts was as much to regulate as to promote the arts; when Proust was Minister (1881-1882) and looked for the realisation of the social ideal within the project of popular theatre,[1922] he was combining both these duties, and it is notable than for most of the period the ministry was subsumed into the Ministry of Public Instruction: in 1885 René Goblet as Minister banned the stage version of Zola's *Germinal* by William Busnach[1923] for what was deemed its socialistic content and it was not until April 1888 that it was licensed by the more sympathetic Edouard Lockroy. The duty could be exercised in a number of ways: in 1902 the Under Secretary for Fine Arts conveyed to Debussy that the references to bed by Yniold in *Pelléas et Mélisande* were unsuited to the subsidised theatre: there is a suggestion that he was put up to this by Catulle Mendès because Debussy had rejected a libretto of his,[1924] presumably a reference to Debussy's abandoned *Rodrigue et Chimène*. Only a year before the banning of *Salomé*, Goncourt's stage version of *La Fille Elisa* (Théâtre Libre, December 1890) was banned in Paris by the Board of Censors (this caused three hundred thousand copies to be sold[1925]). As in England, managements resorted to theatre clubs, subscription performances that could be regarded as private entertainments, not public spectacles, but innovative directors like Antoine and Lugné-Poë with their predilection for plays by foreigners, Jews, anarchists, Dreyfusards, anticlericals and freemasons (or so said their enemies), were the subject of correspondence between the Prefecture of Police and the Ministry. As mentioned in Chapter VI, Théodore de Chirac was sentenced to fifteen months for outraging public decency.[1926] In 1890 Sarah Bernhardt herself had initially been prevented from playing the Virgin Mary in *La Passion* by Edmond Haraucourt[1927] when the Minister for Fine Arts (Armand Fallières) invoked a decree dating to the time of Henri IV.

In 1893 Bal des Quatz' Arts, organized by Jules Roques of the *Courrier français* at the Moulin Rouge fell foul of René Béranger,[1928] a Senator and a moral crusader known as the 'Father of Decency' ('Père Pudeur'[1929]), whose committee included Jules Ferry and Jules Simon,[1930] both former conservative prime ministers who had also, as Ministers of Public Instruction, been the ultimate political masters of the arts. The organisers were prosecuted for indecency (the first nude appearance outside the ateliers, by a model called Mona[1931]), a proceeding which led to student riots[1932] in July, assisted by roughs from Belleville. The Quatz' Arts was banned again in 1900, this time by the Paris authorities, who disapproved of the Inquisition theme of the previous year's ball, again held at the Moulin Rouge; and it was held instead in Brussels. The Cabaret des Décadents, which opened in February 1893 near Rothenstein's studio in the rue Fontaine,[1933] was closed for political reasons by the censor in 1894.[1934] Nor should it be forgotten that Sargent left Paris in dismay after the controversy that surrounded his portrait of Madame Gautreau in 1884.[1935]

Political censorship took many forms. For a republic dedicated to the memory of the Revolution of 1789, there was a strange reluctance to licence plays dealing unconventionally with revolutionary subjects. In January 1891 even Victorien Sardou's *Thermidor* was banned by the government from the boards of the Comédie Française itself as insufficiently sympathetic to the Revolution. *Fructidor*, by Gaston Arman de Caillavet and Robert de Flers was similarly banned. Dedication to the Revolution and the Republic had its ambivalent side, like everything else. While the centenary of 1789 was greatly celebrated (there was even a free matinée of Beaumarchais' 'Le Mariage de Figaro' at the Odéon to mark the centenary of the calling of the States General), that of the declaration of the First Republic, which fell on 21st September 1892, was strangely muted (the naming of a new Paris bridge after Mirabeau indicated no great revolutionary enthusiasm); while the half-centenary of the declaration of the Second Republic (4th May 1898) went unregarded.

In 1885 Maurice Boutet de Monvel's provocatively titled 'Apothéose, ou le Triomphe de la Canaille' was barred from the Salon on the explicit ground that it would create a political fracas. In *La Société mourante et l'Anarchie,* Jean Grave argued for the overthrow of the state; the state in reply jailed him for two years. After the bomb which cost the eye of Laurent Tailhade, on 4th April 1894 at Foyot's, the police took the avant-garde writers and artists as their first suspects. They arrested Félix Fénéon, who was the subject of a miscarriage of justice when he was unjustly acquitted. The royalist marquis de Fages spent five days in jail in 1883 for calling the Marseillaise a filthy song. Alexander Cohen, who translated Hauptmann's *Lonely Lives* into French, was expelled from France for his anarchist sympathies, while an attempt was made to ban the play itself when Lugné-Poë produced it in December 1893 (Stuart Merrill distributed leaflets protesting against the ban). Hauptmann's *The Weavers* was banned for political reasons in May 1893.

Paris audiences were also inclined to make their feelings felt: the Hernani[1936] and Ubu Roi disturbances became causes célèbres, but disturbances were only just avoided at the first night of Erckmann-Chatrian's *L'Ami Fritz* (Comédie Française, 4th December 1876), the Goncourts' *Germinie Lacerteux* (from their prostitute novel of 1865) was howled down at the Odéon in December 1888 and fights broke out in the audience during the Théâtre d'Art's production of Maeterlinck's *Les Aveugles* in December 1891. The first performance of Lalo's *Namouna* had a stormy reception. The public protests at Dujardin's *La fin d'Antonia* at the Vaudeville were severe enough to cause Jacques-Émile Blanche to take refuge in Tortoni's.[1937] At the opening of Chirac's *Prostituée* at the Théâtre d'Art Symbolists and Naturalists came near to fisticuffs. One does not read of such events in London: small wonder Francisque Sarcey thought London audiences easier to please than Paris ones (though Antoine's production of Tolstoy's *The Power of Darkness,* allowed in Paris, was banned in London).

There was editorial and directorial censorship as well: Théodore de Banville,[1938] François Coppée and Anatole France had refused to print anything by Verlaine in *Le Parnasse Contemporain* in 1866; subsequently François Magnard of *Le Figaro* refused an article on Verlaine by Rodenbach: 'il porte trop de la pédérastie en bandoulière'.[1939] Maurice Emmanuel was excluded by Delibes from the Prix de Rome 'for exhibiting model tendencies',[1940] a censorship that sounds positively Stalinist. Ten years later, the journal wittily called *Le Bien Public* discontinued publishing Zola's *L'Assommoir* after adverse public reaction, and it was

Catulle Mendès who continued to bring it out in *La République des Lettres*. *Le Figaro* refused to accept even the advertisements for Maupassant's *La Maison Tellier*. As in England, there could also be censorship from the bookshops, such as Hachette, which had the monopoly on railway bookstalls. André Antoine, prepared to risk plays by Goncourt and Méténier, thought that Gabriel Mourey's play *Lawn-Tennis*, with its lesbian theme, was 'overbold for public presentation' at his Théâtre Libre.[1941] And while London may have had philistine theatre critics like Clement Scott,[1942] Paris had the ultra-conservative Albert Wolff, who once walked out in a rage of a Théâtre Libre production of *Jacques Bouchard* by his own nephew Pierre Wolff,[1943] as well the powerful and long-lived Francisque Sarcey, 'the gentleman who, of the whole journalistic fraternity, holds the fortune of a play in the hollow of his hand'.[1944] Theatre critics were powerful figures, and managements sent their complimentary tickets to their private homes, not to their offices, with the implication that it was the gentleman man of letters, not the professional journalist, whose opinions were being sought.[1945]

Sarcey, described as 'a glorified Clement Scott type of critic',[1946] was said to go a play every night of his life, and was 'the epitome of bourgeois self-satisfaction' according to one authority,[1947] but also 'rondelet, bedonnant, de joyeux humour', according to *Le Chat Noir*, which, I suggest, identifies the drama critic at the beginning of *Nana* as Sarcey.[1948] That Sarcey attracted the nickname of 'L'Oncle' also suggests something of the bonhomme. Goncourt, however, was sarcastic about Sarcey: 'If a Frenchman wants to succeed [in the theatre] he has to fill his play with vulgar things which a Sarcey is capable of understanding and appreciating', while René Ghil, casting about for insult to apply to Wyzewa, called him 'le Sarcey-de-la-Décadence'.[1949] It says much for the prevailing atmosphere of metamorphosis that, for all that he supported the moral purity campaign of Senator Béranger, Sarcey appeared at the 1893 Bal des Quatz'Arts as Bacchus.

Other aspects of English censoriousness also had their French counterpart. Bosie Douglas decided that 'in the long run *l'hypocrasie française* did not appear to differ very much from the English variety' (this was inspired by his unsuccessful attempt to persuade French men of letters to sign a protest against Wilde's sentence).[1950] The notorious burning of Sir Richard Burton's manuscripts by his widow is echoed by the bonfire of Toulouse-Lautrec's paintings made by his scandalised uncle: that Lady Burton was acting at the direct behest of her husband's ghost somehow fails to make this easier to forgive.

If one survived all of this, there was always the possibility of censorship by the sword or pistol. Although not all enmities included duelling in their expression (the impresarios of leisure, men like Zidler, Oller, Salis, and Bruant, preferred lawsuits with one another and their artistes over breaches of contract, imitation and other business disputes), the propensity of the French for duelling was notorious. As Richard Whiteing observed 'the art of giving offence is carried to much perfection'.[1951]   There was a duel between the duc d'Orléans and the count of Turin in 1897, but the vogue spread far beyond aristocratic circles. Cecil Lowther took a military man's interest, listing the types in order of frequency:

> Journalists' duels; duels which are the outcome of a tongue too well hung or of one lubricated by an overdose of alcohol; and thirdly those where the opponents are out to kill if they can [...] The journalist's chief object is to get talked about.[1952]

In 1862 the duc de Gramont-Caderousse had killed a journalist called Dillon on foot of some articles at which the former had taken offence. Another critic, Pierre Veber, was challenged by Robert de Flers. Hostile criticism by Georges Vanor of Bernhardt's 1899 Hamlet brought a challenge from Catulle Mendès, and Bernhardt's son Maurice challenged the caricaturist Langlois for an offensive sketch of his mother, Paul Alexis[1953] for an article deemed insulting, and Edmond Pelletier for a disagreeable review.[1954] Mendès fought duels with Vielé-Griffin and Jules Huret[1955]; Henri Mercier wounded Jean Moréas and Charles Vignier killed Robert Caze.[1956] Léon Daudet[1957] challenged the editor of L'Écho de Paris to a duel for publishing a cartoon that he found offensive, and was himself challenged by the playwright Henri Bernstein[1958] for his adverse criticism – Marie Belloc thought Léon Daudet 'a caricature of his father [and who] often betrayed an extreme violence of nature'.[1959] In a quarrel over Salammbô in 1892 a M. Roulez, 'a prominent member of the École d'Escrime Française, and who in the business world is well known as an inventor of telephone apparatus',[1960] fought and defeated three opponents in the Bois de Boulogne, a feat that all the world must have recognised as surpassing that of D'Artagnan when he challenged Athos, Porthos and Aramis.

'I declare the Cassagnacs unworthy of my pen and of my sword,' said the former Communard Prosper Lissagaray, founder of La Bataille. This was ill-judged, for the Gascon Paul de Cassagnac, editor of Le Pays, fought twenty-two duels between 1880 and 1889. 'I will make you swallow the one and the other,' was Cassagnac's reply, and he did so. Cassagnac's duelling proclivities are alluded to in Chapter Eight of Mark Twain's *A Tramp Abroad* of 1880, 'The Great French Duel'.

Certain duels were *causes célèbres*, going back to 1836 when Émile de Girardin killed Armand Carrel, or when Prince Pierre Bonaparte killed Victor Noir in 1870, an incident characterised as murder in cold blood.[1961] Most duels, however, were more farcical than fierce. The courtesans Cora Pearl and Marthe de Vere fought a duel with riding whips. Gabriel d'Yturri challenged Jacques-Émile Blanche for spreading tales about his relationship with Montesquiou, but Blanche got out of this by convincing Henri de Régnier (Yturri's second) that the tales had been spread by the comtesse Potocka. Antonin Proust quarrelled with Monet in a dispute that arose obscurely from the public subscription to buy Manet's 'Olympia' and challenged him.[1962] After a quarrel at the Café de la Rochefoucauld ('un café assez exigue mais plein de vie'[1963]), a duel between Charles Conder and Edouard Dujardin had to be averted. Michel Ephrussi offered to give a million francs to the poor of Paris rather than fight a duel with the marquis de Breteuil (Proust's marquis de Bréauté). Leconte de Lisle challenged Paul Bourget, who replied that he would do nothing as absurd as he was young and Leconte was old. George Moore refused to accept a challenge from Whistler, brought to him by Vielé-Griffin and Mirbeau.

Manet fought a duel with Duranty, Daudet with Albert Delpit who himself challenged Brunetière. Other duels were even more theatrical, such as the one between Montesquiou and de Régnier, or that between Jean Lorrain and Marcel Proust whose seconds were, respectively, Paul Adam and Octave Uzanne, and Jean Béraud and Gustave de Borda, known as Sword Thrust. Hardly less absurd were Toulouse-Lautrec's challenge to the Belgian painter de Groux; or Erik Satie's to Eugène Bertrand. Mirbeau himself was a man of strong opinions and having become a partisan of Sarah Bernhardt fought a duel with the novelist Paul Bonnetain whom he supposed to have insulted her, wounding him in the left hand, which is odd; he also fought with Paul Déroulède and Catulle Mendès. 'There are three things about [Clemenceau] which you fear,' Déroulède once told the Chamber of Deputies, 'his rapier, his pistol and his tongue. I am prepared to face all three'[1964] – although it was in fact an affair of pistols that followed (Déroulède, founder of the Ligue des Patriotes, was an enthusiastic practitioner of target shooting). Politicians always seemed ready to exchange shots: with a strange sense of occasion, Louis Barthou and Jean Jaurès fought a duel on Christmas Day 1894; but that was not yet the day appointed for the assassination of either.

The theatrical element in all this would not have been lost on Déroulède, a nephew of Émile Augier[1965], and perhaps it was not lost on Wilde, as one version of his celebrated wallpaper *mot* begins 'My wallpaper and I are fighting a duel to the death'.[1966] The opéra-bouffe aspect of many of these duels was replicated both as parody (Rimbaud attacking Carjat with a sword *stick* or when Satie attacked Willy with his fists, and Willy defended himself with his cane) and as masquerade, as in Léon Gérôme's picture 'Duel after a Masked Ball'. The duel between Floquet and General Boulanger also partook of the comedic, when the military hero was wounded by the elderly civilian.

An unusual weapon was the bottle of champagne which the marquis de Dion once broke over the head of Aurélien Scholl for allegedly slandering the concert pianist Madame Roger-Miclos,[1967] though we do not know whether the insult was about her playing, or about her profile like that on a medallion, or for denying that she had the most beautiful arms in the world, or which champagne was deemed fit for the purpose.

CHAPTER TWELVE

PARIS AND THE GOOD AMERICAN

'…that saying by one of the wittiest of men: "Good Americans, when they
die, go to Paris."'
– Oliver Wendell Holmes.[1968]

'One often hears it said here "After death good Americans go to Paris"; we
love your city so much.'
– Francis Parkman to Pierre Margry 9th February 1892.[1969]

'Good Americans.'
– Novel by Mrs. Burton Harrison 1898.[1970]

WILDE was being gnomic rather than original when he said that good
Americans go to Paris when they die. Paris was a reward for being good,
but by adding that bad Americans go to America, he indicated that he also
meant to convey the idea of punishing the dead for being Americans or
rewarding Americans for being dead: it is ironic that Wilde's own reward
for being dead was to stay in Paris. Although he had enjoyed a measure of
social success in the United States (he 'won the regard of some of our
representative Americans, among whom were General Grant, Henry Ward
Beecher, Oliver Wendell Holmes, General and Mrs McClellan, Louisa
Alcott, Henry Wadsworth Longfellow [and] Joaquin Miller'[1971]), Wilde
did not much take to America or Americans. His strictures on the 'land
out of breath with its greed for gain'[1972] are severe, and serve to locate him
firmly on the eastern side not only of the Atlantic Ocean but also of the
Irish Sea: 'English people are far more interested in American barbarism
than they are in American civilisation'[1973]. Although he contrived to wrap
his meaning carefully, he was equally contemptuous of the American in
Paris: 'Americans, according to their own explanation, visit France in
order to complete their education, and the French have to tolerate people
who are so fascinatingly unreasonable as to attempt to finish in a foreign
land what they have never had the courage to begin in their own'. It is
fortunate that this never came before the Americans whose devotion to
Wilde's æstheticism has been so fully documented by Mary Warner
Blanchard.[1974]

The punishment of the dead bad Americans when they got to America was presumably to live in 'some of your simpler cities [with] bad wallpapers horribly designed',[1975] wallpaper being a subject on which Wilde held strong views to his dying day. Wilde's praise of Longfellow is also revealing, for it not only shows his contempt for America but also his notion (by way of contrast) of the artist that he wished himself to be. Longfellow, he wrote, 'deserves a high place in any history of American civilisation', but how did he earn that high place? 'His lectures, though not by any means brilliant, were still productive of much good; he had a most charming and gracious personality, and he wrote some pretty poems. But his poems are not the kind that call for intellectual analysis, or indeed for any serious discussion at all'.[1976] This is praise that seems not so much faint as in a swoon.

It was a pleasant compliment to Lillie Langtry when he said 'I would rather have discovered Mrs Langtry than have discovered America', but to have said it to an American interviewer was not perhaps the best example of tact. 'The discovery of America was the beginning of the death of Art'[1977] is a not untypical remark, and although a silver lode was named Oscar in his honour when he was in Nevada, in *The Picture of Dorian Gray* he sends James Vane to Australia, not to America, to make his fortune. In Paris in 1883 'he spoke little of his American tour and I gathered that it had not been the source of much satisfaction, and that the ugliness of American cities had distressed him'.[1978] Four years later he was still recalling that

> The cities of America are inexpressibly tedious. Boston [...] is [...] the paradise of prigs. Chicago is a sort of monster-shop, full of bustles and bores. Political life at Washington is like political life in a suburban vestry. Baltimore is amusing for a week, but Philadelphia is dreadfully provincial; and though one can dine in New York one could not dwell there.[1979]

Praising the Far West after this was hardly mollifying, especially as he was doing so specifically to commend Buffalo Bill's Wild West Show. This note of metropolitan superiority, which Americans must have found insufferable, extends to his 'praise' of American women, who 'take their dresses from Paris and their manners from Piccadilly, and wear both charmingly' – that is to say, the less they are American the more acceptable Wilde finds them, with their 'quaint pertness, delightful conceit, native self assertion'.[1980] This goes on for some time, culminating in another of Wilde's attacks on older women, 'the dull, dowdy or dyspeptic' American mothers, growing old gracelessly.[1981]

The desire to be acculturated in Europe that Wilde commends made Americans peculiarly susceptible to the lure of Paris, a lure which he himself shared.

> There is no human being to whom [Paris] is so dangerous and so lasting as the man and woman who is everywhere and nowhere at home – which is why rootless Americans and vagrant Irishmen find Paris so much more irresistible than do the parochial English.[1982]

Henry James, a frequent visitor, noted in 1875 that 'the American who comes to Paris [...] takes to the French capital, generally speaking, like a duck to water' and assigned his compatriots to 'the classic region, about a square mile in extent, which is bounded on the south by the rue de Rivoli, and on the north by the rue Scribe, and of which the most sacred spot is the corner of the boulevard des Capucines, which basks in the smile of the Grand Hôtel'.[1983] If that was the place, the time was spring, when 'Paris seemed the playground of every American that claimed to be in society.'[1984] In Jamesian and Parisian fashion, however, by 1884 this has shifted.

> It had been a common reflection for the author of these light pages that the fondness for France (throughout the company of strangers more or less qualified) was oddly apt to feed only on such grounds for it as made shift to spread their surface between the Arc de Triomphe and the Gymnase Theatre.[1985]

This was the Jamesian territory both off and on the page: Sheldon Novick has called James 'the gatekeeper to Europe for two generations of Americans' although James himself soon found wearisome the 'rather languorous and dissipated' American colony.[1986] Colm Tóibín has glossed this, giving James the line 'We must be ready for change, especially when we go to Paris, and that no one who has known the sweetness of Paris can properly return to the sweetness of the United States'.[1987] This presumably is James's version of the destination of bad Americans. His Maria Gostrey remarks 'the name of the good American is as easily given as taken away!'[1988]

The 'nice little hotel' in which Bret Harte stayed in July 1878 on his way to Crefeld was also in Jamesian Paris, the Hôtel Bellevue in the avenue de l'Opéra.[1989] Harte stayed here again on his way home and it was to become his regular lodging when in the city. At the time, he wrote to his wife mock-humorously:

> I did not write to you from that wicked place, for I was so thoroughly
> steeped in iniquity and dissipation while there that I did not wish to write
> to you.[1990]

Harte in fact did not much like Paris, so the comment that he looked like
an actor made up as a French marquis of the *ancien régime* belongs to the
fantasy of its inventor, rather than to any francophilia of Harte's own.[1991]
Harte's comment of 1880 that 'To-day in this bright sunshine and dry
warmth [...] I feel another man'[1992] shows that he too was infected by the
transformations that Paris wrought. He was also there long enough to
experience what must have been the normal occurrence among Parisians:
'Every day I meet people we know or have met in California, in Boston, in
New York, in Chicago even!'[1993] James, on the other hand, felt naturally
Parisian even on his first visit at the age of twelve, overnighting with his
parents in a hotel in the rue de la Paix on the way to Geneva. To this part
of Paris he was always to return, as an adult for the first time in January
1870 when the Louvre claimed him by day and the Théâtre Français by
night.[1994] The play was *The Adventuress*, with Favart; and it became *The
Europeans*. In 1877 he saw Dumas' *Le Demi-Monde*, and it inspired his
Siege of London. Twelve years on, and he visited the dressing room of
Julia Bartet, playing in *L'École des Maris*; it became a scene in *The Tragic
Muse*. The Français, 'an ideal and exemplary world',[1995] was forever
exempt from the acerbic criticism that James brought to so much of his
theatre-going.

If James was at home in Paris, he did notice that the Americans who went
there fluctuated in number, and were unstable in quality.[1996]

> Though the good city of Paris appears to be less in fashion than in other
> days with those representatives of our race – not always, perhaps
> acknowledged as the soundest and stiffest – curious of foreign opportunity
> and addicted to foreign sojourns, it probably none the less remains true that
> such frequentations of France as may be said still to flourish among us
> have as much as ever, the wondrous capital and the wondrous capital
> alone, for their object. The taste for Paris at all events, is – or perhaps I
> should say was, alluding as I do, I fear, to a vanished order – a taste by
> itself; singularly little bound up, of necessity, with such an interest in the
> country at large as would be supplied by an equal devotion, in other
> countries, to other capitals.[1997]

Other American writers found that there was also a risk of alienation.
Thomas Bailey Aldrich in 1875, for example,

before coming to Paris [...] had taken the optimistic view that as he read French with the same fluency as he read English, there could be but little difficulty in both speaking and understanding that language, and was totally unprepared for his precipitous fall when he realised, when surrounded by French voices, that he was both deaf and mute to the speech about him.[1998]

The recovered histories of Americans in Paris suggest that acculturation was more usual than alienation. Iza, or Georgette, de Coëtlogon of the place des Vosges was 'American by birth but utterly French in her manners.'[1999] André de Fouquières says of James Hyde that he loved France as only a foreigner could love it, furnishing his house in the rue Adolphe-Yvon in the eighteenth-century manner, and although he married an American, she was at any rate the widow of comte Louis de Gontaut-Biron.[2000]

Richard Harding Davis, in a chapter devoted to Americans in Paris, said of his countrymen

> Americans go to London for social triumph, or to float railroad shares; to Rome, for art's sake; and to Berlin to study music and economise; but they go to Paris to enjoy themselves.

> Americans who go to Paris might be divided into two classes – those who use Paris for their own improvement, and those who find her too strong for them, and who go down before her and worship her, and whom she either fashions after her own liking, or rides underfoot and neglects until they lose heart and disappear for ever.[2001]

This is very much the 'Paris qui consomme', to give the title of Émile Goudeau's work of 1893, or Paris as described by Felicien Rops in the phrase quoted at the beginning of this work: 'Paris vous agriffe par mille côtés et l'on ne sait jamais quitter cette ville diablée.'[2002] Davis, however, was doing the Americans in Paris less than justice. The French Exhibition in the United States of 1876, the first showing of French art there on any large scale, had greatly increased American interest in Paris, stimulated by concerts conducted by Offenbach and, in Philadelphia, a great panorama of Paris by night. The production of La Bohème at the Metropolitan Opera House, New York, in December 1900 (with Melba as Mimi) was a depiction of what by then had become a familiar representation.

Americans continued to go to Julian's, perhaps most notably in view of his future success in the United States, Frederick Childe Hassam[2003] in 1887. Roger Fry wrote of the Académie Julian in 1892 that there was 'so large a preponderance of Americans that I've not had much to do with French students'.[2004] It has been estimated that by 1888 Paris had an American population of seven thousand, of whom a thousand were art students. Of these, a hundred and fifty were or had been pupils of Léon Gérôme;[2005] the others were chiefly divided between the ateliers of Bonnat and Carolus-Duran, with the Académie Julian accounting for yet others, sometimes simultanæously,[2006] and some stayed on for shorter or longer times ('on no class of visitor does Paris lay her spell more heavily than on the American art student'[2007]), returning home to success or failure, or moving on, like Elihu Vedder, to Rome and elsewhere. Many, perhaps most, seem hardly recoverable, such as the painter Fales of the impasse Hélène, or the lithographer Gortelmeyer, a friend of Saint-Gaudens.

In 1892 the United States Minister reckoned that there were about five hundred American girls studying art or music, and the model named as Alice Brisbane by Marie Bashkirtseff may be included in any reckoning for the previous decade. Among the Americans, Fanny Osbourne, who married Robert Louis Stevenson, for a while lived in the same house as Margaret Wright from Illinois and her daughter, both painters. Anna Klumpke[2008] was at Julian's in 1883-4 and became the protégée of Rosa Bonheur, while Celia Beaux studied there and at the Colarossi in 1888/9 under Bouguereau, Robert-Fleury, Dagnan-Bouveret, and Gustave Courtois, as well as privately with Benjamin-Constant. Edith Catlin, daughter of Julius Catlin of New York and a friend of Rudyard and Carrie Kipling, also studied there, and her sister Julia, wife of Trevor Park, a millionaire industrialist, settled in Paris. Alice Barney brought her daughter Natalie with her, the future 'Amazon of Letters'. Of these, Mary Cassatt now has probably the greatest reputation.

Antony Ludovici met E.M. Ward and Aubrey Hunt at the studio of Gérôme when they were all at the École des Beaux-Arts and thought that they were among the first to go there. This was in 1869/70, and by 1873/4, we find at Carolus-Duran's the Americans Robert Hinckley, Birge Harrison (brother of Alexander Harrison), Theodore Robinson and Walter Laurent Palmer. Even earlier William Hunt from Boston and John La Farge, from New York but of French parentage, had been painting in Paris, the first returning with a velvet jacket, while the second 'when out of doors wore the wide-brimmed black hat and carried the furled black umbrella that were the badges of the Parisian art student'.[2009] At a crémerie in the boulevard Montparnasse, Martin Ross noted an American who 'has formed himself as nearly as possible on the model of the French art student by the simple device of allowing his hair to grow, brushing up his moustache, and abjuring soap [...] A little more, and he will tuck a napkin into his collar at meals, and wear a short frock coat with his blue velvet tam-o'-shanter'.[2010] This was long before the influx of Americans into Montparnasse drove up studio prices and augmented the colonisation of Montmartre, a turn-of-the century phenomenon noted by Paul Henry.[2011] A gap seems to have opened up between the art students whose Mecca was Montmartre, where life was steadily becoming more lurid (as accurately recaptured by Jacques Becker in his 1951 film *Casque d'Or*[2012]) and those who remained true to the Latin Quarter and Montparnasse. Chris Healy in the late 1890s defined 'the American Bohemia' as lying between the avenue de Maine and the Observatory, 'distinguished by some poverty and much knowledge of poker and of art [...] I must confess that the American Bohemia was more lovable than its English neighbour'.[2013]

Hinckley was Carolus-Duran's first pupil and this started the painter's teaching life. Hinckley returned to a successful career as a portrait painter in Washington. Will Low, also of the Carolus-Duran circle, knew yet other Americans, John Love from Indiana, Olin J. Warner, Ridgeway Knight, a rather chocolate box sort of artist. Edwin H. Blashfield was a pupil of Bonnat's. John H. Twachtman of Cincinnati was at the Académie Julian early in the 1870s; the Philadelphian Mike Ramsay was in Paris at the end of the 1870s. John T. Coolidge (son of the United States Minister) exhibited a portrait of his wife Katherine (the daughter of Francis Parkman) in the Salon of 1884, but left in September of that year. Henry Bacon, on the other hand, a pupil of Edouard Frère, remained in Paris, 'leading the life of a happy artist and littérateur'[2014] in the rue Newton, from about 1870 to about 1900, while Frederick Carl Frieseke went to France in 1898 (Académie Julian, atelier of Constant and Laurens) and remained there until his death in 1939. Maurice Brazil Prendergast attended the Académie Julian and Colarossi's from 1886 to 1889, coinciding at the latter with the illustrator Alice Havers, 'a charming English lady' whose 'real name was Mrs Fred Morgan, but, owing to incompatibility of disposition, was no longer living with her husband.'[2015] Prendergast, whose name bespeaks an Irish origin, evidently stayed in Paris for his painting 'Jardin du Luxembourg'[2016] dates to 1892-4.

Sometimes friends went together, such as Frank Weston Benson and Edmund C. Tarbell in 1883 followed by their Boston classmates Robert Reid, William Paxton and Philip Leslie Hale. All of these studied at the Académie Julian and Hale, who moved to Paris from Boston in 1887, at the École des Beaux-Arts as well, becoming an Impressionist under the influence of Monet. Paxton studied at the Boston Museum School with

Tarbell, the Cowles Art School (Boston) with Dennis Miller Bunker, and Benson; the Académie Julian and the École des Beaux-Arts with Gérôme, and became a well-known portrait painter when he moved to Philadelphia.

Richard Whiteing was greatly struck by this colony:

> The Americans are legion [...] With the Americans it is Paris or Munich or nothing [...] Ridgeway Knight [...] Bridgman [...] Mosler [...] Dannat [...] Sargent [...] Bacon [...] Healy and May are the doyens of American art in Paris – the first in portraiture, the last chiefly in genre. Miss Gardner has a marked preference in style and subject for the art of Bouguereau, her master; and among the still numerous admirers of his school, her works are held in high esteem. Blackman, Alexander, Harrison, Reinhart and Stewart are among the younger generation of painters settled here who have made their mark[2017].

He could have added Frank Boggs, Kenyon Cox, William DeLeftwich Dodge, Robert Lee MacCameron, Siddons Mowbray, Harper Pennington who painted one of the few portraits of Wilde, William Picknell, Julius Stewart, Douglas Volk, Wyatt Eaton and Lawton Parker, all of whom were pupils of Gérôme.

This all suggests a camaraderie of pleasant company. Frederick Bridgman, a friend of Will Low's, had spent two summers in Pont Aven before moving to Paris and the studio of Gérôme in 1866. This was arranged by Thomas Eakins who secured the entry of a group of American students, amongst whom were Eakins himself, Earl Shinn, the future Orientalist Harry Humphrey Moore, and Bridgman. Eakins remained in Paris until 1870. Bridgman remained there for four years, spending his summers at Pont-Aven with another American painter, Robert Wylie.[2018] After this Bridgman divided his time between Paris and North Africa, and it was as an Orientalist that he achieved both fame and fortune: his house on the boulevard Malesherbes was said by John Singer Sargent that it and the Eiffel Tower were two sights worth visiting Paris to see. Bridgman also rented an atelier in the same building as two other Americans in Paris, Bonnat's pupil Charles Sprague Pearce and E.H. Blashfield. In 1874, William Lippincott travelled to Paris where he shared an apartment with Blashfield, Pearce and Milne Ramsey, studying under Bonnat. Lippincott stayed in Paris for eight years, a regular exhibitor at the Paris Salons. In the Eakins' set we also catch a glimpse of Joseph R. Woodwell.[2019]

To Whiteing's list can be added the Boston painter Robert Vonnoh,[2020] who attended the Académie Julian in Paris from 1881 to 1883 and again in

1887, spending much of the next three or four years in Grez. Frederick Childe Hassam applied the Impressionism he learned in Paris between 1886 and 1889 to his Boston and New York street scenes, and his friend Abbot Fueller Graves studied figure painting at the Académie Julian under Cormon, Laurens and Gervex from 1887 to 1891, returning frequently thereafter. While in Paris, Hassam showed successfully at a number of exhibitions, including the Paris Salon, the Exposition Universelle (where he received a bronze medal) and at Georges Petit's gallery. Robert Henri and William Glackens shared a studio in 1896/7; on his return to New York, Glackens continued to paint as if he were still in Paris, to which he and Henri returned frequently.[2021]

Another American who did 'go down before Paris and worship her', and whom Paris fashioned after her own liking, was Dennis Miller Bunker, who returned to America with his first name spelled Denis and declaring that his surname was originally Bon Cœur. He did not quite disappear, however, for although he died aged twenty-nine in 1890, he is portrayed in Sargent's 'Denis Miller Bunker at Chalcot' and commemorated in the poem by Robert Frost 'Two Painters: Willard Metcalf and Dennis Bunker'.

Aubrey Hunt continued to spend time in Paris and was painted by Lavery, but his friend Herbert Coop thought that this too was an act of refashioning: 'Having him looking like a missionary that never made a convert, just won't do!'[2022] Sylvia Beach's parents were similarly dislocated by the experience of Paris:

> Father and Mother loved France and the French, though we knew very few French people [...] I think he was a Latin at heart [...] Paris was a Paradise to Mother.[2023]

The preoccupations of American art students indicated a strong interest in academic teaching, traditional skills to do with anatomy, perspective, tonal values; and little in the art that enthused the Parisian *jeunes*. What would Maillol have made of the statue of Shakespeare in accurate Elizabethan dress with a lap for children to climb into, made in Paris in 1892 by William Ordway Partridge for Chicago? What would Matisse have thought of Gustave Cimiotti, who went in 1899 to both the Académie Julian and the atelier of Delescluse before making a career in his native New York as a painter of placid and Romantic landscapes?

American concern for the value of the dollar prevailed over the pioneer spirit, and this was noted as a displeasing characteristic by the Irish artist

Henry Jones Thaddeus – that and their tendency to be disdainful about French ways. Not only Gérôme but even Bouguereau were their models,[2024] and choosing the former may also have indicated a certain Yankee shrewdness for he presided over a committee[2025] that had in its gift annual bursaries of nine hundred dollars for American art students[2026] from Boston and New York. Both Alexander Harrison and Eugene Vail[2027] were students under Gérôme. In 1891 the award went to John Briggs Potter (Boston) and H. Bryson Burroughs (New York). Thomas Buford Meteyard, however, was rich enough to paint in Paris or Giverny whenever he chose, living there continuously from 1888 to 1893 and having a spell at the École des Beaux Arts, before settling down in Rye as a neighbour of Henry James, while his aunt Francesca Lunt preferred life in Paris as the comtesse d'Aulby, at least until the painterly connection was marred by the count's imprisonment for passing off fake old masters to the widow of C.H. Paine, the Boston Copper King.

There can be no final reckoning of the American artists in Paris, and even an interim tally leaves little room for constructing their lives. Certainly local enthusiasm will bring into the light the occasional 'native son' or daughter, but the task of examining their remains is likely to be at worst futile, at best elusive. Can we learn more about the Paris life of John Leslie Breck, for instance, whose 'Giverny Winter' is in the Carnegie Museum in Pittsburgh?[2028] Here is the necessary background for Henry James's John Little Bilham, so 'notoriously not from Boston',[2029] and with a name too reminiscent of du Maurier's Little Billee for comfort: Bilham is almost always referred to as 'little Bilham'.[2030] One is tantalised by such glimpses, just as one is by the passing through Paris in April 1895 of Mary Smith, a Philadelphia Quaker who had married the London Irish Catholic barrister Frank Costelloe in 1885, and left him six years later for Bernard (then Bernhard) Berenson. Her life, like Berenson's, was fixed in Italy.

There was also a strong tradition of Americans studying architecture in Paris: Richard Morris Hunt, for example had been at the École des Beaux-Arts in the early 1850s, Henry Hobson Richardson in the late 1850s, Stanford White's early colleague Charles McKim in the last years of the Second Empire, Louis Sullivan in the early 1870s, Richard Watson Gilder at the end of the 1870s, Ernest Flagg at the École des Beaux Arts in the 1880s. Indeed the firm which White entered in New York, McKim, Mead and Bigelow, greatly reflected French education, William Mead having gone to Paris in the spring of 1879. Their draughtsman Joseph Merrill Wells was in Paris from August 1880 to January 1881 and compiled a sketchbook of impressions. John Ames Mitchell, the founder of *Life* magazine, also studied art and architecture in Paris at the end of the 1870s. Whitney Warren, co-founder of the New York firm Warren & Wetmore in 1896, went to the École des Beaux Arts in 1892 and stayed in Paris for ten years, absorbing the influences that led to the art nouveau design he produced for a number of American buildings, notably Grand Central Station in New York. The other influence he absorbed was a fifteen year 'mystical love affair'[2031] with the actress Cécile Sorel.

The sculptor Augustus Saint-Gaudens was no stranger to Paris, for he too had studied at the École des Beaux Arts, from 1868 to 1870. He had come to Paris from New York in February 1867, and stayed first with his uncle François in the avenue de la Grande Armée, moving on to the rue des Trois Frères in Montmartre where he worked for an Italian cameo cutter called Lupi, and when defeated by the distance to the Beaux Arts, first to the rue des Écoles then to the rue Jacob. Saint-Gaudens returned to Paris in July 1877 and stayed till the end of the year, taking a studio in rue Notre-Dame-des-Champs, and living first in the rue du Faubourg Saint-Honoré and then in the rue Herschel, where Stanford White climbed to the fourth floor to visit him: 'For young White, accustomed to the grime and dirt, the mostly narrow and crowded streets, and the commercial bustle of New York, Paris was a revelation'.[2032] In a few days, White (the nephew of a Paris-based American called Charles Clinch Smith) saw the Louvre, the Exhibition, the Salon, the Musée de Cluny; and went to the Cirque d'Hiver, the Opéra, and the Comédie Française where he saw *Phèdre*. He returned for his honeymoon in March 1884.

Saint-Gaudens was again in Paris in 1878 (he and Stanford White dined at Foyot's on 13th August) and in 1879 (until the summer of 1880), exhibiting at the Salon. By then he and his wife were known in both the artistic and the American colonies, especially at their intersection: he was 'well acquainted with Will H. Low, Carol Beckwith, Kenyon Cox,[2033] Edwin H. Blashfield, and John S. Sargent',[2034] as well as knowing Joseph Evans and William Gedney Bunce, the latter living in Paris since 1867. Mrs Saint-Gaudens was named Augusta, and the couple were known as Gus and Gussie. Born Augusta Homer, she was herself a painter and she and many of her family were familiar with Paris – she had shared a flat with her friend Amey Goodwin in the rue Castiglione in 1875, and her cousin Annie Bunker Homer lived in Paris for most of her life. Another cousin, the song composer Sydney Homer moved to Paris in 1890, where his wife, the contralto Louise Beatty Homer, made her operatic début in 1898. But Camille Sidney abandoned the New York ballet and was taken into keeping in the rue de Rome.[2035]

Gus met Mark Twain (who was staying at the Hôtel Normandy) at this time, and executed a bas-relief medallion of Bastien-Lepage, whom he had known at the Beaux Arts and 'disliked for his general cockiness'.[2036] The Louvre on Sunday afternoons was his recreation, followed by a classical concert at the Cirque d'Hiver;[2037] he occasionally went to the Opéra (his favourite was *Le Pré aux clercs*[2038] by Hérold) or to the Comédie Française. Henry Adams, with perhaps some irony considering the heavy Parisian involvement of Saint-Gaudens, thought that 'Of all the American artists who gave to American art whatever life it breathed in the seventies, Saint-Gaudens was perhaps the most sympathetic, but certainly the most inarticulate'.[2039] Low found him a man of layered identities: 'born in Dublin, of mixed French and Irish parentage, he was not only American but one of the very few genuine New Yorkers that I have ever found'[2040] – his biographer adds fittingly that Saint-Gaudens was a born mimic.[2041] For a long time, Saint-Gaudens had been unaware of his Dublin birth, and French speaker though he was, preferred to be called Saint-Gawdens in the anglophone manner. His small pointed beard was, however, very much that of the French artist.

Saint-Gaudens then spent two weeks in Paris in 1889, staying with Frederick (Willie) MacMonnies, who had once been Saint-Gaudens' studio assistant but had moved to Paris in 1884 to study sculpture at the École des Beaux Arts. MacMonnies lived in the rue de Sèvres (number 44), not far from Huysmans at number 13.[2042] In 1895 another of Saint-Gaudens' pupils, Clio Hinton[2043] (subsequently Clio Huneker, and then Clio Bracken) moved from New York to become a pupil of MacMonnies. Another, Mary Lawrence, was a promising sculptor who gave up the art when she married Tonetti, MacMonnies' assistant ('Half Italian, half French Faun'[2044]) and they moved to the United States. Saint-Gaudens did not care much for MacMonnies' work, an antipathy picked up by his biographer, who sees MacMonnies' portraits in terms not so much of shape-changing but positively of deformation: 'Some of his men [were] so exaggeratedly muscular, his women so voluptuous, that they all looked as though made of rubber and inflated like balloons.'[2045] Indeed, MacMonnies' self-portrait of 1896[2046] shows him in the worst style of Sargent as Velasquez and Carolus-Duran combined. When Saint-Gaudens was made Officier of the Légion d'Honneur, and thus outranked MacMonnies who was Chevalier, he remarked of his friend 'I'm wicked enough to wish to make him feel uncomfortable. It's impossible to make him feel small.'[2047]

Saint-Gaudens returned to Paris at the century's end, living in the boulevard Péreire[2048] from November 1897 to June 1900, and finding a studio 'after the usual inevitable agony of a dreary, maddening and useless search in a charming little garden-like passage in the rue de Bagneux'.[2049] Here Henry Adams visited him, and carried him off to stroll in the Bois (but 'a walk in the Bois is no fun unless you're with a woman'[2050]), or was himself taken to meet others of the sculptor's friends.

It was MacMonnies, however, who introduced Saint-Gaudens to Whistler 'whom I found much more human than I imagined him to be'.[2051] The three dined occasionally together at Foyot's, and it was Saint-Gaudens, commissioned by Charles Freer, who executed the Whistler Memorial at West Point.[2052] But to know Whistler was to avoid Wilde, of whose presence in Paris Saint-Gaudens can hardly have been unaware, although Wilde is unlikely to have been attracted to Saint-Gaudens' sculpture of General Sherman, which won a gold medal in the Salon of 1900. A conjunction might otherwise have been expected: it was after all Saint-Gaudens who was to be responsible for the Parnell Monument in the Irish capital, and his son records that his father 'declared that he felt in his element with anything Irish',[2053] a tribute doubtless to his Irish mother, for Augustus was six months old when his parents emigrated from Dublin. If this serves to dislocate Saint-Gaudens geographically, Henry Adams also supplies a temporal dislocation: 'In mind and person Saint-Gaudens was a survival of the 1500s'[2054]. The sculptor was thus another fugitive in Paris.

The position of Irish-Americans in Paris needs study: were they popular because they were Irish or unpopular because they were American? We have little to go on. Of Thomas Walsh, a member of the American Commission for the 1900 Exhibition, a colleague wrote 'Everybody liked this honest, kindly, generous Irishman.' His daughter Evalayn became a Bright Young Thing *avant la lettre* in the Paris of the new century.[2055] The Irish American sculptor John Donoghue, who became a friend of the Wildes in Paris, is almost as ephemeral a figure.

Bourke Cockran, also living in Paris at that time, was the constant companion at the theatre of Lady Randolph Churchill, the American Jennie Jerome; in turn she introduced him into Paris Society. Cockran, from the Co. Sligo, had a distinguished political career in the United States. Having been educated by the Marist Fathers at Beauchamp, near Lille, he spoke fluent French and should prove an interesting conduit of information both political and social. Unfortunately, neither of his biographers[2056] refer to this Paris period, although James McGurrin records

that when after Cockran's father's death, his mother moved the family to
Dublin (Leinster Road, Rathmines) and held Sunday afternoon 'at homes',
an occasional visitor was Lady Wilde, remembered by Bourke Cockran as
'a huge terrifying person with a regal personality and a thunderous
voice'.[2057]

Many of these Americans lived on very little, on far less indeed than they
regarded as the minimum required at home; but it was easy to incorporate
this into the beguiling fantasy of being an art student in Paris. When
Isadora Duncan went to join her brother in Paris in the spring of 1900

> Raymond met us at the station. He had let his hair grow long over his ears,
> and wore a turned down collar and a flowing tie. We were somewhat
> astonished at his metamorphosis [...] We had no money, we had no friends
> in Paris, but we wanted nothing. The Louvre was our Paradise [...] When
> we had dined off white beans, salad and red wine, we were about as happy
> as anyone could be.[2058]

The presence of American girls was particularly significant, as they seem
to have been more like Hester Worsley than Anna Klumpke, let alone the
courtesan Elisa Parker,[2059] from Ohio, who became Madame Mussard.
Madame Foinet, wife of the supplier of painters' materials of the rue Notre
Dame-des-Champs became a sort of unofficial protector of the American
girls. Rothenstein names as studying painting 'Miss McGinnes, who
became Mrs Albert Herter, and Mrs Frederick MacMonnies, the centre of
an attractive circle';[2060] in the early 1890s, Anne Douglas Sedgwick,[2061]
the future novelist, also studied painting in Paris. They were all
remarkably conspicuous.

> The great Anglo-Saxon colony of students clustering round the Gare
> Montparnasse and scattered over the Quartier, are responsible for many
> changes. The most aggressive amongst them are the art students of the
> United States [...] They organize exhibitions by groups [...] American girl
> students [...] If they go to a café or restaurant they usually sit together in
> corners, forming little groups apart [...] American girls usually live in
> boarding houses and always go to church [...] The influence of the
> American Girls' Club and of the Student Hostel are distinctly visible
> throughout the Quarter. These institutions have introduced a new tone.[2062]

In 1891 assembly rooms were opened in the rue Vavin for young
American women students.

> There were a great many of them without friends or money, and this was to
> give them a place where they could meet together, read, become

acquainted with one another, and find a home. [...] I made a short address, in which I warned them not to be carried away by their enthusiasm, but to eat regularly and take the proper number of hours of sleep and exercise.[2063]

In fact, there had always been concern for the protection of foreign girls in Paris, and Miss Leigh's Home for English Girls in the avenue de Wagram had long been an institution in both senses of the word. Americans, of all ages and both sexes, who distrusted foreign accommodation could choose between Miss Ellis' boarding house in the rue de Bassano and that of Miss Herring in the boulevard Haussmann. The tone was, however, clearly visible. Dorothy Menpes noted that

> One can nearly always distinguish an English or an American girl, especially an art student. There is an indescribable something about the hang of her skirt, the angle at which her hat is set; she has that clean healthy groomed well-set up appearance which one knows so well but cannot easily be put into words.[2064]

Americans in any case were free-er spirits than their English counterparts, the women more autonomous.[2065] As her biographer remarks of the actress Elizabeth Robins 'Her American background gave her perspectives and even freedoms denied to her British counterparts',[2066] while D.S. MacColl thought that the Kinsella sisters displayed 'the double social freedom and vivacity of their Irish-American birthright'.[2067] Lucy Martin Donnelly studied at the Sorbonne in the early 'nineties before returning to a distinguished career at her alma mater, Bryn Mawr.[2068] The sisters Helen and Mary Mears, from Oshkosh, Wisconsin, took to Bohemian life in the cafés of the Left Bank, Mary gathering material for a novel,[2069] Helen working (1896-1898) with Saint-Gaudens as a sculptor; while Annette Johnson from Ohio, also in Paris to study sculpture, moved in with Saint-Gaudens' brother Louis, married though he was. Mary Mears caught the prevailing spirit when she described the customers in the Café de la Paix: 'The rifts of smoke seemed to sever the heads from the bodies and they floated on it'.[2070]

The United States Minister, noting a number of women students at his Independence Day reception in 1892, commented that

> These poor girls are generally without means, and devote the best years of their lives to music or painting. I am afraid that nine out of ten do not succeed, and have to find some other occupation on their return to America; but you cannot help admiring their indomitable courage.[2071]

The American students were coherent enough to form in May 1890 the American Art Association with rooms in an 'old, tumble down building'[2072] in the boulevard Montparnasse, coherent enough to have their own journal, *Le Quartier Latin*, edited by Trist Wood.[2073] This survived for nearly three years between July 1896 and March 1899.[2074] It was not long before they discovered Montmartre. Apart from its erotic allure, Bonnat's studio was in the rue Laval, although by the time the Chat Noir opened next door he had moved to the impasse Hélène off the boulevard de Clichy. This latter studio was subsequently acquired by Benjamin-Constant, who transformed it into 'a very good imitation of an Oriental interior'.[2075] A number of painters 'good, bad and mediocre',[2076] had studios here, J.P. Russell, A.S. Hartrick, Henry Ryland, Jan van Beers. That of the Irish playwright and painter W.G. Wills is described by his biographer:

> Paris never lost its spell upon my brother. For part of the year he made it his headquarters [...] It is not a savoury part of the town, and the studio looked out on a dreary piece of waste ground where skeletons of omnibuses took their last repose.[2077]

One may also conclude that American girls chaperoned one another: these were the predecessors of the 'bachelor girl'. An account has been left[2078] of the adventures of three young women ('Gene', 'Marjorie' and 'the Duke'), written chiefly by Enid Yandell, a pupil of Rodin's, who became known for a large scale public statues and monuments, including that of the seventeenth century Indian chief Ninigret for whom the model was a member of Buffalo Bill's Wild West Show in Paris. Chapter II is set in Paris in 1891, and starts artlessly enough: 'We beg to assure our readers that we do not consider this little book in any way a literary effort. It is a simple story which really wrote itself, and it is with great modesty and hesitation that we cast it upon the sea of public opinion.'[2079] The Paris chapter, from the diary of 'Marjorie', is a factual account of the stay in Paris of Mrs Potter Palmer, there to study the lessons of Expo of 1889 in order to prepare the Women's Pavilion for the World's Columbian Exhibition. She holds a meeting at the Grand Hôtel for women who do:

> First, Madame Guyot, the bright and progressive wife of M. Yves Guyot,[2080] who was at that time minister of public works, and a member of the Cabinet. She was accompanied by her daughter, who was charming, and a perfect type of the jeune fille, sweet and modest as a blush-rose bud. Then Madame Siegfried, Madame Bogelot, who has done such magnificent work for women in the dreadful prison of St. Lazare, and our own Mrs Logan, whose earnest black eyes, under the halo of snowy hair,

watched every movement of the speaker with great interest. Mrs. Logan was accompanied by her son and his wife, who were both very pleasant and entertaining. Next to them sat Mrs. Harrison and Mrs McKee, who were visiting Mrs. Whitelaw Reid, and who made so many friends abroad where ever they appeared. One of the Americans residing in Paris spoke of them as 'our American Princesses,' and the name soon became popular. Next to them sat Mrs. Palmer and by her side Miss Hallowell, who is one of the most widely acquainted of our countrywomen in Paris. Her opinion is sought and respected on everything connected with art, and she has a warm personal acquaintance with all the painters and sculptors who constitute the charmed inner circle in the famous art life of the gay capital. Last of all was Mrs. May Wright Sewell of Indianapolis, who was the American delegate to the Exposition Congress of Women in Paris in 1889, and who consequently has an acquaintance with numbers of prominent workers among the French people.[2081]

Mrs Potter Palmer herself is described in terms which she suggest that she was not so much transformed by being in Paris as transfigured.

> I shall never forget how she looked as she stood in the middle of the large salon, explaining to these distinguished French people in their own language the difficult points that would require an unusual vocabulary and a judicious choice of words in one's own tongue. Sometimes she was at a loss for a moment, and then she would stop and appeal to M. Siegfried, or change her way of phrasing, for it was quite a different thing to talking the ordinary French of shop or drawing-room, which she speaks with fluency. She never for an instant lost the perfect self-poise and charming dignity that lent an added impressiveness to her every word.
>
> As I saw the interest deepening on every face, turned to this slender young woman, and noted the deferential attention given, not to her beauty or her position, or to the grace of her manner, but to her wonderful intelligence, and to the clear reasoning that dominated her hesitating speech, I felt a strange sense of emotion. Miss Hallowell leaned over to me and whispered, 'I never expected to see such a sight as this,' and I noticed the moisture in her eyes.[2082]

The sort of life that young women involved in the arts might lead in America could have habituated them for a Bohemian existence in Paris. Another who shared a flat (or, rather, an attic) in New York was Elizabeth Robins. This cost her eight dollars (two pounds, fifty francs) a week including meals, before she moved to another room which cost four dollars per week, without meals, which she replaced with oatmeal and cream at twenty cents, buns and soup. Paris could provide a more agreeable atmosphere even on this sort of money. 'Nowadays,' observed Mathilde

Marchesi, 'young girls who come to Paris from abroad to study […] may go about alone without fear of annoyance provided their dress and bearing are modest and reserved.'[2083] How this would have appealed to Hadria, the New Woman in Mona Caird's *Daughters of Danaus*, in Paris to study music, may be doubted.

Respectability was, it will be recalled, a concept that found no favour in the Wilde household. It may have coloured Wilde's views of Americans in Paris, many of whom professed a respectability that amounted to hauteur. Ralph Martin has written that the salons of the Americans Mrs Richard Haight, in the place Vendôme, and Mrs Ridgeway, in the rue François Premier ('a highly fashionable part of Paris'[2084]), were among the most exclusive in Paris;[2085] one may add the name of the American duchesse de Choiseul, married in Paris in 1891, or of the comtesse Chandon de Briailles of the avenue Marceau, formerly a Miss Garrison. There was some frontier crossing, such as that of the Société des Américainistes, a learned body. Sometimes marriage blurred boundaries: Mrs Charles Moulton, an American whose husband and his parents all lived in Paris, married *en secondes noces* J.H. de Hegermann-Lindencrone, who was Danish Minister in Washington.

Entertaining was as important to the Americans who could afford it as it was to the French though it was said that champagne was served more lavishly by Americans than by the French.[2086] This was established even before the end of the Empire. The Harrimans took a house in the Champs Elysées, where there was an enclave of 'American and Anglo-Irish gentry',[2087] and hired Waldteufel's players for a ball; an invitation to any one of the Pringles' weekly dances was good for every succeeding one. Mrs John Mackay, the wife of the 'Bonanza King', the Dublin born exploiter of the Comstock lode who had made a fortune in Virginia City, preferred to live in Paris, and took an interest in the rising star when Emma Nevada sang in Paris, lavishing expensive gifts upon her. Mrs Mackay also entertained extravagantly, was reputed to have offered a million francs for a box at the Opera and, with no more success, tried to buy the Arc de Triomphe. A friend of Wilfrid Blunt's whom he calls Lady C., told him that Mrs Mackay also financed General Boulanger.[2088] Madame Courval 'who was a Ray from New York',[2089] did have a box. Mrs Charles Livermore with even greater persistence married baron Raymond de Seillière, committed by his family to a lunatic asylum in 1887. In his biography of Proust, George Painter names Mrs Meredith Howland[2090] as 'one of the very few Americans then admitted to high society'.[2091] She was one of Montesquiou's few women friends and had ties with Charles Haas and Degas, but the sources are chiefly silent, reflecting her own exclusiveness as 'une des personnalités les plus recherchées du Faubourg Saint-Germain'.[2092]

Mrs Sumner, whom Henry James knew in Rome, moved to Paris and became Mrs Mason; James also met in Paris Lilly von Hoffman, sister of 'Uncle Sam' Ward, and Mrs Strong of New York with whom he heard Verdi's *Requiem*[2093] and *Aïda*, conducted by Verdi himself. Mrs von Hoffmann was regarded by Thomas Coolidge as having some the finest pearls he had ever seen, and as being very clever;[2094] perhaps the two were connected. Mrs Ayer ('of great wealth and hospitality'[2095]) had Van Dyck and Sibyl Sanderson sing at her receptions, and Reichenberg and Bartet recite. Mrs Livermore and Mrs Frederick Pierson both acted as chaperones for the young Elsie de Wolfe in 1890, who was in Paris for much of that year. (Mrs Pierson should not be confused with Blanche Pierson, 'a queen of tragedy'[2096] of the Comédie Française, who both painted and appears in Henri Gervex' 'Le Mariage civil' of 1881.) Rather less exclusive was the American comtesse d'Aunay, who is said to have given Clemenceau a son; rather more reclusive was Mrs Lily Coit, an old American lady living at the Grand Hôtel as a permanent resident at the turn of the century.

> I think the American nationality is the most convenient in the world. The Americans do just as they like, and no one is ever surprised. The explanation is quite simple: 'They are Americans'.[2097]

Another American *salonnière*, whom Wilde and Constance met on their honeymoon in Paris, was Henrietta Reubell, to whom Henry James formed a great attachment. James introduced her to Margaret L. Woods, the poet wife of an Oxford don, in Paris to gather material for a book intended to include scenes of artist life[2098]; this led Mrs Woods to William Rothenstein, who recalled her as 'a delicate Shelley-like person, who talked delightfully in a clear, silvery incisive voice'.[2099] Rothenstein thought Henrietta Reubell 'the most notable personality among the Americans I met with in Paris'.

> In face and figure she reminded me of Queen Elizabeth, if one can imagine an Elizabeth with an American accent and a high shrill voice like a parrot's. She was also a close friend and admirer of Oscar Wilde's, to whom she was constantly loyal, despite Whistler's jibes.[2100]

Langlade, giving her address as 42 avenue Gabriel, adds her name to those of Sargent and Bourget at the dinner party Wilde and Constance gave on the 4th June at the Hôtel Wagram. It is the more surprising that references to her are scarce, especially as at one time 'it seemed very likely' that she and Henry James would marry for all that 'she was too tall and too thin'.[2101]

The duchesse de Choiseul[2102] was only one of many American women who transformed themselves by marriage into French aristocrats: Anna Gould did this twice, marrying the duc de Sagan and Boni de Castellane. 'I was surprised at the number of American women in the Faubourg,' wrote T.J. Coolidge, who became United States Minister in 1892. 'They are all beautiful; most of them are rich. They became French immediately.'[2103] American marriages were well-established, for Caroline Georgina Fraser had married Prince Murat, son of Napoléon's marshal and Napoléon's sister, as long before as 1831. The comtesse d'Aramon, the marquise de Talleyrand (née Elizabeth Beers Curtis) were both Americans. The wife of the comte de Sartiges, sometime French ambassador in Rome, was the former Miss Thorndike of Boston 'who always retained the simple, natural manner of the well-born American'.[2104] The comtesse de Lansay, however, invented the title for herself – she was a Mrs Jackson – when her lover, a Levantine banker, installed her in the Château de Louveciennes. Grace Wilson, the daughter of a contractor enriched by the American Civil War, though later to marry Cornelius Vanderbilt II rather than an impoverished aristocrat as one of her sisters did, seems to have assimilated to the type to an almost heroic degree:

> Accustomed to spending her summers abroad since her eleventh year, she was an accepted member of the most discriminating circles of London and Paris [...] Her French was flawless, her German good [...] She knew by heart every aria from every great opera [...] Jean de Reszke had given her both singing lessons and his slavish devotion.[2105]

In 1894, this paragon attended the Dublin Horse Show in the company of the duc and duchesse de Luynes, the duc d'Aosta and the conte di Torino (son of the King of Italy): but there were no longer Wildes in Merrion Square.[2106]

Excluded from the most snobbish houses of the French aristocracy unless they married into them, Americans retaliated. Of the Warrens of the Boulevard Haussmann, George Greville Moore wrote 'I never met a Frenchmen in their house, and like many of the best Americans, they never invited any Frenchman to visit them', also noting that the English Mrs Willington only asked English people to her dances. 'The American colony was small and exclusive,' wrote Colonel Mott, *en poste* at the U.S. Embassy in 1900. The Warrens' daughter Minnie, who later married a

Vanderbilt, was painted by Chaplin in a portrait 'which hardly rendered justice to her beauty'.[2107]

> Mrs Munroe, surrounded by her sons and her two daughters, Mrs Ridgeway and Madame Hottinguer, reigned for long years by right of intelligence and dignity as well as of seniority. Mrs Griswold Gray's salons, when spring arrived, were filled with Burdens and Bradley Martins on their annual visit to Europe, and old Mr Joe Peabody as he sipped his brandy (after champagne and burgundy) invariably recalled some incident of his earliest trips. The Tucks, the Winslows, the Wilmerdings, the Harjes, Miss Fanny Reed, Mrs Ingraham, Arthur Kemp, Persifer Gibson, kept things going in the winter.[2108]

It all sounds rather grim.

Sometimes Americans over-assimilated. Mary Waddington once 'heard one of my friends, an American born, married to a Frenchman of very good family, [say] "Toute la canaille est Républicaine".'[2109] Sometimes it was their fortunes that were assimilated: Boni de Castellane invited three thousand guests to his wife's twenty-first birthday party in the Bois de Boulogne where the entire corps de ballet of the Palais Garnier performed and twenty-five swans were released: it cost eighty-seven thousand dollars of her money, but later he was divorced from both wife and fortune in 1906. In 1912 Beerbohm drew him sitting a bare room.[2110]

Sometimes, however, assimilation proved beyond the American grasp:

> The more I try to converse in French, the more difficult it becomes. A few months suffice to learn to understand and to speak French, but to do it well is so difficult that I have never known more than one or two foreigners to succeed.[2111]

Tony Allen, in his study of Americans in Paris between 1918 and 1939, noted that they met with disapproval from the older colony, which had been 'fairly cohesive as a group, tending to seek out each other's company. Their relations with the French were generally cordial but not close'[2112]. They were also diluted by transients, like Abigail Pankhurst, who when widowed by Edward Wright in the 1880s, travelled in Europe and lived in Paris until she married Prince Alexis Karageorgevitch.[2113] Others seemed to live as they might have done if still in the United (or indeed the Confederate) States. The Green family, moving from Savannah, Georgia, viâ Le Havre to Paris in 1898 not only brought their furniture with them, 'to the French eye a spectacle of horror,[2114] but a Confederate flag as well.

Ex-Senator and Mrs. Gwin, of California, maintained much of their accustomed elegance in a large apartment where they gave many parties; Dr. and Mrs. Marion Sims, with their handsome daughters, Mrs. Pratt (who appeared at a fancy ball, as an American Indian princess, with great éclat), Carrie, and Florence; and the Slidells, one of whom went to the same ball as 'Rain' under a wonderful umbrella dripping with a shower of silver drops, were Southerners much admired in the society of the day. Mr. and Mrs. John Bigelow, to be our good friends and neighbors in Gramercy Park in later years, were just leaving Paris to yield their place to General and Mrs. Dix when we arrived. Mr. Parke Godwin, our future neighbor at Bar Harbor, made the speech of the evening at the farewell banquet given to Mr. Bigelow at the Grand Hôtel in December.[2115]

This separation was challenged by the increasing number of American marriages, so that the Faubourg was divided between those who came to an accommodation and those who became yet more isolated. Although in the 1870s few Americans were living as spouses in Paris, by 1914 they were 'legions of all kinds' there, though 'I think all Americans remain American no matter where they marry'.[2116]

~~~~~~~

Of the American students, not all were art students. George du Maurier has a brief description of an American medical student whom he calls Vincent and who 'is now one of greatest oculists in the world and Europeans cross the Atlantic to consult him'.[2117] Geneviève Ward studied acting under Régnier and played Lady Macbeth at the Porte St-Martin, experience which served her when she came to play the wicked siren Stephanie de Mohrivart in *Forget-Me-Not* in London; she also became the comtesse de Guerbel. Many Americans came to Paris to study singing, whether like Kate Bensberg, Nevada, Eames or Sanderson to turn professional, whether like Rose Stewart and Eleanore Everest to become teachers in their turn (in Philadelphia and Boston respectively) or whether like Tess (Therissa) Porter of Bridgeport, Connecticut, to pursue a lady-like accomplishment – although even then, this was not always the realm of the ingénue.

As our winter in Paris was avowedly for the purpose of giving my education the 'finishing' touches sadly omitted in [American Civil] war experience, I was forthwith started in lessons of various kinds, including a training of the voice by M. Archaimbaud, of the Paris Conservatoire. To meet exigencies of foreign opinion, I was transformed back into the conventional *jeune fille,* accompanied everywhere by my mother. I often wondered what my testy little maître de chant would think if I told him I had sung war songs to marching troops, or played accompaniments for a chorus of soldiers surrounding me at the piano? I believe he would have fainted, then and there![2118]

Blanche Roosevelt, daughter of a successful prospector in Montana (or of Senator Tucker from Wisconsin) and but doubtfully related to the presidential family, studied under Pauline Viardot. The summit of her operatic career was only as high as Josephine in *H.M.S. Pinafore* and Mabel in *The Pirates of Penzance* during the D'Oyley Carte American tour of 1879, and she found that such talent as she possessed lay in writing 'hectic murky novels like *Stage-Struck, or, She WOULD be an Opera-Singer*',[2119] and, between 1884 and 1886, in being the mistress of Maupassant, a dangerous thing to be. Despite or perhaps because of this, she married the marchese Macchetta d'Allegri. Victor Hugo is said to have called her 'the beauty and genius of the New World'. According to the palmist Cheiro, it was at her house in London that he read Wilde's hand: this is noted by Ellmann without inquiry about her, but she contributed articles to *Woman's World* when Wilde was editor, including one on Maupassant. Neither Maupassant's biographers nor Wilde's show much curiosity about her, and the latter seem to have missed that she lived at 69 Oakley Street, making her a near neighbour of Lady Wilde at 146. Whatever about Cheiro and Oscar, she gave a dinner party there for Maupassant, du Maurier, Henry James and Bret Harte.[2120] She also wrote biographies of popular figures such as Longfellow, Sardou and Verdi, and died at the age of forty[2121] in 1898, either comprehensively of cerebral thrombosis, Bright's disease and cirrhosis of the liver[2122], or simply in a carriage accident in Monte Carlo.[2123]

Some American music students even studied music seriously. It was her singing career that turned Claire O'Connolly, born in Paris on 14 September 1882, the daughter of the expatriate American Colonel John Townsend O'Connolly, into Claire Croiza, who after lessons with Jean de Reszke made her debut at Nancy in de Lara's *Messaline*[2124] in 1905. The Californian Emma Ramsey studied singing and later won enough engagements to enable her to send for her brother Lewis and help pay for him at Académie Julian, where he studied under Bouguereau and Jean-Paul Laurens from 1901 to 1903. The American soprano Clara Louise Kellogg, on the other hand, retired to Paris and turned impresario, although there was certainly one occasion when she sang at a reception given by the Waddingtons, accompanied by Arthur Sullivan. Mary Garden, born in Scotland but brought up in the United States, also studied singing in Paris, her lessons in 1896 paid for by one of Marchesi's former pupils Sarah Robinson-Duff of Chicago, a woman who 'had a manner that was wonderfully French'.[2125] Garden also took lessons with another Italian, Giovanni Sbriglia, who had taught Felia Litvinne and Sibyl Sanderson. There was also the niece of the United States Minister James B. Eustis, Mrs Keenan, a high contralto, whose voice was 'thought by many to surpass Mrs Story's and Sibyl Sanderson's.'[2126] (Two other Eustis nieces also lived in Paris, Lydia Eustis and Mrs du Bois.)

Garden in these early years led a very Parisian life. In the spring of 1899 she met Edward Mayer of the Chicago firm Schlesinger & Mayer, which had a Paris branch at 56 rue des Petites Écuries. The Mayers had been giving Garden an allowance which they now stopped, disapproving of dinners at the Café de Paris. Garden was then befriended by Sibyl Sanderson; there is an atmosphere in the accounts of exploitation here. According to her father 'It was Paris did it for her. When Mary went over there she was a jolly, laughing girl who never used her head unless she had to [...] Paris has made my daughter cold and calculating'.[2127] When Sanderson moved to Nice, Garden took a room in a pension in the rue Chalgrin.

Although she sang Marie in Lucien Lambert's *La Marseillaise*, it was Charpentier's *Louise* that was the making of Garden's reputation. Originally, Marthe Riotan was to have sung the heroine, but she was not up to the part and her understudy was ill, so Garden took her place on 10th April 1900 and was an instant success. She went on to sing Diane in *La fille de Tabarin* by Pierné,[2128] with libretto by Sardou, conducted by Messager (with whom she was perhaps having an affaire), and of course Mélisande and Salomé. Garden 'believed Salomé to be a paradox. She was complex. She was Vice and yet she was the archetypal woman. In Mary's view, Salomé was a child of nature, thin and very young and very red-headed'.[2129] After singing in the United States, Garden was conducted in the rôle by Messager in Paris in May 1910. Willy said of this that it was the Salomé of Wilde and Moreau. Garden herself gave a curious judgment: 'I have never heard anyone conduct the opera as Messager does. Strauss conducted Salomé for me and I assure you the opera was scarcely recognisable'.[2130]

The American Clarence Whitehill (Iokanaan in Thomas Beecham's première of Strauss's *Salomé* at Covent Garden in 1912) was also a music student in Paris and came to the fore singing in Massenet's *Thaïs* and *Manon*. James Huneker arrived to study at the Conservatoire in 1878/9 dressed in a velveteen jacket, open-neck shirt and a Tam o'Shanter: his biographer remarks drily that he was 'determined not to be taken for a bourgeois tourist'.[2131] Huneker, who was a Yiddish speaking American Irish Catholic Fenian with a Hungarian name, was later described in the New York *Press* as having 'the wit of an Irishman, the grace of a Frenchman, the power of a German and the versatility of an American'.[2132] This composite figure went to pay homage to the Café Guerbois, and claims not only that he saw Manet and Degas there but also 'heard some of the bizarre and beautiful stories improvised so charmingly by Villiers de l'Isle Adam'[2133] – 'claims' because 1878 was very late for the Café Guerbois. He was also thrilled to see Flaubert passing in the street. Later he was to seek out Ibsen, Shaw, Strindberg, Strauss, Debussy, Schönberg, Cézanne and Matisse, but when he met Wilde in 1890, he described him as 'beginning to fall off […] a peach too long in the sunshine'.[2134] Picking up a commission to write articles for the Philadelphia *Evening Bulletin*, Huneker's first despatch[2135] was titled 'Paris! Beautiful Paris!'

Huneker's fellow American, the future composer Edward MacDowell was a contemporary at the Conservatoire, but not many Americans went there. In 1881 the American singer Emma Thursby who sang at Pasdeloup's concerts at the Cirque d'Hiver, was awarded the medal of the Société des Concerts of the Paris Conservatoire, even though her reputation was almost entirely transatlantic, as was that of Emma Juch. Marchesi's American students included Mdlle Elliot, subsequently 'a concert singer in New York, I believe',[2136] Frances Saville, Emma Eames, Emma Nevada, Emma Silvania,[2137] and Sybil Sanderson,

Distinguished from all the Emmas was Marchesi's pupil Maud Starkweather, but this splendid name became transmuted first into Maud Starkvetta and then into Maria Duma.[2138]

Sibyl Sanderson, with whom Massenet became infatuated, became the great American Paris favourite. She had been introduced to Marchesi by Fanny Reed, 'one of the most esteemed members of the American colony in Paris', but Sanderson thought Marchesi's training too rigorous until Massenet persuaded her. She made her debut in The Hague / La Haye / Den Haag in *Manon* in January 1888, singing under the name Ada Palmer. Massenet then wrote *Esclarmonde* specifically for her, from the French romance *Partenopeus de Blois*.

For five weeks the composer and his muse worked on the score of *Esclarmonde* together, Sibyl wondering if she could possibly sing a role that was becoming more and more elaborate as Massenet became more and more infatuated. Only the presence of Mrs. Sanderson, suffering from an eye infection, seems to have prevented him from taking the ultimate step. Comments scribbled on his manuscripts reveal Massenet's troubled state of mind during these touchy days: 'A painful evening last night...Sad end to the S evening...Sleepless night, a sad future...' When the opera was finished at last, Massenet insisted that Sanderson add her own signature on the last page of the manuscript – the opera was hers, he felt, as much as his, and the first audiences seemed to agree. When the soprano made her entrance in the prologue and unveiled her face, 'there was,' according to Mary Garden, 'a gasp of adoration from one end of the house to the other.'[2139]

Esclarmonde was written for the Exposition Universelle of 1889 and opened on the 14th May 1889: 'Sanderson's Esclarmonde became one of the season's most admired physical objects, second only to the Eiffel Tower, the 1889 Exhibition's other major attraction. All Paris, in fact, was talking about the diva's cadenzas and high G – the "sol d'Eiffel" as her fans dubbed it.'

Esclarmonde, however, was savaged by the critics, as was Massenet's next opera for her, *Le Mage*, and Saint-Saëns' *Phryné* (1893), which was also written for her. She sang Manon again in the 1891 revival, and the United States Minister Coolidge, visiting her in her dressing-room, found Massenet fussing over her. 'Her schooling is said to be most admirable, and her voice much admired by the French,' Coolidge recorded in his diary.[2140] It was, however, in *Thaïs* (16th May 1894) that Sanderson's moment came, in more than one way, when at one point during the first performance, Thaïs' dress became unhooked, perhaps by accident. The audience was stunned and delighted 'to see Mademoiselle Seinderson naked to the waist,' as Willy reported, punning on the soprano's name (*sein* is French for breast).

At first, Sanderson had lived with her mother and sisters in the rue Lincoln, 'a short but fashionable street',[2141] when she was brought to study music and language at the age of fifteen. At that time, the family remained for two years (1881-1883), but returned in 1886, when she studied with Marchesi and Sbriglia. They had been left well off by Silas Woodruff Sanderson, a justice of the California Supreme Court, so Sanderson always remained something of an independent, and private engagements (such as the one on 17th December 1892 when she sang with the wife of Henry Austin Lee of the British Embassy) must have been for pleasure not from necessity. When she sang in St Petersburg the Tsarevitch (later Nicholas II) went every night and 'showered her with jewels'. She was sufficiently

Bohemian to have a stormy private life, which may have included lesbian affairs and certainly included a tragic marriage, to a Cuban millionaire called Antonio Terry, who died suddenly, as did their small daughter. Her death in 1903 prevented a second marriage to Count Paul Tolstoy, and curiously echoed that of Nana:

> Mary Garden visited her friend shortly before her death and was horrified at the sight of a woman whose beauty once had all Paris agape. The poor woman had baskets over her because she couldn't stand a sheet touching her body, which was all swollen and discolored. In the corner sat a man with a cigar. 'Don't you think you should smoke somewhere else?' Garden politely suggested, but Sanderson motioned her friend to her side. 'No, Mary,' she whispered, 'let him smoke; he's my fiancé.'

> Sanderson died two days later. Garden was summoned, but refused to view the corpse—'I'm glad,' reported Sanderson's maid, 'because she's frightening to look at.' Badly shaken, Garden attended the funeral and afterward wrote, 'I thought I never would get out of the church for pain and sorrow. I could feel something tearing and tearing within me...After Sibyl was cremated, they put her ashes in a box, and they put the box into the wall of the Paris crematory. Then they gave her a number, and there we leave my beautiful friend in her thirty-seventh year.'[2142]

Paris was divided between her admirers and those of her rival, Emma Eames. Mary Waddington heard both of them when on leave in Paris between September 1888 and May 1889, Eames as Juliet 'very handsome, fresh young voice', Sanderson, 'also very handsome, but in a quite different style'. 'Massenet has taught her everything,' she adds of her *Esclarmonde*.[2143] Eames, another pupil of Marchesi's, achieved success singing with Jean de Reszke in Gounod's *Roméo et Juliette*, but it is her partnership with the bass singer Pol Plançon (another of Sbriglia's pupils) that is chiefly remembered. Plançon first sang at the Paris Opéra in 1883 as Gounod's Mephistofélès, and remained for ten seasons.[2144] As well as in Paris, both sang at Covent Garden, Plançon every year from 1891 to1904.

Lilian Nordica (whose real name was Norton), from Farmington, Maine, made her Paris Opéra debut in 1882 as Marguerite in Gounod's *Faust*. Less well-known perhaps is Emma Nevada, another pupil of Marchesi's, whose real name was Emma Wixom (she was born in Nevada City, California). She made her debut at the Opéra-Comique in September 1883 as Zora in Félicien David's *La Perle de Brésil*, which so impressed Verdi that he engaged her for La Scala in Milan, where she sang in twenty-one performances. She also played Mignon in the eponymous opera during the autumn season at the same theatre. In 1884, after a dispute over costumes with Carvalho, the director of the Opéra-Comique, she moved to the Théâtre Italien where she sang the role of Lucia in Donizetti's *Lucia di Lammermoor*. The dispute was over whether Nevada should wear a black or white dress.

In March 1884 Nevada converted to Catholicism, most likely under the influence of Mrs John Mackay. On marrying Dr Robert Palmer in October 1885, Nevada presided over a musical salon at her house in the avenue de Wagram; she named their daughter Mignon.

Also American were Mrs Stone-Pyne and her sister Blanche Barton who sang for charity concerts. Another American amateur who sang at charity concerts under her own name, such as it was, was Mrs Joe Riggs (and she subsequently became the Principessa Ruspoli), who sang in the church of Saint Roch. Born Rosalie Van Zandt, she was the wife of Joseph Karrick Riggs 'long a resident of Paris and a man of intelligence and honour and respectability',[2145] and there may be a recollection of her name in that of madame Vanzade, the employer of Christine Hallegrain in Zola's *L'Œuvre*. The American singer Marie van Zandt,[2146] who created the rôle of Lakmé in April 1883, was perhaps related. George Painter falls into unwonted dislocation when identifying her as a constituent of Odette de Crécy's creation 'Miss Sacripant'.

> A certain Marie van Zandt [...] was no doubt either a relative of the Amélie van Zandt who sang Mignon and created the part of Lakmé [...] or the same person using a different Christian name.[2147]

Marie Van Zandt had been brought to Paris when a small child by her mother, also an opera singer who used the name Madame Vanzini. Her début was at the Opéra-Comique in 1882 when she was a great success, but her career was badly damaged when her voiced failed during a performance of *The Barber of Seville* in 1894 and it was put about (perhaps by Emma Nevada) that she was drunk. There was a riot at her next performance. She did not sing again in Paris until 1896, and retired when she married Mikhail de Tscherinoff in 1898, eventually moving to Cannes.

Sibyl Sanderson lent something to Carlotta Peel in Arnold Bennett's *Sacred and Profane Love* of 1905. This fictionalisation of an American singer came to haunt Bennett when he became briefly engaged to the singer Eleanor Green in the following year. Green (elder sister of the future novelist Julian Green) was the daughter of an American family who had lived in Paris since 1898,[2148] part of a set of Americans such as the painter George Ullman, the novelist Mrs Roy Devereux, the dentist William Farley and his Irish wife Agnes, 'easy-going, outspoken, informal people, interested in the arts, amusing sociable' who lived in the rue de la Paix. Clearly they did not sneer at Bennett's provincial clothes and accent in the way that Clive Bell did, and they offer glimpses of Americans in Paris, not particularly distinguished for wealth or talent, who bridged the old-established American colony and the new twentieth century influx.

Margaret Drabble's description of Agnes Farley as 'an expert gossip, matchmaker and hostess' seems to acknowledge this rôle; both this description and Violet Hunt's description of her 'as just mad enough to be charming' seem to combine satisfactorily characteristics from her background and her place of residence.[2149] Julian Green remembered her as 'a stout woman with an ugly face and a charming smile. A small cigar was perpetually burning between her fingers'.[2150] Farley, also 'quite mad' according to Hunt, was himself sufficiently Parisian: 'He was a trick dentist […] it was said that he could take a tooth out of your head and it put it back again the wrong way up.'[2151] He was also a very rich one, charging eight pounds for a single crown. Wilde must have had a dentist in Paris, for where else would he come by his dentures, but it can hardly have been Farley.

~~~~~

In the early nineties Isabella Stewart Gardner, having inherited $1.6 million upon her father's death, came twice a year and 'entertained lavishly at her small and modest-looking hotel in the rue de la Paix'.[2152] She was no stranger to Paris, having been to school there in the 1850s. She bought her first Worth dress in 1867, and came to Paris every few years. In 1879 she went with Henry James to see Mademoiselle Juton at the Cirque, and with her husband Jack, Henry James and the Henry Adamses went to the theatre. This was the Westminster, and the entertainment 'a round of dinners, luncheons and theatre parties'.[2153] Well-seen at the American Legation, she brought the Minister, Thomas Jefferson Coolidge, to Whistler's studio in November 1892, for Americans came to Paris to be painted[2154] as well as to paint and buy paintings. (In December 1891 Gardner bought Vermeer's 'The Concert' at the Hôtel Drouot.)

Gertrude Atherton, the American novelist and friend of Sibyl Sanderson, was in a good position to view Parisian life, as she stayed with her relatives the American Consul General and his wife, Major and Mrs

Lawrence Rathbone, in the Champs Elysées. Major Rathbone was a friend of Gordon Bennett, and thanks to the illness of the wife of Robert McLane, the United States Minister, Alex Rathbone was responsible for official entertaining, but although 'their Thursdays were crowded, I met no one who interested me'. Instead, 'I enjoyed the springtime in Paris, the galleries, all else that delights the wandering novice visiting for the first time in that historic treasure laden city' recalled Atherton of 1889, identifying the predominant mode of exploration and one that Wilde's *nom-de-ruse* of Melmoth 'the wanderer' also recalls.[2155] Atherton did however find her way to the literary salon of an American married to a French baron (chaperoned by Major Rathbone, for whom '"literary salon" had an ominous sound'). Here she was introduced to George Moore, 'anything but handsome: tall and blond, with a long colourless face that looked like a codfish crossed by a satyr' who gave her the impression that 'most of his life had been spent in Paris'.[2156] For his part, Moore recalled that Atherton wore a head dress that she 'fondly believed made [her] look like Pauline Bonaparte'.[2157] Each was deceived in the other.

The Legation[2158] may not have been a social centre under McLane, but there were still diplomatic dinners, such as the one Maurice de Bunsen attended in March 1886, where the Austrian Ambassador (Count Hoyos), the Swedish and Dutch Ministers (Leuwenhaupt and Stuers), and their wives, were there with the Freycinets. De Bunsen and Stuers went on to see *Les Diamants de la Couronne* at the Opéra-Comique, apparently without their wives. De Bunsen's colleague Lister thought Mevr. De Stuers the nicest woman he had yet seen in Paris: 'I have seen a lot of her and quite lost my heart.'[2159] Dining visiting dignitaries was always a part of diplomatic life. When Elihu Washburne was United States Minister in the early 1870s he gave a dinner party at Voisin's for former Secretary of State Seward, Lord Lyons, the marquis de Montholon, ex-Minister Moustier, and Governor Banks of Massachusetts.

It was not only Major Rathbone who was dubious about Paris life, however. James Russell Lowell, epitome of the Boston Brahmin, was of the opinion that 'a walk along Brattle Street was vastly preferable to one along the Champs Elysées'.[2160] This seems to have been a common attitude among conservative Americans, but this lofty detachment was not consistently maintained by Lowell, who having previously visited Paris in 1852 and 1855, spent several months in Paris between August 1872 and March 1873, staying in the Hôtel de France et de Lorraine, 'decidedly French rather than tourist', in the rue de Beaune. Here he was occasionally joined for dinner (at three francs fifty) by Henry James, staying at the

Hôtel Rastadt. Other American acquaintances, Chauncey Wright and the painter Samuel Rowse, were staying at the Grand Hôtel: 'Henry met Wright in the boulevard de l'Opéra, trundling along as if on tiptoe'.[2161]

Lowell took rather a high-toned line with the French. Of *La Tosca* he said (in the recollection of Mary Anderson) 'I have not seen it. I refuse to have my mind dragged in the gutter. If madame Bernhardt will appear in such plays, I for one will forgo the pleasure of seeing her act.'[2162] Lowell might have been the better for Wilde's 'We are all in the gutter, but some of us are looking at the stars.' The *mot* spoken of the American Consul-General John Meredith Read that 'to the frivolous he was known as a man of fashion'[2163] also suggests a certain superior disapproval. This could be reciprocated. 'I don't like the English,' said Willette, 'but I detest the Americans.'[2164]

John Holmes, 'that specimen of Cambridge incarnate',[2165] was also in Paris, at the same hotel as Lowell. Together they seemed to have created a life both Parisian and foreign. 'The days were uniforM. [Lowell] would walk by the river before breakfast, or hunt for bargains in the bookstalls [...] another walk before dinner, preferably with a friend who might share cigars and a walk in the Tuileries Gardens (and almost certainly share Lowell's opinion about Brattle Street). Yet he enjoyed his Paris walks and [...] covered almost every inch of it by foot.'[2166] He described his itinerary to Charles Eliot Norton as 'a walk before breakfast round the parallelogram formed by the Pont de Solférino at one end and the Pont des Beaux Arts at the other, then a walk after breakfast up to the Pont Neuf and across the courtyard of the Tuileries'. This he repeated at dusk.[2167] Lowell returned to Paris in late September 1881[2168] and for two weeks in October 1883.

Oliver Wendell Holmes, who had studied medicine in Paris between May 1833 and October 1835, living at 50 rue Monsieur-le-Prince, returned to Paris for a week in August 1886, staying in the Hôtel d'Orient, rue Daunou, as convenient for the place Vendôme and the rue de la Paix (he had his daughter with him). He too found the city transformed. 'It was the dead season of Paris, and everything had the air of suspended animation. The solitude of the place Vendôme was something oppressive; I felt, as I trod its lonely sidewalk, as if I were wandering through Tadmor in the Desert'. Indeed, when he had last been in Paris, the rue Daunou had been rue Neuve-Saint-Augustin. Anthony Ludovici lodged there in 1872, but when he went back, not only had the street changed its name but his lodgings had been incorporated into the Hôtel Chatham. For Holmes, however, even pleasant afternoon drives in the Champs Elysées and the Bois de Boulogne provoked a feeling of *tout lasse*. 'The drive in the Bois was what made Paris tolerable […] I must say that the whole appearance of the city was dull and dreary. London out of season seemed still full of life; Paris out of season looked vacuous and torpid.'[2169]

He went sight-seeing – St Etienne du Mont, the Louvre, the Musée de Cluny, the Vendôme Column – and called at the American Legation and on Pasteur, but 'I did not see the three objects which a popular saying alleges are always to be found on the Pont Neuf: a priest, a soldier and a white horse.'[2170] The Café Procope, where Holmes had breakfasted as a student, 'had been much altered and improved';[2171] he was charged five sous for coffee, and had a poor meal at a restaurant in the Palais Royal, a disappointing one 'at a very celebrated restaurant on the boulevard' and a good one at the Café Anglais.[2172]

John Hay,[2173] who had been Secretary of Legation from 1865 to 1867, returned to Paris in March 1883 and commented that it was 'a poor place to live in'.[2174] Hay spent a year in Britain and on the Continent in 1893/4, and was three times in Paris, in November and December 1893 and again in the following April, but took no more pleasure than earlier. His published correspondence only refers to a visit to *Madame San-Gêne* on the first occasion, and he told Henry Adams, whom he had hoped to meet in Paris, 'We are going to skedaddle from this gay and wicked city (this is the formula – for my part I found it as dull as a dead rat and vitreous as a mugwump'.[2175]

He was no better pleased on the second occasion with a visit to

> the Champs de Mars Salon, with its wilderness of impressions and nudities, and dirty-looking Frenchmen smoking the cigarette. Why they cannot paint a Frenchman doing something else – blowing his nose, combing his hair, or performing some other natural function – puzzles me. Even a Frenchman must do other things occasionally […] The Salon of the Champs Elysées opens Tuesday, and on Wednesday we ship for London, having seen more pictures than in any previous year.[2176]

In June 1896, the theatre pleased him more, going to Hervé's opera bouffe *L'Œil Crevé* and to the Comédie Française to see Mounet-Sully in *Hamlet*, 'a magnificent performance. The translation is very close to Shakespeare and is given entire'.[2177] He also went to the Ambigu and saw 'an old fashioned melodrama of murders and noble sentiments. The whole house wept, and blew their noses in chorus.'[2178] Nevertheless, despite (or even because of) visits to St Germain, the Louvre and Fontainebleau, Paris filled him with ennui.

> We fill the days with different kinds of idleness. I called at the Londres to Mrs N– but she was not at home. W– T– asked us to dine at the Restaurant L– in the Champs Elysées, a big place, half garden, half house [...] Beside ourselves F– B– and Mrs and Mrs McV–, the artist [...] very chatty and cheery young people.

> We leave tomorrow [...] We have been doing nothing worth telling since last writing.[2179]

Back in Paris in January 1898, Hay only recorded 'a very pretty little dinner' at the B– A–'s, 'only ourselves, in a quaint little maisonette in the Latin Quarter' and a visit *to Cyrano de Bergerac* at the Porte St-Martin 'a most tremendous tour de force of Coquelin.'[2180]

Almost as scathing as John Hay, and from a rarer perspective, was Booker Washington, in Paris in late May 1899. He spent nearly a month there, and 'passed harsh judgment on the French character. Frenchmen might be ahead of black Americans in thoroughness because of the intense competition of their lives, he admitted, but in "morality and moral earnestness", in "truth and high honour, and certainly in "mercy and kindness to dumb animals" the French were far inferior to American blacks'.[2181] It would seem that it was his own countrymen who made most of Washington, the Ambassador (General Porter) calling on him at his hotel. Washington became *persona grata* at the Embassy and Porter presided over at the American University Club where the guests were Washington, ex-President Benjamin Harrison and Archbishop Ireland of New York. Theodore Stanton had arranged accommodation for Washington and his wife,[2182] and they had dinner with Theodore Tilton, but among the French intellectuals they had to make do with August Laugel. He also noted that 'fashion seems to sway everything in this great city',[2183] which sounds as if Margaret Washington was occupying her time.

Stanton was also responsible for the visit to Paris of another civil rights activist, Susan B. Anthony, in May 1883. Stanton's research for his book *The Woman Question in Europe*,[2184] which contains a chapter on France, had brought him touch with Hubertine Auclert, and he introduced the two women. It was an emblematic moment on two counts: it was a meeting of two dedicated feminists from opposite sides of the Atlantic and one also one of mutual incomprehension, for Auclert spoke no English and Anthony spoke no French.

~~~~~~

Henry Adams saw something of Henry James in Paris in 1879, but avoided the literary coteries. Despite a number of visits he never really cared for the place: 'At the best of times Paris is to me a fraud and a snare; I dislike it, protest against it, despise its stage, condemn its literature, and have only a moderate regard for its cooking'.[2185] This prejudice may have been exacerbated by the intense cold that December, and a shortage of firewood in the city, but when he went to Paris in 1897, he said it was because 'like other dead Americans, he could go nowhere else'.[2186] Even so, he stayed until January 1898. The prejudice had been formed a long time before, since it was in 1860 that he first 'squandered two or three months on Paris. From the first he had avoided Paris, and had wanted no French influence in his education. He disapproved of Paris in the lump [...] he disliked most the French mind [...] France was not serious, and he was not serious in going there'. Nevertheless a number of things penetrated his defences: a few idioms, a moderate taste for red wine, a modest liking for the café and Voisin's. 'In a month or six weeks he even forgot to disapprove of it.'[2187] With Will Low, the process was reversed, for the *plaisirs de bohème* faded for him and he only remembered them to disapprove.

> Many lived unwittingly la vie de Bohème; some few, perhaps, consciously, if unwillingly, did so; and fewer still tried with a brave show to flaunt their indifference to conventionality before the world – in a world that was placidly indifferent to their existence.[2188]

~~~~~~

It was not only the American students who would gravitate towards Montmartre. It was inevitable that more established artists should also do so. Will Rothenstein names Alexander Harrison (whose studio in the boulevard Berthier was nearer Clichy than Montmartre), MacMonnies, J.W. Alexander,[2189] Gari Melchers,[2190] the sculptor Paul Bartlett and Walter Gay. Harrison, Rothenstein recalled, 'enjoyed a great reputation among Frenchmen [...] on intimate terms with Manet and Rodin [...] spoke French and understood the French character', while J.W. Alexander 'was more typically American'.[2191] Harrison had been in Paris since 1879, a pupil of Gérôme's at the Académie Julian. He painted in Barbizon and Pont Aven and in 1889 started taking pupils, chiefly American, in Paris where he resided until his death. Kenneth McConkey has observed that Harrison's 'naked females, naturally portrayed "in arcadia', verge on improbability'.[2192] This is a very Parisian usage of 'naturally'. As

Reynaldo Hahn's cousin Marie Nordlinger took tea with him in 1897, one may suggest a wide acquaintance. So far, however, we have an incomplete picture of these artists in their social relations, although this must offer an insight into the engines of change.

Stanford White usually combined business and pleasure when meeting other American artists on his frequent visits between 1884 and 1900: he met J. Alden Weir[2193] in July 1889, MacMonnies in January 1893, Whistler in August 1895, as well as Richard Harding Davis in 1893. The painter Edwin Lord Weeks, whose favourite resort was the Cercle Artistique et Littéraire in the rue Volney,[2194] spent the whole of his artistic life in Paris, living appropriately in the rue Léonard-de-Vinci, where he died in 1903. Edward Darley Boit, another artist and a friend of Sargent's, was a prominent member of the American community, with a house in the avenue Friedland. Mary Repington, a friend of the Boit daughter Florence, stayed there in 1886, being taken to a ball at some other Americans called Munro, in a ballgown by Madame Gloria.[2195]

The artists aside, the names of resident American men are less well-known than those of the women. Apart from the newspaper magnate James Gordon Bennett who lived at 120 Champs Elysées,[2196] the most familiar one is that of Thomas Evans, the dentist to the Imperial court who had helped the Empress Eugénie to escape from Paris in 1870. Curiously, his rival in dentistry was also an American, Dr Bennett of the avenue de l'Opéra; one also notes the American dentist Charles Williams at 102 boulevard Haussmann (where Proust also lived from 1907-1919), and the American doctors Johnston, in Paris for at least twenty-five years from 1850, Robert Palmer, and Henry Schiff, of Montmartre, whose portrait was painted by Saint-Gaudens.[2197] Evans was still in practice in 1890, by which time 'he was reputed to have more decorations than any other man in Europe', living in 'un veritable palais où il exposait ses tableaux, ses tapis, ses objets d'art' at 15 rue de la Paix.[2198] He was the protector of Méry Laurent,[2199] whom he maintained with an allowance of fifty thousand francs a year, some of which she used to support Villiers de l'Isle Adam. George Moore once asked her why she did not leave Evans, to which she replied 'That would be a base thing to do. I content myself by deceiving him.'[2200] Dr Evans, owner of the *American Register*, was vestryman with that other godly man Jimmy Whistler at the American Episcopal Church in the rue Bayard.

The newspaper magnate Joseph Pulitzer also maintained 'a palatial mansion' near the parc Monceau for a time; while Gordon Bennett kept his yacht, the *Noumea*, on the Seine,[2201] using it and its successor the *Lysistrata* (and how did he come to that name, one wonders?) to take his aristocratic friends on cruises as well as hangers-on like Henri Gervex, who painted his portrait in 1903. Bennett thought Pulitzer a 'poor, misguided, selfish vulgarian' and in his turn is described by one of his editors as

> A strange, fascinating, enigmatical figure. If he had not been born rich and had to earn his living he would have been the world's greatest journalist. But he has been hopelessly spoiled for many years, and is now just like an Eastern potentate. His word is law.[2202]

Bennett also helped set up an Anglophone newspaper, *The Morning News* and its sister *Le Matin* in 1884, with the participation of John Mackay and the journalist Samuel Selwyn Chamberlain (1851-1916), who moved from New York to Paris in 1883.

A number of Americans belonged to the intellectual and cultural world of Paris, not all as obscure as the American professors at the Collège de France, or even more obscure such as Mr Pell of New York, living in the rue de St-Petersbourg. The military historian Colonel Theodore Dodge also made his home in Paris for many years. The business world was obviously full of Americans, enough for an American Chamber of Commerce to be founded in 1894 by Dr Stephen Higginson Tyng of New York, who had been Manager of Equitable Life in Paris since 1881.[2203] Nor were culture and shopping the only reasons for visiting Paris: in 1872 the politician Charles Sumner of Massachusetts was a patient of Dr Brown-Séquard, as was President Garfield, whom Brown-Séquard treated by telegram (he died).

While Francis Vielé-Griffin and Stuart Merrill feature prominently as Franco-Americans, they were not the only American writers who made Paris their home. Albert Delpit, a journalist, historian of the Commune, novelist, and playwright, was born in New Orleans but settled in Paris where in 1880 he was awarded the Vitet Prize by the Académie Française. Theodore Tilton was known as 'the most picturesque man in Paris' – which, given Whistler, Barbey d'Aurevilley, Wilde, Villiers de l'Isle Adam, Paderewski, Samuel Pozzi and many others, was no small achievement. Tilton moved from the United States in the wake of his charges against Henry Ward Beecher for adultery with Mrs Tilton, and lived in Paris from 1883 until his death, his complete poetical works being published by the Clarendon Press in 1897 – these included a sonnet sequence in memory of Marie Bashkirtseff. Francis Grierson, essayist,

singer and pianist, was one of Mallarmé's Mardistes from 1889, but he had
frequented Paris since before the fall of the Second Empire. Grierson also
wrote a study of Mallarmé and his books *Modern Mysticism* and *The
Celtic Temperament* were praised by Maeterlinck.[2204]

Stuart Merrill, the American closest to Wilde, was also the link to W.D.
Howells, who wrote a preface to Merrill's *Pastels in Prose* of 1890. These
were translations by Merrill of prose poems by Baudelaire, Mallarmé,
Huysmans and others; Merrill also dedicated a volume of his own poems
to Howells. Howells himself, despite having been married in Paris in
1862, undertook no protracted stay until 1894, when he proclaimed it 'the
wonderful place, the only real capital of the world'. Unfortunately, he
hardly had a chance to undertake more than a visit to Whistler (where he
met Jonathan Sturgis and Henry James) when his father's mortal illness
summoned him home. 'Perhaps it was as well I was recalled home,' he
wrote to his son John, who was studying architecture at the École des
Beaux Arts. 'The poison of Europe was getting into my soul. You must
look out for that. They live much more fully than we do.'[2205] This worry
was shared by James Huneker, who in 1896 fled from Paris because 'I
might become a lotus eater and dream my life away under the rhythmic
winged cathedrals and palaces of marble'.[2206] This is a far cry from Henry
James' triumphal 'I take possession of the old world – I inhale it – I
appropriate it!'[2207]

Compared to the artists, however, American writers did not at this time
stay in any number in Paris, and Henry James is the exception. Even Edith
Wharton, who was there as a child when her parents lived in the avenue
Joséphine (1868-1870), spent no protracted time in Paris until the new
century, although her brother Frederic Jones moved to Paris in October
1894 with his mistress Elsie West and calling himself Mr West; they never
returned to America. Wharton's other brother, Harry, also lived in Paris
from 1896 to 1900, at 146 avenue du Champs Elysées; while their mother
Lucretia settled at 50 avenue du Bois de Boulogne in late 1896 (or early
1897: there is an obscurity[2208]). Before 1900, Edith Wharton visited Paris
on her way to and from Italy: in late 1893 and early 1895, in May and
September 1896, for a few days in July 1899. There was a more protracted
visit to see the Exposition Universelle in June 1900, when she stayed with
Paul Bourget in the rue Barbet-de-Jouy. Bourget's wife Minnie (whom
Wharton thought resembled a Tanagra Madonna[2209]) translated Wharton's
The Muse's Tragedy. This appeared in the *Revue hebdomedaire* in July
1900. Bourget was an old friend from his Boston days,[2210] where he had

also met Isabella Stewart Gardner, with letters of introduction from Henry James.

The novelists whom we do find in fin-de-siècle Paris and writing Parisian novels are Guy Wetman Carryl, who lived in Paris from 1896 to 1902, Robert W. Chambers, there from 1886 to 1893 and Frank Berkeley Smith, author of *The Real Latin Quarter*, *How Paris Amuses Itself* and *Parisians Out of Doors*, there from 1892 to 1912. Chambers had initially gone to Paris to study at the École des Beaux-Arts, and at Académie Julian.

Lawyers, surprisingly, were thin on the ground. Coudert Brothers of New York set up a Paris office in 1879, and this survives at 52 avenue des Champs Elysées although the New York firm was dissolved in 2006. The somewhat ambiguous Edmond Kelly, born in France of American parentage, English upbringing, and Columbia Law School graduation, was employed by Coudert, which he used as a cover while developing his own practice, including an attempt to extricate Seillière from his asylum. Kelly returned to New York from 1891 until the decade's end, and stayed in Paris until 1907.

Certain Americans had moved to Paris from the defeated Confederacy, and these formed a self-created aristocracy. Mrs Burton Harrison was one of these, and somewhat artlessly captured a note of self-reflexive social exclusiveness in her memoirs.

> In October, 1866, my mother and I sailed in the ship *Arago* for Havre, the passenger list made up of many New Yorkers known to each other, including the family of the new United States Minister to the Court of Napoleon III, General Dix. Other people we knew on board were Mr Martin Zborowski, of New York – whose wife had been a Morris – with his sons, John, or 'Laddie', and Elliot, and his young daughter Anna, now the Countess de Montsaulnin, of Paris. A young Southern widow, Mrs. Hewitt, formerly Miss Belle Key, of Mississippi (sister-in-law of Mrs. Walker Fearn), was taking a little blonde daughter, Marie Hewitt, subsequently the handsome Mme. Wilkinson, of Paris, to be put at Mme. Grenfell's school in Paris.[2211]

We get a later glimpse of two of these passengers, which suggests that things did not quite turn out so romantically.

> There were two American beauties, half-sisters [...] Miss Hewett and Miss Zobrowski; the former made a very good marriage to a French count,[2212] because her father gave her twenty thousand pounds as a *dot*, but to her half-sister he said he would give nothing at all, and told her that she must

marry an old Englishman living in Paris, very rich [...] Miss Zobrowski
was desperately in love at the time with a French marquis, but he was not
well enough off, he said, to marry her without a *dot*, so she married the old
Englishman; and the day after the wedding her stepfather gave her the
same dot as he had given to his own daughter [...] The marriage with the
Englishman was far from being a happy one [...] They never spoke to each
other unless actually obliged to do so.[2213]

The two Confederate ladies first moved into the Hôtel de Lille et d'Albion,
and then into the Ville au Bois, a villa of apartments at the Porte Maillot in
Neuilly, where they were joined by a General and Mrs. Myers. They also
met two of the three daughters of General John S. Preston, of Columbia,
South Carolina, 'like goddesses upon a heaven-kissing hill, tall and stately,
with brilliant fresh complexions, altogether the embodiment of vigorous
health [who] occupied, with their parents, a residence in the rue Lord
Byron, receiving and received by the best of French society, with the same
grace they brought to our happy-go-lucky refugee existence in
Richmond.'[2214] The Villa was destroyed in the Franco-Prussian War, but it
remains in Mrs Burton Harrison's pages as a sort of Arcadia.

> ...as pretty a place as could be, with ivy-grown buildings surrounding a
> paved courtyard, where in fine weather the tables for meals were set out of
> doors under the shade of great old trees. A high brick wall, overhung with
> creepers, divided us from the Bois de Boulogne. There, in a small but
> daintily furnished rez de chaussée, consisting of two bedrooms and a
> sitting-room, the latter upholstered in a warm crimson moreen stuff,
> opening upon a wee garden of our own, we spent the winter. We grew so
> attached to our French home that when, during the Franco-Prussian war,
> we heard it had been destroyed by shot and shell – the second abode of
> mine laid low through war's necessities – we were genuinely grieved.[2215]

One of the inhabitants of the Villa was the sister of Alexandre Dumas
père, who took pride in an ancestry that the ladies from the Old South
found distinctly ambiguous.

> Old Mme. Letellier [...] who had an apartment all rosy chintz and growing
> plants, showed me a lock of their 'sainted father's' hair (we called it wool
> in our part of the world), asking me if that was not like the hair of our
> people, generally. She pointed with pride to the deep tinting of blood
> underneath her finger nails, and said: 'I, too, am of your race,
> mademoiselle.' To all of them, to be of the South meant to be off color in
> complexion!
>
> She was a dear little old person, who lent me books, gave me one of the
> great Alexandre's MS. and petted me extravagantly. She adored her

nephew, Dumas fils, whose *Les Idées de Mme. Aubray* had just made its
success at the Gymnase Theatre, and showed me the photograph of her
famous brother sitting with Adah Isaacs Menken on his knee, saying,
indulgently, 'He was always an imprudent boy, ce bon gros Alexandre.'[2216]

Quite in the Paris manner, they embarked upon a salon.

Our little red salon, with its 'feu d'enfer,' as Jean, our attendant, called our
generous fire, opened to some interesting people. Prince Camille de
Polignac and M. de St. Martin were very kind in coming, also dear old Mr.
Francis Corbin, whose family were hereditary friends of the Fairfaxes.
The Preston girls came from rue Lord Byron; Mrs. Myers, with her rosy
young face, bright eyes, and dark hair powdered with white, and the
Amaron Ledoux's, originally from New Orleans, long resident in Paris,
aunt and cousins of Burton Harrison. It was hard to tell which was lovelier
in this family – the mother, renowned since her youth for good looks and
gracious manners; Alice, who died young; Anina, now the Baronne Brin,
of Chateau Beausoleil; or Gabrielle, the present Marquise de Valori.[2217]

The 1889 Exposition Universelle was as great a draw for the Americans as
it was for the English. Whitelaw Reid, who had presented his credentials
as United States Minister on the 22nd May wrote to John Bigelow that
'Americans have been swarming here as if Paris were a new
Oklahoma'.[2218] Visitors, however, could be as naïve then as they can be
now. Mary Anderson noted that Sarah Bernhardt 'acted even better in
Paris than in London'; that Massenet 'always spoke in French'; and that
'much of Massenet's music is too typically French for my taste'.[2219] One
of Reid's first official duties was to attend the unveiling a bronze replica
of the Statue of Liberty (considerably reduced in size) on the Île aux
Cygnes, subscribed by the American colony. It stands there to this to this
day, implicitly inviting the Bois de Boulogne to send its tired, poor and
huddled masses to Paris.[2220]

Although in the view of H. Wayne Morgan, Paris in 1889 'was the proper
spot for Reid, whose cosmopolitan tastes fitted perfectly with the French
capital',[2221] Reid's other cultural needs seem largely to have been satisfied
by riding and wintering abroad (the Riviera and Naples in 1889/90, Turkey
and Egypt in 1890/91). Reid corresponded with Bonnat and Gérôme, and
commissioned murals for his house in New York from Galland. Perhaps
more usefully, he helped Whistler in his campaign against a pirate edition
of *The Gentle Art of Making Enemies* brought out by the American
journalist Sheridan Ford.[2222] Reid's biographer suggests that the 'balls,

dinner and receptions' the Reids gave made their house in the avenue Hoche (rented from the comtesse de Grammont) 'brilliant in the season', but the names that are given (the duc de Broglie, Jules Simon, Alexandre Dumas, John Sargent) indicates a conventional invitation list rather than star gazing, as is also suggested by the dinner party that he gave for Charles A. Dana in November or December 1890, where the guests included Clemenceau (whom he had first met while passing through Paris on his honeymoon in June 1881), Joseph Reinach, de Blowitz, Bonnat, Gérôme and Carolus-Duran. Moreover, 'among the Americans always present there were often old friends, men like Evarts and [John] Hay, Speaker Reed, W.E. Chandler, Wayne McVeagh,[2223] James Gordon Bennett and Thomas Bailey Aldrich'.[2224]

These entertainments sound rather less than scintillating, although the list of guests of the dinner party that Reid attended at Blowitz' house in the rue de Tilsit shows what these all-male power-broking entertainments could rise to: Joseph Reinach, Lord Lytton, Señor Léon y Castillo (the Spanish ambassador), Claretie of the Comédie Française, the playwrights Pailleron and Meilhac, Massenet, Alphonse Daudet's brother Ernest, Gustav Eiffel, the banker Henri Germain, Jules Simon, the painter Munkáczy, Henry Austin Lee of the British Embassy, the marquis d'Autun and a General Nazare-Agha.[2225] The Waddingtons, when Mary was hostess at the Quai d'Orsay, gave small private dinners as well as official ones: eight or ten guests (male) who would include Lord Houghton ('a delightful talker'), Lord Dufferin, Sir Henry Layard (who had 'been everywhere and seen and known everybody worth knowing') and others.[2226]

Reid left Paris in March 1891, returning for a visit in May 1894, but also returning in September 1898 as a Commissioner at the peace conference that met in Paris at the end of the Spanish-American War. This opened on 1st October, the treaty being signed on 10th December. By this time the Legation had been raised to an Embassy and General Horace Porter was ambassador. Reid stayed at the Hôtel Continental and all private meetings of the commission were held there,[2227] his fellow commissioners being Judge William Rufus Day, Senator Cushnahan K. Davis, Senator William P. Frye, Senator George Gray and John Bassett Moore,[2228] secretary. General Wesley Merritt and Colonel (then Lieutenant) Bentley Mott also attended, on leave from Manila. Nor should 'Eddie', the black doorkeeper from the State Department who accompanied them as a sort of majordomo, be forgotten although I fear we shall never hear his story.[2229] What these worthy gentlemen did by way of relaxation will no doubt be uncovered by further research: the 'occasional drives, the inevitable dinners and luncheons, sightseeing in the cold of a Paris winter' sound less than the whole tale.[2230] The Americans appear somewhat dim compared to the Spanish delegation, men 'stiff with formality and mournful dignity [...] with titles that flowed behind them like ribbons in the wind'.[2231]

One official entertainment laid on for them was an evening (12th October) at the Figaro Theatre ('a great many members of the American colony were present, and a number of Frenchmen with American wives'). The Coquelins recited, there was 'some graceful and unusually risqué Spanish dancing', and Loïe Fuller 'told us in bad French [...] one or two little anecdotes about on the intellectual level of a rather vulgar child's newspaper', following these with an appeal that the hostility between the United States and Spain might be settled by arbitration, 'a gratuitous and incredible piece of folly and bad taste'.[2232] It is unlikely that the subsequent dinner at the German Embassy, where the Ambassadress was pro-Spanish, would have restored Reid's temper.

A number of visitors called, including James Gordon Bennett, looking 'perceptibly older',[2233] and on another occasion the American wife of Alexandre Ribot, Prime Minister for ten months in 1895. 'She was not the wife of a Minister at present, she said; besides, she was an American and had a right to talk' – and proceeded to give her views on the Dreyfus case.

> She had no doubt of the innocence of Dreyfus, considered the whole persecution monstrous, and the present intense and proscriptive excitement throughout the country as disgraceful. The whole motive, she said, was a reckless determination to force Jews out of the army, and especially out of the État Major [...] Ribot himself said little on the subject.[2234]

On 8th December, most of the remains of the Spanish Empire were handed over to the United States, and imperialism, twenty-five years after last being identified with Napoléon III, took on a new significance. The negotiations brought to Paris a Cuban delegation, whom Chris Healy met in 'a little hotel off the boulevard Lafayette [...] some almost pure negroes'.[2235] It was clever of them to get themselves identified with Lafayette, but it was without any notable consequences.

~~~~~~~~~

The Yellow Book's editor, Henry Harland, who was from New York where he liked to be thought of as Jewish,[2236] was also a frequent visitor to Paris, where he liked to be thought of as English; but, as Katherine Lyon Mix observes sardonically 'people who were not American sometimes took him for an American'. Harland spent some time at the Sorbonne in 1881, returning with his wife in 1886 and meeting French writers, with the result that his models became Prosper Merimée, Maupassant and Daudet. He returned again in September and October 1889 and again in early March 1893, staying long enough to meet Edmund Gosse when the latter came over in April. 'For three days Gosse and Harland successfully captured Symbolist and Decadent butterflies in their natural habitats', writes Karl Beckson, who rather censoriously refers to this as 'cavorting'.[2237] They visited the Latin Quarter every day with the acquaintances they made, including 'Bobinette', described by Gosse as 'delicate and innocent-looking and playful as if no such thing as the marriage bond ever existed', and 'la Reine de Golconda' who Gosse noted with apparent surprise was 'not painted or powdered in the least degree'.[2238] Harland dined at the Harcourt and met Verlaine at a meeting of La Plume, the fortnightly gathering of writers at the Soleil d'Or, of which Gosse recorded a description.

> Moréas collected us round a table, and we ordered drinks. Suddenly, at the side door, something flopped up out of the darkness like a moth – a timid, shambling figure, in a soft black hat, with jerking hands, and peeped with the intention to disappear again. But there were cries of 'Venez donc, Maître,' and by and by Verlaine appeared and was induced to sit by me [...] Recitations were called for and Verlaine repeated one of his lyrics, in a low voices, with gesticulation, very delicately. Then Moréas, in exactly the opposite manner, with roaring of a bull and modulated sawings of the air with his head.[2239]

As Ann Thwaite comments, for Gosse, who gave a breakfast party at St Germain, this was rather more living the life of Paris than eating sole vin blanc with Hamo Thornycroft before a visit to the Salon. On Easter Sunday, he dined with the Harlands at St Cloud and danced on the bridge. The Harlands delighted in Paris, in that age when travellers' glasses were tinted pink: 'Paris the bright, Paris the beautiful, Paris where the sun shines even while the Heavens pour' exclaimed Aline Harland.[2240] 'This enchanted town, where the sun shines, and the coffee-houses prosper, and everybody has the Artistic Temperament' was how Henry Harland described the city to Richard Le Gallienne.[2241] Le Gallienne reciprocated:

> Paris, half Angel, half Grisette,
> I would that I were with thee yet,
> Where the long boulevard at even
> Stretches its starry lamps to heaven,

And whispers from a thousand trees
Vague hints of the Hesperides.

Once more, once more, my heart, to sit
With Aline's smile and Harry's wit,
To sit and sip the cloudy green,
With dreamy hints of speech between;
[…]

The while the merry crowd slips by
Glitterng and glancing to the eye,
All happy lovers on their way
To make a golden end of day—
O! Café truly called *La Paix*![2242]

Although Harland and Wilde did not care for one another, we read of them dining together at Pousset's in late April 1898,[2243] when presumably Harland footed the bill. Equally hospitably, Harland also once taught a peacock in the Bois de Boulogne to eat cake soaked in absinthe, which was probably the waste of a good peacock. On another of their visits the Harlands were joined for a week by Netta Syrett and they saw Réjane in *Madame Sans Gêne*.[2244]

Often taking a young writer in whose work he was interested (and Syrett was one of these), Harland constituted himself a guide to the Chat Noir, the Mirliton, the Moulin Rouge, 'dining with Dauphin Meunier, supping with Verlaine and breakfasting with the Muses'.[2245] The phrase in fact is part of Harland's invitation, written in the Café de la Paix, asking Le Gallienne to join him and Hubert Crackenthorpe in Paris, which Le Gallienne did on the 14th or 15th October 1894, staying to the 22nd.[2246] Le Gallienne also spent a night in Paris between Davos and London in 1896, and in 1900 spent three more days there (12th to 15th March): 'Paris enchanted him and he suddenly felt more at home there than in any city of the world.'[2247] It was this Paris where Harland could fully realise his 'self-created image of Bohemian, dandy and wit'.[2248] An enchanted town? Certainly, and the enchanter was called Pygmalion – but a Pygmalion in the local mode, reversing the turning of statues into people. One summer Harland and Beardsley played Living Statues against the broken columns at St Cloud for all the world as if they had stepped out of a painting by Puvis de Chavannes; and at five o'clock on summer mornings in 1900 an early stroller would have found Isadora Duncan dancing in the Luxembourg Gardens. No wonder Leonard Merrick caught this when he wrote of his character M. Blotto of Montbonne, 'Had it been Montbonne, he would have seen only a gaunt garret and the need for soap and water – but it was Paris and he saw the shade of Murger and was charmed'.[2249]

Another, American, associate of Harland's who visited Paris was Stephen Crane, there in mid-September 1899. Crane, despite being associated with *The Yellow Book*, was not the man to view with enthusiasm any possible encounter with Wilde. Harland told Crane that 'terrible things might happen if the collapsed dandy found a publisher for his book of memories'; for his part Crane thought that Yeats was the only person who talked sense about Wilde – 'The others talk like a lot of little girls at a Sunday School party when a kid says a wicked word in a corner'.[2250]

> About Wilde and his troubles, a mere stranger and runaway dog like myself can't be supposed to care. I met him once. We stood at looked at each other and he bleated like a sheep. With those bad manners that are so awfully much mine I laughed in his face. He tried to borrow money from Dick Davis when he was being tried, after insulting Davis all across London. Something pretty poor I think. And I owe my brothers too much money to bother about helping with subscriptions for a mildewed chump like Wilde. Blood, &c. If Harris and the rest of Wilde's friends really want to help him, they ought to send him express to Weir Mitchell or some specialist in his kind of malady.[2251]

Far more influential than any of these, but equally in thrall to the Impressionists and the theatre, was Winnaretta Singer. Although born in the United States, she returned with her French mother to Paris in 1878 at the age of thirteen, three years after her father's death. 'During her adolescent years Manet became an object of hero worship.'[2252] This was despite the disapproval of her godfather Edward May, the Paris-based American artist who had been a pupil of Thomas Couture. Winnaretta's art teacher, however, was Félix Barrias, who took over Manet's studio in the rue d'Amsterdam, and through him she became a close friend of Forain: the influence of Thomas Couture could not flow into such an adept, who also collected the work of Monet and befriended the painters Ernest Duez, Roger Jourdain, the Chilean José-Thomas Errazuris, and (more surprising), Sarah Bernhardt's tame painter Georges Clairin. In 1887, already a princess of industry as the Singer heiress, Winnaretta undertook her first transformation, into the princesse de Scey-Montbéliard. This marriage ended in a civil divorce in March 1891 and was annulled in February 1892. As the prince's title was a suspect one, Winnaretta's claim to it became somewhat hypothetical. This was rectified in December 1893 when she married prince Edmond de Polignac. George Painter is rather tactful when he says that 'a single point of difference marred their union:

the princess loved fresh air, and the prince hated drafts',[2253] as one should say as well that a single point of similarity made their union, for as the prince was, like Winnaretta, homosexual, the marriage may also to be said have been somewhat hypothetical. It is, however, as the princesse de Polignac that she became a patron of the arts.

Through Forain, the princess came to know a young architect called Grand'Pierre, who had designed a house for the painter and also for Jean de Reszke. This was perhaps the house in the rue de la Faisanderie which contained a small theatre. The princess commissioned Grand'Pierre to re-model the house that she bought, number 57 avenue Henri-Martin, on the corner of the rue Cortambert. In May 1888 she held two concert performances of Chabrier's *Gwendoline* here, with Chabrier himself at the piano, Fauré at the harmonium and d'Indy playing percussion.   John Singer Sargent painted her portrait in 1889, and in the same year Fauré dedicated to her his setting of 'Larmes', poems by Jean Richepin. This led to her trying to promote a collaboration between Fauré and Verlaine, approaching the latter through Mallarmé and the journalist Robert de Bonnières. This hung fire for a period, neither of the two principals finding the other's approach satisfactory. The princess then tried Maurice Bouchor, whose poems 'Les Symboles' had been published in 1888, and failing to interest him, turned to Albert Samain. Samain wrote seven hundred and fifty verses which Fauré found unsuitable, although he later set many of Samain's poems. By 1892 the princesse was 'beginning to gain a reputation as the guiding spirit behind an increasingly avant-garde salon'.[2254] Before the century was over, Ravel had dedicated his 'Pavane pour une infante défunte' to her. In 1913 she was painted by Jacques-Émile Blanche.[2255]

Her marriage may well have been one of convenience, but it was also one of considerable conveniences. Her husband's mother, Maria, was English, with a sister married to Sir William Rumbold, whose son Sir Horace was subsequently British Minister in Berne. Her husband's sister, Yolande, married Sosthène de la Rochefoucauld, duc de Doudeauville, and was the mother of the duchesse de Luynes. This constituted a formidable cousinage.

~~~~~~~~~

The American in Paris did not escape the critical gaze of the Parisian, a reversal of the rôle of tourist and host. We may see the visitors through the eyes of their hosts, madame Bentzon in her social studies, Dumas *fils* in the play *L'Étrangère*. And there was one bad American, Edward Deacon who one day in February 1892, on finding a Frenchman in his wife's hotel bedroom showed he was sufficiently acculturated to murder him – while the French court was obviously flattered by the imitation of French manners by only sentencing to him a year in prison. 'The sentence did not seem to me to be a severe one,' remarked the United States Minister;[2256] for all that, the American colony wanted the man released and the Government acquiesced. After all, Deacon was very rich, and even though the marriage foundered a year later, the Deacons' daughter Gladys (then Marie-Gladys) became Duchess of Marlborough and her sister Dorothy became Princess Anton Radziwill. Both daughters, and a third called Audrey, had been born in Paris, Gladys at the Hôtel Brighton in February 1881, Dorothy at her parents' house in the rue de Grenelle in April 1891. Edward Deacon returned to Boston, but his wife remained in Paris in the rue Jean Goujon. Gladys, sketched by Boldini in 1899, was absorbed into the circle of Robert de Montesquiou. (The dead Frenchman was Émile Abeille, of the rue de Penthièvre, who under the name of Adam, kept a love nest in the rue d'Anjou.)

Not all were critical of Americans: Alphonse Mucha preferred American women to French ones, even though he had played a notable part in creating the image of the latter.

> The American woman is the most superb creature under the sun, infinitely superior to the most beautiful women of Europe. The anæmic type of Parisian beauty in which all our artists find their ideals, is a false one. Here [New York] the women are strong, solid, vigorous – at once svelte and solid […] The Parisian woman, cloistered between four walls is anæmic. Her smile, her walk, her every movement betrays weakness, feebleness. Here the women are large and robust.[2257]

It would seem that compared to the Americans, the Parisienne was as vaporous as an art nouveau decorative motif.

CHAPTER THIRTEEN

A QUESTION OF GENDER

'The fatherland which is the mother of us all.'
– René Viviani.[2258]

'I used to say when I was young: "I must go over to Paris to be made to feel that I am a woman."'
– Lady Duff Gordon.[2259]

'No women in the world enter so fully into the real spirit of carnival as the French.'
– Ralph Nevill.[2260]

Part 1: Paris is a Lady

'Paris on a wet day is like a woman with draggled skirts.'
– Katherine Cecil Thurston.[2261]

ZOLA'S description of the approach along the Champs Elysées to the Arc de Triomphe[2262] is a specific invitation to see Paris as a feminised topos far beyond the ordinary notion of a female persona in the sense that, say, Berlin was endowed with a male persona: it is a gendering of the very streetscape of the city. It is this that permits such descriptions as that of Arsène Houssaye: 'To Paris he remained devoted as to no other woman in his life'.[2263] At the heart of Arthur Symons' fascination with the repellent side of Parisian life lay a simultanæous, a coterminous, fascination/ repulsion with women, as becomes clear in his chapter on Constantin Guys, himself an artist attracted towards squalor.[2264] Zola's Octave Mouret sees his success in business as 'Paris yielding in a kiss to the boldest man'.[2265] Madame de Vionnet, in *The Ambassadors*, makes a complex link between the city, the concept of *la donna è mobile*, and feminine solidarity, directly challenging the concept of *l'éternel féminin*: 'Ah, but a woman, in this tiresome place where everything is always changing, a woman of goodwill, can always help a woman.'[2266] For Christine Lantier, Paris is the first of her successful rivals for Claude's love, as his picture – the masterpiece of the novel's title – becomes the second. 'Paris haunted him [...] For a long time Claude had been able to hide his longing for Paris but now he talked about it from morning to night [...] He was trembling with emotion, for Paris was calling him'.[2267] Paris exercises *exactly* the power over him that his half-sister Nana exercises over her lovers. This feminisation transgresses the strict grammatical gendering of Paris as masculine: it is, literally, *la France* that is feminine, allowing the concept of Paris dominating France to be given a reading more complex than its simple administrative or economic one. 'French is a dreadfully unsexing language,' reflects one of Saki's characters.[2268]

If Paris herself was sexuality incarnate, so within Paris the position of women was bound up not merely with their social status as women, but with their sexual nature. The most highly visible women were actresses and courtesans. It is necessary to distinguish between courtesans who 'acted' and actresses who bedded, but it is not always easy to make firm divisions. Indeed, at times there seem to have been none: one can consult the directory *The Pretty Women of Paris,* from which, for all its salaciousness, much useful information can be gathered, including the names of theatres where might be found certain named light women – one, known as Kalb, at the Comédie Française itself, although this might have been a confusion with the actress Mary Kalb, who joined the company in 1882, became a *sociétaire* in 1894 and stayed until 1905. Even if that source is somewhat tainted, much other evidence concerning the half-world and its shadows supports the point. Charlotte Kinceler 'achieved briefly her ambition to act, occasionally made money as a prostitute, treated rich or famous men badly, opened a herbalist's shop, was suddenly overwhelmed with religion and, at twenty-six, shot herself'.[2269] Cora Pearl appeared as Cupid in the five-hundredth performance of *Orphée aux Enfers.* Jeanne Forestier, the mother of Paul Léautaud, seems to have been a border line case; Adèle Moutot, who used the name Mirecourt, another.[2270] The actress Henriette Maréchale married her lover, the military painter Alphonse de Neuville, only on his death bed in 1885. Lia Félix[2271] had a daughter by Paul de Saint-Victor, drama critic of *Le Moniteur*. Hortense Schneider pursued both careers with equal success, Grande Duchesse de Gérolstein on the boards (and sometimes off them), and (from 1881) comtesse de Bionne in private life: the conjunction perhaps marked by her ribald nickname 'Le Passage des Princes'.[2272] Irma de Montigny appeared on stage at the Olympia, Caroline Otero at the Alcazar d'Été. Emilienne d'Alençon[2273] first appeared at the Cirque d'Été in 1889, and subsequently at the Casino de Paris and the Menus-Plaisirs. In 1893 she appeared in 'Emilienne aux Quatz'Arts' at the Folies Bergère, and even had a London season at the Alhambra. Of Louise Tautin, James Harding has written 'both as a stage personality and as a mistress, Offenbach found her equally adroit'.[2274] Nana appears on stage and Zola also created 'Sylvaine d'Aulnay', a light comedy actress who contrives to make her lover, the Baron Duvillard, pull enough strings to get her the part of Pauline in *Polyeucte* at the Comédie Française.[2275] The United States Minister used a curiously revealing phrase à propos a meeting with the throat specialist Charles Fauvel, whose practice lay among actresses and singers: 'He offered to procure me any singers I wanted for my receptions.'[2276]

> 'I wouldn't have missed this première for anything. I knew that your theatre...'

> 'You mean my brothel,' Bordenave interrupted, with the cold obstinacy of a man of conviction.[2277]

Zola aside, Georges Ohnet drew a very hostile portrait of an actress he calls Clémence Villa in his novel *The Rival Actresses*, set in the early 1880s. Although she acts well, her success is derived from her lover, a Portuguese banker called Sélim Nuño of the firm Nuño and Grameda, Ohnet's equivalent of Baron Steiner in *Nana*, from whom she has an income and a house, and it is implied that the first lover who took her into keeping was a wealthy woman. 'She was included now amongst the most notorious women in Paris.'[2278] Although it is Henry James's *The Tragic Muse* that has attracted all the critical attention, *The Rival Actresses*, although of scant literary quality, offers details about Paris theatre life, and many insights into the tropes of its representation, although there is little evidence for the novel's being à *clef* save in a very general sense. (Clémence's rival, Lise Fleuron, seems to have many of the characteristics of Jeanne Samary, the theatre manager Rombaud perhaps something of Antoine. There are a few references to Desclées, and one to Bartet as the young lady leading in grace in Paris. The mansion and stables of Nuño in the avenue Hoche, said to have formerly belonged to the Spanish ambassador, are described in terms that suggest those of Felipe Yturbe.) It is however notable for anticipating Warhol in referring to an old violinist as having had 'his quarter of an hour of celebrity'.[2279]

The most notable of those who floated between these worlds was Liane de Pougy. Despite her profession either as a courtesan or actress (she appeared in Jean Lorrain's *L'Arraignée d'Or* at the Folies Bergère, a title that surely recalls the article on Nana by Faucherry in *Le Figaro* titled 'The Golden Fly',[2280]) by the turn of the century Pougy's social position had become unassailable. We find her, for example at the opening of the Paris Ritz in June 1898, with Lita marquise de Breteuil,[2281] James Gordon Bennett, Anna Gould (the marquise de Castellane[2282]), the comtesse de Pourtalès, Kate Moore (known as 'la Mère Moore'), Lady de Grey, Marcel Proust, Arthur Meyer and the Grand Duke Michael, admittedly a somewhat mixed bag.[2283] Kate Moore, in particular, also known as 'Plush', though much mentioned in contemporary memoirs for her dinner parties and her love of the titled, is omitted from later studies.

Within this convention, the fictitious Marie Léonie, mistress-companion of Sir Mark Tietjens, picked up by him outside the Apollo Music Hall in the Edgware Road in London when she was a coryphée with a visiting Paris opera troupe, is a perfectly recognisable figure.[2284] Marie Léonie is a worthy person, but Sylvaine d'Aulnay, as one might expect, is Nana come again, another woman of disordered personality, polarised between outward appearance and inner reality:

> Her great attraction lay in the circumstance that with her virginal countenance and her air of ideal purity was coupled the most monstrous depravity ever displayed by any shameless woman. Despite her innocent blue eyes and lily-like candour, she would give rein, particularly when she was drunk, to the most diabolical of fancies.[2285]

The concept of the actress as incarnate sexuality was recognised within the profession. According to Cécile Sorel, Paul Porel, Réjane's manager-husband, 'used to repeat to Réjane "Produce your voice from the most secret part of yourself; thinks of the spasm which tears it. The words in which your character lives must be acts of love." He even said that another way.'[2286] When the old actress Judith of the Comédie Française remonstrated with her pupil Jeanne Samary (a niece of Madeleine Brohan) that the amount of make-up she wore made her look like a cocotte, Samary replied 'To succeed nowadays you must look like a cocotte'.[2287] But to look like a cocotte, it was not required to behave like one, nor to be treated as one.

> One evening a very rich young man, the son of a well-known banker, who had the entrée of the Comédie Française, was standing in the green room when Samary entered it. He made a profound bow. The actress slightly inclined her head, looked at him frigidly, and said, 'May I give one so young as yourself a little advice? I was surprised, monsieur, when we met yesterday at the Salon – on varnishing day, too – to see you in the company of a woman of no reputation.' 'Madame,' the young man replied indignantly – 'Madame, that lady was my sister.' 'Indeed, monsieur, I could not possibly have guessed it. In this theatre, to which I have the

honour to belong, I always receive you as in my house. I knew you saw
me at the Salon, but declined to recognise me; and so I concluded that your
companion could only be one whose presence at your side made you
pretend not to know me.[2288]

When actresses assumed the manners of *grandes dames*, clearly there was
room for confusion between the two. Harold Kurtz recounts the story of
an admirer telling a famous courtesan '"You look like a Duchess tonight."
"How do you know I am not one?" she replied coldly.'[2289]

It is not clear how far Samary succeeded as an actress – she was called 'la
reine des soubrettes'; dying young, her acting was not what was
memorable. 'Samary, dont le rire sonnait les fanfares à travers les
couloirs', is Jenny Thénard's description.[2290] Frederick Pollock after half a
century remembered her 'irresistible laugh – not even Ellen Terry could
laugh quite like that.'[2291] 'I laugh as much as Mlle. Samary of the Théâtre
Français,' wrote Marie Bashkirtseff.[2292] According to Richard Whiteing,
her 'laugh alone has made her fortune'.[2293]

Sir George Arthur says of Jeanne Samary that it was on her 'delicious
lines Miss Marie Tempest may be thought to have modelled herself'.[2294]
Curiously, the rather straitlaced Marie Tempest herself came to an
interesting conclusion concerning the interaction between actress and
cocotte that also bears upon the construction of Paris as Parisienne.

> I absorb atmosphere, and taste, from others. A French cocotte can rise
> above her simple surroundings, on the wings of her patron, and learn
> manners, learn to absorb the culture of the man who influences her [...] I
> am a little like that [...] Cosmo [Gordon-Lennox, her husband] was
> devoted to the Comédie Française school and I listened to him and went to
> Paris so often during that impressionable time when I was learning to act
> [...] I have never forgotten Réjane's willingness to learn.[2295]

How far this persistent feminisation of France in general and Paris in
particular enhanced the commodification of women is to be speculated
upon; as well as how far such commodification was acceptable to the
commodified.

> 'Who are all these ladies?' enquired a Russian Grand Duke of a friend at
> Longchamps.
> 'They are all *gay* ladies,' replied the friend meaningfully.
> 'And where are the respectable ones?'
> 'There are none left.'[2296]

The author of *The Pretty Women of Paris* describes one brothel in the rue Montlyon as if it were a greengrocer's: 'Another good house, rather cheaper than the first two we have mentioned, but with a fine selection of girls of all sizes and colours'.[2297] Even a journal title which in English would be the innocuous 'Women of the Day', when founded as *Les Femmes du Jour* in 1886 could hardly have not suggested to Parisian men 'plats du jour', a conceit picked up in Buñuel's 1967 film 'Belle du Jour',[2298] in which Catherine Deneuve played Séverine, a woman with a double life as respectable wife at night, and in a brothel by day: how far the choice of the name Séverine was deliberate may be considered.

Dorothy Menpes, however, was thinking in terms of artifice as a means to transformation:

> The Parisian [...] uses poudre de riz, rouge and hair dye freely [...] Men sanction and admire this habit. They may know that the earnest expression of a woman's eyes is caused principally by pencillings; that the carmine of her lips is due to the frequent use of rouge; that the delicate bloom on her face, spiritualising and refining, is from poudre de riz pure and simple; he knows that the glorious auburn, or golden, or blue-black tint of her hair is not brought about by nature alone: but men regard all this as an exquisite feminine weakness, admirable. In their opinion, feminine beauty reaches perfection only when it is aided by art.[2299]

It is possible to see here fascination and disapproval at odds with each other, indicated by the shift from reportage into offering a postulated male perspective. 'I do not wish to mention the subject of women in Bohemia,' wrote Chris Healy with either Irish chivalry or uncharacteristic primness. 'One has to observe the conventions.'[2300] 'By what magic is it that Paris takes possession of you, holds you, fascinates?' Menpes had asked earlier. 'What, then, the mysterious charm? It is not easy to say.'[2301] The answer here, surely, lies in the ability to unseat the visitor's grip on rational narratives of observation. 'Paris is a city that disturbs one's moral values,' reflected Lucy Duff Gordon, referring not to questions of sex, but to reductionist social values. 'To a woman only the fact of being a woman counts in Paris'.[2302] Obviously, implicit in Dorothy Menpes' account is the idea that the origin of this effect lay in the Parisians themselves and their mutations of nature and the natural order. This reached its apogee in a vogue not yet exhausted:

> An absurd craze among Parisian women is the dressing, decorating, trimming and coddling of their dogs. There are actually tailors who earn their living making costumes for the pampered beasts [...] Nowadays it is

necessary that a 'smart' woman's pet should be as well dressed as her coachman or her butler.[2303]

'I am constantly told by the friends who desire to say the prettiest thing they can,' says the narrator of Constance E. Maud's *An English Girl in Paris*, noting conflicting local senses of constructed identity, 'that I am not *tout à fait française – mais tout à fait Parisienne*. A statement of doubtful veracity, but I see what they mean.'[2304] From the emblem of France 'Marie-Claire', to the fifteen foot high statue 'La Parisienne' that stood on the Porte Binet[2305] to welcome visitors to the Exposition Universelle of 1900, her dress designed by Patou, Paris and the Parisienne are intertwined concepts. Arthur Lynch called Sarah Bernhardt 'the most exquisite example of the *fin-de-siècle* Parisienne',[2306] and 'Je chante la gloire de la Parisienne,' sang Jules Berny, but who was the Parisienne and who notre dame de Paris? The duchesse de la Rochefoucauld or Gervaise Coupeau? Jeanne Samary or the Samaritan Woman?[2307] Louise Michel or Jeanne d'Arc? Hubertine Auclert or Liane de Pougy? Juliette Adam or Suzanne Valadon? Réjane or Rachilde? The lorette or the chérette? Marianne or Marie Mère de Dieu? And who was Suppé's *Pariserin*[2308]? This may have been easier to decide at a time when so many people who had thought that they were Berber or Touareg, Annamite or Tonkinois, Shango or Fon, were being told that they were 'French', 'nos ancêtres, les Gaulois'. One might decide that it was not until the homosexual Jean Cocteau designed an image of Marianne for the postage stamps that the ambiguities implicit reached their most symbolic level, a 'caprice de Marianne' unforeseen by Alfred de Musset; but perhaps after all, it was Bernhardt, who was the most representative: the woman who every evening changed into other women and sometimes into men.

A fifteen-foot statue, an artefact so closely associated with patriarchal triumphalism, thus readily became a specifically feminine sex symbol, but fourteen years earlier Richard Whiteing was already catching the element if not of artefact then at least of artifice in the concept of 'Parisienne'.

> With the French the word stands for the ultimate thing to wonder at in civilisation; and they are right, whether one wonders with them or against them. There has been no such work of mere art, as distinct from purely natural growth, in human societies, since man learned to fashion himself.[2309]

The dairymaid of Maupassant's 'Two Little Soldiers'[2310] is described as 'a tall, strapping girl, freckled and tanned by the open air – a girl typical of the Parisian suburbs' – but not typical, by implication, of the city: here is simplicity versus sophistication in the construction of the Parisienne. For Zola, Clarisse Bocquet chatters 'like a true Parisienne, with her superficial borrowed wit and her droll manner'.[2311] The narrator of *An English Girl in Paris* says of a character, 'Odille, though Parisian to her finger-tips, is only one third French. Equipped with a German mother and an Irish grandmother, she can justly claim to be *cosmopolite*'.[2312] One is reminded of the duchesse de Clermont-Tonnerre saying that Tristan Bernard being Parisian and Jewish was doubly Parisian; just as it was said of Albert Wolff that he was called 'the most Parisian of Parisians', even though a German.[2313] James Laver has noted of Huysmans that Paris

> was the only mistress from whom he was never estranged, and one might call her the only wife he ever had. He, the son of an immigrant, was a Parisian of Parisians [...] and of all Paris, he knew best and love most deeply his own *quartier*, the little square of earth enclosed by the rue St Jacques, the boulevard St Germain, the rue du Bac and the river.[2314]

This was *parisianisme*, the exaggerated 'Parisness' adopted by those who came from the provinces,[2315] and can be read against Henry James' Jeanne de Vionnet (daughter of the comte and comtesse de Vionnet), who says 'Oh, but I am not a little foreign girl, I am just as English as I can be [...] but I'm almost American too'.[2316] Here identities shift and reform.

~~~~~~~~~

Though courtesans at the higher degree may well have been able to retain control, they were still exchanged. But then so were their lovers, and clearly the market value of either to other was established in Parisian interchange. 'In Paris the lovers of any celebrated courtesan see each other every day' wrote Alexandre Dumas *fils,*[2317] and English rules of 'kiss but do not tell' did not apply. Considering the position of women in transformative terms, Brian Reade advances the view that 'Some of the liveliest and earliest and more essentially female trustees of the New Woman, from Giselle (or Gisèle) de l'Estoc,[2318] Maupassant's Androgyne, to the Divine Sarah herself, the Woman Who Did in apotheosis, could only have thrived in Paris where culture and commerce combined more than in any other place to occupy men with women and women with each other'.[2319] Here one may oppose the simultanæous cultivation of the asexual virgin Jeanne d'Arc, the pucelle *toute simple*, against the vogue for the highly sexualised virgin Salomé, the pucelle/putain (or Salomé/ salope), the courtesan or even the 'petroleuse' against the *bonne femme*, decadence against the moral order, the anarchist outrages of the early 'nineties bringing the head on a platter close to the fears of heads on pikes, the guillotined heads of Vaillant or Henry as important in the mythopœia of anarchism as was that of the Baptist among Catholics.

~~~~~

Life on the boulevards indicates the locus where the beau monde faded into the demi monde, the *flâneur* into the *rastaquouère*, the songs of Fauré into those of Paulus or Aristide Bruant, *grandes horizontales* with euphonious or pseudo-aristocratic names (or noms de guerre) like Emilienne d'Alençon, Delphine de Lizy (or Delizy), or Léa d'Asco, 'whose high-sounding name hides some very plebeian denomination',[2320] *viâ* Pomme d'Amour, Océana,[2321] Signoret, Vif d'Argent, Fil der Fer, Clair de Lune or Galipette, into *lorettes* with vulgar names like 'La Môme Fromage' (at one time the lover of La Goulue), 'Les Œufs sur le Plat' or Nini 'Gueule de Raie',[2322] down as far as 'Peau de Chien', 'Fleur-de-Bidet',[2323] 'Demi-Siphon' and 'Môme Caca'. Here too were distinctions, the courtesan Léonie de Cloménil of the avenue Malakoff having her imitator, known as 'la fausse Cloménil', of the rue de Rome; and la belle Otero being mimicked or parodied by 'la jolie Théro'. Galipette may have intended a reference to the actor Galipaux, drawn with Réjane by Lautrec. Louise Balthy seems to have been put together from elements of Yvette Guilbert, Jane Avril and Sarah Bernhardt. Maupassant's famous 'Boule de Suif' may have been based on a Rouennaise called Adrienne Legay, who asphyxiated herself with a charcoal brazier in 1893 for want of seven francs to pay her rent.[2324]

It is little surprising that the actress Marie Pigeonnier preferred to be called Marie Colombier: this did not stop her writing a very undovelike lampoon on Sarah Bernhardt, nor Edmond de Goncourt referring to her as 'a notorious whore'.[2325] This may not have been mere vulgar abuse, for according to *The Pretty Women of Paris* 'her cleverness in bed is undeniable [...] Marie is very fond of women'.[2326]

Arthur Symons recorded that

> I used to meet [...] the greater part of these extraordinary women, from Nini-Patte-en-l'Air, the oldest and most learned of them, whose roving eyes had a curious and intent glitter, who I named the 'Mænad of Decadence', to the gamine who was then La Goulue, and whose was supposed, wrongly, to have genius, and from these to Grille-d'Égout, who deserved her nickname; and from her – apart from La Sauterelle, Étoile Filante, La Macarona – who had an extraordinary effrontery – Églantine, Épi-d'Or, La Ténébreuse (who was tenebrous); from these to the adorable,

the fascinating beyond all imaginable fascination, La Mélinite, whose name in the world was Jane Avril [...] La Goulue was a strange and tall girl, with a vampire's face, the profile of a bird of prey, a tortured mouth and metallic eyes.[2327]

Symons also names 'Esmé Lescot, with her too evident hips; Mary Hamilton, profound and pagan; Paula Brébion, disagreeable and luxurious'.[2328] Épi-d'Or was English, as were Dolly du Star, and Ida Heath, and Mary Hamilton, of whom there is a lithograph by Lautrec, 1890. Phillip Cate refers to Georgette la Vadrouille, Nana la Sauterelle, Brise du Sœur and La Torpille as dancers at the Elysée-Montmartre; and la Tonkinoise, la Môme Cri-Cri, la Sauterelle, Reine-des-Prés, l'Etoile filante and Fin-de-siècle as dancers at the Moulin Rouge.[2329] Lautrec painted La Macarona, whose Christian name and date of death have survived (Georgette, and 1895); and La Sauterelle and Rayon d'Or are identified as the companions of William Tom Warrener in Lautrec's 'The Englishman at the Moulin Rouge'.[2330] Whether these were all different people may be doubted: 'elles avaient des noms aussi curieux que leurs figures'.[2331] André de Fouquières mentions the 'very seductive' Mylo d'Arcylle, whose charms were possibly less false than her name, and Eugénie Fougère, 'danseuse excentrique', whose diamonds were famous, and unlikely to have been earned by dancing, unless the eccentricity was greater than customary.[2332] There is also a trace of an 'artiste' called Aline Delvano of the avenue de la Grande Armée in the memoirs of Sir Edward Malet;[2333] and one may imagine how that address might have been used. *Mais où sont les dames d'antan?* as de Fouquières sighs.

Other courtesans whose names may or may not have been their own were Berthe d'Égreville, Nanette Stanley, Nelly Nieuwstratten, this last presumably being also the Nelly Neustretter whom Willie Vanderbilt took into keeping in the spring of 1894. As a result his wife (neé Alva Smith) was the first of the 'New York Four Hundred' to enter the divorce court.[2334] This seems to have been the origin of Henry James' short story *The Special Type*, published in 1903.

Their names of these ladies of the night seem as interchangeable as their bodies, as tenuous as their zoomorphic descriptions. This I think is the thrust of a highly-charged passage by André de Fouquières.

Emilienne, Caroline, Lina, Liane, dont la gloire est devenue poussière dès avant les os, aujourd'hui il ne reste plus d'elles que leurs noms, et ceux qui les prononcent encore sont bien incapables d'imaginer ce que furent ces femmes de chair. Pour moi, qui vis briller tous ces radieux visages au temps où ma jeunesse s'enchantait des longues, des très longues soirées de Paris, les voici toutes confondues, coulées dans un même moule: de grandes poupées empanachés, emperlés, et que rien ne distingue plus les unes des autres.[2335]

Zola plays with this confusion of names when in *Nana* he creates a courtesan called Blanche de Sivry (evoking the name of Charles de Sivry), and then says that her 'real' name was Jacqueline Baudu, also giving the name Baudu to the virtuous and unbawdy Denise Baudu of *Au Bonheur des Dames*, who is based on Marguerite Boucicaut and Marie Jay. This interaction between the real and the novelesque with its wordplay was a (protopostmodernist?) device that appealed to him, for referring to another *fille de joie* in *L'Œuvre* 'Sandoz [Zola himself] said her name, Irma Bécot, would sound well in a novel'.[2336] One can play here with Baudu, Sivry and the play by Auguste Vacquerie *Jean Baudry* (Comédie Française 4th December 1880). Vacquerie was editor of *Le Rappel*, and once met Wilde when the latter made his visit to the house of Victor Hugo.[2337] Baud is a unit of speed in telegraphic or Morse transmission: something coded, intangible: Baud de l'air, perhaps?[2338]

In naming Irma Bécot, there may be another level also implied by Zola. Irma was the name used by the courtesans Irma de Bury and Irma de Montigny, and Bécot is surely only there to suggest *bécotter*? This is reinforced by the fact that Zola gives Bécot an address in the rue de Moscou, where Marie Colombier was also living at about the time of the book was written. Zola also used the name in *Nana* for Irma d'Anglars, introduced as a courtesan of the first Empire still alive in 1868,[2339] and like Nana, Irma Bécot acquires a mansion in the avenue de Villiers, 'an avenue which is almost fashionable',[2340] in which Dumas *fils* and Sarah Bernhardt also had houses. There is much in Irma Bécot of the grande cocotte Méry Laurent, although one cannot imagine the feather-brained Irma being, like Méry Laurent, a friend and mistress of Coppée, Mallarmé,[2341] and Manet and also of Gervex, a circumstance that viâ Irma Bécot helps fix the identity of Gervex as Zola's Fagerolles.[2342] She also became a friend of Proust.

Zola used her surname, Laurent, for that of the painter/murderer in *Thérèse Raquin*; more disconcertingly, in the original production of *Thérèse Raquin* at the Théâtre de la Renaissance in July 1873, old madame Raquin was played by *Marie* Laurent, who also played in *Le ventre de Paris* (adapted by Busnach) at the Théâtre des Nations[2343] in 1887. Marie Laurent (1825-1904) had become famous for her rôle in the double part of the marquise de Rouvéry and the secondhand clothes dealer La Mère Rémy in Victor Séjour's *Les Mystères du Temple*, with its climactic murder of 'La Râleuse' in the rue de la Vieille Lanterne, the street where Gérard de Nerval hanged himself, to which Wilde made pilgrimage with Sherard in 1883. Here was a confusion of life and literature, but who was Marie Laurent, the 'strange little Englishwoman who like [Jane Avril] herself, had become a castaway in Jouy-en-Josas after a life of adventure and distress'?[2344]

The Théâtre de la Renaissance, built in 1871 in the boulevard St-Martin on the site of the restaurant Deffieux (burnt in the Commune), was itself subject to more than one rebirth, as originally it was devoted to serious drama which nearly killed it; then under a new manager, Victor Koning, 'the drama was ignominiously shown the door and the lightsome music of M. Lecocq and his fellows took its place';[2345] then it became a venue for Sarah Bernhardt.

~~~~~~~

The tale of Cora Pearl, the 'pearl from Plymouth' whose real name was Emma Crouch belongs more to the Second Empire than to the Third Republic although she lived until July 1886. She nevertheless exemplifies what the Japanese call the floating world. She had been brought to Paris by Robert Bignell ('Bill Blinkwell' in her memoirs) of the Argyle Rooms in London and installed in the Hôtel de Lille et d'Albion (223-5 rue St Honoré – du Maurier's Robert Maurice stays there in 1856[2346]), whereupon she declined to return to London. In her heyday she was kept more or less serially by the duc de Rivoli,[2347] the duc de Morny, prince Napoléon, prince Achille Murat and prince Willem of Orange[2348] (known as 'Citron', a title conferred by the Prince of Wales at a luncheon party given by Isabella II). She also relieved an Irishman called James Whelpley of £80,000 in two months. Yet her biography, at least, is hard to grasp. Polly Binder has written that 'Biographies of this lady, nearly all written by men, contrive to be snobbish, prurient and boring all at the same time. Indeed, it might be said that they tell us more about the writers than about their subject. Her own autobiography, written in French in her last years […] is sadly muddled and confused; fading reminiscences of a vanished era, outmoded slang, merry anecdotes no longer merry.'[2349] This is promising start to a book called *The Truth about Cora Pearl*, although when Binder tells us that in 1871 Cora Pearl in London contemplated staying at either the Carlton or the Ritz, one realises how elusive the truth can be, for the Carlton did not open its doors until July 1899, nor the Ritz, that section of the rue de Rivoli transposed to Piccadilly, until May 1906. It seems apposite enough that in her last years, Cora Pearl, the woman who introduced hair dye to Paris and was the first of her contemporary sisterhood to alter her eyelashes, should have devoted herself to the study of Volapük;[2350] and hardly less so that whereas Polly Binder gives the date of her death as July 1886, according to W.H. Holden her funeral was on the 10th May.[2351]

> Had pointed out to me in the Champs Elysées the Oh!-no-we-never-mention-her-Cora Pearl, with a lap-dog dyed to match her yellow hair. She is a common-looking thing![2352]

One catches a glimpse of a potential Cora Pearl in Eustacia Vye in Thomas Hardy's *Return of the Native* of 1878. Eustacia is no English bread-and-butter-miss (much of her name is eau de vie), but a sensuous woman of Corfiote descent, set on conquering Paris, 'the capital beauty spot of the world' – here we may move 'beauty spot' on from its touristic meaning to convey Paris as a place of female adornment. 'She hopes for the time when, as the mistress of some pretty establishment, near a Parisian Boulevard, she would be passing her days on the skirts at least of the gay world, and catching stray wafts from those town pleasures she was so fitted to enjoy'.[2353] It is clear that it is as a courtesan that she sees herself.

> Mademoiselle Musette was a pretty girl of twenty, who soon after arriving in Paris had become what pretty girls tend to become when they have good figures, plenty of flirtatiousness, a little ambition and no education to speak of.[2354]

The appropriate analogy here is with von Sacher-Masoch's Wanda, who ends in Paris 'like an Aspasia' – that is, a courtesan, but again the reference is Greek – whose experience in employing the whip could doubtless be put to gainful use.

The sexually charged Lady Constantine in Hardy's *Two on a Tower* (1882) is called with equal significance Viviette, and she clearly has a French strain even though this is not explicit. Her brother is called Louis and their surname is Glanville. With the even more sexualised Felice Charmond in *The Woodlanders*, Hardy offers no suggestion of a French strain but her name is so very nearly French (Félice Charmante?) that it comes as no surprise to find her described in that language: 'She might almost have been taken for the typical *femme de trente ans*, even though she was really not more than seven or eight and twenty. But the *édition définitive* of her beauty had been reached [...]'[2355] Here one is returned to Wilde's description of Madame de Ferrol as 'looking like an edition de luxe of a bad French novel' (*The Picture of Dorian Gray*) and Mr Dumby's description of Mrs Erlynne 'Looks like an édition de luxe of a wicked French novel, meant specially for the English market' (*Lady Windermere's Fan*). Another Hardy woman, Marcia Bencomb, on being widowed moves to Paris and brings up her son there, in at least outward respectability, for he becomes a schoolmaster in England. Here Paris serves as a place of invisible exile where the means of subsistence need not be specified. What is hinted, however, may be discerned. Marcia tries to arrest the marks of time: 'I became as skilled in beautifying artifices as any *passée* wife of the Faubourg St Germain'.[2356]

It is possible to take a real situation against which to read this. Emmeline de Horne was an Englishwoman (of Dutch descent) who married Edmond Morel de Ville, a *fonctionnaire* in the Ministry of Finance. Widowed, she left the family home in the avenue d'Eylau with her young son, Georges, and managed to earn a living by giving piano and English lessons in a city she grew to loathe. This downward mobility was marked by her dropping both the name Morel and the *particule*. Her work provided enough money for Georges to be sent to English schools, where he became Edmund. He returned to Paris in 1888 and worked for the American bankers Drexel, Hayes and Co. An opening with the Elder Dempster Line allowed both mother and son to return to England in 1891, where Edmund Deville became known as E.D. Morel and famous for his political work.[2357]

Hardy's attitude towards the French was always cautious: the unsatisfactory Sergeant Troy has a Parisian mother of light morals, his father putatively Lord Severn (which would make Lady Britomart Undershaft a distant relation) and inherits from her 'that blindness to the line where sentiment verges on mawkishness, characteristic of the French'. In Chapter XXIV of *Far from the Madding Crowd*, his sudden appearance is described as being 'what the sound of a trumpet is to silence', trumpets being, as we have seen, associated in Hardy's mind with Paris. Hardy set no story in Paris, but had taken his honeymoon there in September 1874, staying at the Hôtel St Petersbourg in the rue Caumartin and visiting the place de la Concorde (with its statue of Strasbourg shrouded in crape), the Louvre, the Tuileries Gardens, Versailles, Notre Dame, the Invalides and the Morgue.[2358]

~~~~~~

There is some notion that while at the top and bottom of the scale of daughters of joy, the women were grasping and exploitative, the middle ranks were as keen on pleasure as on money. Jeanne Baldy, once painted by Rochegrosse as Aphrodite, increased her income by reporting to the police any political indiscretions she learned in bed. Of course, not only were there no clear lines dividing the categories, but there was also confusion in the minds of observers: 'You can't tell nowadays, they all have the airs of refined ladies'.[2359] The spectrum ran from Rose d'Avaray who was born a Mercy-Argenteau and had escaped from a narrow upper crust milieu to become 'a courtesan and an expensive one [...] Lovers came in at the doors and jumped out at the windows',[2360] to the most famous of the lower class, thanks to Toulouse-Lautrec, Louise Weber the Glutton – 'La Goulou'. On a tangent one might place Suzanne, the daughter of Anatole France, who ran away from home to become a prostitute, accosted Jean de Tinan, and was returned to her family.

One who had the air of a refined lady was Laure Hayman, born in Chile of English descent, who received from Marcel Proust a copy of his *Les plaisirs et les jours* inscribed 'To Madame Laure Hayman, for the infinite delicacy of her heart, her beauty and her incomparable wit. Her friend, Marcel Proust. June 1896'. George Painter remarks that 'she seems to have been an intelligent, sensible, witty and cultured woman'.[2361] Her bed had been shared by the King of Greece and Prince Karageorgevitch, by Prince Karl von Fürstenberg[2362] and the duc d'Orléans, by the banker Rafael Bischoffsheim and the diplomatist Michael Herbert and Proust's uncle Louis Weil, as well as by the comtesse Mimi Pegère with whom she lived,[2363] but, unlike Nana, she clearly made her mark in her drawing room in the rue La Pérouse as well. As there is something of her in Proust's bisexual Odette de Crécy (lover of 'Sir Michael Linton', the British ambassador, among others, and who also lives in the rue Le Pérouse) – she certainly thought so, and was much put out – and a good deal of her in Paul Bourget's Gladys Harvey (in *Pastels: dix portraits de femmes*, a copy of which she sent to Proust bound in silk from one of her petticoats), as well as, I believe, in Zola's Lucy Stewart,[2364] she remains part of *fin-de-siècle* Paris.

Clearly, with courtesanship at this level such exploitation as occurred was by the woman of the man: choosing her lovers from the rich and famous, she was both financially and sexually autonomous. This explains some of the attraction of such women for 'respectable women', for whom the assertion of autonomy was more difficult, clandestine. This can be represented in terms of personal, rather than political, emancipation, as perhaps the assertion of agency must imply. The anti-feminist comtesse de Martel, for instance, not only believed that her husband's infidelities validated her own, but that 'I considered myself entirely authorised to use my body as I saw fit.'[2365] Maupassant's Madeleine Forestier, contemplating marriage with Georges Duroy, strikes a note of defiance for herself, not for other women:

> Marriage, for me, is not a bond, but a partnership. I expect to be free, completely free, in what I do, whom I see, where I go, always. I could not tolerate either supervision, or jealousy, or any discussion of my behaviour. I would of course undertake never to compromise the name of the man I had married, never to make him seem hateful or ridiculous. But that man would also have to see me as an equal, an ally, not as an inferior or an obedient submissive wife. I know my ideas are not shared by everyone [...][2366]

This is a message to which Maupassant seems sympathetic, subversive as it is of the conventional view of marriage, more unusual in its forthrightness of expression, perhaps, than in its practice. Later, when Duroy catches Madeleine in bed with her lover, it is the latter whom Maupassant ridicules, and by also subverting the comedic representation of the cuckold, allows Madeleine her dignity too. For Madeleine is also a very conventional woman: it is she who transforms George Duroy into Georges du Roy de Cantel in order to have an impressive wedding invitation.

Colette defines cocotte as 'a lady who generally manages to give more than she receives'.[2367] Larousse defines grisette as 'ouvrière jeune et coquette' – the original grisettes were grey-dress-wearing seamstresses[2368] – and distinguishes midinettes, 'jeunes ouvrières parisiennes de la couture et de la mode', celebrated in Zola's *Au Bonheur des Dames* of 1883.[2369] One of these, employed by 'one of the leading *modistes*' became the *petite amie* of 'An English Officer'. Calling her Renée Leclerc, he describes how she read Balzac and Rochefort's paper *La Lanterne*, gave him good advice about affairs of the heart (which he did not take) and 'said that she had no desire to live after thirty, and that she considered that a woman's life was then quite at an end'.[2370] Another dressmaker's employée was Toulouse-Lautrec's last inamorata – Louise Blouet, known as Louise Margouin.[2371] Rosalie (Lilly) Texier worked in the establishment of the Sœurs Callot in the rue Taitbout and lived with 'a nice fellow who dabbled in stocks' before marrying Debussy.[2372] In Maupassant, the type is represented by Henriette in 'Monsieur Parent': 'Pretty, pink and fair, a part flirtatious, part respectable Parisienne who had been born in the back of a shop and raised in the front to catch the eye of passers-by, and having duly hooked one, had married him'.[2373] The courtesan Laure Decroze, whose real name was Laure Broye, began as a grisette in the Latin Quarter, living with a medical student whose family bought her off; she then founded a fortune as a 'kept woman' in the rue de Rome.

The true grisette is a shifting and mutable concept, usually assigned to elsewhen.

> They are a type apart, the modern grisettes, so quiet and well-behaved as to be almost respectable. One always hears that the Quartier Latin doesn't exist anymore – the students are more serious, less turbulent, and that the hard-working little grisette, quite content with her simple life and pleasure, has degenerated into the danseuse of the music-halls and barrière theatres. I don't think so. A certain class of young, impecunious students will always live in that quarter and will always amuse themselves, and they will also find girls quite ready and happy to enjoy life a little while they are young enough to live in the present, and have no cares for the future.[2374]

Writing in 1889, Madame van der Velde regarded the grisette as a thing of the past[2375] though there seems to be no agreement on how long past. Marie Bashkirtseff refers to 'the now vanished Grisette' in her diary entry for 29th December 1881.[2376] F. Adolphus in 1895 thought that the true grisette had vanished around 1870 'with the narrow streets, the paving stones and the cheapnesses that had made her possible'[2377] but Henry Jones Thaddeus recalled that 'in the early eighties the grisette still existed in the Latin Quarter, and was a very captivating and helpful little body' and it was only from the perspective of 1912 that 'she is now a memory of the past'.[2378] Will Rothenstein uses the phrase when looking back on Paris in 1891,[2379] but Jerrold Siegel suggests that they had been replaced or displaced by *lorettes* as early as 1846, these being 'much more mercenary and hard-bitten' than their predecessors, and cites Alfred Delvau's *Grandeur et Décadences des Grisettes* of 1848 as 'claiming to tell the story of the very last' grisette.[2380] Certainly, Barbey d'Aurevilly writing in 1874 of the 1840s reported that 'At that time the Parisian prostitutes, who did not think the pretty name of *lorette*, which literature had bestowed upon them, and which [Paul] Gavarni had immortalised, was sufficiently serious, had adopted the Oriental sobriquet of "panthers"',[2381] though who feasted with them Barbey does not say. 1848 was not entirely a year of revolutions, however. Antony Ludovici, studying art in Paris as the Empire ended, thought that the Latin Quarter was much as his father had described it in the 1840s. 'The Mimi Pinsons were still to be found'.[2382] More than twenty years later, Robert Sherard wrote

The days of 'la Vie de Bohème' are, by no means, as has been said over and over again, past, and Doppelgängers of every one of the famous characters in Murger's book, not excepting Mimi Pinson, could be found to-day over and over again in the hôtels meublés of [the Latin] quarter. They dress a little less raggedly perhaps, and have on the whole more luxurious tastes, for Bohemia has marched with the times also, but there they are just the same.[2383]

Laurent Tailhade disagrees. Writing as early as 1875, he lamented 'pour les poètes d'à présent, il n'est plus de Mimi ni de Musette', and the love had become a fake commodity.[2384] Certainly 'grisettes' became constructs of the imaginary Paris, Lehár writing a 'Grisetten-lied' for *Die Lustige Witwe* in 1905.

The grisette *in* fiction seems to have been finally laid to rest by John Dos Passos in *Three Soldiers* (1921) and *Chosen Country* (1951), but Dos Passos himself had only experienced the grisette *of* fiction. This blurring of the longevity of the grisette is paralleled in that of Montmartre itself. When in July 1930 Carl van Vechten wrote 'the old Montmartre has completely disappeared'[2385] he was referring to the Montmartre of *Louise*, but *Louise* itself marked the passing of the transplanted Quartier Latin of *La Vie de Bohème*, and so on back – in 1895, du Maurier referred to 'what still remains' of the Quartier Latin.[2386]

It is also true that in no area of Parisian life was the difference between fiction and reality so marked. The charming grisette flirting with her student in the Jardin du Luxembourg was doing so in the tiny free time and on the 'pitifully low'[2387] wages of the fashion trade, whether it was that of the seamstress or maker of artificial flowers. An enquiry of 1895 found women with as little as sixty-five centimes (or five pence – 5d) a day to feed themselves. A seamstress was one of the poor who is helped by the Happy Prince and the Swallow (though the concept is as much English as French – Wilde knew Tom Hood's 'Song of the Shirt'), but one seamstress employed in the rue de Rivoli preferred to jump from a seventh storey window than continue to feed herself on three sous (fifteen centimes) a day. 'All sections of opinion, from the Catholic social reformer Albert de Mun on the Right through to the Socialists on the Left, were agreed that it was a matter of deliberate policy on the part of employers not to pay women a living wage'.[2388] Between working for a wage in a sweatshop or working at home on piece rates there can have been little difference. The sort of home a woman could keep on piece rates (and there is an implication that she was single, widowed or the partner of an unemployed man) was hardly a bower: McMillan thinks that 'of all working women,

these were, generally speaking the most hideously exploited'.[2389] Zola's
Denise Baudu budgets one franc fifty a day, which included rent, dry
bread for herself and a little meat for her young brother.[2390]   If the
seamstress who had fifteen centimes a day for food had only managed to
put the money aside and eat nothing at all, in five and a half months she
could have saved enough to buy a tie from Charvet for her beau; or she
might have a bought a newspaper and read of the four hundred thousand
francs that was the divorce settlement obtained by the marquise
d'Osmond[2391] from her husband in November 1885, which at fifteen
centimes a day would have lasted her seven hundred and thirty years.

Grisette was not the only evanescent term. One may also note the
'oiseilles', 'pert little creatures with thin voices and shapely calves'.[2392]
There were also innumerable slang or argot terms, those most used being
'dégrafée', 'agenouillée' or 'grenouille'. Musette, while at one level a
pretty name (originally used by Murger), at another means a horse's nose-
bag.

That said, it would be wrong to ignore the new possibilities opening up for
working women. In 1877 women first became employed at the Central
Télégraphique – Proust's demoiselles de téléphone –, and the emergence
of women as clerical workers is a feature of the time.[2393]   The sewing
machine, once hailed as a liberating instrument for women, might have
failed in this regard, but the typewriting machine renewed the idea, and
'the lady typewriter' soon became a feature of commerce and of literature,
even if in French, 'dactylographe', she sounded more like the pre-historic
flying reptile than the secretary bird. One is not inclined to see it as
coincidence that

> the year 1878 saw for the first time the invasion of the tops of tramcars by
> women. Until that time no Frenchwoman would have […] thought have
> mounting the outside of a tramcar […] but when foreign ladies from
> England or America insisted […] their French sisters were not slow to
> follow suit […] although for a long while […] many Frenchwomen still
> considered it not at all nice or proper to ride upon the outside.[2394]

This greater freedom led to new forms of social exchange. If the café
remained predominantly a male preserve, women could have recourse to
the salon de thé. Credit for the first of these was claimed by Louis Ernest
Ladurée, when after a fire in 1871 he changed the boulangerie he had
opened in 1862 in the rue Royale into a patisserie, and then blended these
two aspects into a tea room with a décor by Chéret. This establishment,

and its similar branch in the Champs Elysées, remain to-day much as they were, a chance to revisit the ambience that Ladurée exploited.[2395]

~~~~~~

The virtues of the Parisienne were admired by Arnold Bennett, who married a Frenchwoman, Margaret Soulié[2396] in the new century. These were listed by Marie Belloc as 'her good humour, her thrift, the way she stands up to the hard things of life'. This is surely the *bonne bourgeoise*, but to become such was at least in literature the ambition of the class below: *L'Assommoir* ('that excellent novel'[2397]) not only charts the fall of Gervaise Coupeau, but also celebrates her earlier if transitory rise. Mathilde Marchesi, who had lived in London (where she remembered 'the formal stuffiness which characterises the English nation'[2398]), Cologne, Vienna, Frankfort and Venice, echoes Renan's remark to Herbert Fisher that Paris was 'the hardest working place in the world' when she describes these bourgeoises.

> As to Frenchwomen, so often misunderstood abroad, I do not think I exaggerate when I state that in no other country do women of the middle classes work so unflaggingly and so intelligently as in France, taking, as many of them do, an active part in business, helping their husbands, and often spending the whole day behind the desk or counter.[2399]

In this view, the Parisian herself forms part of the definition of Paris herself.[2400] The tone is caught in Maupassant's description in 'Boule de suif' of M. and Madame Loiseau, wholesale wine merchants: she 'tall, powerfully built and determined, with a shrill voice and a decisive manner, was responsible for the organisation and accountancy of the firm, while he kept it alive with his cheery energy. This was well observed by contemporaries.

> Women, in France, play a most important part in business and family affairs. Their keenness in the former is remarkable, and although *Monsieur* may be nominally head of the firm, it is very often *Madame* who is really the more active partner. Possibly it is this very knowledge of the power they possess which makes them indifferent to any recognised political rights, for the fact remains that so far, they have shown very little disposition to demand the vote.[2401]

As for thrift, it was often ridiculed as parsimony. Madame Oreille in Maupassant's 'La Parapluie' may stand for many fictional representations, but Will Low saw it as part of the nature of the city.

> With all allowances for the common change in the point of view that
> comes with middle age, no one who knew Paris thirty years ago will deny
> that, in the flaunting outward aspect of certain alleged 'attractions', the
> capital, realising their market value, and with typical thriftiness desiring to
> add to the hoard in the long stocking, has become far more sophisticated
> than in earlier times.[2402]

This American view was also held in England. 'In my long life,' wrote
Marie Belloc, who was brought up at La Celle St Cloud near Bougival,
'one of the things that has often irritated and angered me is the belief, so
constantly expressed in England, that the French are so fond of money that
they will do anything to procure it, and to keep it'.[2403] That the English
should believe this, and that the French should believe that the English
believed it, clearly forms part of the expectation of character upon
encounter, especially when that encounter was one of foreigners who were
in Paris to spend money (seeing themselves as open-handed) with those of
Paris who received it (being seen as close-fisted). Oscar Wilde, spending
lavishly when he had money to spend and credit when he had not, must
have fallen within this confrontation. Sherard turned his phrase in *De
Profundis* about being the spendthrift of his own genius and called him a
spendthrift of genius.

Thrift was, however, not much practised much among the higher income
groups, and certainly not by the women who came to Paris to shop,
however much they thought that Paris fashions might confer upon them
something of the Parisienne. Thomas Coolidge, viewing Parisian women
from his round of diplomatic receptions, thought that middle class women
were often prim and dowdy, but a reception at the duc de Gramont's in the
week of his recall prompted an unusual reflection about the elegance of the
upper class by celebrating the older women:

> I was again struck by the style, dress and beauty of French society [...] The
> principal reason, I think, is the fairness and stoutness of their necks, there
> being no young girls present with scraggy outlines and unformed manners.
> Every neck is covered with superb jewels, pearls, I think, being the
> favourite.[2404]

The English view of the independent woman, however, was not always
favourable. Thomas March, describing in 1896 the Communard women,
fell into the worst form of stereotyping. These women, motivated by the
desire to join the men on equal terms, and exercise such political activity
as was open to them, automatically become 'generally of a vile and brutal
character – there were young women amongst them, but they were neither

pretty nor gentle. These females were more like men, for they were entirely devoid of the charms with which one usually associates womanhood'.[2405] In the context, such women were not merely 'desexing' themselves, but were abandoning all that made the *Parisienne*.

Part 2: Paris Lesbos

WHEN André Antoine, prepared to risk prostitute plays by Goncourt, thought that Gabriel Mourey's lesbian play *Lawn-Tennis*, was 'overbold for public presentation' at his Théâtre Libre,[2406] he was expressing the tensions set up by the more or less open nature of Parisian lesbianism. 'If the frontier between the haut and the demi-monde was being obliterated,' writes Harold Kurtz, 'a new vogue of transvestism, the wide popularity of male and female impersonation, a half-hidden spreading of homosexual self-absorption and similar cults seemed to herald the vanishing of hitherto accepted lines of demarcation.'[2407] Parisians were on the whole tolerant of lesbianism – indeed, Enid Starkie, who had experience of the passion and perhaps of the pleasure, suggests that from *Mademoiselle de Maupin* onwards they had a *culte* for it,[2408] sometimes rather innocently expressed as concern with the writings of the historical Sappho, whose name at least was constantly in vogue. Gounod's 1851 opera *Sapho* was produced in a revised version in April 1884; Alphonse Belot adapted Daudet's *Sapho* for the Théâtre du Gymnase in the same year. Charles Gleyre painted 'Sappho going to bed'.[2409] The comte d'Haussonville called madame Ackermann 'the Sappho of Atheism', and can hardly have meant it as praise: Haussonville's quarrel with the Church was because the Pope had recognised the Republic. The Irish painter and dramatist, W.G. Wills, who spent much time in Paris, wrote a play called *Sapho* which was produced at the Theatre Royal, Dublin in 1875. How long this lasted, and its other manifestations, deserve study. Antoine Bourdelle's bronze 'Sapho' dates to 1925.

Lesbianism is suggested in *À Rebours*,[2410] Laforgue meditated writing a lesbian novel in conjunction with the poet Sanda Mahali,[2411] and in Zola's *Nana* (1880) and Maupassant's 'La femme de Paul' (1881) it is quite explicit. It is, however, part of the contradiction of Rachilde, self-described as 'homme de lettres', author of *Monsieur Vénus* and *La Marquise de Sade*, that she disdained lesbianism, 'the crime of schoolgirls and the weakness of prostitutes'.[2412] Indeed, if the anonymous author of *The Pretty Women of Paris* is to be believed, it was very common amongst prostitutes, either with each other or as a service to clients, and

distinguishable as either active or passive 'tribadism': thus Juliette
Grandville was 'often Sappho by day and Messalina by night'.[2413]   A
prostitute who dressed as a man and even sported a blond beard was
known as 'le bel Ernest'. There appears to have been a lesbian brothel for
Society women in the rue Chabanais.[2414] Catherine van Casselaer accepts
Julian Chevalier's statement that 'at any one time there may have been
upwards of nine hundred lesbians among registered prostitutes'.[2415] It was
frequently close to the surface in both Courbet's and Rodin's depiction of
women and naturally even closer in Rops'; I do not think it entirely
fanciful to see it in a chair of 1893 by Carabin.[2416] Edmond Aman-Jean's
'In the Theatre Box' of 1898 shows two women enjoying an embrace;
Lautrec's 'Le Lit' shows two women gazing tenderly at each other while
tucked up in bed.[2417] In 'Eclogue' by Jean-Jacques Henner (1879) a nymph
is being serenaded on a pipe in usual classical fashion, but the piper is not
Pan or a satyr but another nymph.

In a survey of upper class lesbian Paris Michael de Cossart has listed
Elisabeth duchesse de Gramont (Elisabeth de Clermont-Tonnerre,[2418]
princesse Catherine Poniatowska, the baronne van Zuylen[2419] and
princesse Violet Murat[2420] – this last being described by Proust as more
like a truffle than a violet.[2421] Catherine van Casselaer adds Martine
comtesse de Béarn, Francesca Notabartolo who was comtesse Maximilian
d'Orsay, and the even more exotic Jeanne (or Jeannot) Perrin de Bellune,
granddaughter of Marshal Victor, duc de Bellune, who turned his coat in
1814, supported the Restoration and voted for the execution of Marshal
Ney. Jeannot, at the behest of her Portuguese lover Maria Conceiço do
Valle de Sousa e Menezes Botelho Mexia, condessa de Sarmento, was
created Viscondessa de Juromenha by King Luis of Portugal in 1888. The
many-sided Jeannot was also the lover of princesse Catherine
Poniatowska.[2422]

Sarah Bernhardt is said to have explored the possibilities and Alice
Regnault and Emilienne d'Alençon certainly did. The poetry of Renée
Vivien celebrated it. Catherine van Casselaer also names Suzanne Derval,
once described by the singer Paulus as 'an intermittent actress'.[2423]

The Allée des Poteux in the Bois was a cruising ground at mid-morning –
and perhaps in the evening too, if one can trust Proust's Odette de Crécy.
Proust indeed had a voyeuristic obsession with lesbianism throughout the
Recherche, but his first reference to it was in his short story 'Violante, ou
la Mondanité', published in *Le Banquet* in February 1893. In 1896 two
lesbian novels were published, Jean Lorrain's *Une Femme par Jour* and

Les Demi-Sexes, by madame Gaston Crapez who preferred to write under the rather more high-sounding name of Jane de la Vaudère. Mirbeau nonchalantly introduces an English lesbian housekeeper, known as 'Miss', into the *Journal d'une Femme de Chambre*.[2424] The spread or alleged spread of lesbianism was attacked in 1891 by the controversialist Léon Taxil, in a book called *La Corruption fin-de-siècle*, intended to sell copies rather than analyse trends.

Although her biographers scout any notion of lesbian *affaires*, the dancer Loïe Fuller had an adoring circle of female admirers; while the actress Judith attracted an unwelcome 'pash' on the part of Céleste Mogador. According to Cécile Sorel, Réjane once told her 'What a pity you're a woman. You'd make a lovely lover' and on one occasion 'tightly clad in white satin trousers [...] Madame Lara in *Chérubin* leapt at me with such enthusiasm that Croisset's play was not repeated on the following day on the pretext that this scene was scandalous.'

'Decidedly these reversals of sex are dangerous,' Sorel concludes rather ambiguously.[2425] This was perhaps a little naïve: the Club des Rieuses was a lesbian association the members of which were all actresses. When Jill Davis writes 'The social "persona" of the lesbian had not issued from the discourse of sexology into the cultural reality',[2426] she may be defining the English position, but it was clearly very different in France.

Occasionally, one has to offer a passage that may require a tentative decoding, such as Baroness Orczy's reference to the Grand Duchess Anastasia's being surrounded by a 'bevy of young girls, among whom I was really sorry to note a few English ones' (the Grand Duchess lived chiefly in Cannes, but kept a flat in Paris).[2427] Bernhardt's friend the painter Louise Abbéma 'was a short, tailored lady with cropped hair upon whom the wiser mothers with young daughters kept a wary eye'[2428] – Jean Lorrain used to call her 'the Rajah's son' or 'the old Japanese admiral', but Marie Bashkirtseff thought her 'a very nice girl'.[2429] The comtesse de Jolival also adopted masculine mannerisms, but perhaps the opportunity for transformation was most exploited by the marquise de Belbœuf, Colette's lover. This was (Sophie) Mathilde, daughter of the duc de Morny and therefore related to the Bonapartes. Known as 'Missy', she dressed as a man and called her/himself the marquis de Moira when she did not call herself the marquise de Morny; when she appeared on stage she called herself Yssim. (Her father had also had his fictitious counterparts, M. de Marsy in Zola's *Son Excellence Eugène Rougon*, duc de Mora in Daudet's novel of that name.) André de Fouquières, who knew her well, refers kindly to her taste for drugs and her 'curious loves' as her 'extravagances', the memory of each scandal only effaced by the next.[2430] Her affaire with Colette seems to have been a *ménage à quatre* which included Willy and his then mistress, the singer Polaire (the stage name of Émile-Marie Bouchard), who not only played Colette's Claudine on stage, but did so off stage as well, though was unusual in hating lesbianism.[2431] Marcel Boulestin wrote that 'dressed as a woman [Missy] succeeded in looking like a nice middle-aged man; and [...] dressed as a man she looked exactly the same', although to be sure, this so confused Frank Richardson that he asked 'Who is that old pederast?'[2432]

Clearly being a lesbian, or posing as one, was no bar to advancement or success, at any level, although Margaret Crosland is surely correct is pointing out the difficulties of defining the shades of *amitié amoureuse*.[2433] Rosa Bonheur, the animal painter who lived entirely outside the circles that I have been depicting, became the first woman *officier* of the Légion d'Honneur in 1894. In earlier days she was widely supposed to be lesbian, and is now accepted to have been so. 'Rosa Bonheur is shy in spite of her now somewhat advanced age. She likes to dress as a man, and when she expects visitors she has to dress as a woman. It may turn out that the short, square-set "fellow" in shooting velveteens, of whom you have asked your way in the forest to Rosa Bonheur's place, is the hostess in disguise.'[2434] Equally indicative, and somewhat less illuminating, of her shifting persona is Max Nordau's description of her as 'a Rudyard Kipling of the brush'.[2435] The appropriation of masculine signifiers was widespread. Augustine Brohan, sister of the actress Madeleine, used to affect a monocle and is described by one contemporary as 'masculine-minded'.[2436] The cigar smoking, short haired Jane Dieulafoy, born Jeanne Marge, archæologist, explorer, folklorist, novelist, playwright, and journalist, the wife of the archæologist Marcel Dieulafoy, also preferred trousers, once causing the marquis de Gallifet[2437] unwittingly to address this ardent feminist as 'mon cher'; conversely Dumas once mistook Pierre Loti for her. It is said that 'All Paris laughed at the story of how the commissionaire at the *Revue de Paris* announced to the literary editor Louis Gunderax [*sic*] "There is a gentleman downstairs who says he is a lady".'[2438]

In 1901 Liane de Pougy published a novel entitled *Idylle Sapphique*, which revealed her affaire with Natalie Clifford Barney. Subsequently Natalie Barney became engaged to Lord Alfred Douglas, fell in love with Olive Custance (who married Bosie), and went on to have a long affaire with Wilde's niece Dorothy. This daughter of Willie Wilde in later life would refer to herself as Oscaria[2439] and once said 'I am more Oscar-like than he was like himself': in 1930 she appeared as Oscar at the duchesse de Clermont-Tonnerre's costume ball.[2440] Barney, Douglas and the duchess all dined together in Paris in the autumn of 1911. The poet Lucie Delarue-Mardrus, who was later to write a book on Oscar Wilde,[2441] also fell in love with Natalie Barney; while Dolly Wilde in 1925 had a brief affaire with Alla Nazimova, who three years before had produced a film of *Salomé* in which she starred. Born in 1877, Barney had been brought to Paris from her native United States in 1886 when her mother Alice Barney wanted to study painting there, and Carolus-Duran painted her as Wilde's Happy Prince. They returned to Paris from July 1896 to May 1897 and again from the summer of 1898 to the spring of 1899, staying in a pension next door to Whistler's academy in the rue de Grande Chaumière. (Alice Barney enrolled in the Académie Julian in 1900, and painted a portrait of Whistler.[2442]) Natalie was to remain in Paris, from 1909 in the rue Jacob[2443] (number 20), until her death in 1972, having affaires with as many women as she could, including Elisabeth de Clermont-Tonnerre and Emma Calvé, but Dolly Wilde, with Clermont-Tonnerre, Romaine Brooks and Renée Vivien, was one of her four great loves: two of these were 'preternaturally drawn towards death'.[2444]

Barney's acculturation was remarked upon by Sybille Bedford, who recalled that her 'toughness disguised as femininity [was] heartless and artificial, like all the French'; Dolly Wilde, more ambiguously, once addressed her as 'my dear little Jew boy'.[2445] In the early years of the new century she struck up a friendship with Pierre Louÿs after reading his lesbian collection *Chansons de Bilitis*. This led to acquaintance[2446] with Gide, Schwob, Valéry, Paul Claudel, but takes us beyond the period of Oscar Wilde's Paris into the period where the cast changes, and one enters the Paris of Djuna Barnes and James Joyce, of 'Kiki de Montparnasse' and Max Jacob, of Marie Laurencin and Maurice Utrillo, of Jules Depaquit and 'Frédé', the Paris whose historians are Francis Carco[2447] and Pierre Mac-Orlan.[2448] Bohemia thus renewed itself and the plaint that

> Villon qu'on chercherait céans
> N'est plus là ni Verlaine

was to miss the constant transmutation, even though this was as often from gold into base metal as from base metal into gold.

Much of this subserves the construction of Paris as a female gendered city, but there is another dimension to it. Male fascination, apart from the merely prurient, meant that men had under their notice women who were setting their own sexual agenda, while by noticing this, men were altering themselves from participants in sexual expression to voyeurs of it. Sarah Bernhardt's explicit infusing of sexuality into the drive to power of heroines previously understood by their interpreters as owing more to position than to personality may be seen as contributing to this. The male dominant relationship, already challenged by foregrounding Bernhardt as the eponymous heroine, was thus reversed. This was exaggerated by the fact that when she was not appearing opposite Mounet-Sully or Coquelin, her leading men were usually actors of no great talent, or at any rate of talent that would not overshadow her own: who can name the men who played her Antony or Giovanni, Scarpia or Justinian? Bernhardt's own view that women were 'suited to androgynous asexual rôles, but not to those which require manliness and virility'[2449] poses a further disturbance by feminising Hamlet,[2450] Lorenzaccio, Romeo and the duc de Reichstadt, for while *travesti* can be read as investing the actor with a trans-sexual meaning, it also desexualises the actor. The casting becomes not transgressive but congressive, merging the actor with the part, the dancer with the dance.

Part 3: A Woman's Place

THE women writers of Paris were more numerous than the artists, but are frequently as elusive. Richard Whiteing surveyed them in his 1886 study. 'Henri Gréville stands at the head of the women writers of the day, but she may not hold the place for her lifetime if she writes so much [...] Madame Bentzon comes next [...] then Jacques Vincent [...] The comtesse Dash, Mesdames Louis Figuier, Caro, Craven and Andouard follow, in any order in which you may happen to place them'.[2451] Whiteing is here being mischievous: no one would categorise Pauline Craven in any order that contained, say, madame de Montifaud of whom he had already written that she 'goes to prison for every book she writes'[2452] – this was Marie-Amélie Chartroule de Montifaud who wrote under the name Marc de Montifaud. Whiteing was exaggerating, but it is true that Montifaud's *Madame Ducroisy* was banned. A further list of some two hundred was compiled by Han Ryner in *Le Massacre Des Amazones*.[2453] It says much for the volatility of the canon that not a single one of these women is discussed by Rachel Mesch in her study of the subject.[2454]

Marie-Thérèse Bentzon shared nothing with Montifaud save multiple identity. She seems to have been known as madame Bentzon, although

'Th. Bentzon' was her *nom-de-plume*. She was born Marie-Thérèse de Solms and became madame Blanc. Robert Underwood Johnson, who knew her in both Paris and New York, calls her 'one of the most refined and intellectual women I have ever known […] I never knew a better listener or talker'[2455] – her article 'Conversation in France' appeared in *The Century Magazine*,[2456] which Johnson edited. Bentzon translated Mark Twain and the stories of Thomas Bailey Aldrich[2457] into French and wrote two books on contemporary Americans, *Les nouveaux romanciers américains*[2458] and *Les Américaines chez elles*[2459]; she also wrote for the *Revue des Deux Mondes*, perhaps the most prestigious of the Paris journals, called by Théodore de Banville 'the road to the Academy […] as directly as a straight line goes from one point to another'.[2460]

'Comtesse Dash' was also a *nom de plume*. Her real name was Gabrielle-Anne de Courtiras, vicomtesse Saint-Mars, so while demoting her name, she was upgrading her title. She was a friend of Dumas *père* and is said to be the true author of some of the novels published under his name, such as *Les mémoires d'une aveugle* or *La dame de volupté*. She also published some tales of travel, which are likely not to be true. Nor is it surprising to learn that Henri Gréville was also an adopted name: she was a madame Durand-Fleury.

~~~~~~

Although the relaxed attitude of the French towards morals assumed a certain élan, notably for the repressed English and Americans, the balance of power between the sexes was complex. This was understood by Zola, who explored the theme in *Au Bonheur des Dames*. Mouret, owner-manager of the great department store 'Au Bonheur des Dames' invites sales girls upon whom he sets his eye to dinner, and in the store these are known as the desserts. Such exploitation was of course widespread and Woman-as-commodity paid her price. What is now known in the theatre profession as the casting couch was then called in England 'producer's privilege' but in France was called rather more bluntly 'droit de cuissage'. There was certainly a coarsening of sensibility among men. What Mistinguett wrote of the actor Max Dearly no doubt could be replicated a great many times: 'Women adored him. He treated them abominably of course. He was simply not interested.' [2461] It was said that amongst his other fanaticisms, Charles Maurras 'considered women with the greatest contempt and used them to satisfy his desires without expressing the slightest spark of affection for them'.[2462]

Women paid the price in other ways, too. When Lord Lytton and the marquis de Breteuil (Proust's 'marquis de Bréauté') visited the Salpétrière Hospital in June 1888, they found that six thousand women were undergoing treatment for 'hysteria'. Known as 'les Grandes Hystériques', they represent a Paris of illusions, certainly, but even more of nightmare. The very description parodies the sobriquet 'Grandes Horizontales'.

It was to the Salpétrière that Freud came to study under Charcot in October 1885. While Freud went to plays by Molière, Hugo and Sardou by night,[2463] he was aware that plays of another sort were being enacted by day. 'Charcot,' writes Peter Gay, 'was no doubt theatrical [...] These performances [...] Charcot was far more than an actor [...] Charcot had rescued hypnosis from mountebanks and charlatans.'[2464] But even therapeutic hypnosis, which involves a dissociation of self, added to the prevailing loosening of identic certainty, and it is little wonder that psychiatrists were known as alienists.   Subsequently, Freud himself became aware of a 'mystical element' in hypnosis, and it was their consciousness of this aspect that made it so attractive to the charlatans and mountebanks (and earnest inquirers) who infested the esoteric movements of Paris.

The hysteria, even if imperfectly understood or defined, was certainly noticed, and forms part of both the gendering of Paris as feminine, and the characterisation of Paris as decadent. Although Brian Reade has seen this as an expression of *ennui* (the 'mal de siècle') rather than feverishness, he does so in terms that, though interesting in their associations, seem to deny any notion of languor – although Reade's is a near-Marxist definition of decadence that is now outmoded:

> The ennui was expressed as keenly in the sick Catholicism and mysticism of the intellectuals as in the fatalism of the café songs. Ruthless commerce took on an equally grey face of astuteness. One of the obvious values to be exploited by trade was the one that distinguished Paris most, and some of the easiest profits were to be made in propagating the whole dainty racket of sex and food and art, in reducing the variety of these pleasures to the level of snobbish connoisseurship. It was perhaps a successful form of psychological warfare, and even the most artful people began to suspend in the city of Taste.[2465]

The vigour, the sense of the need to accomplish, coupled with a sense of the unbalanced, is captured in a phrase about Mary Cassatt by Vollard: 'It was with a sort of frenzy that generous Mary Cassatt laboured for the success of her comrades'.[2466]

~~~~~~

When in 1878, G.A. Sala marked the Paris exhibition with a book called *Paris Herself Again*, he was not merely referring to the physical and economic recovery of the city, but also the restoration of la gaieté parisienne. *Paris Herself Again*, noted Arnold Bennett, 'ought to have been paid for in gold by the hotel and pension-keepers of Paris. [It] awakened English curiosity'.[2467] Three years before, Henry James had already told his New York readers that Paris seems 'more than ever, superficially, a vast fairy bazaar, a huge city of shop fronts'.[2468] 'Superficially', one notes, and 'fairy' and shop *fronts*, not shops: Paris was disappearing into 'Paris'.

The openness with which so many lived with, or showed off, their mistresses (their *petites distractions*) removed the necessity for the double life so associated with English prudery (the second family in the suburbs discovered after death, as in the case of Sir Herbert Tree), but the double life did have its place amongst the rest of the make-believe. It was not for nothing that Sarah Bernhardt called her memoirs *Ma Double Vie*. After all, there are two candidates for the paternity of Sarah Bernhardt, and her mother, who was Dutch, was called either Judith or Julia and either Bernardt or van Hard. Manet passed off his son Léon as his mistress's brother; when they married Léon was introduced as his brother-in-law. Another man who had a double life was Zola himself, installing Jeanne Rozerot in a flat in rue St Lazare, thus implicating him in his own world of the Rougon and Macquart. For Zola, if the working class lived a life of domestic violence and animal-like promiscuity, it was because of the disgusting conditions under which they lived,[2469] but the starched shirts and formal uniforms of the upper classes only covered hypocrisy: 'The most distinguished-looking men were the most obscene. The varnish cracked and the beast showed itself, exacting in its monstrous tastes, subtle in its perversions.'[2470]

This was echoed by Octave Mirbeau's *femme de chambre*, whose motives were, however, more overtly political than Zola's.

> I simply love waiting at table. That is where your employers give themselves away, revealing all the beastliness, all the squalor of their inner natures [...] Collecting these revelations, classifying and labelling them against the day of reckoning when they will become a terrible weapon in our hands, is one of the great pleasures of our job, a precious revenge for all the humiliations we endure [...] You would never imagine how many of them are really crazily indecent in their private lives, even those who, in

society, are regarded as being most circumspect and severe in their behaviour, most inaccessibly virtuous. But in their dressing-rooms, when they let their masks fall, even the impressive façades reveal themselves as cracked and crumbling […] Those only see humanity from the outside, and allow themselves to be dazzled by appearances, can have no idea how filthy and corrupt the great world, 'high society', really is. It is no exaggeration to say that the main of aim of its existence is to enjoy the filthiest kinds of amusement.[2471]

~~~~~~

The fascination with Sapphism did not create quite the same atmosphere of inquiry into or intellectual vogue for male homosexuality, and one may cautiously urge that a society that was so stimulated by female sexuality kept its store of tolerance for the various forms of this, from the blatancy of the *poules de luxes* of the Faubourg to the *grisettes* and *cocottes* of the Quartier. Male homosexuality is virtually unknown in the work of Zola, and although one is lavishly treated to scenes of 'goatish copulation, frustrated rape, actual rape, incest and sadistic murder',[2472] the reference to Mme Chanteau's grandfather the Chevalier de la Vignière, who 'had such white skin that he used to go to fancy-dress balls as a woman, in a low-necked dress',[2473] is despite its echo of the Chevalier d'Éon left undeveloped.

One might have supposed that the green carnation, 'the badge of the Parisian homosexual', 'the badge of Parisian homosexuals', 'among Parisian homosexuals a symbol of sexual inversion', 'the insignia of homosexuals'[2474] would have made such men conspicuous, but I have discovered no reference in the French sources either in prose or in paintings to green carnations in Paris. This is a story that, true or false, was always likely to acquire its own accretions. We have Tydeman and Price's dogmatic statement that 'the notorious green carnation [was] much favoured as a badge of identification by homosexuals of the period', and this has been enlarged by Neil McKenna: Wilde, he writes, 'borrowed the idea from the Paris Uranians who had in the summer of 1891 begun a craze for wearing carnations, artificially dyed green, as a badge, a secret symbol, of their sexual preferences. Just a few years earlier, in Paris, green cravats had been the rage among men who loved men.'[2475] Jacques de Langlade, on the other hand, credited its invention to Wilde early on, in his Langtry phase, suggesting that he wore one on the first night of *Patience*, 23rd April 1881, and says it was Wilde who started the Paris fashion, not the other way round, so that in April 1892 these bloomed ('épanouissent') in the windows of Parisian florists.[2476] As red carnations were the badge of the Boulangists, and the 'White Carnation' ('l'Œillet Blanc') was a royalist organisation that in the estimate of the Sûreté was 'an association of snobs, without intelligence or will',[2477] there is room for confusion here. One may add the comte de Montesquiou's *culte* for blue hydrangeas.

Nevertheless, in the city of Jean Lorrain, Pierre Loti, Robert de Montesquiou, Edouard de Max (to whom Gide dedicated *Saül* and who figures in Colette's *Le pur et l'impur*) and Paul Bourget (who when young was 'blatantly homosexual'[2478], one could with some immunity pose as a sodomite, or even as a somdomite. One who cautiously did so was the Cambridge don Goldsworthy Lowes Dickinson, who found the female carnality overwhelming: 'Few young men,' he wrote of visits in December 1888 and 1892, 'ever got less out of Paris than I did. For to get anything out of it, it seems to be essential to approach it by the route of women, and that was no route for me. I am amused, as I look back, to remember a visit to one of the dancing places (was it the Moulin Rouge?) and my boredom for the short time I could stay [...] The principal interest of Paris, women, was no interest to me'.[2479] Pierre Loti posed rather more blatantly: when J.E.C. Bodley and the painter Bonnat met him travelling on the Franco-Spanish border 'his summer costume included a mauve silk shirt buttoned with black pearls, in his manicured hands he held a pair of lavender gloves and his face was slightly rouged'.[2480]

~~~~~~~~

English fantasy about Frenchwomen was matched by the rather different ideas of the French about Englishwomen.

> Voilà les Englishes! Aoh yes! Very well!
> Tra la la la, la la la la la!
> Plats comm' des sandwiches. Aoh yes! Very well![2481]

The flatness refers to the bosoms of Englishwomen, which aligns the verse with Miss Bentson, the comic English governess in Delibes' *Lakmé* (performed at the Opéra-Comique in April 1883), Maupassant's Miss Harriet, and other French fantasies about the English female ('Anglaises pour rire' was a French phrase). Miss Harriet is one of

> the sort England produces in large numbers, one of those straight-backed, unbearable old maids who are seen in the dining-rooms of hotels throughout Europe, spoil Italy, poison Switzerland, make the lovely towns of the Mediterranæan quite uninhabitable, and wherever they go, import

their ghastly fads, the morals of fossilised virgins, ghastly clothes and that
faint odour of rubber which makes you suspect that at night they are put
away in a box.[2482]

Perhaps one discerns another such in Thomas Mann's 'lean English Miss
Brown, with her sourish smile'.[2483] Of English pilgrims at Lourdes,
Huysmans wrote 'None of them sings, but a few of the women, with
spectacles and protruding teeth, croak'.[2484]   At the English tavern
(Austin's) in the rue d'Amsterdam, des Esseintes encounters 'a crowd of
islanders [...] there were some women among the rest, unaccompanied by
male escort, dining by themselves – sturdy English dames with boys'
faces, teeth as big as tombstones, fresh, apple-red cheeks, long hands and
feet. They were attacking with unfeigned enthusiasm a rumpsteak pie –
meat served hot in mushroom sauce and covered with crust like a fruit
tart.'[2485]

V. Sackville West was to describe her father's mistress, Lady Constance
Hatch, as 'a stringy, wispy, French-music-hall Englishwoman'.[2486] As
Lady Constance visited Paris annually, she would have served very well
this aspect of caricature for the French. The English cocotte Nesta
Needham is described as 'the type of a thin English lady [...]', also flat-
chested and looking 'something like a man in woman's clothes'.[2487]
Georges Ohnet noted outside Thomas Cook's that among the English
tourists were 'various elderly ladies with flat figures.'[2488] The French
caricature of Englishwomen was so well established that it was inevitable
that when Maurras wished to describe an Englishwoman in unflattering
terms he should refer to her 'skinny breasts',[2489] and it had also to be
assimilated by English writers who were representing the French to
English readers. The 'elderly Englishwoman of sour aspect [...] a long
toothed English old maid' of W.J. Locke[2490] is an example of this double
reflection, Locke being an author who consistently contrasts French *joie
de vivre* with English *sang froid*.[2491] Elizabeth Robins also picked this up,
when the anti-feminist Greatorex mock-humorously identifies English
women who are engaged in good works as of a piece with 'the sort of
woman who smells of india rubber [...] The typical English spinster.
Italy's full of her. She never goes anywhere without a mackintosh and a
collapsible bath. [...] She doesn't only smell of rubber. *She*'s rubber
too.'[2492] Just such a woman even finds her way into *Teleny*: 'a real
specimen of a wandering English old maid, clad in a waterproof coat'.[2493]
This forms something of the hinterland to Proust's associating
governessses with waterproofs.[2494]

Nor did the Englishwoman in Paris escape the ridicule of the Irish Martin Ross.

> The grocer's shop at the corner is doing a steady and arduous trade [...] In the thronged interior may be discerned at intervals a bonnet, with plumage agitated by conversation, and by violent shocks received from convolutions in the ruck of buyers. By virtue of the compactness of trimming, and a certain cautiousness in the shade of lavender of the ribbon, it is recognisable as an English bonnet, and its wearer as one of a class whose sufferings have too long remained uncommiserated. She is one of the English mothers who have uprooted themselves from home and the tried and trusted suburban tradesmen, to live in Paris with an art-student daughter, to create for her a faint and famished semblance of the Kensington *ménage*, to endure torments of anxiety about damp linen, to nourish for the garçon of her hotel the strongest hatred of her life. The French of her peaceful schoolroom days has little in common with the clipped commercial slang of her uncongenial marketings [...] The workmen at a *cabaret* door call out 'Oh yess! Engleesh spoken!' as she passes with her discomfited face, and a boy thrusts into her hand a gratuitously distributed supplement of a halfpenny newspaper, with a coloured picture of a *décolletée* lady breaking open a grave. It seems [...] the completion of an antagonism and strangeness of all things.

The accompanying illustration by Edith Somerville is no more complimentary.[2495]

'Plats comm' des sandwiches' also conveys how the French esteemed the 'belle poitrine', with their own construction on why Paris was so popular with the English male. Dumas had noted of the courtesan Olympe at a ball that she was 'displaying a dazzling pair of shoulders and much of her magnificent breasts. She was a beautiful girl, more beautiful in terms of her figure, than Marguerite'.[2496] This was clearly what was expected. Peter de Polnay in his lament for the passing of Les Halles refers to 'the girls of the rue de Cygne, who for generations were famous for their large breasts'.[2497] The French had plenty of opportunity to observe Englishwomen and their bosoms, for while it was chic for French men to buy English clothes, it was no less so for English women to buy French ones. Clayton Glyn brought his wife to Paris 'two or three times a year' (notably at Easter) for this purpose: she had smart French cousins, the Fouquet Lemaîtres, with a house in the Champs Elysées and a readiness to tell her where to shop (she is one of the first English women of whom we read to have had her hair waved by Marcel Gautreau, on a visit in 1888)[2498] and Eleanor Glyn created for English fiction the nearest approach to the Parisian coquette yet published.

Robert Louis Stevenson once knowledgeably reversed the usual identification of French women with the ideal: 'The Lord was on his metal when He made the French woman. In America and England, at their best, they're often angels and goddesses, but here they're real women'.[2499] Debussy regretted that he could not get a decent cup of tea in England, certainly not the sort that his wife could make: 'In England, there no such wives as that [...] they are wives for horseguards with their complexions of raw ham.[2500] Marie Belloc, when approaching eighty, reflected that 'I have remained *toute Française de cœur*', which would suggest an unusual constancy were it not for her adding 'more so now, if that were possible, than ever before',[2501] which makes one wonder at the different grades of the absolute that being completely French implied.

> Miss Wilkinson [...] began to talk of Paris. She loved the boulevards and the Bois. There was grace in every street, and the trees in the Champs Elysées had a distinction which trees had not elsewhere. [...] And the theatres: the plays were brilliant, and the acting was incomparable. She often went with Madame Foyot, the mother of the girls she was educating, when she was trying on clothes.
>
> 'Oh, what a misery to be poor!' she cried. 'These beautiful things, it's only in Paris they know how to dress, and not to be able to afford them! Poor Madame Foyot, she had no figure. Sometimes the dressmaker used to whisper to me: "Ah, Mademoiselle, if she only had your figure."[...] Men are so stupid in England. They only think of the face. The French, who are a nation of lovers, know how much more important the figure is.' [...]
>
> Philip noticed then that Miss Wilkinson had a robust form and was proud of it.[2502]

The process of ogling and being ogled, drew upon and contributed to deeper constructions. Zola's Madame Hédouin, proprietor of Au Bonheur des Dames, 'loved the shop, and imagined it expanding, swallowing up the neighbouring shops, and displaying a magnificent frontage'. Here the 'Ladies' Paradise' becomes itself a magnificent woman, pregnant, hungry, full-bosomed – the belle vitrine and the belle poitrine coalescing. Zola goes on 'It was a dream that suited her keen intelligence, her strong will, her woman's intuition of the Paris of the future.'[2503] She is, in short, Haussmann as hausfrau, with all Paris to be swept up.

CHAPTER FOURTEEN

PHASES OF THE MOON –
OSCAR WILDE, SALOMÉ
AND SARAH BERNHARDT

> 'It is I who must bow to you.'
> – Tsar Alexander III to Sarah Bernhardt.[2504]

> 'I shall die upon the stage. It is my field of battle.'
> – Sarah Bernhardt.[2505]

> '*Salomé*, that terrible coloured little tragedy I once wrote.'
> – Oscar Wilde to Frances Forbes-Robertson.[2506]

Part 1: Gitanes

JUST as Maeterlinck's created an Arthurian universe for his symbolist drama *Pelléas et Mélisande*, so Wilde constructed an imaginary ancient Judæa for his symbolist drama *Salomé*. Here too we find a liminal world, the terrace, governed not by the spare dry argument of the rational world, but by reference to the moon, to angels, to the dominion of lust, to magic, to portents, to mystery, whether of love or death. Wilde's Jerusalem is far from Shaw's Alexandria, although the latter's Cleopatra borrows a few plumes from Salomé. The 'sphere of the far away and the archaic,' has been seen by Jürgen Habermas as neo-conservative anti-modernism, where, 'in Manichæan fashion, instrumental reason' is juxtaposed with principle 'only accessible through evocation, be it the will to power or sovereignty, Being or the Dionysiac force of the poetical'.[2507] This is not far to seek in *Salomé*, and reconstructing the circumstances that surround the play tells us why.

'Remarkably,' write Tydeman and Price, 'the protracted emergence of *Salomé* apparently left no detectable traces among Wilde's formal utterances, or extant writings. In their absence, we are forced to glean what enlightenment we can concerning the play's evolution and composition from casual allusions, codicological evidence and from not necessarily reliable remarks culled from the assorted memoirs of Wilde's contemporaries.'[2508] The work of Tydeman and Price, coupled with that of Derrick Puffett,[2509] provided a then exhaustive list of Wilde's sources, actual or speculative, now superseded as Salomé studies proliferate.[2510] As Wilde's engagement with Parisian theatre was bound up not with Réjane or Bartet, Antoine or Rivière, but with Bernhardt, perhaps the chief instance where detailed knowledge of Wilde's engagements in Paris is desirable concerns the highly coloured tale of *Salomé* being exoticised by a *tzigane* band led by Jancsi Rigo in the Grand Café, in 1891.[2511] This was the Rigo who, having come to Paris for the 1889 Exhibition, subsequently eloped with Princess Clara de Caraman-Chimay, known as 'Clara Soleil'.[2512] Here, too, we enter a world of multiple and disputed origins. We learn from Ralph Nevill that the *tzigane* band was inaugurated at Maire's in the boulevard de Strasbourg in the 'nineties, and that it was led by 'the well-known Boldi'; J.-P. Goujon says that Rigo was the violinist at Maxim's, but Maxim's did not open until 1899.[2513] Albert, a later maître d'hôtel at Maxim's, says that it was there that 'le grand Boldi […] faisait frissonner nos petites dames, ensorcelait aussi péremptoirement qu'une Liane de Pougy ou une Otero'; and Isidore de Lara says that Rigo played at Paillard's in the rue de la Chaussée d'Antin, 'the ambiguous Chaussée d'Antin' – perhaps doubly ambiguous, for Colonel Newnham-Davis gives Paillard's address as 38 boulevard des Italiens, which was the address of Bignon's.[2514] Chris Healy opts for both the Grand Café and Paillard's, but dates this to the late 1890s.[2515] Du Maurier, in an authorial aside, has his three 'Angliches' visit a Hungarian Band ('the first that had yet appeared in Western Europe, I believe'[2516]) in the 'Cirque des Bashibazoucks': this must have been towards the end of the 1860s for the word bashibazouck was not current before then, and really only entered general use with the Bulgarian Massacres carried out by these irregular cavalry in 1876. George Painter comes down in favour of Maxim's, but says that Rigo was a violinist in the band of Boldi and dates the elopement to 1896, while Véronique Hartmann gives 1897.[2517] Baroness Orczy, herself Hungarian, says that the three best gipsy leaders of 'exceptionally admirable bands' were Berkes, Rigo and Racz.[2518] Berkes, the first of these, played in London: it is to his band perhaps that Lord Goring is referring in *An Ideal Husband*. Maud Tree thought that the first Hungarian band to perform in London was when Lady Ardilaun hired one for an evening garden party in July 1890.[2519] Gypsies, at least in the operatic sense, returned to Paris in December 1895, when Johan Strauss II's *Zigeuner Baron* had a two month run at the Folies-Dramatiques as *Le Baron Tzigane*. Boldi went on to the

Ritz, 'where he was a well known figure, preening himself and bowing like an elderly peacock'.[2520]

Clara de Caraman-Chimay was also seen in other identities: in the park at Chimay 'she looked like Aurora in her chariot in the fresco by Guido Reni at the Rospigliosi Palace in Rome',[2521] but one night at the Café Procope in 1896 'she seemed to possess the barbaric splendour of an Eastern Sultana painted by Gérôme, while the diners whispered '"Voilà la reine d'Amour"'.[2522]

According to Stuart Merrill, it was seeing a young Roumanian dancing on her hands at the Moulin Rouge that started Wilde's thoughts towards Salomé: 'I want to make her an offer to play or still more to dance the part of Salomé in a play I am going to write'.[2523] This perhaps owes more to Flaubert than to history, but whatever about Rigo helping to inspire Wilde, it would seem that Salomé helped to inspire his mistress. That Wilde may have added the finishing touches to *Salomé* in Torquay is something of an anticlimax, but does serve to remind us that the author was not always on stilts. One senses something of the need to ground *Salomé* in knowable experience in Ellmann's spirited attempt to offer the play as a parable of Wilde's reconciling the influences upon him of Ruskin and Pater, but here Ellmann himself retreated from fully realising his argument, admitting rather naively 'It is Salomé, and not Pater, who dances the dance of the seven veils […] the play takes place in Judaea, not Oxford'.[2524] Even so, once Ellmann's idea takes root, it is tempting to view the disputes at Herod's banquet as mirroring those at Magdalen High Table, even if Dionysiac music was less customary at the latter.

We do not know that Wilde used Maire's ('the connecting link between the smart restaurant and the bourgeois one'[2525]) before his exile, unless a reference to dining there with Frank Harris can so be dated,[2526] but whether all these statements are true, or whether any or none is true, the first must be viewed in the light of the second, and if invented, either as a welcome or as an unwelcome invention. As M. Paillard was the proprietor of Maire's in the days when Escoffier was chef there, there is room for some interplay. Boldi made Maire's fashionable for such *horizontales* as Liane de Pougy, Irma de Montigny and Caroline Otero.[2527] Once described as 'that ambulating jeweller's shop',[2528] Otero suggests another Wildean conceit, la sainte courtisane, the woman covered with jewels.[2529] The drinking in of this ambience by Wilde is perhaps why Robert Sayre finds that it is *Salomé*, and not *The Picture of Dorian Gray*, that was largely inspired by current French decadence, and by Huysmans in particular.[2530]

Much of this rather over-heated atmosphere is caught in the account of
Wilde's gestation of *Salomé* by the Guatemalan diplomat Gomez Carrillo,
who turns the process of creation into obsession: 'A day never went by
when he didn't speak to me of Salomé [...] He used to stand for hours in
the main streets, looking at jewellers' windows and imagining the perfect
jewellery for the adornment of his idol's body [...] There were ten, no, a
hundred Salomés that he imagined'.[2531]   This is part of the mythology of
Salomé, the Wildean trick of not doing something but making people
believe he had done it, as Elizabeth Robins came to believe that 'like a
magnesium light Wilde flashed into the Theatre with "Salomé" in
Paris.'[2532]   Carrillo asserts that Wilde considered all the pictorial Salomés
known to him, but says nothing of Roumanian dancers or Romany bands,
whether at the Moulin Rouge or at Maire's.   Puffett accepts that Carillo
'saw much of Wilde during the composition of the play' and Ellmann also
takes Carillo's statements at face value, as well as attributing to Wilde
knowledge of the Salomé paintings by Rubens, Leonardo, Dürer,
Ghirlandaio, and van Thulden.[2533]   All needs to be viewed more critically:
none of Wilde's other friends mention Carillo.   Pascal Aquien has drawn
attention to other representations of Salomé by Memling, Cranach,
Botticelli, Luini, Tiepolo and Titian, but without suggesting that Wilde
was familiar with them.[2534]

One need not confine oneself to the work of such masters.   Arthur
Symons' 'Abdala, who seems to be doing the *danse du ventre* as one saw
her in the French Exhibition' and Emma d'Auban, who danced in a sort of
harem costume in London in 1881, both suggest the belly dancer that
Beardsley was to draw.[2535]   Given that much of our conception of *Salomé*
derives from Beardsley's 'illustrations', it is as well to note that the
commission to illustrate the play flowed from his 'Salomé and the Head of
St John the Baptist', not the other way round.   Beardsley also offered
Wilde a translation which Wilde found as unsatisfactory as that of Lord
Alfred Douglas (and as unsatisfactory as Beardsley's illustrations, offering
to write a play one day that would go with them).   Wilde himself refers to
a translation by 'one of Dowson's friends' that he hints Smithers might
publish.[2536]   Information on all this is scanty, and Vyvyan Holland's
statement that 'before the English translation was published, it passed
through several hands [...] The result was inevitably a somewhat
patchwork affair', serves more to tantalise than to elucidate.[2537]   Certainly,
Douglas was left in a position where he no longer regarded the translation
as his: 'Wilde revised the translation to the extent of taking out from it
most of the elements of original work on my part [...] I do not claim it as
my translation'.[2538]

Part 2: A Severed Head

ATTENTION to representations of Salomé and the Baptist has been the valuable work of Virginie Pouzet-Duzer,[2539] valuable not least because it deflects attention away from the post-Wilde *culte* of the Salomé dance towards the more interesting task of identifying why the theme had such a hold on the Victorian imagination[2540] – in George Moore's *A Modern Lover* (1883), for example, the painter 'Lewis Seymour' (a cross between Lewis Hawkins and Alma-Tadema or Gérôme) paints a 'Salomé', and Pascal Aquien states that in the second half of the nineteenth century, five or six Salomés were offered to the Salon every year.[2541] Aquien, like most scholars, dates the *culte* to Heine's *Atta Troll* of 1842, which contains the stanza

> In her hands she carries ever
> That sad charger, with the head of
> John the Baptist, which she kisses:
> Yes, the head with fervour kisses.[2542]

'She' here is, however, Herodias, not her daughter. One must be grateful that Wilde did not adopt this Hiawathan metre for *Salomé*.

Concentration on the 'Salomé' of Moreau (or, rather on all fifteen Salomés of Moreau[2543]) has obscured such Salomés as that of Frederick Leighton, rejected by the Royal Academy in 1864 but admired by du Maurier. It is clearly necessary to distinguish between depictions of the severed head of the Baptist, and those rarer works that feature Salomé herself.

I think, too, that it is necessary to conflate with Moreau's Salomé his 'Orphée' of 1865, where a young woman is gently gazing on the head of Orpheus resting not on a charger but on what is perhaps his lyre. She, like Salomé, is in the specifically rich and exotic costume that marks the marriage of æstheticism with orientalism. This was acquired for the French national collection in 1866, and is at least as suggestive of Wilde's Salomé as any of Moreau's Salomé paintings,[2544] and certainly more so that Henri Regnault's success of the Paris Salon of 1870, his rather blowsy gypsy Salomé with a dish yet to receive the head on her knees,[2545] while the same barbaric orientalism of Moreau's Salomé, that so appealed to Graham Robertson, can also be found in his 'Galatée' of 1880.[2546] Moreover, direct and consequent familiarity between Wilde and Moreau seems to be implicitly denied by Gomez Carillo's account, and is not established until Graham Robertson's stage designs. Wilde did acknowledge the connection by sending Moreau a copy of the play. We can ignore Laurent Crozier's

idea that Wilde had become fascinated with Moreau's Salomé pictures
while visiting Paris in 1876: Wilde was not in Paris in that year.[2547]
Lucien Lévy-Dhurmer's 'Salomé kissing the head of John the Baptist'
seems to refer to Mallarmé rather than Wilde.

In fact, 'tête coupé' pictures, such as Bonnat's 'Beheading of St Denis',
were never far away: and, indeed, severed heads are part of Parisian
history, although more usually presented on pikes than on chargers.[2548]
Rubens' painting of Thomyris plunging the head of Cyrus the Great into a
vase full of blood, which had been in the Louvre since the reign of Louis
XV,[2549] certainly ought to have been known to Wilde. Closer to Wilde's
imagery is another painting by Regnault, 'Summary Execution under the
Moorish kings of Granada'.   This very large canvas depicts the
executioner wiping his sword after decapitating a man whose sprawled
body lies on a flight of steps, down which the head has rolled. This was
painted in 1870, and exhibited in the Salon of 1878.[2550]   Both Rodin's
'Head of John the Baptist' and Henner's 'Head of John the Baptist' were
shown at the Salon of 1879 (noting also Rodin's 'Head of John the
Baptist' of 1887[2551]) and there is one passage in *Nana* that a *post hoc*
reading seems to align with the imagery. This is a scene at the Théâtre des
Variétés, where Nana is on stage 'with her back arched and her arms
outspread', while the head of the prompter, seated below stage, was 'level
with her feet [...] resting on the floor looking as if it had been severed
from the body.'[2552]

The Gustave Doré bible illustration of the head being presented to Salomé
(1865) was also easily accessible (it should hardly be necessary at this
point to recall that the two biblical accounts, Matthew 14:1-12 and Mark
6: 14-29, neither name Salomé nor refer to the Dance of the Seven Veils).
Paul Baudry's 'La Danse de Salomé' was painted for the Palais Garnier,
and one must suppose it certain that Wilde knew it. One cannot be as
confident about his acquaintance with Henner's 'Hérodiade' of 1887 or
Georges Rochegrosse's 'Salomé danse devant le roi Hérode' of the same
year; but at least they form part of the Salomé *culte* that Wilde was
drawing upon. Otherwise, 'All the pictorial Salomés known to Wilde' may
not take one beyond the National Galleries of Dublin and London, and the
Louvre: and these certainly do not take one into the Dance of the Seven
Veils, or the sexual passion of Salomé for Iokanaan. It is no doubt
because of this that the later 'Salomé' of Klimt (which is also a version of
a Judith and Holofernes severed head) has been the resource for theatre
programmes when an image has been needed. The Dance and the passion
are inextricable: in a Yeatsian key, Monique Dubar writes 'Ces neuf

minutes trente secondes de musique sont liées de la manière la plus intime et nécessaire au personnage: sans la danse, Salomé n'existerait pas, ni dans l'histoire, ni dans l'histoire de son histoire'.[2553]

~~~~~~

Paris also provided other images. Just as one would wish to be quite sure about Wilde and Rigo, one would also need to know if Wilde ever found his way into, or heard an account of, that strange performance seen by Captain Lennox Berkeley, later Lord Berkeley,

> on the boulevards in a kind of small theatre, which he could not make out at all, and advised my going to see it also. I went, and saw a man who held on a plate the head of a woman, and underneath on the ground was the body of the woman lying flat on her back without a head. The man, who held the plate on his hand, though it was at the same time suspended from above by two strings, for what reason I know not, kept passing his hand underneath the plate to show one that there was no possible connection between the head and the body on the ground. At times he swung the plate to and fro, and the head looked very ghastly indeed.[2554]

This was probably Georges Méliès at the Théâtre Robert-Houdin,[2555] who had an obsession with severed heads. Later, as a film-maker, he produced *L'homme à la tête de caoutchouc* (1902), where a head is displaced from its body, and his *Le Mélomane* of 1903 and *Le bourreau Turc* (1904) also included trick decapitations. Here we find a junction between the magic practised by the occultists, the conjuring practised by the tricksters, and the stage effects managed by the theatres, between Paris of the illumination and Paris of the illusions.

Part 3: Herodians

THERE is, however, another dimension. Is it possible that Wilde had no need of first hand acquaintance with any of these elementals? George Moore arrived at a mysterious wild-eyed bohemian fiddle player in Paris and conferred the status of Wagner's spirit upon him through the exercise of his literary imagination: the exercise of his literary imagination or the general *on-dits* of Parisian café society, or the one acting upon the other. This Adrian Frazier has characterised as a '*symboliste* homo-erotic fantasy';[2556] once more we see the Parisian Moore as an anti-Wilde. That Wilde was aware of the exotic in music can be seen in *The Picture of Dorian Gray*:

At another time he devoted himself entirely to music, and in a long latticed room, with a vermilion-and-gold ceiling and walls of olive-green lacquer, he used to give curious concerts in which mad gipsies tore wild music from little zithers, or grave, yellow-shawled Tunisians plucked at the strained strings of monstrous lutes, while grinning Negroes beat monotonously upon copper drums and, crouching upon scarlet mats, slim turbaned Indians blew through long pipes of reed or brass and charmed – or feigned to charm – great hooded snakes and horrible horned adders.

Two years before the publication of *Dorian Gray*, Maupassant had given a musical evening in Paris:

He entertained in his apartment a troop of Arab dancers, acrobats and musicians who were in Paris for the Exposition – four men, twelve women [...] Stomach dancing, oriental cacophonies, and champagne [...] made up into a wild evening [...] *un méli-mélo fantastique*.[2557]

And if Rigo and other exotic musicians or dancers may have provided some origin for the conception of Salomé and the Dance of the Seven Veils, so Paris could furnish ideas for much else in *Salomé*. There is no reason not to insert into Wilde's vocabulary of poesis Gautier's 'Variations sur le Carnival de Venise' from *Emaux et Camées*, with its evocation of Paganini's frantic bowing, its references to faded veils and golden arabesques, a parataxis, perhaps, between *The Harlot's House* and *Salomé*.[2558] Flaubert's *Hérodias*,[2559] also, offers a number of clues. The erotic Dance of the Bee, which Flaubert had seen in Egypt in 1850, had been performed to harps whose players were blindfolded, that is, veiled. It was probably well-enough known that Flaubert had also taken inspiration from the haut-relief of Salomé dancing on her hands on the tympanum of Rouen Cathedral, which returns us to Merrill's young Roumanian. Flaubert does not quite use the name Iokanaan, as Wilde was to do – the pictorial representations always refer to him as St John the Baptist – although this is used in Baldick's translation. Flaubert's own spelling is Ioakanann.[2560] The moon, so important in Wilde's *Salomé*, has it place, for Ioakanann compares himself and the coming Messiah to the waning and waxing moon. Here too we find Herod's curious ambivalence towards Ioakanann. Na'aman is common to both *Hérodias* and *Salomé*, and the setting for both is the terrace of the palace. The placing of Iokanaan in the cistern seems to have originated with Flaubert – it is not original to Wilde, although he makes better use of it. The enumeration of Herod's treasures lacks the hyperbole that Wilde introduces, but this is a stylistic difference that one would expect. What are unique to Wilde are the lust of Salomé for Iokanaan and the Dance of the Seven Veils, but if one turns from

Salomé to *Salammbô* rather than *Hérodias*, one may see that the doffing of the veils, which gives Salomé power over Herod, has as its parallel the donning and doffing of the mantle of Tanit, and the power this confers upon Salammbô: the similarity of the two names plays its part in this reading, as much as the tragic ends both of the men they destroy through their love, and in consequence, of themselves; and Herod's offering Salomé the mantle of the High Priest. Wilde gives the Executioner the name of Naaman, but Strauss seems to have contemplated returning to Flaubert's Mannaëi as Mannai.[2561] Nor is the dissimilarity of the names Narr'Havas and Narraboth (the Young Syrian) too great to serve as referent.[2562]

Massenet, who composed his *Hérodiade* from the *Hérodias* of Flaubert, did however invest Salomé with sexuality – to the disgust of Saint-Saëns, who accused Massenet of changing her into Mary Magdalen.[2563] *Hérodiade* opened in Brussels in December 1881 in the presence of the Belgian queen and many Parisians, and appeared briefly at the Théâtre des Italiens[2564] in Paris in February 1884. Herodias was sung by Wilhelmina Tremelli,[2565] Salomé by Fidès Devriès; John the Baptist by Jean de Reszke; Herod by Victor Maurel; and Phanuel, Edouard de Reszke – but Wilde did not much care for Massenet's music. After attending a performance of Massenet's *Sapho*, Wilde wrote 'The music meandered aimlessly about, as Massenet's usually does, with endless false alarms of a real melody, and incessant posing of themes that are not resolved into any development'.[2566] The key phrase is 'as Massenet's usually does'. There is no other reference to Massenet in *The Complete Letters*, and Ellmann does not refer to Massenet at all, so Wilde's acquaintance with Massenet's music therefore has to be inferred. Possibilities include *Manon* at the Theatre Royal, Drury Lane, in May 1885; *Le Mage*, Palais Garnier, March 1891; *Manon*, Opéra-Comique, November 1891; *Manon*, Royal Opera House, Covent Garden, May 1892; *Thaïs*, Palais Garnier, March/April 1894; *La Navarraise*, Royal Opera House, Covent Garden, June 1894.[2567] As far as I have been able to ascertain, *Hérodiade* was not produced in London and Wilde was not in Paris when it was playing there. For the rest, perhaps *Thaïs* is the opera most likely to have attracted Wilde, but he was no operamane. Yet if the *Hérodiade* of Massenet was ignored by, or even unknown to, Wilde, it was certainly not the same case with Strauss when he turned to *Salomé*. 'L'une est la mère, l'autre la fille,' is how Pierre Cedars begins his study of the two works.[2568] The linkage was made plain when *Hérodiade* was first performed at Covent Garden on 6th July 1904, when it was renamed *Salomé*, and again when *Hérodiade* was performed in repertory with *Salomé* at the Vienna State Opera, 8th, 12th and 15th

March 1999, but long before that Hector Dufranne sang both Vitellius in
Hérodiade and Iokanaan in *Salomé*.

Evidently research into the staging and reception of *Hérodiade* is
necessary in order to examine Wilde's conception of his own play. Of this
much is known, thanks to Graham Robertson, to which a lesser known
description by Charles Holmes, Director of the National Gallery, may be
added, the result of a discussion one evening at The Vale with Wilde,
Ricketts and Shannon.

> A more instructive evening was spent in discussing *Salomé*. This was
> conceived as a fantastic *jeu d'esprit*, in which elements suggested by
> Maeterlinck, Flaubert and Gustave Moreau were paraded and parodied [...]
> Then he talked of the appropriate stage-setting, with the Jews all in yellow,
> Iokanaan in white, Herod in deep blood-red, and Salomé herself in pale
> green like a snake. On another evening, he brought round Beardsley's
> newly completed drawings. Ricketts was enthusiastic about their
> accomplishment, praising the more generously perhaps because he would
> have liked to have illustrated the play himself.[2569]

Ricketts' ambition was realised in his set designs for the Literary Theatre
Society's production in London and 1906, but it was Graham Robertson
that Wilde chose for his aborted production of 1892. The comment that
Salomé contains an element of parody is a curious one, and if Holmes is
correctly reporting the conversation (he is usually pedestrian enough to be
regarded as reliable), much may be made of it, not least the lack of any
real mutual understanding between Maeterlinck and Wilde.

Holmes goes on to comment that Ricketts was a closer interpreter of
Wilde's intention than Beardsley 'whose Salomé is no idolised, wilful
princess in a remote Oriental palace, but a jaded Cyprian *apache* from a
music-hall promenade', and we know that Wilde never cared for
Beardsley's illustrations. Holmes is perceptive in adding that their
suggestion of 'veiled priapism', of 'hidden depravities', of the substitution
of 'a Grand Guignol animalism' for the play's 'hieratic atmosphere',[2570]
rebounded on Wilde. They have remained to haunt such productions as
that by Steven Berkoff.

Part 4: Oscar's Sarah

WHEN Wilde breakfasted in Paris with Wilfrid Blunt, George Curzon and
Willy Peel at the end of October 1891, he told his friends that 'he was
writing a play in French to be acted for the [Théâtre] Français', that is, the

Comédie Française. This was apparently met with some scepticism, for they promised to go to the opening night with 'George Curzon as Prime Minister', that is as it were on the Greek Kalends.[2571] Curzon, appointed Viceroy of India while Wilde was an outcast in Paris, had been an M.P. only since 1886: in 1891 even he could not have supposed that he would become Prime Minister until the far distant future, and indeed his chance only came (and went) in 1923. A further confusion is introduced by a footnote in *The Complete Letters* that suggests that Wilde spent 'at least two weeks' in Paris in the *spring* of 1891, and might have written much of *Salomé* at that time.[2572]

~~~~~~

If springtide in Paris is time carried in the footfall of the *flâneur*, with something trivial in one's buttonhole, autumn is the season for reflection in the mist, coupled forever in the English literary imagination with mellow fruitfulness, *vendémiaire* not quite over, *brumaire* not quite begun, an interesting time in which to write an Eastern play. Only a few days after his conversation with Curzon (2nd November), Wilde called at the British Embassy and told the Lyttons that 'he had *just written* a play which he wants to have translated into French and acted at the Français'.[2573] Wilde also wrote to Ettie Grenfell that 'Paris is so charming that I think of becoming a French poet'.[2574] Could he never resist the desire to boast? From his own description of *The Importance of being Earnest* ('The first act is ingenious, the second beautiful, the third abominably clever'[2575]) to the time when down on his luck in Paris in 1900 he is said to have told Elizabeth Marbury that he 'had just staged a miracle play in the Latin Quarter'[2576] – though this is perhaps capable of more than one interpretation – he rarely took a less than favourable view of himself. Lady Emily Lytton, then sixteen years old, thought Wilde 'not so odious as we expected, though he is evidently fearfully conceited',[2577] and Wilde was certainly unscrupulous in inflating his connection, dedicating *Lady Windermere's Fan* in 1893 'To the dear memory of Robert, Lord Lytton in affection and admiration.'[2578] One wonders what Lytton's predecessor Lord Lyons, whose watchwords were 'fidelity, reticence, self-effacement',[2579] would have made of Wilde.

Wilde was at least a consistent (if repetitive) believer in his own destiny and genius. In March 1883, with all the assurance of an Oxford man with a Double First, he had told Mary Anderson, to whom he was sending *The Duchess of Padua*, that it was 'the masterpiece of my literary work, the chef d'œuvre of my youth'. As his literary work at the time consisted of his poorly received poems and the even more poorly received play *Vera*, this may be thought something of any empty claim. Despite the very moderate success *The Duchess* had in New York, he decided that he would ask Irving to put it on at the Lyceum. It would have had to be a very much better play to have justified Irving's taking it, but the point needs to be remembered in the context of his belief in *Salomé* as a vehicle for the Français, for Bernhardt and/or for Duse.

The Comédie Française was then under the direction of Jules Clarétie. According to Catulle Mendès, Wilde said that *Salomé* was the working out of the *idée psychologique*, following in reverse the dramatic theories of Ibsen as he had found them in *Hedda Gabler*.[2580] It hardly sounds the sort of material with which the House of Molière[2581] was at ease, especially as at this time Wilde's reputation as a playwright, such as it was, rested on *Vera* and *The Duchess of Padua,* as *A Florentine Tragedy* was neither performed nor published until after Wilde's death.[2582] The Comédie Française's conservatism mirrored that of the École des Beaux Arts. 'After the 1830s the Comédie Française still produced new works, but it became more exclusively the repository of the great works of the past. Hugo was the last important dramatist of the century to create his major works there.'[2583] It is possible that Wilde was trailing his coat before Lord Lytton, who frequented the Français, and was rather stage struck – or perhaps actress-struck. As Sarah Bernhardt was no longer a member of the Comédie Française, having quitted it in April 1880, at least at this point in 1891 Wilde was writing without that actress in mind, and although at the Comédie Wilde (or whoever directed the piece) would have been able to cast the play from Jean Mounet-Sully, Edmond Got, Coquelin *cadet*, Suzanne Reichenberg and others, these actors are difficult to think of in relation to *Salomé*. Would Julia Bartet, known as 'la divine'[2584] before Bernhardt was accorded this apotheosis, have played the title rôle? Moreover, if *Salomé* had been submitted to the Comédie Française, it would have had to be accepted by Claretie and 'the most difficult body of censors'[2585] the Comité de lecture, and this too is not easy to imagine.

The Français may, however, have been a red herring. On 25th November 1891, the *Gazette des Théâtres* reported that 'M. Oscar Wilde, le poète anglais, vient de lire au Théâtre de l'Art *Salomé*, pièce en une acte en prose, qu'il a écrite en français. Cette pièce sera jouée le février prochain.'[2586] While this takes us away from Sarah Bernhardt, it does advance us towards Lugné-Poë and the production of 1896.

When Wilde saw *Salomé* as a possible play for the Comédie Française, he was indicating how far removed he was from the concerns of his younger contemporaries. Frantisek Deak has written that

> Baudelaire, Villiers de l'Isle Adam, Banville and even the young Mallarmé still believed in the possibilities of making a life in theatre, even if Banville was the only one partially to succeed. Toward the end of the 1880s, there were no such illusions on the part of the young poets. Beside frequenting some popular theatres, their theatre going was mostly limited to literary cabarets. It was even fashionable to say that one did not go to the theatre any more, that theatre as an artistic genre was dead. In *L'École décadente*,[2587] which summarised some of the attitudes of the time toward literature and the theatre, Anatole Baju wanted to get rid of theatre completely. For Baju, 'life itself was theatre, or at very best circus'.[2588]

Only slightly differently phrased this might have been a *bon mot* by Wilde himself, yet Wilde, who put his genius into his life, still devoted his talents to the West End stage. There is a final point to be made about the Lugné-Poë production of *Salomé*, namely the identity of Lina Munte. The sources are remarkably silent upon this: the rôle clearly did not sweep her to fame (even Vyvyan Holland calls her Lina Muntz),[2589] and the contemporary critical reaction to the play must be reviewed in the light of this. Even to discover how she played the rôle is difficult enough, Mireille Dottin-Orsini, for example, merely recording (despite her deep knowledge of all to do with Salomé) that her veils caught fire in the wings and were extinguished by Lugné-Poë, while Monique Dubar only cites a contemporary critic (unnamed) who thought that the music Munte danced to was written for dancing bears.[2590] The picture of her playing Salomé reproduced by Melissa Knox[2591] and sourced from the William Andrews Clark Library, is actually of Emmy Destinn. Nor has much been discovered about Munte's career in general. She played Virginie in the adaptation of *L'Assommoir* at the Ambigu, Aquilina in the Théâtre de l'Œuvre production of Auguste Villeray's *Hérakléa*[2592] and also acted at the Gymnase: one contemporary called her thinnest woman in Paris after Bernhardt.[2593] Her name also occurs in the course of some verses by Henri Beauclair in order to provide a rather forced play on words:

> Tout est désert. – On fait le vide autour de lui.
> Seule, une enfant, dont l'œil noir et profond reluit,
> Approche Koning et l'affronte.
> Elle va, court et rit, et cela sans trembler.
> Mais, pour ne point la voir et ne point lui parler,
> Marais descend quand Lina Munte.[2594]

Salomé played for two nights (10th and 11th February 1896) and was reprised in October. One cannot find evidence for Pascal Aquien's claim that the production was 'triomphale',[2595] and he says nothing more concerning the production. It was never revived, unlike Lugné-Poë's *Pelléas et Mélisande*, which the Théâtre de l'Œuvre toured to London, The Netherlands and Scandinavia. The décor was by M.H. Séruzier, the music (which is apparently lost) by René Lardé. Lugné-Poë played Herod and Gina Barbieri played Herodias. Iokanaan was Max Barbier, possibly a connection of Jules Barbier's; his head was commissioned from the Musée Grévin, broken during rehearsal but mended in time for the performance.[2596] The similarity of Barbieri and Barbier make one wonder if one or other of them was a stage name. Narraboth (the Young Syrian) was played by an actor whose name is only given in the programme as Nerey (and not, as Tydeman and Price say, 'a M. Lerey'[2597]). Nerey also played the title rôle in Coolus' *Raphaël*, which played with *Salomé*. The following month he played the king of the barbarians in the Théâtre de l'Œuvre production of Villaray's *Hérakléa*. Suzanne Auclair was also in both *Raphaël* and *Salomé,* as Rita in the first and as the Page in the second, beginning the tradition of a woman playing this part, to which Wilde objected strongly. *Salomé* itself 'scandalised respectable public opinion', the core of this being the 'jeune esclave éffeminé, dont les graces équivoques faisaient scandale'.[2598] In turn, Wilde benefitted from the production, telling André Gide 'You cannot imagine how much good it did me in prison that *Salomé* was being played in Paris'.[2599] Apparently he was treated with a new respect and his book allowance increased: if so, it casts a slightly different light on the martinet régime of Colonel Isaacson.

The play in which Bernhardt did appear in 1893 was *Les Rois* by Jules Lemaître, who became her lover and was to say of her 'She is not an individual but a complex of individuals'.[2600] The play was based on the Mayerling tragedy of 1889, with Edouard de Max playing opposite Bernhardt. This is so much more like Bernhardt's usual style that although she had been prepared to play Salomé in 1892 – had even been enthusiastic – one wonders about the working out of this enthusiasm. The narrative of Bernhardt's involvement with the play, and with Wilde, has been taken too superficially by biographers of both. Her early reputation had been made as a classical actress with the Comédie Française; after that it was as the great exponent of Romantic drama that she made her name. She usually was aware of her limitations: she only ventured Molière on seven occasions and only once (as Dorinne in *Tartuffe*) with success. Even more rarely did she venture into the contemporary avant-garde, in plays such as Octave Mirbeau's *Les mauvais Bergers* of 1898,

Sudermann's *Heimat* (played as *Magda*) and Maeterlinck's *Pelléas et Mélisande*. *Les mauvais Bergers* was not a success, being damned by Sarcey even though Bernhardt was partnered by Lucien Guitry, while *Magda* failed in Paris and in London had to stand comparison with other productions starring Eleonora Duse and Mrs Patrick Campbell (this translated by Louis N. Parker[2601]). The comparison was well made by Shaw: 'The contrast between the two Magdas is as strong as any contrast could possibly be.'[2602] Bernhardt's Ellida Wangel in *The Lady from the Sea*, which she played in Geneva in 1906, was a disaster. It was the orchids and hortensia in the hair of Gismonda, not the vine leaves in the hair of Hedda Gabler, that attracted the divine Sarah. Equally, plays that she expressly asked for from Zola (*La Curée, La Faute de l'Abbé Mouret*) were never performed.[2603]

Wilde was to deny that he had written Salomé for Sarah as though he feared the imputation that he was working with an object in mind; but of course he wanted her for Salomé and was perfectly happy to write *The Duchess of Padua* with Mary Anderson in mind and *Vera* with Mrs Bernard Beere, 'the lovely lady who had risen from a flower stall in the Alhambra to become the English Bernhardt'.[2604] When Sarah Bernhardt took time off from high drama, it had been for pieces like *Nana Sahib* by Richepin (at the Théâtre Porte St-Martin on the 20th December 1883), *Adrienne Lecouvreur*[2605] by Scribe or even *Frou-Frou*[2606] by Meilhac and Halévy with its seven changes of costume for her rôle as Gilberte. Although she produced Maurice Donnay's *Amants*, it was Jeanne Granier who played Claudine. Bernhardt's playwrights were Victor Hugo and Dumas *fils*, even Alfred de Musset; when she discovered Edmond Rostand, it was to proclaim him the new Victor Hugo. (Max Beerbohm wrote that the general view was that Rostand was thought to be a Mallarmé but if you scratched him you only discovered a Sardou.[2607])

In 1879, when she first appeared in London, Bernhardt was already seventeen years into her career, and ten years on from her first success *en travesti* as Zanetto in *Le Passant* 'a lovely little play [by] the then unknown'[2608] Coppée. One anecdote of Bernhardt, told by Jules Renard and recounted by Maurice Baring, captures the effect her acting, indeed her presence, could have – that when she descended a spiral staircase, it was as if she stayed still and the staircase revolved round her.[2609] This works well as not simply as metaphor for her life but also for that of Paris, where the numbering of the arrondissements form a cartographical spiral. Maurice Baring's tribute was as florid as Wilde's, if less floral than Wilde's casting of lilies at her feet. He too produced a sonnet 'Her gesture

is as the soaring of a hymn'; he assisted at the first nights of Bernhardt's
Hamlet and *L'Aiglon*; and his admiration was boundless:

> Eliminate [the best of Bernhardt] and you eliminate one of the sources of
> inspiration of modern art. You take away something from d'Annunzio's
> poetry, from Maeterlinck's prose, from Moreau's pictures; you destroy one
> of the mainsprings of Rostand's work; you annihilate some of the colours
> of modern painting, and you stifle some of the notes of modern music
> (Fauré and Hahn), for in all these you trace the subtle and unconscious
> influence of Sarah Bernhardt.[2610]

This is a different Sarah from the one who was at home in the works of
Scribe and Dumas *fils*, to say nothing of Sardou. For above all in
Bernhardt's repertoire, there was Sardou, Sardou who wrote five plays for
her,[2611] Sardou from whom Wilde was forever trying to disentangle
himself and charges of plagiarism, but was himself once unsuccessfully
sued for plagiarism by Mario Uchard, who alleged that *Odette* was a crib
of his *La Fiammina*.[2612] Indeed, the duchesse de Clermont-Tonnerre,
having seen Bernhardt's Théodora, Tosca, Fédora, Marguérite Gautier and
Phèdre, thought her better suited to Sardou than to Racine.[2613] This is
damning enough, if one agrees with Marie Belloc that Sardou should be
judged by *La Famille Benoîton*, *Divorçons* and *Rabagas*, and not by his
plays for Sarah which were pot boilers written because he had a tendresse
for her.[2614] Be that as it may, his reputation was then sufficient for him to
be elected to fauteuil IX of the Académie Française in 1877 in preference
to Leconte de Lisle and the duc d'Audiffret-Pasquier, and if Sardou is
forever damned by Shaw's description of his works as Sardoudledom, they
were immensely successful at the time. *Théodora* played for two hundred
nights in England. *Fédora* was staged by the Bancrofts in 1883, and
revived in 1893 with Mrs Patrick Campbell and Herbert Beerbohm Tree.
In the United States, from its opening in New York in 1883 and in tours
lasting until 1887, it was an equally great and lucrative success for Fanny
Davenport,[2615] being followed by *La Tosca* in 1888,[2616] *Cleopatra* in 1890,
and *Gismonda* in 1894. On the whole, however, the view of Robert
Burnand is the prevailing one: 'Le clinquant de Sardou, papillonant dans le
bric-à-brac du décor historique.'[2617]

It was the poster for Bernhardt's production in December 1894 of
Sardou's *Gismonda* that launched the career of Alphonse Mucha:2618 in
best Paris fashion, the original design was sketched by Mucha on the
marble table-top of a café. Of *Théodora*, Freud, who was studying in Paris
at the time wrote that 'I can't say anything good. But how that Sarah
plays!' This also gave him the chance to make (or more likely, repeat) a

joke: 'Sardou, who has already written a Dora and Fédora and is said to be occupied at present with a Thermidora, Ecuadora and Torreadora'.2619 Freudian jokes have an alternative life of their own: *Thermidor* was a play by Sardou, *Messidor* one by Zola with music by the Wagnerite composer Alfred Bruneau, 12th February 1897 at the Académie Nationale de la Musique.

J.L. Toole produced a parody of *Fédora* by F.C. Burnand called *Stage Dora*. while 'Musidora' was, presumably unknown to Freud, the heroine of Théophile Gautier's 1837 novel *Fortunio, ou l'Eldorado* and a character in Louis Feuillade's play *Judex*; Pierre Louÿs then bestowed the name on the actress Jeanne Roques, who in turn adopted it as her screen name, while *Floradora* became a successful musical comedy, by James Davis under the name 'Owen Hall', a pun on 'owing all'.

If Phèdre was, in Maurice Baring's phrase, Bernhardt's 'supreme achievement',[2620] it should be remembered that her second greatest was Lorenzaccio; while A.S. Hartrick, who saw her often and thought her the greatest actress he had ever seen, recorded that he had only once seen her at her best and that was as Marguérite Gautier in 1887.[2621] Baring was not necessarily referring to her Phèdre of 1879, seen by Wilde in London, (after all, he was only five at the time) but to what one may perhaps call her cumulative Phèdre which climaxed in 1893.[2622] When it came to individual productions, approval of Bernhardt's interpretation was not unhesitating, and this must be kept in mind when assessing Wilde's enthusiasm. Johnston Forbes-Robertson, who is rather dismissive of Bernhardt, quotes Marie Bancroft's comparison of her Dame aux Camélias with Modjeska's: 'Well, Forby, we've seen something better than this, haven't we?'[2623]

Sir George Arthur puts the point fairly: 'Sarah must now measure herself with Rachel and on Rachel's special terrain[2624], and one must fairly admit that posterity, not perhaps, without hesitation, has given its decision in favour of Sarah'.[2625] But among those who did hesitate are numbered Matthew Arnold and Maurice Donnay. For the latter the cry of his youth 'Ah, if only you had seen Rachel' was now superseded by 'If only you had seen Bartet!'[2626] Judith, an actress of the Comédie Française who admittedly did not like Bernhardt, wrote 'I appeal to all who were able to see both [Rachel and Bernhardt] in that rôle. One was a statue, the other but a statuette,' she wrote.[2627] Of course as Rachel had died in 1858, the ears upon which this appeal fell were almost certainly deaf, although even in 1923 General Sir George Higginson was still able to give clear recollections of her,[2628] and another who saw both women as Phèdre, W. Graham Robertson's mother, 'much preferred Sarah Bernhardt, who, she said, softened by nobility and beauty a part which her great forerunner had made almost unbelievably horrible. Rachel had been an incarnate devil, Sarah was the victim of Fate, the sport of the gods, a noble nature in overthrow.'[2629] This is to bring Phèdre very clearly into *fin-de-siècle* conceptions of the *femme fatale*.

Of one comparison, however, we have been deprived, for the version of *Phèdre* that John Davidson wrote for Mrs Patrick Campbell was never staged.

In imagining a possible Salomé by Bernhardt, it must be remembered that she was the mistress of the great deathbed scene. How far would she have accepted being crushed beneath the shields of Herod's guard, she who had died all over the stage as Cleopatra,[2630] as Doña Sol, as Joan of Arc,[2631] as Adrienne Lecouvreur, as Blanche de Chelles in Feuillet's *Le Sphinx*, as Marguérite Gautier in *La Dame aux Camélias*, and even as Frou-Frou ('For the only time in my life, I think, I wept salt tears in a theatre over the death of Frou-Frou'[2632]). Her *Lysiane* (an unmemorable piece by Romain Coolus) in London in June 1898 made Beerbohm invoke the description of her as 'cette déesse riante et terrible'.[2633] Her death scene could redeem even a woeful play like Pierre Berton's *Léna*. Of this last, Maurice Baring, who saw it, wrote

> As a play no greater rubbish was ever written [...] The low water mark of all the plays she ever produced [...] It gave her the opportunity of a great death-scene, which she was perhaps right in thinking was one of her very greatest achievements.[2634]

Philippe Jullian implies that Bernhardt saw *Salomé* as another grand vehicle for herself,[2635] and one suspects that had she played it, she would have left us with a very different view of the piece, much modified and even transmogrified to suit her. She certainly insisted that the hair powdered with blue that Wilde had conceived for Herodias was transferred to herself. She did make substantial changes to *La Dame aux Camélias*, some with, others without, Dumas' knowledge or approval. If we take George Taylor's view that 'the Bohemian was a law unto himself, a complete individualist for whom beauty was the only virtue [...] thus Wilde's Salomé, thus du Maurier's Svengali',[2636] we can see that its application by Bernhardt could have taken her some way from Wilde conception. Vyvyan Holland appears to lend support to this view, writing that 'she [Bernhardt] put [Salomé] into rehearsal', which, if it is more than merely a *façon de parler*, gives her a directing rôle, not unfamiliar to her.[2637]

Subsequently, Bernhardt has been much criticised for failing to buy the play when Wilde offered it her, with the rider that this would have rescued Wilde from financial embarrassment and provided a great vehicle for the actress. She certainly did not see it that way. If it is true that in the late summer of 1891 Paul Fort intended producing *Salomé*, his conception would certainly have been very different from anything with which Bernhardt would have been comfortable.[2638] Gerda Taranow, in her elaborate study of Bernhardt's stage technique, comes to the same conclusion, although for slightly different reasons.

> Sarah's unwillingness to produce *Salomé* is inherent in the nature of the heroine. The character neither possesses charm nor generates pity. Rather than a chaste courtesan, *Salomé* is a lustful virgin. The disparity between the two is great: one is pure, the other is corrupt; one is redeemed, the other doomed; one is romantic, the other decadent.[2639]

That is to say, Salomé as she is was simply not a Bernhardt part, and Taranow believes that further thought brought her to the realisation that this was so. When Lugné-Poë did produce *Salomé* at the Théâtre de l'Œuvre in a double bill with *Raphaël* by Romain Coolus, there was no question of Bernhardt taking the part (she was then appearing in Molière's *Amphitryon* with Lucien Guitry and both Coquelins, and the contrast between the two productions makes sufficient point).

One must assume from her friendship with Charles Cros, Pierre Loti, Reynaldo Hahn (who wrote the incidental music for her *Dalila* of 1899), Graham Robertson and Edouard de Max that her detachment from Wilde was not because she had a prejudice against homosexuals; indeed, 'il est le fait que tous les dandys pederasts adoraient la déesse Sarah, de Montesquiou à Lorrain jusqu'à Oscar Wilde'.[2640] De Max indeed, with his pearl grey gloves, pearl grey hat, pearl grey boots, pearl grey electric brougham and pearl grey powder on his chin, seems to have outshone even Jean Lorrain in decadence, his fingers loaded with Oriental rings, and giving (it was said) parties in which the guests were naked. 'In appearance,' says Cornelia Otis Skinner, 'he was a mixture of Persian prince, boulevard dandy and gypsy,[2641] and so was perfectly cast as Herod to Ida Rubinstein's Salomé at the Châtelet in June 1912.

Although Edward Wagenknecht has noted that Bernhardt was repelled by the coarse and the wastrel and 'abhorred drug addiction and perversion',[2642] her studio in the boulevard de Clichy and association with les Hydropathes brought her in touch with some of the more louche denizens of Bohemian Paris – more than one would expect from somebody of her fame and fortune, even though she took her lovers, from Mounet-Sully to Lou Tellegen,[2643] from the stage rather than the upper classes. The exception was her early lover Henri, Prince de Ligne, apparently the father of her son Maurice[2644] – although it would appear that she once improbably claimed that the Duke of Clarence was the father.[2645] This would not have gone down well in London, where she was wont to describe Maurice as 'une petite caprice de ma jeunesse', a phrase which, given the context of a baby, rather brings to mind Miss Prism's remark about her handbag, 'Yes, here is the injury it received through the upsetting of a Gower Street omnibus in younger and happier days'.

Bernhardt was

> a mass of contradictions [...] unscrupulous and honest [...] in spite of occasions of cheerfully harbouring hatred, malice and all uncharitableness, a generous rival, a loyal friend and a good sort.[2646]

One such contradiction was that although she refused to play in *La Fille Elisa* because her character was described smoking in the novel on which the play was based, she did play la dame aux camélias even though in the parent novel Marguerite is described as 'accustomed to a life of dissipation, balls and even orgies'.[2647] Sarah frequently helped lame dogs over stiles, but although among these disinterested actions, Bernhardt occasionally helped Lugné-Poë, she thought that his entourage of writers and painters[2648] 'would all come to nothing if they continued to write nonsense and cover canvasses with unintelligible daubs'.[2649] There are no portraits of the most celebrated of all French actresses by any of the Impressionists. Her preferred artists were Georges Clairin, Alfred Stevens, Louise Abbéma[2650] and Gustav Doré; Benjamin-Constant painted her as Théodora, and Gérôme sculpted her in 1895.[2651] Graham Robertson, who knew her well, was scathing about the mediocrity of those who painted her, unable to capture her elusive personality: 'Clairin's immense canvas, full of frills, flounces, fringes, dogs and cushions, like an odd lot at a jumble sale, is of no value as a likeness; Gandara's portrait is a clever study of a pink dress, but Sarah is not inside it.' Robertson thought Burne-Jones would have painted her perfectly, but though he adored Bernhardt, he never did, and when Whistler began a portrait 'she was unable or unwilling to give the artist the allegiance that he required from a sitter'.[2652] What did she wish to conceal?

> I believe that Sargent only narrowly escaped being asked to paint her [...]
> but that he did escape was perhaps fortunate. They were not sympathetic;
> Sargent as a painter of facts was unrivalled, but Sarah Bernhardt was
> embodied Fantasy and was only well and truly seen through the golden
> mist of dreams.[2653]

Bernhardt's conservatism is not startling given her taste in interior decoration and her choice of plays; in the new century despite friendship with Ellen Terry she took no interest in Gordon Craig. It does add to the idea that in her hands, *Salomé* would not have made a mark as Symbolist drama, especially as given her friendship with Alfred Stevens, she was probably aware of his 'Salomé' paintings.[2654] Once, indeed, two worlds met when on 9th December 1896[2655] there occurred 'la journée Sarah Bernhardt', when five hundred guests sat down to a luncheon in her honour in the Salle de Zodiaque of the Grand Hôtel, followed by a matinée at the Théâtre de la Renaissance[2656] where five poets read sonnets to Sarah (Rostand's hailed her as 'Reine de l'attitude et Princesse des Gestes') and scenes from *Phèdre* and *Rome vaincue* were acted. The menus were designed by Bernhardt's friend Louise Abbéma and the poster designers Chéret and Mucha. A 'Golden Book' commemorated the occasion with a gauffrage design by the medallist Alexandre Charpentier on the cover, a medallion by René Lalique[2657] in gold reproduced as the frontispiece, and pictures and poems by Carolus-Duran, Henri Gervex, Mucha, Benjamin-Constant, Antonio de La Gandara,[2658] Joseph Granie, Rochegrosse, Coppée, Rostand, Heredia and Catulle Mendès. After this, many of the company went on to the Théâtre de l'Œuvre for the opening of *Ubu Roi*, as did Yeats and Arthur Symons, in Paris at the time. This was an open dress rehearsal for the performance that followed on the 10th. Deak gives the figure of 'slightly over one thousand' for the audience and Gide seems to have been among them.[2659] Nevertheless, it was in the end Duse, not Bernhardt, who gave a season at the Théâtre de l'Œuvre.[2660]

There is one other piece of evidence that Wilde saw *Salomé* as possible in Paris independently of Bernhardt. As it comes from Charles Ricketts it is worth considering, but as with so much circumstantial evidence, there is too much circumstance and too little evidence for conviction. Ricketts, referring to his designs for *Salomé*, wrote that the play 'at that time had a chance of being given in Paris, that is before madame Sarah Bernhardt thought of giving it in London. I do not remember if it was M. Lugné-Poë who contemplated the production, but I rather fancy it was, since he produced the play some years later'.[2661] This vagueness does not quite sit with Tydeman and Price's statement that Ricketts 'had been approached by Wilde to design a projected production in Paris, probably under the direction of Lugné-Poë.'[2662] There seems to be no evidence for this.

Part 5: Sarah's Oscar

CONVERSELY, what was the connection between Wilde and Bernhardt? What took Wilde to meet her at Folkestone, when in May 1879 she arrived, 'rather sick and very sorry for herself', with the Comédie Française company for their first London season?[2663] Here too the myths that each of these flamboyant characters created or attracted encrust the record, the more thickly in conjunction. It must be remembered that up to this time, Wilde had never seen Bernhardt on stage. Could he have hoped that the company would repeat a play that had featured in their 1871 London season, called *Oscar*? That may be far-fetched, but certainly not more so than Cornelia Otis Skinner's assertion that 'Oscar Wilde and Sarah Bernhardt were already friends. They had met in Paris and in his extravagant fashion he adored her both as a consummate artist and as the irresistible woman she could be when she chose'.[2664] As far as can be ascertained, Wilde had only been twice in Paris, once with his mother in 1867 at the age of thirteen, the other time when he passed through on his way from Italy to London in August 1875. Bernhardt's rôles that year were Berthe in de Bornier's *La Fille de Roland* and the name part in Augier's *Gabrielle*. Neither of these were staged in August.

To Skinner's myth-making can be added (reluctantly) that of the absurd Michel Peyramaure. In his account, Wilde greets Bernhardt with the words 'L'Angleterre vous salue par ma voix, mademoiselle. Je m'appelle Oscar Wilde. J'aimerais que...' Peyramaure says that what Wilde wished to say was drowned by a wave, but we can suppose what he (Peyramaure, that is) would have us believe what Wilde wanted to say from a subsequent passage. Here Wilde attends Bernhardt's exhibition of sculpture in Piccadilly, attended by an entourage of beautiful young men ('ephèbes'), and approaches the actress not to pay court but to talk of the play he was engaged upon writing, namely *Salomé*. This in June 1879![2665]

Wilde of course was an assiduous collector of other men's tinsel. In December 1878 Henry Nevinson was in Paris, staying at the Hôtel Corneille, when Bernhardt played Doña Sol in Hugo's *Hernani*, the production which finally established her with the public. 'Night after night I went, and day after day I walked up and down the railings of the parc Monceau where she then lived, carrying a big bunch of violets which I had not the courage either to leave at the door or throw into the kitchen window.'[2666] That was when Nevinson was at Oxford, a university where stories like that got about. We do not know if it reached Magdalen, but at the end of the following May, Wilde, more daring than Nevinson and known to the latter at least by sight, was at Folkestone to throw lilies at her feet.

The Folkestone episode presents certain difficulties, as it seems to derive solely from Bernhardt's own account.[2667] The company was a strong one, containing, among the women, Reichenberg, Dudlay, and Baretta: it should not be assumed that Bernhardt at this time dominated the company. The account of their arrival by Jenny Thénard says nothing of the scene, although 'de ma vie, je n'oublierai la spectacle de notre débarquement'. While Thénard might not have been ready to record a tribute to a fellow-actress, she says other pleasant things about Bernhardt, and in general recalls many of the social occasions when the company or individual members of it were fêted in London. Wilde does not feature in her chapter at all.[2668] Sir George Arthur makes no mention of Wilde, or indeed of *Salomé*, in his brief and personal memoir of Bernhardt; and nor does Suze Rueff in her recollections.[2669] The *only* mention of Wilde by Elaine Aston in her detailed study *Sarah Bernhardt: A French Actress on the London Stage*[2670] is a reference to his having been at Folkestone. Joanna Richardson in her *Sarah Bernhardt*[2671] also mentions Folkestone, but not *Salomé*.

> It was in Folkestone, not the rue de Richelieu, that she first heard the cry of 'Vive Sarah Bernhardt!' It came from a young man who looked like Hamlet and handed her a gardenia. It was Forbes-Robertson. 'They will soon be making you a carpet of flowers,' said a jealous colleague. 'Here it is,' cried another worshipper [...] It was Oscar Wilde, and Wilde led the cheers as the Comédie boarded the train for London.[2672]

This is in fact only a paraphrase of Bernhardt's account: 'It was the first time I had ever heard the cry of "Vive Sarah Bernhardt!". I turned my head and saw before me a pale young man, the ideal face of Hamlet. I was destined to admire him later on as Hamlet.' This episode is not mentioned by Forbes-Robertson in his autobiography;[2673] that he looked like Hamlet may have been inspired by the recollection of Forbes-Robertson's success in that part. Of course there were the other Forbes-Robertsons, Norman and Eric and Ian, and Ruth Brandon believes that it was Norman at Folkestone,[2674] but after all Johnston is the most likely. J.C. Trewin in his essay on Bernhardt in London accepts the presence of Johnston Forbes-Robertson ('not yet with a hyphen in his name').[2675] Wilde's letter to

Norman, tentatively dated March 1880, carries no implication of a
Folkestone meeting, and is memorable because it suggests that they should
go together to, of all events, the Boat Race. At least Wilde, and whichever
Forbes-Robertson brother it was, were more engaging admirers than the
man who met Bernhardt in 1910 at Folkestone, the elderly Sir Squire
Bancroft.[2676]

A *culte* for actresses was not unbecoming or unusual in a young man at the
end of an Oxford education, even if Wilde (who rarely did things by
halves) was rather more showy than most: more showy, and less
discriminating, for he seems to have been as enthusiastic about Lillie
Langtry as about Bernhardt, and more so than he was to be about Duse.
(Richard Whiteing thought that French equivalent of Langtry was madame
Pasca,[2677] whose reputation has faded away.) Wilde apparently went on to
work as a sort of unpaid secretary to Bernhardt for a few subsequent
weeks when she was appearing in London in *Phèdre*, *Andromaque*,
Voltaire's *Zaïre*,[2678] Dumas' *L'Etrangère* (as Mrs Clarkson[2679]), Feuillet's
Le Sphinx (as Berthe de Savigny)*, Hernani* and *Ruy Blas* at the Gaiety
Theatre. Bernhardt herself says only that 'he was a devoted attendant, and
did much to make things pleasant and easy for me in London, but he never
appeared to pay court'.[2680] Philippe Jullian tells of a dinner party which
Wilde gave in her honour, pawning his gold medal in order to pay for it;
but Jullian also has Wilde, and not Forbes-Robertson, crying 'Long live
Sarah, Long live the Goddess'.[2681] But how could all this have come
about? Bernhardt was famous, Wilde in 1879 a very minor figure.

What exactly were Wilde's services to Bernhardt in London? Robert
Keith Miller in his 1982 study of Wilde[2682] asserts roundly and without a
source that Wilde acted as her 'interpreter and advisor': this is typical of
how accounts get passed on down through the biographies. Moreover,
such a rôle ignores the involvement with Bernhardt of Mayer, the
impresario who arranged the visit, or Edward Jarrett, Bernhardt's own
agent and impresario with whom she had been connected since early
spring, or madame Guérard, her companion and social secretary, or
Claude, her 'faithful factotum'.[2683] It should not be overlooked that Wilde
was also dancing attendance on Lillie Langtry that summer – his poem to
her, 'The New Helen', was published that July – and he must have been of
some help to his mother who gave up her house in Merrion Square in May
and moved to London. If he was indeed acting in some sort of secretarial
capacity to Bernhardt — and Langlade says he organised for her parties
('fêtes') 'avec les *beautiful people*',[2684] he took his duties lightly enough,
given her need for them. Sir George Arthur refers to Bernhardt receiving

'hundreds of letters which she never answered [...] She accepted invitations, and at the last moment failed to appear, or disturbed all arrangements by preposterous unpunctuality'.[2685]   There was an evening arranged by Lady Brassey at which the Prince of Wales was present, and Sarah sent a late message to say that it was too hot and she would not be coming, leaving the other members of the Comédie Française to carry on without her.[2686]

Wilde is never mentioned in connection with the menagerie that Bernhardt established at 77 Chester Square where she was staying, and nor does he ever refer to this remarkable and Rossetti-like extravaganza by Bernhardt. One may use as a measure Henry James using this same visit to London by the Comédie Française to strike up an admiring friendship with Coquelin. Did Wilde see her in *L'Etrangère*, when she lost a hundred and sixty-six lines of a crucial scene through stage fright?   Bernhardt's Phèdre in London in June was only Act II played as an entr'acte (with scenes from *Le Misanthrope* and *Les Précieuses Ridicules*), and according to Max Beerbohm the audience had some difficulty understanding the text,[2687] but Wilde published the sonnet 'To Sarah Bernhardt' to her in *The World* on 11th June 1879.

> How vain and dull this common world must seem
> To such a One as thou, who should'st have talked
> At Florence with Mirandola, or walked
> Through the cool olives of the Academe:
> Thou should'st have gathered reeds from a green stream
> For Goat-foot Pan's shrill piping, and have played
> With the white girls in that Phæacian glade
> Where grave Odysseus wakened from his dream.
> Ah! surely once some urn of Attic clay
> Held thy wan dust, and thou hast come again
> Back to this common world so dull and vain,
> For thou wert weary of the sunless day,
> The heavy fields of scentless asphodel,
> The loveless lips with which men kiss in Hell.

One wonders what was the relevance of much of this to Bernhardt. Versatile as she was, to have conversed with a neo-Platonist in Florence, and with Socrates in Athens, while being at the same time the reincarnation of a Greek nymph, a handmaid of Nausicaa's and a mixture of Eurydice and Persephone, might have been puzzling enough, given the sketchiness of her education. She might even, as somebody in some sense Jewish, in some sense Roman Catholic, have found this offensive. The poem was reprinted in the *Biograph and Review*[2688] in August 1880 retitled oddly as 'Sara [*sic*] Bernhardt' – descriptive rather than dedicatory – but in the volume *Poems* of 1881, the poem is called 'Phèdre', the actress merging into the part.[2689]

In fact, Bernhardt could have made nothing of the poem, unless it was translated for her. Her English at this time was even less than sketchy, having taken only one lesson and that from a Dutch lady. 'The first time I met her was at one of Irving's first night suppers on the stage of the Lyceum: a forlorn, somewhat insignificant figure without a word of English', remembered Jerome K. Jerome.[2690] Maurice Baring asserts that English was a language that Bernhardt 'never possessed, and of which she never succeeded in mastering the rudiments'.[2691] Alice Comyns Carr thought it was better than this but still regarded it as 'quaint';[2692] her granddaughter refers to 'that pronounced French accent of which she was never able to rid herself' when speaking English.[2693] Bernhardt herself was prepared to admit that 'I was ashamed of my ignorance of the English language';[2694] when in July 1889 she wrote a letter to *The Standard*, protesting against the circumstances under which she had been forced to present *Lena*, she did so in French.[2695] As late as 1899, when introduced to Bernhardt in New York by Elsie de Wolfe and Elizabeth Marbury, Jessie Millward asked her why she had never learned English, although she adds that Bernhardt 'at all events knew enough English to make herself understood' – no very great accomplishment in a talented actress one might suppose.[2696] Finally, in 1904, playing to British audiences, she preferred Mrs Patrick Campbell to play Mélisande in her halting French rather than essay Pelléas in English. Even when in 1910 she was asked to send a telegram on the occasion of the unveiling of Sir Henry Irving's statue, Cyril Maude had to write the telegram himself.

One must, however, commend Wilde's foresight in determining that Sarah Bernhardt was the actress to watch, although the sources do not make it clear why this should have been so. It was at that time by no means obvious that Bernhardt was the natural successor of Mars and Rachel, and it was perfectly possible to see Arnould-Plessy or Jouassain or Reichenberg as that, while Sophie Croizette was thought by Brander Matthews to be Bernhardt's equal. There was no 'star' system at the Comédie Française – billing was in order of seniority – so Bernhardt was not particularly 'puffed'. Brander Matthews disliked her, and for a reason which perhaps unconsciously suggests her appeal for Wilde. This was the 'evidence of conscious self-advertisement, not to say a distinct trace of charlatanry. This unpleasant flavour was most prominent during the visit of the Comédie Française to London in 1879.'[2697]

Oxford also had its demands on Wilde that summer, and on 17th June he attended the Ball given by the Apollo Lodge of the University freemasons, where the music was provided by the band of the Coldstream Guards, and guests included Lord and Lady Dufferin, the novelist Margaret Oliphant, and, something of a cynosure, Ivan Turgenev.

> The probability that Turgenev spoke with Oscar Wilde [...] is most attractive and exciting. [...] Two possible consequences of his encounter with Turgenev (or at the very least of his coming into the novelist's sphere) may be suggested here as leads for further research. The first is that his play called *Vera*, written in 1880, shows considerable interest in and knowledge of Russia and things Russian, in spite of many far-fetched elements. The climax is a potential union of nihilists and Tsar, between whom Vera is the living – and dying – link. Turgenev would have thoroughly approved of this, one feels – had he known. The second sequel is six years later still, in 1886, Oscar Wilde translated for Macmillan's *Magazine* the sketch 'A Fire at Sea', dictated by Turgenev on his deathbed. Turgenev himself, meanwhile, could have thought just about anything of Wilde.[2698]

One engagement that Bernhardt did keep was at Lord Wilton's in Grosvenor Square, in the presence of the Prince of Wales. The evening was memorable because the Prince was handed a telegram with the news of the death of the Prince Imperial in Zululand.[2699] If Wilde had any hand in the arrangements, they may be seen as returning to Wilde later, for John Worthing's house was in the first version of *The Importance of being Earnest* called Wilton, and both Sir Robert Chiltern and Dorian Gray live in Grosvenor Square, where, indeed, Lady Bracknell fears scenes of disorder; and of course he was moved to write an ode. One other recollection Wilde could have taken from the visit of the Comédie Française. The senior actress in the company at the time was not Sarah Bernhardt, but Madeleine Brohan, described as 'perhaps the greatest "grande dame" who ever trod the boards'.[2700] Such a recollection might have served to help Wilde envisage Rose Leclercq as Lady Bracknell.

Maurice Baring's description of Bernhardt at this time is less stilted than Wilde's, less reminiscent of a picture by Puvis de Chavannes.

> She had poetry, passion, and grace and youth, and first love to express. She expressed it easily, with unerring poetical tact; there was no strain, not a harsh note, it was a symphony of golden flutes and muted strings; a

summer dawn lit by lambent lightnings, soft stars and a clear-cut crescent moon.[2701]

With or without Wilde's assistance, Bernhardt also held an exhibition in Piccadilly of sixteen of her oil paintings and nine of her sculptures, visited by Gladstone and the Prince and Princess of Wales;[2702] and staffed a stall at the fête held to raise money for the French Hospital in London. She certainly visited the flat that Wilde shared with Frank Miles in Salisbury Street, as Harry Marillier had a clear memory of her signature made with a carpenter's pencil all across one white wooden panel.[2703] There is a final glimpse offered by Joyce Bentley. A Magdalen friend of Wilde's, 'Gussy' Cresswell, wanted to meet Bernhardt 'and Oscar promised to bring about an introduction if Gussy would, in his turn, introduce him to some girls'.[2704] Bentley does not source any of her assertions,[2705] and Cresswell is not mentioned by Ellmann; moreover she appears to date this anecdote to 1878 or even 1876.

~~~~~~

While staying in Paris in 1883, Wilde and Robert Sherard called at the Vaudeville[2706] where Bernhardt was playing in *Fédora*, and later called at her house on the corner of the rue Fortuny and the avenue de Villiers,[2707] as we learn from Ellmann, following Sherard's account.[2708] This house, built for Bernhardt in 1875 by the fashionable architect Félix Escalier,[2709] had ceilings and murals by Clairin, Duez, Picard, Butin, Jadin and Parrot, and one would give much to know if Wilde exercised his wit about this opulence on his way out.

The timing of Wilde's meetings with Bernhardt is quite tight, and Ellmann may have been wrong to rely on Sherard. *Fédora* had opened in the December 1882 and Wilde met Sherard in April 1883, on the twenty-eighth of which Bernhardt opened in Richepin's *Pierrot Assassin*[2710] with Réjane at the Trocadéro. Could the meeting have been at the Trocadéro, not the Vaudeville? The encounter is the occasion of one of Ellmann's most trivial anecdotes, namely that Bernhardt smiled at Wilde and 'Jean Richepin was less pleased'.[2711] This seems a futile way of introducing Richepin, who was Bernhardt's lover for about fifteen months from 1883,[2712] when she had produced his *La Glu* at the Ambigu, with Réjane, 'a new and brilliant young actress who lit up the gray skies of Paris with her ineffable charm and pathos. The piece had a certain success, but its grim realism frightened the public.'[2713] Moreover, it was Richepin's song 'La Glu' that Arthur Symons thought the most remarkable in the repertoire of Yvette Guilbert, 'the one woman of genius, of a new and startling kind, among many notable and remarkable persons of talent'.[2714] Described by Cornelia Otis Skinner as 'a sort of Prince of Bohemia, [who] looked like an actor impersonating one of the romantic vagabonds of whom he wrote',[2715] he had been soldier, sailor, boxer. He would hardly have seen Wilde as a rival for Bernhardt's affections.

One is left with the idea that Ellmann had less than a good grasp of who exactly Richepin was (he might have looked at Beerbohm's 1898 drawing of him in the Victoria and Albert Museum[2716]), and this again weakens our idea of his over-all understanding of Wilde's Paris. Yet 'more than one contemporary remarked that Richepin seemed to be a succession of different personalities, each one living a different life',[2717] and this may also be true of his plays – his *Le Chemineau* was adapted for the English stage by Louis N. Parker[2718] as *Ragged Robin*, which was put on by Tree. Sherard came to view Richepin, despite his anglophobia, as 'one of the most delightful and sympathetic men I had ever met'.[2719] (Sherard knew another Richepin, too, for he was for a while the lover of Jane Avril, whose real name was Jeanne Richepin. She remembered him as 'a tall golden-haired youth with frank grey-blue eyes and an enchanting smile',[2720] no doubt part of his appeal for Wilde.)

Jonathan Fryer's suggestion that Wilde 'paid court' to Bernhardt in Paris in 1883 is unsourced and, if it is meant to indicate more than what Ellmann wrote, of doubtful authenticity:[2721] the wallflowers that Sherard says were bought from a street seller[2722] to give to Bernhardt were hardly in the same class as the Folkestone lilies. This apart, there is nothing to suggest that Wilde encountered Bernhardt again in person despite the fact that 'she seldom failed to visit London during May or June',[2723] until the rehearsals for *Salomé* in 1893. We do not read of lilies or secretarial help when Bernhardt opened in *Adrienne Lecouvreur* at the Gaiety Theatre in May 1880,[2724] nor during her three weeks in London in the June 1881 (where she played in *La Dame aux Camélias*, its first London production, in the presence of the Prince and Princess of Wales). In 1882 Wilde was in the United States when Bernhardt was in London[2725] but she played *Fédora* in London in 1883[2726] and again we have no account of the meetings in Paris earlier in the year being renewed. Wilde admired Bernhardt in *Macbeth*, which he saw in Paris on his honeymoon, as well as seeing Judic in *Lili*.[2727] His liking for *Macbeth* was eccentric, for it found favour neither in Paris nor in London in 1884 ('a complete failure',[2728] and only given three performances) and there is no indication that Wilde and Bernhardt met. Marie Bashkirtseff, seeing it on 16th June 1884, thought that Marais as Macbeth was 'pitiful' and Bernhardt while 'always admirable', had exchanged her golden voice for an ordinary one.[2729] This opinion about Bernhardt's voice at this time was shared by Laurent Tailhade when he saw her in *Théodora* (either December 1884 or January 1885), that it was less and less golden and that whomever she played it was always with the same voluptuous fits and swooning ('même épilepsie voluptueuse et la même pâmoison').[2730] One need not take Bashkirtseff's or Tailhade's view over that of Wilde, but neither is there a need to take an uncritical view of Wilde's opinion. The other plays of Bernhardt's 1884 London season were *Fédora*, *Frou-frou*, *Ruy Blas* and *Adrienne Lecouvreur*, but it was her *Phèdre* that Wilde chose to praise that year, declaring that 'It was not until I heard Sarah Bernhardt in *Phèdre* that I realised the sweetness of the music of Racine', which certainly suggests either the golden voice or the resurgence of lying.

We do not find Wilde at *Théodora* in London, where it ran for a hundred performances in 1885, nor at her brief seasons there on the way to tour America in April 1886 and on her way back in 1887. Bernhardt contributed an article 'The History of My Tea-Gown' to the *Woman's World* but declined Wilde's invitation to contribute again.[2731] Jessie Millward went to see Bernhardt's Tosca three times in one week, but there is no report of Wilde having seen her either in *La Tosca* or in *Françillon* in 1888 or *Lena* or *Théodora* in July 1889, or in *Jeanne d'Arc* with music by Gounod in 1890 (from 23rd June to 5th July), followed by single performances of *Adrienne Lecouvreur* and *La Dame aux Camélias* and four of *La Tosca* (indeed, on 8th July Wilde preferred to go to the Annual Dinner of the Society of Authors at the Criterion Restaurant). This compares to John Boon's making 'a point of going to see her performances whenever it was possible' and being 'always warmly received'.[2732] *Théodora* had incidental music by Massenet[2733], and Bernhardt's performance ('walking on like one of Burne-Jones' dreams come to life'[2734]) was described prophetically by Jules Lemaître as 'a Salomé, a Salammbô' – Wilde himself saw his Salomé as a sister of Salammbô.[2735]

According to Jacques de Langlade, Wilde went to see *La Femme de Claude* by Dumas *fils* 'surtout pour embrasser Sarah et serrer la main de Lucien Guitry'.[2736] This is an important addition to our knowledge of their relations, or would be if it happened. Langlade does not source this, and it is not clear from the context whether the meeting took place in Paris or London. *La Femme de Claude* opened in Paris on the 27th September 1894 and in London on the 5th June 1895. Unless Wilde made a special dash for Paris, we have no other information that suggest he was in France in either that September or October; by June 1895 he was in prison.

When, and how was Bernhardt engaged to play Salomé? We have to dismiss Skinner's statement that Wilde wrote the play 'in French expressly for Sarah Bernhardt, and when he read the script aloud to her she was madly enthusiastic and all for putting it on the following season in London'. During Wilde's stay in Paris in 1891, Bernhardt was on a world tour, only returning in May 1892. What was the rôle of Bernhardt's English manager, the almost invisible C.J. Abud, whose strange name Granville Barker put into *The Marrying of Ann Leete*? As rehearsals for *Salomé* began in June, there had been little time for negotiation and casting and we know it was going to be necessary for Bernhardt to re-use her Cleopatra costumes. Indeed, the concept of rehearsal must itself be questioned. The note in Holland and Hart-Davis that 'rehearsals were in full swing' must surely be exaggerated, even though it names Albert Darmont as Herod.[2737] Langlade adds only that Henry Bauër helped (or possibly just attended – *assisté*) at the rehearsals.[2738] Bernhardt also played *Léah* and *Pauline Blanchard* in London that season[2739], the latter opening on the 16th June, and Darmont appeared in these, which does not leave much of a window for *Salomé*. In August Bernhardt was engaged in Paris, in September touring Belgium and the Netherlands. Although she was capable of breaking agreements upon a whim, it is difficult to see when she would have been free for Wilde.

No producer has been named, nor a cast for the other parts, though Tydeman and Price say that it is a 'reasonable conjecture' that Jane Méa was 'earmarked' for Herodias and that [Maurice] Fleury would have played Iokanaan, but apparently on no other evidence that they too were members of Bernhardt's company: I suspect that the rehearsal was only a read-through. The casting of the Baptist would have been particularly important, for Sarah of the 'voix d'or' would have addressed to him the line 'Parle encore, Iokanaan. Ta voix m'enivre', a challenge of direction and interpretation.

This all adds to the impression that the Bernhardt Salomé was a very *ad hoc* project, with Bernhardt suited neither to the part nor the play. Had Wilde even seen *Cleopatra*? Lord Lytton said of Bernhardt's performance that 'Sarah and Sardou between them have created a most improbable Cleopatra', while Ernest Constans said that it had the effect of *Aïda* – if the music had been written by Sardou instead of Verdi.[2740] The first night had been on 20th October 1890, and Wilde was certainly in Paris (he called on William Rothenstein) during that month, though no correspondence survives. His reference to Bernhardt as 'the only person in the world who could act Salomé' dates to 1900 and one is uncertain how far Bernhardt would have been flattered by Wilde's adding that she was 'the serpent of Old Nile, older than the pyramids'.[2741] This advocacy of Sarah and its apposition again give us an odd insight into Wilde's conception of the part of the Hebrew princess, the Egyptian queen. His remark is a strange conflation of Mona Lisa, Salomé, Cleopatra, and her asp – the relationship between Sarah and the asp had already been the subject of a bawdy song by Xanrof – (and something of the same conflation occurred when Ackté sang Salomé at Covent Garden in 1912, wearing two jewelled snakes, one twined round her upper arm, the other rising to strike her from the air.)[2742] More, the description was not an original usage by Wilde, for in his poem 'Camma', dedicated to Ellen Terry, he had already used 'serpent of old Nile' (the phrase is of course Shakespeare's), 'methinks I'd rather see thee play / That serpent of old Nile, whose witchery / made Emperors drunken'.[2743] There is a further linguistic point to be made that may have lain within Wilde's literary subconscious: the sinuousness of the snake is repeated in the initial letter of both Sarah and Salomé, and famously in the favoured posture captured in the portrait by Clairin of Bernhardt, so often likened to a corkscrew; nor does one ignore the sinuousness of line favoured in art nouveau.[2744]

London, even without *Salomé*, remained a lure for Bernhardt. Although in 1893 she was touring further afield (Duse played Marguerite Gautier in London that year), in 1894 she and Lucien Guitry played *Izéyl* by Armand Silvestre and Eugène Morand (with incidental music by Pierné) at Daly's Theatre, as well as Lemaître's *Les Rois*, although this feeble play was only given two performances, buttressed by *La Dame aux Camélias*, *Fédora* and Dumas' *La femme de Claude*. Elizabeth von Arnim and Maud Ritchie (daughter of the Tory politician) went 'night after night' to see *Dame*.[2745] The following year Bernhardt brought *Magda* and Rostand's *La Princesse lointaine* (also with incidental music by Pierné) to London: but Wilde, now paying the penalty of his own love-quest, seems to have been far from her thoughts. Part of the context of Bernhardt's attitude towards Wilde is that she, like Wilde himself, liked the admiration of young men (in 1879 Wilde was only twenty-five). Later Maurice Baring danced attendance on her, and when in the new century Marcel Schwob introduced Gerald Kelly to her, she became one of the 'glowing Parisian memories'[2746] Kelly owed to the Schwobs, who had earlier similarly befriended Rothenstein and were later to befriend Arnold Bennett.[2747] There is no reason to suggest that Bernhardt's liking for Wilde was anything other than sincere (she 'always had a high regard for Oscar Wilde'[2748]), but it is wrong to assume that Wilde was especially favoured, or that beyond the failed attempt to stage *Salomé* in London, she had any special commitment to Wilde. Indeed, the failure must surely have been exasperating to Bernhardt, no longer used to the rough-and-tumble of theatrical productions. Jullian affirms that 'Sarah, furious, saw a superb part and *a lot of capital already invested in it*, escaping her'.[2749]

According to Robert Sherard, when the rehearsals for *Salomé* in London were discontinued in June 1892, Bernhardt 'brought the play to Paris with her, and had promised to produce it at her own theatre of the Porte St-Martin as soon as opportunity should permit'.[2750]   Even if this were true (the Porte St-Martin was not her own theatre[2751]), she did not of course find the opportunity, despite the interest generated by the simultanæous publication of the play in Paris and London by the Librairie de l'Art Indépendant and John Lane in February 1893.   One is left with the conclusion is that this great actress, and Sarah was a very great actress, once back in Paris, simply did not see Salomé as a rôle for her repertoire. Is this not reinforced by the fact that whereas the part of Salomé has been *sung* by many of the greatest names of twentieth century opera, the part of Salomé has been *played* by hardly any (one is tempted to say none) of the great names of the stage?[2752]

The aftermath is the story of Wilde's attempt to persuade her to buy the rights in the play after his imprisonment. This has come down in various versions, but the ur-source is again Sherard. According to his account,[2753] Wilde asked him to negotiate the rights and he waited on the actress several times in an unsuccessful attempt to talk business, even tracking her to the *vernissage* at the Salon.   Each time he was fobbed off.   The implication, and this followed by most of Wilde's biographers, was that Bernhardt deserted Wilde in his hour of need, sobbing a few crocodile tears. In any event, by the end of November the moment had passed, for any money that Bernhardt might have paid would have gone to the Official Receiver following Wilde's bankruptcy. Sherard grew fanciful in later years about this, saying that *Salomé* was offered to Bernhardt for $1500–$2000 and that she 'threw away the certitude of a large fortune – certainly more than half a million dollars'.[2754]   Yet after all, Bernhardt was not an entrepreneur, buying rights in unproduced plays as a business proposition, and given Wilde's slippery dealings with the rights to *Mr and Mrs Daventry*, she was probably justified.

There is no record of Bernhardt having seen Lina Munte in Lugné-Poë's production; nor the opera when it was produced at the Théâtre de Châtelet in 1907 with Emmy Destinn as Salomé and Strauss himself conducting, or again in 1910 when Messager conducted and Mary Garden sang the rôle. Would she have come to the same conclusion that Peter Raby has come to, that Wilde's play was but 'the scenario' for Strauss?[2755] Nor did she see Loïe Fuller's *Salomé* in 1895, although she was curious enough to meet the dancer after the close of the production at the end of April, in the rather untheatrical milieu of Manchester. What I argue here is that it is more than possible to urge that Bernhardt only took to *Salomé* in a momentary burst of enthusiasm, perhaps as much because she was as fond of the designer Graham Robertson as she was of the play or its author, and this was an enthusiasm that rapidly evaporated. It would be interesting to establish a relationship between Ellen Terry's description of Bernhardt that 'Her body was not the prison of her soul, but its shadow' and the phrase in Wilde's *The Fisherman and his Soul* that 'What men call the shadow of the body is not the shadow of the body, but is the body of the soul'[2756], although, not to be high-falutin', Terry's remark probably refers more to Bernhardt's preternatural thinness than to any spiritual quality. Terry's other remark about Bernhardt, that she was 'more symbol than woman',[2757] may, however, help to suggest the essence of Wilde's attraction to her.

It is worth noting that Maurice Baring, who knew Bernhardt well, makes no mention of *Salomé* at all. He calls Bernhardt's life one of 'fiction and sideshows',[2758] and her involvement with Wilde fits into that view. No sluggard herself at seeking and receiving what we would call media attention, Bernhardt, already, in the phrase of Henry James, 'simply, at present, in Paris, one of the great figures of the day',[2759] was not the woman to allow an association with the aspirant celebrity Wilde to serve any purposes other than her own. Bernhardt's grand-daughter only lists him as a name among others of those who came to receptions at the rue Fortuny: '[…] Oscar Wilde (whom she had known in London and always defended)'. Nothing here of Folkestone and lilies, secretarial services and Salomé, omissions more acute for the book having been translated by into English by Wilde's son.[2760]

Unless one can establish more substantial contact between Bernhardt and Wilde, it would appears only that Wilde, less than a year down from Oxford, saw something of Sarah Bernhardt in 1879, met her briefly twice in 1883, saw her in *Macbeth* (perhaps more than once), corresponded at no great length to obtain material for the *Woman's World*, and offered her the part of Salomé sometime in 1892, having in his haste forgotten to submit the play for licensing before engaging her. One must add that according to Joanna Richardson, Wilde gave or sent Bernhardt a copy of his poems inscribed 'Comme la princesse Salomé est belle ce soir', which is the first line of the play, although which poems and when this took place is not stated.[2761] There is also Wilde's own account[2762] of the reconciliation that he effected with Sarah Bernhardt in Nice in 1899 when he went round to see her after attending a performance of *La Tosca* (although *none* of the Bernhardt sources here cited refer to this, except Skinner, who merely cites Wilde; or even to her having been in Nice). But the rest is hyperbole.

There is one other intermingling of Wilde and Sarah Bernhardt. Wilde had offered the part of the Nihilist Vera to Mrs Bernard Beere, just as he offered the parts of the Duchess of Padua and of Salomé to Mary Anderson and to Sarah Bernhardt. In Lemaître's *Les Rois,* a Prince Hermann is shot by his wife (played by Bernhardt) when she discovers him in the arms of his lover, a Nihilist called Frida. In 1887, Mrs Beere created the part of Lena Despard in an adaptation of F.C. Philips' novel *As in a Looking Glass*; this was also adapted by Pierre Berton[2763] and Mme van de Velde[2764] as *Léna*, which Bernhardt played in London in July 1889. Mrs Beere, 'heralded as "the English Sarah Bernhardt" [...] from whom she took her cue for her method and style',[2765] went on to play Mrs Arbuthnot in *A Woman of No Importance*. Although her first name was Fanny, Wilde used to call her Bernie, and one can be quite, quite sure that this was not a diminutive he ever addressed to Sarah.[2766]

The final word can be left to Bernhardt herself. When she published her autobiography in 1907, it would have been acceptable enough for her to have extended herself on the subject of Wilde: her embroideries are not exactly petit point. But this is all she did write, in the passage that refers to the young Irishman's throwing the lilies at her feet at Folkestone:

> He had luminous eyes and long hair, and looked like a German student. He was an English poet, though, and one of the greatest of the century, a poet who was a genius, but who was alas! later tortured and finally vanquished by madness. It was Oscar Wilde.[2767]

Few would claim that Wilde was one of the greatest poets of the century. Even in retrospect, Wilde was less important in the story of Bernhardt than Bernhardt has become in the story of Wilde.

CHAPTER FIFTEEN:

PARIS AS WILDERNESS

'There is no city like Paris, no crowd like a Parisian crowd, to make you
feel your solitude if you are alone in its midst!'
– George du Maurier.[2768]

'J'ai peur de souvenirs.'
– Francis Vielé-Griffin[2769]

Part 1: Last Acts

'I am frightened of Paris.'
– Oscar Wilde to Robert Ross.[2770]

IT was not just in London that Wilde's fall was welcome to purveyors of
the burlesque. The wits of the boulevards and music-hall came up with
skits such as 'Oscar, ou les dangers de l'esthète-à-tête' or 'Coucher
d'Oscar',[2771] and these gave him a new and unwelcome celebrity when he
settled in Paris in 1898. Nevertheless, Montgomery Hyde's opinion was
that 'the last three years of Oscar Wilde's life were by no means unhappy.
It is true that he led a somewhat aimless existence […] However, he
remained a brilliant conversationalist and, if anything, was more brilliant
than in the earlier period of his social success'.[2772] Although one must
defer to Montgomery Hyde's deep knowledge of things Wildean, this goes
far too far, just as a number of accounts are over-weighted in the opposite
sense. Stuart Merrill was one of the first in print, in *La Plume* on the 15th
December 1900,[2773] which begins startlingly 'I knew Oscar Wilde *in
London* [my italics] at the height of his fame', and then gets the date
muddled up, first saying that it was when Wilde had three (itself a mistake
for two) plays running – that is, 1895 – and then that *Dorian Gray* was
about to be published – that is, 1891. This is followed by a recollection of
Wilde at the Garrick Club trembling 'like a mere beginning writer' in the
presence of – Walter Pater! This is about as likely as the further mention
of secret visits to his sons in Geneva. The account ends with the
remarkable invocation 'May the work of Oscar Wilde appear to us
henceforth in the serene beauty of anonymity. Let us at least be as merciful

as the tomb'. Elsewhere Merrill dates Wilde's American tour to '1888 or 1889' and his own London visit to 1890, with Jonathan Sturges[2774] and Clarence McIlvaine, saying that Wilde at this time 'was so to speak king of London'. In this passage, from the perspective of 1912, the Pater story has grown – it has become a dinner at the Garrick, with Wilde addressing that most easily embarrassed of men as 'Sir Walter'. Merrill goes on to say that Wilde's last scene, 'drinking beyond measure' and his financial resources dried up, dates to his boredom after the close of the 1900 Expo, although this was only three weeks before Wilde died. 'Moreover, whether from bravado or genuine inclination, he frequented quarters where his presence was extremely disagreeable to those who considered themselves compromised in such company'.[2775] This was Sherard's view as well, though distant from Wilde at this time: 'I was away from Paris for the whole of 1900, and the stories that reached me about Oscar's situation on all sides were appalling'.[2776] Bosie Douglas's view, not entirely trustworthy, was that 'The stories of his [Wilde's] supposed privations, his frequent inability to obtain a square meal, his lonely and tragic death in a sordid lodging, and his cheap funeral, are all grotesquely false […] I give it as my firm opinion that Oscar Wilde was, on the whole, fairly happy during the last years of his life.'[2777]

The opposite point of view is also well established. Gide refers to Wilde as 'The enfeebled and crushed being given back to us from prison, as Ernest La Jeunesse paints him in the best, or rather the only passable article on the great reprobate which any one had the talent or the courage to write […] Nothing remained in his shattered life but a mouldy ruin, painful to contemplate.'[2778] Mason, in his introduction to Gide's memoir, refers to Wilde enduring 'several weeks of intense suffering' towards the end, and dying 'in poverty and almost alone', which seems to be more Chatterton than Wilde.[2779] This was rapidly followed by Robert Sherard's first biography:

> There were times when [Wilde] suffered actual want […] and but for the hospitality of friends would have passed the night in the streets.

> His last years were supremely unhappy. Poor, lonely, abandoned, he had little company but of those who hoped to prey upon him.[2780]

Our view of this has been reinforced by the much-repeated tale of his begging recounted by that *monstre sacré*, Nellie Melba, the veracity of which is questioned by Melba's biographer,[2781] and which may even owe something to Elizabeth Marbury, who wrote that Wilde sought her out in Paris 'unkempt, forlorn, penniless'.[2782] Melba's story is also given the lie by Sherard, although, as usual, he overstates the case: 'Not on one single occasion in the whole of his life – even in the starveling years after his release from prison – did he obtain or attempt to obtain resources by any means unworthy of proper pride, of self-respect, of delicacy.'[2783] It is possible that tales of Wilde's scrounging reached the ears of his admirer Hector Munro – 'Saki' – for the only one of his stories set in Paris, 'The Soul of Laploshka', turns on the begging and owing of two francs.[2784]

Gustave Le Rouge, who is not altogether to be trusted, says (apparently without irony) of the Wilde of this period

> He was familiar with the literary cafés, the wine-cellars frequented by amateur songwriters and even the dens of ill-repute. He greatly enjoyed the company of these as yet unpublished poets. He would take long strolls with them along the quiet streets near the place Saint-Sulpice, gladly stopping before antique dealers' windows to study the trinkets whose price and origin he knew wonderfully well.

> He had quickly become popular with the people in the wine-cellars because of his generosity in offering drinks to first-comers.[2785]

This is hardly the picture drawn by Ernest La Jeunesse, of a Paris 'gradually closing against him, a deaf Paris, bloodless, heartless, a city without eternity and without legend'[2786] – whatever that may have meant. Although Vance Thompson, claiming a drinking acquaintance with Wilde, paints a grim picture of Wilde in decay, Vincent O'Sullivan refers to the way that Wilde remained spruce and well-groomed and so indeed said La Jeunesse: 'He remained to the very last day the perfect, well-groomed Englishman – and he did not beg'.[2787] Of course we do not know what 'well-groomed' meant to La Jeunesse, 'réputé pour sa physiognomie ingrate',[2788] and according to Sisley Huddleston 'brimming over with malice',[2789] who was known for being 'as filthy as he was erudite'.[2790]). Commenting on his physical appearance, the *Candid Friend* wrote on 21st June 1901 that he combined 'the voice of a Vatican soprano [with] the effulgence of a Levite. He has the facial expression of the missing link. He is proud to be the ugliest man in France.' La Jeunesse is described by George Painter as 'a malicious, falsetto-voiced Jewish homosexual, unwashed, deformed, and notorious for his physical resemblance to a body-louse'.[2791] Although Bosie Douglas calls him 'an accomplished critic and essayist',[2792] he was one of Wilde's less attractive companions.

Robert Ross distanced himself from Sherard: 'His view of Wilde is not MY view, especially in regard to Wilde's unhappiness after his release'.[2793] This is nowhere better expressed by Sherard than in his reference to Melmoth being 'the name under which [Wilde] was to drag out the remaining agony of his years', but Sherard was to go on defending Wilde at the peril of Wilde's life throughout his days – and beyond, for Boris Brasol was to write

> I wish to express my sincere thanks [...] particularly to Mr Robert Harborough Sherard, the valiant friend of Oscar Wilde. By conveying to me many first-hand data on the life drama of the English poet, Mr Sherard has greatly facilitated my work.[2794]

Frequently Sherard's defence of Wilde is as embarrassing as any attack:

> It should be added here that although Oscar Wilde was in no sense a hard drinker, and never by his most intimate friends once seen in a state of intoxication, it is on record that every single foolish and mad act which he did in his life, acts which had for him the most disastrous consequences, was done under the influence of liquor.

> [His homosexual adventures were] committed, not when he was drunk, for he was never drunk, but when he had developed an epileptic crisis in his head.

> Oscar Wilde was the beau idéal of an English gentleman. That is to say the sane Oscar Wilde. What he may have been when his epileptiform fits took him it is for the outcasts to say who saw him on those rare and mournful occasions.

> The writing of some of his letters [...] is the writing of a neuropath [...] He does not appear to have written during the paroxysms of his dementia.[2795]

Chris Healy, who claims to have met Wilde frequently in Paris 'a few weeks after he finally left England' (that is, when he was en route for Naples in September 1897), also declares that 'despite the splendour of his intellect, Oscar Wilde on one point was as mad as the proverbial hatter. To the many, Wilde was an unspeakable person, but to the few he was an accomplished scholar and gentleman, suffering from one of the most terrible and loathsome forms of insanity.'[2796] The measure of this is that Healy also claims to have read *The Ballad of Reading Gaol* in manuscript *before* meeting Wilde, whom he calls 'the greatest sonneteer since the days of Rossetti and John Keats'.[2797]

There is a good deal here of Wilde's circle casting dice for the custody of his reputation in a somewhat self-serving way. Robert Sherard wrote of Robbie Ross 'The truth was not in Ross, and sordid self-interest seems to

have been the *leit-motif* of his life':[2798] this the man to whom Sherard had
dedicated his *Oscar Wilde, The Story of an Unhappy Friendship* for his
'elevation of heart and loyalty of character'! Stuart Mason called André
Gide's *Oscar Wilde* 'perhaps the best account of the poet's latter days';[2799]
Sherard called the same work 'Gide's mischievous memoir of Oscar
Wilde'.[2800] Ross thought Gide's 'not only the best account of Oscar Wilde
at every stage of his career, but the only true and accurate impression of
him that I have ever read'.[2801] St John Ervine described Sherard as 'A man
of small, ox-like mind, liable to fall into unreasonable rages and as
unreasonable admirations [...] His judgment was as feeble as his literary
style. The man was full of commonplace opinions and jejune beliefs and
febrile emotion'.[2802] Stuart Merrill thought Arthur Ransome's biography
of Wilde (for which he supplied a chapter) the best, but could not
remember the name of the publisher;[2803] Lord Alfred Douglas sued
Ransome for libel over it. Gide (and many others, including eventually
Douglas himself) attacked Douglas's *Oscar Wilde and Myself* as
'abominable [...] a villainy'.[2804] Reggie Turner fell out with Ross over
Ransome's use of *De Profundis*, and resumed a severed friendship with
Bosie. Frank Harris rightly thought that some of Wilde's French friends
'were determined to make him out a martyr'[2805] – but of course, so was
Harris, even if Philippa Pullar, writing in 1975, thought that Harris has not
really been given credit for the number of times he was generous to
Wilde.[2806] Henri de Régnier described Harris's portrayal of Wilde as 'the
truest and most lifelike portrait which has been drawn of him',[2807] but
Régnier's own acquaintance with Wilde hardly gave him authority for this,
and he is listed by Langlade with Schwob, Mirbeau and Anatole France as
one of those who dropped Wilde in 1898.[2808]

Oscar once more vanishes behind a mist of words.

> Certain soir, dans un bar du boulevard des Italiens, un homme pauvrement
> vêtu me demanda la permission de s'asseoir à la table voisine de la mienne.
> C'était M. Wilde [...] Je le revis plusieurs fois en le même lieu. Il manquait
> d'argent, de vêtements, d'amis vrais.[2809]

This bar might have been the Kalisaya, for Wilde told Reggie Turner that
it was 'now the literary resort of myself and my friends: and we all gather
there at five o'clock – Moréas, La Jeunesse, and all the young poets'.[2810]
Gustave Le Rouge met him there with La Jeunesse and Maurice Du
Plessys 'who detested one another'.[2811] This bar, which Marcel Boulestin
and Gustave Le Rouge spell 'Calisaya' and Vincent O'Sullivan spells
'Calsaya', was, says O'Sullivan, a place that Wilde 'would never have

dreamed of entering in his best days'[2812] — yet the Guatemalan diplomat Gomez Carillo introduced Wilde to the Nicaraguan consul Ruben Dario there. Dario, who was impressed by Wilde, recorded in his autobiography that La Jeunesse was also there as a friend of Carillo's.[2813] If Wilde had been reconciled with Moréas, other social encounters would have been a matter of course, for the Greek was an inveterate stroller – he spent the afternoons promenading the boulevard Saint-Michel – and did his writing at the Vachette. This friendship would also have brought Wilde to the Café Procope, still frequented by Bibi-la-Purée after Verlaine's death: Gustave Le Rouge speaks of meeting Wilde there. Paul Henry, studying art in Paris at the century's end, remembered that 'the Café Procope was always crowded and full of the most colourful people to be met with even in Paris'. Henry took there the English journalist and future novelist Ladbroke Black[2814] who wanted to write something there for the sake of having done so. That night not only was Bibi present but Cléo de Mérode was there also.[2815] Paul Henry actually liked Bibi, that 'very common ruffian, who was not only a bore but smelt',[2816] so he would hardly have turned away from Wilde. Nevertheless, his fellow-Irishman is not mentioned in Henry's book.

Barbara Belford says that Wilde used the Brasserie Lipp (151 boulevard Saint-Germain) and the Deux Magots (170 boulevard St Germain).[2817] The former was founded in 1880 by the Alsatian Léonard Lipp when he took over the Brasserie des Bords du Rhin, but, like so much else, it tends to dissolve under scrutiny. Its own historian[2818] states that it began to make a stir in the world only in 1920 ('C'est en juillet 1920 que la famille Cazes [...] devient propriétaire de cette brasserie qui commençait à faire quelque bruit') with a clientèle that included Verlaine, Alfred Jarry, Max Jacob, and Guillaume Apollinaire, three of whom were still dead. Nor can one recreate the pre-1914 atmosphere there, for its décor dates to 1926. The Deux Magots opened in 1885[2819] and its brochure claims rather improbably that it was used by Verlaine, Rimbaud and Mallarmé. If Wilde used either of them (and they were close enough to the hotels in which he lived after 1897), it was because they were cheap and unknown, and as yet undiscovered by Ernest Hemingway.

Another possible Left Bank haunt of Wilde's is mentioned by Irene Vanbrugh, who had played Gwendolen Fairfax in the original production of *The Importance of being Earnest*. Her account is sufficiently striking:

Not very long after his death I had gone over there to choose some costumes for a new play and was taken one evening by a Secretary of the

French [*sic*, perhaps a slip for British?] and my friend Mrs Handley Seymour to see some of the haunts of the underworld in Paris [...].

We [...] made our way down a little dark street where I noticed that the gendarmes walked in threes. [...] We found ourselves in a large, stable-like apartment with a rough bar along one side and people sitting about on little stools. The proprietor, who was serving behind the bar, looked up quickly as we came in but knowing my host by sight, he nodded and said 'Passez, monsieur'.

There was a complete absence of interest in us or indeed in anybody, and we went down some dirty stone stairs to another apartment which might have been disused vaults. Here there was very little light and at the far end a man was singing to his own accompaniment on a poor piano, which, from an occasional leer on the faces round, I took to be a very obscene song. Some men were at tables drinking a rough kind of pink cider out of earthenware bowls and eating fried chip potatoes. The women were strangely unattractive; rather old, untidy, unkempt; heavily powdered with crimson lips, and dressed for the most part in coats and skirts which were rather obviously their only garments.

It was to this haunt that Oscar Wilde came during the last months of his life – an exile and penniless. It was here he held court, heralded by this underworld as 'Master' just as he had been in other worlds. Here a small coterie would cluster round him and hang on his words and they would pay for his company by standing him a meal; his only lasting tribute being that his name is among the very few deemed worthy to be carved on a pillar which stands on a pillar in the middle of one of the vaults. The only other name I recognized was that of Gabriele d'Annunzio.[2820]

This perhaps is a little too circumstantial – from whom did Vanbrugh learn the details? – and she does not name the bar, but Arlen Hansen mentions that the *wall* in the Bol de Cidre in or off the rue Gît-le-Cœur was autographed by Wilde,[2821] and this may identify the place. D'Annunzio scholars may be able to confirm this.

The bar in the boulevard des Italiens might also have been Pousset's at number 14 which was 'one of his favourite haunts', and Wilde would write letters there.[2822] Reggie Turner dined there in 1897 on 'un bon petit bœuftec saignant et une demie bouteille de vin, rouge comme le sang de mes ancêtres';[2823] it was also well-known for its Munich beer.[2824] (But Manet put two bottles of Bass on the bar of the Folies Bergère.) Henri Ghéon used it as a coign of vantage to look for male pick-ups. Other habitués of Pousset's were Henri Mercier the translator of Keats, and the painter Lewis Weldon Hawkins. Wilde had his last, silent, encounter with

Whistler there in April 1898: Wilde was dining with Frits Thaulow.[2825] In the summer of 1900 Wilde was also to be found in the Grand Café, where he had been a regular visitor in pre-lapsarian days,[2826] though history does not relate whether he ever played billiards in the basement below (as E.V. Lucas used to do – there were thirty billiard tables[2827]) on the days when his enthusiasm for outdoor games was not satisfied by playing dominoes. Otherwise, a restaurant surely open to him was Viel's (or the Restaurant de la Madeleine), in the boulevard de la Madeleine, a quiet and modest establishment favoured by the theatrical profession.

If Wilde really was 'pauvrement vêtu' when on the Right Bank, his standards had certainly slipped: earlier he had been known for his dislike of slovenliness and prison had inflicted an obsessive tidiness upon him. He did tell Harris at the end of September 1898 that the only clothes he had were ones given him by Harris seventeen months before, but such letters were written to obtain money and it is difficult to suppose that Wilde was not exaggerating to serve his purpose.[2828] Sos Eltis has made an interesting point that bears upon this. In the summer of 1899, Wilde was working up *An Ideal Husband* for publication. It is only in this version that the stage direction appears referring to Lord Goring as a philosopher:

> Enter LORD GORING in evening dress with a buttonhole. He is wearing a silk hat and Inverness cape. White-gloved, he carries a Louis Seize cane. His are all the delicate fopperies of Fashion. One sees that he stands in immediate relation to modern life, makes it indeed, and so masters it. *He is the first well-dressed philosopher in the history of thought.* [2829]

Eltis glosses this. 'The grooming of the dandy may thus have been an attempt by Wilde, destitute and shunned, to present the impeccable dandy as an infallible figure, an idealised version of himself before the fall […] The validation which the stage direction gives to Lord Goring's speech could be the result of bitter personal experience breeding the wish for a perfect and unconditionally charitable wife'.[2830]

~~~~~~

Sherard's rôle in all this is obfuscated by Sherard himself. In *Oscar Wilde, the Story of an Unhappy Friendship*, he makes some play with the way he was vilified in Paris for his friendship with Wilde, including the tale of his being publicly insulted by a 'highly-placed' member of the English colony, leading to the latter's being prosecuted and fined[2831]: this should be retrievable. When Wilde left Naples for Paris, Sherard (then in London) went to see him, but as between Wilde and Dowson, whom Sherard was now befriending, the old ease was no longer present. This was despite Sherard's having visited Wilde twice in Wandsworth and three times in Reading, as well as his service to Wilde in having secured the suppression of a damaging article that Douglas had tried to get published in the *Mercure de France*.

> Towards me he became more and more distant; the verminous parasites that clung to him fostered the wrong idea that I had condemned him. In melancholy and solitary peregrinations on the boulevards, which fifteen years earlier we had trod so triumphantly, we sometimes passed each other in silence, with only a faint wave of the hand – like two wrecked ships that pass in the night.[2832]

Apart from the curious simile, this passage is notable for its reference back to their earliest acquaintance in 1883 rather than to their times together in 1891. 'Verminous parasites' may be taken as a reference to Rowland Strong or Ernest La Jeunesse, but it also indicates how little Sherard was aware of (or if aware, willing to acknowledge) the support Wilde was receiving from Robert Ross, Reggie Turner and others. Writing less than two years after Wilde's death, Sherard was laying down his version for posterity, complete with the misleading reference to the Hôtel d'Alsace: 'After leaving Naples he came to Paris and took a room in the fourth rate hotel in an obscure street in the Latin Quarter, where he died.'[2833] This is backed by an even stranger remark that the proprietor of the Alsace, M. Dupoirier, had known Wilde in his prosperous days.[2834] One can fall into quibbling, but this is a most unlikely acquaintance, and the rue des Beaux-Arts, running parallel to the rue Jacob and debouching into the rue Bonaparte opposite the École des Beaux-Arts, does not deserve the appellation 'obscure'. Gérard de Nerval (whose real name was Labrunie) had lived at number five, Fantin-Latour at number eight, Corot at number ten and Atget at number twelve. The Hôtel d'Alsace was, and is, number thirteen. The area (rue Bonaparte, rue du Bac) was favoured by artists as different as Strindberg, Whistler and Eileen Gray. This is not to say that the street was entirely salubrious. Shirley Fox describes there a 'horrible little eating house', kept by mère Naile, 'skinny and wizened as a witch', immediately opposite the gates of the École des Beaux Arts. 'The cookery was of the most savage description, and the atmosphere close and reeking of grease.[2835] But it was cheap' and much patronised by the art students. Mère Naile may not have survived till Wilde's day, but her establishment probably did.[2836]

In any case, Wilde stayed in many places before his final residence in the Alsace, including Switzerland with Harold Mellor and Monte Carlo with Frank Harris. Sherard also plants a dart in Harris: 'I know for a fact that *at least* two plays which were produced in London and which were great successes, were almost entirely written by [Wilde]'.[2837] If one of these was *Mr & Mrs Daventry* (not that it was written 'almost entirely' by Wilde), what was the other? Surely not Haddon Chambers' *Tyranny of Tears*,[2838] which rumour attributed to Wilde, although whether this was by way of praising Chambers or damning Wilde it is difficult to say. The attribution of an English translation of Barbey d'Aurevilly's *Ce qui ne meurt pas* to Wilde or even to Melmoth is similarly incorrect. Indeed, the picture of a Wilde hard at work hardly squares with the rest of Sherard's account, or indeed, any other account.

Nor does any of this square with Wilfred Chesson's account of his visit to Wilde at Nogent-sur-Marne in July 1898 on 'a perfect summer day', when Wilde was in remarkably good form, even praising Dickens and being witty at the expense of John Butler Yeats ('"Could he paint?" I asked. "Not in the least".'). He also recounted Maupassant's story 'Deux Amis' and called Verhaeren 'the greatest living poet'. This was a remarkable judgment and suggests a flicker of the Wilde of long ago. Twelve years later Stefan Zweig was to write that Verhaeren was 'the greatest of modern poets, and perhaps the only one who has been conscious of what is poetical in contemporary feeling, the only one who has shaped that feeling in verse, the first poet who with skill incomparably inspired, has chiselled our epoch into a mighty monument of rhyme'.[2839] Perhaps there are references to Wilde by Verhaeren yet to be excavated.

With a good deal of insight Wilde also recommended Chesson to read Georges Eekhoud[2840] (whom Chesson, or Chesson's printer, unfortunately calls Eekhond), for it was Eekhoud who ten years later was the first to write about the homoerotic implications of the iconography of St Sebastian.[2841]

> I said that [Wilde's] life was a harmony of two extremes, very rare and I thought very valuable. With a level suavity that, like the lawns of Oxford, had centuries of culture behind it, he replied 'yes, artistically it is perfect; socially, most inconvenient'.[2842]

Nevertheless, one convenient social occasion is mentioned by Langlade, a visit by Wilde to Versailles and 'his friend Lady Plunket' who had rented a large house there.[2843] Langlade adds that he was joined there by Esterhazy. This is rather startling if true. Lady Plunket was Lady Victoria

Blackwood, daughter of the Marquess of Dufferin; her husband was a diplomatist who in 1904 was appointed Governor-General of New Zealand. This was the Anglo-Irish *haute monde*, access to which even in Merrion Square days would have been beyond the Wildes.

Part 2: Final Call

> 'What clever plays he wrote: might still be writing! What clever things he said: might still be saying!'
> – Sir Squire Bancroft.[2844]

> 'There is not a single degradation of the body which I must not try and make into a spiritualising of the soul.'
> —Oscar Wilde: *De Profundis*.

> 'I hate Paris! […] Towns, like persons, are either sympathetic or antipathetic to me.'
> – Marie Bashkirtseff.[2845]

THE *vie de Bohème*, the romanticisation of which had begun by Murger as long before as 1848, was still being celebrated in du Maurier's Trilby of 1894 (put on stage with Dorothea Baird as Trilby and Tree as Svengali in 1896[2846]), Puccini's *La Bohème* of 1896[2847] (at Covent Garden with Melba in July 1899), Leoncavallo's *La Bohème* of 1897 (performed at the Théâtre de la Renaissance in October 1899), and even in Bernhardt's production of Miguel Zumacois' *Bohèmos*, when she played the penniless poet of that name in Monte Carlo and London in 1903. Massenet's *Sapho*, from a novel by Daudet,[2848] which was produced at the Opéra-Comique also in 1897, had an artist's model as its leading part (she is called Fanny Legrand), sung first by Calvé and then by Georgette Leblanc. Wilde went to see *Sapho* early in June 1898 (which means that he still had dress clothes[2849]). The last of this group was Gustave Charpentier's *Louise* of 1900, a four act opera with Mary Garden, later to sing Salomé, in the title rôle. *Louise* was written between 1890 and 1894 when Charpentier lived in Montmartre[2850] and attempted to review Montmartre in terms of social Realism. In 1921, Mary Garden wrote of Charpentier that he 'was the King of Montmartre, a real Bohemian to whom money and fame meant nothing. He was satisfied if he had enough to pay for drinks for himself and his friends at the Rat Mort. He lived in a dirty little garret[2851] up on the butte, and while he was writing this realistic picture of his own life, he was slowly starving to death. The production of his opera brought him nearly half a million francs, but he spent it all on the working girls of Montmartre'.[2852] Having little to eat, Charpentier consumed himself in writing, and the sequel to *Louise, Julien ou La vie du poète,* a four act 'poème lyrique' was a failure when produced in 1913 at the Opéra-Comique, while his third opera or 'drame lyrique' *L'amour au faubourg* in two acts, has never been produced at all.[2853]

The first night of *Louise* was attended by President Loubet.[2854]   Zola approved of it. Saki's 'Lord Carrywood' saw it three times.[2855]   Carl van Vechten queued an hour and half for one-franc tickets. Debussy loathed it. The poster by Georges Rochegrosse showed the exchange of vows between Louise and Julien. 'I always recalled this scene as intensely as when I watched Mary Garden and Léon Beyle from the topmost gallery', wrote van Vechten.[2856]

For those who could not have seen *Louise*, of course, Murger could still exercise an enchantment, Maugham's Philip Carey

> began to read Murger's fascinating, ill-written, absurd masterpiece, and fell at once under its spell. His soul danced with joy at that picture of starvation which is so good-humoured, of squalor which is so picturesque, of sordid love which is so romantic, of bathos which is so moving. Rodolphe and Mimi, Musette and Schaunard! They wander through the grey streets of the Latin Quarter, finding refuge now in one attic, now in another, in their quaint costumes of Louis Philippe, with their tears and their smiles, happy-go-lucky and reckless. Who can resist them? It is only when you return to the book with a sounder judgment that you find how gross their pleasures were, how vulgar their minds; and you feel the utter worthlessness, as artists and as human beings, of that gay procession. Philip was enraptured.[2857]

Should this have appealed to Wilde? The romantic view of the Bohemian life now held few charms for him: admiration for a garret does not survive two years in a cell, when what Virginia Woolf called 'the delicious society of my own body'[2858] ceases to have its attractions. And he could have afforded a one franc ticket.

Wilde did not of course have only himself for society. Apart from Wilde's sexual encounters, Conder for one was living in the rue St Honoré from December 1898 to February 1899 and in the rue Amsterdam in the autumn of 1900. Conder saw something of Wilde and if he did not go to Wilde's funeral it was perhaps because he was busy with his wedding, which took place two days later – Robbie Ross put Conder's name on the funeral wreath. Wilde also saw his London friend George Ives in March 1898, and in April dined with Henry and Aline Harland at Pousset's and with Frank Harris at Foyot's.

Harris at this time was maintaining a ménage at St-Cloud with an actress
called May Congden, and he should have been at home in Paris, this Irish-
born Englishman, whose name was really James and who 'in England
passed as an American and in America was believed to be an English
Jew'.[2859] He was certainly no stranger to the city, having spent some time
there from early September 1875 to January 1876 with an American friend
called Ned Bancroft. Harris found his way to lectures, read *Hernani* and
Madame Bovary, went to the Opéra and frequented the Café Anglais and
the Trois Frères Provençaux.[2860] In October 1878 he had married his first
wife, Florence Adams, at the British Embassy, and perhaps tactlessly (but
tact was not Harris's chief frailty) nine years later took his second wife on
honeymoon to the Hôtel Meurice. In May and June 1900 Harris was again
in Paris, and entertained Wilde 'sumptuously'[2861] while discussing *Mr and
Mrs Daventry*.

Lord Alfred Douglas was occasionally in Paris (in August, September and
October 1898, and in May 1899) and would give Wilde dinner at
Paillard's, Maire's or the Café de la Paix as of old (or sometimes, not quite
as of old: his dinner with George Ives at the Café de la Paix, where Ives
'drank glass after glass of hot milk, while Wilde demolished endless
whisky and sodas', hardly sounds alluring[2862]). To dine in fashionable
restaurants, even if it was Wilde's only meal of the day, does not indicate
any very great loss of self-confidence. How far away really was he from
the chance of an invitation to that dinner party of Proust's on 25th April,
attended by Montesquiou, Anatole France, Mathieu and Anna de Noailles,
madame Arman de Cavaillet, and madame Lemaire? Not as far, surely, as
those exiles who really did become down and out in Paris, like Captain
James Shaw.

Wilde and Douglas also stayed together at the well-named inn L'Idée in
Nogent-sur-Marne in June 1898.[2863] Unfortunately, this association with
Douglas cut Wilde off from Carlos Blacker, who lived in Paris from
February 1898 and had been urged by Constance Wilde[2864] to visit her
husband. Blacker had quarrelled with Wilde specifically over Oscar's
post-Berneval reconciliation with Douglas; and his wife, Carrie, was even
more hostile to Wilde on more general grounds. Nevertheless for a while
the breach between Wilde and Blacker was healed, despite reservations by
Blacker concerning Wilde's relationship with Maurice Gilbert. This
resulted in Constance restoring Wilde's allowance, while the cost of
friendship for Blacker himself was four hundred fifty francs (£18/-/-). It
was, however, Carrie's intervention that began a new estrangement
between the two, leading to Wilde's informing Chris Healy of Blacker's

plans to discredit Esterhazy. This Blacker regarded as a betrayal. A reconciliation when Constance died proved transitory, and ended when Blacker visited Wilde at Nogent-sur-Marne and found Douglas there.

> [Blacker] came down to see me about a fortnight ago–enquired affectionately into my financial position – actually wept floods of tears – begged me to let him pay the balance of my hotel bill – a request that I did not think it right to refuse – and left me with violent protestations of devotion. A week later he wrote me a Nonconformist conscience letter in which he said that as he did not approve of my knowing Bosie [Douglas] he thought it would be morally wrong of him to help me in any way except by advice! He also added that his wife disapproved of my knowing Bosie!! So Tartuffe goes out of my life[2865].

The letter, and Wilde's reply, finally ruptured the friendship between the two men, Blacker coming to the view that Wilde 'would finish in the gutter as he deserves', Wilde that Blacker was a Tartuffe from whom nothing better could be expected as he was a Jew on his father's side.[2866]

A more welcome meeting was one with Alexander Teixeira de Mattos, who had married Wilde's brother's widow Lily in October 1900. 'Tex' reported back to Margot Asquith that 'Wilde was a complete invalid at the time, and Teixeira found him lying on a sofa surrounded by books, fruit and flowers. He looked up when he saw his friend, and said: "You see I am dying beyond my means".'[2867] This is perhaps the most authentic record we are likely to have of this famous saying. The meeting was probably at the same time as one elsewhere recorded, when Alec Ross (Robbie's brother) and Lily Teixeira de Mattos called on Oscar (25th October).

Vincent O'Sullivan was a perhaps more level-headed friend than most: 'I have known people I have liked better than I did Wilde. But never one it was such a happiness to see or be going to see. You never felt that he felt very much for you but you felt he was glad to see you then and there [...] He was good-natured, kind-hearted, but not large-hearted. He probably never cared for anyone as much as some cared for him. Lord Alfred Douglas was essentially and practically far kinder to Wilde than Wilde ever was to Douglas. This was Lionel Johnson's opinion too.'[2868] For all that much detail of Vincent O'Sullivan's life is lost to us,[2869] he has as much claim as Stuart Merrill or James Whistler and almost as much as Francis Viélé-Griffin[2870] to be regarded as a Paris American and knowledgeable about what he wrote: it is, however, Merrill who has a square named after him, into which the avenue Stéphane Mallarmé leads.

He refers to Henry-D. Davray as 'a friend of my youth in the Latin Quarter'[2871] and this alone would serve to place him among the more serious acquaintances of Wilde's final two years. As a friend of Wilde's he attended the dinner given for Robbie Ross on the publication of Wilde's *Complete Works* in December 1908. Dowson and Beardsley were two of his closest friends. He was also a friend of Leonard Smithers, which argues a larger heart, a narrower judgment.

What clearly did tell on Wilde was the continual uncertainty about how he would be received, either by friends or strangers who recognised him; as a man 'remarkably free from malice'[2872] himself, the spiteful attitude of others would have been not only hurtful but incomprehensible. Those who supported him may have made it harder, not easier, for Wilde to have borne slights, although Wilde himself occasionally added to the difficulty – his constantly touching his friends for money cannot have endeared, and there were other embarrassments. Ford Madox Ford, not a particularly reliable autobiographer (he even manages to call Bibi-la-Purée 'Bibi La Touche or something of the sort'), tells how he twice shared and paid for cabs in Paris with Wilde: 'the memory is one of long-continued discomfort. It was humiliating to dislike so much one so unfortunate'. Ford admits to having always disliked Wilde, and recounts a disobliging anecdote when Robert de la Sizeranne is with him in the Chat Noir and says to Ford 'Vous voyez cet homme-là. Il péchait par pur snobisme. Cela me faisait chaque fois vomir'.[2873]

Rothenstein was in Paris in 1899 with Augustus John and dined with Wilde 'more than once. [Wilde] was greatly taken with John, though John was very silent'[2874]. This sounds as if Rothenstein was put out of countenance. The encounters were not entirely to John's liking.

> Though appreciative of [Wilde] as 'a great man of inaction' and a 'big, good-natured fellow with an enormous sense of fun, impeccable bad taste, and deeply religious apprehension of the Devil', Augustus felt embarrassed by his elaborate performances of wit [...] The unnatural deference, the trained astonishment put on by the rest of his audience sickened him [...] Augustus felt stifled by these long, unspontanæous lunches at the Café de la Régence and the Café Procope, and was always on the look-out to escape with Conder and seek 'easier and less distinguished company' [...] in Montmartre.[2875]

Certainly in 1900, when William and Alice Rothenstein were staying with Rodin, there was an awkward moment.

Usually they would ask Oscar Wilde to dine with them, but on a previous
occasion Wilde had annoyed William by showing too much interest in one
of the musicians playing in the restaurant where they were dining en plein
air: he had resolved therefore not to see him again. But they met on the
boulevards and it was only too plain that Wilde thought William had meant
to avoid him. The Rothensteins at once asked him to join them, but the
crackle of wit had by now became mechanical and was only sustained by
absinthe. They never saw him again.[2876]

Could the musician in fact have been Rothenstein's attempt to disguise the
identity of the painter? John returned to France, to Le Puy-en-Verlay, in
September 1900 and stayed to November, making a visit to Paris to see the
Expo and Rothenstein's picture 'A Doll's House', which won a silver
medal. He made no attempt to renew acquaintance with Wilde, who by
then, according to Robert Ross, was actually dying.   Another whose
interest in Wilde had clearly waned was, very surprisingly, Ada Leverson,
who only mentions in passing that she called once at the Hôtel d'Alsace
and found Wilde 'leading the life of a student in a tiny room'.[2877] Was this
the Sphinx who had put him up in her own house when he was on bail and
visited him at Stewart Headlam's house on the day of his release? Only
one anecdote remains to mark this occasion, one that Leverson herself told
Harold Acton.

She told me a latterday anecdote about Oscar in Paris. He had romanced to
her somewhat fulsomely about a beautiful young apache, who was so
attached to Oscar that he always accompanied him with a knife in one
hand. 'I'm sure he had a fork in the other,' said the Sphinx. I left her
chuckling to herself in the dim lounge of a frigid hotel.[2878]

Rather more creditable is the account, unfortunately unconfirmed, that
Bram Stoker visited Wilde in Paris and gave him some financial
assistance.[2879] As told by Daniel Farson, this has the air of a family
legend; when embroidered by Barbara Belford it becomes more
fantasticated.

A story still circulates that Stoker brought money to Wilde when he was
destitute in Paris. It is pleasant to imagine Stoker arriving at the Hôtel
d'Alsace and Wilde's surprise and pleasure at seeing him. They would go
first to the Café de la Régence for Courvoisier, and Wilde would order a
box of gold-tipped cigarettes. They would dine at the Café de Paris and
talk of Trinity, of Florence and her beauty. That one evening they would
be Dubliners.[2880]

There were others whom Wilde might have seen in the distance and placed himself out of their way. In June 1899 George Gissing moved to Passy with his new French wife and lived there (13 rue de Siam) to April 1900. A closer examination of his days would show whether his path might have intersected with Wilde's, although we would know if they had actually met – and this is true for many others in Paris at that time. Gissing indeed might have had reason equally to avoid or to look out for Wilde, for after his estrangement from his second wife Edith, 'she spread the rumour that she refused to live with me because *I was a disciple of Oscar Wilde!*'[2881]

Edwin Lutyens, since 1897 married to that Emily Lytton who six years earlier had found Wilde so fearfully conceited, was also in and out of Paris from May 1898, having duties concerning the British Pavilion. This in itself was something of an illusion, being the reproduction of Kingston House, Bradford-on-Avon, and filled with pictures lent by the American J.P. Morgan. Lutyens recorded that the city was 'like a mad-woman whose hair was full of straw and plaster'.[2882] On one occasion some of the Commissioners of the British Section[2883] visited the Moulin Rouge, which Lutyens found 'beastly'.[2884]

Baroness Orczy, with her husband Montague Barstow, spent six months in Paris between 1900 and 1901. Barstow painted, and exhibited in the 1901 Salon, but the Baroness (it was an Hungarian title) spent her time writing *The Old Man in the Corner* and exploring the city, and in particular the Quartier Latin for the sense of place which she was to bring to the writing of *The Scarlet Pimpernel*: 'In writing of Paris or Boulogne, they were always Paris or Boulogne'.[2885] Less static was one of the exhibits in the Hungarian section of the Expo, a stuffed Russian bear, shot in the Carpathians by Orczy's uncle Count Wass and bought by a rich Armenian for his house in Alexandria.

Lord Rosebery and Lady Warwick were at the first night of *L'Aiglon* on 17th March (they had to be smuggled out the theatre when there was a Pro-Boer demonstration). W.T. Stead, once imprisoned for the 'Maiden Tribute' affair, was in Paris at a peace conference in October 1900; Lady de Grey in November to see *L'Aiglon*. E.F. Benson visited Paris for the Exposition Universelle, as did Charles Ricketts in May 1900, and Frederick Pollock, who took the opportunity to discuss *Hamlet* with Mounet-Sully, and Wilfrid Blunt, who was later to re-introduce Lord Alfred Douglas into society, in September.

A fatiguing affair. I went through the Pavillons Etrangers, of which incomparably the best is the Spanish, most of the others are cluttered up with the rubbish of modern manufactures, and even the English pavilion, which represents a Victorian Gothic country house, has a certain vulgarity, but here in the Spanish section there is an incomparable dignity.[2886]

Henri Mazel (whose accuracy of recollection is not beyond suspicion) mentions that the months of the Exposition Universelle of 1900 were ones in which Wilde enjoyed especially some happy days, amusing himself 'like a fat child', says Stuart Merrill.[2887] This Mazel ascribes to the fact he was not deserted 'in his troubles' by André Gide, Henry Davray and Edouard Julia.[2888] Whatever about Davray, whose motives cannot have been unmixed by pecuniary considerations, Gide had in fact abandoned Wilde (they only met twice in Paris, each time by chance and to Gide's embarrassment); and if Wilde had to depend on Edouard Julia for his happiness, he had certainly descended in the ranks of the intellectually demanding. A sketch by Jean Matet of Wilde in a cabaret in the rue de Dunkerque, probably dating to this period, shows him holding forth to three very young men.[2889] If these were the friends whom Mazel says 'delighted to compare [Wilde] to a grand priest of the Moon Goddess in the days of Heliogabalus', Wilde's company was more admiring than admirable.

The months of the Exposition Universelle in fact must have been difficult ones for Wilde as the English came to visit. Although this was slow to start, from August the railway companies serving the Channel Ports were putting on extra carriages. The extraordinary number[2890] of conferences and congresses held in Paris that year also boosted the numbers of English people, many of whom, if not personally known to Wilde, would certainly have been in the audience for *A Woman of No Importance*, *Lady Windermere's Fan*, *An Ideal Husband* or *The Importance of being Earnest*. One who was personally known to Wilde was the Irish-American Anna Dunphy, comtesse de Brémont, a friend of Wilde's mother, or at least 'a hanger-on at Lady Wilde's soirées'.[2891] Little enough seems to have been researched about this novelist, who had been in the public eye when she sued W.S. Gilbert for libel. This took place in 1895, and Sir Edward Clarke appeared for Gilbert with more success than he had had defending Wilde, and William Bowen-Rowlands for de Brémont. Lord Russell of Killowen presided. Gilbert had referred to her as 'a lady who styles herself the comtesse de Brémont'. Bowen-Rowlands' son gave a brief account of the case which perhaps can be read as a covert warning not to take this woman too seriously, for he had sufficient doubt about his father's client to place her title in inverted commas, adding 'it was a peculiar case, and if I may say so, the parties were not altogether free from the imputation of peculiarity.'[2892] At any other time, Wilde might have appreciated the case.

The encounter between de Brémont and Wilde, in the Spanish Café in October 1900, was an unfortunate one. In order not to embarrass her hostess when Wilde walked in, the countess covered her face with her fan. Unfortunately, Wilde had recognised her. Some reparation was possible when they met by chance the next morning on a bateau-mouche. Wilde said that he had been happy enough not to have been introduced to de Brémont's friends as he did not care to meet strangers.[2893] Did he recall (as all his biographers recall) his remark to his Oxford friend David Hunter Blair, that if he could not be famous, he would be notorious? The bill was now being proffered.

De Brémont asked him why he did not write and he replied that it was 'Because I have written all there was to write. I wrote when I did not know life. Now that I know the meaning of life, I have no more to write; life cannot be written, live can only be lived. I have lived'.[2894] This major reconsideration of the Wildean æsthetic, as especially as Gide records it, coheres with what Robert Ross said of Wilde's re-assessing his achievements.[2895] 'My work is done,' Wilde went on, 'and when I cease to write, that work will begin to live. Ah! My work will live as long as men live to read it; my work will be my great monument'.[2896] In this at least Wilde prophesied truly: not for him the fate of Enoch Soames. Wilde had once said 'Whoever observes himself arrests his development.'[2897] In ceasing to develop himself, Wilde left the field clear for others to reinvent him.

~~~~~~~~

Another man who was down on his luck in Paris at this time was Robert Sherard. I have cited his remark concerning the way that in 1898 and 1899 Wilde 'used to frequent people whom it was impossible for me to meet, men classed in Paris as social outcasts'.[2898] (It may be recalled that Yeats, no great stickler for what was *comme il faut*, would not have Leonard Smithers in his house; and Gide too was unhappy about being seen in the company that Wilde was keeping.) Sherard does, however, palter somewhat with the truth, as we know from Wilde's meeting him in Campbell's Bar in May 1898, unshaven and 'all covered with cigar ash, stains of spilt whiskey and mud'.[2899] According to Wilde, Sherard attacked another customer, shouting 'À bas les juifs' and trying to provoke an anti-Dreyfusard brawl.

It is not easy to evaluate this incident. Sherard had been living in England since 1893, returning to Paris in February 1898 to cover the Zola trial. It would seem that his book *The White Slaves*, about working class conditions in England, had cost him dear. As the author of a study of Zola[2900] he was the obvious choice to send, yet 'il ne tarda pas à se ranger parmi les anti-dreyfusards'.[2901] Sherard rather glossed over his anti-Dreyfusard feelings, while at the same time recalling a number of Jewish people with respect or, in the case of Ernest La Jeunesse, admiration – he calls La Jeunesse 'that wonderful writer'.[2902] He was also keen to exculpate Wilde from any suspicion of anti-Semitism,[2903] and blamed Rowland Strong for involving Wilde with Esterhazy. It was Sherard who first introduced Strong to Esterhazy (in the offices of Drumont's *Libre Parole*), but fell out with him some time in the early summer of 1899[2904]. 'I met severally and separately yesterday afternoon Oscar, Strong and Sherard all inveighing bitterly against one another', wrote Dowson to Frank Harris,[2905] though Strong had liked Wilde well enough to lend him his dog, Snatcher, when Wilde was staying in Nogent-sur-Marne. Strong's position was equivocal, anti-semitic but publishing an article in the *New York Times* in which he declared his belief in Dreyfus' innocence, Esterhazy's guilt.

Not surprisingly, Esterhazy too quarrelled with Strong, whom he was to recall as

> A little man with a red beard [...] whose cuffs were frayed and very dirty, [and who] smelled of alcohol ten feet away [...] A contemptible clown [...] an absolute swine [...] a despicable scoundrel.[2906]

For a time, they had been inseparable.

~~~~~~

Quarrels in Campbell's Bar apart, life was sustainable in Paris. It was not so much that Wilde was without resources, rather that he was no more able to manage slender resources than he had been able to manage large ones a few years earlier.[2907] It was part of Wilde's loss of place that in Paris at the end of the 1890s he preferred to follow his own sexual inclinations once more among the rent boys of the streets, rather than attempt to reconstruct his earlier æstheticisation of 'the love that dare not speak its name'. This might have given us an encounter between Wilde and Giovanni Costa, a Parisian Apollo much sought after by both sexes, whose Irish mother had been stabbed on her husband's grave by a rejected suitor.[2908]   What a subject for Wilde at his most rococo!

According to Robert Ross, however, Wilde even began to re-assess what he had already created: 'Many people hardly believe that in his last years he was the severest critic of his own achievements.'[2909] Once Paris was where he had been 'deep in literary work, and cannot stir from my little rooms over the Seine until I finish two plays. This sounds ambitious, but we live in an age of inordinate personal ambition and I am determined that the world will understand me.'[2910] Paris was where Wilde had sought out the Parnassians and honeymooned in the Hôtel de Wagram ('of the highest class' said Baedeker), and thought about living after the censor had refused to licence *Salomé*. Paris too was where he been received by the British Ambassador, re-reading *The Decay of Lying* although dying at his post.[2911]   It was a dramatic reversal that the Embassy doctor, Maurice a'Court Tucker, attended the dying Wilde, but one does note that it was the Embassy doctor.[2912]

This all forms a desperately ironic background to Wilde's experience in this last return to Paris, exchanging the Right Bank of his earlier visits for St Germain and the Quartier Latin. Even so, had Wilde not undertaken a voluntary self-effacement, the Sunday morning organ recitals by Charles-Marie Widor at Saint-Sulpice would have offered great escape at no great distance. These were a rendez-vous 'of the whole aristocratic and artistic Paris world'[2913] and beyond – when the American Senator Hoar was in Paris for his health in 1892, he was taken there by the United States Minister, Coolidge, both almost certainly unaware that the bell tower was the setting of much of Huysmans' novel *Là-bas*, published the previous year. Widor, of course, had his own idiosyncrasy. Claiming to believe in metempsychosis, he once announced remembering that in a previous life he had been a duck.[2914]

Robbie Ross's suggestion that Wilde was re-assessing himself, for all that it fits both Wilde's continual remaking of himself and into Paris as a *mise-en-scène* for such a process, cannot however be let pass without drawing attention to Ross' consistent attempt to 'improve' his friend. It was after all Ross who engineered Wilde's final remaking, from lapsed Irish Protestant to Roman Catholicism, at a time when Wilde can have hardly, if at all, understood was taking place, so that the odour of sanctity was not quite enough to mask the odour of humbug. At no time in Paris did Wilde hold himself out to be a repentant sinner, and his conduct and attitude is measurable against that of Aubrey Beardsley. As Wilde sauntered along the boulevards or sat outside a café did his eye ever catch in recognition that of any of his Catholic compatriots on their way to or from Lourdes, as it might have done of old? Mrs Craven had noted Lord Denbigh and Lady Mary Howard passing through Paris on their way to Lourdes in May 1883: the exact date is not given, but Wilde was in Paris that month. He was certainly in Paris at the end of October 1898 when Count Arthur Moore of Mooresfort, Co. Tipperary, a former M.P., went to Lourdes 'to ask the recovery of his son from a long illness and that his wife might be cured and thus saved from a serious operation'.[2915] Both died.

Arthur Moore was long enough in Paris (either then or upon another occasion – the source does not specify which) to visit the Chambre de Deputés. 'How many of these men do you think believe in God and prayer?' he asked his friend the comte de Franqueville, who recalled the 'unutterable look of sorrow [that] passed over his handsome face' when he, Franqueville, replied 'At least half of them believe in nothing'.[2916] Believing in nothing, distinguished from not believing in anything, is a position that coheres well with Wilde's way of life in Paris.

Of course, one must not understate the embarrassments and humiliations that this way of life forced Wilde to undergo – for example, the barman in the Chatham Bar, 'a snivelling little Yankee', once refused to serve Wilde while willing to serve Bosie[2917] – yet the picture of Wilde as chiffonnier or clochard has been overdrawn, by himself as well as by others. Undoubtedly from time to time Wilde was the worse for wear (or drink), as we know from Jean de Mitty's description of him at the Chatham;[2918] but at other times Wilde's residuum of good humour and the care of friends uplifted his spirits and self-esteem. Simon Callow's remark about the 'desperate rag-picking of Wilde's last years'[2919] cannot be substantiated, while Wilde's own statement made to Frances Forbes-Robertson, 'You don't know how poor I am: I have no money at all: I live or am supposed to live on a few francs a day: a bare remnant saved from shipwreck',[2920] has to be set in context. Unlike Simeon Solomon in the East End of London, Wilde was not reduced to selling matches and shoe laces; nor, like a derelict artist with whom Paul Henry once fell into conversation on the Paris quays, to earning money by collecting cigarette ends for recycling. Indeed, Paul Henry noted that even among his student companions, 'some of us were miserably poor and were glad to pick up discarded butts of cigarettes on the boulevard or a neglected croissant from a table'.[2921] (There were two or three hundred such *ramasseurs de mégots*, and they collected three hundred pounds weight of tobacco each day[2922]). Did Wilde ever reflect on the Bohemian code attributed to Henri Murger's friend, the painter Antoine Fauchery? '1) Rent should never be paid, 2) all moves are made through the window, and 3) tailors, bootmakers, hatters and restaurateurs are relatives of Monsieur Crédit.'[2923]   After all, Wilde had once put into the mouth of John Worthing the sentences 'Why is it that we all despise the middle classes? Simply because they invariably pay what they owe.' Bohemian insouciance allied with aristocratic disdain in anti-bourgeois coalition. What does not seem to have occurred to Wilde was to attempt to earn money, except from the sales of *The Ballad of Reading Gaol*. He could surely have found a market for the stories he was still capable of narrating.[2924]

Bob Stevenson once remarked 'I find that being hard up in London is not attended with amusement as it often is in Paris',[2925] but this sentiment was probably not shared by the clochards whom Chris Healy saw on a bench between La Madeleine and the Théâtre de la Renaissance, despite the *féeresque* effect of the street lamps.[2926]   Wilde was still capable of rousing himself occasionally.   In July 1899 he returned to Chennevières-sur-Marne, to a place well-named the Île d'Amour, 'a lovely spot – an island, with trees and a little inn. 6.50 francs a day tout compris'.[2927]

Paris in a hot summer amalgamated Zola-esque moral decay with physical corruption.

> It was one of those summer evenings when Paris is completely airless. The city, hot as an oven, seemed to swelter in the stifling night atmosphere. The stench of sewage rose up from the granite mouths of the drains, and through the low windows of basement kitchens the foul vapours of dishwater and stale sauces belched into the streets.[2928]

> The last days of August in Paris! A deadly oppression of heat; a brooding inertia that lay upon the city like a cloak![2929]

But as with Claude Lantier, so with Wilde: he returned to Paris to be devoured.

> Paris is burning hot – streets of brass in which the passers – few in number – crawl like black flies. I wish I had the means to go away, but I am in dreadful want – no money at all. I wonder would you lend me £5? If you could I think you would. I have been passing through a terrible time.[2930]

~~~~~~~

In discussing Parisian poverty, Ambrose Vollard gives a picture of Alfred Jarry that commands respect: 'There never was a nobler figure in the

world of letters. Though very poor, he never made a show of his poverty.
He even avoided those he thought capable of helping him. And so
scrupulous!'[2931] (Wilde only managed to say of him 'In person he is most
attractive. He looks just like a very nice renter.'[2932]) Vollard himself,
before he prospered, could relish 'a plate of York ham, a pint of dark beer
and a generous slice of cheese' for three francs fifty, *service compris*, at
the Café Weber in the rue Royale,[2933] while Arthur Symons once
encountered Jean Moréas in a Bouillon Duval where, according to
Baedeker, the food 'is generally good, but the portions are rather small,
and the cost of a meal amounts to $2^1/2 - 3$ fr., including wine and coffee'.
Maupassant's Duroy, when reduced to his last six francs fifty, lunches at a
Duval[2934] and Duvals may be to what Wilde was referring when he told
Robbie Ross that he dined 'in modest restaurants at two or three
francs'[2935]; lunch at the Rat Mort was two francs, a price justified by the
badness of the food, according to Wilde, who only ate there once.[2936] This
would have been about half a crown at the then rate of exchange, which
remained stable until 1919: if Wilde had his £5 he could have had forty
such meals. In 1900, Bentley Mott noted that you could lunch at the Rat
Mort for two francs twenty-five or dine at the Abbaye de Thélème for
three-fifty.[2937]

While at the Académie Julian in 1893-4, Violet Maxse lunched every day
at a Duval ('cutlets or beefsteak aux pommes, a vegetable, cheese and
coffee for 1fr.50'[2938]); and in 1909 Dorothy Menpes mentioned 'certain
dishes, costing no more than ninety-five centimes and quite a good wine
[…] for one franc fifty'[2939]. One wonders what she would have thought a
bad wine. Beardsley remarked, however, that 'Duvals end by becoming
loathsome and impossible'. Augustus Saint-Gaudens presumably thought
the same, for he varied dining at a Duval with dining at Foyot's, and then
compromising 'in some two-franc eating house at the top of
Montmartre'[2940]. Sherard was dismayed on meeting an American publisher
who had done well out of pirating his work to be offered dinner at a Duval
which cost four francs.[2941] Huysmans describes the sort of cheap meal that
one would prefer to miss: 'an extremely dead fish, a piece of meat, flabby
and cold, a few lentils stiff with insecticide, some ancient prunes, whose
juice smelt of mould'.[2942] Perhaps the one advantage of the Duvals was
that smoking was permitted, unlike in regular restaurants.[2943]

One could also dine cheaply, if frequently repulsively, in *crémeries*, as
described by Martin Ross, admittedly from the point of view of Anglo-
Irish Co Galway, rather than that of a Dubliner newly released from an
English prison.

It is possible to dine sufficiently for a single franc; satiatingly, with three courses and a bottle of *ordinaire*, for eighteenpence; it is also possible, when there is *bouilli* at threepence, to stay one's appetite for that sum. But in any case the forks and spoons will be more than dubious, the *serviettes* like pieces of coarse sheeting, and the eyes must be averted at the unescapable moment when the prune juice or the soup washes over Angélique's thumb as she puts down the plate. A memory rises of the *soup à l'oiseille*, that seductively named potion, that looked like water in which the breakfast things had been washed, leaving tea-leaves and crusts of bread floating about in it. What is tasted like is a thing that its victim will struggle long and anxiously to forget. But how to remove the recollection of a slab of something that was entitled *tête de veau à la sauce Ravigote*, and resembled the unshaven cheek of an elderly gentleman? It is a matter too recent and poignant to dwell upon[2944]

This coheres with Ralph Nevill's view: 'The cheap dinners, two francs and upwards, which attracted unwary tourists, were in the number of their component parts wretched imitations of the lordly feasts of the Café Anglais and other noted shrines of gastronomy. All things in these terrible and strange meals wore an aspect not their own.'[2945]

There were, however, perils other than the food, for Arnold Bennett was inspired over a meal in the boulevard de Clichy to write *The Old Wives Tale*[2946] and Arthur Symons once heard Jean Moréas 'thunder out some verses of his own in a Bouillon Duval, to a waitress whose name was Célimène, who pretended to understand them'[2947]. Was her name really Célimène? Symons doubtless heard Moréas call her that, but Célimène is not only the name of a character in *Le Misanthrope* (revived in 1890, with Célimène played by Marie-Louise Marsy, and again with Cécile Sorel) but also of one in Alfred de Musset's *On ne badine pas avec l'amour*. It was also the name that Jean de Tinan used when contributing his chronicle 'La Ghirlande de Célimène' to *La Presse*. But doubtless even the verses of Moréas were preferable to the Salvation Army songs that Catherine Booth, Blanche Young and Kate Patrick would sing in boulevard cafés, once even taking their praise of Paradise into the Café de l'Enfer[2948].

What Aubrey Beardsley had saved in the Duvals, he apparently spent in the Café Anglais[2949], for he left Paris without paying his hotel bill, not doubt using one of his favourite expressions 'Je suis stoné'.[2950]

Another peril had been an uncultured one – after relieving Alexandre Duval of his considerable fortune inherited by Alexandre from his father Baptiste-Adolphe Duval, founder of the Bouillon Duval chain, Cora Pearl refused to receive him further, and he shot himself. Although this was not fatal[2951] clearly no one thought of him as Armand Duval brought to life. Duval was in any case something of a figure of fun — after the death of the comte de Paris, said Arthur Meyer, Duval only ate crêpes and he was nicknamed Godefroy de Bouillon, gentilhomme consommé[2952] — but the jest here is that much of the Duval fortune had been made through the low wages paid to the twelve hundred employés – not that Cora Pearl had any idea of redistributive justice. Moreover 'Duval aspired […] to fashion a pliant personnel by hiring women to wait on tables'[2953], tables that were now turned. In 1900 the waitresses (only the Duval in the rue Montesquieu employed waiters) struck for a twelve hour day and against giving some of their tips back to the management; in 1909 Dorothy Menpes reckoned that they earned between four and eight francs a day. It is difficult to credit that in their survey of living conditions among the working class in the XIIIème arrondissment in 1899, Octave du Mesnil and Charles Mangent suggested that 'one franc was the minimum per capita income needed by a household each day to subsist without want or without assistance'; nor with Berlanstein's conclusion that this figure is 'all things considered, quite defensible'.[2954]

~~~~~~

Dowson's friend William Theodore Peters, a young American poet who could not afford fabulous or any other expense, died in Paris of starvation;[2955] and, rather than starve, the poet René Leclerc, known as René de la Villoyo, dined on cyanide of potassium in his garret in the rue Gay-Lussac. This gives its hollow ring to Robert Sherard's dictum that 'there is no city in the world where one can starve with less discomfort than in Paris'[2956]. 'In no part of the world,' wrote Robert Louis Stevenson, 'is starvation an agreeable business, but I believe it is admitted that there is no worse place to starve in than this city of Paris.'[2957]

Henry Lucy's budget when a young journalist relates to the last year of the Second Empire, but it gives one a benchmark. He relates that, friendless and alone, he lived on 2/- a day, chiefly eating at an estaminet near the Bon Marché kept by Père Camie. Here his breakfast of a bowl of hot chocolate and a roll cost 2½d; lunch, usually a cutlet or steak, and bread and cheese and beer, was 9d. 'Dinner, taken about half-past six, cost from 10d to 1s. Supper cost nothing, as I did not have any.'[2958] In his impoverished days in the rue de Londres, Debussy would lunch off a 'petit pain' at one sou and a small bar of chocolate.

When a student at the Conservatoire in 1878, James Huneker had a weekly income of thirty-five francs, of which his room in the rue Puteaux took fifteen. The £1/-/- a day that Grant Richards budgeted when he visited Paris in the early spring of 1892 was quite indulgent – Heinrich Felbermann claims to have lived on 7d a day, at which rate Richards' pound would have lasted more than a month, but 7d – less than a franc (ninepence ha'penny) – would have been virtual destitution: a franc would only buy café-au-lait, petits croissants and butter at the Gare du Nord, though near the Gare de Lyons was a small café frequented by cabmen where in 1888 Edgar Jepson found 'a very good meal' for two francs, and at Carron in the avenue Victor Hugo one could have a 'gargantuan' meal for five or six francs.[2959] Eighteen francs was what Colonel Newnham-Davis found 'a moderate sum for quite a good meal' at the Restaurant Volney.[2960] Wilde told Charles Wyndham in the spring of 1900 that he had £2/10/- (62 francs 50 centimes) a week 'which only just enables me to drag on in endless anxiety about the necessaries of daily life'.[2961] He did not confide his idea of the necessaries.

Even more impoverished than Felbermann were Paul Léautaud and Adolphe van Bever[2962] who, it is said, 'for several months shared a room'[2963] and contrived to live on two francs a week'[2964]: I do not find this probable (at least without stealing) at a time when the average male wage in Paris was five francs a day.[2965] The meal at thirty centimes that Verlaine would eat at the restaurant de la Huchette[2966] can hardly have been distinguishable from starving, but starving was not unfamiliar to Verlaine. Jean Émile Bayard, who 'was not unacquainted with this literary Bohemia of the period 1886 to 1896', says that Verlaine 'took his meals, when he could get any, at the Restaurant Tarle, known as the "Ancien Cocher", in the rue Soufflot'[2967], but the poet was sitting outside the Café Mahieu when Léautaud saw him on Friday 24th August 1894, and had violets sent over from a nearby florist's. 'I may assure you,' wrote Theodore Child in 1886, 'that as prices run in Paris, it is impossible for a restaurateur to serve you a healthy and honest plate of meat for less than one and a half francs'. This seems to be what Mme Bechet charged for Wilde's regular meals Chez Bechet at 42 rue Jacob, where he was occasionally joined by Ernest La Jeunesse.[2968]

Yeats found an anarchist restaurant in the boulevard Saint-Jacques where he could dine for 1/-[2969]; perhaps the same one where Arthur Lynch used to lunch for the same sum on three courses with wine, perhaps the same one where Gwen Salmond, Ida Nettleship and Gwen John took their meals, 'where beautiful, grubbily dressed girls fetched their own food to avoid being waited upon'.[2970]

The American art student Abbot Handerson Thayer lived at the Hôtel Britannique in the avenue Victoria from July 1875 to late 1878 at an annual rent of $144.00 (£36/-/-)[2971] – but his fellow Americans Mr and Mrs Warren paid for a furnished house in the boulevard Haussmann five thousand francs a month. Lillie Langtry paid eleven hundred francs a month in 1880 for her flat in the Champs Elysées: 'I don't think it is much, do you?'[2972] she wrote to a friend. Five years earlier, Fanny Stevenson paid seventy-five francs or $15 a month (plus $2 for the concierge) for two large bedrooms, a 'pretty little salon', small entrance hall, 'large elegant dining room' and kitchen in the rue de Naples;[2973] for his single room at 6 rue Cortot Satie paid eight francs *a year*. Fifty-five francs a month was what Freud paid at the Hôtel de la Paix, in the impasse Royer-Collard (rue Gay-Lussac), where he stayed for six weeks at the end of 1885, eating out twice a day at two francs a meal;[2974] and fifty francs a month was what Norman Angell paid in 1898 for a room at the Hôtel de l'Univers et de Portugal in the rue Croix des Petits Champs, behind the Banque de France, where Beardsley had stayed five years before. Gerald Kelly, attracted by the name,[2975] was to stay there on first arriving in Paris in 1901,[2976] Duncan Grant and Marius Forestier in 1906. (This 'curious haunt' was run by M. and Mme Troulet, whose receptionist, Rosalie, 'an old peasant woman in a white Berrichon cap' told anti-German tales dating back to 1870.[2977]) The brothel opposite was modest in its charges, while the *prix fixe* dinner in the restaurant next door was only 1 fr.15: soup, hors d'œuvre, meat, vegetables, sweet, wine and 'a napkin as large as a table cloth'.[2978]

By 1912 it was said to be possible to construct a French cabinet from former boarders at the Pension Laveur in the rue des Poitevins, just behind the fountain in the place St-Michel. Dinner here was two francs. Such a cabinet would have included Raymond Poincaré, Gabriel Hanotaux, Alexandre Millerand and many others, once students at the Sorbonne. Daudet and Coppée had also lodged there. It was presided over by Mdlle Marie Rosalie Losset, 'tante Marie' to her boarders but once christened 'the Greek statue' by Gambetta himself. [2979]

Lord Russell of Killowen demanded six guineas a day expenses when in Paris for the Venezuela Arbitration in June 1899 'as he could not live in Paris in matter befitting his high station [as Lord Chief Justice] on five guineas a day', which was what the Treasury had allotted him but Baedeker suggested fifteen to twenty francs a day pocket money for

tourists.[2980]   One could after all go to the cheapest seats at the Comédie
Française for 2fr.50 (the prices of the rest were from eight to twelve francs
if bought before the evening, or from six to ten francs if bought at the
door); the cheapest seats at the Opéra were four francs. Both were free on
national holidays. From the death of his wife in April 1898 Wilde enjoyed
a small bequest of an annual £150, or six months pocket money in
Baedeker's terms. Wilde himself told a friend who was thinking of moving
from London to Paris 'On £25 a month you should be able to manage'.[2981]
In 1885/6, Freud managed on three hundred francs (or £12) 'including
books and the money he sent to his mother'.[2982]   In 1900 Wilde received
some £1,000[2983] or 25,000 francs from Lord Alfred Douglas alone.
Equivalencing values is always difficult, but in her 1995 biography of the
actress Elizabeth Robins, Angela John calculated that to match the
purchasing power of £1,000 in 1907, one would need an income of
£160,000.[2984]   This gives a view of Cecily Cardew's fortune, with a capital
value of £130,000 in 1895.

This is not to say that everything in Paris was cheap. Although a few
years earlier one might have bought a donkey called Modestine for sixty-
five francs and a glass of brandy, Meissonier's battle picture 'Friedland-
1807' was bought by Alexander T. Stewart of New York at the Club des
Mirlitons exhibition of 1875 for 300,000 francs[2985] and the New York
Metropolitan Museum of Art in 1887 paid 250,000 francs for Rosa
Bonheur's 'The Horse Fair'.[2986] This compares with the flower piece by
van Gogh that the publisher T. Fisher Unwin was persuaded by Joseph
Pennell to buy from Tanguy or Portier, which cost twenty-five francs. A
simple frock from Worth such as Lillie Langtry favoured would have cost
not less than twenty-five thousand francs, or a thousand pounds. (Lord
Lyons thought that the appropriate dress allowance for an ambassador's
wife was £1,000 a year – but then, Lyons was a bachelor). At the Hôtel
Drouot in 1882, the pearl necklace of Marie Blanc fetched 360,000 francs.
Maurice Ephrussi, married to Béatrice, daughter of baron Alphonse de
Rothschild, whose very hair was silver, paid the duc de Nemours for his
house in the avenue du Bois de Boulogne three million four hundred
thousand francs.[2987]

We do not know what resources Wilde had at his disposal on his pre-1895
visits, though doubtless they were as inadequate as usual for the demands
he would place on them. Certainly when he stayed at the Hôtel Voltaire in
the spring of 1883,[2988] he would have needed a deep purse. In October of
that year, Strindberg complained that twenty francs a day were insufficient
yet John Lavery, while at the Académie Julian in 1881, paid forty francs a

month for board and lodging at the Hôtel de Saxe in the rue Jacob, and in 1897 and 1898 Feodor Ivanovich Chaliapin paid eleven francs full board at Madame Chalmel's in the rue Copernic. Finally, one may cite the opinion of Nathaniel Newnham-Davis, that

> My experience is that an Englishman who is in Paris to enjoy himself, going to the best restaurants, and neither stinting himself, nor launching out into extravagance, spends about fifteen to sixteen francs on his breakfast and from eighteen to twenty francs on his dinner.

This does not include tips, for waiter, *maître d'hôtel*, cloakroom attendant and the *chasseur* who calls a cab. Newnham-Davis may have intended 'luncheon' for 'breakfast', and his idea of 'a very simple dinner' that cost him eighteen francs at the Café Anglais may not have been generally followed: six Ostend oysters, *Potages Laitues et Quenelles*, *Merlans Frits*, *Cuisse de Poularde Rôtie*, *Salade Romaine*, cheese, half a bottle of Graves premier cru and a bottle of St Galmier (i.e. Badoit). 'I did not want an elaborate dinner, as I was going to the theatre'.[2989]

~~~~~

In his last year in Paris, Wilde again took up his acquaintance with Jean Moréas, despite the earlier lack of sympathy between the two[2990]. After his Symbolist period Moréas had returned to classicism[2991], associating with Charles Maurras, and classicism or even mediævalism marked the post-Symbolist work of de Régnier, Samain, Vielé-Griffin and others, who now 'produced some of the most uninteresting poetry in the French language', leaving Émile Verhaeren to be considered 'the greatest poet in the world writing in French'.[2992] When Harold Nicolson makes the æsthete Lambert Orme fall into abstraction and says 'He was thinking, probably of Albert Samain and Henri de Régnier',[2993] he was suggesting the persistence of these poets in the æsthetic imagination. That Wilde was unable to respond intellectually even to this attenuated literature shows how much of his force was spent.

If Wilde now lost touch with the French literary men for whose company he had once been so eager, equally poignant is his avoidance of theatre. As far as I can tell, the author of *Salomé* was not to be seen at the Théâtre de l'Œuvre, nor did the admirer of Bernhardt's Phèdre and Lady Macbeth see her in Catulle Mendès' *Medée* at the Théâtre de la Renaissance in October 1898, or her Hamlet (played in French, a heavily cut, prose translation by Eugène Morand and Marcel Schwob, with incidental music by Pierné) when it opened at the Théâtre Sarah Bernhardt in May 1899 with a second run there in the following December.[2994] Nor did Wilde, who had once written a poem on the death of the Prince Imperial, witness Bernhardt's triumph in Rostand's *L'Aiglon*, the part that ensured the survival of her legend in March 1900 – and effaced that of Jeanne Granier in a breeches part in *Le petit Duc* (Théâtre de la Renaissance, 1878). Her granddaughter calls *L'Aiglon*, with *Phèdre* and *La Dame aux Camélias*, 'the mainstays of Sarah Bernhardt's dramatic and lyrical career'.[2995] One may also say that without Bernhardt, *L'Aiglon* (Napoléon II) would not be remembered, any more than are remembered *Le Roi de Rome* by Émile Pouvillon (1840-1906) and Armand d'Artois (1788-1867), which Gide saw in January 1899, or *Le Fils de l'Étrangère*, a play about the Prince Imperial by the baron Sipière under the pen name Desmirail. (*L'Aiglon* also ensured the survival of Napoléon II, that 'pale young man, whom the imagination of a poet and the genius of a great actress have conspired to present to posterity as a stoutish woman in a white uniform with a queer haunting voice'.[2996]) All the most notable people in the literary and social world were at the opening on the 17th: Prince Murat, Anatole France, Jules Lemaître, Halévy, Sardou, Montesquiou, the historian Albert Vandal, Henry Houssaye[2997], Paul Hervieu[2998], Coquelin, 'and many beautiful women'[2999]. Wilde no longer had lilies to throw at Bernhardt's feet, and perhaps instead he went to Blanche Marot's première of Louÿs' *Les Chansons de Bilitis*, or perhaps he merely got drunk (it was St Patrick's Day).

Wilde's claim to have effected a reconciliation with Sarah Bernhardt in Nice in December 1898 has neither been questioned by biographers of Wilde nor substantiated by biographers of Bernhardt. The one actress who says she befriended Wilde towards the end in Paris is Cécile Sorel, who was sufficiently moved by reading *The Ballad of Reading Gaol* as to want meet its author, and was encouraged by friends to seek him out. The question might be put, why did Sorel wait to the autumn of 1900 to do so? She called, she tells us, at the Hôtel d'Alsace and was introduced to 'a stout, bowed man who looked like a wounded bull. His eyes were glassy, his mouth slack. [He] appeared the most wretched of beings. You felt that springs within him had irrevocably snapped. Gravely, before this twilight of an idol, I heard Oscar Wilde stammer 'I am happy – to see – Cécile Sorel – before I die'[3000]. This, or at least the telling of it, was doubtless gratifying: after all, Sorel did not enter the Comédie Française until the year after Wilde's death. 'I knew how much he had suffered,' says Sorel, 'and admired him above all because out of his evil fortune, he had made an immortal work of art'. As she makes it clear that she is here referring, not to the *Ballad* but to *De Profundis*, her admiration, like his, was of the proleptic variety.

Her imagination continues to serve her when she tells how she invited him to her house.

> An invisible orchestra was to play throughout dinner. Lackeys holding torches stood on the steps of the broad stone staircase. Others in white stockings and knee breeches, with gold epaulettes, awaited the guest they were to announce […] To greet Wilde I had put on diadem, necklace, bracelet and rings of emerald. My gown moulded me in gold like an Egyptian statue […] 'Why did you never come to see me before?' I asked.[3001]

If this sounds rather like Sarah Bernhardt as Cleopatra, it sounds even more like Elizabeth Taylor. Where did this remarkable dinner take place? Here one thinks of Shaw's remark about Mary Anderson's autobiography: 'This book is an actress's confessions: consequently I should not, under ordinary circumstances, dream of believing a word of it'[3002]. In the late 1890s Cécile Sorel lived on the corner of the avenue de l'Alma and the avenue des Champs Elysées,[3003] but I doubt whether this ran to a broad stone staircase. The remark of the theatre writer M. Willson Disher about her – 'there never was an actress so radiant' – seems to take on less the aspect of praise, more that of recognition that there was more make up to her than there should have been. The view of her parents, her aunts and her uncle the Archbishop of Rheims that she should not go on stage was clearly a mistaken one.[3004]

~~~~~~~

Vyvyan Holland gives the traditional view that it was prison that had killed his father's creativity.

> The spark of genius in him was extinguished by prison life, and it could never be rekindled. He constantly spoke of work which he had in mind, but when it came to actual writing he would be assailed by doubts and problems; doubts as to whether it was humanly possible for him to reconstruct his literary life[3005].

Richard Ellmann rather spoiled his own identification of this by assimilating Wilde to Bunbury: 'Cramped to one myth, and that sombre and depleted, Wilde could not extricate himself. There was nothing to do but die, which accordingly he did'.[3006] Kerry Powell regards the London theatre as the vital support system for Wilde's creativity: 'absent from the turmoil of that scene, separated by barriers of time and distance, Oscar Wilde was left with nothing to answer, nothing to contend with, and alas, nothing to say'.[3007] This of course fails to explain why he was unable to draw strength from the Paris theatre – there were seventy-eight playhouses of all sorts at this time. One can perhaps understand that Berneval should have not provided stimulus sufficient for creation, and neither Switzerland nor Italy provided Wilde with the milieu in which he could write, but his eventual return to Paris should have altered the case, Paris where the idea of the artist in the garret was so firmly entrenched. 'One can only write in cities,' Wilde told Sherard, 'the country hanging on one's walls in the grey mists of Corot, or the opal mornings that Daubigny has given us',[3008] a notable admission that Wilde was still clutching at Barbizon for the art which life was imitating.

If we can follow Laurence Housman's account, Wilde came to the conclusion that having enjoyed success, it was necessary to experience failure in order to have achieved 'the complete life necessary to the artist'.[3009] This fits very well with his project of realisation of self. Unfortunately there is a flavour about it of *post hoc, propter hoc*, a thought out and therefore specious reason for not creating. All we do know is that deprived of money and audience, he was unable to create, nor even to mix much with those who did.

Apart from the *Ballad*, the very sketchy ideas that have come down to us of what Wilde was contemplating after *The Importance of Being Earnest* suggest that so far from developing the critique of Society that he had begun with *Lady Windermere's Fan*, he was returning to the poetic dramas that he had abandoned after *Salomé*. Could he have given us 'the Epic of the Cross, the Iliad of Christianity, which shall live for all time', as he once told Coulson Kernahan that he hoped to do before he died?[3010] Clearly, his trials and imprisonment would have made writing society comedies impossible, but had Wilde returned to verse drama and biblical epics, the comedies would have been an interlude. Melissa Knox reflects that 'the life into which Wilde put his genius was not comedy but the great tragedy he never wrote about a martyred prophet',[3011] but equally he might now have only been known to us as another Stephen Phillips. Wilde knew Phillips and admired his poetry, but we do not know whether news came to him of Tree's production of *Herod* (31st October 1900) with Tree as Herod and Eleanor Calhoun as Salomé. Phillips' verse dramas – *Paola and Francesca* (1899), *Herod* (1900) and *Ulysses* (1902) were in fact highly successful flashes in the pan[3012], and their dismissal from subsequent critical attention does not speak well for any possibility of success by Wilde in this vein: his idea in 1897 of rewriting *A Florentine Tragedy* shows how unrealistic he could be. Although it is tempting to contemplate Wilde turning again to Symbolism, *pace* Katharine Worth[3013] one does not descry the possibility of another Yeats. The form was certainly safer with Yeats, and one can only shudder at the plot of Wilde's *The Cardinal of Avignon*: 'the Cardinal of the title, newly elected Pope, is his son's rival in love, a conflict which leads the Pope to tell the son for the first time of their real relation [...] The girl whom they both love, forbidden to wed the son, kills herself, whereupon the Pope's son throws himself on her bier and stabs himself'.[3014] We can therefore be thankful that we have been spared Wilde's *Pharaoh* or his *Ahab and Jezebel*, this last apparently considered as a vehicle for Sarah Bernhardt.

It is also quite difficult to see this as the way forward from *The Importance of Being Earnest*, a way that in other hands led to *The Admirable Crichton* or *The Madras House*. Kate Terry the younger, viewing a revival of *Lady Windermere's Fan* at the Kensington Theatre in October 1900, noted that 'this play has grown very quickly *démodé*'.[3015] The Italian critic Mario Borsa, writing in 1908, was of the opinion that

> If Oscar Wilde had not disappeared ignominiously from the face of the earth, he might have given to the English theatre new elegances of thought and form, fresh refinements of psychological observation, more epigrams, more witticisms – but not the drama or the comedy which would have re-created the English stage. Not because Wilde lacked the dramatic instinct, but because this instinct, instead of developing freely and rising to further and loftier creative heights, had been gradually distorted by the hypercritical attitude and the æsthetic vanity of this artist.[3016]

Ellmann tells how for a while Wilde took up his unfinished play 'La Sainte Courtisane' but dropped it again. The suggestion is that he was unable to return to the cast of thought that had enabled him to begin this piece early in 1894. 'La Sainte Courtisane' is one of Wilde's highly charged purple prose works, and it is easy to accept the implication that the sense of luxury that it projects was hard to recover in more Spartan days, but the play also concerns an anchorite and this is a theme that Wilde could now have undertaken with a good deal more experience than in 1894. The piece, as Ellmann notices, is a re-working of Anatole France's *Thaïs*, but what Ellmann does not seem to have noticed is that Massenet had 'scooped' Wilde with his operatic version of *Thaïs*, which opened in Paris on the 16th March 1894, making Wilde's version *de trop*. The rôle of Thaïs appealed to sopranos such as Cavalieri, Ackté and Garden who also sang Salomé.

In any case, if he were to out-reach Massenet by making something new of
'La Sainte Courtisane', he would have needed far greater powers of
invention than those that he could now command. Only a man in whom
sensibility had decayed would have developed a taste for drinking
Advokaat, or the company of Major Esterhazy. Thus was fulfilled Wilde's
own line in *The Duchess of Padua* 'We are each our own devil and we
make this world our hell'.

~~~~~~~~

Early in June 1899, Wilde was dining in a Paris restaurant when the
actress Ada Rehan came in with the Augustin Dalys. Each recognised the
other.

> 'I didn't know what to do,' she told me. 'Mr and Mrs Daly were with me
> and I could not tell how they would feel about it. You never *do* know with
> men when they are going to feel very proper and when they are not.'

> 'And – *was* Mr Daly feeling proper?' I enquired.

> 'No,' said Ada, 'he wasn't. It was such a relief: if I could not have bowed,
> I should have cried.'[3017]

Daly, the proprietor of Daly's Theatre, might in fact have been justified in
feeling proper as far as Wilde was concerned, for the opium den in *The
Picture of Dorian Gray*, 'which looked as if it had once been a third-rate
dancing-saloon', is called Daly's[3018]. The restaurant is not named: good
enough for the Dalys but not too expensive for Wilde, he must have been
in some funds that week, or else being treated – Sherard thought that
Wilde was with another man, possibly Harris.[3019] Wilde was clearly
touched by his reception for when Daly died unexpectedly on 7th June, he
wrote his condolences to Ada Rehan in generous terms.[3020]   Graham
Robertson noted Daly's death in a different, but familiar, manner, saying
of Daly and Rehan 'Just as *in real life* they played the Trilby-Svengali
drama of du Maurier's romance, so did Ada Rehan, the actress, vanish for
ever after the death of Augustin Daly.'[3021]

It was not always so pleasant for Wilde, although again one must be wary
of exaggeration. Cosmo Gordon Lennox and Harry Melvill cut Wilde in
Paris: 'I felt as I had been cut by two Piccadilly renters. For people whom
one has had to give themselves social or moral airs is childish. I was very
much hurt. But have quite recovered'.[3022] If this means that Wilde and the
two men had been lovers (not usually noted by Wilde's biographers) one

might understand that a certain embarrassment might have arisen, as they were in the company of Gordon Lennox's wife, the actress Marie Tempest whom he had only recently married (summer 1898). The marriage, perhaps unsurprisingly, was not a success. 'His peculiar nature and her magic existed on a different sides of a wide, wide gap'[3023]. Marie Tempest herself 'remembered seeing Wilde in Paris, a few weeks before his death, sitting outside the Pavillon Bleu in the Champs Elysées'. She did not like Wilde[3024] but how far she is a trustworthy witness is difficult to assess. Did Wilde really write to her 'self-revealing letters, almost every fortnight when he was in prison'? These she claims to have torn up, as she tore up her letters from Sarah Bernhardt, Réjane and Eleonora Duse.[3025] An American critic called her 'the English Réjane', and she was admired by Yvette Guilbert.[3026] Tempest was working in the United States in the early 'nineties when Wilde was casting his plays, but in her long life, she never played in Wilde.

Others of Wilde's former associates behaved either badly or well, according to their measure of Wilde (or their own) but, again, not all is patent. One who made no attempt to see Wilde while in Paris in March 1900 was Richard Le Gallienne, to whom Wilde had been a lodestone after hearing him lecture in Birkenhead in 1883, and to whose circle he gravitated when setting up in London in 1891 at Staple Inn, receiving an author's complimentary copy of *Salomé*. Wilde also sent him and his first wife, Mildred, tickets for the first night of *Lady Windermere's Fan* and they stepped round to see Wilde after the performance. This provided Wilde with the opportunity for a little gentle teasing of his admirer, complaining of Le Gallienne's unkindness to him in his recently published *Bookbills of Narcissus*. Le Gallienne, puzzled, protested that there had been no unkindness, that he had not indeed mentioned Oscar. 'That was the unkindness,' said Wilde.[3027]

In 1895, Le Gallienne was to attempt an act of kindness, for he was in New York with John Lane when the news of Wilde's arrest was known.

> Lane, who had never much time for Wilde, was all for yielding to the barrage of demands that his name should be erased from the Bodley Head lists, and it is to Richard's credit that he persuaded the dithering little publisher that Oscar was much too good a writer to drop.[3028]

What kept Le Gallienne from an act of kindness in 1900? He was staying at the Grand Hôtel and found time to revisit the Café de la Paix and for a stroll round the Quartier where he found that 'the cafés were as full of light-hearted young people as ever'[3029]. Once he had had a dream in which he saw Wilde approaching his house, 'toiling up the hill, bedraggled and wretched [...] When I came to the door he said "Richard, the whole world has forsaken me. Will you take me in?" and I answered "Of course I will, Oscar".'[3030] Unfortunately, dark dreams vanished in the Paris sunshine, resurfacing when Wilde died ('Poor Oscar! His death made a dark day for me. I shall never forget him. He was a great original personality, say what they will, and I believe time will confirm his value'[3031]), and again when he read Sherard's first book on Wilde[3032], 'not a great book, but for all its weakness and sentimentality, it had a ring of sincerity that somehow managed to convey that goodness and simplicity of Oscar that I saw long ago'. This prompted a further reflection that perhaps indicates an unease with his own part in this tale: 'I often wish I had made some sign to him in those days [...] but God knows my own hill needed climbing, and doubtless I could have done little with him with that crew around him, and that *folie des grandeurs* in his brain'[3033]. Could their contrary opinions about Dreyfus have played a part in this?

Writing in 1926, Le Gallienne's memories of Wilde included descriptions that were less than flattering, 'a sort of caricature Dionysius disguised as a rather heavy dandy of the Regency period [...] He made one think of an enormous doll, a preposterous, exaggerated puppet [with hands that were] soft and plushy.' [3034] Perhaps recollection of Wilde once writing 'I hope your laurels are not too thick across your brow for me to kiss your eyelids'[3035] served only to embarrass. As for Le Gallienne himself, he seems to have fallen foul of Chris Healy who, usually coy enough about putting names to people, calls him 'a poor little poetling', and quotes Arthur Lynch's description of him as a 'sugar-coated prig [...] He has a good forehead, but then he has the prim, mean mouth of a parlourmaid'[3036]. There seems to be something especially malicious in Healy's recounting a conversation with Wilde: 'Then he referred to English writers, and his opinions on these I forbear from quoting, except in the case of Richard Le Gallienne. "Poor Richard!" he said. "He is an absurdity, but he is a graceful absurdity."'[3037]

Another graceful absurdity who became disconnected from Wilde was his friend John Audley of the avenue Montaigne. Described as 'a curious individual who wished to be taken for an æsthete, dilettante, original whatever it cost', he called himself English, but de Fouquières believed him to be a German.[3038] Unfortunately, Wilde's biographers say nothing of him.

Social intercourse, even when uncomplicated with a man with such a past as Wilde's, was heavy with nuances almost impossible now to recreate. Rothenstein tells, for example, that Arthur Studd 'was a little suspicious of [Conder's] influence, and was inclined to persuade me from seeing too much of him', and having overcome his dislike of Conder, transferred his distrust to Wilde[3039]. But what was that influence? The social line that Conder himself drew suggests a certain squeamishness: 'It's hardly fair to inflict a man who's just served a sentence of hard labour on your family'. This homage to Victorian sensibilities may be judged by the way that it was accepted by Wilde himself, although he must have reflected that he himself had not been quite so exclusive in his Tite Street days, reflected too on the days when his acceptance of invitations was a cause of pleasure: reflected, but, apparently, rarely recalled out loud[3040] In Paris in 1899, Wilde encountered his old friend J.E.C. Bodley. 'Humbled by prison, he pretended not to recognise him, but Bodley insisted on recalling his old friendship and drew him towards his house. At the door Wilde hesitated, and on hearing that Bodley had a family waiting within, hesitated again and then fled forever'.[3041] Similarly, when Wilde crossed paths with de Régnier, it was Wilde who turned away.[3042]

Yet other motives came into play. Robert Ross noted that 'Many people were kind to him, but he was too proud, or too vain, to be forgiven by those whom he regarded as his social and intellectual inferiors [...] He chose therefore a Bohemian existence, entirely out of note with his genius and temperament'.[3043] Whistler, cutting Wilde when they chanced to meet in the entrance of Pousset's, is generally held to have been maintaining ancient grudges, but it must be remembered that Whistler was grieving for his wife, who hated Wilde, and to have greeted the Irishman would have been a betrayal.[3044] Douglas Ainslie, who had lunched with the Wildes 'on two or three occasions' in Tite Street but had severed the connection when he 'began to hear stories of an unpleasant nature about him', visited Beardsley in Dieppe and was shown the Mademoiselle de Maupin drawings, but he did not see Wilde, perhaps because he was attached to the Paris Embassy at the time. Later, in the autumn of 1898 in Paris, even Robbie Ross and Reggie Turner on their way to Italy viâ Paris 'deliberately by-passed Wilde's headquarters, probably fearing that, depressed and lonely for English companionship, he would soften them into not going any further'.[3045]

To this period belongs the story, recounted by Félix Fénéon, that Wilde 'one night had decided to make an end of it and went to the Seine. He passed another rather strange-looking person, gazing down at the water from the parapet of the Pont Neuf. Thinking it was a fellow sufferer, the poet stopped and asked: "Are you also a candidate for suicide?" – "No," the other replied, "I am a hairdresser!" This non sequitur, F.F. later recounted, convinced Wilde that life was still comical enough to be endured' – and, obviously, comical enough to tell, for it is also recounted by J. Joseph Renaud, who transfers it to the Pont des Arts.[3046] It was from the parapet of the Pont Neuf that Coupeau leaped into the Seine 'in the belief that a bearded man was barring his way'[3047]; and from the same parapet Claude Lantier had leaned 'over towards the great, chill, unfathomable moat, with the dangerous mystery of its lights, drawn by the melancholy sound of its waters, ready – so deep was his despair – to respond to their call'[3048]. 'If you saw a man throw himself into the river here,' said Sherard to Wilde as they crossed the Pont des Arts, 'would you go after him?' 'I should consider it an act of gross impertinence to do so,' was the reply.[3049] Ohnet's Lise Fleuron chose the Pont de la Concorde.[3050]

If Wilde really contemplated suicide, it was an aberration, for he usually made the best of his situation, and accepted his own agency in it. There is a characteristic tale of a lunch at the Café de la Paix with Robbie Ross's elder brother Aleck in March 1900, when he convinced Ross that he was going straight.

> All went well until an unlucky event occurred [...] Dear Aleck passed before the little café behind the Madeleine, and saw me with a beautiful boy in grey velvet – half rough, all Hylas. Alas, the eye he turned on me was not the sightless one. His smile was terrible.[3051]

Aleck Ross, though well affected towards Wilde, saw him clearly enough even with one eye. Later he was to tell Siegfried Sassoon that he attributed Wilde's downfall 'largely to hock and seltzer. In the preceding years he was seldom sober.'[3052]

~~~~~~~~

One result of Wilde's self-effacement was that the death of the man who used to say that the only thing worse than being talked about was not being talked about, went almost unnoticed, 'un bien mince événement', as Léon Lemonnier called it. Even Proust, who marked the death of Ruskin in January 1900 with an article in *Le Figaro* 'Pélerinages Ruskiniens en France', seems to have left the death of Wilde unnoticed. Lemonnier thought typical the four lines devoted to Wilde's passing in *Le Petit Parisien*:

> Oscar Wilde, le littérateur anglais bien connu à cause de ses démêlées avec la justice de son pays est mort après-midi, à deux heures, des suites d'une méningite, au numéro 13 de la rue des Beaux-Arts.

Lemonnier continues, with considerable ambiguity, 'La précision et l'exactitude des informations montrent bien qu'Oscar Wilde était une figure parisienne. Mais on ne se rappelait de lui que son procès scandaleux'.[3053].

Arthur Symons relates this last Wilde period to the final wearing out of his æsthetic:

> In Wilde we see a great spectacular intellect, to which, at last, pity and terror have come in their own person, and no longer as puppets in a play. In its sight, human life has always been something created on the stage; a comedy in which it is the wise man's part to sit aside and laugh, but in which he may also disdainfully take part, as in a carnival, under any mask. The unbiased, scornful intellect, to which humanity has never been a burden, comes now unable to sit aside and laugh, and it has worn and looked behind so many masks that there is nothing left desirable in illusion.[3054]

This is a passage of notable insight, as well as being one that ties together so many of the themes I have been discussing. In that loss of creativity lies the answer to all the speculations about a Wilde, after the fashion of Melmoth the Wanderer, with a life prolonged to 1914, to 2000 or to 2004. Late in 1898 Max Beerbohm, who tried to say kindly things about Wilde when he could, wrote as if Oscar were already dead: 'Mr Jones has always seemed to me the only dramatist of any intellectual force [...] except in that too brief period when the genius of Mr Oscar Wilde shone, a comet, in the theatrical firmament.'[3055] Speculation about what might have been is futile, not because it belongs to the 'what if?' idea of history as a panorama of alternative anecdotes or even because one can dignify it with counterfactual theory, but because we have the example of Wilde himself – Wilde who had once said 'I think a man should invent his own myth'[3056] – unable to adapt, going downhill and dying as his century died.[3057] Even many-mirrored Paris could not for ever maintain a life that depended upon the maintenance of fictive relationships, of shimmering reflections, of the multiplicity of his own identity.

> Oscar Wilde came to our house [in London] now and again, but my mother could not bear him, especially his mannerism of standing on the hearthrug in front of the fire with his back to the company, and there he would pose until he got his huge heavy face in the cheval glass above, directly in line

with the cheval glass at the end of the room, and thus he would get rows and rows of himself.[3058]

Mirror, mirror on the wall? The actress Judith in old age wrote that it seemed to her that 'the little bent old woman I see in the mirror is but an imaginary vision, and that the brilliant intoxicating memory is the only reality'.[3059] 'Alas!' wrote Francis Carco of his life as a Montmartrois, 'with time, how many illusions have I left behind!'[3060]   Even that pragmatic Scot, Thomas Barclay, who quaintly reflected that 'my long connection with France has never diminished my admiration for her people', wrote of it as a land of 'illusions of friendship, illusions of kindness misunderstood, illusions of good purposes misrepresented, illusions of affection and sacrifice requited with ingratitude and treachery'.[3061] What illusions were left for Wilde?   Henri de Régnier, on the twenty-fifth anniversary of Wilde's death, wrote that 'Wilde had keen insight into his age. It is this clearsightedness which led him to create the character he portrayed so completely and with such outstanding success',[3062] but that age – the Yellow Nineties, the Beardsley Period – was over.

> 'Fin de siècle,' murmured Lord Henry.
> 'Fin du globe,' answered his hostess.
> 'I wish it were fin du globe,' said Dorian with a sigh. 'Life is a great disappointment.'

'It is not only the Queen who has disappeared,' Mary Waddington remarked on the 29th of December 1901, 'it is the century. England will enter on a new phase, but it must be different from the chapter that has just closed.'[3063]

~~~~~~~

One may invoke the list of those who attended the funeral of Mallarmé on 11th September 1898: Valéry, Heredia, Toulouse-Lautrec, Renoir, Vuillard, Rodin, Bonnard, Octave Mirbeau, the Natansons and de Régnier, just as Villiers de l'Isle Adam's funeral had been attended by Mallarmé, Huysmans, Alexis, Coquelin *cadet*, Leconte de Lisle, Hervieu, Lavedan, and Maurice Fleury. One may gain some understanding of Wilde's ruined position by contrasting these galaxies with Ellmann's list of those who called to offer condolences when Wilde was dead, noble as the gesture was: Raymond 'de Tailhade', Eugène Tardieu, Charles Sibleigh, Jehan Rictus, Robert d'Humières, George Sinclair and Henry Davray.[3064] Stuart Merrill was in bed with influenza. Gide was in Algeria: 'en vain me désolai-je que mon absence semblât diminuer encore le nombre si petit des amis durés fidèles'.[3065]

In this list, Raymond de Tailhade is a conflation of Laurent Tailhade and Raymond de la Tailhède. Jehan Rictus, whose real name was Gabriel Randon, wrote ballads and poems of Parisian low life, two volumes of which had been published.[3066] Wilde met him at the beginning of July 1899 at the Montmartre café where he recited (hitherto unidentified, but perhaps La Bosse, although Philippe Jullian says that Rictus 'opère tous les soirs aux Quatz'Arts'[3067]). Rictus actually lived rough and his songs reflect no humour – it was Rictus, not Bruant, who was the contemporary François Villon; it says much for Wilde that he made the gesture of sending him an inscribed copy of *The Ballad of Reading Gaol*.[3068] Davray is mentioned elsewhere, and Tardieu was the translator of *The Picture of Dorian Gray*. As for Sinclair and Sibleigh, the former is so obscure as almost to be unidentifiable. Katherine Lyon Mix makes two passing references to a Charles Sibley,[3069] and Ellmann calls what is presumably the same person 'Gibleigh [?]'. Vance Thompson refers simply to a Sibleigh as a friend of Wilde's whose visits dropped off towards the end, but who attended the funeral.[3070] My best guess is this is the writer whom Paul Henry encountered in Paris at this time, 'a man I knew slightly through seeing in cafés'.

> I told him how perplexed I was at some of the things I saw in the 'Caillebotte Collection'. He was a good talker and helped me clarify my ideas. He talked brilliantly and at great length about the growth and function of new ideas in painting and literature. He said that once art failed to be revolutionary it ceased to have any meaning for him, and he implored me, in my future, which was just opening, to break all traditions [...] This talk with Charles Sibley was the point of departure, so to speak, of the opening and enlarging of my mind at this time.[3071]

Whether this man could have a meeting of minds with Wilde is, however, questionable. Ellmann tells us that Tailhède and Rictus 'are said to have come every day to see Wilde in his last illness',[3072] but does not offer a suggestion as to who said so. Carlos Blacker, who had become completely estranged from Wilde in the course of the Dreyfus Case, arrived on the 1st December with flowers on behalf of Wilde's sons to go into the coffin.[3073] Blacker had arrived in Paris a few days before but had held back from calling.

The vicomte Robert d'Humières, not otherwise mentioned by Ellmann, is identified by Sir Rupert Hart-Davis only as a collaborator with Louis

Fabulet as a translator of Kipling (Wilde mentions dining with him in May 1898)[3074]: room might have been found for d'Humières' belief, at least as retold by Sherard, that Wilde had committed suicide because of his ill-treatment by Harris over *Mr & Mrs Daventry*.[3075] His connection with Wilde needs to be explored. Mauclair wrote of him 'non moins noble, non moins chevalesque était l'âme de Robert d'Humières,'[3076] and in paying tribute to Wilde d'Humières showed both qualities (the point is especially forceful as Mauclair himself once left the Café Weber because of his disapproval of Wilde's behaviour there with Lord Alfred Douglas[3077]). D'Humières was the director of the Théâtre des Arts — his *La Belle au Bois Dormant* has been mentioned. He also translated *The Second Mrs Tanqueray* into French. More to the point, he wrote a scenario for a stage work about Salomé. This version, *La Tragédie de Salomé* with music by Florent Schmitt, was the one danced by Loïe Fuller at the Théâtre des Arts in 1907, with Briand and Clemenceau in the audience, and by Karsavina in 1913.[3078] Stravinsky called it 'a work of genius'.[3079]

Another who called was Anna de Brémont, who as soon as she heard that Wilde was dying hurried to the hotel, which she noticed was painted 'a light "shrill green", Oscar's favourite colour'[3080], contrasting with the 'raw, sad-coloured November day'. She arrived only just too late, soon after two o'clock, and saw the dead man: 'The beauty of his youth had returned,' she reports, disposing of the tale that Wilde's body had exploded. She believed that the cause of death was 'a cerebral inflammation brought on by an attack of influenza'. Robert Ross told her that Wilde had been received into the Catholic Church four days previously.[3081]

While the good people trooped to the Hôtel d'Alsace, three minutes away at the Hôtel Seine John O'Leary, Stephen Mac Kenna and John Mac Bride were attending upon President Kruger. Which of those bold Fenian men spared a thought for Speranza's son? And what had happened to those friends like Bodley or O'Sullivan or Rowland Strong who still knew Wilde, or those whom Langlade calls the 'nouveaux fidèles', Jean de Tinan, Fénéon, Antoine, La Jeunesse?[3082] Instead, Langlade lists Harris, Blacker and Merrill, who were not there;[3083] and Léonard Sarluis, the gay Dutch painter who became 'un admirateur exuberant et unconditionnel' and whom Langlade transforms into Sar Luis?[3084]

Wilde was buried on 3rd December after a requiem mass at the Church of St Germain-des-Prés, where twelve of Bosie Douglas's ancestors are buried. Ten thousand people had followed Verlaine to his grave and Fauré

played the organ at the obsequies; but those who attended Wilde's are
curiously difficult to number or identify – a final tribute to Parisian
ambiguity. Vance Thompson says thirteen attended the mass, not counting
three reporters 'bored but benevolent'. Implying that he himself was
there, he names 'if memory serves' Davray, Ross, Turner, Sibleigh,
Tavera, Brunot, Jean de Mitty, La Tailhade and Charles Lucas, as well as a
mysterious veiled woman whom Thompson suggests without naming was
the wife of Stuart Merrill. Who Tavera and Brunot were are unexplained,
but Thompson says that all the men he names went on to the interment at
Bagneux. Gustave Le Rouge, who may or may not have been there, says
that 'only four or five' people followed the coffin to Bagneux, and names
Ross and J.B. de Bucé, the director of a small literary paper whom I have
not been able to identify further. De Brémont, who was there, says that
the mourners numbered about fifty, and Langlade gives the same number,
'une cinquantaine', at the funeral service, including Paul Fort, Jehan
Rictus, Laurence Housman, La Jeunesse and Sarluis. Ernest La Jeunesse
declares for thirteen mourners at Bagneux. Simon Callow's statement that
there were 'about twenty people' at Bagneux cannot be substantiated.
According to Gide, seven people followed Wilde's hearse. 'And even
they did not all accompany the funeral procession to the end.'[3085]

~~~~~~

The time now came for the tragedy to enter its final scene, well marked by
tragic irony. *Mr and Mrs Daventry* opened at the Royalty Theatre in
London on the 25th October 1900 for a three-month run and it would not
have been beyond Wilde to have wrung more money out of Frank Harris
than he actually did. Yeats and George Moore went to the first night.
Max Beerbohm gave it a favourable review in *The Saturday Review* on the
3rd November[3086] The Prince of Wales' attendance at the play would also
have meant much to Wilde, who, although he wrote not a single line of it,
regarded it as his own in the way that Whistler tended to regard his
paintings: gone out of his possession but still subject to his artistic control.
A circle was completed when the part of Gerald Ashurst was taken by
Gerald du Maurier, the son of Wilde's old foe, of whom it was said that
'his only obvious asset [as an actor] was that he knew how a gentleman
should behave in a club or drawing-room'.[3087]

Wilde, who had once burned with a soft, gem-like flame, in the end was
consumed by it, dying on the 30th November: transformation as
dissolution. That night Hennique's play *La Mort du duc d'Enghien* opened
at the Théâtre Antoine. Antoine records that 'ce titre, un peu lugubre pour

l'affiche, est modifié; desormais l'œuvre s'appelle *Monsieur le duc d'Enghien*, concession que je n'aime guère, mais souhaitée par l'auteur',[3088] but of the passing of Wilde, Antoine makes no mention. On the 7th of that month, the first revival of *Patience* had opened at the Savoy Theatre. Gilbert attended, but Sullivan was too ill, dying on the 22nd. He was buried in St Paul's Cathedral, the cortège passing the house where Richard D'Oyley Carte was also lying in his final illness. '*Patience* owed its existence to the notoriety of Oscar Wilde, and it repaid the debt by making him even more notorious'.[3089] Now death cancelled all the debts.

CONCLUSION

'My (secret) aim is to disconcert the reader to such a point that he goes
crazy.'– Gustave Flaubert.[3090]

'If Wilde were only alive to see you.'
– James Joyce: *Ulysses*.

IN his study of J.-K. Huysmans, James Laver offered his own classification of Paris. 'Paris is one; it has to be accepted as a single experience. It has the unity of a work of art.'[3091] Does this view of Paris survive my critique? I think not. Paris is experience fractured, diversified. It can be re-assembled in interlocking parts, but the parts are the points of light of the Divisionists, its ethos the destruction of the concept of a work of art's unity. Therefore in this work I have suggested that the City of Paris itself was unstable in its social and spatial forms, that its institutions shared and contributed to this, and that its inhabitants did likewise. This formed a broken elision between the City and its inhabitants, a discontinuum wherein new movements and new people consistently were given birth and necessarily were subsumed, and into which exiles of unstable personality and flawed histories could insert themselves and were in turn 'recycled'. In its fracturing of form, it anticipates the intellectual confusion that was to derive from Einstein, Heisenberg, Mandelbrot, Joyce, Picasso, Ionesco, Beckett and others whose work emphasises randomness and discontinuity: in this reading, *fin-de-siècle* Paris was not the capital of the nineteenth century but of the late twentieth. From this flowed the creativity of Paris, and its resilience, renewed after the trauma of the Siege and the Commune, and to be renewed again after that of the Great War in attenuated form, the conflict between the moral order and the artist as crisis by then transposed to lesser modes as the scenes for such struggle shifted elsewhere.

This provides a method of reading Paris through superimposed physical and metaphysical maps, which can be used to scrutinise in greater detail any of the themes and case studies that I have introduced.

Within this reading, Paris was for Oscar Wilde the essential other site, not merely a place for cultural tourism or tolerated exile, but the city in which his multiple and multiplied selves were in harmony with their surroundings, where he was no longer an outsider. In a world of floating signifiers, his paradoxes could take shape and sharpen. In his last phase, however, he was too weakened to avail himself of the symbiosis. As he himself recognised, he and the background could no longer co-exist. One of them had to go.

Notes

[1] Mona Caird: *The Daughters of Danaus.* London: Bliss, Sands & Foster 1894 p.302. Hereafter cited as Caird.

[2] Thomas Hardy: *Far From the Madding Crowd* (1874) Chapter XXII.

[3] G.H. Fleming: *Lady Colin Campbell, Victorian 'Sex Goddess'.* Adlestrop: Windrush Press 1989 p.215. Hereafter cited as Fleming 1989.

[4] George Moore: *Memoirs of My Dead Life.* London: William Heinemann 1906. Revised edition 1928 p.16. Hereafter cited as Moore/Memoirs.

[5] This is what Marie Bashkirtseff (or her translator) refers to rather oddly as 'the circular train'. Diary entry for 14th July 1880. Marie Bashkirtseff: *The Journal of Marie Bashkirtseff.* Translated by Mathilde Blind. London: Cassell & Co 1890. With a new Introduction by Rozsika Parker and Griselda Pollock. London: Virago 1985 p.413, hereafter cited as Bashkirtseff. Constructed under the Second Empire, the line was slighted in 1934.

[6] By 1890, only London had the greater population, at 2,362,000. Berlin, Vienna and Naples were the only European cities with more than 400,000 inhabitants; Liverpool, Glasgow and Manchester more than 300,000, Birmingham 200,000; Rome, Palermo, Milan and Turin 150,000; Lyons, Marseille, Bordeaux, Venice, Genoa, Messina, Florence, Bologna, Leeds, Sheffield, Edinburgh, Bristol and Bradford 100,000.

[7] Guy de Maupassant: 'A Picnic in the Country' in *The Mountain Inn and Other Stories*. A New Translation by H.N.P. Sloman. Harmondsworth: Penguin Books 1955 p.203, hereafter cited as Maupassant/Inn. The family are at La Grande Jatte, painted by Seurat.

[8] John F. MacDonald: *The Amazing City.* London: Grant Richards 1918 p.52; hereafter cited as Macdonald. The Gare St Lazare opened in 1842, replacing a smaller station in the place de l'Europe, from which the first train to leave Paris had travelled to St Germain, 26th August 1837. The present Gare St Lazare was completed in 1889.

[9] Guy de Maupassant: *Miss Harriet and Other Stories.* A New Translation by H.N.P. Sloman. Harmondsworth: Penguin Books 1951 p.43. Hereafter cited as Maupasssant/Harriet.

[10] There were twenty-two of these completed by 1914, but the boulevard Haussmann itself was not completed until January 1927 and had ended at the rue Taitbout. Generally, however, the title 'grand boulevard' is only applied to the boulevard des Capucines and the boulevard des Italiens.

[11] His authority was as Prefect of the Department of the Seine, that is all Paris outside the fortifications. Haussmann was born in the rue Faubourg le Roule, which was later buried under the boulevard Haussmann; the Department of the Seine has also vanished, having been divided in 1920.

[12] Philip Guedalla: *The Second Empire*. London: Hodder & Stoughton 1922. Uniform edition 1946 p.203. Hereafter cited as Guedalla.

[13] Minister for Public Works, whose statue by Dalou and Formigé (1899) is in the avenue Foch (then the avenue du Bois de Boulogne (1875-1930), but before that

(1870-1875) the avenue du Général Ulrich, and before that (1854-1870) the avenue de l'Impératrice). Instabilities of place names have their counterpart in similarities of personal names. Adolphe Alphand, for example, should not be confused with Alphonse Allais. Such similarities can be *faux amis*, involving a good deal of verifying of references. The avenue Henri Martin is named after the historian of that name, not the painter. Who can be sure that a reference one finds to the critic Roger Marx should not be ascribed to his son Claude Roger-Marx, the critic, or vice-versa? There are times when one is thankful for names like Aurélien-Marie Lugné-Poë or Tristan Klingsor – although these carry their own associations, as both are adopted names, as is 'Pierre Louÿs', taken by Pierre Louis presumably to distinguish himself from 'Pierre Louis', which was the pen name of Maurice Denis. If my insistence on saying throughout this work that so-and-so should not be confused with so-and-so becomes a little tiresome, this is because confusions do arise. Mary Ann Stevens twice asserts that Maurice Denis' *nom-de-plume* was Pierre Louÿs. Stevens 1990 pp.18,23, hereafter cited as Stevens 1990. Maurice Peyramaure in his biography of Sarah Bernhardt confuses the poet Auguste Barbier (1805-1882) with Jules Barbier (1825-1901), the dramatist and librettist of Gounod's *Faust*. To point this out is not merely to engage in scholarly one-upmanship, satisfying as that is. Such similarities of names help establish the interlocking system of referents, associations, and ideas, and beyond this merely biographical point lies the deeper semantic of verbal association.

[14] 7000 metres^3 were removed and used to raise the level of Champs de Mars. The avenue de l'Opéra was known as the avenue Napoléon until 1873.

[15] Harold P. Clunn: *The Face of Paris*. London: Spring Books n.d. p.9. Hereafter cited as Clunn.

[16] André de Fouquières: *Mon Paris et ses Parisiens*. Paris: Éditions Pierre Horay 1953 p.5; hereafter cited as Fouquières. Fouquières was the quintessential Parisian man-about-town. 'It was a proud moment when Monsieur André de Fouquières, the "Cotillon King" of a dozen *plages*, piloted me through Montmartre.' John Evelyn Wrench: *Uphill, The First Stage in a Strenuous Life*. London: Ivor Nicholson & Watson 1934 p.185. Hereafter cited as Wrench.

[17] Bonnie Blackburn and Leofranc Holford-Strevens: *The Oxford Companion to the Year*. Oxford: Oxford University Press 1999 pp.664-5. The metallic strip marking this meridian can still be seen in the church of Saint-Sulpice.

[18] Quoted by Lawrence Housman: *Echo de Paris*. London: Jonathan Cape 1923.

[19] Alexandre Dumas *fils*: *La Dame aux Camélias*. 1848. Translated by David Coward. Oxford: Oxford University Press 2000 p.6. Hereafter cited as Dumas.

[20] Carolyn Steedman: 'New Times, Mignon and Her Meanings', in John Stokes (ed.): *Fin-de-siècle / fin du Globe, Fears and Fantasies of the late Nineteenth Century*. Basingstoke: Macmillan 1992 p.102. Hereafter cited as Stokes.

[21] Arthur D. Trottenberg (ed.): *A Vision of Paris – The Photographs of Eugène Atget, the Words of Marcel Proust*. New York: Macmillan 1963 p.11. Hereafter cited as Trottenberg.

[22] Edmund Wilson: *Axel's Castle, A Study in the Imaginative Culture of 1870-1930*. New York: Charles Scribner's Sons 1940, hereafter cited as Wilson 1940;

Charles Rearick: *Pleasures of the Belle Époque, Entertainment and Festivity in Turn-of-the Century France*. New Haven & London: Yale University Press 1985 p.3, hereafter cited as Rearick; Raymond Rudorff: *Belle Époque – Paris in the 1890s*. London: Hamish Hamilton 1972, hereafter cited as Rudorff; Dominique Lejeune: *La France de la belle époque 1896-1914*. Paris: Armand Colin 1991.

[23] Serge Pacaud: *Chroniques mémorables de la Belle Epoque*. Paris: Éditions CPE 2004.

[24] Jean-Jacques Leveque: *Les années de la Belle Époque: 1890-1914*. Paris: ACR Edition 1991; Michel Winock: *La Belle Époque*. Paris: Perrin 2002.

[25] Jean-Paul Crespelle: *La Vie quotidienne à Montparnasse à la grande époque*. Paris: Hachette 1976. The Edwardian Age too is a slippery concept. While it is obviously centred on the reign of Edward VII (1900 to 1910), it is usual to prolong it to 1914, while its beginning can be pushed back at least as far as 1881 ('l'ére victorienne s'est terminée avant la mort de la reine en 1901, au moment de celle de Disraeli.' Delbourg-Delphis p.55.

[26] Malcolm Bradbury: Essay on Marcel Proust in Malcolm Bradbury: *The Modern World, Ten Great Writers*. London: Martin Secker & Warburg 1988 p.131. Even more strangely, Nancy Mitford makes the same slip. Nancy Mitford: *The Blessing*. London: Hamish Hamilton 1951. Harmondsworth: Penguin Books 1957 p.150.

[27] Leonard Merrick: *While Paris Laughed, being Pranks and Passions of the Poet Tricotin*. London: Hodder & Stoughton n.d p.46, hereafter cited as Merrick. Something may perhaps be made of Colette's making the arrival of eight o'clock noticed by having it chimed on an *English* wall clock. Colette: *Chéri*. London: The Folio Society 1963 p.91; hereafter cited as Colette 1963.

[28] Fitzwilliam Museum, Cambridge ref. PD.44-1986. Information about attribution from the accompanying label.

[29] Clive Bell: *Old Friends, Personal Recollections*. London: Chatto & Windus 1956 p.140. Hereafter cited as Bell.

[30] Carl van Vechten: *Sacred and Profane Memories*. London: Cassell and Co 1931 p.51, hereafter cited as Vechten. His novel *Peter Whiffle* (1922), like Henri Pierre Roché's *Jules et Jim* (Paris: Gallimard 1953), is set in the Paris of 1907. Roditi describes it as 'that clearance sale of all the curios that Carl Van Vechten had inherited from the "estates" of Wilde, Edgar Saltus and Ronald Firbank.' Edouard Roditi: *Oscar Wilde*. New York: New Dimensions 1947. New & enlarged edition 1986 p.51. Hereafter cited as Roditi.

[31] Some survived the Great War. The Bal au Printemps was on the ground floor of 74 rue Cardinal Lemoine when Ernest and Hadley Hemingway took a flat *au quatrième* in 1922.

[32] George du Maurier: *The Martian, A Novel*. London & New York: Harper Brothers 1898 p.5. Hereafter cited as Du Maurier/Martian. Du Maurier, brought up in Paris, later insisted, says David Lodge, on speaking French with a strong English accent. David Lodge: *Author, Author*. London: Secker & Warburg 2004 p.53. Hereafter cited as Lodge.

[33] Emile Zola: *Le Rêve*. Translated as *The Dream* by Eliza E.Chase. With eight illustrations by Georges Jeannot. London: Chatto & Windus 1893 p.44. The rue

des Deux-Ecus was the birthplace of Paul Poiret. Jump two generations and lost demesnes, empty houses and filled in lakes form the groundplan of *Le Grand Meaulnes*.

[34] Maurier/Martian p.437. Either this (the 'Mare d'Auteuil'), or another disappearing pool, is described by Shirley Fox as a 'little reedy pond, which has long since disappeared, but used to be in the broad expanse of grass lying between the gardens of the [...] Maison Erard (Château de la Muette) and the Grand Lac'. Shirley Fox: *An Artist's Reminiscences of Paris in the Eighties*. London: Mills & Boon 1909 p.11; hereafter cited as Fox. The Château de Muette was bought by Sébastien Erard in 1820 and was still in the family in the 1950s. There is a picture of it by John Cameron on the same page. Du Maurier searched in vain for his pool when in Paris with Oscar Deutsch of the British Museum in 1867. The area is described in Emile Zola: *Paris*. Translated with a preface by Ernest Alfred Vizetelly. London: Chatto & Windus 1898 pp.255 *seqq.*, hereafter cited as Zola/Paris.

[35] Robert Louis Stevenson and Lloyd Osbourne: *The Wrecker*. London: Cassell & Co 1892 p.293. Hereafter cited as Stevenson/Osbourne. There is justification for seeing these shifts of meaning lurking within words. 'The divine contagion that is religion is traceable in part to the viral quality of language itself [....] contaminating its putative referent with its peculiar and alien inflection. Oddly, the very word inflection seems to carry infection in its very utterance'. Ellis Hanson: *Decadence and Catholicism*. Cambridge, Mass: Harvard University Press 1997 p.21.

[36] This still exists as a night club.

[37] If this was the Hamley's of its day, one can fairly safely assume it was where Wilde bought toy soldiers for his son Cyril in March 1894. 'Au Bonheur des Dames' is translated by Brian Nelson as 'The Ladies' Paradise' which licences frequent references to it in the text simply as 'the Paradise', while the semantic connection with Paris is reinforced by the shop's exclusive silk called 'Paris-Paradise'. Emile Zola: *Au Bonheur des Dames*. 1883. Translated as 'The Ladies' Paradise' with an Introduction and Notes by Brian Nelson. World's Classics 1995; reissued as an Oxford World's Classics. Oxford: Oxford University Press 1998, hereafter cited as Zola/Bonheur. 'Le Paris des Dames' was at 8 rue de Rivoli.

[38] Chris Healy: *Confessions of a Journalist*. London: Chatto & Windus 1904 pp.50,48. Hereafter cited as Healy.

[39] Mrs Belloc Lowndes: *Where Love and Friendship Dwelt*. London: Macmillan 1943 p.160. Hereafter cited as Belloc 1943. Baudelaire's 'Les paradis artficiels', a pæan to hashish, first appeared in 1858; Wilde cites this title in *Pen, Pencil and Poison*.

[40] Zola Paris p.91. Long before, the phrase 'the modern Sodom' had been applied to Paris by Friedrich Schlegel. Pierre Denfert-Rochereau was the Governor of Belfort in the war of 1870.

[41] Quoted in Robert Baldick: *The Siege of Paris*. London 1964 p.26. This sentiment casts a long shadow: 'We shall always have Paris,' says Richard Blaine in the film *Casablanca* of 1942.

[42] James Laver: *The First Decadent, being the Strange Life of J.K. Huysmans*. London: Faber & Faber 1954 pp.47-8, hereafter cited as Laver.

[43] Emile Zola: *Le Débâcle*. Translated with an Introduction by Leonard Tancock. Harmondsworth: Penguin Books 1972 p.27. Hereafter cited as Zola/ Débâcle. This is developed in *Paris*, which suggests that a new débâcle was coming: 'The veil of disaster, which was submerging Paris, now seemed to grow thicker under the gusts of the icy north wind' and even the light has become 'gloomy, livid'. Zola Paris p.20. Many other passages reinforce this idea.

[44] Zola/L'Œuvre p.xxii. Hereafter cited as Zola/L'Œuvre.

[45] Arthur Symons: *From Toulouse-Lautrec to Rodin, with Some Personal Recollections*. London: John Lane The Bodley Head 1929 p.72. Hereafter cited as Symons.

[46] Will H. Low: *A Chronicle of Friendships 1873-1900*. London: Hodder & Stoughton 1908 p.viii. Hereafter cited as Low.

[47] Weber quoted by W. Scott Haine: *The World of the Paris Café – Sociability among the French Working Class 1789-1914*. Baltimore: Johns Hopkins University Press 1996 p.313, hereafter cited as Haine; .E.V. Lucas: *A Wanderer in Paris*. London: Methuen 1909 p.142, hereafter cited as Lucas. My italics. Lucas first visited Paris in 1889, when he encountered Mr Gladstone at the Hippodrome. He describes *A Wanderer in Paris* as 'a book about Paris written wholly from the outside, and only containing so much of that city and its citizens as a foreigner who has no French friends may observe on holiday visits' (p.i). In 1919 Methuen published a Volume of Wilde's reviews edited by Lucas under the title *A Critic in Pall Mall*, and Ellmann credits him with suggesting the title De Profundis to Robert Ross. Ellmann 1987 p.581.

[48] Sir Thomas Barclay: *Thirty Years Anglo-French Reminiscences 1876-1906*. London: Constable & Co 1914 p.334. Hereafter cited as Barclay.

[49] Trottenberg p.11.

[50] Discussions of Baudelaire in relationship to Wilde also surprise by their absence, the most substantial being Karen Tipper's 1975 thesis 'A Study of the Relationship between Charles Baudelaire and Oscar Wilde.' Walter W. Nelson: *Oscar Wilde's Allusions and References to Baudelaire, An Essay* (Lund: The Author 2001) should also be noted. I am most grateful to Dr Nelson for kindly sending me this pamphlet. The distinction between Baudelaire as theoretician of dandyism and as denouncer of the 'puerile utopia' of art for art's sake is clearly worth analysing with reference to Wilde.

[51] Leon Chai: *Æstheticism, The Religion of Art in Post-Romantic Literature*. New York: Columbia University Press 1990 p.ix.

[52] The reference may be to Jehan Valter, an assistant editor on *Le Gaulois*, for which Maupassant wrote, as Francis Steegmuller suggests. Francis Steegmuller: *Maupassant*. London: Collins 1950 p.201, hereafter cited as Steegmuller/ Maupassant. A man as well as informed as Maupassant would have been aware of John Walter, proprietor of *The Times*, who had spent some time in that newspaper's Paris office.

[53] A friend of and writer on most of the Impressionists, Duret was Manet's executor. His portrait by Whistler of 1883 ('Arrangement in Flesh Colour and Black') is in the Metropolitan Museum of Art, New York, ref.13.20; in turn he wrote a book *Histoire de J. McN. Whistler, et de son Œuvre* (Paris: Floury 1904).

[54] Theodore Reff: *Manet and Modern Paris*. Washington DC: National Gallery of Art and Chicago & London: University of Chicago Press 1982 p.13, hereafter cited as Reff. The remark of Berthe Morisot that Manet spent the war of 1870 changing his uniforms has a certain ring to it.

[55] John Augustus O'Shea: *Roundabout Recollections*. London: Ward & Downey 1892 Volume II p.248. O'Shea, who had lived in Paris throughout the Siege, was covering the World Fair, to which he devotes a number of anecdotal chapters. He stayed in a small hotel behind La Madeleine, but then as now that was an area of small hotels and his is not identifiable. In 1892 Grant Richards stayed at the Hôtel Tête, recommended by Phil May, 'in a quiet backwater near the Madeleine'. Grant Richards: *Memories of a Mis-Spent Youth*. London: William Heinemann 1932 p.172; hereafter cited as Richards.

[56] Robert Delevoye, Gilbert Lascault, Jean-Pierre Verheggen and Guy Cuvalier: *Felicien Rops*. Lausanne & Paris: Comos Monographies / Bibliothèque des Arts 1985 p.122, hereafter cited as Delevoye. Rops occupied about a dozen studios or apartments while in Paris.

[57] Sisley Huddleston: *In and About Paris*. London: Methuen 1927 p.1. Hereafter cited as Huddleston.

[58] Although written in 1924, A.E. Morgan's words of caution should not be forgotten: 'In speaking of modern drama I am deliberately giving a qualitative rather than a chronological meaning to the word modern. Modern dramas were written more than thirty years ago, in the sense they are akin to the modern drama of to-day. Contrariwise, Victorian dramas are still being composed'. Morgan instances H.A. Jones' *Saints and Sinners* of 1884 as an example of the first. A.E. Morgan: *Tendencies of Modern English Drama*. London: Constable 1924 p.2. Hereafter cited as Morgan 1924.

[59] Otherwise called in translation 'A Queer Night in Paris', a title that sits well with the master narrative of this book. This is not the Monsieur Saval of Maupassant's 'Regret'.

[60] Guy de Maupassant: *A Parisian Affair and Other Stories*. Translated with an Introduction and Notes by Siân Miles. London: Penguin Books 2004 pp.42-3. Hereafter cited as Maupasssant/Affair.

[61] Séverine was the name adopted by Caroline Rémy, from the heroine of Dumas' *La Princesse Georges* of 1872; confusingly Madame Severine was also the name adopted by Lilian Spencer, the actress wife of the poet and essayist Vance Thompson. The journalist Séverine was ably played by Florence Pernel in the film *Jaurès – Naissance d'un géant*, dir. Jean-Daniel Verhaeghe, 2005. Réjane's real name was Gabrielle Réju. In 1885 she married the actor manager Paul Porel. His real name was Désiré Paul Parfouru. Henri Becque wrote for her the leading part Clotilde in *La parisienne* in the same year. Porel succeeded Charles Rouvenat de La Rounat as Director of the Odéon, December 1884 to May 1892. Colette's Gigi

has a schoolfriend called Lydia Poret [*sic*], niece of an actress at the Comédie Française, presumably Réjane. Rachilde should not be confused with the actress Rachel, whose real name was Elizabeth Félix. Rachilde was married to the publisher Alfred Vallette. Vallette should not be confused with the painter Adolphe Vallette or the painter Adolphe Willette. Willette should not be confused with the writer Willy, who was married to Colette. Willy's real name was Henri Gauthier-Villars. As is well-known, the earliest novels of Colette were published over the name of Willy who passed them off as his. Subsequently, before dropping the name of Willy, Colette published over the name Colette Willy, not of course to be confused with Colette Baudoche, the heroine of a novel by Maurice Barrès. Barrès called Rachilde 'Madame Baudelaire'. Margaret Crosland, in her biography of Colette, declares that Rachilde 'is forgotten'. Margaret Crosland: *Colette, The Difficulty of Loving*. London: Peter Owen 1973 p.170, hereafter cited as Crosland. Colette's very feminine name was in fact her father's surname, her first names being Sidonie-Gabrielle. Sidonie was Colette's mother's name, Adèle-Sidonie *née* Landoy (1835-1912). Colette's mother was known as Sido, and the nickname of Colette's second husband, Henry de Jouvenel, was Sidi. There is a Musée Colette at St-Sauveur-en-Puisaye.

[62] Vincent O'Sullivan: *Aspects of Wilde*. London: Constable 1934 p.198. Hereafter cited as O'Sullivan 1934.

[63] Thomas Hardy: *The Return of the Native*. 1878. Macmillan Library edition 1949 pp.119,201. In *Far from the Madding Crowd*, Cainy Ball, newly come to Bath, is impressed by 'the grand glass windows to the shops'.

[64] Ralph Nevill: *The Gay Victorians*. London: Eveleigh Nash & Grayson 1930 pp.114-5.

[65] The Earl of Dunraven, K.P., C.M.G.: *Past Times and Pastimes*. London: Hodder & Stoughton n.d. [1922] Volume I p.223.

[66] F. Adolphus: *Some Memories of Paris*. Edinburgh: William Blackwood & Sons 1895 p.163. Hereafter cited as Adolphus.

[67] e.g. Emile Zola: *Un Page d'Amour*. Translated as *A Love Affair* by Jean Stewart. London: Elek 1957 pp.39,41.

[68] Delbourg-Delphis p.147.

[69] Quoted by Samuel M. Osgood: *French Royalism since 1870*. 2nd enlarged edition The Hague: Martinus Nijhoff 1970 p.1. The real name of Claretie (1840-1913) was Arsène-Arnaud, not Jules. The drawing of him by Beerbohm dates to 1910. Hereafter cited as Osgood.

[70] Quoted by Robert L. Herbert: *Impressionism, Art, Leisure and Parisian Society*. New Haven & London: Yale University Press 1988 p.294; hereafter cited as Herbert. This expands our notion of the *flâneur*, who as a purely literary construct is never found dozing and only moves on foot.

[71] Guy de Maupassant: *Bel-Ami*. Translated by Margaret Mauldon with an Introduction and Notes by Robert Lethbridge. Oxford: Oxford University Press 2001 p.xxvii. Hereafter cited as Maupassant/Bel Ami.

[72] It was published in March 1883.

[73] This was undertaken by the Compagnie Générale de Traction, headed by the Belgian financier Baron Empain, which for the purpose created the Compagnie du Chemin de Fer Métropolitan de Paris, a name which did not prove popular. The line opened on 19th July 1900, the Exposition Universelle being served by the Champs-Elysées station and a moving pavement from there.

[74] 'Les flâneurs qui se promènent entre la Madeleine et la rue Montmartre ne le prendront pas, c'est évident.' Of course in the upshot Paris has both underground and aerial railways.

[75] It is hotly discussed, however, by a group of men in Maupassant/Bel Ami p.25. The Institut itself is the subject of a painting by Raffaëlli dating to 1897. Musée Carnavalet, Paris, reproduced as plate 27 in Marianne Delafond & Caroline Genet-Bondeville: *Jean-François Raffaëlli.* Paris: Musée Marmotton-Monet 1999.

[76] Major-General Sir C.E. Callwell, K.C.B: *Stray Recollections.* 2 Volumes. London: Edwin Arnold 1923 p.292.

[77] Or in the phrase of a cousin of Baron Haussmann, 'capital of the entire world'. Mathilde Marchesi: *Marchesi and Music, Passages from the Life of a famous Singing Teacher.* With an introduction by Massenet. London & New York: Harper & Brothers 1897 p.266. Hereafter cited as Marchesi. See also Pascal Ory: 'Paris, capitale culturelle de la *fin-de-siècle.' 'Quarante-huit/Quatorze'* 1848-1914, Conférences du Musée d'Orsay 6. Paris: Réunion des Musées Nationaux 1994 pp.14-18.

[78] 2nd June 1896, quoted in Sir Alfred Lyall: *The Life of the Marquess of Dufferin and Ava.* London: John Murray 1905 Volume II p.351.

[79] 25 boulevard des Italiens; here too were the barber Henry and Potel et Chabot the caterers.

[80] Lord Lytton to Mr Justice Stephen 2nd January 1891. Lady Betty Balfour (ed.): *Personal and Literary Letters of Robert, First Earl of Lytton.* London: Longmans, Green & Co. 1906 Volume II p.412. Hereafter cited as Balfour.

[81] The origin is a lecture of 1818: 'Il faut de la religion pour la religion, de la morale pour la morale, comme de l'art. Le beau ne peut être la voie ni de l'utile, ni du bien, ni du saint; il ne conduit qu'à lui-même'. The date may be a surprise. Cousin also provides a different sort of link: his mistress Louise Colet was also the mistress of Flaubert.

[82] Henri Perruchot: *Manet.* Translated by Humphrey Ware. London: Perpetua Books 1962 p.111 has it that the term was invented by the critic Castagnary. Hereafter cited as Perruchot.

[83] Born in Athens, Moréas' original name was, according to most authorities, Iannis Pappadiamantopoulos, although Laurent Tailhade, his friend and collaborator, told his (Tailhade's) mother that 'Jean Moréas s'appelle, *en realité,* Iônnais Pappadiamontopoulos Moréas Lendik'. Laurent Tailhade: *Lettres à sa Mère 1874-1891.* Introduction, Notes et Index par Pierre Dufay. Paris: René van den Berg & Louis Enlart 1926 p.128. My italics; hereafter cited as Tailhade. Once a Symbolist champion and an early practitioner of *vers libre,* Moréas' post-symbolist return to classicism was perhaps better informed than that of his contemporaries.

[84] Maupassant claimed that he shared 'a similar philosophical tendency' to the Naturalists, rather than actually being one. Maupassant/Bel Ami p.xiv.

[85] Marvin Carlson: *The French Stage in the Nineteenth Century.* Metuchen, New Jersey: The Scarecrow Press 1972 p.186. Hereafter cited as Carlson.

[86] John A. Henderson: *The First Avant-Garde 1887-1894.* Sources of Modern French Theatre. London: George G. Harrap & Co 1971 p.10. Hereafter cited as Henderson.

[87] Founder of the *Revue wagnérienne* (1885) and first editor of the *Revue indépendante* (1886). One gathers from Roger Fry that he did not always keep his monologues in his interior (if by Desjardins, Fry means Dujardin): 'Desjardin [...] is a Desjardinist – Desjardin being the general form of which Christianity and Judaism are particular manifestations'. Roger Fry to Lady Fry 1st February 1892. Denys Sutton (ed.): *The Letters of Roger Fry.* London: Chatto & Windus 1972 p.151. Hereafter cited as Sutton/Fry.

[88] Editor, poet and theoretician of Symbolist drama. 'The clearest definition of the theory of *vers libre* is that formulated by Gustave Kahn, in the preface to the second edition of his *Palais Nomades,* in 1897, the first edition of which had appeared in 1887.' Enid Starkie: *From Gautier to Eliot – The Influence of France on English Literature 1851-1939.* London: Hutchinson 1960. New edition 1962 p.99. Hereafter cited as Starkie.

[89] *Joies* (Paris: Tress et Stock 1889) announced the overthrow of the Alexandrine. Edmund Wilson says nastily 'We are surprised to learn that Vielé-Griffin is still considered an important poet'. Wilson 1940 p.16. Although he lived till 1937, he is not mentioned in Arlen J. Hansen: *Expatriate Paris, A Cultural and Literary Guide to the Paris of the 1920s.* New York: Little, Brown & Co 1990; or in Nancy Green: *The Other Americans in Paris 1880-1941.* University of Chicago Press 2014, hereafter cited as Green.

[90] André Gide: *Correspondence avec Francis Vielé-Griffin 1891-1931.* Édition établie, présentée et annotée par Henry de Paysac. Lyon: Presses Universitaires 1986 p.79. Properly Marie-Anne Krysinska de Levila, Krysinska should not be confused with Mathilde Krzesinska, who married the Grand Duke Andrei, nor should Laforgue be confused with Marx' son-in-law Paul Lafargue, or the American painter (who studied in Paris) John La Farge, or the writer Léon-Paul Fargue.

[91] There is virtually no literature on Disdéri. See Sylvie Aubenas: 'Le petit monde de Disdéri. Un fonds d'atelier du Second Empire', *Études photographiques* n° 3, novembre 1997.

[92] Curiously, Richard Traubner, in his discussion of the origins, mentions neither Bovery nor *Madame Mascarille*, but does say that 'operetta is of French extraction'. Richard Traubner: *Operetta, A Theatrical History.* London: Victor Gollancz 1984 p.2; hereafter cited as Traubner. Traubner confines *opéra-bouffe* to the works of Offenbach, and suggests that the rest were *opéras-comiques* (*ibid.* p.x); he also distinguishes *opéra-bouffe* from *opera buffa.* Claude Terrasse (1867-1923) composed forty-six works, one of which was an *opéra-comique,* one an *opéra bouffe* and the rest *opérettes.* He also wrote the music for *Ubu Roi.* All this

is significant for the idea of shifting and dissolving identities in all aspects of Parisian cultural life.

[93] The play was revived in 1877 when Henry James saw it, and, with Réjane, in 1889 at the Théâtre de Vaudeville. Although the term rapidly came to be used for the world of prostitutes, or at best courtesans, Dumas intended a more restricted meaning, women who had 'fallen' from the *beau monde* after a sexual transgression. To Dumas *fils* may also go the credit of the first use of *féministe*, albeit as a term of disparagement (*L'Homme-Femme*, 1872). It is part of the atmosphere of Paris that I wish to convey to mention that Dumas *fils* was the illegitimate son of Alexandre Dumas *père*, and that although the world knows Dumas *père* as Alexandre Dumas, the beau monde would have known him as the marquis Davy de la Pailletière (1802-1870). One may also make some wordplay with Pailletière – a marquess of straw, perhaps?

[94] Julie Speedie: *Wonderful Sphinx, the Biography of Ada Leverson*. London: Virago 1993 p.93. What became of this Ms Speedie does not say. Was it *Paris, fin-de-siècle* by Ernest Blum and Raoul Toché with music by Massenet?

[95] Philippe Cruysmans: 'Vienne-Bruxelles et les origines du Jugendstil'. *L'Œil* no.387 October 1987. One may add that in Italy it was called Stile Liberty.

[96] J.K. Huysmans: *À Rebours.* With an introduction by P.G. Lloyd. London: The Fortune Press n.d. [1946]. p.12. Dr Lloyd suggests 'Against the Grain'; in his later translation, Robert Baldick preferred 'Against Nature'. J.-K. Huysmans: *Against Nature, A new translation of À Rebours.* Translated and introduced by Robert Baldick. Harmondsworth: Penguin 1959, hereafter cited as Huysmans/Baldick. Certainly the literal translation of 'à rebours' – backwards – conveys little meaning.

[97] Parkman visited Paris in 1844, wintered there in 1858/9, retired to Paris after a breakdown in 1869, and visited it again in 1880, 1881 and 1887.

[98] Charles Haight Farnham: *A Life of Francis Parkman.* London: Macmillan 1900 p.89. Hereafter cited as Farnham.

[99] This was a man called Wilson, whose son Daniel cast such darkness in the sale of honours scandal under President Grévy, the daughter of whom Wilson had married.

[100] Ralph Nevill: *Fancies, Fashions and Fads.* London Methuen 1913 p.128; hereafter cited as Nevill 1913. Nevill, a prolific and sturdy commentator on the manners and morals of his time, was also the translator of Courtilz de Sandoz' *Memoirs of d'Artagnan* (London: H.S. Nichols n.d.). He was the son of Lady Dorothy Nevill, briefly a *patronne* of Wilde's.

[101] Emile Zola: *Le ventre de Paris.* Translated as *Savage Paris* by David Hughes & Marie-Jacqueline Mason. Preface by Hugh Shelley. London: Elek Books 1955. p.15. Hereafter cited as Zola/Ventre.

[102] avenue de la Reine-Hortense until 1879.

[103] Zola/Paris p.75.

[104] Gabriela Zapolska: *Madame Zapolska et la scène parisienne.* Textes traduits du polonais par Lisbeth Virol et Arturo Nevill. Paris: Éditions de la Femme Presse 2004 p.23; hereafter cited as Zapolska. My translation from the French.

[105] Henry James: *The Ambassadors*. London: Methuen 1903; Harmondsworth: Penguin Books 1973 p.133. Hereafter cited as James/Ambassadors.

[106] Maupassant/Bel Ami p.9. These offices are in the boulevard Poissonnière.

[107] 'La liberté éclairant le monde'. The statue of Lafayette in Cours-la-Reine by Paul Wayland Bartlett, largely raised by subscription from school children in the United States, was the return gift. Archbishop Ireland of New York came to Paris for its unveiling, an interesting alignment of the Church's authority with a revolutionary hero. Bartholdi, whose workshop was in the rue Guyot, was famous for his monumental sculptures such as the 'Lion of Belfort', the Washington-Lafayette group in the place des Etats-Unis (1895) that Joseph Pulitzer presented to the city of Paris, the statue of Vercingetorix at Clermont-Ferrand or the statue of Rouget de l'Isle at Lons-le-Saulnier; which perhaps explains his obscurity to-day.

[108] Mary King Waddington: *Letters of a Diplomat's Wife 1883-1900*. London: Smith, Elder & Co 1903 p.189. Hereafter cited as Waddington 1903.

[109] Mrs. Burton Harrison: *Recollections Grave and Gay*. New York: Charles Scribner's Sons 1911 p.256. Hereafter cited as Harrison.

[110] Maupassant/Bel Ami p.242; Proust/Ombre p.183.

[111] Lord Frederic Hamilton: *The Days before Yesterday*. London: Hodder & Stoughton 1924, republished as *The Vanished World of Yesterday*. London: Hodder & Stoughton 1950 p.46. Hereafter cited as Hamilton.

[112] Anita Leslie: *Jennie, The Life of Lady Randolph Churchill*. London: Hutchinson & Co 1969 p.180.

[113] Born in Lausanne, he had moved to Paris in 1881.

[114] His name, significantly in terms of the work he produced, means a fête or street festival, but Verlaine nicknamed him Gavroche. He was friend of Toulouse-Lautrec, who painted his portrait.

[115] Lenard R. Berlanstein: *The Working People of Paris 1871-1914*. Baltimore & London: Johns Hopkins University Press 1984 p.8. Hereafter cited as Berlanstein.

[116] H.C.G. Matthew (ed.): *The Gladstone Diaries* Volume XIII. Oxford: The Clarendon Press. 1994 p.10. Diary entry for 26th February 1892. Hereafter cited as Matthew. Gladstone also stayed at the Bristol in December 1887 and September 1889. A less likely occasion at this fashionable hotel than a visit from Gladstone (less likely because the source is the extremely dubious account of Edward Trelawney Backhouse) was a mock marriage there in May 1893 between Wilde and 'a catamite in female attire from the gutter'. Neil McKenna: *The Secret Life of Oscar Wilde*. London: Century/Random House 2003 p.237, hereafter cited as McKenna.

[117] Zola/Ventre p.6.

[118] Born Arsène Housset, Houssaye was editor of *L'Artiste*, Director of the Théâtre Français and the Opéra, and a friend of Princess Mathilde Bonaparte. He gave *Madame Bovary* its first publication in the *Revue de Paris*. His novel *De Profundis* was published in 1852 under the name Alfred Mousse. Houssaye published four Volumes of memoirs in 1885 and a further two in 1891, totalling two thousand four hundred pages. A selection from what is undoubtedly a key guide (chiefly to the period 1850-1870) was published in London in 1887 as *Behind the Scenes at*

the *Comédie Française* in 1887. I have used the selection drawn from all six Volumes, Arsène Houssaye: *Man About Paris. The Confessions of Arsène Houssaye.* Translated and edited by Henry Knepler. London: Victor Gollancz 1972. Hereafter cited as Houssaye.

[119] Gautier's novel *Mademoiselle de Maupin* of 1835 (later illustrated by Beardsley) was one of the formative works of the art for art's sake movement. He should not be confused with the Théophile Gautier who owned a café in the place Clichy, a meeting place for Paul Adam and others; nor with Armand Gautier the painter and Communard whose portrait by Courbet is the Musée des Beaux Arts at Lille.

[120] Houssaye p.319.

[121] In 1908 champagne became the first 'appellation d'origine contrôlée', giving both a legal and a spatial definition to its evanescence. 'In former days it was only rarely that the ordinary Frenchman touched champagne [...] often alluded to contemptuously as "the vin des cocottes" or "le vin des Allemands".' Nevill 1913 p.119.

[122] Zola Paris p.76. A sidelight on this is suggested by Ralph Nevill, 'The decadence of Parisian cooking had already commenced in the early eighties'. Nevill 1913 p.112.

[123] Michael Hamburger: *The Truth of Poetry, Tensions in Modernist Poetry since Baudelaire.* London: Weidenfeld and Nicolson 1968. New edition London: Anvil Press1996 p.59. Hereafter cited as Hamburger.

[124] Mary King Waddington: *My First Years as a Frenchwoman 1876-1879.* London: Smith, Elder & Co 1914 p.87.

[125] Prince Chlodwig von Hohenlohe-Schillingsfürst: *Memoirs.* Edited by Friedrich Curtius for Prince Alexander von Hohenlohe-Schillingsfürst, translated from the first German edition and supervised by George W Chrystal, B.A. London: William Heinemann 1906 p.289. Hereafter cited as Hohenlohe. Diary entry for 13th May 1882. A *Vanity Fair* cartoon of Beust by 'Ape' appeared on 28th August 1875.

[126] Palmer was a partner in Huntley & Palmer, the great biscuit manufacturers of Reading, and a friend of the Wildes.

[127] Olive Schreiner to Edward Carpenter 21st March 1889. 'I am obliged to go to Paris on private business, but don't mention the fact to *anyone*'. Richard Rive (ed.) *Olive Schreiner Letters.* Volume I 1871-1899. Oxford: Oxford University Press 1988 p.152.

[128] The others being the Académie and the asylum.

[129] Eve Adam (ed.): *Mrs J. Comyns Carr's Reminiscences.* London: Hutchinson n.d. p142, hereafter cited as Carr. This essentially other site – that of death itself – was also frequented at one time by Delius.

[130] George du Maurier: *Peter Ibbetson.* London: James R. Osgood, McIlvaine & Co 1896 p.53, hereafter cited as du Maurier 1896; Ralph G. Martin: *Jennie, The Life of Randolph Churchill* Volume I: The Romantic Years 1854-1895. Englewood Cliffs: Prentice-Hall 1969 p.301. Churchill was supposed to be studying French in Paris.

[131] Wrench p.178. I have not been able to identify *La princesse de Flirts*: perhaps Capus' *Mademoiselle Flirt*?

[132] Anderson retired from the stage on her marriage in 1890. She makes no mention of Wilde in her 1896 Volume of banal recollections, which is not surprising, but none either in the second Volume she wrote forty years later.

[133] Mary Anderson: *A Few Memories*. London: Osgood, McIlvaine & Co 1896 p.23. Hereafter cited as Anderson 1896. Anderson had taken an apartment near the Bois de Boulogne for the winter.

[134] Robert Harborough Sherard: *Twenty Years in Paris, being Some Recollections of a Literary Life*. London: Hutchinson 1905 p.230. Hereafter cited as Sherard 1905.

[135] An elusive figure. According to Bayard, Jouy (1855-1896), the son of a butcher of Bercy, was a journalist attached to *La Tintamarre* and wrote songs for Paulus (Jean-Emile Bayard: *The Latin Quarter, Past and Present*. Translated by Percy Mitchell. London: T. Fisher Unwin 1926 p.58; hereafter cited as Bayard). Bayard also quotes Paul Bilhaud on Jouy, that he was 'sarcastic, bitter, terrible' (p.150). Velter adds that Jouy was an anarchist who worked the *Cri du Peuple* (André Velter (ed.): *Les Poètes du Chat Noir*. Paris: Gallimard 1996 p.494, hereafter cited as Velter). Segal says that Jouy (1855-1897) was himself a butcher (Harold B. Segal: *Turn of the Century Cabaret – Paris, Barcelona, Berlin, Munich, Vienna, Cracow, Moscow, St Petersburg, Zürich*. New York: Columbia University Press 1987 p.37, hereafter cited as Segal). Jouy's songs link a number of nodes: his 'Derrière l'Omnibus' with music by Louis Raynard was sung by Paulus at the Alcazar d'Été in 1883, while his 'Marche Lorraine' of 1892 became a Resistance song during the Second World War. One comes across the name again in Jouy-de-Josas, the village to which Jane Avril retired. 'Toile de Jouy' was itself a hybrid, being a mixture of cotton and linen.

[136] Healy p.19.

[137] Wilfred Chesson: 'A Reminiscence of 1898'. New York: *The Bookman* Volume 34 December 1911, hereafter cited as Chesson. Reprinted in E.H. Mikhail (ed.): *Oscar Wilde, Interviews and Recollections*. London: Macmillan 1979 Volume II p.377. Hereafter cited as Mikhail.

[138] Lucas p.54. By 1909 it had been closed to tourists.

[139] Edmund Gosse: *Father & Son, A Study of Two Temperaments*. Edited by Peter Abbs. London: Penguin Books 1983, reprinted 1986 p.82.

[140] Guy de Maupassant: *Mademoiselle Fifi and Other Stories*. Translated with an Introduction and notes by David Coward. Oxford: Oxford University Press 1993 p.103. Hereafter cited as Maupassant/Fifi.

[141] W Somerset Maugham (ed.): T*he Truth at Last, from Charles Hawtrey*. London: Thornton Butterworth 1924 p.169.

[142] Anon: *The Pretty Women of Paris* 1883. New edition with an introduction by Robin de Beaumont. Ware, Herts: Wordsworth Classics 1996 p.84. Hereafter cited as *Pretty Women*.

[143] Violet Hunt: *The Flurried Years*. London: Hurst & Blackett n.d. p. 14, hereafter cited as Hunt. Unfortunately Hunt says nothing of her life in Paris, or even how long was this compulsory exile (which would seem more like reward than punishment). Crackanthorpe I take to be Montague Crackanthorpe QC.

[144] Fleming 1989 pp.209-14.

[145] The daughter, Henriette Riel, later became 'a great friend' (the implication is lover) of the courtsean 'la fausse Cloménil'.

[146] Collected as Eustace Grenville-Murray: *High Life in France under the Republic, Social and Satirical Sketches in Paris and the Provinces*. London: Vizetelly & Co 1884. Hereafter cited as Grenville-Murray.

[147] This was Jeanne-Marie, born on 8th March 1881, and brought up in ignorance of her parentage. She subsequently married Sir Ian Malcolm, M.P.

[148] 'It is one of the saddest recollections of my life in Paris, how one day, walking from the place Jeanne d'Arc under the colonnade of the rue de Rivoli, I noticed coming towards me a tall, fine, soldierly-looking man with utter despair written on his manly countenance. His throat and lips were working as though to suppress cries of anguish and dismay. I said to myself "That man, like Dante, has suddenly been brought face to face with hell". An hour or two later I learned that an Englishman had shot himself in the Hôtel Regina.' Robert Harborough Sherard: *Bernard Shaw, Frank Harris and Oscar Wilde*. With a preface by Lord Alfred Douglas and an additional Chapter by Hugh Kingsmill. London: T. Werner Laurie 1937 p.181; hereafter cited as Sherard 1937. This was on 25th March 1903. The Hotel overlooks the place Jeanne d'Arc. A short way off, the statue of MacDonald's fellow clansman, Marshal MacDonald, duc de Tarentum, looks down from the façade of what is now the Musée des Arts décoratifs on to the rue de Rivoli. For the twentieth-first century stroller, these two military men are separated almost equidistantly by a branch of a cheap restaurant chain called MacDonald.

[149] Countess Marie Larisch: *My Past*. London: Eveleigh Nash 1913 p.91.

[150] A poet, prolific art critic, editor of the Mercure de France edition of the works of Laforgue, and close friend of Maeterlinck.

[151] The full measure of this cannot be realised unless one knows that Juliette Mealy (whose real name was Josserand) starred in *Madame Mephisto* at the Parisiana, that Severin was the stage name of a well-known mime artist as well as of the hero of von Sacher-Masoch's *Venus in Furs*, that Camille is an ambiguously gendered name, and that Mauclair is an oxymoron. Moreover, in *Le Petit Faust*, which ran for a year at the Olympia in 1900, Faust was played by a woman, Julia Seal, Mephistopheles by another, Jane Thylda, and Marguerite was played by the courtesan Emilienne d'Alençon. Mévisto was a member of Lugné-Poë's company.

[152] This was 'un pseudonyme phénoménal qui devait lui fournir une patine d'homme de lettres tout à fait convenable'. Eric Dussert: 'La main dans le sac' in *Le Matricule des Anges* Numéro 22 de janvier-mars 1998. Yet the name is hardly more inherently improbable than that of the Belgian socialist César de Paepe, for whom see Bernard Dandois: *Entre Marx et Bakounine: César de Paepe*. Paris: Maspéro 1974.

[153] Parisians were attached to the concept of *frou-frou*. Not only was it the name of the frequently performed play by Meilhac and Halévy (first performed at the Gymnase in October 1869), but also the name of a portrait of a woman by Georges Clairin shown at the Salon in May 1882. In 1895 a song of the name was written

by Blondeau et Montréal with music by Henri Chatau. A magazine *Frou-Frou* was started in 1900 and was the first twentieth century commercial venture based on the concept of the 'naughty nineties'.

[154] Marie-Sophie André, and Christophe Beaufils: *Papus, biographie, la belle époque d'occultisme*. Paris: Berg International 1995 p.92. Hereafter cited as André/Beaufils. One might also note the critic of the *Gil Blas* who wrote over the name Richard O'Mon Roy, the name of a Royalist song of the Restoration, and of course an evocation of the English King Richard Cœur de Lion. Francis Steegmuller lists him as one of a number of 'remembered and unremembered writers' who wrote successful short stories in the journals, spelling his name O'Monroy. The others so named are Paul Arène, Ludovic Halévy, Gyp de Martel, Coppée, de Banville, Armand Silvestre and Mendès. Steegmuller/Maupassant p.60.

[155] In his autobiographical novel *Sébastien Roch* of 1890.

[156] A. Ludovici: *An Artist's Life in London and Paris 1870-1925*. London: T. Fisher Unwin 1926 p.25. Hereafter cited as Ludovici.

[157] Steegmuller/Maupassant p.68.

[158] Julian Symons (ed.): *Essays and Biographies by A.J.A. Symons*. London: Cassell 1969 p.vii.

[159] A pupil of Bonnat, his dates are given in Grove as 1850-1936, in the Tate Gallery Catalogue as 1849-1935 and by Hartmann as 1849-1936. Véronique Hartmann (ed.): *Le Monde de Proust, Photographies de Paul Nadar*. Paris: Éditions CNMHS 1991 p.78, on which page there is also a photograph of him. Hereafter cited as Hartmann.
http://www.musexpo.com/aage/ag9901/beraud/index.html

[160] Patrick Offenstadt: 'Le Paris Disparu de Jean Béraud'. *L'Œil* n° 380, March 1987. Hereafter cited as Offenstadt.

[161] Fouquières p.93.

[162] Bertrand Lorquin: 'L'exigence de la réalité', in Dina Vierney and others: *Félix Vallotton*. Paris: Réunion des Musées Nationaux 1997 p.28. Hereafter cited as Vierney.

[163] There is a good account of Bonnat as a teacher in H. Barbara Weinberg: *The Lure of Paris – Nineteenth Century American Painters and their French Teachers*. New York: Abbeville Press 1991, Chapter VII: 'Bonnat'. Hereafter cited as Weinberg. One of Bonnat's pupils was Toulouse-Lautrec and each detested the work of the other. At one time Marie Bashkirtseff aspired to be taught by him, which demonstrates the gap between the followers of Bastien-Lepage and the new art. Bashkirtseff p.299. Diary entry for 22nd December 1879. Bonnat bequeathed his own collection to his native Bayonne; a self-portrait of 1905 is in the Galeries des Office, Florence (shown at the exhibition 'Moi! Autoportraits du XXe Siècle', Musée de Luxembourg, spring 2004.

[164] John Milner: *The Studios of Paris, the Capital of Art in the late Nineteenth Century*. New Haven & London: Yale University Press 1988 p.108. Hereafter cited as Milner.

[165] Paul Henry: *An Irish Portrait, the Autobiography of Paul Henry R.H.A.* London: B.T. Batsford Ltd 1951 p.13. Hereafter cited as Henry.

[166] Henry F.T. Rhodes: *Alphonse Bertillon, Father of Scientific Detection.* George G. Harrap 1956 p.94.

[167] Robert Louis Stevenson: *An Inland Voyage.* 1878. New Impression. London: Chatto & Windus 1908 p.112. Hereafter cited as Stevenson.

[168] Herbert Tint: *The Decline of French Patriotism.* London: Weidenfeld & Nicolson 1964 p.144. Hereafter cited as Tint.

[169] John House & Mary-Anne Stevens (edd.): *Post-Impressionism, Cross-Currents in European Painting.* London: Royal Academy of Arts in association with Weidenfeld & Nicolson 1979 p.25. Hereafter cited as House/Stevens.

[170] Paris: Mercure de France.

[171] Trottenberg. New York: Macmillan 1963 p.12. Publication 'passed unnoticed by the Paris newspapers'. Alan Sheridan: *André Gide, A Life in the Present.* London: Hamish Hamilton 1998 p.146, hereafter cited as Sheridan. 1,650 copies were printed, much higher than the print run for any of Wilde's works, but only 329 copies were ordered in its first year, of which 119 were returned. Wilde bought one of the other 210. No sales were recorded in the second year; by 1908 total sales had reached only 500. A similar amount was sold over the enxt seven years, and it was not until 1917 that sales started to be brisk. Enid Starkie was lucky to have found her copy, perhaps the only one in Dublin, or even Ireland.

[172] Poet and theorist of Symbolism.

[173] Symbolist poet and dramatist; dramatic critic of the *Mercure de France*; translator of Æschylus and Euripedes.

[174] I retain the diaresis (or 'tréma') in his name as this seems to be the general usage, although John Henderson has written that 'the second part of Lugné's name is often spelled Poë in reference works, though Poe seems more logical, in view of the connection with Edgar Allan Poe, and is the spelling adopted by Lugné's editors in his autobiography'. Henderson p.11n. Poë occurs on most of the Théâtre de l'Œuvre posters, and was also thus added to his own name by Colonel William Hutcheson. Although most agree that Poe, however spelled, was added by Lugné to his name, Latour and Claval suggest that Poë was his name and that he added the Lugné. Geneviève Latour and Florence Claval (edd.): *Les Théâtres de Paris.* Paris: Délégation de l'action artistique de la ville de Paris, Bibliothèque historique de la ville de Paris, Association de la Régie Théâtrale 1991 p.176, hereafter cited as Latour/Claval. It is less important here to establish the correct version than to suggest that this is another example of the instability of Parisian identities, and the system of nominal signification that was endemic.

[175] The Belgian Symbolist poet who moved to Paris. 'When Verhaeren began to write, Baudelaire was forgotten'. Stefan Zweig: *Emile Verhaeren.* 1910. Translated by Jethro Bithell. London: Constable & Co 1945 p.142. Hereafter cited as Zweig.

[176] A poet completely associated with French literature and literary Paris, but who was born in London (or in Hawai'i according to Catherine van Casselaer: *Lot's Wife, Lesbian Paris 1890-1914.* Liverpool: Janus Press 1986 p.63, hereafter cited

as Casselaer) of an English father and an American mother. Her real name was Pauline Tarn.

[177] A Symbolist and song writer who also experimented in colour photography, as may be seen in the Musée Charles Cros, rue Vivienne, 4, Paris 2. He was the younger brother of the sculptor Henri Cros. A biography of Cros was a project of Enid Starkie's that never eventuated. His popular song 'Le Hareng saur' was translated by George Moore.

[178] Robert Harborough Sherard: The Real Oscar Wilde, to be used as a supplement to, and in illustration of 'The Life of Oscar Wilde'. Philadelphia: David McKay 1911 p.36. Hereafter cited as Sherard 1911.

[179] Zola/L'Œuvre p.64.

[180] Jules Husson *dit* Champfleury, novelist and art historian; director of the Sèvres factory. His *Aventures de Mademoiselle Mariette* (1853) was a novel of the *vie de bohème*. Jerrold Siegel suggests that his real name was Jean Fleury. Jerrold Siegel: *Bohemian Paris – Culture, Politics and the Boundaries of Bourgeois Life 1830-1930*. New York: Viking 1986. Hereafter cited as Siegel.

[181] The painting is titled 'La Peinture Réaliste' (NGI 4220). In the 1850s Manet had been a disaffected pupil of Couture, whose atelier was on the corner of the rue de Laval and the rue Pigalle. Twenty years earlier Couture had been a pupil of Paul Delaroche. His very large canvas, 'Les Romains de la Décadence' of 1847 (Musée d'Orsay, ref. INV 3451) is an early expression of the creeping fear of decadence, and inevitably brings to mind Verlaine's line 'Je suis l'Empire à la fin de la décadence'.

[182] Carlson p.77.

[183] Throughout this text I have avoided using the term Post-Impressionism or Post-Impressionist, as in the period that I cover Impressionists and Post-Impressionists are not particularly to be distinguished as individuals, and it is their social interaction, rather than the form of their art, that is relevant. In any case, Post-Impressionism was not a contemporary term, and Impressionism was, although its use before 1874 is 'art-historical' - if one accepts its derivation from Monet's landscape of 1874, 'Un Impression'.

[184] Emile Zola: *L'Assommoir*. Translated by Leonard Tancock. London: Penguin Books 1970 p.94. This passage comes to take on a much deeper meaning when Zola writes the description of Paris burning at the end of *Le Débâcle*. Hereafter cited as Zola/Assommoir.

[185] Philippe Jullian: *Oscar Wilde*. Translated by Violet Wyndham. London: Constable 1969 Chapter XVII; hereafter cited as Jullian 1969. Jullian (1919-1977) was not really much more than a dilettante whose Wilde is in some sense himself. He has been taken too seriously by those who knew him. Ulick O'Connor, for example, says that Jullian wrote biography as he himself would have liked to do so, and that his *Oscar Wilde* was the first biography 'to make the point that Wilde conquered not only London society with his gift of language and conversation, but the Faubourg St Germain as well'. O'Connor p.201. This reflects Jullian's own position in the rue Jacob, not Wilde's. This would not matter but for the fact that O'Connor has also written on Wilde.

[186] Pascal Aquien: *Oscar Wilde, Les mots et les songes*. Croissy-Beaubourg: Éditions Aden 2006; Xavier Darcos: *Oscar a toujours raison*. Paris: Plon 2013.

[187] Richard Ellmann: *Oscar Wilde*. London: Hamish Hamilton 1987 Chapter XIII. Hereafter cited as Ellmann.

[188] There is a photograph of her in Hartmann p.22.

[189] Journalist and critic and originally included in Bel-Ami (Maupassant subsequently changed the name to Garin). Shirley Fox describes him as 'at once the terror and admiration of rising artists', with a way of making very cutting and bitter comments on work that displeased him. Fox p.280. He should not be confused with Theodor Wolf, Paris correspondent of the *Berliner Tagblat* 1893-1906.

[190] George D. Painter: *Marcel Proust, A Biography* Volume I. London: Chatto & Windus 1959 pp.169,170. Hereafter cited as Painter I.

[191] Painter I p.275.

[192] H.H. the Dayang Muda of Sarawak: *Relations and Complications*. With a foreword by T.P. O'Connor P.C., M.P. London: John Lane: the Bodley Head 1929 p.32. The Dyang Muda was Palmer's daughter Gladys, known as Diana but called 'Snowdrop' by Wilde; Lucien Daudet once hoped to marry her. Sir Walter Palmer, of Huntley & Palmer of Reading, helped Wilde 'both financially and morally' during his trial. This passage seems not to have been known to Painter.

[193] Daudet was once private secretary to the duc de Morny. His reputation as a writer was well-established by the end of the 1870s, but according to David Coward, he is now 'principally remembered as a humourist'. Maupassant/Fifi p.245. There is a Musée Daudet in Fontvieille. A photograph of Daudet is in Hartmann p.83.

[194] 'On the Index in both London and Paris' i.e. was socially inadmissible. This letter also reveals Gide's attitude to Lord Alfred Douglas. Jonathan Fryer: *André and Oscar – Gide, Wilde and the Gay Art of Living*. London: Constable 1997 pp.113,140. Hereafter cited as Fryer 1997.

[195] André Gide: *Oscar Wilde, A Study from the French*. Translated by Stuart Mason. Oxford: Holywell Press 1905 p.44. Frechtman prefers 'strange practices'. André Gide: *Oscar Wilde*. Translated by Bernard Frechtman; London: William Kimber 1951 p.26, hereafter cited as Gide/Frechtman.

[196] Max Beerbohm to William Rothenstein late August 1897. Mary M. Lago and Karl Beckson (edd.): *Max and Will, Max Beerbohm and William Rothenstein Their Friendship and Letters 1893-1945*. London: John Murray 1975 p.38.

[197] Massenet disliked his name Jules, once saying that it was enough to have been the pupil of [Ambroise] Thomas. Pierre Andrieu: *Souvenirs des frères Isola, cinquante ans de vie Parisienne*. Paris: Flammarion 1943 p.117. Hereafter cited as Andrieu.

[198] Gertrude Atherton: *Adventures of a Novelist*. London: Jonathan Cape 1922 p.155. Hereafter cited as Atherton.

[199] Richard Whiteing: *The Life of Paris*. London: John Murray 1900 p.217, hereafter cited as Whiteing 1900.

[200] Robert Harborough Sherard: *The Life of Oscar Wilde*. London: T. Werner Laurie 1906 p.160. Hereafter cited as Sherard 1906.

[201] Farnham p.101.

[202] Sherard 1906 p.419.

[203] Bauër, the dramatist and critic, was a natural son of Dumas *père* who in June 1895 published an article in *L'Echo de Paris* attacking the sentence on Wilde, and the hypocrisy and absurdity of the English in punishing homosexuals. He should not be confused with Henri Bauer, the teacher and friend of Gide, described as 'a "musardeur" with markedly Romantic tastes'. G.W Ireland: *André Gide, A study of his creative writings*. Oxford: Oxford University Press 1970 p.18. Wilde sent him copies of *The Ballad of Reading Gaol* and *An Ideal Husband*, but they do not seem to have established any social relations after Wilde's settling in Paris in 1898. His portrait by Gervex is in the Musée des Beaux Arts, Nice.

[204] Sherard 1937 p.289.

[205] Sherard 1937 pp.26,291,292,293. Sherard rarely let an opportunity slip to distance himself from the subject of homosexuality, which he regarded as unmentionable in English. Discussing Maupassant, he refers to that author's touching 'on horrible sexual aberrations common among the Arabs – *plaies autrement épouvantable*, as Zola would have described them' and says Maupassant in his final illness 'was heard to rave about things *non inter Christianos nominanda*'. 'Poor, clean-minded Guy!' he apostrophises. Robert Harborough Sherard: *The Life, Work and Evil Fate of Guy de Maupassant (Gentilhomme de lettres)*. London: T. Werner Laurie 1926 p.274. Hereafter cited as Sherard/ Maupassant.

[206] His ultimate chief was the Minister of the Interior. Four men held this office during Wilde's post-Berneval residence in Paris: Louis Barthou (29th April 1896 to 28th June 1898), Henri Brisson (28th June 1898 to 1st November 1898), Charles Dupuy (1st November 1898 to 22nd July 1899) and René Waldeck-Rousseau (22nd July 1899 to 7th June 1902).

[207] Alan Schom: *Emile Zola, A Biography*. New York: Henry Holt & Co 1987 p.109.

[208] Lieut.-Colonel H.C. Lowther, C.M.G., M.V.O., D.S.O.: *From Pillar to Post*. London: Edwin Arnold 1911 p.209-10. Hereafter cited as Lowther.

[209] Haine unnumbered page, perhaps p.xx.

[210] Siegel pp.222,291.

[211] Chris Healy asserts the contrary, but I think erroneously, and even he says that 'on the *grands boulevards* one can wander all night' in safety. Healy p.93.

[212] Louis Andrieux 1879-1881; Ernest Camescasse 1881-1885; Arthur Gragnon 1885-1887; Léon Bourgeois 1887-1888; Henri Lozé 1888-1893; Louis Lepine 1893-1897, Marie-Charles Blanc 1897-1899; Louis Lepine 1899-1913.

[213] This was a very senior post, with an official residence at 9 place Vendôme – one military governor, General Saussier, stood against Sadi Carnot in the election for president in December 1887. The Invalides became the headquarters of the Military Governor in January 1898. The involvement of the military in the governance of France was reinforced by the presence of a general in the Cabinet as

Minister of War, with all the implications this has for the affaires of Boulanger and Dreyfus. Between February 1871 and the end of 1900, of the twenty-seven men who held this office (frequently more than once) only two were civilians.

[214] There were also riots in the Latin Quarter on the 24th and 25th April 1881, renewed on the 26th and 27th May.

[215] T. Jefferson Coolidge: *An Autobiography*. Boston: Massachusetts Historical Society 1923 p.176. Hereafter cited as Coolidge.

[216] Macdonald p.255.

[217] Maupassant/Bel Ami pp.261-8.

[218] Louis Lépine: *Mes Souvenirs*. Paris: Payot 1929 p.170.

[219] Maupassant/Bel Ami p.76.In the original this is 'un municipal grave et immobile: "Voilà un agent qui a l'air solide."' The Reine Blanche is the scene of the first few minutes of the Jean Renoir film 'French Cancan' (1954), complete with policeman.

[220] Felix Moscheles: *Fragments of an Autobiography*. London: James Nisbet & Co. 1899 p.110. Hereafter cited as Moscheles.

[221] The Steinlen is reproduced in Phillip Dennis Cate (ed.): *The Graphic Arts and French Society 1871-1914*. New Brunswick & London: Rutgers University Press with the Jane Voorheese Zimmerli Art Museum 1988 fig. 211, hereafter cited as Cate; the Lambeaux is in the sale catalogue '19th Century Continental Pictures Watercolours and Drawings', London: Christie's 20th March 1992 plate 49.

[222] Lépine introduced the white baton for traffic control, and created the Seine river police, which in French has a somewhat ethereal name: la brigade fluviale. When he retired in 1913 he devoted himself to the study of economic and social conditions from his very rare perspective.

[223] http://www.insecula.com/contact/A006306.html

[224] Patricia Mainardi: *The End of the Salon – Art and State in the Early Third Republic*. Cambridge: Cambridge University Press 1993 p.xi. Hereafter cited as Mainardi.

[225] Harold Kurtz: *The Empress Eugénie 1826-1920*. London: Hamish Hamilton 1964 p.290, hereafter cited as Kurtz. 'Sauvez Rome et la France / Au nom du Sacré Cœur' was, says Kurtz, 'the Marseillaise of Ultramontanism', but the lines can be sung following the tune of 'L'internationale / Sera le genre humain'.

[226] François Loyer: *Paris Nineteenth Century, Architecture and Urbanism*. Translated by Charles Lyon Clark. New York: Abbeville Press 1988 pp.376,402. Hereafter cited as Loyer.

[227] Ian Small: 'Literary Radicalism in the British Fin de Siècle', in Stokes p.210.

[228] Octave Mirbeau: *The Diary of a Chambermaid*. Translated by Douglas Jarman and with an Introduction by Richard Ings. Sawtry, Cambs: Dedalus 1991; new edition 2001 p.190. Hereafter cited as Mirbeau.

[229] Miriam R. Levin: *Republican Art & Ideology in Nineteenth Century France*. Ann Arbor: University of Michigan Research Press 1986 p.110. Hereafter cited as Levin.

[230] Levin pp.215,217.

[231] William Rothenstein: *Men and Memories, Recollections*. London: Faber and Faber 1931 Volume I p.123. Hereafter cited as Rothenstein.

[232] Richard Harding Davis: *About Paris*. New York: Harper Brothers 1895 p.192. Hereafter cited as Harding Davis.

[233] Farnham p.35. My italics.

[234] Edmund Gosse: *Aspects and Impressions*. London: Cassell & Co 1922 p.97.

[235] Ann Thwaite: *Edmund Gosse, a Literary Landscape 1859-1928*. London: Secker & Warburg 1984 p.415. Hereafter cited as Thwaite.

[236] Irene Vanbrugh D.B.E.: *To Tell My Tale*. London: Hutchinson 1948 pp.16-17, hereafter cited as Vanbrugh. Six years later Vanbrugh played Gwendolen Fairfax in *The Importance of being Earnest*.

[237] Lord Newton: *Lord Lyons, A Record of British Diplomacy*. London: Edwin Arnold 1913 Volume II p.71. Hereafter cited as Newton.

[238] Du Maurier/Martian p.433.

[239] *Dombey & Son*, serialised in 1846-7, was published in 1848, 'the year of revolutions'. Mrs Skewton's association of 'gay' and 'Paris' suggests a usage already established. Mr Dombey might have had recourse to Francis Coghlan's *A visit to Paris; or, The stranger's guide to every object worthy notice in that gay city, with 20 valuable hints to Englishmen on their first arrival*, published London: Onwhyn 1830.

[240] Thus Arthur Richmond in 1894. Alan Schom may be mistaken when he says that Zola travelled Dover-Calais and St Lazare in June 1899. Schom p.216.

[241] Neil McKenna says that Wilde went to Paris with Fred Atkins by the 2.45 Club Train on 21st November 1892. McKenna p.211.
Passengers on Christmas Day 1891 included the newspapermen Ralph Blumenfeld, Harry Marks (founder of the *Financial News*), and Davison Dalziel (1854-1928). R.D. Blumenfeld: *R.D.B.'s Diary*. London: William Heinemann 1930 p.52, hereafter cited as Blumenfeld. Dalziel was founder of Dalziel's News Agency and came to be chairman of both the Pullman Car Company and the Compagnie Internationale des Wagon Lits. Another of the family, Henry Dalziel, was manager of a French newspaper company and married the proprietor.

[242] Oliver Wendell Holmes: *Our Hundred Days in Europe*. Boston & New York: Houghton. Miflin & Co 1895 p.161, hereafter cited as Holmes 1895. This was not the preferred route, and few references are made to it, e.g. Caird pp.298-9.

[243] Blumenfeld p.141.

[244] Kenneth McConkey has expressed this as 'an increased curiosity for the special prestige of Paris'. Kenneth McConkey: *Impressionism in Britain*. With an essay by Anita Gruetzner Robins. New Haven & London: Yale University Press 1995 p.13. Hereafter cited as McConkey.

[245] Rudyard Kipling: *Something of Myself*. Edited by Robert Hampson with an introduction by Richard Holmes. London: Penguin Books 1977 reprinted 1992 p.47. Hereafter cited as Kipling. Kipling's biographers are very slow to look at Kipling and France.

[246] Oddly miscalled Dagnan-Bouvert in Andrew Lycett: *Rudyard Kipling*. London: Weidenfeld & Nicolson 1999 pp.56,215. Hereafter cited as Lycett. The young André Gide preferred the nudes.

[247] Kipling p.168. The spluttering polysyllables, so rare in Kipling, I think indicate his uneasiness with so intellectual a proposition as that his unconscious should have nurtured a work grounded in a French painting and novel.

[248] Kipling p.75.

[249] Kipling p.47.

[250] There is a notebook in the Berg Library, New York, concerning this visit.

[251] Remy de Gourmont: 'La littérature anglaise en France', reprinted in Remy de Gourmont: *Promenades Littéraires*. Paris: Mercure de France. 17e édition 1919 p.327.

[252] . Lycett p.373.

[253] Frank McLynn: *Robert Louis Stevenson, A Biography*. London: Hutchinson 1993 p.96.

[254] Low p.58.

[255] Louise Hall Tharp: *Saint-Gaudens and the Gilded Era*. Boston: Little, Brown & Co 1969 p.111. Hereafter cited as Tharp.

[256] 'Victor Hugo's Romances', published in *Familiar Studies of Men and Books*.

[257] The trip recorded by Stevenson in *An Inland Voyage* 1878.

[258] Laura Alma-Tadema, *née* Epps, who married Tadema as his second wife in 1871. 'As she also signed her canvases L. Alma-Tadema her paintings are sometimes confused with those of her husband'. Jane Turner (ed.): *Grove Dictionary of Art*. London: Macmillan 1996, hereafter cited as Grove. Laurence and Laura's daughter was called Lawrence.

[259] 'X': *Myself Not Least*. London: Thornton Butterworth 1925 p.167. Hereafter cited as Vivian (the London Library identifies the author as H. Vivian). 'X' met Bouguereau while staying in Paris in the winter of 1894/5. Bouguereau was one of the most successful and now despised of academic painters. Even in 1907 Max Nordau could write 'The contempt of Bouguereau is the beginning of wisdom in art'. Max Nordau: *On Art and Artists*. Translated by W.F. Harvey, M.A. London: T. Fisher Unwin 1907 p.225, hereafter cited as Nordau.

[260] and of Liszt, Rubinstein, Sarasate and Joachim.

[261] Anderson 1936 pp.33-5.

[262] Jerusha Hull McCormack: *John Gray, Poet, Dandy and Priest*. Hanover NH: Brandeis University Press 1991 pp.22,23. Hereafter cited as McCormack.

[263] Léon Vanier published Verlaine, Moréas, Laforgue and Vielé-Griffin from his premises at 10 quai St Michel. Described as 'a rascal with a love of literature', he is said to have been the Parisian counterpart of the non-rascally John Lane. David Arkell: *Looking for Laforgue, An Informal Biography*. Manchester: Carcanet Press 1979 p.158, hereafter cited as Arkell. Matisse had a studio at the same address (n. 19).

[264] McCormack pp.27,31.

[265] De Régnier was the brother-in-law of Pierre Louÿs and the son-in-law of Heredia. Should not be confused with the actor Regnier, whose real name was François-Joseph-Philoclès Regnier de la Brière (d.1885)

[266] Brother-in-law of Lucien Muhlfeld, chiefly remembered as a social novelist.

[267] There was another American painter called Sargent, a contemporary at the École des Beaux Arts of Shirely Fox, who supposed him to be a cousin of John S.

[268] There is a photograph of Pozzi, Cottard in *À La Recherche*, in Hartmann p.63.

[269] Sherard 1905 p.415. Langlade adds that this was at La Coupole, which opened in 1927. Jacques de Langlade: *Oscar Wilde, ou la vérité des masques*. Préface de Robert Merle. Paris: Mazarine 1987 p.97. Hereafter cited as Langlade. I cannot substantiate Simon Callow's statement that Paul Bourget and Sargent were guests at Constance Wilde's 'very first dinner party' (4th June 1884). Simon Callow: *Oscar Wilde and His Circle*. London: National Portrait Gallery Publications 2000 p.49; hereafter cited as Callow

[270] In 1906 Sherard noted that it had already 'long since disappeared'. Sherard 1906 p.242.

[271] A journalist, head of the French Union of Decorative Arts, and a deputy who was the only Cabinet Minister for the Arts in this period (1881-1882), Antonin Proust was not related to Marcel Proust. He shot himself in 1905.

[272] It went in fact to the Luxembourg and it was not until 1907 that at the urging of Clemenceau it was accepted by the Louvre. Further urging got it hung – in 1917, when Clemenceau was Prime Minister.

[273] Tate Gallery, London.

[274] McConkey p.43.

[275] Jacques-Emile Blanche: *Portraits of a Lifetime – The Late Victorian Era, the Edwardian Pageant*. Translated and edited by Walter Clement. Introduction by Harley Granville Barker. London: J.M. Dent & Sons 1937 p.157. Hereafter cited as Blanche.

[276] Margot Asquith and Wilde had once been friends enough for Wilde to have dedicated 'The Star Child' to her, but as her husband had been Home Secretary when Wilde went to prison, one would hardly have expected a meeting. Nevertheless, both the Asquiths remained friends with Robbie Ross and Margot must have known that Wilde was in Paris. Ribblesdale by his marriage was on the fringes of 'the Souls', and was acquainted thus with Wilde, although one cannot accept that Wilde was, in Langlade's phrase 'pape des *Souls'*. Langlade p.65. 'A brilliant luncheon with Margot and her husband at 30 Upper Grosvenor Street . . . The other guests were Mrs Grenfell, Mrs Daisy White, Ribblesdale, his brother Reggie Lister, and Oscar Wilde, all immensely talkative, so that it was almost like a breakfast in France.' Wilfrid Scawen Blunt: *My Diaries, being a Personal Narrative of Events 1880-1914* Volume I: 1880-1900. New York: Alfred A. Knopf 1921 p.145. Diary entry for 17th July 1894. Hereafter cited as Blunt. An anecdote of an epigrammatic exchange over lunch at Lady de Grey's between Ribblesdale and Wilde is given in H. Montgomery Hyde: *Oscar Wilde. A Biography*. London: Eyre Methuen 1976 p.178 (hereafter cited as Hyde 1976),

giving Lady Randolph Churchill as the source. It is dated to 2nd March 1895 in Langlade pp.209,210.

[277] *née* Jeanne-Marguerite Seillière. The prince de Sagan is a component of Proust's duc de Guermantes, both being named Boson.

[278] There is a photograph of Mme de Pourtalès in Hartmann p.61.

[279] To remove to France for purposes of economy was so common as to be a trope of fiction. Thus the widowed and impoverished Lady Constantine contemplates Versailles, Boulogne and Dinan as refuges. Thomas Hardy: *Two on a Tower*. Edited by Sally Shuttleworth. London: Penguin 1999 p.76.

[280] His discreet memoirs make no mention of his social acquaintances, though one learns something of official life in Paris. Sir Charles Rivers Wilson G.C.M.G., C.B.: *Chapters from My Official Life*. Edited by Everilda McAlister. London: Edwin Arnold 1916, hereafter cited as Wilson.

[281] Wilson p.223.

[282] Low p.ix. It is an insight into the manners of the times that while Low refers to Stevenson as Louis, the letters of R.L.S. to Low begin 'My dear Low'.

[283] J.G.P. Delaney: *Charles Ricketts – A Biography*. Oxford: Clarendon Press 1990 p.144. Hereafter cited as Delaney.

[284] Michael Steinman: *Yeats's Heroic Figures: Wilde, Parnell, Swift, Casement*. London: Macmillan 1983 p.17.

[285] Middleton Jameson seems to have remained in Paris. The only record of his brother there is in the first weeks of November 1898, when he saw *Cyrano de Bergerac* and an unspecified play of Bernhardt's. Ian Colvin: *The Life of Jameson*. London: Edwin Arnold 1932. Vol. II p.182. This was probably *La Dame aux Camélias* at the Théâtre de la Renaissance, which opened on the 18th November.

[286] This is spelled Julien almost as often as it is Julian, perhaps because of confusion with the Académie Julien in Montréal and the Australian Académie Julien, later the Sydney Art School, founded in 1896 by Julian Ashton, after studying in London and Paris. Contemporaries may also have had the spellings to confuse them of the historian Camille Jullian (1859-1933) and Jean Jullien (1854-1919), associated with the Théâtre Libre. I have silently standardised the spelling of the Academy and its owner as Julian. As the Académie Julian expanded, further branches were opened. The surviving records are in the Archives Nationales, 63AS 1-9. One should also be wary: a contemporary reference to, say, meeting at Julian's, might in fact indicate the Restaurant Julian in the rue du Faubourg St Denis, or the patisserie of the same name in the rue de la Bourse. Shirley Fox calls the impasse des Panoramas the passage des Panoramas, which gives a significant shift in meaning. Fox p.34. The men's atelier at this time was in the rue d'Uzès, presided over by Bouguereau and Tony Robert-Fleury, although the latter gave instruction at the women's atelier as well – Marie Bashkirtseff was a protégée of his.

[287] Julian, originally from Marseilles, was an entrepreneur, not a professional artist, though he had exhibited at the Salon and Shirley Fox calls him 'by no means a bad draughtsman'. Fox p.52. Marie Bashkirtseff's *Journal* suggests that he was frequently able to offer sound advice to students.

[288] Adrian Frazier: *George Moore, 1852-1933*. New Haven & London: Yale University Press 2000 p.29. Hereafter cited as Frazier.

[289] Alexandra Lapierre: *Fanny Stevenson, Muse, Adventuress and Romantic Enigma*. Translated from the French by Carol Cosman. London: Fourth Estate 1995 pp.133,134. Hereafter cited as Lapierre.

[290] Bashkirtseff p.275. Diary entry for 4th October 1877. Names such as Delsarte, Wick, Bang, Nordtlander, Forschammer and Zilhardt, given by Bashkirtseff, indicate the range of nationalities. *Ibidem* p.295. Diary entry for 27th November 1877.

[291] Flo Garrard and Mabel Price lived off the avenue d'Iéna, where they arranged amateur theatricals with Nigel Playfair, who went on to an acting career. Kipling has their fictitious counterparts study under 'Kami of Paris', not in Paris but at Vitry-sur-Marne, a displacement which perhaps indicates his own unease about his relationship with Flo and hers with Mabel. The first part of Chapter XIII is set in Vitry. Dick Heldar is also described by Kipling as having studied under Kami for two years: could Kami be intended for Lami?

[292] Mann was a Scot who became an American. Beerbohm exhibited a drawing of him in 1913.

[293] Emanuel's *Illustrators of Montmartre* was published in 1904.

[294] A.S. Hartrick, R.W.S.: *A Painter's Pilgrimage through Fifty Years*. Cambridge: Cambridge University Press 1939 p.11. Hereafter cited as Hartrick.

[295] Anita Gruetzner: 'Great Britain and Ireland, Two Reactions to French Painting in Britain'. House/Stevens p.178.

[296] W Somerset Maugham: *Of Human Bondage*. London: William Heinemann 1915. Harmondsworth: Penguin Books 1963 p.176. Hereafter cited as Maugham. If Amitrano's is intended for the Académie Julian, it was not the latter's only appearance in fiction, for it is also 'Daveau's' in George Moore's story 'Mildred Lawson'.

[297] Opposite the Gare St Lazare. The Restaurant Mollard and the Restaurant de la Pépinière were also opposite the station, favoured by travellers, the latter especially by the English.

[298] Fox.

[299] Fox p.286.

[300] A pupil of Aimé Morot's in 1882, Joseph Crawhall should not be confused with Joseph Crowhall.

[301] At the Académie Julian 1899-1903.

[302] S.B. Kennedy: *Paul Henry*. New Haven & London: Yale University Press 2000 p.18. Hereafter cited as Kennedy 2000.

[303] Oscar Wilde to Eric Forbes-Robertson 5th May 1893. Holland & Hart-Davis p.563. He met Wilde by chance in Paris in late spring 1899 and kept in touch. Another brother, Ian who used the surname Robertson by itself, was married to a daughter of the critic Joseph Knight, who was hostile to Wilde. Ian was an actor in America, and Wilde called on him and his wife in New York in January 1882. They later returned to England, where Ian worked as a manager for Johnston. Mrs

Ian was a friend of Beardsley and saw something of him in Paris in 1897, while staying with an American called Mrs Meygenberg.

[304] Painter of historical and religious subjects. Should not be confused with his son Jean-Pierre Laurens (1875-1933), who painted a portrait of the wife of Charles Péguy, or with the Montpellier artist Jean-Joseph Laurens (1801-1890), or with J. Albert Laurens, the illustrator of the 1907 limited edition of *Monna Vanna* published in Paris by the Imprimerie Nationale, or with Paul-Albert Laurens, another painter son of Jean-Paul and André Gide's companion on Gide's first North African visit It was the fate of Jean-Paul Laurens to teach painting to artists who far outshone him. In 1906, Duncan Grant found that Laurens' work 'filled him with horror'. Frances Spalding: *Duncan Grant*. London: Chatto & Windus 1997 p.45; hererafter cited as Spalding 1997. There is a bust (1882) by Rodin in the Musée d'Orsay, ref. RF 1049.

[305] A.S. Hartrick R.W.S.: *A Painter's Pilgrimage through Fifty Years*. Cambridge: Cambridge University Press 1939 pp.10,13. Hereafter cited as Hartrick.

[306] Paris: Gallimard 1953 pp.7,61. The action of the novel begins 'vers 1907', but its depiction of Paris (and of course its film version by Truffaut) rings true for the pre-century years as well.

[307] D.S. MacColl: *Life, Work and Setting of Philip Wilson Steer*, with a full catalogue of paintings and list of watercolours in public collections by Alfred Yockney. London: Faber & Faber 1945 p.20. Hereafter cited as MacColl.

[308] This was run by two ladies, Miss Scott (who was English) and Madame Perret (who was Swiss).

[309] Stott studied art with Carolus-Duran (1880-1882) then with Alexandre Cabanel at the École des Beaux Arts, 1882-1884.

[310] Bruce Laughton: *Philip Wilson Steer 1860-1942*. Oxford: Clarendon Press 1971 p.3.

[311] The nature of the homage is itself ambivalent. The others depicted are Tonks, MacColl, and Hugh Lane, with George Moore reading his article on Manet. Gonzalez, hung rather high, seems to be aloof from the clannish gathering of middle-aged men.

[312] Shown at the Nicholson exhibition, Royal Academy, London 2004, as was Nicholson's Whistlerian 'Lady in Yellow' of 1893.

[313] According to McConkey, who describes him as 'a slick classicist by 1900', Arthur Hacker (1856-1919), a late Pre-Raphaelite, lived in a Parisian garret next to that of Stanhope Forbes. McConkey p.36.

[314] According to the label on one of his paintings in the Crawford Municipal Art Gallery, Cork, he 'appears to have died in the South of France', a suitably ephemeral end.

[315] Carmen Collell, Francis Greenacre, Gillian Hedley, and Maria Mendes-Murao: *An Anthology of Victorian and Edwardian paintings from the collection of the City Art Gallery, Bristol*. Swansea: The Glynn Vivian Art Gallery, Bristol: The City Art Gallery 1975 p.49. Gotch, like many of the English artists here mentioned, went on to Newlyn. See for example information relating to the exhibition 'Thomas Cooper Gotch (1854-1931)', Penlee House, Gallery, Penzance, 6th

Oscar Wilde's Elegant Republic   451

November 2004 – 8th January 2005. Curated by Alfred East Gallery, Kettering, to celebrate the 150th anniversary of Gotch's birth, this coincided with the launch of a book about the painter, *The Golden Dream*: *A Biography of Thomas Cooper Gotch* by Pamela Lomax (Sansom & Co).

[316] Here the model Zoe Piedefer, in Zola's *L'Œuvre*, lives at number 7; and Whistler had a studio in the 1850s at number 3. Zola liked this name, for there is a Laure de Piedéfer in *Nana*.

[317] Fox p.195. The rue Notre Dames des Champs was much favoured by artists, Whistler, Carolus-Duran, Gérôme, Camille Claudel and Saint-Gaudens all having studios there at one time or another.

[318] N.B. also 'Afternoon at Grez' by the American Edward Hamilton, 1889, in the Musée de l'Art américain, Giverny.

[319] Lapierre p.78.

[320] A.S. Hartrick, R.W.S.: *A Painter's Pilgrimage through Fifty Years*. Cambridge: Cambridge University Press 1939 p.154. Hereafter cited as Hartrick.

[321] Should not be confused with F.W. Sullivan, secretary of the Society of Illustrators.

[322] Hartrick p.156.

[323] Desmond McCarthy in Max Beerbohm (ed.): *Herbert Beerbohm Tree, Some Memories of Him and His Art*. London: Hutchinson n.d p.228. Hereafter cited as Beerbohm/Tree.

[324] Laurence des Cars: 'Burne-Jones and France' in Stephen Wildman and John Christian: *Edward Burne Jones, Victorian Artist-Dreamer*. New York: Metropolitan Museum of Art 1998 p.27.

[325] Carr. p.89.

[326] Alma, née Strettell, produced the Volume *Poems* by Emile Verhaeren, 'selected and rendered into English by Alma Strettell'. London: John Lane 1899. Laurence Harrison was known as Peter.

[327] Six of his works are in the Tate Gallery.

[328] Barry Duncan: *The St James' Theatre, Its Strange and Complete History*. London: Barrie & Rockcliff 1964 p.156, hereafter cited as Duncan 1964; Traubner p.22.

[329] Thwaite p.210.

[330] Thwaite p.20. Coppel is presumably a confusion of Coppée and Curel, though one cannot tell if the mistake is Gosse's or Thwaite's.

[331] Thwaite pp.207,208,355.

[332] Barlas was later bound over for firing a revolver near the House of Commons, and Wilde stood surety. Sherard, a friend of Barlas when both had been at New College, Oxford, suggested that this 'act of pure kindness' of Wilde's was 'prompted, I think, by his friendship for me'. Robert H Sherard: *Oscar Wilde, the Story of an Unhappy Friendship*. London: Greening & Co. 1905. Popular edition 1908 p.104; hereafter cited as Sherard 1908. Sherard also suggests that Wilde subsequently distanced himself from Barlas. *Ibidem* p.109. See also Sherard 1911 pp.112-4,121.

[333] Healy p.238.

[334] London: William Heinemann 1898.

[335] Painter I pp.123-4.

[336] Chesson p.379; Hart-Davis 1962 p.76n.

[337] J.A. Spender: *The Life of the Right Hon. Sir Henry Campbell-Bannerman G.C.B.* London: Hodder & Stoughton n.d. [1923?].

[338] General the Right Hon. Sir Henry Brackenbury, G.C.B., K.C.S.I: *Some Memories of My Spare Time*. Edinburgh & London: William Blackwood & Sons 1909 p.293.

[339] Lord Rathcreedan: *Memories of a Long Life*. London: John Lane, The Bodley Head 1931 pp.110,128. Hereafter cited as Rathcreedan.

[340] Lord Redesdale: *Further Memories*. With an Introduction by Edmund Gosse C.B. London: Hutchinson 1917 p.156. Hereafter cited as Redesdale.

[341] This should be a warning to illustrators and set designers who like to incorporate Klimt's 'Judith with the Head of Holofernes' into their imagery of Salomé. For the Vienna-Brussels link see Philippe Cruysmans: 'Vienne-Bruxelles et les origines du Jugendstil'. *L'Œil* no.387 October 1987.

[342] This may be further explored through Anne Pingeot & Robert Hoozee: *Paris-Bruxelles / Bruxelles-Paris, les relations artistiques entre la France et la Belgique 1848-1914*. Paris: Réunion des musées nationaux 1997.

[343] Oscar Wilde to A.D. Hansell 12th April 1897. Sir Rupert Hart-Davis (ed.): *More Letters of Oscar Wilde*. London: John Murray 1985 p.139, hereafter cited as Hart-Davis 1985; Holland & Hart-Davis p.800.

[344] Jean Paul Bouillon: *Art Nouveau 1870-1914*. London: Weidenfeld & Nicolson 1985 p.69. One must wryly admit that the chapter 'The Intellectual and Social Climate of Belgium in in the 1880s' in Roger van Gindertael's biography of Ensor is not the longest chapter in the book. Roger van Gindertael: *Ensor*. Translated from the French by Vivienne Menkes. London: Studio Vista 1975. Hereafter cited as Gindertael.

[345] Pretty Women p.79.

[346] Zweig 1945 p.16. Verhaeren, Maeterlinck, Georges Rodenbach and Charles van Lerberghe were all from Ghent, educated by the Jesuits at Ste Barbe, a 'somewhat squalid school. No music was taught, and modern French literature was forbidden.' Roger Nichols & Richard Langham Smith: *Claude Debussy, Pelléas et Mélisande*. Cambridge: Cambridge University Press 1989 p.8.

[347] Verhaeren lived at St Cloud, in 'a little flat full of pictures and books and usually of good friends as well' – Rodin, Maeterlinck, Mockel, Vielé-Griffin, Signac, Rysselberghe, Rilke, Rolland. Zweig p.249.
Stevens should not be confused with the English sculptor of the same name who had died in 1875, and whose statue is on the façade of the Victoria and Albert Museum. Stevens' portrait by Henri Gervex is in the Musée royale des Beaux Arts, Brussels.
Although Rysselberghe's name constantly occurs, biographical information has been surprisingly meagre, despite his friendship with Gide. In 1930, in a book on James Ensor, André Ridder dismissed van Rysselberghe as 'insignificant' (cited in Gindertael p.61). This has probably been put right by Russell T. Clement and

Annick Houze: *Neo-Impressionist Painters : A Sourcebook on Georges Seurat, Camille Pissarro, Paul Signac, Theo Van Rysselberghe, Henri Edmond Cross, Charles Angrand.* Greenwood Publishing Group 1999. I have not yet consulted this work. Rysselberghe designed the programme for Verhaeren's *La Cloître*, Théâtre de l'Œuvre, February 1900.

[348] Antoine read it to the end of the first act, and then telegraphed to Berrnstein to say that he would produce it. It opened on 12th June 1900. Antoine pp.152-3.

[349] Stevenson p.5.

[350] House/Stevens p.23.

[351] John Hetherington: *Melba, A Biography.* London: Faber & Faber London 1967 p.67. Hereafter cited as Hetherington.

[352] Henri Bataille's portrait 'Catulle Mendès en 1895' is in the Musée Carnavalet, ref. P.2509.

[353] O'Sullivan 1934 p.165.

[354] Sherard 1906 p.31. According to Sherard Sir William had learned German to while away train journeys in England in 1834, rather an early date for extended rail journeys.

[355] Anita Roittinger: *Oscar Wilde's Life as Reflected in his Correspondence and His Autobiography.* Salzburg: Institut für Anglistik und Amerikanistik, Universität Salzburg 1980 p.12. Hereafter cited as Roittinger.

[356] Painter and printmaker who lived in Paris 1881 to 1891, particularly associated with Signac. His real name was Henri-Edmond-Joseph Delacroix and he took the name Henri Cross to distinguish himself from Eugène Delacroix. Unfortunately this then led to confusion with the sculptor Henri Cros, who had dropped his first names of César-Isidore. Cross consequently added Edmond to his name. Cros was the elder brother of the Zutiste poet Charles Cros.

[357] Denis, who once said that 'art is a caricature,' was knocked down and killed by a lorry in avenue de l'Observatoire while dressed in the habit of the Third Order of Franciscans. His best memorial is the Musée Départemental Maurice Denis in St-Germain-en-Laye, in the house where he once lived.

[358] 'Alb' [Richard Whiteing]: *Living Paris and France, A Guide to the Manners, Monuments, Institutions and the Life of the People.* London: Ward & Downey; Paris: Galignani 1886 p.147, hereafter cited as Whiteing 1886. McConkey p.22. Lhermitte was Léon Lhermitte, a close friend of Zola's. Gabriel Weisberg: *The Realist Tradition, French Painting and Drawing 1830-1900.* Cleveland, Ohio: Cleveland Museum of Art and Indiana University Press 1980 p.17, hereafter cited as Weisberg. Stott (1857-1900) went to the École des Beaux Arts in 1879 and studied under Gérôme and Bonnat, as well as painting at Grez-sur Loing. There are sympathetic references to him in Fox.

[359] Paul Adam quoted by Bayard p.141.

[360] Paris 1892.

[361] Pierre Coustillas: *Gissing's Writings on Dickens.* London: Enitharmon Press, 1969, quoted at www.lang.nagoya-u.ac.jp/~matsuoka/GG-Coustillas-CD.html. The reference is to Wyzewa's review of Gissing's edition of Forster's *Life* of

Dickens, in the *Revue des Deux Mondes* 15th November 1902, which suggests that Wyzewa could read English with some fluency.

[362] Jose Shercliff: *Jane Avril of the Moulin Rouge*. London: Jarrolds 1952 p.89. Hereafter cited as Shercliff.

[363] Mary-Anne Stevens: 'Innovation and Consolidation in French Painting', in House/Stevens p.19.

[364] E. L. Duval: *Théodor de Wyzewa, Critic without a Country*. Geneva: Librairie Droz 1961, hereafter cited as Duval.

[365] Lemmen was in London in 1892, and painted views of the Thames.

.[366] Louis Lépine: *Mes Souvenirs*. Paris: Payot 1929 p.129.

[367] James/Ambassadors p.60.

[368] Nancy Mitford: *The Blessing*. London: Hamish Hamilton 1951. Harmondsworth: Penguin Books 1957 p.8. The quotation is not the only nod towards Wilde – Mitford also invents a house called Bunbury Court.

[369] Langlade p.163.

[370] The French Ambassador in London from 28th August 1874 to 8th May 1875 was the comte de Jarnac. Raymond de Nanjac is a character in Dumas' *Le Demi-Monde*. The comte de Nangis is a character in Chabrier's opera *Le Roi malgré lui*, performed in Paris on the 18th May 1887; the comtesse de Najac was a friend of Sarah Bernhardt. Wilde is here drawing upon an established system of nomenclature.

[371] Guy de Maupassant: 'The Wreck' in Maupassant/Inn p.104.

[372] Maupassant/Fifi pp.71, 74-5.

[373] Rudorff p.298.

[374] Delbourg-Delphis p.135. According to the same source (p.111), 'Pool', the leading London tailor of the day, also had a Paris establishment, behind the Madeleine, but 'Pool' is a mistake for Poole.

[375] Delbourg-Delphis pp.16, 35. Delbourg-Delphis distinguishes between Brummell and Wilde: 'Brummell n'est jamais amusant. Oscar Wilde l'est presque toujours'. *Ibidem* p.48. She dates French dandyism to the 'Muscadins' and 'Incroyables' of the Counter-Revolution following Thermidor, part of her hypothesis that dandyism is non-democratic. She also draws attention to the affectation of lisping (or omitting) the letter 'r' among the Muscadins, a fashion followed by the English 'heavy swells' of the 1860s and still current at the end of the century: General Sir Henry Brackenbury pronounced his name 'Bwackenbway' and General Sir John Brabazon was known as 'Bwab' to the end of his days, which did not come until 1922.

[376] Delbourg-Delphis p.52. This may also be applied to Wilde.

[377] Grenville-Murray p.48.

[378] *Pretty Women* pp.32, 44.

[379] Paul Léautaud: *Le Petit Ami*, with *In Memoriam* and *Amours*. Translated by Humphrey Hare as *The Child of Man*. London: The Bodley Head 1959 p.52.

[380] Healy p.91.

[381] G.M. Sugana: *The Complete Paintings of Toulouse-Lautrec*. London: Weidenfeld & Nicolson 1973 p.85. Hereafter cited as Sugana.

[382] Huysmans/Baldick p. 131.

[383] Davis 1895 p.18.

[384] The photograph of Willie Heath in Hartmann p.46 also shows a dandy as the sum of his appurtenances.

[385] Whiteing p.58.

[386] Sir Harold Hobson: *French Theatre since 1830*. London: John Calder 1978 p.67. Hereafter cited as Hobson.

[387] Barclay p.93.

[388] Maya Slater (ed.): *Three Pre-Surrealist Plays*. Oxford: Oxford University Press 1997 p.xlv. Bordure may be a scabrous descendant of Offenbach's fire-eating General Boum in *La Grande Duchesse de Gérolstein*, where a war is won with by covering the battlefield with champagne bottles that the enemy drink. Baron Puck and Baron Grog in the same operetta also anticipate Jarry's names.

[389] George Bernard Shaw: *Fanny's First Play*. 1911. London: Penguin Books 1987 p.139, hereafter cited as Shaw 1911. Shaw was not at this time a well-travelled man in any sense other than that he had exchanged a metropolitan life in Dublin for a provincial one in London.

[390] J.-K. Huysmans: *Là-Bas*. 1891. Translated by Keene Wallace, Paris 1928. New edition: New York: Dover Publications 1972 pp.125, 128. Hereafter cited as Huysmans 1891.

[391] e.g. at Avignon, Montpellier, Chalons, Grenoble, Arras. The Hôtel de la Plage et d'Angleterre at Royan in the Charente-Maritime dates to 1910.

[392] Fox p.142.

[393] Both Association Football and Rugby were introduced in this period. A soccer club called the White Rovers was formed in 1890, and goalposts brought over from England. The Standard Athletic Club had so many English members, however, that it became known as 'les Anglais de Paris'. Fox p.257.

[394] Delbourg-Delphis pp.179, 16; Langlade p.188.

[395] Marchesi p.223.

[396] Rathcreedan p.134.

[397] Merrick p.66.

[398] First performed 28th November 1905. First published 1907.

[399] Whiteing p.40. One must be careful with the very Parisian concept of chic, which Philippe Jullian says was a creation of French Jews. Philippe Jullian: *De Meyer*. Edited by Robert Brandau. London: Thames & Hudson 1976 p.9. 'Nobody had even heard of the word in English until I brought it in later, although it has been sadly overworked since.' Lucy Lady Duff Gordon: *Discretions and Indiscretions*. London: Jarrolds 1932 p.26, hereafter cited as Duff Gordon. The word was apparently much favoured by Tristan Corbière. Hamburger p.51.

[400] Merrick p.196.

[401] Nevill 1913 p.124.

[402] Levin p.86. But Proust also says, confusingly, 'what the English call a lavabo, and the French, in their misguided anglomania, water closets'. Proust/Grieve p.67.

[403] W Graham Robertson: *Time Was, being Reminiscences*. London: Hamish Hamilton 1931 p.124. Hereafter cited as Robertson.

---

[404] Obituary for Sir Charles Dilke in *Le Figaro* 28th January 1911, reprinted in Joseph Reinach: *Récits et Portraits Contemporains*. Paris: Librairie Félix Alcan 1915 p.201.

[405] 'John, the English coachman, never overturned, nor in a collision.' Mary King Waddington: *My First Years as a Frenchwoman 1876-1879*. London: Smith, Elder & Co 1914 p.27. Hereafter cited as Waddington.

[406] Barclay p.40.

[407] Jules Barbey d'Aurevilly: *Les Diaboliques*. Introduction by Peter Quennell (no translator named). London: Paul Elek 1947 p.133.

[408] This became the dominant *culte* under the Occupation, promoted by Vichy for its moral values, accepted by Collaborators as anti-English, and by the Resistance as anti-German.

[409] Newton Volume II; Lord Newton, P.C.: *Retrospection*. London: John Murray 1941 p.35.

[410] Roittinger p.285.

[411] E. Malcolm Carroll: *French Public Opinion and Foreign Affairs 1870-1914*. London: Frank Cass & Co 1936 p.198.

[412] March pp.322, 339, 346, 347, 354. March states the whole of the losses incurred by those loyal to the National Government amounted to 877 killed, 6454 wounded and 183 missing, while 'the lowest computation' for those killed on the side of the Commune was 6,500 with 'much reason to believe that this figure is greatly inaccurate. From ten to twenty thousand more probably covers the total.'

[413] Harry de Windt: *My Restless Life*. London: Grant Richards 1909 p.278.

[414] Jerome K. Jerome: *My Life and Times*. John Murray 1926. New edition 1983 p.208. Hereafter cited as Jerome.

[415] Baroness Orczy: *Links in the Chain of Life*. London: Hutchinson & Co 1947 p.86. Hereafter cited as Orczy.

[416] Giles St Aubyn: *Edward VII, Prince and King*. London: Collins 1979 p.269. Hereafter cited as St Aubyn.

[417] Anstey pp.206-9.

[418] 'The French appear to take every opportunity to show their affection for Russia'. Coolidge p.176. This was particularly à propos a fête held in aid of Russian famine relief. Coolidge recognised that Russomania was the political response to the Triple Alliance.

[419] Lord Newton, P.C.: *Retrospection*. London: John Murray 1941 p.15.

[420] On the corner of the rue Chauchet and the rue de Provence (on another corner of which 'Nana' had once had her beat).

[421] Debora L. Silverman: *Art Nouveau in fin-de-siècle France – Politics, Psychology and Style*. Berkeley: University of California Press 1989 p.278. I have not found the original of this incendiary remark. Jean Paul Bouillon translates it with an interestingly different emphasis: 'All this smacks of English viciousness, Jewish morphinomania or Belgian cunning, or an agreeable mixture of all three poisons'. Jean Paul Bouillon: *Art Nouveau 1870-1914*. London: Weidenfeld & Nicolson 1985 p.98. Hereafter cited as Bouillon.

[422] Martin Battersby: *The World of Art Nouveau*. London: Arlington Books 1968 p.125. Liberty's supplied the dresses Antonia and her companions wore in Dujardin's *La Légende d'Antonia*. Hereafter cited as Battersby.

[423] Elizabeth Ann Coleman: *The Opulent Era – Fashions of Worth, Doucet and Pingat*. London & New York: Thames & Hudson and the Brooklyn Museum 1989 p.162.

[424] Nordau p.217.

[425] There is a photograph of Hayman in Hartmann p.47.

[426] Philippe Jullian: *Edouard VII*. Paris: Hachette 1962. Translated as *Edward and the Edwardians* by Peter Dawnay. London: Sidgwick & Jackson 1967 p.102. Following fashion, de Pougy and other courtesans also set it. Colette, with perhaps satirical intent, says of the motor cars of 1899 that they were higher in their coachwork to take account of the wider hats worn that year by de Pougy and Otero. Colette: *Gigi*. Lausanne: La Guild du Livre 1944. New edition, with a foreword by Alain Brunet. Paris: Hachette n.d p.33. Hereafter cited as Colette 1944.

[427] Shercliff p.133. Colette 1944.

[428] Lautrec's poster for this depicts Avril, with three other dancers known as Cleopâtre, Eglantine and Gazelle.

[429] Relph's stage name was a reference to the Tichborne Claimant, the massive Arthur Orton. Little Tich was greatly admired in Paris, and his success at the Folies-Bergères in 1898 led to an engagement at the Théâtre des Mathurins, appearing with Marguerite Deval, appropriately described as 'chanteuse, danseuse, et fantaisiste'. Latour/Claval p.192. Was her name part of her fantasy? It seems to echo rather too closely Marguerite Gautier and Armand Duval.

[430] Lord Winterton: *Pre-War*. London: Macmillan 1932 p.68.

[431] Steven Moore Whiting: *Satie the Bohemian, from Cabaret to Concert Hall*. Oxford: Oxford University Press 1999 p.15.

[432] Sidney Dark: *Mainly About Other People*. London: Hodder & Stoughton 1925 p.105.

[433] Her real name was Alice Lapize (1889-1979), and she made her début in Paris in *The Belle of New York* (Moulin Rouge, 1903). Possibly better remembered for her title rôle as 'She' in the 1916 film of Rider Haggard's novel, she should not be confused with Gaby Deslys, whose real name was Gabrielle Caire (1881-1920).

[434] Sir Harry Preston: *Leaves from My Unwritten Diary*. London: Hutchinson & Co, n.d. p.294. For more on Fragson, see http://www.chanson.udenap.org/fiches_bio/fragson/fragson.htm.

[435] Midge Gillies: *Marie Lloyd, the One and Only*. London: Victor Gollancz 1999 p.185.

[436] Theodore Child: 'Dining in Paris', Chapter VIII (hereafter cited as Child) of Whiteing p.23; Maureen Borland: *Wilde's Devoted Friend – A Life of Robert Ross 1869-1918*. Oxford: Lennard Publishing 1990 p.144; Marcel Proust: *A l'ombre des jeunes filles en fleur*. 1919. Translated by James Grieve as *In the Shadow of Young Girls in Flower*. London: Penguin 2002 p.60. Wilde liked especially œufs Weber, poached egg in aspic on ham with tarragon leaves. Vyvyan Holland: *Time*

Remembered, After Père Lachaise. London: Gollancz 1966 p.13. Hereafter Holland 1966.

'Everyone in the arts had been there at one time or another.' Edward Lockspeiser: *Debussy, His Life and Mind.* Volume I 1862-1902. London: Cassell 1962 p.135; hereafter cited as Lockspeiser. Marcel Dietschy affirms that Debussy had 'nothing in common' with Proust. Marcel Dietschy: *La Passion de Claude Debussy.* Neuchâtel: Éditions de la Baconnière 1962. Translated and revised by William Ashbrook and Margaret G. Cobb as *A Portrait of Claude Debussy.* Oxford: Oxford University Press 1990 p.51. Hereafter cited as Dietschy.

Weber's was at 21 rue Royale and closed in 1961. Not unfittingly it is now a branch of Villeroy & Boch, the tableware retailers Henri Raczymow says that it became an English pub, 'taverne anglaise', and again not unfittingly it was known for its cocktail '333', 1/3 champagne, 1/3 gin, 1/3 orange juice, served in a long glass. Henri Raczymow: *Le Paris littéraire et intime de Marcel Proust.* Paris: Parigramme 1997.

'Richard Lucas', in the place de la Madeleine, was a quiet bourgeois restaurant, noted for its herrings.

[437] Lt.-Col. Newnham-Davis: *The Gourmet's Guide to Europe.* London: Grant Richards 1903. Third edition 1911 p.33. Hereafter cited as Newnham-Davis.

[438] Orczy p.89. The owners lived in the boulevard Diderot.

[439] Lord Lytton to Lady Salisbury 10th April 1888. Balfour Volume II p.345. The Paris 'Season' began in October or November and ended with the Grand Prix at Longchamp in July.

[440] Whiteing p.v.

[441] Arnold Bennett: *The Old Wives' Tale.* Introduced by Dudley Barker. London: Dent Everyman 1966 p.377. Hereafter cited as Bennett/Barker.

[442] Healy p.92.

[443] Healy pp.92-3.

[444] du Maurier p.54. My italics. The paradox of the 'New Bridge' being the oldest in Paris would not have been overlooked.

[445] One might begin with Charles Stuart Fielding: *The Illustrated English and American Paris-Guide.* Paris: Hachette July 1855. The postcard was both the scenic and the 'dirty'. The part the latter played in the construction of Paris as a haven of lubricity is important and lasted long. This all comes together with *Oo-la-la: a collection of the naughtiest cartoon post cards ever imported from gay Paree!!.* New York: Skyline Features Syndicate 1957.

[446] Quoted by Rearick p.vi. My italics.

[447] Starkie p.130.

[448] Kurtz p.217.

[449] Ralph Nevill: *Night Life, London and Paris Past and Present.* London: Cassell & Co 1926 p.271. Hereafter Nevill 1926.

[450] Healy p.237-8.

[451] Farnham p.86. This refers to Rome but crossing the Alps rarely implies a sea-change.

[452] Peter de Polnay: *Aspects of Paris*. London: W.H. Allen 1968 p.229, hereafter cited as Polnay. 'All Englishmen are supposed in France to suffer from a mysterious disease known as "le spleen". Lord Frederic Hamilton: *Here, There and Everywhere*. London: Hodder & Stoughton n.d. p.59.

[453] Davis 1895 p.27.

[454] Jean Méral: *Paris dans le littérature américaine*. Translated as *Paris in American Literature* by Laurette Long. Chapel Hill & London: University of North Caroline Press 1989 pp.47-8. Hereafter cited as Méral.

[455] Healy p.206.

[456] Sheldon M. Novick: *Henry James, the Young Master*. New York: Random House 1996 p.316. Hereafter cited as Novick.

[457] Tony Allen: *An American in Paris*. London: Linkline Publications/Bison Books 1977 p.9. Hereafter cited as Allen.

[458] Or so says Bodley's biographer, Shane Leslie. The Castle Leslie school of historiography, although always entertaining, has also tended to play fast and loose with facts and figures: Thiers had died in 1877, Gambetta in 1882.

[459] Shane Leslie: *Memoir of John Edward Courtenay Bodley*. London: Jonathan Cape 1930. Hereafter cited as Leslie.

[460] John Edward Courtenay Bodley: *France*. London: Macmillan 1898; new edition revised 1899.

[461] John Lane's wife was an American, Anna or Amie Eichberg, veuve King. Swiss born, she spent time in Paris during her widowhood. In 1886 or 1887 Lane discussed with Robert Sherard (suitably, over lunch at the Café Royal) the possibility of a book on Maupassant. This eventually surfaced as Sherard/Maupassant.

[462] Or almost of his own contriving: Richard and Gallienne were his own. Wilde is sometimes credited with the additional 'Le', but in fact Gallienne added it to his name before he left his native Liverpool. It is true that Wilde, never one to waste a good thing, suggested to Althea Gyles she should re-work her surname as Le Gys.

[463] Richard Whittington-Egan and Geoffrey Smerdon: *The Quest of the Golden Boy, the Life and Letters of Richard Le Gallienne*. London: The Unicorn Press 1960 pp.262-3. Hereafter cited as Whittington-Egan.

[464] London: John Lane 1895.

[465] 13 rue des Beaux-Arts.

[466] 'An English Officer': *Society Recollections in Paris and Vienna 1879-1904*. London: John Long 1907 p.35. Hereafter cited as English Officer.

[467] Among whom may be include Thackeray's stepfather, Major Carmichael-Smyth, on whom Colonel Newcome was based.

[468] He is omitted from the 1999 edition of Burke's *Peerage*.
— JACK: I have carefully preserved the Court Guides of the period. They are open to your inspection, Lady Bracknell.
— LADY BRACKNELL: [Grimly.] I have known strange errors in that publication.

[469] Tharp p.132.

[470] Lord Howard of Penrith: *Theatre of Life* Volume I: Life seen from the Pit 1863-1905. London: Hodder & Stoughton 1935 p.41. Hereafter cited as Howard.

[471] 'Almost a separate class in France [...] very earnest, religious, honourable, narrow-minded people. They give a great deal in charity and good works of all kinds. In Paris the Protestant coterie is very rich [...] They live among themselves and never intermarry'. Waddington 1914 p.263. .

[472] Barclay pp.92,93.

[473] Newton Volume II p.201.

[474] Newton Volume II p.314.

[475] Wilson p.60.

[476] Newton Volume II p.201.

[477] Andrieu p.40.

[478] Colm Tóibín: *The Master*. London: Picador 2004 p.5. Hereafter cited as Tóibín.

[479] Gloria Groom: *Edouard Vuillard, Painter Decorator. Patrons and Projects 1892-1912.* New Haven: Yale University Press 1993 p.8; herafter cited as Groom. Dr Groom also notes that Vuillard was 'an intensely private person' who 'was unable to accept unreservedly the Nabis' theoretical excesses' (pp.5,8). Vuillard's sister married Ker-Xavier Roussel.

[480] Leon Chai: *Æstheticism, The Religion of Art in Post-Romantic Literature.* New York: Columbia University Press 1990 p.112.

[481] Alphonse Daudet: *Twenty Years of Paris and of My Literary Life.* Translated by Laura Ensor. London: George Routledge & Sons 1888 p.324. Hereafter cited as Daudet. Lady Bracknell's reference to Lord Bracknell's health seems to echo this sentence.

[482] Daudet p.339. The restaurant in the place de l'Opéra-Comique was called Byron. Huysmans, on the fringe of this group, listed Flaubert, Goncourt and Zola as the three masters who, after Baudelaire, were most read by des Esseintes. J.-K. Husymans: *À Rebours.* London: The Fortune Press n.d. [1946] pp.150-1.

[483] Not of course to be confused with the group of designers of the 1890s also called Les Cinq: Félix Aubert, Alexandre Charpentier, Jean Dampt, Henri Nocq and Charles Plumet. These became 'Les Six' when Tony Selmersheim joined them. Battersby *passim.* Even this grouping is malleable. Jean Paul Bouillon substitutes the name of Étienne Moreau-Nélaton (1859-1927) for that of Henri Nocq, and says that Selmersheim was one of the original five with Plumet making up the sixth. Bouillon *passim.* Nor should these Six be confused with 'Les Six' – Auric, Poulenc, Cocteau, Milhaud, Honegger and Geneviève Taillefer; although properly speaking, Cocteau was their spokesman rather than one of them. In his painting 'Les Six' of 1924, Jacque-Emile Blanche included Marcelle Meyer-Bertin and Jean Wiener (Musée des Beaux-Arts, Rouen), while in a photograph in the Satie Museum in Harfleur, Louis Durez replaces Cocteau. Once again, identities are confused, multiplied.

[484] Daudet p.339. It is clear that Daudet intended a description of something rather more than the plats du jour, but these men were certainly gourmands. Flaubert knew what he was doing: in *L'Education sentimentale* he sets a short scene in the

restaurant Les Trois Frères Provençaux, 'Le repas fut long, délicat'. When Turgenev sent Flaubert a salmon and a pot of caviare, the latter addressed him as 'St Vincent de Paul des Comestibles' and said that he could eat it like jam. Steegmuller/Flaubert p.264, hereafter cited as Steegmuller/Flaubert. Zola reveals his own gastronomic passions in *Pot-Bouille*, and attracted the nickname 'le ventre de Paris'. Emile Zola: *Pot-Bouille*. Translated as *Pot Luck* with an introduction and notes by Brian Nelson. Oxford: Oxford University Press 1999 p.185. Hereafter cited as Zola/Pot-Bouille. For these dinners, see also Schom pp.102-3, where he says that Emile de Girardin tried to join them, but was blackballed by the others.

[485] Gustave Flaubert: *Trois Contes*. Paris: Charpentier 1877. Translated as *Three Tales* with an Introduction by Robert Baldick. London: Penguin Books 1961 p.117.

[486] Maupassant listed a number of other regulars: Taine, Frédéric Baudry, Georges Pouchet, Claudius Popelin, Burty, Charpentier (the publisher, not the composer), Emile Bergerat, Heredia, Huysmans, Céard, Hennique, Gustave Toudouze, Cladel'the obscure and refined stylist' and, inevitably, Mendès 'with his face of a sensual and seductive Christ'. Henry James was also a visitor. Steegmuller/Flaubert p.224. Robert Sherard compared the prelapsarian Wilde to Vitellius

[487] A group of five friends also form a sort of club in Maupassant's story 'Mouche'.

[488] Anatole France: *On Life and Letters*. First series. Translated by A.W Evans. London: John Lane The Bodley Head 1910. New edition 1924 p.197. Hereafter cited as France. The presence of Bonnetain in this group is especially remarkable, for in 1883 he had published a novel about what Robert Lethbridge rather primly calls 'onanism', *Charlot s'amuse*. Maupassant/Bel Ami p.299. Alan Schom, who says that the five were friends or followers not of Zola but of Daudet and Goncourt, gives Guiche a final 's'. Margueritte eventually apologised in decent terms. Schom pp.118, 128.

[489] Kathleen Adler and Tamar Garb: *Berthe Morisot*. Oxford: Phaidon 1987 p.33. Hereafter cited as Adler, Garb.

[490] Edward Lucie-Smith: *Fantin-Latour*. Oxford: Phaidon 1977 p.16.

[491] Adler, Garb p.37; Anne Higonnet: *Berthe Morisot, A Biography*. London: Collins 1990 p.181; hereafter cited as Higonnet. Mauclair's *Puvis de Chavannes* was published Paris: Plon n.d.

[492] Now in the Courtauld Institute, London.

[493] Rollo Myers: *Emmanuel Chabrier and His Circle*. London: J.M. Dent & Sons 1969 pp.5,7. Hereafter cited as Myers. Myers refers the reader to Roger Delage: 'Chabrier et ses amis Impressionists', *L'Œil*, December 1963. Chabrier's Monet, 'Rue St Denis, Festivities of 30th June 1878' is now in the Musée des Beaux-Arts, Rouen. Paul Vidal also noted Debussy's 'marked predeliction' for Verlaine. Roger Nichols (ed.) *Debussy Remembered*. London: Faber & Faber 1997 p.8. Hereafter cited as Nichols 1997.

[494] Myers p.28.

[495] One thinks also of Flaubert's name for Thiers, Pignouf I. *L'Étoile* was staged by the Glimmerglass Opera Company, Cooperstown, NY, in their 2001 season.

[496] James Harding: *Folies de Paris, The Rise and Fall of French Operetta.* London: Chappell & Co / Elm Tree Books 1979 p.91. Hereafter cited as Harding.

[497] Printed in Francis Poulenc: *Emmanuel Chabrier.* Translated by Cynthia Jolly. London: Denis Dobson 1981. Hereafter cited as Poulenc.

[498] Jules Renard: *The Journal of Jules Renard.* Edited and translated by Louise Bogan and Elizabeth Royat. New York: George Brazillier 1964 p.46. Hereafter cited as Renard.

[499] Huddleston p.156. This a rare reference to d'Esparbès.

[500] Bayard p.33.

[501] The rue du Départ had arrived in 1849.

[502] Robert W Service: *Ballads of a Bohemian.* http://www.gutenberg.org/files/995/995-h/995-h.htm#link2H_4_0002

[503] Moore/Confessions p.50.

[504] H.P. Clive: *Pierre Louÿs (1870-1925), A Biography.* Oxford: Clarendon Press 1978 p.99, hereafter cited as Clive; Lockspeiser p.160. This was one of many works that Debussy failed to effect, but a stage version by Pierre Frondaie was produced at the Renaissance and it was turned into an opera by Camille Erlanger with a libretto by Louis Ferdinand de Gramont, which opened 27th March 1906 at the Opéra-Comique, Garden singing Chrysis.

[505] The limited edition of 1891.

[506] Paris: Ollendorff 1901.

[507] John Warrack and Ewan West: *The Oxford Dictionary of Opera.* Oxford: Oxford University Press. 1992.

[508] James Harding: *Gounod.* London: George Allen & Unwin 1973 p.217.

[509] Francis Grierson: *Parisian Portraits.* London: Stephen Swift 1911 p.162. Hereafter cited as Grierson. There is also a bust of Gounod by Carpeaux in the Fitzwilliam Museum, Cambridge; Carpeaux himself is represented by a bust by Auguste de Niederhäusen, *dit* Rodo, in the Musée de l'Art et de l'Histoire, Geneva (1897, bronze, ref Inv. 1925-19) and 'Carpeaux en travail' by Antoine Bourdelle, Musée Bourdelle, Paris.

[510] Grierson pp.168-9.

[511] Princess Helena von Racowitza: *An Autobiography.* Authorised Translation from the German by Cecil Mar. London: Constable & Co 1910. Hereafter cited as Racowitza.

[512] Siegfried Sassoon: *Meredith.* London: Constable 1948 p.155.

[513] Grierson p.147.

[514] Deak p.146.

[515] Camille Pissarro to Lucien Pissarro 22nd January 1899. François Daulte: *Alfred Sisley, Catalogue Raisonné de l'Œuvre Peint.* Paris: Éditions Durand-Ruel 1959 p.9.

[516] The portrait head in the Musée d'Orsay is the result.

[517] Rothenstein Volume I p.159. Rothenstein made two lithograph portraits of Goncourt in March 1894, as well as drawing Zola. In 1895, when he spent most of the summer in Paris, Rothenstein also drew Huysmans.

[518] Kirk Varnedoe: *Gustave Caillebotte.* New Haven & London: Yale University Press 1987 p.10. Hereafter cited as Varnedoe.

[519] Nigel Gosling: *Nadar.* Amsterdam: Meulenhoff; London: Secker & Warburg 1976 p.208. Hereafter cited as Gosling.

[520] Paris: Charpentier 1877.

[521] Stevens 1990 p.21.

[522] Musée d'Orsay ref. RF 2834; Musée d'Orsay ref. RF 1959-8.

[523] Rothenstein Volume I p.90. Time, preoccupied with other reputations, has not endorsed Swan's opinion of Dagnan-Bouveret, and the title of his exhibition at the Dahesh Museum in New York in 2002 indicates his ambiguous relationship with critics to-day: 'Against the Modern, Dagnan-Bouveret and the Transformation of the Academic Tradition'. I am grateful to Dr Maureen E. Mulvihill of the Princeton Research Forum for drawing my attention to this.

[524] Joan Ungersma Halperin: *Félix Fénéon, Æsthete & Anarchist in fin-de-siècle Paris.* New Haven: Yale University Press. 1988 p.136. Hereafter cited as Halperin.

[525] Frederic V. Grunfeld: *Rodin, A Biography.* London: Hutchinson 1987 p.196. Hereafter cited as Grunfeld.

[526] Healy p.66.

[527] Albert Mockel: *Emile Verhaeren,* avec une note biographique par F. Vielé-Griffin. Paris: Mercure de France 1895.

[528] David Arkell: *Looking for Laforgue, An Informal Biography.* Manchester: Carcanet Press 1979 p.239; hereafter cited as Arkell.

[529] All the texts and libretti for which Debussy wrote have been collected in the Volume *Claude Debussy, Textes,* edited by Martine Kaufmann. Paris: Radio France 1999. I am very grateful indeed to madame Danielle Guérin, Direction de la Musique, Radio France, for the gift of this important Volume.

[530] Painter I p.144.

[531] This was performed in Béziers in August 1900.

[532] Anon [Julian Osgood Field]: *More Uncensored Recollections.* London: Eveleigh Nash & Grayson. 1926 p.147. Hereafter cited as Field. The would-be composer is identified by Gustave Le Rouge as Maurice Legay. Gustave Le Rouge in *Nouvelles Littéraires* 3rd and 10th November 1928, reprinted in Mikhail Volume II p.462. Hereafter cited as Le Rouge. The translation is by E.H. Mikhail.

[533] Albert Dubeux: *Julia Bartet.* Préface de Maurice Donnay. Paris: Plon 1938 p.70; hereafter cited as Dubeux. This is to be distinguished from Albert du Bois: *Julia Bartet.* Essai critique. Sansot, 1920. Albert du Bois (1872-1940) was a Belgian critic and playwright who wanted Wallonie to be joined to France. His *L'Hérodienne* of 1913 was produced at the Comédie Française in 1919, with Bartet as Bérénice, her last part.

[534] Gerald M. Ackerman: *The Life and Work of Jean Léon Gérôme, with a catalogue raisonné*. London: Sotheby's 1986 p.42. Hereafter cited as Ackerman.

[535] Dietschy p.121; talk on Massenet, BBC Radio 3, 2nd October 2004.

[536] Nichols 1997 p.ix.

[537] Belloc 1943 p.198.

[538] Vivian p.165.

[539] Dubeux p.95.

[540] Philippe Jullian: *Montmartre*. Translated by Anne Carter. Oxford: Phaidon 1977 p.66. Hereafter cited as Jullian 1977.

[541] Higonnet p.185.

[542] Perruchot p.88.

[543] Halperin p.75.

[544] Symons p.104.

[545] Rothenstein Volume I p.111.

[546] Manet's portrait of Zola in the Musée d'Orsay dates to 1868.

[547] Zola/L'Œuvre p.vii. The incident where Fagerolles insists on Lantier's picture of his dead child being accepted by the Salon does seem to have been suggested by Guillemet's patronage of Cézanne in similar circumstances in 1879.

[548] Bruno Foaurt: 'Gervex le Maudit, ou l'ombre de Fagerolles' in Francis Robinat, Bernard Montgolfier and Béatrice Debrandère-Descamps: *Henri Gervex 1852-1929*. Paris: Paris-Musées 1992, hereafter cited as Robinat. Page unnumbered but identifiable as p.10.

[549] Kathleen Adler: *Camille Pissarro, A Biography*. London: B.T. Batsford 1978 p.117, hereafter cited as Adler. The regulars of this group were Antoine Guillemet, Fantin-Latour and Frédéric Bazille, who was killed in 1870. The literary figures were led by Duranty. F.W.J. Hemmings: *The Life and Times of Emile Zola*. London: Paul Elek 1977 p.53. Hereafter Hemmings 1977.

[550] Moore/Memoirs p.86.

[551] Antoine p.7. Diary entry for 7th October 1895. My translation.

[552] Quoted in Katharine Worth: *The Irish Drama of Europe from Yeats to Beckett*. London: Athlone Press 1986 p.142, hereafter cited as Worth. This must have been in the second half of February 1894.

[553] Elizabeth de Gramont, ex-duchesse de Clermont-Tonnerre: *Au temps des Equipages*. Translated as *Pomp and Circumstance* by Brian W Downs, with an Introduction by Louis Bromfield. London: Jonathan Cape 1929 p.164. Hereafter cited as Gramont.

[554] Adler p.85.

[555] Adler p.106.

[556] Ludovici pp.129, 201.

[557] John Rewald (ed.): *Paul Cézanne, Letters*. Oxford: Bruno Cassirer 1941. 4th edition revised and enlarged 1976 p.150 note c. Hereafter cited as Rewald.

[558] George Moore: *Impressions and Memories*. London: T. Werner Laurie 1914 p.226, hereafter cited as Moore/Impressions; Jean Adhémar and others: *Toulouse-Lautrec*. Paris: Hachette 1963 p.195, hereafter cited as Adhémar; Rothenstein

Volume I p.106. Rothenstein does not make it clear if by 'Rodin' he means the man, the work, or both.

[559] Rothenstein Volume I p.60.

[560] Ludovici p.200.

[561] Christopher Lloyd: *J.-K. Huysmans and the fin-de-siècle Novel.* Edinburgh: Edinburgh University Press 1990 p.10; cp Tennyson's remark about Churton Collins, that he was 'a louse in the locks of literature'. For Bloy, see Marie-Joseph Lory: *Léon Bloy et son époque.* Paris: Desclée de Brouwer 1944.

[562] Bayard p.89.

[563] Antoine p.26.

[564] Antoine p.143.

[565] Perruchot p.183.

[566] Belloc 1943 pp.22,178; Healy p.63.

[567] Reproduced in Lee Revens (ed.): *The Graphic Work of Felicien Rops.* New York: Léon Amiel 1975 p.15. Coppée first work was in the Parnassian manner. In 1892 he quitted Paris for Brunoy, and later became a fervent Catholic and member of the anti-Semitic Ligue de la patrie française. He refused to sign a petition asking for clemency for Wilde. His head in bronze bas-relief decorates a column in the place André Tardieu (formerly the place St-François Xavier), but the brasserie named after him is in the place Léon-Paul Fargue. The plays recorded on the column are *Le Passant, Le Luthier de Cremorne, Severo Torelli, Pour la Couronne,* and *Les Jacobites.*

[568] Robert H. Sherard: 'Notes from Paris', *The Author* October 1892 p.163.

[569] Maurice Baring: *French Literature.* London: Ernest Benn 1927 p.75. Hereafter cited as Baring 1927. Robert Lethbridge regards him as 'the leading critic of the day'. Maupassant/Bel Ami p.vii.

[570] Gosse 1922 pp.203-4.

[571] Duval p.46.

[572] Antoine p.14.

[573] Belloc 1943 p.196.

[574] Renard p.42.

[575] Edmond & Jules de Goncourt: *Pages from the Goncourt Journal.* Edited, Translated and Introduced by Robert Baldick. London: Oxford University Press 1962 p.311; hereafter cited as Goncourt/Baldick. Diary entry for Christmas Eve 1885.

[576] Belloc 1943 p.153.

[577] Belloc 1943 p.167.

[578] Renard p.45. This was one evening at Daudet's in January 1892.

[579] Goncourt/Baldick p.334. Diary entry for Monday 9th January 1888.

[580] Whiteing p.188.

[581] Renard p.39.

[582] Belloc 1943 p.182.

[583] Belloc 1943 p.117.

[584] At the Chalet des Îles in the Bois, 20th June 1893.

[585] Hemmings 1977 p.89; George Moore: *Impressions and Memories.* London: T. Werner Laurie 1914 p.44, hereafter cited as Moore 1914. According to Moore, Turgenev spoke well of *L'Assommoir*; the counter view is in Patrick Waddington: *Turgenev and England.* New York: New York University Press 1981 p.223. Moore wrote 'An idea has been improvided from his long residence in France that he is more western that his illustrious compeers Tolstoy and Dostoievsky; but it would be hard to point out to a trace of this denaturalisation in his works. Tolstoy I have not read...' *Ibidem* p.48.

[586] Daudet pp.347-8.

[587] February 1891. Renard p.39.

[588] Renard pp.55,51.

[589] Ernest Dimnet: *My New World.* London: Jonathan Cape 1938 p.41. Hereafter cited as Dimnet 1938.

[590] Perruchot p.169. One would give much for a list of these.

[591] Rothenstein Volume I p.243.

[592] His real name was Ernest Rey. He also wrote with Camille du Locle the opera of Flaubert's *Salammbô.* Du Locle later moved to Capri, where he was known as 'the Englishman'.

[593] Myers p.58. *Gwendoline* was published by Enoch et Cie, the leading Paris publisher of music.

[594] Poulenc pp.17,18,50. I regret I do not know what word Ms Jolly translates as 'balderdash'.

[595] Lockspeiser p.98; Dietschy p.65. The version of *Le Cid*, called *Rodrigue et Chimène*, was neither published nor performed and the MS was lost for many years. It was given its first performance only in June 1987.

[596] Poulenc p.17. *Isoline* was written by Mendès' estranged wife, Judith Gautier. He himself collaborated with Massenet on *Ariane.*

[597] Moore/Confessions pp.47-8. Dorian Gray drinks just such a wine *for breakfast*, the morning after he has learned of Sibyl Vane's death.

[598] Renée Felbermann (ed.): *The Memoirs of a Cosmopolitan.* By Heinrich Felbermann. London: Chapman & Hall 1936 p.113. Hereafter cited as Felbermann.

[599] According to Narcisse Lebeau. Nichols 1992 p.40. Debussy was best man at Lebeau's wedding, which Alphonse Allais also attended. 'Narcisse Lebeau' may be thought to be a somewhat self-regarding name: his real one was Vital Hocquet (1865-1931) – as 'hoquet' means hiccough, the change is excusable for all its vanity. Satie was perhaps having a joke at Hocquet's expense when he wrote articles under the name of Virginie Lebeau.

[600] James Harding: *Massenet.* London: J.M. Dent & Sons 1970 p.156. Mendès wrote the libretti for Massenet's *Ariane* (1905) and *Bacchus* (1909); one may also relate the reference to Alfred Roll's painting 'Festival of Silenus' of 1880, now in the Musée des Beaux-Arts, Gand / Museum voor Schone Kunsten, Ghent, and to Jacques Dalou's sculpture of Silenus, installed in the Luxembourg Gardens in 1898. The Roll is reproduced in Aleksa Celebonovic: *Chefs d'Œuvres du réalisme bourgeois.* Adapted and edited by Sacha Tolstoî and translated by Peter Willis as

The Heyday of Salon Painting, Masterpieces of Bourgeois Realism. London: Thames & Hudson 1974.

[601] Felbermann p.238.

[602] Douglas Ainslie: *Adventures Literary and Social.* London: T. Fisher Unwin 1922 p.102. Hereafter cited as Ainslie.

[603] Ainslie p.177.

[604] 'La fille aux cheveux de lin', 'La cathédrale engloutie'. Monet's Rouen Cathedral series was exhibited at Durand-Ruel in 1894. 'Rouen Cathedral: the Portal in Grey Weather' was bought by the Rouen industrialist François Depeaux, and is now in the Musée des Beaux-Arts, Rouen (ref. 909.1.8). Leonard Tancock has compared Zola's descriptions of Paris as seen from Auteuil in *Une Page d'Amour* to these Monets. Leonard Tancock: Introduction to Zola/Assommoir p.13.

[605] Quoted by Linda Ormiston, BBC Radio 3, 28th September 2004.

[606] Niamh Burns: 'The Imagery of Debussy', unpublished lecture given at the National Gallery of Ireland 29th June 1999. My contemporary note.

[607] From *I Kamp og Fest* (1908), quoted by Ragna Stang: *Edvard Munch, the Man and the Artist.* London: Gordon Fraser 1979 p.55.

[608] Louis would have had his own English acquaintants, for he was a member of the Egyptian Caisse de la dette, governed by nominees of both the French and British Governments.

[609] The Montebello's only son, Louis, was dressed by his mother until well into his childhood à la Little Lord Fauntleroy. He was saved as a young man from whatever fate for which this might have destined him when he was killed by lightning.

[610] Lockspeiser p.177. Bourgeois was an amateur sculptor, which shows that to be engaged in the arts is not necessarily to have an open mind. D.W Brogan calls him 'a new and inferior Victor Cousin', which is to start from a low base. D.W Brogan: *The French Nation, from Napoléon to Pétain 1814-1940.* London: Hamish Hamilton 1957 p.194. Hereafter cited as Brogan.

[611] Nichols 1992 p.xix.

[612] Oscar Wilde to Robert Ross, June 1898. Hart-Davis 1962 p.753; Holland & Hart-Davis p.1083.

[613] For an extended account of this see Michael de Cossart: *Ida Rubinstein (1885-1960), A Theatrical Life.* Liverpool: Liverpool University Press 1987. Chapter I: 'The Baptist's Head'. Jacques-Emile Blanche's portrait of Rubinstein (1909) shows her as Scheherazade, which may give some idea of her as Salomé. It is reproduced in Mireille Bialek: *Jacques-Emile Blanche à Offranville, peintre-écrivain.* Offranville: Musée Jacques-Emile Blanche 1997 p.57. Clearly a comparative study of the orientalism of the Wilde/Strauss *Salomé* and the Rimsky-Korsakov/Ballets Russes *Schérérazade* needs to be undertaken.

[614] Paul Cézanne to his son 15th October 1906. Rewald p.336.

[615] Bashkirtseff p.510. Diary entry for 5th November 1881.

[616] Quoted in Mikhail Volume I p170.

[617] Joy Melville: *Mother of Oscar, The Life of Jane Francesca Wilde*. London: John Murray 1994 p.110. Hereafter cited as Melville. This is ignored by Jonathan Fryer, who dates Wilde's first visit, with Speranza, to 1874. Fryer 1997 p.14.

[618] Burke's *Irish Family Records*. London: Burke's Peerage 1976 p.1217.

[619] Melville p.124.

[620] Lowther p.196.

[621] Francisque Sarcey (1827-1899, not, as given in James/Sketches, 1828-1889). Sarcey was the successor as leading theatre critic of the even more conservative Jules Janin (1804-1874), who came to Paris in 1859, though even Janin had his lighter moments, for he once as a hoax convinced le tout Paris that the *cabotin* Debureau of Théâtre des Funambules was a great actor. Sarcey himself was succeeded by Henry Bordeaux, who dated the decline in moral seriousness of the French theatre to *Amoureuse* by Georges Porto-Riche in 1891. Bordeaux' position, as understood by Harold Hobson [Hobson.p.76], was one of antagonism to any work, whether lubricious or cynical, that challenged the moral order, perhaps oblivious to the fact that a moral order that was only represented in its full rigour on the stage, was not a moral order at all.

[622] Henry James: *French Poets and Novelists*. 1878. New edition London: Macmillan 1893 p.37, hereafter cited as James/Poets. It was endorsement by Sarcey that substantiated the success of the Isola brothers.

[623] As Cole Porter was to write
You come to Paris, you come to play;
You have a wonderful time, you go away.
And from then on, you talk of Paris knowingly,
You may know Paris, you don't know Paree.

[624] Filson Young: *The Sands of Pleasure*. London: Grant Richards 1905 p.125. Hereafter cited as Young.

[625] Spencer Leigh Hughes: *Press, Platform and Parliament*. London: Nisbet & Co 1918 pp.237-8. Hereafter cited as Hughes.

[626] Henry James: 'Rouen 1876' in *Portraits of Places*. London: Macmillan 1883 p.131, hereafter cited as James/Portraits.

[627] Caroline Jebb: *The Life and Letters of Richard Claverhouse Jebb O.M., Litt.D.* Cambridge: Cambridge University Press 1907 p. 221, hereafter cited as Jebb. My italics.

[628] *The Author,* August 1890 p.98. This was part of an eulogy to Jebb made by Wilde in proposing his health at the annual dinner of the Society of Authors at the Criterion Restaurant in London on 8th July. I am most grateful to Ms Kate Peel of the Society for this information.

[629] These were in 1886. Andrieu p.38.

[630] Novick p. 330.

[631] Tint p.80.

[632] Oscar Wilde to W.E. Gladstone 17th May 1877. Hart-Davis 1962 p.38; Holland & Hart-Davis p.48. This would seem to be supported by Wilde's reference to Renan in *De Profundis*. Hart-Davis 1962 p.479; Holland & Hart-Davis p.743.

Oscar Wilde to the Editor of the *St James' Gazette* 23rd June 1890. Hart-Davis 1962 p.262; Holland & Hart-Davis p.435.

[633] Robert H. Sherard: 'Notes from Paris' in *The Author* Volume II/11, April 1892 p.360. Sherard/Maupassant. London: T. Werner Laurie 1926 p.185, hereafter cited as Sherard April 1892. This is based on an interview that Renan gave to 'an English writer in Paris': connoisseurs of Sherard will realise that Sherard means himself. He found Renan 'sleek, bland and unctuous'.

[634] There is a bust of Larroumet by Paul Roussel (1906) in the Galérie du Théâtre Francais. He should not be confused with Gaston Larroumet, directeur des Beaux-Arts, as does Mainardi p.147.

[635] Born Céline Seure, Cécile Sorel (1873-1966) became comtesse de Ségur.

[636] Cécile Sorel: *An Autobiography*. Translated by Philip John Stead. Foreword by M. Willson Disher. London: Staples 1953 p.39. Hereafter cited as Sorel.

[637] W.W Vaughan was also staying there.

[638] Edgar T.S. Dugdale: *Maurice de Bunsen, Diplomat and Friend*. London: John Murray 1934 p.19. De Bunsen stayed at the Casaubons' when learning French for the diplomatic service in 1875.

[639] They seem not to have been aware that this was the house in which Voltaire died (30th May 1778). It is now (March 2004) reduced to the groundfloor Restaurant Voltaire, the upper floors, at least on the outside, being in some dilapidation.

[640] Tint p.70.

[641] Hereafter cited as Baring 1927 p.70. Numa Denis *Fustel de Coulanges* (1830-1889) was a mediæval historian. His *La cité antique : étude sur le culte, le droit, les institutions de la Grèce et de Rome* (Paris: Hachette 1872), and should have been known to Wilde, as a copy is in the library of Trinity College Dublin. An English translation (*The Ancient City: A Study on the Religion, Laws and Institutions of Greece and Rome*) was published in 1874 and is in the Bodleian.

[642] Charles Péguy, at the time of *l'affaire* a socialist of the left who wrote for the *Revue blanche* under the name Jacques Laubier, was perhaps the most subtle of the those of his generation who moved to the right. He was killed on the Marne. There is a Centre Charles Péguy in Orléans.

[643] Hereafter cited as Baring 1927 p.70.

[644] John Viscount Morley: *Recollections* Volume I. London: Macmillan & Co. 1917 pp.300-1. My italics. Hereafter cited as Morley.

[645] De Mun's position was strengthened when in 1892 the Church came to a rapprochement with the Republic, although this drove a wedge between the Church and the more Royalist of its devotees.

[646] H.A.L. Fisher: *A History of Europe*. London: Eyre & Spottiswoode 1935. New and enlarged edition 1938, republished 1952 Volume II: From the Beginning of the Eighteenth Century to 1937 p.1001.

[647] Taine became increasingly pessimistic as he wrote his *Origines de la France Contemporaine* – origins that concluded with Taine's death– revealing the pessimism rooted in Naturalism as well as in disenchantment with the way the world was going.

[648] H.A.L. Fisher: *An Unfinished Biography.* London: Oxford University Press 1941 pp.60,62,65,72,75. David Ogg: *Herbert Fisher 1865-1940, A Short Biography.* London: Edward Arnold 1947 adds nothing to Fisher's own account.

[649] Waddington 1903 p.163.

[650] Rod was Swiss but lived in Paris from 1878 to 1886. A writer of Naturalist and psychological novels and a friend of Zola, Richard Whiteing thought him 'one of the most interesting figures of the day'. Whiteing 1900p.113.

[651] Philip Gilbert Hamerton: *An Autobiography 1834-1858*, and a Memoir by His Wife 1858-1894. London: Seely & Co 1897 p.622. Hereafter cited as Hamerton.

[652] Huysmans 1891 pp.22-3.

[653] Frederic Harrison: *Autobiographic Memoirs.* London: 1911 Volume II pp.64-5.

[654] Oscar Browning: *Memories of Sixty Years, at Eton, Cambridge and Elsewhere.* London: John Lane: The Bodley Head 1910 p.294. Browning adds 'I must not omit my dear friends the Raoul Duvals in the rue François Premier' – presumably because these were aristocrats and the rue François Premier was one of the most fashionable in Paris.

[655] Renan's funeral (7th October 1892) was boycotted by the Nuncio and the ambassadors of Catholic countries. Coolidge pp.182-3.

[656] Maspero unwrapped Rameses II in June 1886, contributing to the incorporation of the mummy into late Victorian gothic.

[657] Edmund Gosse: *Aspects & Impressions.* London: Cassell & Co 1922 p.212. Hereafter cited as Gosse 1922.

[658] Havelock Ellis: introduction to Emil Zola: *Germinal.* http://www.ibiblio.org/eldritch/ez/gin.html.

[659] G.P. Gooch: *Court and Cabinets.* London: Longmans, Green & Co 1944 Chapters XXV, XXVI.

[660] G.P. Gooch: *Under Six Reigns.* London: Longmans, Green & Co 1958, Chapter V 'Paris in the Nineties'.

[661] Lautrec, thirty-seven when he died, produced six hundred paintings, three hundred and thirty lithographs, perhaps thirty posters ('une trentaine') and thousands ('milliers') of drawings. Henri Perruchot: 'Une vie ardente' in Adhémar p.28.

[662] Fouquières pp.190-1. Fouquières says that Delarue was known as the Hermit of La Muette, but to whom?

[663] Sorel p.44.

[664] Francisque Sarcey: *Quarante Ans de Théâtre.* Paris: Bibliothèque des Annales 1900-1902.

[665] Paris: Michel 1922-28.

[666] Dietschy p.31.

[667] Her deliberately ungendered *nom-de-plume* was taken from Jip, Dora's dog in *David Copperfield.* Belloc 1943 p.218. Martel is credited with the invention of the dialogue novel, appropriately crossing over between art forms. Gerald Ackermann refers to 'a Monsieur Gyp' who supported the acquistion by the State of the Caillebotte bequest. I take this to be a further example of multi-identity among Parisians. Ackerman p.142. One may note the title of one Gyp's novels

was *Sans Voiles* (1885). Her work does not seem to have attracted English attention, however, at least until 1900 when the Pioneer series published *Little Bob*, translated by A. Hallard. There is a photograph of her in Hartmann p.43; her portrait by Boldini is in the Musée des Beaux Arts, Dijon.

[668] The cycle is enumerated below, those underlined being referred to in the text, with double underlining indicating extensive citation. Dates are those of publication in book form.

La Fortune des Rougon (October 1871); *La Curée* (1872; originally translated into English as *The Rush for Spoil*, translated by Vizetelly); *Le Ventre de Paris* (April 1873); *La Conquête de Plassans* (May 1874); *La Faute de l'abbé Mouret* (April 1875); *Son excellence Eugène Rougon* (February 1876); *L'Assommoir* (February 1877), originally translated into English as *Drunk* by Arthur Symons; *Un Page d'amour* (June 1878); *Nana* (March 1880); *Pot-Bouille* (April 1882; originally translated into English as *Piping Hot!* Introduction by George Moore 1885); *Au Bonheur des Dames* (March 1883); *La Joie de Vivre* (March 1884); *Germinal* (March 1885); *L'Œuvre* (April 1886); *La Terre* (November 1887, originally translated into English as *The Soil*); Le Rêve (October 1887); *La Bête humaine* (March 1890); *L'Argent* (March 1891); *La Débâcle* (June 1892); *Le docteur Pascal* (July 1893).

[669] Vivian p.163. Adrian Frazier has pointed out that in the five years between the publication of *Mike Fletcher* and that of *Esther Waters* (1889 to 1894), George Moore wrote at least a hundred and sixty-nine articles ('the best journalism in London'), a play and a novel. This is more than Wilde's output. Frazier pp.200,215.

[670] 'While Lang knew French literature very well, James was pleased to find that he knew Paris better […] He conducted Lang and Hamilton Aïdé to Berneval, and introduced them to Turgenev'. Novick p.400.

[671] George Moore: *Confessions of a Young Man*. London: Swann, Sonnenschein 1889. I have used the Ebury Edition, published by William Heinemann in 1937, hereafter cited as Moore/Confessions. Blanche himself had been a pupil of Mallarmé's at the Lycée Fontane.

[672] Playwright, whose first work was in the Parnassian manner. In 1892 he quitted Paris for Brunoy, and later became a fervent Catholic and member of the anti-Semitic Ligue de la patrie française. His head in bronze bas-relief decorates a column in the place André Tardieu (formerly the place St-François Xavier), but the brasserie named after him is in the place Léon-Paul Fargue. The plays recorded on the column are *Le Passant, Le Luthier de Cremorne, Severo Torelli, Pour la Couronne,* and *Les Jacobites.*

[673] Moore/Confessions pp.47,48.

[674] There is a photograph of Anatole France in Hartmann p.90.

[675] Katherine Lyon Mix: *A Study in Yellow, The Yellow Book and Its Contributors.* Lawrence: University of Kansas Press and London: Constable 1960 p.118, hereafter cited as Mix. Heredia was a poet of Cuban origin whose sonnets were the epitome of the Parnassian ideal of beauty. The spelling of his name here is as given by Larousse, and I have standardised to this form throughout the variants

that different writers favour: I have seen Héredia, Hérédia (Margaret Crosland's, Philippe Jullian's and André de Fouquière's spelling), Herédia and Hérèdia. Even Anatole France and Anthony Hartley call him Hérédia. France p.264; Anthony Hartley (ed.): *The Penguin Book of French Verse* Volume III: The Nineteenth Century. Harmondsworth: Penguin 1957 pp.viii, 181; hereafter cited as Hartley. Hartley says that Heredia 'can be said to be the best of the Parnassians'. The republican deputy Severiano de Hérédia is spelled thus by Stephen C. Hause: *Hubertine Auclert, the French Suffragette.* New Haven & London: Yale Univeristy Press 1987 p.83. Heredia's portrait by Émile Lévy, dating to 1881, is in the Musée d'Orsay; one of his wife, née Louise Despaigne, by the same artist and dating to 1995, is in the Musée des Beaux Arts, Rouen, as is another by de Nittis.

[676] George Moore: *Ave.* London: William Heinemann 1911 p.8; hereafter Moore 1911. Capoul is the tenor Victor Capoul.

[677] Edouard Colonne, who conducted concerts at the Théâtre de Châtelet from 1873 to his death in 1910 (Bizet, Saint-Saëns, Lalo, Massenet, Ravel, Mendelssohn, Wagner, Liszt, Schumann, Brahms).

[678] Constant Benoît Coquelin, called Coquelin *aîné*; Ernest Alexandre Honoré Coquelin ,called Coquelin *cadet*. It is not always possible to distinguish which Coquelin is being referred to, but generally speaking one may assume the elder. Max Beerbohm, a man somewhat given to hyperbole, wrote 'The death of Coquelin may without hyperbole be described as a blow to the whole educated world'. Beerbohm 1953 p.534. There is a portrait of Constant Coquelin by Charles Giron in the Musée Carnavalet, ref. P.1604, and both Coquelins were sculpted by Bourdelle (1891, *cadet*; 1893; *aîne*), Musée Bourdelle.

[679] This was the Charles Le Bargy whose rehearsing so disturbed Proust in the rue Laurent-Pichat. Known as the Brummel of the Comédie Française thanks to his clothes from the fashionable tailor Wasse of the rue Auber, he played Cyrano de Bergerac in the second production (1913). His wife was Simone Le Bargy, of whose performance in *The Man of the Moment* at the St James's Theatre in 1905, Beerbohm remarked 'not a heaven-born genius'. Beerbohm 1953 p.381. After madame Le Bargy divorced her husband, she preferred to be known simply as Madame Simone. The Duchess of Sermoneta thought her (like Jeanne Granier) 'excessively talkative and unlike my dear Duse'. Vittoria Colonna Duchess of Sermoneta: *Things Past.* With a foreword by Robert Hichens. London: Hutchinson n.d. p.91. Hereafter cited as Sermoneta.

[680] Violet Markham: *Return Passage, The Autobiography of Violet R. Markham, C.H.* London: Oxford University Press 1953 p.44. Henry James thought little of Adeline Dudlay: 'As far as the interests of art are concerned, Mdlle Dudlay had much better have remained in the Flemish capital, of whose language she is apparently a perfect mistress'. James/Poets p.330. Dudlay played Hermione to Bernhardt's Andromaque in London in June 1879.

[681] Mortimer Menpes: *Paris.* With text by Dorothy Menpes. London: Adam & Charles Black 1909 pp.143-5. Hereafter cited as Menpes.

[682] John Joseph Conway: *Footprints of Famous Americans in Paris.* With an Introduction by Mrs John Lane. London: John Lane The Bodley Head 1912 p.247. Hereafter cited as Conway.

[683] E.C. Bentley: *Trent's Last Case.* London 1912. Harmondsworth: Penguin Books 1937 pp.143-4.

[684] Sherard 1906 p.340. This is strange stuff from the man who had only a few years before succoured Ernest Dowson.

[685] Shercliff p.189.

[686] Robert W Service: *Ballads of a Bohemian.* Toronto: G.J. McLeod 1921. One supposes 'windmill land and crescent moon' to refer to the Moulin Rouge and Père Lunette. http://www.gutenberg.org/files/995/995-h/995-h.htm#link2H_4_0002.

[687] In this monograph, Mercure de France refers to the publishing house; *Mercure de France* to the journal. The first issue of the journal, dated January 1890, in fact was published on Christmas Day 1889, another instance of Parisian elision of real time.

[688] André Antoine (1858-1943), the theatre director, not to be confused with the hairdresser Antoine (1885-1976), who did not arrive in Paris from his native Poland until 1902. Nor was the hairdresser's name really Antoine, but Antek Cierplikowski.

[689] Roumanian born, his real name was Eduard-Alexandru Max. Notable parts included ones in *Britannicus* (1891) and *The Persians* (1896), both at the Odéon. Beerbohm drew de Max, c.1904.

[690] There is a portrait by Edouard Vuillard of Desprez, who was the wife of Lugné-Poë, in the Musée de Beaux-Arts, Caen, ref. D.75.1.21. Bernard Shaw gives her name as Despres and Jean Chothia gives Després. George Bernard Shaw: *Our Theatres in the Nineties.* London: Constable 1932 p.78, hereafter Shaw 1932; Jean Chothia: *André Antoine.* Cambridge: Cambridge University Press 1991 p.122, hereafter cited as Chothia. Isabelle Cahn, curating the exhibition 'Théâtre de l'Œuvre', Musée d'Orsay, spring 2005, preferred Desprès. However spelled, she joined the Théâtre de l'Œuvre in 1895.

[691] Pretty Women p.72.

[692] In the rue Scribe, owned by Volpini, and presumably that 'luxurious café' outside which 'two tall, shabbily clad and very dirty fellows' sell the scandal sheet *Voix du Peuple.* Zola/Paris p.93.

[693] Isadora Duncan: *My Life.* London: Victor Gollancz 1928 p.77, hereafter cited as Duncan. Her first performance as a serious actress was in Donnay's *Les Amants* at the Renaissance in November 1895. Sada Yacco川上 貞奴 was a Japanese who took Paris and London by storm. See Antoine p.167. Gide went to see Yacco seven times (but his wife, it seems, went only once).

[694] Turner had an ancestral connection with Paris as his grandfather Lionel Lawson had owned an ink factory there and kept a *pied-à-terre* in the boulevard des Italiens.

[695] X.-M. Boulestin: *Myself, My Two Countries.* London: Cassell & Co 1936 pp.33,40,67,82,115. Hereafter cited as Boulestin.

[696] Paul Poiret: *My First Fifty Years*. Translated by Stephen Haden Guest. London: Victor Gollancz 1933 p.20. Hereafter cited as Poiret.

[697] Paul Léautaud: *Le Petit Ami*, with *In Memoriam* and *Amours*. Translated by Humphrey Hare as *The Child of Man*. London: The Bodley Head 1959 p.233. He was regarded as a passé figure even in 1889. Joanna Richardson: *Judith Gautier, A Biography*. London: Quartet Books 1986 p.165, hereafter cited as Richardson/ Gautier. Mendès may also be said to be an 'ancestor' of Georges Duroy, Maupassant's Bel-Ami.

[698] Fouquières p.95.

[699] Bell p.124. This refers to 1904.

[700] Pierre Louÿs et Jean de Tinan: *Correspondance 1894-1898*. Présentée et annotée par Jean-Paul Goujon. Ouvrage publié avec le concours de Centre national du livre. Paris: Éditions du Limon 1995 pp.54n,62. Hereafter cited as Louÿs/Tinan.

[701] Rothenstein Volume I pp.92,94.

[702] Robert H. Sherard: 'Notes from Paris' in *The Author* Volume III/2 1st July 1892 p.62.

[703] Many years later Poulenc set Moréas' 'Airs chantés' to music, causing his biographer to comment 'It is perhaps surprising that these mediocre poems inspired this musician'. Pierre Bernac: *Poulenc, The Man and His Songs*. Translated by Winifred Radford. London: Victor Gollancz 1977 p.202. Apparently Poulenc did it as a tease.

[704] Arthur Symons: *Dramatis Personæ*. London: Faber & Gwyer 1925 p.98. Hereafter Symons 1925.

[705] Starkie p.107. The implication is that he superseded Wilde, whose time in this regard was the 1880s. One cannot altogether follow this, especially as Starkie says, erroneously, that between 1881 and 1883, Wilde paid 'several visits to France'. *Ibidem* p.102.

[706] Lord Ronald Sutherland Gower: *Old Diaries 1881-1901*. London: John Murray 1902 p.279. My italics.

[707] London: John Lane 1929. This contains essays on Henri de Toulouse-Lautrec; Degas; Constantin Guys; Daumier; Forain; Henry de Groux; Simeon Solomon; Monticelli; Gustave Moreau; Odilon Redon; Beardsley; Whistler and Manet; and Rodin.

[708] Moore 1911 p.62.

[709] And perhaps with that of the actor Paul Taillade. Tailhade is called Teilharde by Elizabeth Wilson: *Bohemians, the Glamorous Outcasts*. London & New York: I.B. Tauris 2000 p.68; Richard Ings calls him Tailharde. Mirbeau p.ix. Paul Taillade fell on hard times, reduced to appearing at Le Fourmi, a caf'conc' in the boulevard Barbès, 'à trainer dans les bouisbouis de banlieu'. Antoine p.32.

[710] Rothenstein Volume I p.92. Anthony Hartley thought de Tailhède 'one of the more presentable members' of the École Romane. Hartley p.xxxvii.

[711] Lucas p.180. *Sic* indicates my supposition that the reference is to the artists' models of the Académie Julian, but it could conceivably refer to the characters

upon whom the dramatist Jean Jullien drew in such plays as *L'Echéance* for the Théâtre Libre.

[712] Conway p.238.

[713] Davis 1895 pp.55,61,63.

[714] Sherard/Maupassant. London: T. Werner Laurie 1926 p.344.

[715] Baju's list is given by Harold Nicolson: *Verlaine*. London: Constable n.d. pp.181-2 and is as follows:

(1) *Decadents*: Verlaine, Maurice du Plessys (first manner), Ernest Raynaud, Arthur Rimbaud, Jules Laforgue, Stuart Merrill, Fernand Gregh.

(2) Symbolists: Mallarmé, Jean Moréas (first manner), Charles Morice, Maurice *Barrès*, Paul Adam, Henri de Régnier, Vielé-Griffin, Jean Lorrain.

(3) *Instrumentalists*: René Ghil, Verhaeren.

(4) *École romane*: Jean Moréas (second manner), Maurice du Plessys (second manner), Raymond de la Tailhède, Charles Maurras.

(5) *Anarchists*: Paterne Berrichon, Octave Mirbeau, André Gide.

(6) *Neo-Decadents* & *Neo-Symbolists*: Camille Mauclair, Oscar Wilde.

(7) *Independents*: Albert Samain, Pierre Louÿs.

The absentees from this list are as striking as those present.

[716] This should not be confused with the literary review *La Décadence*.

[717] His real name was Paul Duval, and he used the pen-name Raitif de la Bretonne. Lorrain also wrote a novel based on the life of Sarah Bernhardt, *Le Tréteau*. A portrait by La Gandara is in the Musée Carnavalet, ref. P.1818.

[718] Tailhade p.xxx.

[719] Tailhade p.177n.

[720] Delbourg-Delphis p.155.

[721] Falguière, 1885 (?), Maison Victor Hugo, Paris, inv. MVH-S-O/1998; Rodin 1897, Musée d'Orsay ref.4066.

[722] Healy p71.

[723] Healy p.72.

[724] Nordau pp.275,279,280.

[725] Mary Ann Caws: *Marcel Proust*. Woodstock, NY: The Overlook Press 2003 p.7.

[726] De Flers collaborated with de Caillavet on a number of boulevard comedies (including the French version of Lehar's *Merry Widow*), later becoming a director of *Le Figaro*. His novel *Ilsée, Princesse de Tripoli* (1897) was illustrated by Mucha. In 1901 he married Eveline, daughter of Victorien Sardou.

[727] Trarieux' 'Une nuit d'avril à Céos' was produced at the Théâtre de l'Œuvre, 27th February 1894, programme by Vuillard.

[728] Here Zola locates Mademoiselle Tatin's lingerie shop in *Au Bonheur des Dames* and here too du Maurier locates a restaurant called Carmagnol's 'where they gave you hors-d'œuvres, potage, three courses and dessert and a bottle of wine' for two francs fifty'. Du Maurier/Martian p.179. The soup cannot have been up to much.

[729] Streets named after them are in the XVe arrondissement, at Beaugrennelle.

[730] For more on *Le Banquet* see William Logue: *Léon Blum, The Formative Years 1872-1914*. DeKalb: Northern Illinois University Press 1973 p.30. Hereafter cited as Logue.

[731] Grenville-Murray pp.224-7. 'Giroflée' is a wallflower, or gilly-flower, and served like hortensia as one of the emblematic flowers of the period. Eugène Sue's Arthur, hero of the novel of that name of 1839, bore a name which became a generic one for romantics, like Werther and Rodolphe. For a discussion of this, see Delbourg-Delphis pp.67-8. Arthur is used by Wilde not only for Lord Arthur Savile but also for Lord Goring and Lord Windermere.

[732] Robert H. Sherard: 'Notes from Paris' in *The Author* Volume III/11 April 1893 p.404. As late as 1911, Bernard Shaw was able to suggest that the English were still uncomfortable with the idea of the word having become anglicised. 'Vaughan: Youre dekkadent. Gunn: Decādent! How I love that early Victorian word!' Shaw 1911 p.180. The spelling is Shaw's.

[733] Retté, like Gustave Kahn, was an editor of the Symbolist review *La Vogue*, and another called *L'Ermitage*, in which Gide was to publish his memories of Wilde (June 1902). His article on Maeterlinck in *Art et Critique* (4th January 1890) was the first critical assessment written on that author.

[734] October 1893. Quoted in Deak p.185.

[735] Edgar Jepson: *Memories of a Victorian*. London: Victor Gollancz 1933 p.247, hereafter cited as Jepson; Henri Perruchot: 'Une vie ardente' in Adhémar p.7.

[736] Low p.71.

[737] Should not be confused with Maurice Hennequin, the writer of farces, still less with the dramatist Hennique or the architect Hennequet. George du Maurier names a sculptor Hennequin. George du Maurier: *Trilby, A Novel*. London: Osgood, McIlvaine & Co 1895 p. 121. Hereafter cited as du Maurier/Trilby.

[738] If Evenepoel (1872-1899) is the painter whom Roditi calls Evenpoël, his work may have been known to Wilde: '*The Sphinx without a Secret,* Wilde himself calls an "etching"; it is a fictional elaboration, in terms of magazine art almost reminiscent of the Parisian drawings of Steinlen or Evenpoël.' Roditi p.76.

[739] Aurier founded *Le Moderniste Illustré* in 1889 when he was twenty-four. He may be followed up in the thesis 'G.-Albert Aurier, critic and theorist of Symbolist art' by Margaret Rauschenbach Lunn, for details of which see http://theses.mit.edu/Dienst/UI/2.0/Describe/0018.mit.theses/1982-128.

[740] Editor of *Le Minerve*, which appeared six times in 1885. Pierre Dufay did not think much of him: 'Le falot et calamateux Charles Buet, ce porte-coton Barbey d'Aurevilly, auquel son drame de *Prêtre* vault une éphémère notoriété, a fondé une revue non moins éphémère, *La Minerve*.' Tailhade p.xvii.

[741] http://www.providenceproductions.com/ccros/ccros.html.

[742] Moore 1914 p.88.

[743] Richard Le Gallienne: *The Romantic '90s*. London: John Lane 1925 p.143.

[744] W Somerset Maugham: *The Moon and Sixpence*. London: William Heinemann 1919. Harmondsworth: Penguin Books 1944 p.38.

[745] Harold Nicolson: *Helen's Tower*. London: Constable 1937 p.241.

[746] Bell p.161. For more on Morrice (1865-1934), see Lucie Dorais: *J.W Morrice*. Toronto: National Gallery of Canada, Canadian Artists Series 1985.

[747] Nordau pp.107-8. This may perhaps be taken as having particular reference to Gustave Geffroy, whose articles about contemporary art were collected in the eight Volumes of *La Vie artistique*, published between 1892 and 1903. Volume III, *Histoire de l'impressionisme*, consists of a historical introduction followed by individual chapters on each artist.

[748] Symons 1925 p.229. Admittedly Symons, no stranger to mental disturbance himself, was rather over inclined to express himself in such terms.

[749] Zweig p.141.

[750] Quoted (or, rather, misquoted) by Geraldine Harris: 'Yvette Guilbert' in Viv Gardner & Susan Rutherford (edd.): *The New Woman and Her Sisters, Feminism and Theatre 1850-1914*. Hemel Hempstead: Harvester Wheatsheaf 1992 p.121. Harris suggests that black indicated the Bohemian, 'an alternative, slightly seedy elegance, perverse, provocative sexuality, the satanic, death, dadacence, the outsider – the modernist'. *Ibidem*. One runs that against the Yellow Nineties, and its place in the dandyism of Baudelaire. The misquotations: Donnay does not say 'Pantheism' but 'panamisme', the brouhaha over the Panama Canal scandal; Mme Marnier is in fact Mme Moraines, and la vie en rose is just that, seeing life through rose tinted spectacles, not a play as implied by italicisation. The passage is longer than the one given here. Maurice Donnay: *Autour du Chat Noir*. Paris: Bernard Grasset 1926 pp.43-4. Hereafter cited as Donnay.

[751] Emile Zola: *Madeleine Férat*. 1868. Translated by Alec Brown. London: Elek 1957.

[752] Zola/Paris p.30.

[753] Edmund Gosse: *Leaves and Fruit*. London: William Heinemann 1927 p.268. Not that one associates Edmund Gosse with high animal spirits in any very feral quantity.

[754] Rearick p.165.

[755] Stevenson/Osbourne p.66.

[756] Louis R. Harlan: *Booker T. Washington, The Making of a Black Leader*. New York Oxford University Press 1972 p.241. Hereafter cited as Harlan.

[757] March pp.21,45,150. One feels that 'gesticulating' merits March's particular disdain, but these and other passages are freighted with class, gender and xenophobic prejudice.

[758] March p.115.

[759] Steven Moore Whiting: *Satie the Bohemian, from Cabaret to Concert Hall*. Oxford: Oxford University Press 1999 p.57.

[760] Thwaite p.256.

[761] Quoted in Rudorff p.140.

[762] Marie-Sophie André and Christophe Beaufils: *Papus, biographie, la belle époque d'occultisme*. Paris: Berg International 1995 p.52. Hereafter cited as André/Beaufils.

[763] André/Beaufils p.56.

[764] Whiteing 1900 p.15.

[765] Ernest Dimnet: *France Herself Again*. London: Chatto & Windus 1913 p.135.

[766] Zola 1883 p.66.

[767] 2nd April 1887. Quoted in Isidore de Lara: *Many Tales of Many Cities*. London: Hutchinson & Co n.d. [1926] p.218. Hereafter cited as de Lara.

[768] Levin p.104.

[769] Symons pp.50-1. 'Plus fin que Pachmann,' cries the ghost of Chopin on hearing the Duke of Dorset play his Marche Funèbre. Max Beerbohm: *Zuleika Dobson*. London: The Bodley Head 1911. New edition London: The Folio Society 1966 p.99.

[770] Symons p.70.

[771] Emile Zola: *Nana*. 1880. Translated with an introduction by Douglas Parmée. World's Classics 1992; reissued as an Oxford World's Classics. Oxford: Oxford University Press 1998 p.114. Hereafter cited as Zola/Nana/Parmée.

[772] Vivian p.167.

[773] Casselaer p.5.

[774] Louis-Arsène Delaunay, who retired in May 1887. Should not be confused with the painter Jules Élie Delaunay. There was also an actress-cum-courtesan called Blanche Delaunay of the Théâtre Athénée.

[775] J.E.C. Welldon, D.D.: *Recollections and Reflections*. London: Cassell 1915 p.57.

[776] Sir Frederick Pollock: *For My Grandson, Remembrances of an Ancient Victorian*. London: John Murray 1933 pp.142-3. Hereafter cited as Pollock 1933.

[777] Beerbohm 1953 p.437.

[778] Howard p.45.

[779] Howard p.46.

[780] Coolidge p.89.

[781] James 1878 p.316. The Odéon was officially called the 'Le Deuxième Théâtre-Français'; the title 'Le Troisième Théâtre-Français' was adopted by Hilarion Bellande for the Théâtre Déjazet when he was director there.

[782] Maupassant/Bel Ami p.92. A *cabanon* is a padded cell. There may be a slight reference also to another version of Don Quixote, *Don Quichotte et Sancho Pança*, an operetta by Hervé.

[783] James 1878 p.326.

[784] James 1878 p.326. The Gymnase acquired a new façade in 1887, a re-assertion of the power of surface over substance. Desclées is Aimée Desclées (1836-1874), of whom there is a picture in 'An English Officer': *More Society Recollections*. London: John Long 1908, facing p.208. Hereafter cited as English Officer 1908.

[785] Raymond Recouly: *The Third Republic*. 1928. New edition, translated by E.F. Buckley. New York: AMS Press 1967 p.35.

[786] Deak p. 248. Dr Deak states (p.250) that audiences would often dress in costume (presumably appropriate to the play) rather than in ordinary evening dress.

[787] Grenville-Murray p.68.

[788] Lucas p.228.

[789] Haine p.2.

[790] Alexandre Benois: *Memoirs*. Translated by Moura Budberg. London: Chatto & Windus Volume II 1964 pp.144-5. Hereafter cited as Benois.

[791] Henderson p.74.

[792] Shaw 1932 p.248.

[793] See Gérard-Denis Farcy: 'Shaw et la scène française', in Paul Brennan & Thierry Dubost (edd.): *G. B. Shaw: un dramaturge engagé*. Caen: Presses Universitaires de Caen 1998 pp.121-37.

[794] J.P. Wearing (ed.): *The Collected Letters of Sir Arthur Wing Pinero*. Minneapolis: University of Minnesota Press 1974 p.93. Hereafter cited as Wearing. Letter to Henry Arthur Jones 17th April 1887.

[795] By Pierre Decourcelle (1856-1929) and Edmond Tarbe (1838-1900).

[796] By Albin Valebrèque (1853-1934).

[797] Wearing pp.131,154. Letters to Augustin Daly 21st November 1891 and William Archer 27th December 1893.

[798] *Les Viveurs* is also the name Georges Ohnet gives to a play by 'Claude La Barre' in his novel *The Rival Actresses*. Edited by G.F. Monkshood. London: Greening & Co 1909. This was originally published as *Lise Fleuron* in 1884. Hereafter cited as Ohnet.

[799] Wearing pp.169-70. Letter to William Archer 16th January 1896.

[800] Wearing p.180. Letter to Henry Irving 13th April 1898.

[801] 'When you have seen one, you have seen all,' was Marie Bashkirtseff's dismissive view in 1878. Bashkirtseff p.318. Diary entry for 31st May 1878. Dion Boucicault tried to import the genre into London with *Babil and Bijou* in 1873. This was set in 'Lutetia', an imaginary version of France, costumed in the time of Louis XIV. For a lengthy discussion of this piece see Sir Osbert Sitwell: *Left Hand, Right Hand! An Autobiography* Volume I: The Cruel Month. London: Macmillan 1945 (hereafter cited as Sitwell) Appendix C.

[802] Chothia p.64.

[803] I have silently corrected the variant forms of this theatre's name to conform to the above usage which is that in Latour/Claval p.123. After the destruction of 25th May 1871, it re-opened on the 2th December 1873.

[804] Lilian Browse (ed.): *Constantin Guys*. London: Faber & Faber 1946 plate 42, unfortunately undated. Hereafter cited as Browse.

[805] Now in the Courtauld Gallery, London. The man is Renoir's brother Edouard, the woman next to him the courtesan 'Nini Gueule de Raie'.

[806] Now in the Boston Museum of Fine Arts, The Hayden Collection–Charles Henry Hayden Fund 10.35.

[807] Salon of 1879. Now in the Musée d'Orsay, ref. RF 2645.

[808] L. Charrel Collection, New York, reproduced in [Anon]:*Toulouse-Lautrec*. Bergamo: Istituto Italiano d'Arti Grafiche n.d. plate V and in Claire and José Frèches: *Toulouse-Lautrec, Painter of the Night*. Translated by Alexandra Campbell. London: Thames & Hudson 1994 p.83, hereafter cited as Frèches. The Frèches suggest that one of the women is the proprietor of the lesbian bar Le Hanneton.

[809] The man in the box is Charles Conder.

[810] Susan Griffin: The Book of the Courtesans, A Catalogue of their Virtues. New York: Broadway Books 2001 p.61.

[811] 'A Cosmopolitan' [Madame v.d. Velde]: *Random Recollections of Courts & Society*. London: Ward & Downey 1888 p.256-7, hereafter cited as van der Velde. Madame van der Velde was the daughter of Count de Launay, sometime Italian Ambassador in Berlin.

[812] Joanna Richardson: *Sarah Bernhardt*. London: Max Reinhardt 1959 p.11. Hereafter cited as Richardson/Bernhardt.

[813] Dubeux p.383.

[814] To say nothing of the reputation of Rousseil whom Eustace Grenville-Murray thought Bernhardt's 'greatest living rival'. Grenville-Murray p.71.

[815] Rôles played by both include ones in Ruy Blas, Mademoiselle de Belle-Isle, Marion de Lorme, Adrienne Lecouvreur, Thermidor, Hernani.

[816] Baring 1935 p.136.

[817] J. Brander Matthews: *The Theatres of Paris*. London: Sampson Low, Marston, Searle & Rivington 1880 p.70. Hereafter cited as Matthews.

[818] Opened 5th January 1875.

[819] Apart from seating capacity, the Palais Garnier was three times the size of the next two biggest opera houses, the Alexandra in St Petersburg and the Munich Opera House. One may also note the Fenice (2,000 seats), the New York Academy of Music (2,000), the Carlo Felice in Genoa (2,000), the San Carlos in Lisbon (2,000), the Royal Theatre in Munich (2,300), the Vienna Opera (2,400) and La Scala (3,000), to say nothing of the Grand Opera House, Belfast (3,500).

[820] F.W.J. Hemmings: *The Theatre Industry in Nineteenth Century France*. Cambridge: Cambridge University Press 1993 p.3. Hereafter cited as Hemmings 1993.

[821] F.W.J. Hemmings: *Theatre and State in France 1760-1905*. Cambridge: Cambridge University Press 1994 pp.195-6, 203. Hereafter cited as Hemmings 1994.

[822] Dumas p.50.

[823] Marie & Squire Bancroft: *Recollections of Sixty Years*. London: John Murray 1909 p.171. Hereafter cited as Bancroft.

[824] Charlotte Leaf (ed.): *Walter Leaf 1852-1927, Some Chapters of Autobiography*. London: John Murray 1932 p.78; hereafter cited as Leaf. Charlotte was another of Symonds' daughters. Leaf was a classical scholar (Harrow and Trinity, Cambridge), a member of the Alpine Club and a banker, with a wide acquaintance among the more established literary men. Wilde had been a guest at the Leafs' house (*ibid.* p.158), and Charlotte Leaf refers to her husband's diary, which needs to be recovered for its references to Wilde. Bancroft (who only ever has the kindliest recollections of his contemporaries) says of Desclées' Frou-Frou that 'the impression left on my memory is that she was one of the finest and most touching actresses who ever adorned the art I love'. Bancroft p.171.

[825] Dumas p.viii. Marie Bashkirtseff thought Desclées superior to Bernhardt. Bashkirtseff p.560. Diary entry for 19th October 1882.

[826] Matthews pp.6-7. The dedication refers to the 'soirées passées dans sa loge'.

[827] Anderson 1936 p.115.

[828] Mary Anderson: *A Few Memories*. London: Osgood, McIlvaine & Co 1896 p.113. Anderson met Ristori again in Paris six years later. Ristori's own recollections stop before this period, but contain discussions of *Medea* and *Phèdre* that bear on the popularity of these plays in Paris in the 1880s and 1890s. Adelaide Ristori: *Ricordi e Studi Artistici.* Torino: L. Roux 1887.

[829] Shaw 1911 p.117. The impresario Cecil Savoyard is speaking, and there is also something false about him, for his real name is William Tinkler, while his assumed name is derived from the two luxury hotels, the Cecil and the Savoy.

[830] Later Master of Christ's College, Cambridge and Clark's biographer.

[831] Rothenstein Volume I p.46. *Le Roi s'amuse* is better known as *Rigoletto*.

[832] A.E. Shipley: *'J'. A Memoir of John Willis Clark*. London: Smith, Elder & Co 1913 p.162. Hereafter cited as Shipley.

[833] Also used by Hilaire Belloc, when he went to Paris in December 1900 to write his book on the city.

[834] Shipley p.151.

[835] Prince Serge Volkonsky: *My Reminiscences*. Translated by A.E. Chamot. London: Hutchinson & Co 1925 Volume I p.1104.

[836] The Lyrique, the Cirque Impérial, the Folies Dramatique, the Gaîté, the Funambules, the Délassements Coques, the Lazari. The Gaîté survived in the Square des Arts.

[837] *Punch*, 5th March 1892.

[838] Shaw 1932 Volume III p.213.

[839] Hobson p.16.

[840] Quoted by Henderson p.96. 1892 saw the fiftieth anniversary of Cambronne's death.

[841] In Paris in a double bill with Bjørnson's *Beyond Human Power*, 13th February 1894, the programme designed by Vuillard.

[842] Oscar Wilde to Reginald Turner 25th May 1898. Hart-Davis 1962 p.746; Holland & Hart-Davis p.1075.

[843] Langlade p.287.

[844] Elizabeth Wilson: *Bohemians, the Glamorous Outcasts*. London & New York: I.B. Tauris 2000 p.77.

[845] Lugné-Poë did direct two plays by Shaw (*The Doctors' Dilemma* in May 1922, and *Mrs Warren's Profession* in October 1924.) His penultimate play was Maugham's *The Circle* in November 1928.

[846] Poster by Vuillard reproduced in Cate fig.98.

[847] Reproduced in Cate fig.99.

[848] Reproduced in Cate fig.100.

[849] Michael Meyer: *Strindberg, A Biography*. London: Secker & Warburg 1985 p.311.

[850] 22nd January and 18th December 1895.

[851] Miscalled Auclare by Shaw, she had played Hilda Wangel in the Théâtre de l'Œuvre London production of *The Master Builder*.

[852] Described by Fouquier of *Le Figaro* as 'les contorsions d'un lièvre qui a reçu un coup de feu dans les reins'. Quoted by Bernard Shaw in his review, *The Saturday Review*, 21st November 1896. Shaw 1932 Volume II p.255.

[853] 15 rue Blanche. Shaw calls this the Théâtre de la Nouveauté, which is a considerable shift in meaning, and describes it as 'nearly as large as [the Theatre Royal] Drury Lane'. Shaw 1932 Volume II p.255. The Nouveau Théâtre, once used for skating, and an annexe of the Casino de Paris subsequently became the Théâtre Réjane (1906-1918), and is now the Théâtre de Paris. In the 1890s it was owned by Alfred Edwards, one of Misia Sert's husbands.

[854] De Max also played Dom Balthazar in the Théâtre de l'Œuvre's production of Verhaeren's *La Cloître* in February 1900. He did not always favour Lugné-Poë, once describing him to André Gide as 'the humbug of Paris'. Gide/O'Brien p.114. Diary entry for 15th October 1906.

[855] Henderson p.141. Henderson consistently refers to the princess by her nom-de-plume Tola Dorian, and occasionally it is unclear that he makes the identification between the two.

[856] 29th and 30th May, as *Les Revenants*.

[857] George Moore: 'Note on *Ghosts*' in *Impressions and Memories*. London: T. Werner Laurie 1914 p.162.

[858] Balfour Volume II p.413.

[859] Exhibited at the Théâtre de l'Œuvre exhibition, Musée d'Orsay 2005.

[860] Brandès, the favourite of Barbey d'Aurevilly, had been a member of the Comédie Française since 1887, becoming Sociétaire in 1896 and remaining until 1903.
Hedda's insistence that Eilet Lovborg should 'die beautifully' had been rehearsed by Zola, when Nana revels in the beautiful death of the comte de Vandeuvres, who sets fire to his stables. But just as Lovborg muffs his suicide attempt, so there are rumours that Vandeuvres faked his death. The Château de Vendeuvre [*sic*] in Normandy is known for the trick jets of water in its grounds, an atmosphere of playfulness and deception. 'Dans une ambiance chaleureuse animée par des automates, vous ressentirez tout le raffinement et l'art de vivre du XVIIIe siècle,' is the remarkable claim of the château's brochure. Whether these refinements extend to the château's collection of kennels from the seventeenth to the nineteenth century is perhaps best left to individual judgment.

[861] Kerry Powell: *Oscar Wilde & the Theatre of the 1890s*. Cambridge: Cambridge University Press 1990, Chapter V. Hereafter cited as Powell 1990. Wilde was one of the seven guarantors of Elizabeth Robins' 1893 Ibsen season at the (London) Opéra Comique, but even so in 1891 he had found that at *Hedda Gabler* the pit was 'full of sad vegetarians and the stalls occupied by men in mackintoshes and women in red shawls', not at all the sort of audience he liked. Oscar Wilde to Mrs Willie Grenfell, late April 1891. Hart-Davis 1985 p.96; Holland & Hart-Davis p.477. Given the status now accorded to Robins, it may be surprising to learn the view of Irene Vanbrugh that Robins was 'afterwards much more famous as an authoress'. Vanbrugh p.23. Vanbrugh played both Hedda and Thea in J.M. Barrie's burlesque *Ibsen's Ghost*.

[862] F.W.J. Hemmings: *Culture and Society in France 1848-1898 – Dissidents and Philistine*s. London: Batsford 1971 pp.240-1. A storyboard at the exhibition 'Théâtre de l'Œuvre', Musée d'Orsay, spring 2005, listed actors closely associated with the Théâtre de l'Œuvre: Avernès, Firmin Gémier (1869-1933), de Max, Mévisto, Louise France, Cora Lapercerie, Marthe Mellot and surprisingly, Sérusier (surprisingly, that is, if Paul Sérusier was intended). Scrutiny of the programmes of the Théâtre de l'Œuvre adds as regular members of Lugné-Poë's cast Suzanne Auclair, Berthe Bady, Marie Samary, Fanny Zaessinger, and an actress called Yellow.

[863] Setting up this theatre had been first proposed in March 1890, but it was not until December that it was launched. It eventually became a commercial theatre. Lugné-Poë played Wangel and Georgette Camée played Ellida.

[864] William Tydeman and Steven Price: *Wilde Salomé*. Cambridge: Cambridge University Press 1996 p.30. Hereafter cited as Tydeman/Price. Ernest Dowson and Aubrey Beardsley were in the audience. Henry Maas, J.L. Duncan and W.G. Good (edd.): *The Letters of Aubrey Beardsley*. London: Cassell 1970 p.96. Hereafter cited as Maas/Duncan/Good.

[865] Maurice Toesca: *Jules Renard*. Paris: Albin Michel 1977 p.140. Journal de Jules Renard. http://abu.cnam.fr/cgi-bin/go?ren93982,5621.

[866] Maurice Rostand was himself gay. José Squinquel played Wilde and Andre Fouché Lord Alfred Douglas. It was a great success.

[867] Programme designed by Henri Bataille.

[868] This piece, in which Berthe Bady was the leading lady, should not be confused with *La Belle au Bois dormant* by Jean Richepin and Henri Cain which Sarah Bernhardt produced at the Théâtre Sarah Bernhardt in December 1907 with herself as the prince. *La Belle au Bois dormant* also became a piece for voice and piano by Debussy to text by Victor Hyspa, 1890, and for piano by Ravel (1908, written while staying with the Godebski family, the first of the 'Cinq pièces enfantines' in his 'Ma mere d'oye' suite. The magical and transformative theme of *La belle au bois dormant* is the characteristic of its appeal at the time.

[869] Deak p.225. Laurence des Cars rejects the influence of Burne-Jones. Laurence des Cars: 'Burne-Jones and France' in Stephen Wildman and John Christian: *Edward Burne-Jones, Victorian Artist-Dreamer.* New York: Metropolitan Museum of Art 1998 p.32. Isabelle Cahn for the exhibition 'Théâtre de l'Œuvre', Musée d'Orsay, spring 2005, only committed herself to 'après Burne-Jones'. The play was a flop.

[870] Daudet p.26. Zola, describing the audience at the Variétés, writes 'This was Paris: the Paris of literature, finance and pleasure; lots of journalists, a few authors, stockbrokers, and more tarts than respectable women; a strangely mixed bunch, comprising very kind of genius, tainted with every kind of vice.' Zola/ Nana/Parmée pp.9-10.

[871] Romain Rolland to Richard Strauss 1st December 1905. Richard Strauss et Romain Rolland: *Correspondance et Fragments de Journal*. Avant-propos de Gustave Samazeuilh. Paris: Albin Michel 1961 p.83. Hereafter cited as Strauss /Rolland.

[872] Mary Daniel: *The French Drama of the Unspoken*. Edinburgh: Edinburgh University Press 1953 p.12.

[873] One of only two plays written by women produced at the Théâtre de l'Œuvre, the other being Judith Cladel's *Le Volant* (28th May 1895), programme by Ker-Xavier Roussel.

[874] This was revived in January 1897, with programmes designed by Denis and Vuillard.

[875] 8th May, with both Max Barbier and Edouard de Max.

[876] Hobson p.58.

[877] This had its origin in a private performance at Daudet's house on 10th February 1887.   The guests included Bonnetain, Descaves, Alexis, Coppée, Heredia, Hennique, Leconte de Lisle, Goncourt and George Moore.   'Moore was in ecstasies over Pierrot, which he saw as the great symbol of French civilisation'. Frazier p.151.

[878] In 1899 'Andrée Alvar', the mother of Colette's Gigi, is singing a secondary rôle at the Opéra-Comique in *Si j'étais roi*, an elderly piece (1852) by d'Ennery and Jules Bresil.

[879] Sherard/Maupassant p.325.   He did see *The Mikado* at the Savoy Theatre in August 1886.

[880] Charles Castle: *The Folies Bergère*.   London: Methuen 1982 p.35, hereafter cited as Castle.   Not to be confused with the Belgian poet Fernand Séverin or the Danish painter Peder Severin Kroyer, nor with Anne Severin, the heroine of a novel by Pauline de Ferronays (Mrs Augustus Craven).

[881] Henderson p.121.

[882] Founded at 18 rue St Lazare by Charles Bodinière, secretary-general of the Comédie Française.   It became known as La Bodinière, the foyer doubling as a gallery. This address is also given as that of the procuress Thecla de Lancry (a Belgian, whose real name was Lorsikoff). *Pretty Women* pp.101-2.

[883] Quoted in Deak p.225.

[884] Deak p.175.

[885] *L'Enfant et les Sortilèges* was not published until 1925 (Paris: Durand et Cie), but had its beginnings much earlier.   While Ravel's name is always associated with it, that of Colette, who wrote the libretto seems not to be.

[886] Offenbach's *Contes d'Hoffmann* opened at the Opéra Comique on 10th February 1881. Susanne Rutherford suggests that this opera 'usefully combines all the major nineteenth century patriarchal interpretations of the meaning, possession and voice in the single figure of Stella [who] appears only briefly and mutely in the final scene.' Susan Rutherford; 'The voice of freedom' in Viv Gardner & Susan Rutherford (edd.): *The New Woman and Her Sisters, Feminism and Theatre 1850-1914*. Hemel Hempstead: Harvester Wheatsheaf 1992 p.96. Well, perhaps.

[887] F. Novotny: *Cézanne*. London: Phaidon 1961; 3rd edition 1972 p.4.

[888] Reproduced in, e.g., Vierney p.50.

[889] Carlson p.210.

[890] Arthur Gold & Robert Fizdale: *Misia, The Life of Misia Sert*.   London: Macmillan 1980 p.42.

[891] This is the basis of the 1911 opera *Conchita* by Riccardo Zandonai. The soprano part was sung by his wife, Tarquinia Tarquini 51882-1976), one of the first Salomés to perform the Dance of the Seven Veils. The English translation by G.F. Monkshood (*Woman and Puppet*) was published by Greening & Co in their Lotus Library series.

[892] Matthews p.195. The Vrai Guignol should not be confused with the Grand Guignol, directed by Max Maurey, the macabre theatre established in 1898 in the impasse Chaptal, Montmartre (now the Cité Chaptal). This closed in 1962. It was originally a chapel, then a shop for religious goods, then the studio of Rochegrosse, mutations that would hardly have been lost on the audience. Subsequently it became the Theatre 347 and then the International Visual Theatre), a company devoted in this interplay of semiotics to presenting plays in sign language.

[893] Oscar Wilde to the Editor of the *Daily Telegraph* 19th February 1892. Holland & Hart-Davis pp.518-20.

[894] Sherard 1906 p.239.

[895] Bourdelle had already executed bas-reliefs for the Théâtre de Champs-Elysées. Maquettes and drawings can be seen in the Musée Bourdelle, Montparnasse.

[896] In 1932 John Dickson Carr published a novel, *The Waxworks Murders*, where the possibilities of the 'Musée Augustin', somewhere off the boulevard de Sébastopol, were exploited.

[897] George Moore thought it could be done on £150-£200. George Moore: *'Théâtre Libre'* and *'On the Necessity of an English Théâtre Libre'* in *Impressions and Memories.* London: T. Werner Laurie 1914 p.176.

[898] Camille Pissarro and Octave Mirbeau saw this. W.S. Meadmore: *Lucien Pissarro, Un Cœur Simple.* London: Constable 1962 p.63, but John Henderson says March 1892, with the production of Jules Bois' *Les noces de Sathan.* Henderson p.100. The exact date is given as 30th March 1892 by Deak p.162. Deak agrees about *Les noces* and adds two scenes from Scheré's *Vercingétorix* and *Le premier Chant de l'Iliade.*

[899] In November 1906 Colette appeared as Paniska in his play *Pan* (music by Robert Haas) at the Théâtre Marigny.

[900] Latour/Claval p.141. For more on Fort and Wilde, see Paul Medina: 'Zum 25 Todestag Oscar Wildes am 30 November, Ein Gesprach mit dem "Dichterfürsten" Paul Fort, dem letzen Freund Oscar Wildes'. Berlin: *Die Literarische Welt* 17th November 1925.

[901] The Déjazet was owned at one time by Blanche Querette, 'a very wretched actress' whose lover managed it 'but he is on the verge of bankruptcy'. *Pretty Women* p.154. Ballande gave up the theatre in 1879 when a M. Desmottes took it over, being succeeded in his turn in 1881 by Henri Luguet. In 1882 the director was Marcel Villars. The theatre was named in honour of 'the frivolous but accomplished' Virginie Déjazet (1798-1875), who even in her old age anticipated Sarah Bernhardt in playing young men on stage: the Chevalier de Belle-Isle in *Monsieur de Belle-Isle* (1865) and the Chevalier de Garsac in *Les Pistoles de mon père* (1870). The description of Déjazet is that of Guedalla p.105.

[902] Fouquières p.44.

[903] Carlson p.210.

[904] MacDonald p.123.

[905] Henderson pp.14, 44.

[906] At Firmin Didot in the rue Jacob.

[907] Henderson p.44. But few are the arts administrators who have never done this.

[908] Edmond Got: *Journal*. Publiée par son fils Médéric Got. Paris: Plon 1910 p.248. Hereafter cited as Got.

[909] Richardson/Gautier pp.96,205.

[910] George Moore: Essays 'Théâtre Libre' and 'On the Necessity of an English Théâtre Libre' in *Impressions and Memories*. London: T. Werner Laurie 1914 pp.167,173. We now have accessible two important essays on the Théâtre Libre by Gabriela Zapolska who worked with Antoine in these early days, 'Antoine et le Théâtre Libre' and 'Credo Théâtral de Zapolska'. In Zapolska q.v.

[911] Goncourt/Baldick p.332.

[912] Goncourt/Baldick p.333. Diary entry for 320th October 1887.

[913] Chothia 1991 p.2.

[914] 30th March 1887.

[915] Poster by Sérusier reproduced in Cate fig.97.

[916] Argot for a police informer.

[917] Henderson p.54.

[918] Until 1899, when the prison was pulled down and streets built over its site.

[919] Or Trolliet, un 'géant habillé d'un tricot de laine, coiffé d'une calotte plantée de travers sur des cheveux qui frisent; il mâche un cigare d'un sou, crache sec, hérisse une dure moustache sur une bouche piquée de bleu par des points de poudre. [...] Trolliet marié à une géante au teint couperosé et aux cheveux couleur d'acajou, un type d'ogresse alsacienne.' J.-K. Huysmans: *La Bièvre et Saint Séverin*. http://www.huysmans.org/betsseverin/severin.htm; unnumbered pages.

[920] Lucas p.183.

[921] 24th April 1894; poster by Toulouse-Lautrec.

[922] Hobson p.26.

[923] One may note Raffaëlli's designs for *La patrie en danger* (Goncourt) when Antoine produced it at the Théâtre Libre, 1889. These were more akin to his illustrations for such books as *Les Sœurs Vatard* or *Germinie Lacerteux*, than to his undemanding topographical Paris street scenes.

[924] Symons p.84.

[925] Symons p.45.

[926] Arnold Bennett: 'Henri Becque' in *Books and Persons, being Comments on a Past Epoch*. London: Chatto & Windus 1917 p.257. Hereafter cited as Bennett 1917.

[927] I am much indebted to Ms Helka Maria Mäkinen of the Department of Theatre Research, University of Helsinki for sending me a TS copy of her article 'Politics, Sexuality and Emancipated Women: The Reception of Oscar Wilde's Salomé in Finland 1905 and 1919', published in *Nordic Theatre Studies* 1999; together with much information about Wilde productions in Finland.

[928] Harris p.265.

[929] Antoine p.10. The Gymnase was under the direction of Albert Carré and of Porel, Réjane's husband, who regarded Antoine as an amateur and ensured that he did not direct there again.

[930] Henderson p.84.

[931] Antoine p.10.

[932] *La Plume* March 1891, quoted in Henderson p.88.

[933] Henderson p.88.

[934] Maurice Bouchor, chiefly a song writer, not to be confused with Joseph-Félix Bouchor who shared a studio with Antonio de La Gandara at 22 Monsieur-le-Prince, rented at one time by Whistler.

[935] Henderson p.116.

[936] Reginald Lister to his mother June 1891. Emma Lady Ribblesdale: *Letters and Diaries*. Collected by her daughter Beatrix Lister. London: Private printed at the Chiswick Press 1930 p.96. Hereafter cited as Ribblesdale 1930.

[937] Relocated to the 25th/26th in Marchesi p.255; and to 1886 in Fox pp.62-4.

[938] Hemmings 1994 p.xii. There is no source for this assertion, but it is also given by Ralph Nevill, who witnessed the fire, adding that 'For days afterwards people declared that the vicinity of the theatre smelt like a kitchen after dinner had been cooked'. Nevill 1913 p.118. Clunn temporises: 'more than a hundred'. Clunn p.51.

[939] This was well covered in the exhibition 'Carmen à Mélisande' at the Petit Palais, 2015.

[940] The history of the Paris theatres is a history of fire in Paris, as few theatres seem to have escaped it at one time or another. The fire at the Odéon on Good Friday 1818 burned for a week; the Ambigu was destroyed in 1827; the Gaîté in 1835. The Trianon-Concert, boulevard Rochechouart, was destroyed by a fire towards the end of the century. The Elysée-Montmartre burned in 1900; the Opéra in Lille in 1903. The twenty-year old actress Jane (or Jeanne) Henriot was killed in the Théâtre Français fire.

[941] Segal 1987 p.69.

[942] Dauphin, a friend of Laurent Tailhade who composed for Jules Jouy, also wrote poems under the name Pimpinelli. The pension of madame Vauquier, where Père Goriot lives, was in the rue Neuve-Sainte-Geneviève.

[943] His real name was François Sommier. There is a portrait of him by Lautrec.

[944] The texts are printed in Donnay. *Ailleurs* is dedicated to Verlaine.

[945] Ralph Nevill: *Days and Nights in Montmartre and the Latin Quarter*. London: Herbert Jenkins 1927 p.118. Hereafter cited as Nevill 1927.

[946] Diary entry for 30th October 1897. Newman Flower (ed.): *The Journals of Arnold Bennett 1896-1910*. London: Cassell 1952 p.60. Hereafter cited as Flower/Bennett.

[947] Belloc 1943 p.295.

[948] Belloc 1943 p.295.

[949] I take this from Painter I p.213, who does not say how far the title was borrowed from Dujardin.

[950] In 2004/5 Marey's work was the basis of an exhibition at the Musée d'Orsay, 'Etienne-Jules Marey, photographie des mouvements'. He should not be confused with Jules Marey, who was a patron of Muybridge's.

[951] A list of these is printed in Andrieu p.57.

[952] If both the name of the man and the nature of his invention feed the sense of fantasy, one may also throw in a small joke played by the only result for his name that the Internet throws up: 'ce maudit Jules! (terme d'abus)'.
http://web.uvic.ca/lancenrd/french/topics/adj02/note01.htm.

[953] Richard Abel: *The Cine Goes to Town, French Cinema 1896-1914.* Berkeley: University of California Press 1994 p.61. Hereafter cited as Abel.

[954] 28th December 1895, in the Salon Indien before an audience of thirty-three people. The Grand Café was then under the direction of Volpini, so influential in the establishment of the Symbolist painters. The Lumières' programme was 'Sortie d'Usine', 'Le Bocal au Poisson', 'L'arroseur'', 'Tramways de Lyon', and 'L'arrivée du train'. While Jean Joseph-Renaud could by 1898 title a work *Le cinématographie de marriage*, Wilde, conversely, seems to have shown no interest in moving images, even when fashionable.

[955] 'Brain of Britain 2004', BBC Radio 4 23rd October 2004.

[956] Auguste and Louis Lumière: *Letters.* Edited and Annotated by Jacques Rittaud-Hutinet with the collaboration of Yvelise Dentzer, preface by Maurice Trarieux-Lumière. Translation by Pierre Hodgson. London: Faber & Faber 1995 p.84. Hereafter cited as Lumière.

[957] The name Pitou comes from *La Fille de Madame Angot.*

[958] I am not sure whether this was the same Trewey who became a performance artist using different hats, or whether either was the man described as 'the celebrated Trewey, the French fantaisiste' (Henry Ridgely Evans: 'A Day With Alexander the Great', *The Sphinx*, Kansas City, Volume 4, Nos. 3 & 4, May and June 1905 http://www.uelectric.com/pastimes/hermann.htm), or even whether this was his real name, Trewy being a town in Cornwall.

[959] David E. Bordwell and Kristin Thompson: 'The power of Mise-en-scene' in *Film Art, an Introduction.* McGraw Hill 1997 pp.171-2.

[960] 'L'Affaire Dreyfus', 1899.

[961] His real name was the more prosaic Edward Muggeridge.

[962] Morot's depiction of the cavalry charge at Rezonville was one of the first to adopt the correct position.

[963] Gordon Hendricks: *Eadweard Muybridge, The Father of the Motion Picture.* London: Secker & Warburg 1975.

[964] The Bonnat is reproduced as fig.3.7 in Elizabeth Ann Coleman: *The Opulent Era – Fashions of Worth, Doucet and Pingat.* London & New York: Thames & Hudson and the Brooklyn Museum 1989.

[965] Abel p.17.

[966] Lumière p.46n2. Curiously, the same editors state (p.67n) that the fire was caused 'by someone lighting a match too close to a bottle of ether'. Possibly the fact that the Securitas lamp was fuelled by ether allows both explanations to be true.

[967] Abel p.61.

[968] 1887/8. Now in the Winthrop Collection, Harvard.

[969] One Seurat painting of a circus sideshow has been identified as that of the Cirque Corvi, in the place de la Nation in the spring of 1887. Metropolitan Museum of Art, New York ref. 61.10.17; the Cirque Fernando is the setting for Degas' 'Miss La' in the National Gallery, London.

[970] The theme of the disturbing exhibition on the Clown, 'La Grande Parade, Portrait de l'artiste en clown', at the Grand Palais, 11th March to 31st May 2004. One can add that 'Parade' is the name of the bourgeois vulgarian in Sardou's *Nos Intimes*.

[971] Should not be confused with Gaston Leroux, author of *Le Fantôme de l'Opéra*, who studied law in Paris towards the end of the 1880s and contrived to spend in six months the million francs his father left him in 1889. Gaston Leroux, a Norman like Maupassant's Bel-Ami, also like Bel-Ami became a successful journalist on *L'Echo de Paris* and then *Le Matin*.

[972] Helen Day: 'Female daredevils' in Viv Gardner & Susan Rutherford (edd.): *The New Woman and Her Sisters, Feminism and Theatre 1850-1914*. Hemel Hempstead: Harvester Wheatsheaf 1992 p.139.

[973] In 'London Models', Wyse Jackson p.34.

[974] Stevenson p.182

[975] This may be the Cirque des Bashibazoucks of the rue St-Honoré in *Trilby*. Du Maurier/Trilby p.281.

[976] Kröller-Müller Museum, Otterlo.

[977] e.g. 'L'Equestrienne' of 1888, now in the Art Institute of Chicago.

[978] Richard R. Brettell: *French Impressionists*. Chicago: The Art Institute of Chicago 1987 p.55. This was one of Bertha Potter Palmer's acquisitions. Hereafter cited as Brettell.

[979] Colette: *Gigi*. Translated by Roger Senhouse 1949. Harmondsworth: Penguin Books 1958 p.27; hereafter cited as Colette 1958. The original at Colette 1944 p.52. She later (1910) married the writer Henri Duvernois.

[980] Brettell p.65. 'The Tightrope Walker' is reproduced on p.64.

[981] Musée d'Orsay, ref. 2511,

[982] See, for example, Raffaëlli's 'Georges Clemenceau prononçant un discours au cirque Fernando', 1883, Musée national du Château de Versailles, reproduced as plate 11 in Marianne Delafond & Caroline Genet-Bondeville: *Jean-François Raffaëlli*. Paris: Musée Marmottan-Monet 1999.

[983] Matthew p.229. Diary entry for 5th September 1889.

[984] van de Velde Vol. II pp.234-6.
http://www.mle.asso.fr/banquet/97/n28/inedits5.htm

[985] Pretty Women p.90.

[986] Field p.124.

[987] Corner of the rue du 4 septembre / place de l'Opéra. Whiteing p.57.

[988] Thomas was Director of the Conservatoire. *Mignon* was first performed in Paris on the 17th November 1866. Albani visited Paris for two weeks in 1871 to study Mignon with Thomas; Marie Tempest played Mignon on her American tour

in 1891 and Charlotte Wyns made her debut in the rôle at the Opéra-Comique in 1893.
[989] Carolyn Steedman: 'New Times, Mignon and Her Meanings', in Stokes.
[990] Gramont p.246. Could she have taken her name from that of the restaurant? This acquisition gives some piquancy to the account that in Paris the Grand Duke Vladimir 'did not *merely* engage in in reckless extravagance, *but* [...] spent many hours at museums and art galleries, collecting paintings and antiques' (my italics). Meriel Buchanan: 'The Grand Duchess Vladimir' in *Victorian Gallery*. London: Cassell & Co 1956 p.50.
[991] Barbara Wilson: *Dear Youth*. London: Macmillan & Co 1937 p.34. Hereafter cited as Wilson.
[992] English Officer p.62. Just as Nana engaged the attention of the 'Prince of Scotland', so Massin engaged that of the Prince of Wales. Pretty Women p.130.
[993] Harding p.100.
[994] Quoted in Leslie p.61.
[995] Blunt p.176. For the Halévy family, see Henri Loyrette: *Entre le théâtre et l'histoire. La famille Halévy (1790-1960)*. Paris: Coédition Réunion des musées nationaux, Fayard 1996 (catalogue of the exhibition of the same name, Musée d'Orsay, March - June 1996).
[996] Balfour Volume II p.388. Richard Whiteing, in a remark of studied ambiguity, calls Hading (whose theatre was the Vaudeville), 'an actress of the first class, and in her peculiar style no living woman is quite her equal'. Whiteing 1886 p.213.
[997] Now in the Museum of Art, Rhode Island School of Design.
[998] Herbert p.109.
[999] 1878/9. Now in the Musée d'Orsay.
[1000] And not only for Parisians. Cabanel's 'The Birth of Venus', a piece of chocolate box art at its most sickly, was painted for the American collector John Wolfe in 1875, who passed it on sixteen years later to the Metropolitan Museum of Art, New York (ref.94.24.1). There is another in the Musée d'Orsay, as is a similar work by Bouguereau. Wolfe was chiefly a patron of Pierre-Auguste Cot of whom Marie Bashkirtseff was a pupil. She describes Cot as 'quite forty-seven, but neither stout nor bald'. Bashkirtseff p.451. Diary entry for 15th January 1881.
[1001] Carlson p.226. Rostand's *Cyrano de Bergerac* opened on the 28th December 1897 with Coquelin *cadet* in the title part. It took forty curtain calls and Sarcey called it 'the joyous sun of old Gaul rising again after a long night.' Rudorff p.319. *L'Aiglon* opened at the Théâtre Sarah Bernhardt on the 15th March 1900. Beerbohm's drawing of Rostand (1910) features in the background Bernhardt as l'Aiglon and Coquelin as Cyrano; reproduced as plate 31 in Rupert Hart-Davis (compiler): *A Catalogue of the Caricatures of Max Beerbohm*. London: Macmillan 1972, hereafter cited as Hart-Davis 1972. There is a Musée Edmond Rostand in Cambo-les-Bains. Lemaître was 'one of the most acute observers of the scene in the 1890s'. Henderson pp.131-2; 'an illustrious critic and essayist respected in academic, social and theatrical circles'. Arthur Gold & Robert Fizdale: *The Divine Sarah, A Life of Sarah Bernhardt*.New York: Alfred A. Knopf 1991 p.249. Hereafter cited as Gold/Fizdale 1991.

[1002] Oscar Wilde to Robbie Ross July 1898; Oscar Wilde to Robert Ross 10th March 1896. Holland & Hart-Davis pp.190,653.

[1003] Harding p.107. This is followed by Traubner p.91. The racehorse named after her was called Jane Hading.

[1004] Fouquières p.99, 263. My italics.

[1005] Got p.171. Entry for 3rd March 1872.

[1006] van der Velde p.253; Symons p.92; Vivian p.168. Vivian spent the winter of 1894/5 in Paris. Judic was born Anna Damiens, and had made her debut at the Eldorado in 1867.

[1007] Belloc 1943 p.232.

[1008] Traubner p.20. The London version of *Nitouche* starred May Yohé.

[1009] At her peak, she was earning a million francs (£40,000) a year, perhaps £1,000,000 in the currency of a century later. Harding p.69. Zola lived in the rue de Boulogne 1877-1889, copying his own art, for he had given the comte and comtesse de Viargue a house there in *Madeleine Férat* (1868).

[1010] Whiteing p.212.

[1011] Whiteing 1900 p.208.

[1012] Young p.14. Noel Peters was in the passage des Princes (no.24), and may be the Peters referred to in *Nana* (Douglas Parmée describes it vaguely as 'a well-known restaurant on the *grands boulevards'* (Zola/Nana/Parmée p.428) – although the latter 'Peters' may be the one referred to as 'a well-known night-house'. Pretty Women p.121. Or the two descriptions may not be incompatible. The Café de Paris was in the Avenue de l'Opéra. Wilde lunched Sherard there in 1883.

[1013] Various sources, most recently McKenna p.1.

[1014] 'L'étrange symbiose de la galanterie et de la littérature'. Anon: *Paris et ses cafés*. Catalogue of the exhibition of the same name. Paris: Action artistique de la Ville de Paris. Paris 2004 p.9; James/Ambassadors p.271.

[1015] Moore 1914 p.1.

[1016] Silvestre (1837-1901) was known for his rather Rabelaisian stories. 'Armand Silvestre? Well, yes ... I suppose so ... Pretty smutty of course ... I wouldn't exactly swap him for the *Imitation of Christ,*' says a priest who questions Célestine about her reading. Mirbeau p.207. Silvestre was a mécène of Laurent Tailhade when the latter first came to Paris, and there is a statuette of him by Théodore Rivière in the Musée d'Orsay, ref. RF 4064

[1017] Félicien Rops' biographers add Rops but he is not referred to in the other lists of Guerbois habitués. Delevoye p.120. A list is also given in Raymond Cogniat: *Sisley*. Translated by Alice Sachs. Naefels: Bonfini Press 1978 p.37, hereafter cited as Cogniat. The names I give here have been compiled from a number of sources, and may be the most comprehensive so far assembled. Bazille was killed in 1870. Paul Guigou (1834-1871), not to be confused with Paul Gauguin, was an Impressionist painter from Provence, a friend of Monticelli and Frédéric Mistral, whose work was collected by Dr Gachet.

[1018] Felbermann p.113.

[1019] Musée d'Orsay, ref. RF 729. This is (surely?) a composite, rather than a group portrait; the same being true of Fantin's 'Un coin de table' of 1872 (Musée d'Orsay, ref. RF 1959), which shows Verlaine, Rimbaud, Ernest d'Hervilley, Camille Pelletan, Elzéar Bonnier, Emile Blémont and Jean Aicard. This was bought by Blémont, whose real name was L.-E. Petitdidier.

[1020] Zweig p.93.

[1021] Perruchot p.71.

[1022] National Gallery, London.

[1023] The father of the Gothic revival in France.

[1024] Perruchot p.144.

[1025] Cogniat p.37.

[1026] On the corner, 18 rue Saint-Rustique / 12 rue des Saules in Montmartre. I have not in fact found a single contemporary reference to it for the period 1870-1900. Up to 1890 it was called Aux Billards en Bois, and as such is the subject of van Gogh's 'La Guingette', painted in October 1886 when he was living nearby in the rue Lepic with his brother Theo, 1886-8.

[1027] Huysmans 1891 p.20.

[1028] Sherard/Maupassant. London: T. Werner Laurie 1926 p.319.

[1029] Haine pp.ix,2.

[1030] Nubar became prime minister of Egypt that year and again from 1884 to 1888 and 1894 to 1895, when ill-health obliged him to resign. He died in Paris in 1899.

[1031] 4th April 1878.

[1032] The results were not quite as straightforward as they should have been, always a risk with secret manœuvres. 'I cannot help thinking,' wrote the Prince of Wales to Lord Beaconsfield, 'that though Mr Rivers Wilson is a man of undoubted ability, and acted from the best of motives, he has managed to lose instead of gaining the confidence of the Khedive, and has been in the pocket of Nubar Pasha, who is the Khedive's sworn foe.' Sir Sidney Lee: *King Edward VII, A Biography* Volume I: From Birth to Accession. London: Macmillan 1925 p.449. Hereafter cited as Lee.

[1033] Son-in-law of Georges Charpentier, president of the Société des Gens de Lettres, novelist of Parisian life, and contributor, under the name Lancelot, of articles on correct French in *Le Temps*. With less correctitude he was a collaborator during the Occupation.

[1034] Sorel p.28. It is described in Newnham-Davis pp.18-19, where it is called La Rue. 'In one corner a band plays quite inoffensively.' Closed in 1955.

[1035] Tailhade p.79. Dufay does not identify Yeu-Yeu.

[1036] Haine p.2.

[1037] Rothenstein Volume I p.94.

[1038] Rothenstein Volume I p.121.

[1039] Richardson/Gautier p.134.

[1040] Moore/Impressions p.225.

[1041] From the exhibition 'Paris et ses Cafés', Mairie du XVe arrondissement, June/July 2004.

[1042] Moore/Memoirs p.74. Moore quotes his aphorism 'Three military bands would be necessary to give the impression of silence in music'. He died of tuberculosis, and should not be confused with Alexandre Cabanel the painter whose real name was Cabaner.

[1043] The description, from Moore's *Avowals*, is in Frazier p.33.

[1044] Frazier p.56. This sounds very like Wilde, but Wilde preferred to dominate a table, rather than participate in cut and thrust. Joyce knew, of course: Bloom and Stephen walking back to Eccles Street were clearly 'æstheticising':
Of what did the duumvirate deliberate during their itinerary?
Music, literature, Ireland, Dublin, Paris, friendship, woman, prostitution, diet, the influence of gaslight or the light of arc and glow-lamps on the growth of adjoining paraheliotropic trees, exposed corporation emergency dustbuckets, the Roman catholic church, ecclesiastical celibacy, the Irish nation, jesuit education, careers, the study of medicine, the past day, the male-cent influence of the presabbath, Stephen's collapse.

[1045] Moore/Confessions p.68; Hemmings 1977 p.129.

[1046] George Moore to Jacques-Emile Blanche 2nd December 1887. Blanche p.67.

[1047] Belloc 1943 p.184.

[1048] Gosling p.21.

[1049] Georges Boudaille: *Gauguin*. Translated by Alise Jaffa. London: Thames & Hudson 1964 p.141. My italics.

[1050] Fouquières p.223.

[1051] This was one of three well-known English restaurants in Paris, the others being Richard Lucas in the place de la Madeleine and Hill's, 39 boulevard des Capucines. It was only at the Café de la Madeleine, however, that Hodgson's East India Ale could be procured, at four francs the pint bottle. English groceries were at one time only procurable at Cuvillier's in the rue de la Paix. The duc des Esseintes spends part of an evening in the Bodega, which is minutely described. J.-K. Huysmans: *À Rebours*. London: The Fortune Press n.d. [1946] pp.111-3.

[1052] Klaus Bergner: *Odilon Redon – Fantasy and Colour*. London: Weidenfeld & Nicolson 1964 p.41.

[1053] Officers were forbidden cheap cafés.

[1054] Reff p.73; Rearick p.28; Haine pp.3-4. Dr Haine suggests that the number fluctuated between thirty and thirty-three thousand between 1885 and 1905, and there are obvious problems of definition, but the point is well-made. Borsi and Godoli give the astonishingly inconsistent number of two thousand cafés, and five hundred restaurants. Franco Borsi & Ezio Godoli: *Paris 1900*. London: Granada Publishing 1978 p.61. Hereafter cited as Borsi/Godoli.

[1055] Haine p.126.

[1056] Henry W Lucy: *Sixty Years in the Wilderness, Some Passages By the Way*. London: Smith, Elder & Co 1909 p.77. Hereafter cited as Lucy.

[1057] Newnham-Davis p.44.

[1058] W.J. Locke: *The Joyous Adventures of Aristide Pujol*. Illustrations by Alec Ball. London: John Lane The Bodley Head 1912 pp.30-1. Hereafter cited as Locke.

[1059] Mirbeau p.312.

[1060] Low pp.45-6.

[1061] Berlanstein p.36.

[1062] Anon: *Kings, Courts & Society, Recollections of a Veteran*. London: Jarrolds n.d. pp.106-10.

[1063] Sheridan p.159.

[1064] Sisley Huddleston: *Poincaré, A Biographical Portrait*. London: T. Fisher Unwin 1924.

[1065] Child p.232. The other chain of cheap eating houses, the Bouillons Boulant, does not figure in the literature as do the Duvals.

[1066] G. di San Lazzaro: *Painting in France 1895-1949*. Translated by Baptista Gilliatt-Smith and Bernard Wall. London: Harvill Press 1950 p.38. Hereafter cited as Lazzaro.

[1067] Moore/Confessions p. 68; George Moore to Jacques-Emile Blanche 2nd December 1887. Blanche p.67; George Moore: *Salve*. London: William Heinemann 1912 p.241. Hereafter cited as Moore 1912.

[1068] John Rewald: *Cézanne*. London: Thames & Hudson 1986 p.140.

[1069] Renoir's portrait 'Monet lisant' dates to 1872. Musée Marmottant-Monet, Paris.

[1070] Murer sold this and bought the Hôtel du Dauphin in Rouen (4 place de la République). Sisley spent much of the summer of 1894 there.

[1071] Frazier p.47. These were the five disciples of Zola. Francis Steegmuller reckoned that by the late 1940's only Huysmans remained well-known. Steegmuller/Maupassant p.96.

[1072] Katherine Cecil Thurston: *Max*. London: Hutchinson 1910 p.173. The dislocation of space and time is wisely observed. Hereafter cited as Thurston.

[1073] Guy de Maupassant: 'Monsieur Parent' in Maupassant/Harriet pp.247,248.

[1074] Guy de Maupassant: 'Monsieur Parent' in Maupassant/Harriet p.441.

[1075] The iconography becomes important in establishing the number, nature and behaviour of women in cafés.

[1076] 'An attempt to unite impeccable social form with cakes and ale', it had a 1040 franc entrance fee and a 450 franc subscription. Whiteing p.47. Sir Henry Hoare was a member ('he was a great deal in Paris, knew everybody') but was careful not to utter any liberal opinions there. Waddington p.246.

[1077] Jacques-Emile Blanche became a member in 1884, proposed by Georges Ohnet (a cousin) and the marquis de Massa.

[1078] Barclay p.160; Andrieu p.43. The Épatant was on the corner of the rue Boissy-d'Anglas and the avenue Gabriel, where the United Sates Embassy now stands. Its proprietor was called Henri Wallet. A charity fête was organised here each year by Martell of the cognac family. The Mortigny was for rich Bohemians, though the subscription was what one could afford. Colonel T. Bentley Mott: *Twenty Years as a Military Attaché*. New York: Oxford University Press 1937 pp.175-6. Hereafter cited as Mott.

[1079] Whiteing p.53.

[1080] Whiteing p.56.

[1081] Sir Horace Rumbold: *Recollections of a Diplomatist*. London: Edwin Arnold 1902 Volume I p.162.

Oscar Wilde's Elegant Republic

495

[1082] Above the barber Lespès, angle of the boulevard Montmartre and the rue Vivienne.

[1083] On the corner of the boulevard des Capucines / place de l'Opéra.

[1084] Fittingly, it is now the Paris branch of Burberry's.

[1085] Whiteing p.47; Dietschy p.31. Dietschy lists as members Paul Bert, Denfert-Rochereau, Scheurer-Kestner, both Coquelins, Claretie, Goudeau, Bartholdi. The most English of the clubs, the Travellers', was not founded until the new century, despite D.W Brogan's belief that it dated to the Second Empire. Brogan p.112.

[1086] Not the original café of that name, which had in this period become the Bonvalet (boulevard du Temple).

[1087] Not the existing Rotonde at 105 boulevard de Montparnasse, which only opened in 1911.

[1088] Hobson p.73. André de Fouquières also notes the rings of La Jeunesse (and the toupet of Henri Rochet). Fouquières p.95. Pierre Mac-Orlan, miscalling the café 'la Napolitaine', says that La Jeunesse was one of its attractions and that it gave 'le ton au boulevard'. This is to stretch the sense of 'ton'. Pierre Mac-Orlan: 'De Montmartre à Buffalo', in Adhémar p.79; hereafter Mac-Orlan. He adds 'Ce n'était pas le genre d'établissement qui semblait séduire Lautrec.' Bannefroi is surely a mistake for Bonnefon.

[1089] Low p.131.

[1090] Newnham-Davis p.44; Rothenstein Volume I p.44. Rothenstein names Humphrys Johnston, Philip Hale, Sargent Kendall and Howard Hart. In their time both Thackeray and Dickens had been frequent customers.

[1091] Polnay p.55.

[1092] Properly the Taverne Alsacienne, but known as Clarisse from the name of the proprietor. Zola twice uses the name for characters, Clarisse Bocquet in *Pot Bouille* and Clarisse in *Nana*.

[1093] Delbourg-Delphis p.49. Delbourg-Delphis adds the Bibesco brothers, Fénélon de Salignac and the Spanish marquis Illan de Casa-Fuerte, a great-nephew of the Empress Eugénie. To such as these Delbourg-Delphis applies Stendhal's description 'the happy few' (in English, the dedication of *Le Rouge et le Noir*), apparently without realising its origin in *Henry V. Ibidem* p.71. Casa-Fuerte was also a friend of Lucien Daudet, and d'Annunzio, who knew him through Montesquiou, put him into *Forse che si* as Aldo. Salignac was killed at Mametz in December 1914.

[1094] Colette 1944 p.40; Colette: *Gigi*. Translated by Roger Senhouse 1949. Harmondsworth: Penguin Books 1958.

[1095] This was announced in an article in *L'Éclair* by one of the group, Maurice Pujo, on the 19th December. His co-founder was Henri Vaugeois, but the name most associated with the Action Française is that of Charles Maurras. The Café Flore, which opened in 1885, was said by Virgil Thomson to be 'a dreary place till bought by a progressive management and done over to look less nineteenth century'. Quoted in Hansen p.75. Of the café society of the fin-de-siècle Latin Quarter, only Remy de Gourmont seems to have favoured it. Laver p.121.

[1096] Grenville-Murray p.46.

[1097] Charles H.E. Brookfield: *Random Reminiscences*. London: Edwin Arnold. 2nd impression 1902 p.21. Mazagran is cold coffee served with ice cubes and rum. Pierre Andrieu notes that one could eat at the Palais Royal for two francs in the outer room, while for five francs in the inner room one could eat like a nabob ('menu de nawab').

[1098] Nevill 1913 p.110.

[1099] It was Mildé who installed the electric light chez Mme Verdurin. Proust/Ombre p.183.

[1100] On 5th February 1892 William Terris telephoned Jessie Millward at her hotel in Paris. 'I was told that I was "wanted on the telephone". As I had never in my life used a telephone, I quivered with nervousness. A polite clerk told me how to use the terrible instrument, and assured me that there was not the slightest danger of electrocution.' Jessie Millward: *Myself and Others*. In Collaboration with J.B. Booth. London: Hutchinson & Co 1923 p.177; hereafter cited as Millward. 'The idea fascinates me,' says Mme Cottard, 'but only in some one else's house, not my own.' Proust/Ombre p.183.

[1101] André Gide to Paul Valéry 28th November 1891. Fryer 1997 p.28; Langlade p.149. There is no mention of Merrill in André Gide: *Journals 1889-1949*. Translated, selected and edited by Justin O'Brien. London: Secker & Warburg 1947. Hereafter cited as Gide/O'Brien.

[1102] Haine p.88.

[1103] Comte Jean de Kegourlay was eloquent in the ear of Whitelaw Reid about the increasingly spendthrift habits of the working class, the men spending ever more on drink, the women on fripperies. H. Wayne Morgan (ed.): *Making Peace with Spain, The Diary of Whitelaw Reid September - December 1898*. Austin: University of Texas Press 1965 pp.152-3. Hereafter cited as Morgan 1965.

[1104] Berlanstein p.149.

[1105] Herbert p.74.

[1106] Berlanstein p.134.

[1107] Art Institute of Chicago.

[1108] 1880. Musée d'art moderne et d'art contemporaine de la ville de Liège; reproduced as plate 6 in Marianne Delafond & Caroline Genet-Bondeville: *Jean-François Raffaëlli*. Paris: Musée Marmottan-Monet 1999.

[1109] Emile Zola: *Nana*. Translated with an introduction by George Holden. Harmondsworth: Penguin Books 1972. New edition 1982 pp.216-9. Hereafter cited as Zola/Nana/Holden.

[1110] Zola/Pot-Bouille pp.185-6. A menu is described in detail at p.185.

[1111] Marylène Delbourg-Delphis says 1815. Delbourg-Delphis p.178. It disappeared in 1913. The original Café Anglais, on the corner of the quai Conti and the rue Dauphine, had been founded in the eighteenth century by an Englishman called Becket. Were his footfalls ever heard, one wonders?

[1112] Pretty Women pp.67-8.

[1113] Newnham-Davis p.7. Newnham-Davis describes the discreet way in which the Anglais presented itself, so that the casual passer-by might not even realise that a restaurant operated on the premises, in a manner that could not have been surpassed had he been describing a fashionable brothel. *Ibidem* pp.8-9.

[1114] Bashkirtseff p.348. Diary entry for 10th January 1879.

[1115] Du Maurier/Trilby p.433. Nor should one forget that it was at the Café Anglais that Babette prepared her blinis Demidoff, her cailles en sarcophages'.

[1116] Giles St Aubyn gives Dugleré's name as Duclere, Ralph Nevill calls him Ducléré and Marylène Delbourg-Delphis has Dugléré. St Aubyn p.266; Ralph Nevill: *The Man of Pleasure*. London: Chatto & Windus 1912 p.228; Delbourg-Delphis p.178. I follow Newnham-Davis p.9.

[1117] http://www.cuisineaz.com/tournedos_rossini.htm. James de Rothschild, known to his English friends as 'Jimmy', is the unattractive 'Gundermann' in Zola's *L'Argent*.

[1118] Menpes p.136.

[1119] Mortimer Menpes was also the godfather of Vyvyan Wilde (he is the 'Mortimer Mempis' of Bentley 1983 p.69).

[1120] Menpes pp.140-1.

[1121] Fitzwilliam Museum, Cambridge. There is also his 'Dans un café' of 1880, Musée des Beaux Arts, Rouen ref.D.946-1.

[1122] Kröller-Müller Museum, Otterlo.

[1123] Detroit Institute of Art.

[1124] The former is in the New York Museum of Modern Art; the latter features the Gaîté-Rochechouart.

[1125] Daniel J. Terra Collection, Giverny.

[1126] Musée d'Orsay.

[1127] Private collection, but shown in the exhibition 'De Vallotton à Desnos', Musée Jensch, Vevey, 24th July to 3rd October 1965.

[1128] Musée de la Carnavalet ref. P.2682, used as the poster for the exhibition 'Paris et ses Cafés', Mairies des 9e et 6e arrondissements, 20th April to 22nd May and 10th June to 11th July 2004.

[1129] National Gallery, Washington.

[1130] Cleveland Museum of Art, 1895. I suspect M. Boileau of being a type rather than a person. There was a café called Boileau in the rue Cujas, and the name suggests (ironically) a water-drinker. 'Gens chic' is reproduced in Adhémar p.219.

[1131] The van Gogh is in the Kröller-Müller Museum, Otterlo. The identification is in the catalogue, p.65. The Raffaëlli is in the Musée des Beaux Arts, Bordeaux, reproduced as plate 48 in Marianne Delafond & Caroline Genet-Bondeville: *Jean-François Raffaëlli*. Paris: Musée Marmottan-Monet 1999; and as fig. 166 in Weisberg.

[1132] Daniel J. Terra Collection, Giverny.

[1133] Jean-Paul Crespelle: La vie quotidienne à Montmartre à la Grande Epoque 1905-1930. Paris: Hachette 1976 p.43.

[1134] Sherard 1908 p.110.

[1135] Coolidge p.236.

[1136] Holland & Hart-Davis p.493.

[1137] 1863-1934. His real name was George Goursat. Beerbohm drew him 1907.

[1138] Walkley's theatre criticism, compared to that of Shaw, Archer, Scott, Agate or Beerbohm, appears little known. He was sufficiently in France to know the work of Daguet and Brunetière, and to be familiar with the writings of Maeterlinck.

[1139] 7 boulevard Montmartre (although Douglas Parmée locates it in the boulevard des Italiens. Zola/Nana/Parmée p.426), 'excellent for [...] lively pieces in the French taste' (Baedeker) and called by Mistinguett 'the Comédie Française of the Boulevards'. Mistinguett: *Mistinguett, Queen of the Night*. Translated by Lucienne Hill. London: Elek Books 1954 p.55; hereafter cited as Mistinguett. A number of chapters of *Nana* are set here. The Café des Variétés was next door.

[1140] Brother of the future founder of the Boy Scouts, and pupil of Carolus-Duran and Rodin, who exhibited both at the Royal Academy and the Paris Salon.

[1141] It was at a dance at the Hôtel Continental in the autumn of 1890 that André Poniatowksi encountered the curious group of Catulle Mendès, Georges Courteline, Debussy and Pierre Louÿs. Dietschy p.66.

[1142] Lee pp.359-60.

[1143] March p.51.

[1144] The date is also given as 22nd September. Robinat p.192. The caterers were Potel et Chabot.

[1145] Trapp in Stanley Jackson: *Guy de Maupassant*. London: Duckworth 1938 p.100. Trop in Steegmuller/Flaubert p.242; André Billy: *The Goncourt Brothers*. Translated by Margaret Shaw. London: André Deutsch 1960 p.257.

[1146] The reclusive Huysmans had been introduced to Céard by his friend Ludovic de Vente de Francmésnil, a pupil of the Polish law tutor Chodsko.

[1147] Goncourt/Baldick p.231n. Dishes included Potage purée Bovary, Truite saumonée à la Fille Elisa, Poularde truffée à la Saint-Antoine, Artichaut au cœur simple.

[1148] Musée d'Orsay, ref. RF 2239.

[1149] These unregarded men should have had their chronicler. The brothers Michel and Calmann Lévy of the great publishing house of Calmann Lévy began as bouquinistes.

[1150] Antoine p.30.

[1151] 18 rue Gaillon, founded in 1880 and still (May 2004) a smart restaurant.

[1152] Moore 1914 p.218.

[1153] Roger Shattuck: *The Banquet Years – The Arts in France 1885-1918*. New York: Anchor Books 1961 p.3.

[1154] Whiteing pp.7-8.

[1155] In 1880 Lemerre published Laurent Tailhade's *Le Jardin des Rêves*, with a preface by Théodore de Banville.

[1156] Whiteing p.65. Was there a confusion in the taxonomy here, the French for seahorse being hippocamp?

[1157] Healy p.105.

[1158] MacDonald p.96.

[1159] Menpes p.137.

[1160] Healy p.81.

[1161] Hartley p.vii.

[1162] Joanna Richardson: *The Bohemians, La Vie Bohème in Paris 1830-1914*. London: Macmillan 1969 p.166. For Bibi, whose real namewas André Salis, see Christian Gury: *Bibi-la-Purée, Compagnon de Verlaine*. Paris: Editions Kimé 2004.

[1163] Bayard p.88.

[1164] James repaid the compliment by sending Strether and Waymarsh there. James/Ambassadors p.51. This is one of the few references to an actual place in the novel, all the more striking for James's declining to name the 'delightful house of entertainment on the left bank – a place of pilgrimage for the knowing' to which Strether goes with Miss Gostrey, and again with Chad Newsome, and yet again with Newsome, Waymarsh and Bilham. *Ibidem* p.191. Significantly, it is other restaurants that are named: Bignon, and Brébant. *Ibidem* p.269.

[1165] This much used maxim long outlasted the Hardy (or Hardi, so-called after its proprietor), which was renamed the Maison Dorée in 1835. It was the first restaurant to offer dining 'à la fourchette', or fork suppers. Delbourg-Delphis p.180.

[1166] Novick p.xvii. The Café Riche became a brasserie in 1894, designed by the architect Albert Ballin. It closed in 1916.

[1167] Oscar Wilde to Mrs Allhusen, early 1890, Hart-Davis 1962 p.255, Holland & Hart-Davis p.425.

[1168] Leon Edel: *Henry James, A Life*. London: Collins 1987 p.211. Hereafter cited as Edel.

[1169] Maupassant/Bel Ami pp.xxiii,62. Maupassant also sets 'Imprudence' there. The Café Riche had mosaics by Forain. It closed in 1916 and was pulled down in 1922.

[1170] Child p.233.

[1171] Michael Turnbull: *Mary Garden*. Aldershot: Scolar Press 1997 p.32. Hereafter cited as Turnbull.

[1172] Maupassant/Bel Ami pp.63-4.

[1173] From which perhaps the actress Bade of the Menus-Plaisirs took her name.

[1174] Grenville-Murray p.46.

[1175] Moore/Memoirs p.18.

[1176] Perruchot p.92 One may contrast this with Agnes de Stoeckl's notion that the typical smell of Paris was 'clean linen and fresh bread', and fortify it with Zola's suggestion that on wet nights 'Paris had the stale, damp smell of a bedroom not properly cleaned'. Zola/Nana/Parmée p.239. This was the difference between Notre Dame de Lorette and St Germain-des-Prés.

[1177] This was 'the mincing step of the demirep' that Wilde refers to in 'The Harlot's House'. The French for to strut, *dindonner*, to walk like a turkey-cock, is particularly expressive.

[1178] Zola/Nana/Holden p.271; Zola/Nana/Parmée p.237.

[1179] Young pp.105-6.

[1180] Fitzwilliam Museum, Cambridge ref. 2387; n.d. This should not be confused with the 'Au Café', also known as 'L'Absinthe' (a significant change in emphasis), showing Marcel Desboutin and Ellen Andrée, now in the Musée d'Orsay.

[1181] Private collection n.d. (exhibited in the *1900: Art at the Crossroads* Exhibition, Royal Academy, London 2000).

[1182] Bashkirtseff p.329. Diary entry for 17th August 1878.

[1183] James/Ambassadors p.60.

[1184] Richard Ellmann: 'The mark of the aristocrat', review of A.W Raitt: *The Life of Villiers de Lisle Adam.* Oxford: Clarendon Press 1981. *Times Literary Supplement* 23rd October 1981. There is no mention of Villiers in Ellmann.

[1185] Sherard 1906 p.287.

[1186] J. Joseph-Renaud: Preface to Oscar Wilde: *Intentions.* Paris: Stock 1905; reprinted in Mikhail vol. I pp.167-8.

[1187] Moore/Memoirs pp.76,75.

[1188] André Gide: *Oscar Wilde, A Study from the French.* Translated by Stuart Mason. Oxford: Holywell Press 1905 p.23. Hereafter cited as Gide/Mason.

[1189] André Gide: *Oscar Wilde.* Translated by Bernard Frechtman. London: William Kimber 1951. Hereafter cited as Gide/Frechtman p.71.

[1190] Sherard 1911 p.360.

[1191] Hyde 1976 p.83.

[1192] Oscar Wilde: Petition to the Home Secretary, 2nd July 1896, printed in Holland & Hart-Davis p.657.

[1193] Quoted in Steegmuller/Maupassant p.199.

[1194] James Harding: *Lost Illusions, Paul Léautaud and His World.* London: George Allen & Unwin 1971 p.55. Hereafter cited as Harding 1971. Langlade lists these (in 1883) as Bourget, Verlaine, Hugo, Daudet, Richepin, Goncourt, Coquelin *ainé*, Bernhardt and Alexandre Parodi. He might even be right. Langlade p.93.

[1195] Groom p.48, citing 'contemporary accounts'.

[1196] This had been founded in Belgium (in Spa) in 1889 by the Belgians Auguste Jeunhomme and Joe Högge, and the Frenchmen Charles and Paul Leclercq. The Natansons were associates of the Leclercqs and assisted the review's first move to the Leclercqs' apartment in an hôtel particulier in the rue Marbeuf in 1891. This street had a certain reputation for raffishness – 'habitée par beaucoup des cocottes'. Fouquières p.98.

[1197] Alfred Natanson used the name Alfred Athis.

[1198] Sherard 1906 p.231.

[1199] Sherard 1906 p.233.

[1200] Langlade p.95.

[1201] Sherard 1908 p.462.

[1202] Sherard 1908 p.17.

[1203] McCormack p.76. This is almost certainly the 'public meeting' at which Conal O'Riordan made his 'first public speech, to be snubbed by the chairman for my simplicity'. Conal O'Riordan: *Bloomsbury and Beyond in the 1890s.* The Tredegar Memorial Lecture. Printed as an off-print from *Essays by Divers Hands, The Transactions of the Royal Literary Society*, New series XXIV. London: Oxford University Press 1948.

[1204] Fryer 1997 pp.29,81,204.

[1205] For a discussion of this point see Guy de Maupassant: *A Life*. Translated with an Introduction and notes by Roger Pearson. Oxford: Oxford University Press 1999 p.xi.

[1206] McCormack p.58. This extended to confusion as to their own agenda, and there was no Rhymers manifesto, as there certainly would have been in France.

[1207] Kipling p.118.

[1208] Kathleen O'Meara: Madame Mohl, Her Salon and Her Friends, A Study of Social Life in Paris. London: Richard Bentley & Son 1885 p.123.

[1209] e.g. Harris p.79.

[1210] Clive p.71.

[1211] Gide/Mason 1905 p.23.

[1212] Gide/Mason 1905 p.27.

[1213] André Gide: *Oscar Wilde*. Paris: Mercure de France 1989 pp.15-16, hereafter cited as Gide 1989.

[1214] Renard p.47.

[1215] Robert Underwood Johnson: *Remembered Yesterdays*. London: George Allen and Unwin 1923 p.396. Hereafter cited as Johnson. Johnson put his knowledge of Paris at the service of Aubrey Beardsley, and was invited to tea. Beardsley to Johnson 12th and 15th September 1897. Maas/Duncan/Good pp.367,369.

[1216] Max Beerbohm: Tribute read at the unveiling of the Tite Street plaque 16th October 1954, printed in Rupert Hart-Davis (ed.): *Max Beerbohm, A Peep into the Past and other Prose Pieces*. London: Heinemann 1972 p.42.

[1217] McKenna 2003 p.417. This is unsourced, but appears to be from a letter to More Adey.

[1218] W.B. Yeats: *Autobiographies*. London: Macmillan 1955 pp.285,294.

[1219] Sherard 1908 p.17.

[1220] Steegmuller/Maupassant p.95.

[1221] E.F. Benson: *Final Edition*. London: Longmans, Green & Co 1940 p.214.

[1222] David Gilmour: *Curzon, Imperial Statesman 1859–1925*. London: John Murray 1994 p.427.

[1223] Newton Volume II p.99.

[1224] Varnedoe p.9.

[1225] Nigel Lambourne: *Renoir, Paintings, drawings, lithographs and etchings*. London: The Folio Society 1965 unnumbered page.

[1226] Hohenlohe p.114. Diary entry for 6th February 1876.

[1227] Spelling his name in the French fashion Tourgénieff. Reprinted in Patrick Waddington (ed.): *Ivan Turgenev and Britain*. Oxford: Berg Publishers, Anglo-Russian Affinities Series 1995. MS sold at Sotheby's 27th July 1911 and now in the University of Texas.

[1228] Houssaye p.3. He also sowed some confusion about his date of birth, which may have been on either 28th March 1814 or 28th March 1815.

[1229] Houssaye p.7.

[1230] Bowra p.4.

[1231] Brigadier General Sir Douglas Dawson, G.C.V.O., K.C.B., C.B., C.M.G.: *A Soldier-Diplomat*. London: John Murray 1927 p.261.

[1232] Barclay p.1.

[1233] *La Plume*, 15th December 1900.

[1234] Fryer 1997 p.29. Fryer says that Gide instigated Louÿs to arrange this. Another who frequented the Café d'Harcourt at this time was Jane Avril.

[1235] Ellmann p.331.

[1236] J. Joseph-Renaud: Preface to Oscar Wilde *Intentions*. Paris: Stock 1905 p.viii. Reprinted in Mikhail vol. I pp.167-8.

[1237] Fryer 1997 p.19; Langlade p.135 This is a surprising date to visit Paris, and even more surprising that there was a 'foule bruyante' for him to watch in the boulevard Saint-Germain, unless he was watching the tourists. That Langlade also says that Wilde went again to the Mardis of Mallarmé casts further doubt, and one is not re-assured by Langlade's quoting for his source (*ibid.* p.323 n.88) an earlier work of his own.

[1238] Langlade p.143, 181-2.

[1239] The index is sketchy and the bibliography defective.

[1240] Routier also saw Wilde in Wandsworth, described in *L'Écho de Paris* 13th July 1895, according to Langlade p.240. Little can be found about Routier, who wrote a history of Mexico and other forgotten works.

[1241] *L'Écho de Paris* 12th February 1893; *La Plume* March 1893. Langlade pp.178,181.

[1242] Jacques Daurelle in the *Echo de Paris* 6th December 1891, reprinted in Mikhail Volume I p.169.

[1243] My translation. Gide 1989 p.14.

[1244] Léo Lack: 'Avertissement' in Oscar Wilde: *Une Maison de Grenades*. Traduit de l'anglais par Léo Lack. Paris: Mercure de France 1948 p.7. The 1902 edition was limited to three examples on China, seven on Japan Imperial, and fifteen on Van Gelder paper, published by La Plume in their Nouvelle Collection Internationale. The translation was by Georges Khnopff. The first trade edition was not until 1911, when Albert Savine's translation was published by Stock in their 'Bibliothèque Universelle'.

[1245] Quoted by Delbourg-Delphis p.84. Daudet thought that to associate with Wilde would need two existences, one for ordinary life, the other to be kept for Wilde.

[1246] Henry pp.12-13. Lucien Daudet succeeded Reynaldo Hahn as the principal recipient of Proust's affections. He became a close and improbable friend of the Empress Eugénie, and through him, even more improbably, Eugénie met Jean Cocteau. See Lucien Daudet: *L'Impératrice Eugénie*. Paris: Fayard n.d.

[1247] Henry Jones Thaddeus: *Recollections of a Court Painter*. London: John Lane The Bodley Head 1912 p.20. Hereafter cited as Thaddeus.

[1248] He was not mentioned in the Théâtre de l'Œuvre exhibition at the Musée d'Orsay (spring 2005), although there were references to Jean-Marie Gros as administrator, 1893-7.

[1249] Rothenstein Volume I p.94.

[1250] Robert H. Sherard: 'Notes from Paris' in *The Author* Volume III/10 January 1893 p.361. Merrill (1863-1915) was twenty-nine when this was written. See Marjorie Louise Henry: *La contribution d'un Américain au symbolisme français,*

Stuart Merrill. Paris: Honoré Champion 1927, hereafter cited as Henry 1927. For a little more on him, see http://www.poetes.com/merrill/index.php.

[1251] Moore 1912 p.112.

[1252] 1855-1921.

[1253] Author of *Aux beaux temps du Symbolisme, 1890-1895.* Mercure de France & Editions N.R.B. 1943.

[1254] Jules Renard: *Journal.* Paris: Gallimard 30th edition 1935 p.88.

[1255] Jonathan Fryer: *Robbie Ross, Oscar Wilde's True Love.* London: Constable 2000 p.75. Hereafter cited as Fryer 2000.

[1256] Henri Mazel: 'My Recollections of Oscar Wilde', *Everyman* Volume I:1 18th October 1912, reprinted in Mikhail Volume II pp.444-5. Mazel retells some of the Wilde anecdotes that he obtained from Merrill, which casts a better light on his credulity than on his veracity.

[1257] Van Wyck Brooks: *The Confident Years 1885-1915.* New York: E.P. Dutton & Co 1952 p.3. Hereafter cited as Brooks 1952.

[1258] Edgar Saltus: *Oscar Wilde, An Idler's Impression.* Chicago: Brothers of the Book 1917.

[1259] Brooks 1952 p.114.

[1260] Arnold T Schwab: *James Gibbons Huneker, Critic of the Seven Arts.* Stanford: Stanford University Press 1963 p.37. Hereafter cited as Schwab.

[1261] Schwab p.38.

[1262] Robert H. Sherard: 'Notes from Paris' in *The Author* Volume II/10 March 1892; hereafter cited as Sherard March 1892.

[1263] Savine had published George Moore's account of his Paris education *Confessions of a Young Man* as *Confessions d'un jeune anglais* in 1889. He also published Swinburne's *Songs and Ballads* (*Poèmes et Ballades*, translated by Mourey) in 1891, and *An Enemy of the People* in 1892. Tardieu translated Bosie Douglas's poems for the *Mercure de France* edition of 1896.

[1264] Delbourg-Delphis p.8.

[1265] Caspar Wintermans adds the further detail that Carrington was an ex-lavatory attendant. Lord Alfred Douglas: *Oscar Wilde, A Plea and a Reminiscence.* Introduced and annotated by Caspar Wintermans. Woubrugge: Avalon Press 2002 p.12. Hereafter cited as Douglas/Wintermans.

[1266] Sherard 1937 pp.12-13.

[1267] Rothenstein Volume I p.92.

[1268] Sherard 1908 p.67. Parodi wrote *Rome vaincue*, in which Bernhardt had an early success, but later fell out of favour, an eclipse not entirely reversed by the turning of *Rome vaincue* into an opera by Massenet in 1912.

[1269] Robert Keith Miller: *Oscar Wilde.* New York: Frederick Ungar 1982 p.11. Hereafter cited as Miller.

[1270] Ellmann p.341 Langlade p.98.

[1271] McCormack p.72.

[1272] Callow p.7.

[1273] Mark Hichens: *Oscar Wilde's Last Chance – The Dreyfus Connection.* Edinburgh: The Pentland Press 1999 p.3 (hereafter cited as Hichens 1999);

Mireille Dottin-Orsini (ed.): *Salomé*. Collection 'Figures Mythiques'. Paris: Éditions Autrement 1996 p.54. Hereafter cited as Dottin-Orsini.

[1274] Lord Alfred Douglas: *Oscar Wilde, A Summing Up*. London: The Richards Press 1940. Reprinted 1961 p.93. Hereafter cited as Douglas 1940.

[1275] Sherard 1908 p.109.

[1276] Sherard 1908 p.110. The article (in English) is given as an Appendix.

[1277] Sherard 1911 p.360; Sherard 1906 p.292.

[1278] Oscar Wilde to Robert Sherard December 1891. Hart-Davis 1985 p.103.

[1279] Sherard 1908 p.258.

[1280] Rudorff p.241. Laurent Tailhade dedicated a villanelle to Meyer in his *À Travers des Grouins*, and he was a model for 'Monsieur Walter' in Maupassant's *Bel-Ami*, Walter being the name of the proprietor of *The Times*.

[1281] *Le Gaulois* 29th June 1892, reprinted in Mikhail Volume I p189. It was this article that, according to Stuart Merrill 'introduced Wilde to Parisians'. Stuart Merrill: 'Some Unpublished Recollections of Oscar Wilde', translated and partially edited by H. Montgomery Hyde. London: *Adam International Review* nos. 241-3 1954 pp.10-12, reprinted in Mikhail Volume II pp.468-72; hereafter cited as Merrill. June 1892 is rather late for Wilde being introduced, and he was not in Paris in June. Could Wilde have been quoting Comte? 'Paris c'est la France, l'Occident, la Terre' – a notion that as effectively destabilises the Paris of Haussmann into the Paris of Huysmans as any other definition, or indefinition, of the French capital. http://www.chapelle-humanite.fr/.

[1282] Sherard March 1892 p.304; Robert H. Sherard: 'Notes from Paris' in *The Author* Volume III/10 March 1893 p.360.

[1283] Joy Melville: *Mother of Oscar, The Life of Jane Francesca Wilde*. London: John Murray 1994 p.226.

[1284] Quoted in Langlade p.143.

[1285] Maupassant/Bel Ami pp.50-1.

[1286] Lord Lyons to Lord Granville 27th May 1884. Newton Volume II p.329. This contradicts Raymond Rudorff, who calls it the second most serious newspaper in Paris after *Le Temps*. Rudorff p.281.

[1287] Vivian p.170. Vivian met Magnard and his successor Gaston Calmette (1856-1914) while spending the winter of 1894/5 in Paris. There is a photograph of Calmette in Hartmann p.81.

[1288] Sherard 1906 pp.284,342.

[1289] A brief and unsourced account of the latter is in Langlade p.144. The source is probably Ernest Raynaud: *La Mêlée symboliste*. Vol. II 1890-1900. Paris: La Renaissance du Livre 1920 pp.131-2. The Côte d'Or, on the corner of the rue Racine and the rue de Médicis, is not much mentioned, though Raynaud gives a good account of the Côte d'Or and its habitués. Merrill's biographer lists Verlaine, Retté, Clément Bellenger, Julien Le Clerq, Gauguin, Albert Trechsel, Charles Morice as meeting there, and as the café where the école romane was founded in 1891. Henry 1927 p.67. It no longer exists, at least with that name.

[1290] Michael de Cossart: *The Food of Love – Princesse de Polignac (1865-1943) and Her Salon*. London: Hamish Hamilton 1978 p.58. Hereafter cited as Cossart. De Cossart's *particule* was assumed: he began life as a Scot called Cossar.

[1291] *Pace* her biographers, more remains to be discovered about Constance's connections. For example, her kinswoman Mabel Troubridge married Ernest Mallet of the banking family Mallet Frères, a Parisian relationship that research might illuminate. Princess Alice, while sympathising with Wilde's misfortunes, seems not to have interested herself in his fate. It was with the Princess's help that Vyvyan was sent to the Collegio della Visitazione in Monaco in 1897; Constance stayed at the Hotel Bristol, Monte Carlo, for a week in February 1898 and saw Vyvyan for the last time. Alice was also an acquaintance, at least, of Frank Harris.

[1292] Langlade p.180.

[1293] William Freeman: *The Life of Lord Alfred Douglas, Spoilt Child of Genius*. London: Herbert Joseph 1948.

[1294] Rupert Croft-Cooke: *Bosie, The Story of Lord Alfred Douglas*, His Friends and Enemies. London: W.H. Allen 1963 p.96.

[1295] Goncourt p.967.

[1296] Gladys de Grey was the daughter of the Earl of Pembroke (and so sister of Michael Herbert of the British Embassy) and married first, the Earl of Lonsdale, and secondly, Lord de Grey, subsequently second Marquess of Ripon. She became the great patronne of the Ballets Russes in London. Douglas Ainslie wrote 'I saw nothing of [Wilde] for many years, though I occasionally met and heard of him from those who did see him, such as the late Lady Ripon who, as Lady de Grey, stood by him through all his troubles and told me several curious little details about his life in prison and afterwards when he was released.' This unfortunately leads nowhere. Ainslie p.100.

[1297] Nellie Melba: *Melodies & Memories*. London: Hamish Hamilton. New edition 1980 p.49; hereafter cited as Melba. Louÿs' break with Wilde is covered by Sherard 1908 pp.113-4.

[1298] Fryer 1997 p.67. The friendship had only lasted eighteen months.

[1299] McCormack p.72. Wilde's *The Sphinx* was dedicated to Schwob (June 1894) 'in friendship and admiration'.

[1300] Belloc 1943 pp.146-8. For his part, Sherard included Marie Belloc among his protégés, describing her as 'one of the cleverest of the young ladies who make a living by their pens'. Robert H. Sherard: 'Notes from Paris' in *The Author* Volume III/9 February 1893 p.323, hereafter cited as Sherard February 1893. The 'young wife', if beautiful, was not faithful. Hyde 1976 p.183.

[1301] Sherard/Maupassant p.x.

[1302] *Le Gaulois* 17th December 1891, quoted in Sherard 1908 p.269.

[1303] Possibly princesse Cécile Murat, *née* Ney d'Elchingen, who was painted by Boldini in 1910; or Marie de Rohan, who married Prince Lucien Murat in 1897 and was known as 'Distinguett'.

[1304] Née Caraman-Chimay. George Painter, throughout his biography of Proust, spells her name Greffuhle. Painter I. The pronunciation in the Faubourg was 'Greffeuille'. There is a photograph of her in Hartmann p.41.

[1305] de Lara p.90.

[1306] Powell 1990 p.102.

[1307] Sos Eltis, who draws heavily upon Powell, writes that 'The contemporary play which most closely mirrors the radical concerns of *An Ideal Husband* was, perhaps, *Un Journée Parlementaire*'. The 'perhaps' greatly weakens this statement, and Eltis further adds 'Though Wilde was well acquainted with Barrès, there is no evidence that he borrowed from the French writer'. Sos Eltis: *Revising Wilde: Society and Subversion in the Plays of Oscar Wilde*. Oxford: Clarendon Press 1996 p.158, hereafter cited as Eltis. The acquaintance is sourced only from Blanche in Mikhail Volume II pp.35-3.

[1308] Jacques-Emile Blanche: *La Pêche aux souvenirs*. Paris: Flammarion 1949 pp.187-9.

[1309] Sherard 1908 1905 p.258.

[1310] Langlade p.144.

[1311] Sheridan p.xiii.

[1312] Ainslie p.262.

[1313] Sorel p.95. There is a photograph of Barrès that captures this in Hartmann p.76.

[1314] Gramont p.346.

[1315] Daubigny spent some time in London after 1870. The painter Charles Daubigny (1817-1878) should not be confused with the painter Karl Daubigny (1846-1886).

[1316] Sorel Chapter V.

[1317] Sorel says that Barbier had written this for Bernhardt, who was prevented from using it by an American tour, so Sorel took it on. I have not been able to trace any further information.

[1318] Duff Gordon pp.267-8.

[1319] Barclay p.111.

[1320] Thwaite p.226.

[1321] Rothenstein Volume I p.82.

[1322] Rothenstein Volume I p.87.

[1323] Translated as *La Mégère Apprivoisé* by Paul Delair (1849-1894), this opened on the 19th November 1891.

[1324] Rothenstein Volume I p.87. My italics. It is fair to add that Rothenstein also says of Wilde 'He was not only a unique talker and story teller – I have never heard anyone else tell stories as he did – but he had an extraordinarily illuminating intellect'. *Ibid.*

[1325] Leslie p.18. One critic friend of Bodley's was P.G. Hamerton, who hardly sounds as if he would have been impressed by Wilde had Bodley thought of inviting him. Though Bodley is mentioned in the Hamerton biography, Wilde is not. In 1880 the Hamertons' son Richard had committed suicide 'partly due to the influence of unhealthy and pessimist literature on a mind already diseased'. Hamerton p.560.

[1326] Leslie p.18.

[1327] Leslie p.18.

[1328] Robert Harborough Sherard: *Oscar Wilde, Twice Defended (from André Gide's Wicked Lies and Frank Harris's Cruel Libels)*. Chicago: Argus 1934 p.15.

[1329] Ducoté was editor of the little magazine *L'Ermitage*. His correspondence with Gide has been published. *Correspondance (1895-1921) / Edouard Ducoté, André Gide*. Edition établie, présentée et annotée par Pierre Lachasse; [ed. par l'association des amis d'André Gide]. Nantes: Centre d'études gidiennes 2002.

[1330] 'Gide et Edouard Ducoté organisèrent un dîner qui réunit, avec Wilde, quelques-uns de leurs amis.' Léon Pierre-Quint: *André Gide, L'homme, Sa Vie — Son Œuvre. Entretiens Avec Gide et Ses Contemporains*. Paris: Stock 1952 p.25. Quint's book is not cited by Jonathan Fryer.

[1331] Now in the Berg Collection, New York Public Library. It would be instructive to discover whether Tailhède read English.

[1332] Sherard 1906 p.225.

[1333] Roittinger p.114.

[1334] Sherard 1906 p.225.

[1335] Sherard 1906 p.229.

[1336] Gide/Mason 1905 p.23; Rothenstein Volume I p.162. Gide's mature view of Wilde as a writer is ambiguous: he praises *An Ideal Husband*, *Lady Windermere's Fan* and *A Woman of No Importance* without mentioning *The Importance of being Earnest*. Gide 1989 p.8.

[1337] Rothenstein Volume I p.162.

[1338] For Goncourt's rather more terse comments and his reference to Wilde as 'the English poet' – Wilde was not obviously concerned here to establish himself as an Irishman – see Goncourt p.284.

[1339] 'Pas de blague, mon ami – pas de blague' said General Roget to Paul Déroulède when the latter urged him to march on the Elysée.

[1340] Paris: Stock 1905. In his preface Joseph-Renaud refers to encountering Wilde in the boulevard des Italiens, a meeting that Alfred Douglas reckoned 'obviously imaginary'. Douglas/Wintermans p.39.

[1341] Sherard 1906 p.231. But how, save as *blague*, is one to characterise Sherard's dating his book on Maupassant 2nd Germinal, An 134?

[1342] Sherard 1906 p.235.

[1343] Sherard 1906 p.292.

[1344] Was there, indeed, such a person? Edouard Roditi summed up the critics of the day:
To realize Wilde's stature as a critic, we need to return, from his dialogues, to some other critics of the generation or of the next two decades. Saintsbury is but a sensible and reliable scholar; Charles Whibley, a charming enthusiast with exquisite taste but vague principles; Sir Edmund Gosse, a first-class columnist for the Sunday supplements; Sir Arthur Quiller-Couch, an unbelievably sentimental fuddy-duddy who is content to state that a poem is good because, after twenty or more years of knowing it, he is still moved to tears by its beauty.
Roditi p.4. Of these, only Quiller-Couch can really be called a novelist.

[1345] Sherard 1906 p.239.

[1346] Sherard 1906 p.235. The owner of the rights was presumably Mary Anderson, for whom the play was written, or Elizabeth Marbury, the agent. If the latter, it is permissible to wonder if the 'beautiful young American actress' might not have been Marbury's lover, Elsie de Wolfe.

[1347] Sherard 1906 p.288.

[1348] Sherard 1906 p.252. This refers to Wilde's lecture tour of 1884. He was twenty-eight at the time.

[1349] Healy p.74.

[1350] Moscheles p.121. Moscheles knew Wilde: an invitation to him and his wife from Constance Wilde (24th April 1887) is in the Berg Collection, New York Public Library.

[1351] Ernest La Jeunesse, writing in *La Revue Blanche* 15th December 1900. Translated by Perceval Pollard. Reprinted in Mikhail Volume II pp.477-81, hereafter cited as La Jeunesse. La Jeunesse, a minor literary figure, at one time the secretary of Anatole France, was also indeterminate. Sherard, whose original surname was Kennedy, mentions that the original surname of La Jeunesse was Cohen-Cahen. Sherard 1905 p.438. But if La Jeunesse was not the real name of this Ernest, it was the real name of Emma Albani, whose stage name, she would say, was taken from Albany, New York (it was actually suggested by her Italian elocution master). Marie-Louise-Emma-Cécile Lajeunesse was of Breton Canadian descent.

[1352] Barbara Belford: *Oscar Wilde, A Certain Genius*. London: Bloomsbury 2000 p.294. Hereafter cited as Belford.

[1353] Ernest Samuels: *Henry Adams: The Middle Years*. Cambridge, Mass: Harvard University Press 1958 p.121. This is not, I think, to be found in the Bernhardt biographies. Hereafter cited as Samuels.

[1354] Hohenlohe p.170. This Baude is not to be confused with the chief engineer responsible for the Gare Montparnasse, completed in 1852.

[1355] Merlin Holland (ed.): *Oscar Wilde, A Life in Letters*. Selected and edited by Merlin Holland. London: Fourth Estate 2003 p.73. Hereafter cited as Holland 2003.

[1356] Gide 1989 p.17.

[1357] Henry James to his brother William, 1890. Edel 1987 p.300.

[1358] Hector Bolitho: *Marie Tempest*. London: Cobden Sanderson 1936 p.210, hereafter cited as Bolitho. It is true that Tempest's husband once described her 'as a schoolmarm at heart' (*ibid..* p.251), but much the same point was made by Lord Frederic Hamilton: 'Idiocy, whether real or feigned, does not appeal to the French temperament'. Hamilton p.147.

[1359] Princess Catherine Radziwill: *These I Remember*. London: Cassell 1924 pp.101-2. Hereafter cited as Radziwill.

[1360] Sherard 1906 p.230.

[1361] O'Sullivan 1934 p.168.

[1362] Described as a sort of Quilp by Lord Redesdale, 'singularly ugly, even grotesque'. Redesdale p.174. It will be recalled that this was also the description attached to Sir William Wilde.

[1363] Whiteing p.48.

[1364] This was the wicked Lord Hertford, Thackeray's Lord Steyne. Wilde gave the name Hertford (phonetically spelled Harford) to the wicked Lord Illingworth in *A Woman of No Importance*, and Alan Campbell (*The Picture of Dorian Gray*) lives in Hertford Street, Mayfair.

[1365] Donald Mallet: The Great Collector, Lord Hertford and the Founding of the Wallace Collection. London, Macmillan 1979 pp.37-8.

[1366] Polnay p.122. The version De Battut is given in Ralph Nevill: *The Man of Pleasure*. London: Chatto & Windus 1912 p.183. Nevill says de Battut's mother was 'a rich Frenchwoman of good birth', and that he died in obscurity in Naples. Clunn also says that Arsouille was Seymour's nickname, but calls him simply Lord Seymour. Clunn. p.180.

[1367] Mistinguett p.67.

[1368] Delbourg-Delphis pp.33,203.

[1369] Du Maurier/Trilby p.70. The street name is difficult to translate (probably argot) – the street where the wind cuts like a sword blade, perhaps.

[1370] Frederic V. Grunfeld: *Rodin, A Biography*. London: Hutchinson 1987 p.325. Hereafter cited as Grunfeld.

[1371] George Moore to Jacques-Emile Blanche 2nd December 1887. Blanche p.292.

[1372] Edmund Gosse: 'Marcel Schwob', *The Athenæum* 4th March 1905; Sherard 1911 p.243. Child was English and Jewish and Henry James thought of him as a Daniel Deronda. Novick pp.344, 352.

[1373] Harris p.48.

[1374] Derrick Puffett (ed.): *Richard Strauss, Salomé*. Cambridge: Cambridge University Press 1989 p.2, citing an article by Ellmann. Hereafter cited as Puffett.

[1375] Sherard 1906 p.93.

[1376] Douglas/Wintermans p.40.

[1377] Gide/Mason 1905 p.23; Gide/Frechtman p.74.

[1378] Waddington 1914 p.118.

[1379] Harold Nicolson: *Verlaine*. Constable n.d. p.202; Healy p.224; J. Joseph-Renaud: Preface to Oscar Wilde: Intentions. Paris: Stock 1905 p.xxiii; Rothenstein Volume I p.88; Du Maurier/Trilby p.76. 'Ollendorf' is *Ollendorff's New Method of Learning to Read, Write and Speak the French Language*.

[1380] Langlade p.292.

[1381] Le Rouge; Gedeon Spilett in *Gil Blas* 22nd November 1897, both reprinted in Mikhail Volume II, pp.356,459 (translation is by Mikhail); Tydeman/Price p.18. *Gil Blas* was several steps down from *Le Gaulois*, where Sherard had published his interview with Wilde in 1891, indeed Arnold Bennett wrote of it that it would not be easy to underestimate its importance. Bennett 1917. 'Mention of the *Gil-Blas* invariably creates an atmosphere of amiable disreputability'. Steegmuller/Maupassant p.139.

[1382] Max Beerbohm: *Letters to Reggie Turner.* Edited by Rupert Hart-Davis. London: Rupert Hart-Davis 1964 p.36.

[1383] Langlade p.147n.

[1384] Elaine Aston: *Sarah Bernhardt, A French Actress on the London Stage.* Oxford, New York, Munich: Berg Publishing 1989 p.75. Hereafter cited as Aston.

[1385] 'Verlaine knows English very well' was George Moore's view. Moore 1914 p.93.

[1386] Grierson p.51.

[1387] Ellmann pp.316-7.

[1388] Sherard 1906 p.93

[1389] Clive p.73.

[1390] In any case, all agree that Wilde had a profound distaste for vulgar or coarse expressions, to the point which one scholar identifies as 'oral inhibitions'. Roditi p.118.

[1391] My translation. The original reads 'Quelque remarkable que soit la connaissance que Wilde avait du français, il est impossible pourtant de le considérer comme un poète français'. Rolland to Richard Strauss 12th November 1905. Strauss/Rolland p.80. Rolland was hostile to *Salomé.*

[1392] The details are set out in Langlade pp.152-3; and in Tydeman/Price pp.17-19.

[1393] Clive p.73.

[1394] 'Des mièvreries prétentieuses de style.' Romain Rolland to Richard Strauss 14th May 1907; Strauss to Rolland 10th November 1905. Strauss/Rolland pp.87,78. The difficulties posed for Strauss in the retranslation of the text as French libretto are discussed in Stephan Kohler: 'Warum singt der Franzose anders als er spricht?': Richard Strauss und die französische Fassung seiner Oper *Salomé. Jahrbuch der Bayerischen Staatsoper.* Vol. 2 1978/9. Pascal Aquien finds Wilde's French hardly worth criticising, despite certain anglicisms and occasional solecisms. Oscar Wilde: *Salomé.* Présentation de Pascal Aquien. Paris: Flammarion 1993 pp.20-1. Hereafter cited as Aquien/Salomé.

[1395] Roditi goes so far as to say that Louÿs 'probably helped [Wilde] write the original French text'. Roditi p.40. This is not generally followed by Wilde scholars.

[1396] O'Sullivan 1934 p.13.

[1397] Starkie p.106.

[1398] Fryer 1997 p.17. Fryer says that the book had been published 'only weeks before' but it may only have been days.

[1399] G.A. Cevasco: *Oscar Wilde, British Author, Poet & Wit.* Charlotteville, NY: Samhar Press 1972 pp.18-19; Lloyd pp.84,117,vi. See also Cevasco's *J-K Huysmans, A Reference Guide.* Boston: G.K. Hall 1980.

[1400] Laver p.75.

[1401] Oscar Wilde to Robert Ross 6th April 1897.Hart-Davis 1962 pp.520-1. This *En Route* should not be confused with the book of the same name by E. Saxelby and illustrated by Blam (London: Ginn & Co 1937), which is a French primer for young children. Roditi describes Ohnet as 'in those days a very popular French novelist whose style Wilde had good reason to despise, and whose works are now remembered in France, if at all, only as proverbial examples of a truly obsolete kind of *Kitsch.*' Roditi p.181. Roditi also reckons Wilde's views here expressed on Huysmans as less perceptive.

[1402] Joris-Karl Huysmans: *La Cathédrale*. Translated as *The Cathedral* by Clara Bell. London: Kegan Paul, Trench, Trübner & Co 1898; Healy p.136.

[1403] Holland & Hart-Davis p.1022. Why Wilde chose to characterise Healy as a poet is not explained.

[1404] Carlson p.198.

[1405] Ohnet pp.17-18,41.

[1406] Edmond et Jules de Goncourt: *Journal – Mémoires de la Vie Littéraire*. Paris: Robert Laffont 1989. Volume III p.1150 (entry for 6th July 1895).

[1407] Harris p.300.

[1408] Hugues Rebell et al.: *Pour Oscar Wilde, des Écrivains français au secours du condamné*. Rouen: Elisabeth Brunet 1994. The others here are Paul Adam, Henry Bauër, Louis Lormel, Jean Lorrain, Stuart Merrill, Henri de Régnier and Laurent Tailhade

[1409] 'Des lys! Des lys!' 7th April 1895 and 'Toujours des lys!' 28th April 1895 – not, be it noted, œillets verts, green carnations.

[1410] This was later (1964) filmed by Buñuel. 'Sartorys' is also the leading male in *Froufrou*.

[1411] Mirbeau pp.162-6.

[1412] Sherard 1937 p.137.

[1413] Rudorff p.239.

[1414] *Les Cosaques* was a play by Adolph Arnault and Louis Judicis produced at the Théâtre de la Gaîté in 1853.

[1415] Novelist and dramatist of domestic problems. Fittingly, the rue Paul Hervieu debouches into the avenue Émile Zola (XVe arrondissement). Note also the writer, painter and printmaker Louise Hervieu.

[1416] Comte Paul Marie Théodore Vincent d'Indy was a Symbolist disciple of César Franck, creator of the Schola Cantorum, and an enthusiast for Wagner. Paderewski called him 'a great musician'. Ignace Jan Paderewski and Mary Lawton: *The Paderewski Memoirs*. London: Collins 1939 p.151; hereafter cited as Paderewski. Inheriting a fortune from his grandmother, he was a dandy in more than in his name. His bust by Bourdelle (Musée Bourdelle) dates to 1927.

[1417] A picture of Alice Regnault is in English Officer 1908, facing p.46; her portrait by Boldini is reproduced as plate 18 in Carlo L. Ragghianti: *L'Opera completa di Boldini*. Con apparati critici e filologici de Ettore Camesasca. Milano: Rizzoli 1970 (hereafter cited as Ragghianti). She is also the subject of Boldini's equestrian picture 'Amazzone al Bois de Boulogne', Gallery of Modern Art, Milan.

[1418] An embittered and caustic wit, Renard carried a Naturalist's pessimism about human nature and the human condition into Symbolist circles and the aphorisms in his Journal are chiefly sardonic.

[1419] Allais' work has been published in many Volumes in France, but in England he is only represented by the slim Volume *The World of Alphonse Allais*, selected, translated and introduced by Miles Kington. London: Chatto & Windus 1977. Kington calls him 'probably the finest humorous writer France has ever produced'. Material for Allais can be found in the Musée du Vieux-Honfleur. He should not be confused with Adolphe Alphand.

[1420] Logue p.285. For the Octave Mirbeau Society, see
http://mirbeau.asso.fr/societeom.htm.
[1421] Born at 9 rue Edouard-Detaille.
[1422] Oskar Reinhart Sammlung, Winterthur ('La Clownesse'). Although this name
suggests that of one of the Chinese Treaty Ports, it derives from Chahut-Chaos,
which Alexandra Campbell has translated as Hurly-Burly. Frèches p.62. There is
another painting of her by Lautrec in the Musée d'Orsay ('La Clownesse Cha-u-
kao' 1895) and there is a copy of the lithograph 'Female Clown Seated, Mlle Cha-
U-Ka-O' of 1896 in the British Museum, ref. BM PD 1949-4-11-3635. I think it
was her name that Joyce drew upon in the Cyclops chapter of *Ulysses*: 'Li Chi Han
lovey up kissy Cha Pu Chow.' Cha-U-Ka-O was not Chinese.
[1423] Nordau p.70. 'The great palace of art' is obviously a foolish translation of 'le
Grand Palais de l'Art'.
[1424] Du Maurier/Martian p.37. I suggest that 'even' is a misprint for 'ever'.
[1425] Hamilton p.49; Ohnet p.238.
[1426] Emile Zola: *Le Ventre de Paris*. Translated as *Savage Paris* by David Hughes
& Marie-Jacqueline Mason. Preface by Hugh Shelley. London: Elek Books 1955.
pp.229,234. The latter passage presages Huysmans' famous organ of liqueurs.
Unusually Zola finds the smells disgusting.
[1427] 'Paris 1900'. http://tfaoi.com/newsm1/n1m556.htm.
[1428] Henry Adams: *The Education of Henry Adams, an Autobiography*. London:
Constable & Co. n.d. pp.378,379. Hereafter cited as Adams.
[263] Bradford A. Booth and Ernest Mehew (edd.): *The Letters of Robert Louis
Stevenson*. New Haven and London: Yale University Press 1995 Volume V: July
1884 to August 1887 p.304 n.3.
[1430] Derek Hudson*: For Love of Painting, The Life of Sir Gerald Kelly K.C.V.O.,
P.R.A.* London: Peter Davis 1975 p.16. Hereafter cited as Hudson.
[1431] Grunfeld p.148.
[1432] Rollinat also had a link to the theatre through his mistress, whose sister was an
actress in Sarah Bernhardt's company.
[1433] Poet, socialist, editor of *Le Mot d'ordre*, at one time imprisoned for his part in
the Commune at Marseilles, for which city he subsequently became a deputy. His
real name was Hugues Clovis, and he should not be confused with Hugues Rebell,
whose real name was Georges Grassal.
[1434] Bracquemond engraved Manet's bookplate which bore the legend *Manet et
manebit*, and in 1882 painted a portrait of Edmond de Goncourt (now in the British
Museum). Bracquemond's wife Marie was also an Impressionist painter, now it
seems largely overlooked.
[1435] Rodenbach's portrait by Lucien Lévy-Dhurmer (1895, Salon of 1896) is in the
Musée d'Orsay, ref. RF 39677.
[1436] c.1898. Musée Rodin S.1126.
[1437] Interview with Gilbert Burgess 4th January 1895, reprinted in Wyse Jackson
p.xix.
[1438] Ellmann p.543.

[1439] Not, as Langlade states, at the Salon of 1898. Langlade p.282. The site of the Rodin Pavilion is the present place de la Reine Astrid. The Rodin exhibition was part of the Exposition Universelle which opened on the 20th April 1900 and closed on the 10th November. The British Embassy staff attended the opening in uniform. 'I remember little of it'. Maurice Baring: *The Puppet Show of Memory*. London: William Heinemann 1922 p.204. Hereafter cited as Baring 1922.

[1440] Maureen Borland: *D.S. MacColl, Painter, Poet, Art Critic*. Harpenden: Lennard Publishing 1995 p.199. Hereafter cited as Borland 1995.

[1441] Adolphe Retté: *Symbolisme, Anecdotes et Souvenirs*. 1903. Cited in Mikhail Volume II p.471.

[1442] Oscar Wilde to Robert Ross 7th July 1900. Hart-Davis 1962 p.831. 'Quite wonderful' is not a term much used by art critics.

[1443] As early as 1878, Laurent Tailhade said of Charles Hugo's adaptation of *Les Misérables* that the novel was bad, the play execrable. Tailhade p.51.

[1444] Grunfeld p.411. 'Poet' one must guess, indicates Rodin's awareness of Wilde as the author of *The Ballad of Reading Gaol*.

[1445] Grunfeld p.410.

[1446] Steegmuller/Maupassant p.185. She is the 'Princess Peglioso' of Jacques-Emile Blanche's *Aymeris*.

[1447] Whiteing p.15.

[1448] Now in the Musée Carnavalet.

[1449] Jean-Baptiste-Edouard Detaille 'peintre quasi-officiel de l'armée française'. *Dictionnaire des Peintres, Sculpteurs, Dessinateurs et Graveurs*. Paris: Librairie Gründ 1976. The Irish painter Walter Osborne, seeing works by him in the Luxembourg in 1895, described them as 'huge atrocities'. Jeanne Sheehy: *Walter Osborne*. Ballycotton, Co Cork: Gifford and Craven 1974 p.37. The Prince of Wales commissioned from him an equestrian portrait of himself and his brother the Duke of Connaught at the Aldershot Review, which he gave to his mother who had it placed in the State Dining Room at Windsor Castle. This perhaps gives the measure of atrociousness.

[1450] Probably Etienne Dubois de L'Estang (1851-1909), Inspecteur et directeur général des Finances

[1451] Reproduced in Robinat p.46.

[1452] Patrick Offenstadt: 'Le Paris Disparu de Jean Béraud'. *L'Œil* n° 380, March 1987.

[1453] Fouquières p.93. 'Madame Cahen d'Anvers' was Loulia, née Warshawski, wife of the comte Albert Cahen d'Anvers. Her sister Marie Kahn was one of Maupassant's lovers.

[1454] Robinat p.47. By then over ninety, the countess and her last greyhound died of hunger during the German occupation and were somewhat eaten by rats.

[1455] Pretty Women p.154.

[1456] Pretty Women p.153.

[1457] Douglas/Wintermans p.42.

[1458] Dimnet 1938 p.49; Bell p.150.

[1459] From 'Fantaisies Décoratives, I: Le Panneau'. The æsthetic limitations of this verse are discussed by Roditi p.26.

[1460] Richard Buckle: *Diaghilev*. London: Weidenfeld & Nicolson 1979 p.300. Buckle more than once seems to need to validate his understanding of Diaghilev by reference to Wilde, but only demonstrates that he does not understand Wilde.

[1461] Duncan p.78.

[1462] Duncan p.99. There is much to be read in this line.

[1463] Duncan pp.76,77.

[1464] Oscar Wilde to Robert Ross 13th August 1898. Hart-Davis 1962 p.758. Langlade says that Wilde was at the vernissage, 30th April 1898. Langlade p.286.

[1465] Apart from the maquettes and small bronze versions in the Musée Balzac, examples may also be seen in the Musée d'Orsay and the Metropolitan Museum of Art, New York, ref.1984.364.15. The statue itself is now at the intersection of the boulevard Raspail and the boulevard Montparnasse.

[1466] Oscar Wilde to Frank Harris 1st May 1898. Hart-Davis 1962 p.732.

[1467] Robert H. Sherard: 'Notes from Paris' in *The Author* Volume II/9 February 1892 p.265.

[1468] Grunfeld p.574.

[1469] Gramont p.26.

[1470] Leslie pp.251,272.

[1471] Oscar Wilde to Reginald Turner 11th May 1898. Hart-Davis 1962 pp.738-9.

[1472] Sherard 1908 p.193.

[1473] Belloc 1943 p.163.

[1474] 13th September 1886.

[1475] Sherard 1908 p.26. One may also note the description of the painter 'Bongrand': 'One habit he had retained from his Romantic youth was wearing a special costume for working in, which explained why he received his visitors in baggy trousers, a dressing-gown with a cord round the waist like a monk, and the top of his head encased in an ecclesiastical skull-cap'. Zola/ *L'Œuvre* p.203.

[1476] 'S. Bing' is how Bing (1838-1905) always signed his own name, and what the S stood for was long open to conjecture. Battersby p.26. 'Often misnamed Samuel' (Gabriel Weisberg, Article on Bing in Grove). Samuel is given by John Fleming and Hugh Honour: *The Penguin Dictionary of Decorative Arts*. London: Penguin 1977 p.92, and by Borsi/Godoli p.39; by House/Stevens p.23; by Delbourg-Delphis p.190; and by Simon Houfe: *Fin-de-siècle, the Illustrators of the Nineties*. London: Barrie & Jenkins 1992 p.5. His name is now held to have been Siegfried.

[1477] Wilde would also have been exposed to the art nouveau decoration of the Hôtel Chatham, if he ventured beyond the bar. This was by the Belgian Gustav Serrier-Bovy (1858-1910), who had visited England in 1884. France Borel: 'Serrurier-Bovy, entre Art nouveau et Art déco', in *L'Œil* no.387 October 1987.

[1478] Langlade p.306.

[1479] Jonathan Vickers & Peter Copeland: 'The Voice of Oscar Wilde: An Investigation'. *British Association of Sound Collections News* 2, 1987. There were also pirated editions of Wilde published in Paris in the early years of the twentieth century.

[1480] Benois p.193.

[1481] The subtitle of the 1997 film *Wilde*.

[1482] The De Dion-Bouton motor car dates to 1899.

[1483] Ellmann p.326. Ellmann's vagueness here is symptomatic of his unease with the French culture of the period. Moreno (1871-1948), a lifelong friend of Colette and the first actress to play the title rôle in Giraudoux' *The Mad Woman of Chaillot*, was 'probably the best-known French actress of the twentieth century.' Crosland p.60. Her portrait by Joseph Granié, dating to 1899, is in the Musée d'Orsay, ref. RF1977-186. Casselaer p.100. Paul Léautaud was silently infatuated with her, provoking her into saying, 'Well, Léautaud, I'd like to make love before I'm sixty'. Mavis Gallant: 'Paul Léautaud, 1872-1956' in *Paris Notebooks*. London: Hamish Hamilton 1989 p.143.

[1484] Kelly's 'essential Irishness' (Hudson p.ix) was perhaps more obvious in Paris than it was in London, as he was the son of the Vicar of Camberwell and like his father before him had been educated at Eton and Cambridge. Kelly's uncle Richard was M.P. for North Camberwell 1886-1892. Monelle is the eponym of Schwob's *Le Livre de Monelle*, which made Colette cry after reading it.

[1485] De Dion's other engineer, Trépardoux, did not bequeath his name to a motor-car and is accordingly forgotten.

[1486] Blunt p.371. Diary entry for 8th September 1900. Sermoneta p.95.

[1487] Should not be confused with the rue du Caire off the boulevard de Sébastopol in the *quartier des fringues.*

[1488] The Swiss Village remained and was renovated in the 1960s. Still called the Village Suisse, bounded by the avenues Suffren, Motte-Picquet, Paul Déroulède and Champaubert, it is now neither tranquil nor simple, let alone rural, being home to antique dealers with apartments above. The place Lucerne indicates its former tranquillity.

[1489] 'André Gide and His Friends at the Exposition Universelle 1900'. Musée des Beaux-Arts, Rouen. Rouart's collection of Impressionists was important enough to merit an exhibition devoted to it ('Au cœur de l'Impressionisme – La famille Rouart') at the Musée de la Vie Romantique, Paris, 3rd February to 13th June 2004. Athman had been brought to Paris as a factotum by Gide, and remained to create a career of his own.

[1490] Paul Greenhalgh: 'The Paris Exposition Universelle 1900'. Unpublished lecture given at the Royal Academy, London 4th February 2000. My contemporary note. Hereafter cited as Greenhalgh 2000.

[1491] Oscar Wilde to Leonard Smithers 2nd September 1900. Holland & Hart-Davis p.1196. There had also been a rue de Caire in the 1889 Exhibition, complete with belly dancers. Joseph Harriss: *The Eiffel Tower, Symbol of an Age*. London: Paul Elek 1976 p.133. The Dance of the Seven Veils in *Salomé* was illustrated by Beardsley with a picture of a belly dance, and the dancers of the rue de Caire may have played a part in this identification.

[1492] Sherard 1908 p.34.

[1493] Menpes p.81.

[1494] Often ascribed to Charles Coborn, the man being Charles de Ville Wells, but it has also been credited to a Fred Gilbert. Coborn certainly made the song famous. Clearly the line should read 'As I walked along the avenue du Bois de Boulogne', but topography yields to scansion.
http://www.csufresno.edu/folklore/BalladIndex.html

[1495] See J.F. Raffaëlli's 'Marchand d'ail', Museum of Fine Arts, Boston, reproduced as fig. 165 in Weisberg.

[1496] Fox pp.26-7,29.

[1497] Ohnet p.6.

[1498] Hamilton pp.51-2.

[1499] Fouquières p.283. My translation.

[1500] Christopher Hibbert: *King Edward VII, A Portrait*. London: Allen Lane 1976 p.135.

[1501] Wilde asked More Adey for soap from Houbigant, either 'Peau d'Espagne' or 'Sac de Laitue', for his release from prison. Oscar Wilde to More Adey 6th May 1897. Holland & Hart-Davis p.809. The other fashionable parfumiers were Violet (boulevard des Capucines), Pinaud (boulevard des Italiens) and Guerlain (rue de la Paix), whose scent Shalimar was favoured by Dolly Wilde.

[1502] Baroness de Stoeckl: *Not All Vanity*. Edited by George Kinnaird. London: John Murray 1950 p.12. Hereafter cited as Stoeckl. Founded in the rue d'Antin in 1845, it moved to 10 rue Royale in 1900, and to its present address, 103 rue du Faubourg Saint-Honoré, only in 2012. Mme de Stoeckl wrongly sites Lachaume in the boulevard de la Madeleine. Proust, through Odette de Crécy, called Lachaume's prices indecent. Proust/Ombre p.179.

[1503] Proust/Ombre pp.117-9.

[1504] Joanna Richardson: *Princess Mathilde*. London: Weidenfeld & Nicolson 1969 p.301.

[1505] Hohenlohe p.114. Diary entry for 22nd May 1874.

[1506] Gramont p.137.

[1507] Jules Laforgue to Gustave Kahn January 1881. Arkell p.48.

[1508] Sheridan p.14.

[1509] Tailhade p.19. It should be remembered that asphalting was carried out in part to diminish the store of setts and cobblestones available to rioters. The chief asphalt engineer in Paris was British, a man called Delano.

[1510] 1861–1921. A Belgian, his real name was Felix Tillkin. In 1896, George Dance's *The Gay Parisienne*, with music by Ivan Caryll, opened at the Duke of York's Theatre in London, where it ran for 369 performances, transferring to New York at the Herald Square Theatre as *The Girl from Paris*, and having a similar success. Mr. Honeycomb is a conventional Englishman while in England but abroad, he cuts loose and on a trip to Paris he falls into the hands of Mlle Julie Bon-Bon. This musical comedy is a significant example of the Anglo-Saxon construction of Gay Paree.

[1511] Lady Mitchell: *Three Quarters of a Century.* London: Methuen 1940. Florence Mitchell (née Morrison) stayed in a pension in the avenue d'Iéna in January 1882.

[1512] Ernest Jones: *Sigmund Freud, Life and Work* Volume I: The Young Freud 1856-1900. London: Hogarth Press 1953 p.200. Hereafter cited as Jones. Curiously, after leaving Paris the following February Freud only ever returned twice, in 1889 and on his way to exile in England in 1938.

[1513] Laver p.26.

[1514] Shelley Rice: *Parisian Views.* Cambridge, Mass: MIT Press 1997 p.42, quoting Charles Yriarte: 'Les Types parisiens – les clubs' in *Paris Guide* Volume II 1867, as given by T.J. Clark: *The Painting of Modern Life.* New York: Knopf 1984 pp.43-4.

[1515] Maupassant/Bel Ami p.153.

[1516] Émile Zola: *L'Assommoir.* Translated by Margaret Mauldon with an Introduction by Robert Lethbridge. World's Classics 1995; reissued as an Oxford World's Classics. Oxford: Oxford University Press 1998 p.386. Hereafter Zola/L'Assommoir.

[1517] Anne Distel, Douglas W Druick, Gloria Groom, Rodolphe Ropetti: *Gustave Caillebotte, Urban Impressionist.* Paris: La Réunion des Musées Nationaux and the Musée d'Orsay; Chicago: The Art Institute 1995. Hereafter cited as Distel.

[1518] See, for example, 'Young Man at his Window' (1875; private collection) or 'Man on a Balcony' (1880; private collection), reproduced as plates 59 and 67 in Distel.

[1519] Loyer p.354.

[1520] Editor of *La Centaure.*, and translator of *Also Spracht Zarathrustra* (*Ainsi Parlait Zarathoustra.* Paris: Mercure de France 1898). His real name was Henri-Albert Haug.

[1521] Louÿs/Tinan p.111.

[1522] Lord Ribblesdale: *Impressions and Memories.* With a preface by his daughter Lady Wilson. Cassell & Co. 1927 p.xvi. Hereafter cited as Ribblesdale.

[1523] Wilson p.141.

[1524] Ribblesdale p.xvii.

[1525] Wilson p.32. Something of the atmosphere of such markets was caught by Pissarro in his painting 'The Pork Butcher' (1883, National Gallery, London, ref. NG L724. Although this is thought to be the market at Pontoise, Pissarro's use of a model (his niece Eugénie or Nini Estruc) suggests that he had in mind the 'generic' market scene rather than a specific moment. Here the 'butcher' is cutting up meat on a stall. A visit to-day to a Paris street market, such as the one (Tuesday and Friday) in the rue St-Charles will suggest that here at last is one thing in Paris that is constant.

[1526] Laver p.47.

[1527] Hughes pp.236-43. Colonel Newnham-Davis, however, thought the prices at the Bœuf à la Mode moderate, the place itself quiet and comfortable, and says that English ladies lunched there unescorted. Newnham-Davis also recommended the Restaurant Lequen facing the Gare du Nord, which might have fallen under

Hughes' notice. Newnham-Davis pp.41,43. Prunier's was in the rue Duphot, with
an oyster and snail shop attached.
[1528] Diary entry for 24th October 1897. Flower/Bennett p.54. Although the name
of Trocadéro remains in use, the building itself was replaced in 1936/7 by the
Palais de Chaillot.
[1529] Hunt p.29.
[1530] Diary entry for 27th October 1897. Flower/Bennett p.57.
[1531] Diary entry for 27th October 1897. Flower/Bennett p.57.
[1532] Menpes p.6.
[1533] Low p.308. Italics in the original.
[1534] Diary entry for 12th April 1893. Coolidge p.237.
[1535] Lucas p.316.
[1536] Paris: The Author (16 rue Jacques Caillot, VIe) 2002.
[1537] Zola/L'Assommoir pp.74-81. The Colonne Vendôme is really called the
Colonne d'Austerlitz, 'but for some unexplained reason Parisians have always
termed it the Colonne Vendôme'. Clunn p.22.
[1538] Zola/L'Assommoir p.256.
[1539] Zola/L'Œuvre p.82.
[1540] Zola/L'Œuvre p.342.
[1541] Zola 1883 pp.136,149,282.
[1542] Maupassant/Bel Ami p.261.
[1543] no. 90.
[1544] Zola/L'Œuvre p.396. In *Le ventre de Paris*, Lantier also strolls about. Emile
Zola: *Le ventre de Paris*. Translated as *Savage Paris* by David Hughes & Marie-
Jacqueline Mason. Preface by Hugh Shelley. London: Elek Books 1955 p.181.
As a child in the 1870s, Jane Avril shopped in the rue Lepic.
[1545] Reff p.14.
[1546] Ohnet p.238.
[1547] Maupassant/Fifi p.277. 'Monsieur Parent' was written in the autumn of 1885
and published in January 1886.
[1548] Paul Léautaud: *Le Petit Ami*, with *In Memoriam* and *Amours*. Translated by
Humphrey Hare as *The Child of Man*. London: The Bodley Head 1959 p.236.
Hereafter cited as Léautaud.
[1549] Léautaud p.225.
[1550] Young pp.129-30.
[1551] Fox p.19.
[1552] Dumas p.78. Marguerite's original, Marie Duplessis, actually lived at 11 rue
Lafitte, so to seek a window in the rue d'Antin is to fantasise doubly. Moreover,
the 11 rue Lafitte of that time is now number 15; and the rue Mont Blanc no longer
exists.
[1553] Guy de Maupassant: 'Old Vestey' in Maupassant/Harriet p.130.
[1554] Guy de Maupassant: 'Cemetery Walkers' in Maupassant/Harriet p.137.
[1555] Guy de Maupassant: 'Monsieur Parent' in Maupassant/Harriet p.28.

[1556] Harold Nicolson: *Some People*. Constable & Co 1927 p.50. 'Marstock' was a compound of J.R. Parsons, at school with Nicolson, and Harold Duncan, with whom he was at Balliol. The bridge is the Pont Royal.

[1557] Zola/L'Assommoir p.82.

[1558] 1806-1889.

[1559] Alice Diehl: *The True Story of My Life, An Autobiography*. London: John Lane The Bodley Head 1907 p.118

[1560] Hamerton p.189.

[1561] There was also the Denman Tripp gallery in the rue de Provence.

[1562] An artist of the Barbizon School.

[1563] Colette 1963 p.116.

[1564] Colette 1963 p.122.

[1565] Barbara S. Fields: 'J.-F. Raffaëlli' in Grove.

[1566] Raffaëlli's 'Le Chiffonnier' of 1879 is in the Musée St-Denis, Reims, and is reproduced in Weisberg fig.164, and as plate 4 in Marianne Delafond & Caroline Genet-Bondeville: *Jean-François Raffaëlli*. Paris: Musée Marmottan-Monet 1999.

[1567] Maupasssant/Affair p.47.

[1568] Fox pp.64-5. There is a drawing by John Cameron of *chiffonniers* on p.65. 'Le p'tit Fox' had his own ambiguity, beyond the gendering of his name, for on a number of occasions as a practical joke he dressed as a girl and was accepted as such by those he sought to hoax (*ibid.* pp.126-34).

[1569] From Gavroche onwards, the French seemed uncertain whether street urchins should be sentimentalised or treated realistically. See, for example, Marie Bashkirtseff's 'Jean et Jacques' in the Salon of 1883, now in the Newbery Library, Chicago, or Louise Breslau's 'Gamins de Paris', 1885, Kunsthaus, Zürich; while the literary convention is represented by Cadine and Marjolin in Zola's *Le ventre de Paris*.

[1570] c.1882, Petit Palais, Geneva.

[1571] Wadsworth Museum, Hartford, Connecticut.

[1572] 1885, Musée de la Chartreuse, Douai.

[1573] Metropolitan Museum of Art, New York ref. 60.174. The three views of the Jardins des Tuileries, also in the Metropolitan (refs. 66.36, 1992.103.3 and 1979.414) also answer to this point, painted as they were from Pissarro's window at 204 rue de Rivoli, 1899.

[1574] James/Ambassadors p.18.

[1575] David Harvey: *Consciousness and the Urban Experience*. Oxford: Basil Blackwell 1985 p.74.

[1576] Louÿs/Tinan p.296.

[1577] James/Portraits p.131.

[1578] Méral p.111.

[1579] Lucas p.219.

[1580] Zola 1883 pp.155, 270. Zola also saw a movement downward, the marquise de Fontenailles taken on as a shop girl in the Bonheur and marrying one of the porters.

[1581] Carol Clark points out that in the streets of Proust's Paris 'all the young people who bring goods to the house [...] and all messengers except telegram boys are girls', but she regards this as odd. Marcel Proust: *A la recherche du temps perdu / In Search of Lost Time*. Vol. V: *La Prisonnière*, tr. by Carol Clark as *The Prisoner*; London: Penguin Books 2003 p.x.

[1582] Severini's picture 'Le Marchand d'Oubliés [Wafer Vendor], avenue Trudaine' dates to 1908, but the kiosk it shows would be much as it was earlier.

[1583] Oscar Wilde to the Editor of *The Speaker* early December 1891, from 29 boulevard des Capucines. Hart-Davis 1962 p.300.

[1584] Oscar Wilde to William Rothenstein late February 1898 from the Hôtel de Nice. Hart-Davis 1962 p.707.

[1585] Whiteing 1900 pp.202-3, from the Chapter (V) entitled 'Life on the Boulevard'. This aspect of the Paris kiosk at least seems to have transferred itself in our day to the London telephone kiosk.

[1586] Lucy Broido: *The Posters of Jules Chéret*, with a Catalogue Raisonné. New York: Dover Books 1980

[1587] Reproduced in Cate fig. 102.

[1588] The Musée des Beaux-Arts in Nice is also known as the Musée Jules Chéret. His portrait by Jacques-Emile Blanche (1892) is in the Petit Palais.

[1589] Paul Colin: 'Le créateur de l'affiche moderne', Chapter VI of Adhémar.

[1590] There is an excellent contemporary representation by Jean Béraud in the Walters Art Gallery, Baltimore.

[1591] Whiteing 1900 pp.142,147,182.

[1592] Xanrof: *Chansons à rire*. Paris: Flammarion 1891, quoted in Cate p.16.

[1593] Mrs Belloc Lowndes: *"I, too, Have Lived in Arcadia", A Record of Love and Friendship*. London: Macmillan & Co. 1941 p.164. Wingfield worked with the American ambulance run by a Dr Swinburne in 1870.

[1594] Louÿs/Tinan p.81n.

[1595] Lysiane Bernhardt: *Sarah Bernhardt, My Grandmother*. Translated by Vyvyan Holland. London: Hurst & Blackett 1949 p.132. Hereafter cited as Bernhardt.

[1596] Stefan Zweig refers to Emile Verhaeren 'strutting about in fantastic apparel'. Zweig p.141.

[1597] C.W Stamper: *What I Know. Reminiscences of Five Years Attendance upon his late Majesty King Edward the Seventh*. London: Mills & Boon 1913 p.99.

[1598] Poiret p.33.

[1599] The form favoured in Michael G. Lerner: *Maupassant*. London: George Allen & Unwin 1975 p.215.

[1600] de Lara p.99. Could this have been the marquis Macchetta d'Allegri who married Blanche Roosevelt? Marion Mainwaring: *Mysteries of Paris, The Quest for Morton Fullerton*. Hanover & London: University Press of New England 2001 p.98; hereafter cited as Mainwaring. Mainwaring says he was Portuguese but the name is surely Italian, and a plaque in Brompton Cemetery, London, where she is buried, gives her name as Blanche Roosevelt Macchetta, Marchesa d'Allegri.

[1601] Leslie p.253.

[1602] In April 1894 Robert Sherard reported that Dumas was selling his house in the avenue de Villiers and leaving Paris. Sherard April 1892 p.359.

[1603] Moore 1914 p.22.

[1604] O'Sullivan 1934 p.167.

[1605] Mix p.184.

[1606] Lucas p.273.

[1607] Daudet p.211.

[1608] Healy p.189.

[1609] Davis 1895 pp.17,18.

[1610] Nevill 1926 p.240.

[1611] Moscheles p.310.

[1612] Sherard 1905 p.179.

[1613] Berlanstein p.125.

[1614] Menpes p.5

[1615] Berlanstein p.123

[1616] Whiteing 1900p.181.

[1617] Whiteing 1900p.259.

[1618] Maupassant/Bel Ami p.178. Even by day, the Champs-Elysées had its erotic aspect, as Ford Madox Ford noted in disapproval: 'On sunny days, the most horrible, half-nude creatures sunned themselves on the benches.' Ford Madox Ford p.80.

[1619] Symons p.123.

[1620] It had long been possible to visit the sewers, from the place du Châtelet, by underground tramway to the place de la Concorde, and then by boat to the Madeleine, but this was not quite the same thing.

[1621] Merrick p.61.

[1622] Walter Leaf found the rue du Bac 'pitted from end to end' with bullet holes when he went to Paris on 16th June 1871. Leaf p.77. Later still, after 1917, the reader of *Le Débâcle* could hardly have come across without a chill the sentence 'This march to Verdun was a march to death'. Zola/ Débâcle p.79.

[1623] Reproduced in Hemmings 1977 p.85.

[1624] Zola/L'Œuvre p.76.

[1625] James/Ambassadors pp.52-3.

[1626] From 'Causerie'. Monet's 'Les Tuileries' of 1876 (Musée Marmottan-Monet, Paris) captures very well the contrast between the shell of the Palais and the well-maintained gardens.

[1627] Zola/Paris pp.387-8.

[1628] De Profundis.

[1629] Diary entry for 13th March 1892. Goncourt/Baldick p.373.

[1630] Ainslie p.162.

[1631] The Rt. Hon. Sir Austen Chamberlain K.G., P.C., M.P.: *Down the Years*. London: Cassell & Co 1935 p.26.

[1632] Sharon Benstock: *No Gifts from Chance, A Biography of Edith Wharton*. London: Hamish Hamilton 1994 p.75. Hereafter cited as Benstock.

[1633] Radziwill p.120.

[1634] Cossart p.19.

[1635] Jean-Michel Nectoux: *Gabriel Fauré, A Musical Life*. Translated by Roger Nichols. Cambridge: Cambridge University Press 2004 pp.67,150.

[1636] Sorel p.22.

[1637] Letter to Philip Houghton of February 1894. Holland & Hart-Davis p.586.

[1638] Sherard 1908 pp.127-8, 151.

[1639] Henry p.13.

[1640] Arthur W. À Beckett: *London at the Turn of the Century, A Book of Gossip*. London: Hurst & Blackett 1900 p.327.

[1641] Sherard 1905 pp.377-8.

[1642] Borland 1995 pp.81-2.

[1643] Menpes p.102.

[1644] Frances Spalding: *Roger Fry, Art and Life*. London: Paul Elek Granada Publishing 1980 p.42.

[1645] Stevenson/Osbourne p.30.

[1646] Healy p.267.

[1647] Fox pp.55-6. Fox also acted as cicerone to an American musician, identified only as W–. In 1886 the planned to see *Mignon* at the Opéra Comique, but went instead to the Cirque d'Eté, witnessing the fire that destroyed the Opéra Comique as they were returning to the Hôtel de Londres et New York. Fox pp.62-3.

[1648] Ribblesdale 1930 p.47.

[1649] 'The prince of the Boulevard and the most Parisian of journalists'. Perruchot p.82. Originally he was twice included in *Bel-Ami* but Maupassant subsequently changed the name to Montel in one instance and Frevacques in the other, perhaps in awe of Scholl's 'ironie mordante' and propensity for duelling. The description is from Monique Chartier: *Zola, Trois Etés à Royan*. Préface de Colette Becker. Royan: Editions Bonne Anse 2003 p.52.

[1650] Rearick p.72. Gaston Lachaille, in Colette's *Gigi*, which is set in 1899, has 'un nez peu long [...] le commun de mortels croyait grugé', a 'prominent nose, large enough to appear false'. Colette 1944 p.32; Colette 1958 p.18.

[1651] Its heydays were between 1887 and 1896; later it was known as the Trianon-Lyrique.

[1652] Robert Twombly: *Louis Sullivan*. Chicago: University of Chicago Press 1987 p.69. This must have been in November 1874, as Sullivan had arrived in August that year (by an unusual route, Dover-Dieppe) and was back in New York on the 24th May 1875. Twombly discovered (or discloses) little of Sullivan's life save his fondness for window-shopping.

[1653]. The touches of melancholy and the autumnal in his writings was another *fin-de-siècle* characteristic. Anatole France wrote of him 'It was reserved for Pierre Loti to make us taste to intoxication, to delirium, even to stupor, the acrid savour of exotic loves'. France p.313. Loti's real name was Julien Viaud.

[1654] Two men in evening dress with a masked lady, 1886. Now in a private collection in Paris. Reproduced as plate 42 in the catalogue of the 1992/3 Gervex exhibition held in Bordeaux, Nice and Paris. No publication or authorial details are given in this save © Paris-Musées.

[1655] 1873. Bought by Henry Havemeyer of New York, this is now in the National Gallery of Art, Washington.
[1656] Henri de Toulouse-Lautrec: 'Maxime DeThomas at the Bal de l'Opéra', National Gallery of Art, Washington. DeThomas, a painter and draughtsman, was a close friend of Tinan's.
[1657] Nevill 1926 p.252.
[1658] This was Adolphe Willette, not to be confused with the soldier of that name, known as 'the Padré', aide-de-camp to Marshal Bazaine.
[1659] Jules Renard's *Poil de Carotte*, which brought him fame, was staged as a curtain raiser to *The Devil's Disciple* in 1900, as 'Carrots', the English version being by Alfred Sutro, and, according to Forbes-Robertson, who played in the latter, a 'touching and beautiful little picture of French provincial life'. Sir Johnston Forbes-Robertson: *A Player under Three Reigns*. London: T. Fisher Unwin 1925 p.199, hereafter cited as Forbes-Robertson. 'Jules Renard,' says Harold Hobson roundly, 'is the most memorable dramatist of the late nineteenth century'. Hobson p.27.
[1660] The Théâtre Tristan-Bernard in the rue du Rocher honours his name.
[1661] His real name was George Moineaux; his portrait by Leopold Stevens is in the Musée Carnavalet, ref. P.2693. Some authorities, notably the Bibliothèque Electronique de Lisieux, give his birth date as 1859; but Joyce M.H. Reid (ed.): *The Concise Oxford Dictionary of French Literature*. Oxford: Oxford University Press 1976 prefers 1861, while the *Nouveau Petit Larousse*. Paris: Librairie Larousse 1969 has 1858. Wilde's readiness to prevaricate over his own age is given some context by such slippage.
[1662] Symons p.42.
[1663] Clement Scott: From 'The Bells' to 'King Arthur', A Critical Record of the First Night Productions at the Lyceum Theatre from 1871 to 1895. London: John MacQueen 1896 p.187.
[1664] de Lara pp.83-4.
[1665] Robert H. Sherard: 'Notes from Paris' in *The Author* Volume III/7 December 1892 p.239.
[1666] It may be in part from the Parisian tradition of carnivalesque that Joyce took something of his transformation scenes in *Ulysses.*
[1667] Ruth First and Anne Scott: *Olive Schreiner*. London: André Deutsch 1988 p.186. I prefer this to the version given in Ellmann p.243.
[1668] Thwaite p.211. Gosse's wife, Nellie, herself a painter and feminist, was the sister of Alma-Tadema's wife.
[1669] Henley's brother Anthony was a painter at Grez, and his brother E.J. Henley once collaborated with Cyril Maude on a version of *Le Monde où l'on s'amuse*; but du Maurier's friend, 'the boisterous and entertaining' 'Bill' Henley, was not William Ernest but Lionel Charles. Leonée Ormond: *George du Maurier.* London: Routledge 1969 p.79. Hereafter cited as Ormond. Bill Henley died in 1893, while du Maurier was giving 'Taffy' the whiskers that Henley had sported in their salad days.
[1670] Low lived in Paris until the following year (12 rue Vernier).

[1671] Jebb p.222.

[1672] Jules Abels: *The Parnell Tragedy*. London: The Bodley Head 1966 p.114.

[1673] Constance Battersea: *Reminiscences*. London: Macmillan & Co 1922 p.82.

[1674] Sir Francis Burnand: *Records and Reminiscences, Personal and General*. London: Methuen 1904 Volume II p.263.

[1675] Her real name was Alice Prin. http://www.kiki.pp.se/kiki1.htm.

[1676] Merrick p.134.

[1677] Ormond pp.9,92.   David Lodge uses 'Kiki' throughout, but du Maurier's grand-daughter only uses Kicky.   Lodge *passim*; Daphne du Maurier: *Gerald, A Portrait*. London: Victor Gollancz 1934 *passim*.

[1678] London: Smith, Elder & Co 1882. Dramatised by Edward Rose, an associate of Wilde's, at the Strand Theatre summer 1883, Rose playing Dick Bultitude.

[1679] Ormond p.366.

[1680] F. Anstey [Thomas Anstey Guthrie]: *A Long Retrospect*.   London & New York: Oxford University Press 1936 p.163. Hereafter cited as Anstey.

[1681] Ormond p.363.

[1682] Davis 1895 p.217.

[1683] Now the Grand Hôtel Intercontinental.   The hotel covers the entire block bounded by the place de l'Opéra, the boulevard des Capucines, the rue Scribe and the rue Auber.   The entrance is in the rue Scribe.   The peripatetic Bashkirtseff family and their entourage stayed there on their Paris visits until renting a house of their own.

[1684] Enid Yandell, Jean Loughborough, and Laura Hayes: *Three Girls in a Flat*. Chicago: Knight, Leonard & Co. 1892 p.32. This is illustrated on p.231. Hereafter cited as Yandell.

[1685] Letter to James Bryce 12th November 1893, quoted in David Mathew: *Lord Acton and His Times*. London: Eyre & Spottiswood 1968 p.328.

[1686] Du Maurier/Trilby pp.420-1.   The title, the name of the heroine, seems to be derived from *Trilby, le lutin d'Arguill* a tale by Charles Nodier of 1822. 'Arguill' is Argyll in Scotland.

[1687] Plate 17 in Ormond.

[1688] Zola/L'Assommoir p.87.

[1689] The first practical joke of Allais began with his birth, for he shared his birthday with Arthur Rimbaud.

[1690] 'This is the real Bohemia, you know,' remarks Ned Blake in Katherine Thurston's novel *Max*.   'Not the conscious Bohemia but the true one, that is lawless simply because it knows no laws.' Thurston p.83.

[1691] Bofa was a designer, writer, poster artist, printmaker and literary critic.   An exhibition of his work was held at the Musées de la Cour d'Or, Metz, 6th June - 31st August 1997 under the title 'Art and Humour'.

[1692] 'Coucher de Soleil sur l'Adriatique'.

[1693] Perhaps inspired by Alexandre Decamps' 'Le singe peintre', showing a monkey engaged in painting a canvas? This is undated (Decamps died in 1860), but the Louvre acquired it in 1902 (ref. RF 1375), and it seems to have much the same message as Couture's 'La Peinture Réaliste', already referred to.

[1694] Crosland p.58

[1695] Donnay pp.23,41.

[1696] Éric Dussert: 'Les Egarés Les Oubliés', *Le Matricule des Anges*, no 20 July/August 1997. Most of my account of Gabriel Lautrec is derived from this source.

[1697] Not to be confused with Aristide Bruant, this journalist and politician (1862-1932) is only perhaps remembered for the Briand-Kellogg pact and for the hideous sculptural commemoration of this in the quai d'Orsay, but deserving of being remembered in the polymorphous description of him by the American author Elliot Paul as 'an orator with a face that looked like a composite of all the earnest animals in the zoo'. Elliot Paul: *The Narrow Street* (also published as *The Last Time I Saw Paris*). New York: Random House and London: The Cresset Press 1942; Harmondsworth: Penguin p.79; hereafter cited as Paul. This gives Briand his place in this Paris of shape-changing.

[1698] Maurice Agulhon: *The French Republic 1879-1992*. Translated by Antonia Nevill. Oxford: Blackwell 1993 p.107. Hereafter cited as Agulhon.

[1699] Agulhon p.64.

[1700] Bashkirtseff p.266. Diary entry for 18th August 1877. Proust seems to have regarded comte Louis de Turenne as hardly more than the vehicle for his monocle, if one can so read his dedication to Jacques de Lacretelle of *Du côté de chez Swann*.

[1701] 'A slum area of the worst kind'. Hemmings 1977 p.34. Zola lived in a room in the rue Soufflot in 1862/3 and set some of *Madeleine Férat* there.

[1702] Paris: Mercure de France 1914. Schwob himself was the translator of Walt Whitman, and introduced his work to Gide, with that of Stevenson and Meredith.

[1703] Symons p.24. The Jardin was a reincarnation of the Mabille. Seurat's 'Study for "Le Chahut"' c.1889 is in the Courtauld Institute, London.

[1704] Paul Hefting, in the catalogue of the Kröller-Müller Museum, Otterlo, p.81.

[1705] Or, more properly, in the allée des Veuves, now part of the avenue Montaigne. It had been opened by M. Mabille in 1840.

[1706] Ralph Nevill: *The Man of Pleasure*. London: Chatto & Windus 1912 p.183.

[1707] This is the eponymous heroine of the 1936 film when Rigolboche was played by Mistinguett.

[1708] http://www.moulinrouge.fr/hist/home_6.htm

[1709] According to Michael Marrus: 'Modernization and Dancing in Rural France, from "La Bourrée to "Le Fox Trot" in Jacques Beauvoy, Marc Bertrand and Edward T. Gargan (edd.): *The Wolf and the Lamb, Popular Culture in France from the Old Regime to the Twentieth Century*. Stanford French and Italian Studies Volume III. Saratoga, Cal.: Anima Libri 1977 p.153 (hereafter cited as Marrus.), but at the Grande Chaumière in 1843 according to Polnay p.201.

[1710] This may be a starting point for looking more closely at the 'veritable explosion of [clandestine] dancing [...] a complete subculture' that occurred when Vichy banned public dances in both the Occupied and Free Zones. Richard Gildea: *Marianne in Chains, in search of the German Occupation 1940-1945*. London: Macmillan 2002 pp.153-5.

[1711] Polnay p.118.

[1712] James F. McMillan: *Housewife or Harlot, The Place of Women in French Society 1870-1940*. Brighton: Harvester Press 1981 p.70. Hereafter cited as McMillan.

[1713] First danced at a party given by Mme Manuel de Yturbe. Fouquières p.248.

[1714] This Brazilian dance became in France *la mattchiche*. I am grateful to Danielle Guérin for making this point. The sheet music, published by Hachette, sold 240,000 copies and was understandably described by the publisher as 'le grand succès de 1905'. (From the copy displayed at the exhibition of sheet music 'When the Music Stops', Espace Culturel Les Dominicaines, Pont-l'Évèque, summer 2004.) Guy de Bellot says that it was André de Fouquières who introduced the dance to Paris from New York. Guy de Bellet: *Gaby Deslys*. Paris: La Vie Amoureuse n.d. p.76.

[1715] Mott p.90.

[1716] Marrus. p.154

[1717] William J. Locke: *The Belovéd Vagabond*. London: John Lane The Bodley Head 1906 p.184.

[1718] Zola/L'Assommoir p.92.

[1719] Maupassant/Affair p.87.

[1720] This was well established: '"Let's go to Bougival to the Point du Jour. It's run by a widow called the Arnould" […] Oh! Happy days at Bougival! Where are you now?' Dumas pp.120,193.

[1721] Du Maurier/Trilby p.100.

[1722] These went back a long time, and there is a reference to them in Anthony Trollope's novel *La Vendée* of 1850, which is set in 1792. Anthony Trollope: *La Vendée*. Edited with an Introduction by W.J. McCormack. Oxford: Oxford University Press Worlds Classics 1994 p.77 and note p.448, which note being slightly defective. I take it that Constantin Guys' drawing 'La Bastringue' represents a *bal de barrière*. Now in the National Gallery, Capetown, it is reproduced as plate 48 in Browse, where it is miscalled 'La Bastrinque'. The *barrières* were the portals in the old octroi wall, numbering fifty-five. The licensing regulations of Paris did not go beyond them.

[1723] Leonard Merrick: *A Chair on the Boulevard*. London: Hodder & Stoughton n.d. p.197.

[1724] Marrus p.155.

[1725] Richard Nelson Current and Marcia Ewing Current: *Loïe Fuller, Goddess of Light*. Boston: Northeastern University Press 1997 p.122, hereafter cited as Current; Symons p.92.

[1726] Current p.47.

[1727] *National Observer* 13th March 1893.

[1728] Article in *La Revue Encyclopédique*, quoted by Current p.55.

[1729] Current p.125. A list is given as an Appendix, *v. infra*.

[1730] A medal showing Gallé in 1901 by Henri Nocq is the Victoria and Albert Museum, ref. 162-1906. Gallé lived chiefly in Nancy, though he exhibited very successfully in Paris and visited London. He was also fervently pro-Dreyfus. The

New York firm of Tiffany first exhibited in Paris at the 1867 exhibition, and again in 1878, but made a stir in 1887 when Charles Tiffany bought some of the French Crown jewels. It was Charles' son, Louis Comfort Tiffany who established the art jewellery when he took over the firm on his father's death in 1902. 'Tiffany had a great success with the French. Many of my friends bought souvenirs of the [1878] exposition from him. His work was very original, fanciful, and quite different from the rather stiff, heavy, classic silver that one sees in this country. Waddington p.176.

[1731] 'Seems' from the illustration in Abel p.80.

[1732] This must be distinguished from *La Tragédie de Salomé* with music by Florent Schmitt, which Fuller danced at the Théâtre des Arts in 1907. In 1922 (22nd October) Pierné conducted Ibert's 'La Ballade de la Geôle de Reading, d'après le poème d'Oscar Wilde' at the Concerts Colonne.

[1733] Current p.82.

[1734] Current p.107. I refer, naturally, to the American photographer Samuel Joshua Beckett.

[1735] Current p.112.

[1736] 10 boulevard Montmartre.

[1737] Current p.76.

[1738] Current p.129.

[1739] Current p.177.

[1740] Thus Castle; but Raymond Rudorff calls it the Divan Fayouac. The invention of striptease has also been credited to Cléo de Mérode, in the Casino at Royan, in 1895. Robert Colle: *L'Histoire de Royan et de la Côte de Beauté*. Royan: Jeune Chambre Economique 1988 p.15.

[1741] The next, perhaps, was Lina Munte's Dance of the Seven Veils in the 1896 production of *Salomé*, of which we have no account.

[1742] 'Les pudeurs de Monsieur Prudhomme', lithograph of 1893.

[1743] Newton Volume II p.212. This was almost certainly the marquis de Noailles in 1880. Freycinet (1828-1923) was Prime Minister (President of the Council of Ministers) in 1879, 1882, 1886 and 1890. Like his predecessor William Waddington, Freycinet was a Protestant, 'deferential, evasive and highly intelligent', according to Brogan p.168.

[1744] Renard p.71. Diary entry April 1895.

[1745] Anon (Constance E. Maud): *An English Girl in Paris*. John Lane: The Bodley Head 1902 p.4. Hereafter cited as Maud.

[1746] Quoted in Matthews p.208.

[1747] Francis Gribble: *The Tragedy of Isabella II*. London: Chapman & Hall 1913 p.85.

[1748] Mrs Belloc Lowndes: *The Merry Wives of Westminster*. London: Macmillan 1946 p.31. Hereafter cited as Belloc Lowndes1946.

[1749] H. Montgomery Hyde: Introduction to Richard Le Gallienne: *The Romantic '90s*. New edition. London: Putnam & Co 1951 p.xvii; repeated by Hyde ('Actually the book in question was *Aphrodite*, a novel by Wilde's friend Pierre Louÿs') in H. Montgomery Hyde: *Famous Trials 7, Oscar Wilde*. New and enlarged edition. Harmondsworth: Penguin Books 1962 p.154n, and again word

for word in H. Montgomery Hyde: *Oscar Wilde, A Biography*. London: Eyre
Methuen 1975 p.226n., hereafter cited as Hyde 1976. It is not correct to refer to
Louÿs as a friend of Wilde's in the context of 1895.

[1750] Richard Le Gallienne: *The Romantic '90s*. New edition. London: Putnam &
Co 1951 p.96.

[1751] David Pierce: *Yeats's Worlds, Ireland, England and the Poetic Imagination*.
New Haven and London: Yale University Press 1995 p.287.

[1752] Belloc Lowndes 1946 p.177.

[1753] Du Maurier/Trilby p.430. Du Maurier was prudish about this, also referring to
'the famous "esprit Gaulois"' which 'was somewhat precocious in the forties [...]
Perhaps it is now, if it still exists (which I doubt – the dirt remains, but all the fun
seems to have evaporated.' Du Maurier/Martian p.103.

[1754] Maupassant/Bel Ami p.193.

[1755] Matthews p.187.

[1756] Reproduced as plate 23 in the Christie's Catalogue '19th Century Continental
Pictures, Watercolours and Drawings', London, March 1992. There is no
suggestion of the Celt or Scot in the smouldering and exotically jewelled
Bernhardt.

[1757] Aston p.81. This does not of course explain Bernhardt's success in Paris or
Vienna.

[1758] Mistinguett p.22; Laurence Garcia: 'Joséphine Baker, artiste en résistance',
Muze June 2005 p.29.

[1759] Matthews 1880 p.11. The Porte Saint-Martin had re-opened in 1873 after its
destruction during the Commune with Victor Hugo's *Marie Tudor*. The reference
to electric light at this date is the significant point.

[1760] On this occasion Edward stayed at the Club, but we know that he went to the
Folies on another evening (in October 1896) to see Liane de Pougy in Jean
Lorrain's *L'Arraignée d'Or*.

[1761] Diary entry for 24th October 1897. Flower/Bennett p.54.

[1762] Mario Borsa: *The English Stage of To-day*. Translated from the original Italian
and edited with a prefatory note by Selwyn Brinton M.A. London: John Lane The
Bodley Head 1908 p.17. Hereafter cited as Borsa.

[1763] Quoted in Cate p.28.

[1764] Maud pp.143-48, esp. p.133.

[1765] Menpes pp.122-3.

[1766] Zola/Paris p.219n.

[1767] Maupassant/Bel Ami p.11.

[1768] Du Maurier/Trilby pp.430-2

[1769] Guy de Maupassant: 'The Mask' in *The Mountain Inn and Other Stories*. A
New Translation by H.N.P. Sloman. Harmondsworth: Penguin Books 1955 p.189.
Roger Colet prefers 'tarts' to 'girls'. Guy de Maupassant: *Selected Short Stories*.
Translated with an Introduction by Roger Colet. London: Penguin Books 1971
p.345. Hereafter cited as Maupassant/Colet.

[1770] Jullian 1977 p.55. But could there really have been four thousand guests?
Frazier p.61. Alan Schom only refers to 'several hundred'. Schom p.81.

[1771] Zola/Assommoir p.173. Mauldon prefers 'showing her undies like a floozie'. Zola/L'Assommoir p.167. Later this ecstatic dancing and kicking is transferred from the hammer to the dipsomaniac Coupeau, the artisan no longer distinguishable from an artisan's tool.

[1772] Moore/Impressions p.44. This was on the 18th January 1879. According to Moore, Turgenev spoke well of *L'Assommoir*; the counter view is in Patrick Waddington: *Turgenev and England*. New York: New York University Press 1981 p.223. Hereafter cited as Waddington 1981. Moore wrote 'An idea has been improvised from his long residence in France that he is more western that his illustrious compeers Tolstoy and Dostoievsky; but it would be hard to point out to a trace of this denaturalisation in his works. Tolstoy I have not read...' *Ibidem* p.48.

[1773] Cate p.26. His first name is also given as Courtelat. Sugana p.86.

[1774] Shercliff p.97.

[1775] Nevill 1926 pp.244,279.

[1776] Peter Wykeham: *Santos-Dumont, A Study in Obsession*. London: Putnam 1962 p.37. This was also Carl van Vechten's view. Vechten p.55.

[1777] Jullian 1977 pp.134-5. The vogue for ether (methylated spirit) rivalled that of absinthe, whether sprinkled on strawberries or taken in capsules. The decadent Hyacinthe Duvillard eats the latter. Zola/Paris p.41. Max Jacob died in the concentration camp at Drancy, 6th March 1944.

[1778] Augustus Saint-Gaudens: *The Reminiscences of Augustus Saint-Gaudens.* Edited and amplified by Homer Saint-Gaudens. London: Andrew Melrose 1913 Volume II pp.196-7. Hereafter cited as Saint-Gaudens.

[1779] Benois p.147.

[1780] Young p.237. The London equivalent was perhaps 'The Judge and Jury' presided over by 'the Lord Chief Baron' (Renton Nicholson), a low haunt that did not survive the 1870s.

[1781] Zola/L'Assommoir p.456.

[1782] Zola/Paris pp.219, 220. Vizetelly in his footnote locates it on the site of 'La Bagne'. This is Maxim Lisbonne's Taverne du Bagne. Earlier, Zola also offers a perhaps assumed distaste when he describes a place he calls 'Le Papillon' in the rue des Poissonniers, as 'a revolting dive'. Zola/Nana/Parmée p.227.

[1783] For a Freudian discussion of this last point, see Willa Z. Silverman: *Gyp, The Notorious Life of Gyp, Right Wing Anarchist in fin-de-siècle France*. Oxford: Oxford University Press 1983 pp.121-3. Hereafter cited as Silverman.

[1784] Sir Thomas Beecham: *Frederick Delius*. London: Hutchinson 1959; new edition London: Severne Books 1975 p.53. (*Les Mystères de Paris* by Eugène Sue had been published in 1842, but serialised in *Le Petit Lyonnais* in November 1885 with a poster by Jules Chéret).

[1785] Milner p.158. The Lapin Agile (4 rue de Saules) is the subject of the painting 'Le Cabaret du Lapin Agile' by Pierre Prins (1838-1913) in the Musée Carnavalet, ref. P.585.

[1786] Should not be confused with the politician Aristide Briand (1862-1932), who for a while was the lover of la belle Otero. Bruant's real name was in fact Armand.

[1787] Subsequently the place Emile Goudeau. Pierre Mac-Orlan says the Zut was in the place J.-B. Clément. Mac-Orlan p.76. He gives the habitués as Manolo, Picasso, Tiret-Bognet, Léon-Paul Fargue and Charles Maurin.

[1788] Mac-Orlan p.76; Paul p.114.

[1789] Nevill p.142. The site was later occupied by La Cigale.

[1790] 49 rue Vivienne, a dance and concert hall opened in 1873. In 1879 it became the Cercle des Arts Liberaux.

[1791] Augustin Daly to Joseph Francis Daly 26th January 1879. Joseph Francis Daly: *The Life of Augustin Daly.* New York: The Macmillan Company 1917 p.297.

[1792] He meant palingenesis. Whiteing 1900p.212. Mac-Orlan p.74.

[1793] Sherard 1908 p.96.

[1794] Boulestin p.143.

[1795] Scott p.12.

[1796] C.J. Holmes: *Self & Partners (mostly Self).* London: Constable 1936 p.237. Hereafter cited as Holmes.

[1797] Holmes p.165.

[1798] J.W Lambert & Michael Ratcliffe: *The Bodley Head 1887-1987.* London: The Bodley Head 1987 pp.31-2. Hereafter cited as Lambert/Ratcliffe.

[1799] Rothenstein Volume I p.29.

[1800] Hereafter cited as Forbes-Robertson.p.58.

[1801] Rothenstein Volume I p.65.

[1802] Johnson p.395.

[1803] Coolidge pp.187-8.

[1804] Coolidge p.225. The count is only named as Count d'O–.

[1805] on the Salon of 1896, quoted by John House: 'The Legacy of Impressionism in France' in House/Stevens p.13.

[1806] Toulouse-Lautrec to his mother April 1883. Frèches p.137.

[1807] Nordau p.7.

[1808] Lazzaro pp.1,8.

[1809] John Russell: *Seurat.* London: Thames & Hudson 1965 p.13.

[1810] It may be useful to calibrate those who, like F.A. Chéramy, opposed the Caillebotte bequest with those who opposed the Eiffel Tower.

[1811] Nordau p.107

[1812] Hartrick p.11.

[1813] Zola/Pot-Bouille p.133.

[1814] Zola/Bonheur p.8.

[1815] Chapter IV of Levin.

[1816] For Roger Colet, pessimism is Maupassant's defining characteristic. Maupassant/Colet p.15.

[1817] The phrase is Gyp's. Gyp de Martel: *La Joyeuse Enfance de la Troisième République.* Paris: Calmann-Lévy 1931.

[1818] Richard Schiff; 'Ascribing to Manet, Declaring the Author', in Radford R. Collins (ed.): *Twelve Views of Manet's Bar.* Princeton: Princeton University Press 1996 p.1.

[1819] It may be helpful to summarise the Institut and the Académies. The Institut de France, in the Palais Mazarin, houses five Académies, all of which have roots stretching back before the Revolution, but date their current status to the Napoleonic foundation of 1803 and its subsequent reforms. All Academicians are therefore members of the Institut, and entitled at meetings to wear green uniforms, a sort of court dress. The Académies are

(A) The Académie française: forty holders of chairs (fauteuils) elected for their distinction chiefly but not exclusively in literature, and the most prestigious of the académies.

(B) The Académie des Inscriptions et Belles Lettres: for those distinguished in archæology and history.

(C) The Académie des Sciences: for those distinguished in the sciences, including natural history and mathematics.

(D) The Académie des Sciences morales et politiques: for those distinguished in philosophy, political economy and law.

(E) The Académie des beaux Art. :Fourteen of the forty fauteuils were reserved for painters and they formed the Académie des beaux Arts. The Académie des beaux Arts had organic relationships with the official Salons and the École des Beaux-Arts, relationships that shifted from 1863 onwards through various reforms. The Académie nationale de Musique, founded in its contemporary form in 1875, was not part of the Institut de France.

The Palais Mazarin also houses the Bibliothèque Mazarine, the Librarian of which was Silvestre de Sacy from 1836 till his death in 1879, when he was succeeded by Frédéric Baudry. Flaubert hoped to obtain this post when de Sacy died. See Steegmuller/Flaubert pp.252-4.

[1820] 'Immortal' more because they were members until they died than because their reputations were imperishable.

[1821] Nancy Green has noted that the first American woman artist to be awarded the Légion d'Honneur was Cecilia de Wentworth in 1901, ahead of Mary Cassatt (1904), an ordering that history has not sustained. Green p.230. The former came to Paris to the studio of Cabanel in 1883, as Cecile Smith, later marrying Josiah Winslow Wentworth and apparently promoting herself to the title of marquise de Wentworth. Green p.230.

[1822] Antoine Guillemet became a chevalier of the Légion d'Honneur in 1880, officier in 1896 and commandeur in 1910. Not to be confused with Gustave Achille Guillaumet, a precocious orientalist painter who became a chevalier of the Légion d'Honneur in 1878, nor with Armand Guillaumin the Impressionist; nor with Jules Guillemin who, with his American wife, appears in Manet's 'In the Conservatory' of 1879 (now in the National Gallery, Berlin); nor with Alfred Guillon, a pupil of Cabanel and Bouguereau; nor with Albert Guillaume, the cartoonist; nor with Eugène Guillaume, a painter and sculptor who was Director of Fine Arts and Inspecteur-Général de l'Enseignement du Dessin, whose bust by

Rodin is in the Musée d'Orsay, ref. RF 2245; nor with Ernest Guille, a pupil of Gérôme's in the late 1860s. In this context, it is particularly apt that 'guillemets' means 'inverted commas': semantic confusion can lead to semiotic significance.

[1823] (Antoine-Auguste-)Ernest Hébert (1817-1908) was a portrait painter and Lehmann's successor at the École des Beaux Arts, he also served a term (1867-1873) as Director of the Académie de France in Rome. His house, 85 rue du Cherche-Midi, is now the Musée Ernest Hébert.

[1824] One painting of Duez', 'L'heure du bain au bord de la mer', inverts the usual convention by showing two ladies watching the bathers. Musée des Beaux Arts, Rouen ref.D.897.2

[1825] Olga Somech Phillips: *Solomon J. Solomon, A Memoir of Peace and War*. London: Herbert Joseph n.d. [1933] pp.34,39. Hereafter cited as Phillips.

[1826] Although it dates to 1911, Jules Alexandre Grun's 'Un vendredi au Salon des Artistes français' in concept, treatment and subject seems to justify the split. This immense canvas, a monument to painstaking and uninspired endeavour, contains portraits of a hundred and one figures, including Harpignies, Bonnat, Detaille, Robert-Fleury, Flameng, Cormon, Jean-Paul Laurens and so on, the only surprising presence being that of Yvette Guilbert. Musée des Beaux Arts, Rouen. Ref. D.932.1

[1827] Another exhibitor was Alfred Smith, who despite his name was from Bordeaux.

[1828] Herman Lebovics: *True France, The Wars over Cultural Identity*. Ithaca and London: Cornell University Press 1992 pp.21-3.

[1829] Levin, notably p.79.

[1830] The prevailing bourgeois view was adequately and typically expressed by Thomas March, in generic (and xenophobic) description of the Communards (whom he consistently refers to as Communists) after the shooting of Generals Thomas and Lecomte on 18th March 1871: 'Drunken with blood and wine, passionate with hate, delirious with their achievements, mad with the moment's yield, and knowing neither past nor future, these biped brutes, in pandemoniacal array, shrieking and shouting, men, women and children confusedly joined together, many half-nude, and all entirely possessed with an uncontrollable hellish frenzy, danced round their dead victims a dance of victory'. March p.109. This description owes more to the imagination of how a Paris crowd would behave in the circumstances than to any idea of how it actually did behave. 'Half-nude' is particularly telling.

[1831] Claud Cockburn: *Bestseller, The Books that Everyone Read 1900-1939*. London: Sidgwick & Jackson 1972 p.139.

[1832] Laver p.55.

[1833] Philippe Perot: Les Dessus et les Dessous de la bourgeoisie, une histoire du vêtement au XIXe siècle. Paris: Librairie Athène Fayard 1891. Translated with an Introduction by Richard Bienvenu as Fashioning the Bourgeoisie, A History of Clothing in the 19th Century. Princeton: Princeton University Press 1994 p.144.

[1834] Redesdale p.190.

[1835] Zola/Bonheur pp.4,110,250,410.

[1836] Marcel Proust: *A la recherche de temps perdu: Du coté de chez Swann*. Translated by Lydia Davis as *In Search of Lost Time: The Way by Swann's*. London: Penguin 2003 p.200.

[1837] Directeur des Beaux Arts 1887-1888.

[1838] Quoted in Mainardi p.21.

[1839] Agulhon p.31. My italics.

[1840] Albert de Broglie, grandson of madame de Staël and of Benjamin Constant, was twice Prime Minister (President of the Council of Ministers), ambassador in London and a diplomatic historian. 'He had that worst of all faults for a leader, he was unpopular. He was a brilliant, cultured speaker, but he had a curt, dictatorial manner, with an air of looking down upon his public.' Waddington 1914 pp.63-4. The name was pronounced 'Breuil' in the Faubourg.

[1841] Zola/Paris p.249. He may have had in mind Agénor Bardoux (1829-1897), Minister for Public Instruction 1877-1879, who published poems under the name A. Brady.

[1842] Levin p.215.

[1843] 'The French language is particularly rich in words of scorn for this unfortunate class'. Mainardi p.147.

[1844] Timothy J. Clark: 'The Bar at the Folies Bergères' in Jacques Beauvoy, Marc Bertrand and Edward T. Gargan (edd.): *The Wolf and the Lamb, Popular Culture in France from the Old Regime to the Twentieth Century*. Stanford French and Italian Studies Volume III. Saratoga, Cal.: Anima Libri 1977 pp.248-9.

[1845] In Maupassant's short story 'A Night Out'.

[1846] Healy p.99.

[1847] Siegel pp.11,291.

[1848] Healy p.105.

[1849] The Picture of Dorian Gray Chapter XIX.

[1850] Henry Tonks: 'The Vicissitudes of Art' in *Fifty Years, Memories and Contrasts. A Composite Picture of the Period 1882-1932*. By Twenty-Seven Contributors to *The Times*. London: Thornton Butterworth & Co 1932. Keystone Library Edition 1936 p.58.

[1851] Phillips [1933] p.33.

[1852] Orchardson's submission for the Royal Academy Summer Show in 1873 was sent from the Hôtel du Louvre.

[1853] Audrey Williamson: *Gilbert and Sullivan Opera, An Assessment*. London: Marion Boyars 1982 plates 31-4.

[1854] Edith Cooper recorded 'Of course, Ricketts protested he was of the nineteenth century and always would be [...] He had nothing to do with the twentieth century [...] As the new century progressed he was to find it ever more alien and uncongenial, and himself in conflict with many of its leading tendencies.' Delaney p.142.

[1855] Battersby p.14.

[1856] Samuel Hynes: *The Edwardian Turn of Mind* Princeton & London: Princeton University Press 1968 p.330. Ricketts denounced van Gogh's work as rubbish produced by a lunatic. Holmes p.280. D.S. MacColl, once a perceptive advocate of the art of his contemporaries, also rejected later movements and his biography of Wilson Steer includes a gratuitous attack on Seurat. MacColl pp.38-9. Ross's denunciation appeared in the High Tory *Morning Post*, singling out especially Matisse: 'The relation of M. Henri Matisse and his colleagues to painting is more remote than that of the Parisian Black Mass or the necromantic orgies of the Decadents to the religion of Catholics'. Fryer 2000 p.213. Did Wilde stir uneasily in his tomb? Nor was Ross's commendation worth much, writing of Duncan Grant in 1911 that he would 'one day be heard of beyond the walls of the Borough Polytechnic. Perhaps he is the Millais of the New Pre-Raphaelites'. Frances Spalding apparently thinks this was praise. Spalding 1997 p.112.

[1857] Quentin Bell: *Victorian Painters*. London: Routledge 1967 p.78. Presumably Pierre-Edouard Frère (1819-1886), a pupil of Paul Delaroche, who exhibited twenty-eight times at the Royal Academy between 1868 and 1885, but his name is omitted from Geraldine Norman: *Nineteenth Century Painters and Painting, A Dictionary*. London: Thames & Hudson 1977.

[1858] Sherard 1908 p.18. Sherard spells Pissarro 'Pizarro', a confusion with the Conquistador which would hardly have pleased the anarchist painter.

[1859] Roditi p.27.

[1860] My italics. The 'Archaicistes' seem to have been an invention of Wilde's. Jonathan Fryer suggests that it was in 1883 that Wilde acquainted himself with the work of Corot, Monet and Pissarro. Fryer 1997 p.17. 'Symphonie en blanc majeur' is a poem in Théophile Gautier's *Emaux et Camées* (1852).

[1861] One assumes that he is not intending a sly reference to the poster artist Clouet.

[1862] Lord Henry Wotton is depicted as a particularly convincing advocate that progress could be achieved by a 'return to the Hellenic ideal'.

[1863] Langlade p.85.

[1864] Sherard 1906 p.139.

[1865] T.H.S. Escott: *England, Its People, Polity and Pursuits*. London: Chapman & Hall 1884. New and revised edition 1890 p.503.

[1866] I take this to be François Bonvin (1817-1887), the close friend of Courbet, rather than the painter Léon Bonvin (1834-1866) who hanged himself from a cherry tree, breaking the branch – 'the only harm he ever did'. According to the Dictionnaire Bénézit, François Bonvin was 'peut être considéré comme un des meilleurs peintres de genres du XIXe siècle'. *Dictionnaire des Peintres, Sculpteurs, Dessinateurs et Graveurs*. Paris: Librairie Gründ 1976. Neither this, nor the fact that he once worked for the Préfeture de Police, stopped him from starving to death. His 'Kitchen Interior' is in the Fitzwilliam Museum, Cambridge ref. 1591.

[1867] Quentin Bell: *Victorian Painters*. London: Routledge 1967 p.78. In 1918, Charles Holmes went to Paris to look for works by Ingres, Delacroix and others that had been collected by Degas, and came back with the fragments of the Manet 'Maximilian' that are in Trafalgar Square, as well as the Corot that had hung over Degas' bed.

[1868] Diary entry for 27th October 1897. Flower/Bennett p.57.

[1869] Two years earlier, Constance's portrait had been painted by Louis Desange.

[1870] Ludovici p.79. In 1899, Ludovici illustrated Lord Alfred Douglas's book of nonsense verse, *The Duke of Berwick*.

[1871] This could refer either to Jozef Israëls (1824-1911) or to Isaac Lazarus Israëls (1865-1934).

[1872] Whiteing pp.143,145. This is confirmed in Cabanel's case by his portrait (1873) of the comtesse de Keller, later marquise de Saint-Yves d'Alveydre, now in the Musée d'Orsay, ref. RF 2048.

[1873] Sitwell p.207.

[1874] Bashkirtseff p.532. Diary entry for 25th May 1882.

[1875] Bashkirtseff p.602. Diary entry for 6th May 1883.

[1876] Bashkirtseff p.xi.

[1877] The correspondence with Maupassant is published in the volume *The Portable Maupassant* (New York: Viking Press 1947) but is characterised by Francis Steegmuller as 'not very interesting'. Steegmuller/Maupassant p.305.

[1878] Bashkirtseff p.602. Diary entry for 6th May 1883. Although frequently spelled Baschkirtseff, I have silently standardised to this usage. Bashkirtseff died on 31st October 1884, but the exact date of her birth is debated, apparently in 1858 — 28th November according to her father, but perhaps January 1859 or even 11th November 1860. Marie Bashkirtseff was related to Toulouse-Lautrec, for her great-grandfather's sister married the then comte de Toulouse-Lautrec, but she seems to have been unaware of this distant cousin. Bashkirtseff goes on to discuss the resonance of the names of other artists: Georges Rochegrosse, Tony Robert Fleury, Bonnat, Manet, Breslau, Saint-Marceaux, Henner, Carolus-Duran, Dagnan-Bouveret.

[1879] Morley p.302. Diary entry for 15th January 1892.

[1880] Hartrick p.28. Even Rodin produced a funerary statue of Bastien, of which an example is in the Musée Marmottan-Monet, Paris.

[1881] 1877, now in the Louvre. A bust of Dumas by Carpeaux (1873) is in the Musée d'Orsay, ref. RF 1854.

[1882] Belloc 1943 p. 198.

[1883] Marc J. Gottlieb: *The Plight of Emulation, Ernest Meissonier and French Salon Painting*. Princeton: Princeton University Press 1996 p.9. The National Gallery of Ireland has a small collection of these small pictures; Meissonier's 'Friedland 1907', given by Henry Hilton to the Metropolitan Museum of Art, New York (re.87.20.1) is larger in scale if not in the sympathy of the twenty-first century critic.

[1884] Milner p.1.

[1885] Painter I p.52. 'Execrable' is Painter's favourite term of dismissal. As far as Gounod is concerned, perhaps Painter was influenced by the story that the inspiration had come to Gounod for 'Ave Maria' while visiting the studio of Emile Vernet-Lecomte, with whom time has dealt even more mercilessly than with Meissonier. For all that, Shirley Fox, a pupil in the early 1880s, recalled Vernet-Lecomte as 'an artist of no little ability'. Fox p.19.

[1886] Morot's students (including Robert Anning Bell and many of the Glasgow painters) are better known than he.

[1887] Inv.3834.

[1888] Ref. NG 1909, bequeathed by Lord Cheylesmore in 1902.

[1889] Wilde, who apparently preferred to be photographed than painted, does not, I think, anywhere discuss photography either as an art form *per se*, or in conjunction with his exploration of the relationship between nature, art, and the real.

[1890] The sculptor was J.B. Phillip whose daughter Beatrix married first Godwin and then Whistler. Another daughter married Charles Whibley.

[1891] Andrew Lambirth: 'High Art or Pop Culture'. *RA The Royal Academy Magazine* LVII Winter 1997. A Delaroche exhibition was held at Hertford House, London (the Wallace Collection) December 1997 / January 1998.

[1892] Monticelli's 'Shade and Light' ('Ombre et Lumière') was sold in London in 1895 for 9,196 francs. As far as I know, there is no major collection of Monticelli's work, though the Musée Bourdelle has ten oils by him, including a portrait of the comte de Montvallon.

[1893] Julia Frey: *Toulouse-Lautrec, A Life*. London: Weidenfeld & Nicolson 1994 p.125.

[1894] Denys Sutton: *Walter Sickert, A Biography*. London: Michael Joseph 1976 p.66.

[1895] Sir Lionel Cust: *King Edward VII and His Court, Some Reminiscences*. London: John Murray 1930 p.98.

[1896] Lord Caversham, in *An Ideal Husband*, is said to resemble a portrait by Sir Thomas Lawrence. The Panthéon (built as the church of Ste Geneviève) entered its present state with the burial there of Victor Hugo in 1885. Clunn pp.115-6.

[1897] Bell p.150.

[1898] Fouquières p.115. My translation.

[1899] Maison Victor Hugo, Paris, ref. MVH-P-1205. Marie Bashkirtseff saw it at the Salon of 1879 and thought that 'there is some life in what paints'. Bashkirtseff p.367. Diary entry for 12th May 1879.

[1900] Frèches p.136.

[1901] A photograph of the atelier (rue Constance), in which Bernard, Lautrec and Anquetin are seen, is reproduced in Mary Anne Stevens: *Emile Bernard 1868-1941, A Pioneer of Modern Art*. Zwolle: Waanders p.12; and there is a drawing by Hartrick based on a contemporary photograph in Hartrick opp. p.48. 'Par un singulier hasard, son atelier devait devenir un des berceaux de l'art moderne'. Henri Perruchot: 'Une vie ardente' in Adhémar p.12.

[1902] She was also painted by Boldini (1888).

[1903] http://www.npg.org.uk/search/Images/weblg/0/0/mw06900.jpg

[1904] Carolus-Duran also retained the friendship of Batignollais like Fantin-Latour, Manet, Monet, and Zacharie Astruc, as well as of Courbet.

[1905] Weinberg Chapter VI: 'Alexandre Cabanel'.

[1906] See, for example, his 'Mort de Francesca da Rimini et Paol Malatesta' of 1870, Musée d'Orsay ref. RF 69.

[1907] (Divers hands): *Jules Bastien-Lepage*. Verdun & Montmedy: Les Musées de la Meuse n.d. p.111.

[1908] Agulhon p.45.

[1909] Now in the Musée royale des Beaux Arts, Brussels.

[1910] Henry James: *Parisian Sketches – Letters to the New York Tribune 1875-1876.* Edited with an Introduction by Leon Edel and Ilse Desoir Lind. Washington Square: New York University Press 1957 p.131, hereafter cited as James/Sketches. Letter of 22nd April 1876.

[1911] Lady Frances Balfour: *Ne Obliviscaris – Dinna Forget.* London: Hodder and Stoughton n.d Volume II p.202.

[1912] Stoeckl p.163.

[1913] Gustave Flaubert to Edmond de Goncourt 31st December 1876. Steegmuller/ Flaubert p.237; Fouquières p.35; Cossart p.85.

[1914] But not before des Esseintes had acquired a copy and, with Barbey's *Un Prêtre marié*, found it 'particularly enthralling'. Huysmans/Baldick pp.160-2. 'The works of Barbey d'Aurevilly were still the only ones whose matter and style offered those gamey flavours, those stains of disease and decay, that cankered surface, that taste of rotten-ripeness which he so loved to savour'. J-K. Huysmans: *À Rebours.* London: The Fortune Press n.d. [1946] p.135. *Les Diaboliques* was issued in London in 1926 in the Blue Jade Library with an introduction by Edmund Gosse.

[1915] Schom p.158.

[1916] Whiteing p.63. This was Marie-Amélie Chartroule de Montifaud who wrote under the name Marc de Montifaud.

[1917] Halperin p.263.

[1918] Descaves was one of the five disciples of Zola who repudiated Naturalism.

[1919] It had been risqué even under Napoléon III, and casting Hortense Schneider as the Grand Duchess could only have reminded Parisians (had they needed a reminder) that the mother of the Emperor had also been called Hortense and had not been known for her prim virtue. There seems to have been no problem with the next revivals, at the Théâtre des Variétés in May and again in October 1890.

[1920] Hemmings 1994 pp.224-5. Hemmings dates the abolition to 1906, but it was the 'loi des finances' of 17th April 1905 that created the new situation. Latour/ Claval p.18.

[1921] Musée de la préfecture de police.

[1922] Levin p.31.

[1923] Busnach was 'an Italian with names both Germanic and English, born in France of an Algerian father' Harding p.81. This was a sufficiently amorphous identity for him to become a supplier of libretti and an adaptor of other men's works rather than write his own – not only Zola's, but Jules Verne's (*Mathias Sandorf*). He provided libretti for Offenbach (*Polichinelle dans le monde, Pomme d'api*), but the operetta he wrote with Paul Siraudin for Bizet, *Malbrough s'en va-t-en-guerre*, has apparently been lost.
http://rick.stanford.edu/opera/Bizet/main.html

[1924] Nichols 1997 p.83.

[1925] This clearly demonstrates the difference between tolerance for the private act of reading a novel and the public act of portraying immorality on stage. Earlier prostitute novels were Hugo's *Marion Delorme* of 1831, Alfred de Musset's

---

Frédéric et Bernerette of 1838, and *Fernande* by Dumas *père* (1844). *La Fille Elisa* was produced by Antoine on 1st June 1900. Of these, *Marion Delorme* was still being staged as a play.

[1926] There was also a Chirac invented by Arnold Bennett as a journalist on the *Journal des Débats*. For Chirac, says Bennett, 'whatever existed might be admitted and examined by serious persons interested in the study of human nature'. Sophia Baines sees 'France personified in Chirac'. In the siege of Paris he escapes by balloon and is never seen again. Bennett/Barker pp.282,339.

[1927] A post-Parnassian and director first of the Musée Trocadéro and from 1903 of the Musée de Cluny. His *Shylock* was produced at the Odéon in 1889, his *Héro et Léandre* in 1893. He first came to attention in 1882 with *La Légende des Sexes*, a Volume of licentious verse, published under the name Sire de Chambley. Haraucourt's claim to fame is that he is not remembered as the author of the lapidary phrase 'Partir, c'est mourir un peu'.

[1928] This is a name with which Wilde's capacious memory would have been familiar, as another Béranger, the topographical artist Gabriel Béranger, had been the subject of a biography by Sir William Wilde, while Oscar himself reviewed the songs of Pierre-Jean Béranger ('Béranger in England', *Pall Mall Gazette* 21st March 1886, a review of William Toynbee (ed.): *A Selection of the Songs of de Béranger in English Verse*. London: C. Kegan Paul 1886). René Béranger (1830-1915; appointed a life senator in 1875) had instigated a law against immoral commercial displays in 1890, but Berthe Béranger ('Bébé') was a well-known prostitute of the rue Saint-Anne. Pierre-Jean Béranger's popular and sometimes bawdy songs may have been known to Lady Bracknell. The statue by Doublemard which commemorated him in the Square du Temple was melted down by the Germans in 1943.

[1929] The nickname was doubly derisive as it was also that of the bouncer at the Elysée-Montmartre.

[1930] In 1902 a banal statue to him (public subscription) was unveiled in the place Guatemala, boulevard Malesherbes. The name of the sculptor (Denys Peuch) is no longer easy to read. Simon's original name was Jules Suisse, but one could not build a political career on that.

[1931] It was the 9th February, which says much for Mona's hardihood. An alternative version is given by Chris Healy, who names the model as Sarah Brown and says that she rode a white donkey through the ballroom with a rose in her hair, the only departure in her costume from that usually ascribed to Lady Godiva. Healy pp.115-6.

[1932] These are described, apparently as an eyewitness, by Macdonald pp.106-8. Student riots were exceptional, but in May 1895 anti-Dreyfus demonstrations over two days turned riotous.

[1933] No. 23, a rather grand building built in 1884. Maupassant's Georges & Madeleine Forestier in *Bel-Ami* live at number 17 rue Fontaine, the ground floor of which now suitably houses Clairvoy, a theatrical agency.

[1934] It thereupon mutated into the Café du Pendu under the ownership of Marguerite Duclerc, and remained thus for two years before becoming the Concert Duclerc in 1896.

[1935] 'Madame X', now in the Metropolitan Museum of Art, New York, ref.16.53. American born, Virginie Gautreau (neé Avegno), the wife of the banker Pierre Gautreau, was a friend of Gyp de Martel. This is the woman whom D.W Brogan calls Madame Gauthereau. Brogan pp.113, 114.

[1936] By the time Albert Besnard painted his 'La première d'Hernani, avant la bataille', the play had become an established part of the repertoire, so the picture (the most striking figure in which is Théophile Gautier in his red waistcoat) reduces the incident to anecdote. Undated, Maison Victor Hugo, Paris, ref.MVH-P-196.

[1937] Corner of the boulevard des Italiens (number 22) and the rue Taitbout until it closed in 1894. It was famous for its ices (sorbets).

[1938] He is identifiable as the poet Norbert de Varenne in Maupassant's *Bel-Ami*.

[1939] Delbourg-Delphis p.157.

[1940] Nichols 1997 p.21.

[1941] Lockspeiser p.110n.

[1942] 'Lord High Reactionary Pooh Bah […] A scented rogue who would amplify a grain of truth or invent a story to suit himself.' Duncan 1964 pp.298,212.

[1943] Best known as a writer of plays for the théâtre des boulevards (*anglice* Shaftesbury Avenue).

[1944] James 1878 p.316.

[1945] Hemmings 1993 p.25. *Le Figaro*, says Hemmings, could command up to twenty-two free tickets at various theatres.

[1946] Healy p.253.

[1947] Keith Beaumont: *Alfred Jarry – A Critical and Biographical Study*. Leicester: Leicester University Press 1984 p.103, hereafter cited as Beaumont. Alphonse Allais, who relished a practical joke, sometimes wrote under the name Francisque Sarcey, but his unsuccessful pursuit of Jane Avril, to whom he proposed marriage, presumably exhausted his sense of humour.

[1948] 'Well set up, stout, and good humoured.' Cate p.154. The same source says that Sarcey was known as 'notre Oncle'. Zola/Nana/Parmée p.10.

[1949] Diary entry for 20th December 1892. Goncourt/Baldick p.381. Duval p.55.

[1950] Douglas Murray: *Bosie, A Biography of Lord Alfred Douglas.* London: Hodder & Stoughton 2000 p.94.

[1951] Whiteing p.120.

[1952] Lowther p.201. Lowther was British Military Attaché.

[1953] Novelist and dramatist of the Naturalist school, and a friend and acolyte of Zola, who drew on him for the character of Jory in *L'Œuvre*. He was also George Moore's closest friend among the naturalist writers.

[1954] Langlois and Alexis fought; Pelletier preferred to apologise.

[1955] Mendès had taken exception to the way Huret, a journalist and friend of Mirbeau and Maeterlinck, had referred to him as an associate of Wilde (*Le Figaro littéraire*, 13th April 1894; *L'Écho de Paris* 18th April 1895). Huret is also a name included in the Sherlock Holmes story 'The Golden Pince-Nez', as that of 'the boulevard assassin' — c.p. the critic Frank Rich, known as the butcher of Broadway.

[1956] 15th February 1886. Goncourt/Baldick p.312. Vignier's duel with Moréas in 1888 had a happier outcome, if one takes a favourable view of their work.

[1957] Daudet (1868-1942) was the son of Alphonse Daudet and son-in-law of Victor Hugo. Remembered now more for his political journalism than his novels, Daudet was a right-wing extreme 'patriot', a co-founder of the Action Française, who overlooked the possibility of joining the army in 1914 – some said it was because he was too fat to fight. It is unlikely that he and Wilde found much in common, but of his *Souvenirs des milieux littéraires, politiques, artistiques, et médicaux de 1890 à 1905*, Rothenstein wrote 'His prose portraits are sharp and convincing. The book recalled very clearly this period of my life in Paris'. Rothenstein Volume I p.162.

[1958] Bernstein was educated at Cambridge and was attached as interpreter to the British Embassy in 1914. Was he aware of *An Ideal Husband*? In *Après Moi* (1911), there is certainly a resonance of Robert Chiltern when Guillaume Bougade declares that not to succeed in a swindle is the act of a weakling, and that he had no right to not to succeed, a sentiment repeated by the character Mérital in Bernstein's *L'Assouet* of 1912. And did his name strike a chord with Meinhold's novel *Maria Schweidler die Bernsteinhexe* (1838)?

[1959] Belloc 1943 p.167.

[1960] http://www.fencingroom.com/article.html.

[1961] This was certainly the case in 1914 when Gaston Calmette, editor of *Le Figaro*, was killed by the wife of the politician Caillaux for publishing pre-nuptial correspondence (handed him by an earlier madame Caillaux) in which Caillaux confided state secrets. Madame Caillaux was acquitted.

[1962] 27th January 1890.

[1963] Jules Bertout *Henri Gervex Souvenirs receuillis*. Paris: Flammarion 1924 pp.50-1. Citation from Robinat p.41, where it is spelled Rochefoucault. The Café de la Rochefoucauld was on the corner of the rue de la Rochefoucauld and the rue Notre Dame de Lorette, favoured by the painters Gérôme, Reyer, Dupray, Cormon, Humbert, Degas, Lemoine, and by William Busnach and Maupassant, who first met Gervex there.

[1964] Edgar Holt: *The Tiger, the Life of George Clemenceau 1841-1929*. London: Hamish Hamilton 1976 p.85. Clemenceau fought twenty-two duels in all; Déroulède's henchman Millevoye fought thirty-seven.

[1965] Dramatist of the *école de bon sens* who died in 1889 Bernhardt appeared in his verse play *L'Aventurière* in April 1880, but Maurice Baring reckoned that although he was 'an excellent playwright, he was not only not a poet, he had not a spark of poetry in his composition'. Maurice Baring: *Sarah Bernhardt*. London: Peter Davies 1935 p.46, hereafter Baring 1935. It was at the unveiling of a statue to Augier in October 1895 (by Barrias in the place de l'Odéon) that Dumas *fils* caught the chill that killed him at the end of November; even more symbolic was the renaming of the rue Emile-Augier as the rue Jean-Richepin.

[1966] '...One or other of us has to go.' Ellmann p.546. Ellmann quotes this as having been said in a café on 29th October 1900 to Claire de Pratz, as cited in Gilles de Saix' 'Souvenirs Inédits' i.e. *Souvenirs inédits sur Oscar Wilde*. Paris: L'Européen n.d. and this is also given by Frank Harris*: Oscar Wilde: His Life and Confessions*. New York: Crown Publishing Co 1930 p. 572. But who was Claire de Pratz, and why was she drinking with Wilde? If she was the author of *A Frenchwoman's Notes on the War*, her dates are given as (?-1916?) by Agnès Cardinal, Dorothy Goldman, and Judith Hattaway (edd.): *Women's Writing on the First World War*. Oxford: Clarendon Press 1999, but if she was the author of *French Home Cooking*, her death occurred on 27th March 1934. The Claire de Pratz who was a correspondent of Elsa Barker has two letters in the Elsa Barker collection, University of Delaware Library, 1918 and 1920. www.lib.udel.edu/ud/spec/findaids/barker.htm.

[1967] Fouquières p.277.

[1968] Oliver Wendell Holmes: *The Autocrat of the Breakfast Table*. Volume I of the Collected Works. Boston: Houghton, Miflin & Co. 1892 p.125.There is no ascription, but elsewhere it is made clear that the 'wittiest of men' was Thomas Gold Appleton (1812-1884). *The Autocrat* was first published in 1858 and reprinted in 1882. Wilde knew his Holmes, who also quotes his 'friend the Historian, in one of his flashing moments: "Give us the luxuries of life, and we will dispense with its necessities".' The only other phrase, witty or not, ascribed to Appleton (also by Holmes) is "our late friend Mr Appleton [who said of] the real green turtle soup set before him that it was almost as good as mock'. Oliver Wendell Holmes: *Over the Teacups*, Volume IV of the Collected Works. Boston: Houghton, Miflin & Co. 1892 p.27. Appleton was the brother of Longfellow's wife. In 1911 Henry Huntington wrote that 'the much quoted "Good Americans, when they die, go to Paris" was perhaps the best known of his sayings.' Henry G. Huntington: *Memories, Personages, People, Places*. London: Constable 1911 p.166.

[1969] Wilbur R. Jacob (ed.): *Letters of Francis Parkman*. Norman: University of Oklahoma Press 1960 Volume II p.255.

[1970] New York: The Century Company. She also wrote a book called *The Anglomaniacs*.

[1971] Anna, comtesse de Brémont: *Oscar Wilde and His Mother, A Memoir*. London: Everett & Co 1911 p.28. Hereafter cited as Brémont. Brémont also wrote *Sonnets from a Paris Balcony*, and the memoir contains a sonnet to Wilde. Joaquin Miller (1839-1913), known as 'the poet of the Sierras', was much in London and Paris in the 1870s.

[1972] Review of Eric Robertson: *Longfellow, The Pall Mall Gazette* 28th March 1887, Wyse Jackson p.92.

[1973] 'The American Invasion'. *Court and Society Review*, 23rd March 1887, reprinted in Wyse Jackson p.36.

[1974] Mary Warner Blanchard: *Oscar Wilde's America: Counter Culture in the Gilded Age*. Yale University Press: New Haven 1998.

[1975] Lecture on 'The Practical Application of the Principles of Æsthetic Theory to Exterior and Interior House Decoration', delivered in America on 11th May 1882, reprinted in Wyse Jackson p.184.

[1976] Review of Eric Robertson: *Longfellow*, *The Pall Mall Gazette* 28th March 1887, reprinted in Wyse Jackson p.92.

[1977] Laurence Housman: *Echo de Paris*. London: Jonathan Cape 1923 p.26. Hereafter cited as Housman.

[1978] Sherard 1908 p.73.

[1979] Oscar Wilde: 'The American Invasion', *Court and Society Review* 23rd March 1887, reprinted in Wyse Jackson p.36. Compare this to Herbert Tree's delight in New York – 'nor was Chicago too grim for him, nor Boston too prim'. Beerbohm/Tree pp.197-8.

[1980] Oscar Wilde: 'The American Invasion', *Court and Society Review* 23rd March 1887, reprinted in Wyse Jackson p.37.

[1981] Oscar Wilde: 'The American Invasion', *Court and Society Review* 23rd March 1887, reprinted in Wyse Jackson pp.38,39.

[1982] Whittington-Egan p.355.

[1983] James/Sketches pp.3,6. Letter of 22nd November 1875.

[1984] Mott p.82.

[1985] Henry James: *A Little Tour of France*. Boston: James R. Osgood 1884. Edited by Geoffrey Grigson. Oxford: Oxford University Press 1984 p.1. Hereafter cited as James/Tour.

[1986] Novick pp.xii,330.

[1987] Tóibín p.355.

[1988] James/Ambassadors pp.85-6.

[1989] T. Edgar Pemberton: *The Life of Bret Harte*. London: C. Arthur Pearson 1903 p.168.

[1990] Bret Harte to his wife 11th August 1878. Geoffrey Bret Harte (ed.): *The Letters of Bret Harte*. London: Hodder & Stoughton 1926 p.87. Hereafter cited as Harte.

[1991] The comment, unsourced, is given in Van Wyck Brooks: *Howells, His Life and World*. London: J.M. Dent & Sons 1959 p.131. Hereafter cited as Brooks 1959.

[1992] Bret Harte to his wife 28th July 1880. Harte p.185. He goes on 'I otherwise don't like Paris'.

[1993] Bret Harte to his wife 28th July 1880. Harte p.186.

[1994] Four nights out of eight.

[1995] Leon Edel: Introduction to Henry James: *Guy Domville*. London: Rupert Hart-Davis 1961 p.41.

[1996] There may have been some five thousand Americans in Pars in 1870/1 and approaching 30,000 by the century's end. Green p.16.

[1997] James/Tour p.1.

[1998] Mrs Thomas Bailey Aldrich: *Crowding Memories*. London: Constable 1921 p.195.

[1999] Frazier p.41. She and Moore seem to have had some sort of affaire (for with Moore one can rarely be more precise).

[2000] Fouquières pp.212-3.

[2001] Harding Davis pp.4,177.

[2002] Delevoye p.122. Rops occupied about a dozen studios or apartments while in Paris.

[2003] He was also at Pont Aven in 1897.

[2004] Roger Fry to Nathaniel Wedd 21st February 1892. Sutton/Fry p.152.

[2005] A group photograph of Gérôme's students, identifying sixteen of them, is reproduced in Low opp. p.42.

[2006] Weinberg pp.79,93.

[2007] Davis 1895 p.217.

[2008] 1866-1945, or 1856-1942 according to Delia Gaze (ed.): *Dictionary of Women Artists*. London & Chicago: Fitzroy Dearborn 1997. Klumpke first arrived in Paris in 1877, and remained there apart from a period in the United States 1890-1989. Her portrait of Rosa Bonheur (1890) is now in the Metropolitan Museum of Art, New York.

[2009] Novick pp 62, 63. James spent some time studying with them.

[2010] E.Œ. Somerville and Martin Ross: *Stray-Aways, a Volume of Studies and Sketches*. London: Longmans, Green & Co 1920 p.35. This was written in November 1894. Hereafter cited as Somerville/Ross.

[2011] Henry p.18.

[2012] The real Casque d'Or (played in the film by Simone Signoret) was painted by Toulouse-Lautrec in 1891.

[2013] Healy pp.99-100.

[2014] Moncure Daniel Conway: *Autobiography, Memories and Experiences*. London: Cassell & Co. 1904 Volume II p.248.

[2015] Fox p.225.

[2016] Musée de l'Art américain, Giverny.

[2017] Whiteing p.147. Alexander is presumably J.W Alexander, Harrison either Alexander Harrison or his brother Birge, 'Miss Gardner' Elizabeth Gardner who became Madame Bouguereau; Healy is George Healy. I have been unable to identify May.

[2018] Wylie's group portrait 'Les modèles de Pont Aven' (c.1875) is in the Musée d'Art américain, Giverny. Thus the title on the accompanying label, but on the frame it is identified as 'Breton audience'.

[2019] Eakins' portrait of Woodwell of 1904 is now in the Carnegie Museum, Pittsburgh, ref.30.5.

[2020] The lithograph of May Belfort by Toulouse-Lautrec in the Metropolitan Museum of Art, New York was the gift of Bessie Potter Vonnoh.

[2021] Glackens' striking picture of the footbridge at La Villette (Carnegie Museum, Pittsburgh c.1896 ref.56.13) can be said to demonstrate the American painter bringing Paris back home, while his 'Chez Mouguins' (Art Institute of Chicago), demonstrates his lingering Frenchness in this restaurant of New York's Sixth Avenue. (Denys Sutton: *Fads and Fancies*. With an introduction by Kenneth Clark. Salisbury: Michael Russell 1979 Plate I.) Henri, in contrast, shrugged off Impressionism and created the Ashcan realist school.

[2022] http://www.burtonartgallery.co.uk/painting3.htm

[2023] Sylvia Beach: *Shakespeare & Company*. London: Faber & Faber 1960 p.16. Beach's mother was born Carlotta Welles, whose father had been Paris representative of Western Electric.

[2024] Conway p.237. Henri studied under Bouguereau.

[2025] Puvis de Chavannes, Carolus-Duran, Benjamin-Constant and Gérôme.

[2026] Coolidge p.185.

[2027] This French-American settled in Paris at 15 rue Lesueur. Laurence Vail, a husband of Peggy Guggenheim and of Kay Boyle, was his son, brought up in Paris.

[2028] John Leslie Breck, 'Giverny Winter' 1889, ref.2000.51.1. Breck's 'Giverny Autumn' of the same year is in the Musée de l'Art américain, Giverny. It is thanks to the curators of this museum that we can chiefly look for continued recuperation of the American artists, especially those at Giverny, where their presence (notably that of Theodore Robinson and Thomas Earl Butler) substantially antedated that of Monet.

[2029] James/Ambassadors p.70.

[2030] 'Billee' was the nickname bestowed by his friends, borrowed from Thackeray.

[2031] Sorel p.123; Chapter XII.

[2032] Paul R. Barker: *Stanny, The Gilded Life of Stanford White*. New York: The Free Press and London: Collier Macmilllan 1989 p.47.

[2033] Presumably the Cox remembered by Shirley Fox as a 'fine painter [...] a most brilliant caricaturist'. Fox p.115.

[2034] Saint-Gaudens Volume I p.250. 'Blasfield' is an error for Blashfield.

[2035] Another New Yorker whose accomplishments were varied, was Gertrude Stevens, a cocotte of the boulevard des Italiens,

[2036] Saint-Gaudens Volume I p.215.

[2037] Classical concerts seem to have played little part in Parisian life, apart from recitals in private houses and Sunday performances. The Concert Rouge opposite Foyot's was the chief home of classical music, accompanied by cerises au cognac, for which a small shelf was provided on the backs of the seats.

[2038] George du Maurier's Barty Josselin goes to this at the Opéra-Comique. Du Maurier/Martian p.172.

[2039] Adams p.285.

[2040] Low pp.220-1.

[2041] Tharp p.29.

[2042] Huysmans told Chris Healy that he lived there because it was equidistant from St Sulpice, St Sévérin, St Etienne du Mont and St Germain l'Auxerrois. Healy p.141.

[2043] She was in Paris again in 1898.

[2044] Tharp p.305.

[2045] Tharp p.192.

[2046] Musée de l'Art américain, Giverny.

[2047] Tharp p.308. For more on MacMonnies, see Mary Smart and E. Adina Gordon: *A Flight With Fame: The Life & Art of Frederick MacMonnies, 1863-1937*. Madison, Conn.: Sound View Press 1996.

[2048] Florent Schmitt lived at 49, Sarah Bernhardt at 56.

[2049] Saint-Gaudens Volume II p.123.

[2050] Maupassant/Bel Ami p.11.

[2051] Augustus Saint-Gaudens to a correspondent 16th November 1897. Saint-Gaudens Volume II p.180.

[2052] Its base was designed by Stanford White.

[2053] Saint-Gaudens Volume I p.311. Saint-Gaudens' father was a shoemaker, originally from Gascony. The town of Saint Gaudens is in Gascony (department of Gers).

[2054] Adams p.386.

[2055] Mott pp.77-8.

[2056] Ambrose Kennedy: *American Orator, Bourke Cockran, His Life and Politics*. Boston: Bruce Humphries Inc 1958; James McGurrin: *Bourke Cockran, A Free Lance in American Politics*. New York: Charles Scribner's Sons 1948, hereafter cited as McGurrin.

[2057] McGurrin p.16.

[2058] Duncan pp.75, 76.

[2059] Courtesan may be too kind a word. Princess Metternich's biographer roundly calls her a strumpet ('gourgandine'). Emmanuel Haymann: *Pauline Metternich, la jolie laide du Second Empire*. Paris: Perrin 1991 p.114.

[2060] Rothenstein Volume I p.79.

[2061] Though Sedgwick had been living in London since the age of nine, she was from Englewood, New Jersey.

[2062] Conway pp.244-5.

[2063] Coolidge p.186.

[2064] Menpes p.113.

[2065] Green pp.82-4.

[2066] Angela V. John: *Elizabeth Robins, Staging a Life 1862-1932*. London: Routledge 1995 p.1.

[2067] D.S. MacColl: The *London Mercury* January 1939, quoted in Borland 1995 p.89.

[2068] Her bust by Epstein is in the library at Bryn Mawr.

[2069] This was incorporated into a fictionalised life of Saint-Gaudens, *The Breath of Runners*, published in New York in 1906.

[2070] Quoted by Tharp p.285.

[2071] Coolidge p.63.

[2072] Healy p.201. Healy met Whistler there in 1896. Should not be confused with the United States Students' and Artists' Club, boulevard Raspail, which opened in 1920.

[2073] Letters from Trist Wood while he worked as an artist and editor in Paris and London, 1893-1905, are in the Southern Historical Collection, Manuscripts

Department, Academic Affairs Library of the University of North Carolina at Chapel Hill; other papers are in the Special Collections at Tulane University.
[2074] This was subtitled 'A Little Book Devoted to the Arts', published in England by Dent at 6d and in the United States at 10¢.
[2075] Nevill p.102.
[2076] Nevill p.103.
[2077] Freeman Wills: *W.G. Wills, Dramatist and Painter*. London: Longmans, Green & Co 1898 p.213.
[2078] Yandell. Chapter II.
[2079] Yandell p.9.
[2080] It was Yves Guyot who had begun serialising *L'Assommoir* in his paper *Le Bien publique* and then changed his mind. He was the author, inter alia, of *Prostitution under the Regulation System* (1884).
[2081] Yandell pp.34-5.
[2082] Yandell p.35.
[2083] Marchesi p.223.
[2084] A.G. Temple: *Guildhall Memories*. London: John Murray 1918 p.234.
[2085] Ralph G. Martin: *Lady Randolph Churchill, A Biography* Volume II The Dramatic Years 1895-1921. London: Cassell 1971 pp.14,318.
[2086] English Officer p.13.
[2087] Novick p.51. The James family rented a house in the avenue des Champs Elysées in 1856, before moving to the rue d'Angoulême and later to the rue Montaigne.
[2088] Blunt p.3. Diary entry for 11th November 1888. Hereafter cited as Blunt.
[2089] Coolidge p.157.
[2090] *Née* Adelaide Torrance. There is a photograph of her in Hartmann p.49. She should not be confused with Degas' friend Hortense Howland, the Parisian divorçee of an American, who had left her with an annuity and a house in the rue de la Rochefoucauld. It is this 'Madame Howland' whom Francis Steegmuller suggests introduced Degas to Maupassant. Steegmuller/Maupassant p.359.
[2091] Painter I p.135. This refers to 1893.
[2092] Hartmann p.48.
[2093] 30th May 1876.
[2094] Coolidge p.198.
[2095] Coolidge pp.152,227,235.
[2096] Whiteing p.212. A picture of Blanche Pierson is in English Officer 1908, facing p.130. She began at the Vaudeville. 'Blanche Pierson has always had rich keepers and has become a first-rate actress besides'. Pretty Women p.153.
[2097] Waddington 1914 p.160.
[2098] Woods (1856-1945) was the wife of Henry George Woods, President of Trinity College, Oxford 1887-1897. I have not been able to ascertain whether her Paris novel was ever written.
[2099] Rothenstein Volume I p.282.
[2100] Rothenstein Volume I p.81. This goes much further than Ellmann.

[2101] Novick p.330. 'There is almost no agreement among scholars on Reubell's birth date, and few scholars provide citations or other reasons for preferring particular dates. For the most part James scholars have cited Reubell's birth as c. 1839, with the precedent for accepting this date probably beginning with Robert Gale's *A Henry James Encyclopedia*. Reubell was also close friends with Oscar Wilde, and Wilde scholars usually give c. 1849 for her birth date, citing a 3 June 1884 letter from Constance Wilde to Otho Holland Lloyd in which Constance estimates Reubell's age to be forty. Her death is almost unanimously given as 1924, though primary sources confirming this were not forthcoming. She appears to have lived in Paris for most of her life. Her mother, Julia Coster, was an American and her father, Frederic Reubell, was a wealthy French citizen.' Daniel Meyer to the present writer, e-mail 26.iv.2010.

[2102] The duchess (1864-1919) also became Rodin's the last grand passion. Conceived by Rodin as a Bacchante, her bust by him of 1908 made her look like an inebriate charwoman. She was not pleased. Now in the Victoria & Albert Museum A.46-1914.
http://www.musee-rodin.fr/fr/collections/sculptures/la-duchesse-de-choiseul#sthash.70Z740YQ.dpuf

[2103] Coolidge p.151.

[2104] Waddington 1914 p.192.

[2105] Cornelius Vanderbilt Jr: *The Vanderbilt Feud, the Fabulous Story of Grace Wilson Vanderbilt*. London: Hutchinson 1957 p.17. Her sisters were Belle, who married the Hon. Michael Herbert, and May, who married another rich American, Ogden Goelet.

[2106] Aristocratic alliances with money transcended other boundaries. The daughter of the duc de Tancarville even married a German banker, Hermann Hüffer of the rue de Coq, one of the Paris branch of the Hüffer family 'tremendously rich, good Catholics, building churches'. Hunt pp.27,159. Another was Leopold Hüffer (1825-1897), an uncle of Ford Madox Hueffer's.

[2107] English Officer p.4,26.

[2108] Mott p.82. One would need the determination to be a bore of the old Mr Joe Peabody sort to attempt to track down these social nonentities, but Mott tells us that Tuck was Edward Tuck, an intimate friend of General Porter's, who lived somewhere beyond the Bois de Boulogne and was famous for his Major Curley Blue Grass Whisky of 1883.

[2109] Waddington 1914 p.189.

[2110] Hart-Davis 1972 plate 75.

[2111] Coolidge p.172.

[2112] Allen p.9.

[2113] Her daughter married Count Alexander Mercati and their daughter married Michael Arlen.

[2114] Julian Green: *Memories of Happy Days*. London: J.M. Dent & Co. 1944. 3rd impression 1946 p.1. Hereafter cited as Green 1944.

[2115] Harrison pp.250-1.

[2116] Waddington 1914 p.46.

[2117] Du Maurier/Trilby p.134.

[2118] Harrison p.245.

[2119] Mainwaring p.97.

[2120] Michael G. Lerner: *Maupassant*. London: George Allen & Unwin 1975 p.216.

[2121] The Italian Verdi scholar Marcello Conati says that she was born in 1853, which would make her fifty-two or fifty-three; Mainwaring says forty-one; but the plaque in Brompton Cemetery gives her dates as 2nd October 1858 to 10th September 1898 – I am grateful to Ms Connie Nisinger for drawing my attention to this.

[2122] Mainwaring p.98.

[2123] Steegmuller/Maupassant pp.177-82; http://diamond.boisestate.edu/GaS/whowaswho/R/RooseveltBlanche.htm. She is not mentioned in Wilde's letters. http://pinafore.www3.50megs.com/b-roosevelt.html

[2124] This had premièred at Bordeaux on 14th December 1900 with Thérèse Ganne in the title rôle. Toulouse-Lautrec produced a series of drawings and paintings inspired by this production.

[2125] Turnbull p.5.

[2126] Coolidge p.201. Mrs Story was possibly one of the family that included William Wetmore Story (1819-1895), the sculptor and poet, and his sons Julian (1850-1919), the painter, and Thomas Waldo (1854-1915), the sculptor. Julian Story worked in Paris and became a friend of Whistler's. 'A photograph taken in JW's studio in Tite Street in 1881 shows JW with Story, his brother Waldo, the painter Frank Miles and the sculptor Frederick Lawless. Sir Rennell Rodd recalls that particularly in 1882 and 1883 Story, along with his brother Waldo, Frank Miles, Walter Sickert and Harper Pennington were constantly in JW's studio' (http://www.whistler.arts.gla.ac.uk/biog/Stor_J.htm). There are links to Wilde here, for Miles and Wilde shared a flat, Rodd was an early friend of Wilde's, and Pennington painted Wilde.

[2127] Turnbull p.55.

[2128] Should not be confused with *La Femme du Tabarin* by Catulle Mendès, which opened at the Théâtre Montparnasse on 11th November 1887.

[2129] Turnbull p.66. Plates 10, 11 are Garden as Salomé.

[2130] Turnbull p.93.

[2131] Schwab p.20.

[2132] Schwab p.145.

[2133] Schwab p.23.

[2134] Brooks p.158. Huneker had attended Wilde's lecture in Philadelphia in January 1882.

[2135] 14th November 1878.

[2136] Marchesi p.263.

[2137] Born Emma Walter, she subsequently changed her stage name to Esther Palliser.

[2138] Less exotic was the name of Caroline Salla (madame Uhring) which was de Septavaux. Salla sang the title rôles of Ambroise Thomas' *Françoise de Rimini* and Saint-Saëns' *Proserpine.*

[2139] The following references to Sanderson are drawn from Peter G. Davis: *The American Opera Singer, The Lives and Adventures of America's Great Singers in Opera and in Concert from 1825 to the Present.* New York: Doubleday 1997. Davis draws heavily on the recollections of Blanche Marchesi and Mary Garden.

[2140] Diary entry for 15th October 1892. Coolidge p.184.

[2141] Atherton pp.155-60.

[2142] 1997.

[2143] Waddington 1903 p.295.

[2144] Gounod's *Faust*, first performed at the Opéra-Lyrique in 1859 with the recitatives as spoken dialogue, had been part of the repertoire at the Palais Garnier since 1875. Admired by Berlioz, attacked by Wagner, popular acclaim ensured a production in Paris every year except 1912 and the war years until 1924. Shaw grew tired of it, and it was denounced, not surprisingly, by Ernest Newman.

[2145] E.B. Washburne: *Recollections of a Minister to France* vol. II. London: Sampson Low, Marston, Searle & Rivington 1887 p.2. Hereafter cited as Washburne.

[2146] A similar lack of grasp afflicts the author of *The Pretty Women of Paris,* who says she was 'a native of the Dutch colonies belonging to Spain', whatever dystopia these may have been, and spoke English with a Dutch accent and French with an American one. Pretty Women p.179.

[2147] Painter I p.193.

[2148] Edward and Mary Green (d.1927 and 1914) were from Georgia and Virginia, and had gone first to Le Havre in 1895, and then to Paris where Green was European Agent of the Southern Cotton Oil Company, rue du Louvre. They lived at 4 rue Rhumkorff until 1903, when they moved to the rue de Passy. Eleanor married an Englishman and moved to Italy. Julian Green, the fifth child, was born on 6th September 1900.

[2149] Margaret Drabble: *Arnold Bennett, A Biography.* London: Weidenfeld & Nicholson 1974 p.129; Hunt p.75.

[2150] Green 1944 p.26.

[2151] Hunt pp.75, 186.

[2152] Rothenstein Volume I p.95. Another Paris American of the same name, Frank Gardner, spent his money in subventing the steam-powered motor-cars designed by Léon Serpollet first for Peugeot and then on his own. The fuel was paraffin. Serpollet died in 1907, and his designs were then used to develop the Darracq-Serpollet omnibus.

[2153] Louise Hall Tharp: *Mrs Jack, A Biography of Isabella Stewart Gardner.* Boston: Little, Brown & Co 1965 p.160.

[2154] Not only Americans of course. Henry James introduced a Lady Selina Bidwell to Pavel Zhukovsky in order to have her portrait painted.

[2155] Atherton pp.161,154.

[2156] Atherton p.163.

[2157] Frazier p.187.

[2158] At 95 rue de Chaillot until 1881, when it moved to 3 place de la Bitche, which name was changed to the place des États-Unis to avoid embarrassment.

[2159] Ribblesdale p.86.

[2160] Martin Duberman: *James Russell Lowell*. Boston, Mass.: Houghton Miflin Co 1966 p.259. Hereafter cited as Duberman.

[2161] Novick p.253.

[2162] Anderson 1896 p.84.

[2163] Conway pp.224-5. Meredith (1837-1896) lived at 37 avenue d'Antin.

[2164] Healy p.207.

[2165] Duberman 1966 p.259.

[2166] Duberman p.259.

[2167] Horace Elisha Scudder: *James Russell Lowell, A Biography* Volume II. Boston: Houghton, Mifflin & Co 1901 p.153.

[2168] His friend Thornton Lothrop was staying at the Bristol.

[2169] Holmes 1895 pp.162,176.

[2170] Holmes 1895 p.175.

[2171] Holmes 1895 p.167.

[2172] Holmes p.174.

[2173] His Papers are in the Library of Congress.

[2174] John Hay to Amasa Stone 11th March 1883. William Roscoe Thayer: *The Life & Letters of John Hay* Volume I. London: Constable & Co.; Boston: Houghton Miflin Co. 1905 p.412. Hereafter cited as Thayer.

[2175] John Hay to Henry Adams 3rd November 1893. Thayer p.102.

[2176] John Hay to Henry Adams 25th April 1894. Thayer p.110. The translation was that of Paul Meurice and Alexandre Dumas.

[2177] John Hay to Clara Hay 11th June 1896. John Hay: *Letters of John Hay and Extracts from His Diary* Volume III. Washington, D.C.: Privately printed 1908 p.14. Hereafter cited as Hay.

[2178] John Hay to Clara Hay 16th/17th June 1896. Hay p.17.

[2179] John Hay to Clara Hay 15th and 16th/17th June 1896. Hay pp.15,17. The 'Londres' would have been the hotel of that name, rue Bonaparte; the restaurant, Ledoyen.

[2180] John Hay to Henry White 21st January 1898. Hay p.111. The Coquelins had taken over the theatre in 1897, replacing Baduel with Hertz as administrator.

[2181] Harlan p.241.

[2182] I have not been able to establish where.

[2183] Booker T. Washington: 'On the Paris Boulevards', New York *Age* June 1899, reprinted in Louis R. Harlan & Raymond W Smock (edd.): *The Booker T. Washington Papers* Volume V: 1899-1900. Urbana: University of Illinois Press 1976 p.130.

[2184] New York 1884.

[2185] Samuels p.119.

[2186] Adams p.360.

[2187] Adams p.96.

[2188] Low opp. p.71.

[2189] John White Alexander, who had previously worked in Munich, moved to Paris in 1891 and stayed to 1901, coming into Whistler's orbit and exhibiting in the 1900 Expo.

[2190] A prolific painter from Detroit, of German descent, he won a medal in the American painting section at the 1889 Universal Exposition, awarded only to Melchers and Sargent. Melchers was another student at the Académie Julian in Paris and subsequently was accepted at the École des Beaux-Arts, before setting up a studio in Holland, where he chiefly worked. In the late 1880s and the 1890s he was influenced by Symbolism.

[2191] Rothenstein Volume I pp.77,78.

[2192] McConkey p.46.

[2193] Weir was responsible for persuading Puvis de Chavannes to work on the murals in the Boston Public Library. He is represented in the Musée de l'Art américain, Giverny, by his 'Christmas Tree' of 1890.

[2194] I take it that this is the Cercle Volney referred to by Edmund Got. When offered membership, he reflected that 'I hardly think this is the slippery slope to that bogus café society' ('Je ne me sente guère de pente à cette fausse vie de café'). Got p.223. 'The Cercle de la rue Volney, otherwise the *Crêmerie* or the *pieds crottés* follows the Mirlitons at a respectful distance in everything, except perhaps in high play'. Whiteing p.50.

[2195] Mary Repington: *Thanks for the Memory*. London: Constable n.d. p.33.

[2196] Gordon Bennett gave his name to the English language as an expletive and directed the *New York Herald* by cable from his apartment. His secretaries, Charles Inman Barnard and Charles Christiansen, may be glimpsed in Blumenfeld pp.30-1.

[2197] By 1881 there were thirty American dentists in Paris, and in 1890 the American Dental Club of Paris was founded by Thomas Evans and John Spaulding. Green p.125.

[2198] His Honour Judge J.W. Scobell Armstrong C.B.E.: *Yesterday*. London: Hutchinson 1955; Stéphane Mallarmé: *Correspondence*. Receuillée, Classée et Annotée par Henri Mondor et Lloyd James Austin. Paris: Gallimard 1965 Volume IV p.117n. Armstrong had a tooth stopped by Evans when a thirteen year old boy in Paris.

[2199] Née Louviot.

[2200] Moore/Memoirs pp.54-5.

[2201] He had better luck than Hubert Evelyn, who had once got up a touring company in England so that his wife could play La Tosca. Evelyn, who went on to live in a houseboat moored in Paris, fell into the Seine one night from the gangplank 'and thus lost his rather useless life'. Edward Gordon Craig: *Index to the Story of My Days 1872-1907*. London: Hulton Press 1957 pp.170.

[2202] Blumenfeld p.34.

[2203] Conway pp.278,283. Conway lists a number of American painters and sculptors living in Paris at the time of publication, p.294.

[2204] Publisher's advertisement in Grierson.

[2205] Brooks 1959 pp209, 210.

[2206] Schwab p.85. He was also upset by the scarcity of bath tubs.

[2207] Novick p.315.

[2208] Benstock p.82.

[2209] Eugène Melchior de Vogüé also wrote a sonnet to Julia Bartet 'À la vivante Tanagra', while Maurice Donnay, who sometimes remembered that before he became an Academician he had been a Chat Noir poet, addressed a quatrain to 'la Bartet tanagrine'.

[2210] August 1893.

[2211] Harrison 1911 p.244.

[2212] Meeting the comtesse de Montsaulnin many years later, T.J. Coolidge thought that she 'has lived so long in France as to have become in every respect a Frenchwoman'. Coolidge p.151.

[2213] English Officer pp.18-19.

[2214] Harrison p.154.

[2215] Harrison pp.245-6.

[2216] Harrison p.246.

[2217] Harrison p.248.

[2218] Royal Cortissoz: *The Life of Whitelaw Reid*. London: Thornton Butterworth 1921 p.127. Hereafter cited as Cortissoz.

[2219] Mary Anderson de Navarro: *A Few More Memories*. London: Hutchinson 1936 pp.267,44,45. Hereafter cited as Anderson 1936. Massenet was 'a cherished friend' of Anderson's husband (p.36).

[2220] "Give me your tired, your poor, / Your huddled masses yearning to breathe free,/The wretched refuse of your teeming shore.' Originally it faced inwards, towards the pont de Grenelle, being turned round in 1938.

[2221] Morgan 1965 p.9.

[2222] A brief account of the relations between Whistler and Ford is given at http://www.whistler.arts.gla.ac.uk/biog/Ford_S.htm.

[2223] Attorney General under Presidents Garfield and Arthur, and U.S. Ambassador to Rome.

[2224] Cortissoz p.162.

[2225] 5th June 1890. I have yet to identify the general, possibly a Phanariote attached to the Turkish Embassy.

[2226] Waddington 1914 pp.86-7. Houghton was the former Richard Monckton Milnes 'whom men call Baron Houghton / But the gods call Dicky Milnes'.

[2227] The negotiations themselves were held in the Foreign Ministry, quai d'Orsay.

[2228] Papers in the Library of Congress.

[2229] An attempt to reduce the obscurity of the history of black Americans in Paris is made in Green.

[2230] Morgan 1965 p.15.

[2231] Morgan 1965 p.15.

[2232] Morgan 1965 p.70.

[2233] Morgan 1965 p.48. Reid himself was a newspaperman, controlling the *New York Tribune* from the early 1870s until his death in 1912.

2234 Diary for 19th October 1898. Morgan 1965 p.90. John Morley, lunching with the Ribots in 1892, remarked oddly that madame Ribot 'is an American lady whom we have known, and known about, for years'. Morley 1917 p.302.
2235 Healy p.191.
2236 He wrote under the name Sidney Luska and described himself as 'almost a Jew […] all but a Jew myself'. Karl Beckson: *Henry Harland, His Life and Work*. London: The Eighteen Nineties Society 1978 p.2. Hereafter cited as Beckson.
2237 Beckson pp.50,37.
2238 Thwaite p.355.
2239 Edmund Gosse to Nellie Gosse n.d.g. Thwaite p.356.
2240 Beckson p.43. Gosse's expectations were doubtless sharpened by George Moore's recollections, for the two were friends (something of a feat) for forty years. Edmund Gosse: *Books on the Table*. London: William Heinemann 1923 dedication.
2241 Mix p.63.
2242 Extracts from Richard Le Gallienne: 'Paris Day by Day: A Familiar Epistle (To Mrs. Henry Harland)'; from *Robert Louis Stevenson, An Elegy, and Other Poems Mainly Personal*. London: John Lane 1895 pp.29-32.
2243 Oscar Wilde to Robert Ross late April 1898. Hart-Davis 1962 p.731.
2244 Netta Syrett: *The Flowering Tree*. London: Geoffrey Bles 1939 p.77. Netta's sister Kate lived in Paris. She was 'one of the best artists, working for a wealthy firm in England. Her designs for fabrics better judges than I consider remarkable, and if talent always received its deserts, she should still be making an excellent living.' *ibid*. pp.84-5. There is a photograph of Réjane in *Madame Sans-Gêne* in Hartmann p.100. This allows us to date the visit by the Harlands and Syrett to 1893.
2245 Mix p.113. Dauphin Meunier is difficult to identify, but is probably the poet Joseph Dauphin Meunier (1868-1927).
2246 Whittington-Egan pp.262-3.
2247 English Officer p.35.
2248 Beckson p.2.
2249 Merrick p.63.
2250 R.W Stallman: *Stephen Crane, A Biography*. New York: George Brazillier 1968 pp.316-7.
2251 Stephen Crane to H.S. Bennett 29th August 1899 quoted in Stanley Wertheim & Paul Sorento: *The Crane Log, a Documentary Life of Stephen Crane*. New York: G.K. Hall 1994. Dick Davis is Richard Harding Davis and Mitchell is Silas Weir Mitchell, author of *Neurasthenia and Hysteria* (1887), and inventor of a rest cure.
2252 Cossart p.15.
2253 Painter I p.164.
2254 Cossart p.37.
2255 See 'Étude pour le portrait de la princesse Edmond de Polignac', Musée des Beaux Arts, Rouen ref.922.1.6.
2256 Coolidge pp.154-5.

[2257] Quoted by Brian Reade: *Art Nouveau and Alphonse Mucha.* London: Her Majesty's Stationery Office 1963 p.29, hereafter cited as Reade.

[2258] Quoted in Tint p.126. My translation of *la patrie*.

[2259] Duff Gordon p.108.

[2260] Nevill 1913 p.122.

[2261] Thurston p.18.

[2262] Zola/L'Œuvre p.76. In 1881 the group 'La Triomphe de la République' by Jean-Alexandre Falguière, one of the leading realist sculptors, was placed on top of the Arc de Triomphe. In 1886 it was taken down again.

[2263] Houssaye p.319. My italics. It did not stop him having a *secondaire* at Royan.

[2264] Symons Chapter III. Although the best work of the reclusive Guys, born as long before as 1805, was done under the Second Empire, he continued to paint in Paris until incapacitated in a street accident in 1885. It is extraordinary to think that Guys, who had met Byron at Missolonghi, only died in 1892, having outlived all his friends except Nadar. By 1905, the year of the first Guys exhibition in London, Henri Frantz could publish *A Forgotten Artist: Constantin Guys* (London: The Studio), despite having had his portrait painted by Manet.

[2265] Zola/Bonheur p.34.

[2266] James/Ambassadors p.242. This is not the Zola-esque loyalty to each other despite their squabbles that Douglas Permée sees among the prostitutes /actresses in *Nana*, for the specifically Parisian meaning is brought out a few lines later where the quiddity of Vionnet's help is expanded: 'She was ready to advise about dressmakers and shops'. *L'Eternal féminin* was the title of a novel (1881) by Joseph Gayda, to whom Laurent Tailhade dedicated his *Un dizain de Sonnets.* What made James give madame de Vionnet the same name as the couturière Madeleine Vionnet, given his own distance from femininity? David Lodge speculates that 'it was probably the insistent pressure of sexual activity and sexual obsession in French literary life that had driven him from Paris'. Lodge p.57.

[2267] Zola/L'Œuvre pp.182,183,188.

[2268] 'Saki' (H.H. Munro): 'The Boar Pig'. *Beasts and Superbeasts.* London: John Lane, The Bodley Head 1914. Reprinted in *The Complete Short Stories of 'Saki'.* London: The Bodley Head 1930 p.281.

[2269] Crosland p.54. Could Kinceler have been a corruption of the Irish name Kinsella?

[2270] Mainwaring p.88. There was something especially factitious about this name, for Eugène de Mirecourt was the nom-de-plume of Charles Jacquot (1812-1880) who wrote *Les confessions de Marion Delorme* (1849) and an attack on Dumas *père Fabrique de Romans: Maison Alexandre Dumas & Cie* which claimed that most of Dumas' work was written by other writers. Dumas successfully sued Mirecourt, who was sentenced to a fortnight in prison for libel. Théodore de Banville wrote a satire against Mirecourt for this episode. Adèle Moutot is also transformed by R.W.B. Lewis in his life of Edith Wharton into 'Henrietta Mirecourt': the history of this absurdity is told by Marion Mainwaring *loc. cit.* p.244. One presumes that this is the Mirecourt of the Palais Royal mentioned in Pretty Women p.136.

[2271] A sister of Rachel. The third sister, Dinah, was also an actress, member of the Comédie Française 1871-1881. Rachel herself, dead long before the period here covered, had been the mistress of a number of those mentioned, notably the prince de Joinville, 'Plon-Plon' and Napoléon III. Such was her success that, more than Mars, she remained the benchmark against which her successors in the classical drama were measured. Her sisters remain obscure, scantily mentioned even in the substantial exhibition devoted to Rachel, Musée d'Art et d'Histoire du Judaïsme, Paris, 2004.

[2272] Harding p.47. Less amusing was the result of an affaire with the duc de Grammont-Caderousse, a child with Down's syndrome. The passage des Princes is an arcaded street constructed in 1860, leading from the rue de Richelieu to the boulevard des Italiens, notable for the restaurant of Noel Peters. *La grande duchesse de Gérolstein* was successfully revived in 1887 at the Variétés with Judic and in 1890, at the same theatre, with Jeanne Granier.

[2273] Her real name has apparently been lost, although Charles Castle suggests that it was Amilienne André, Pierre Andrieu offers Emilie Andrée, and André de Fouquières settles for Emilienne André. Castle p.47; Andrieu p.75; Fouquières p.17. Alençon was a Bourbon title, and the joke must have turned sour when the duchesse d'Alençon perished in the Bazaar de la Charité fire.

[2274] Harding p.50.

[2275] Zola/Paris p.68. Corneille's *Polyeucte* had been made into an opera by Gounod in 1878; Paul Dukas had written an overture for it in 1891. It may be doubted that there were strings long enough or stout enough for Zola's idea, but Sarah Bernhardt had first been taken on by the Comédie Française when the duc de Morny had a word in the ear of the then Minister, Camille Doucet, who had a word with the administrator Edouard Thierry. Cornelia Otis Skinner: *Madame Sarah*. New York: Houghton Miflin 1966. New edition New York: Paragon 1988 p.35, hereafter cited as Skinner.

[2276] Coolidge p.181.

[2277] Zola/Nana/Holden p.22. Douglas Parmée prefers the more brutal 'knocking shop'. Zola/Nana/Parmée p.4. Bouthemont, in *Au Bonheur des Dames*, refers to the department stores as 'the brothels of business'. Zola/Bonheur p.306

[2278] Ohnet pp.15,58.

[2279] Ohnet p.33. The reference to Bartet is on p.59, to Nuño's stables on p.230.

[2280] Zola/Nana/Parmée p.190.

[2281] Daughter of William Thorn Garner of New York, and sister of Florence Garner, who married Sir William Gordon Cumming, involved in the Tranby Croft Baccarat scandal.

[2282] Anna Gould married Boni de Castellane in New York in March 1895 and left him in January 1905; she subsequently married the duc de Talleyrand-Périgord (d.1937). This fails to explain why Cornelia Otis Skinner characterises her as 'dismal'. Skinner p.297. Bernhardt appeared in Boni de Castellane's *Le Festin de la Mort* in 1904.

[2283] Marie Louise Ritz: *César Ritz, Host to the World*. Paris: Hotel Ritz; London: Bodley Head 1981 p.224. The hotel opened on the 1st June 1898.

http://www.ritz.com/fr/R0100.asp 'I do not think the Ritz for all its modern attractions ever held a hundredth of the charm and elegance of the Hôtel Bristol'. Stoeckl pp.130-1. Ritz had recently returned to Paris after eight years at the Savoy, driven out by the machinations of the housekeeper 'Mrs W', who had given evidence at Wilde's trial. The revelations at the trial and the strictures of Mr Justice Wills – 'It is a condition of things one shudders to contemplate in a first-class hotel' – cannot have endeared Wilde to Ritz, and we may be sure that whereas Liane de Pougy was on the invitation list, Oscar Wilde was not.

[2284] Ford Madox Ford: *Last Post*.   London: The Bodley Head 1928; Harmondsworth: Penguin Books 1948 p.36. The encounter takes place c.1900.

[2285] Zola/Paris p.218.

[2286] Sorel p.25. This was not quite how English actresses expressed it. 'I remember a discussion over a theory Sir Felix Semon, the throat specialist, put forward, that we should act and speak from our stomachs and not from our throats. Mrs Patrick Campbell, with an instinct of true acting but ready at any time to sacrifice what she really thought to a chance of getting a laugh, declared that she refused to act from her stomach, and asked me what I acted with. I said with every bit of my body or not at all.' Vanbrugh pp.94-5.

[2287] Madame Judith: *My Autobiography*. Edited by Paul G'Sell and translated from the French by Mrs Arthur Bell. London: Eveleigh Nash 1912 p.318. Hereafter cited as Judith. Judith (1827-1907), whose real name was Julie Bernat and was nicknamed Blanchette, was the mother of a child by Prince Napoléon. Judith Gautier was named after her.

[2288] Bancroft p.375. The story was related to Squire Bancroft by Louis Delaunay.

[2289] Kurtz p.217.

[2290] Jenny Thénard: *Ma Vie au Théâtre, (choses vues, choses vécues)*. Préface de Jules Clarétie. Paris: Librairie Ambert n.d. p.112. Hereafter cited as Thénard. *Soubrette* is defined in the Larousse de Poche as 'Abigail', which does not I think leave one the wiser.

[2291] Pollock p.143.

[2292] Bashkirtseff p.434. Diary entry for 22nd October 1880.

[2293] Whiteing p.212.

[2294] Sir George Arthur: *Sarah Bernhardt*. London: William Heinemann 1923 p.67. 'Delicious' (délicieuse') is also the description of Samary by André de Fouquières. Fouquières p.190.

[2295] Bolitho p.115.

[2296] Kurtz p.217. It is at Longchamps that Zola's Nana has her greatest triumph.

[2297] Pretty Women p.187. This is misprinted as Monthyon.

[2298] Not to be confused with 'Les Belles de Nuit' (René Clair), starring Gina Lollobrigida, Martine Carol and Gérard Philippe.   (Information from the documentary on Gérard Philippe, France Télévision 2, 16th July 2004.)

[2299] Menpes p.27.

[2300] Healy p.103.

[2301] Menpes p.3.

[2302] Duff Gordon p.108.

[2303] Menpes p.14. The poodle (caniche), known outside France as the French poodle, was obviously the epigone of this. George du Maurier writes of the 'Toutou – a nondescript French lapdog, of no breed known to Englishmen (a regular little beast!) [and the] Loulou – a Pomeranian dog – not much better'. Du Maurier/Trilby p.297n. It was not until the new century, however, that the hairdresser Antoine died his poodle lilac to match the colour of his own hair, and the hair of Lady Mendl (Elsie de Wolfe) blue to match that of her borzoi.

[2304] Maud p.76.

[2305] There is an excellent photograph of this in Borsi/Godoli p.30. Wilde said that it reminded him of Sarah Bernhardt. Hyde 1976 p.361.

[2306] Arthur Lynch: *Human Documents, Character Sketches of Representative Men and Women of the Time*. London: 1896 p.232.

[2307] 'La Samaritaine' was a well, from which Ernest Cognacq took the name of his nearby shop; also a play by Rostand, with Bernhardt, first staged at the Théâtre de la Renaissance 13th April 1897.

[2308] Carltheater, Vienna, January 1898.

[2309] Whiteing p.39.

[2310] Guy de Maupassant: *Best Short Stories*. Ware, Herts: Wordsworth 1997 p.226.

[2311] Zola/Pot-Bouille p.130. Professor Nelson's decision not to translate 'Parisienne' is itself revealing. Nana is also a 'big, sturdy girl'. Zola/Nana/Parmée p.274.

[2312] Maud p.200.

[2313] Racowitza p.291.

[2314] Laver p.49. Huysmans' father was from Breda in the Netherlands. Christened Charles Georges, Huysmans later changed his name first to Karl Joris then to Joris-Karl, an insistence on his Dutch paternity. His French mother remarried a Monsieur Og.

[2315] This is discussed in Maurice Donnay: *Autour du Chat Noir*. Paris: Bernard Grasset 1926 pp.11-12.

[2316] James/Ambassadors pp.165,166.

[2317] Dumas p.vii.

[2318] De l'Estoc wrote under the name Gyz-El and her real name was Marie-Elise Courbe.

[2319] Reade p.2.

[2320] Pretty Women p.16.

[2321] 'It was the correct thing a few years since to have slept at least one night with Océana'. Pretty Women p.146.

[2322] The model in Renoir's 'La Loge' of 1874, now in the Courtauld Institute, London. The mistress of Lhiabaster the newspaper proprietor, who called herself Marie Lhiabaster, was also known as Gueule-de-Raie – perhaps they were the same person? Lhiabaster's fortune was lost in the crash of 1882.

[2323] Elina Denizane, 11 rue de Miromesnil.

[2324] Sherard/Maupassant pp.1-10. Various myths grew up around her, not least that the events of the story never happened. See Steegmuller/Maupassant p.105.

[2325] 'Putain bien connue'. Edmond et Jules de Goncourt: *Journal, Mémoires de la vie littéraire*. Vol. III. Paris: Robert Laffont 1956 p.196.

[2326] *The Life and Memoirs of Sarah Barnum*; Goncourt/Baldick p.339; Pretty Women p.40.

[2327] Symons pp.13,21-2. Zola enters the convention when in *Nana* he names one of his prostitutes Tata Néné, which one might perhaps translate as Auntie Big Tits.

[2328] Symons p.92. Esmé is an error for Edmée.

[2329] Cate p.27. Henri Perruchot also refers to the first two, and adds Rosa la Rouge. Henri Perruchot: 'Une vie ardente' in Adhémar pp.14,18.

[2330] Metropolitan Museum of Art, New York, ref. 67.187.108. Information from the accompanying label.

[2331] Jean-Gabriel Domergue: 'Les femmes et Lautrec', in Adhémar p.155.

[2332] Fouquières pp.87,263.

[2333] Sir Edward Malet: *Shifting Scenes*. London: John Murray 1901 p.311.

[2334] Arthur Vanderbilt II: *Fortune's Children, the Fall of the House of Vanderbilt*. London: Michael Joseph n.d. p.203.

[2335] Fouquières p.19.

[2336] Zola/L'Œuvre p.81. See also pp.288,310,313 for more resemblances between Irma Bécot and Nana Coupeau.

[2337] Sherard 1908 p.17. The Norman poet Charles Frémine also worked for *Le Rappel*, where, said Laurent Tailhade, 'he polishes Vacquerie's boots'. Tailhade p.116.

[2338] Named after the contemporary scientist Émile Baudot (1845-1903). One also notes the architect Anatole de Baudot (1834-1915). The Hôtel Baudy at Giverny was the favourite social space of the local artists.

[2339] Zola/Nana/Holden p.202. Danglars is of course the name of Count of Monte Cristo.

[2340] Low p.315.

[2341] There is a photograph of Méry Laurent with Mallarmé looking like a comfortable bourgeois in Hartmann p.95. This is dated 25th February 1896.

[2342] A photograph of all four is reproduced in Rewald p.52.

[2343] Formerly the Théâtre de Ville until 1880, it was the Théâtre Sarah Bernhardt from 1899 to 1967. It is now the Théâtre de la Ville again.

[2344] Shercliff p.184. I have traced Marie Laurent as far as January 1900 when she appeared with Edouard de Max in Jean Richepin's *La Gitane*, directed by Antoine. Antoine noted that it was a lamentable failure, 'un four épouvantable'. Antoine p.153.

[2345] Matthews p.67.

[2346] Du Maurier/Martian p.187. The name can still be read, but the hotel no longer exists as such, having been absorbed by the Hôtel Saint-James et Albany, which fronts on the parallel rue de Rivoli

[2347] Victor Masséna, subsequently Prince of Essling, was the grandson of Napoléon I's marshal, a man who was also fond of beautiful spoils, but who used them to enrich himself rather than the reverse.

[2348] 'A hare-brained, extravagant, reckless, prodigal but not vicious *viveur*, the type of the Boulevardier, loving theatres for the sake of the pretty actresses, and the hero of countless more or less risqué adventures, one of which was graphically related by Daudet in his *Rois en Exil*'. Van der Velde Volume II p.214. 'Citron', who also kept the cocotte Fanny Robert, predeceased his father Willem III (1817-1890), who was therefore succeeded by the daughter of his old age, good Queen Wilhelmina (1880-1962). Willem III had in own day been a prodigal Paris *viveur*, keeping the American Elisa Parker. The Dutch Court almost exclusively spoke French.

[2349] Polly Binder: *The Truth about Cora Pearl*. London: Weidenfeld & Nicolson 1986 p.10. This book boasts neither footnotes nor bibliography.

[2350] Invented in 1879.

[2351] W.H. Holden: *The Pearl from Plymouth – Eliza Emma Crouch alias Cora Pearl*. With notes on some of her celebrated contemporaries. London: British General & Technical Press 1950. Virginia Rounding says precisely, 8th July, at 8 rue de Bassano. Virginia Rounding: *Grandes Horizontales, The Lives and Legends of Four Nineteenth Century Courtesans*. London: Bloomsbury 2003.

[2352] Harrison p.253.

[2353] Thomas Hardy: *The Return of the Native*. 1878. London: Macmillan Library edition 1949 pp.358,284.

[2354] Henri Murger: *Vie de Bohème*. Translated by Norman Cameron. London: The Folio Society 1960 p.74.

[2355] Thomas Hardy: *The Woodlanders*. 1887. Edited with an introduction and Notes by Patricia Ingham. London: Penguin 1997 p.229. Dr Ingham points out (p.404) that *Une femme de trente ans* refers to Balzac's novel of that name, dating to 1832.

[2356] Thomas Hardy: *The Well-Beloved, A Sketch of a Temperament*. 1897. New Wessex Edition. Introduction by J. Hillis Miller and Notes by Edward Mendelson. London: Macmillan 1975 pp.182,188. This novel played its part in forming Proust's *A la Recherche du Temps Perdu*.

[2357] Catherine Anne Cline: *E.D. Morel 1873-1924, The Strategies of Protest*. Belfast: Blackstaff Press 1980 pp.1-3.

[2358] Before arriving in Paris he and his wife stayed at the Hôtel d'Albion in Rouen. 'All Romances end at marriage,' he reflected in *Far from the Madding Crowd*. The Tuileries Gardens were painted at about this time by Monet (1876).

[2359] Zola/Bonheur p.98.

[2360] Gramont p.168. I take Rose d'Avaray to be the 'Mademoiselle D'Avaray' referred to in Moore/Memoirs pp.18-20, though he calls her 'an actress of the Palais Royal'. Here she is apparently the mistress of the painter Gervex. She seems to have born a great resemblance to the actress Jeanne Samary, but unreliability appears to have run in the family. Fouquières p.93. 'Mme de Mercy-Argenteau's claim to have been '[Napoléon III's] last love' can be taken no more seriously than the other extravagant claims she makes in that work of fiction which she calls her Memoirs.' Kurtz p.186n.

[2361] Painter I p.87.

[2362] I take this to be the 'Prince Charles de Furstemberg' (Karl-Egon von Fürstenberg, married to Dorothée de Talleyrand-Périgord) of the Austrian Embassy and 76 avenue Marceau mentioned by André de Fouquières. Fouquières says of him that he was 'fit parti, avant 1914, de cette brillante phalange de gentilshommes, "coqueluches" de tous salons où l'on appréciait leur élégance, leur prestance de cavalier, leurs qualités de valseurs.' Fouquières p.152. If so, he was probably that 'ultra-Catholic Austrian prince' referred to by Proust, who presided over 'the most brilliant salon in Paris'. Proust/Ombre p.92.

[2363] From Haiti, known as the 'comtesse noire'. Pretty Women pp.83,150. This source describes Hayman (who is spelled Heymann) as 'any age between twenty and thirty […] hailing from the French colonies', but confirms Michael Herbert as her lover.

[2364] This cocotte, whose father is English, specialises in titled lovers. Zola/Nana/Parmée p.88.

[2365] Silverman p.50.

[2366] Maupassant/Bel Ami p.146.

[2367] Colette 1963 p.85.

[2368] See the painting by C. Bouginet (1814-1886): 'The Seamstress', Victoria & Albert Museum ref. 1564-69.

[2369] 'Midinettes' by Steinlen (1900) is reproduced in Cate fig.79. One must assume that Zola derived some of his information from Marie Monnier (1865-1900), the mistress of his disciple Paul Alexis, who worked in a London department store until Alexis brought her home in 1884 and married in 1888.

[2370] English Officer p.83.

[2371] 'Margouin' is argot for milliner. Louise worked for Renée Vert, whom Lautrec had drawn some years before.

[2372] Dietschy p.104. The character Jean de Brive, in Ohnet's *Lise Fleuron* of 1884, is also a nice fellow who dabbles in stocks and lives in the rue Taitbout, as a suitable address for a young fashionable man-about-town who lives on his wits. Ohnet p.69. Lily Texier should not be confused with Marie Texier, the *poule* with whom Charles-Louis Philippe was connected and who appears in his novella, *Bubu de Montparnasse*. Paris: La Revue Blanche 1910; new edition Grasset 2005.

[2373] Maupassant/Fifi p.135.

[2374] Waddington 1914 p.216.

[2375] van der Velde Volume II p.248.

[2376] Bashkirtseff p.516.

[2377] Adolphus p.17.

[2378] Thaddeus pp.19-20.

[2379] Rothenstein Volume I p.92.

[2380] Siegel pp.41-2.

[2381] Jules Barbey d'Aurevilly: *Les Diaboliques*. Introduction by Peter Quennell (no translator named). London: Paul Elek 1947 p.229. They perhaps feasted on, rather than with, those who paid them. This use of the description panther (there was also an anarchist group, les panthères) needs to be remembered when reading that Henri de Jouvenel's lover madame de Comminges was called 'la panthère'.

[2382] Ludovici pp.26-7.

[2383] Robert H. Sherard: 'Notes from Paris', *The Author* October 1892 p.163.

[2384] Tailhade p.11.

[2385] Vechten p.44 and n.

[2386] Du Maurier/Trilby p.80.

[2387] McMillan pp.6-12.

[2388] McMillan pp.63,64,68.

[2389] McMillan p.65.

[2390] Zola/Bonheur p.183.

[2391] George Moore had once set his cap at her, and it is surprising that he did not return to the attempt after her divorce. Her husband was Ranulphe Marie Eustache d'Osmond, a name favoured by Henry James.

[2392] Mistinguett p.22.

[2393] Susan Bachrach: *Dames Employées: The Feminization of Postal Work in Nineteenth-century France.* New York : Institute for Research in History / Haworth Press 1984.

[2394] Fox p.6.

[2395] Ladurée is at 16 rue Royale. The famous Rumpelmayer at 226 rue de Rivoli, next to Galignani, opened in 1903, and is now known as Angelina. It was last 'restored' in May 2005.

[2396] Sometimes spelled Solié.

[2397] Guy de Maupassant: 'The Christening' in Maupassant/Inn p.203.

[2398] Marchesi p.9.

[2399] Marchesi p.223.

[2400] Ironically, this has more force in English than in French, where 'Paris soi-même' is not so explicitly a gendered term.

[2401] Fox p.297.

[2402] Low pp.307-8.

[2403] Belloc 1943 p.125.

[2404] Coolidge p.243. Diary entries for 15th and 23rd May 1893. Would Coolidge have known that an earlier duc de Gramont (Agénor, who died in 1880) had kept Marie Duplessis, Dumas' dame aux camélias?

[2405] March p.233. March nevertheless insists that although 'some women had undoubtedly been *petroleuses* [...] there were no bands of such women as the rumour referred to'. *Ibidem* p.293.

[2406] Lockspeiser p.110n.

[2407] Kurtz p.217.

[2408] Starkie p.44.

[2409] 'Le coucher de Sapho', Musée cantonale des Beaux Arts, Lausanne.

[2410] Huysmans/Baldick p.112.

[2411] Arkell p.112.

[2412] Diana Holmes: *Rachilde, – Decadence, Gender and the Woman Writer.* Oxford and New York: Berg 2001 p.114. The cross-gendered titles of the two books mentioned was echoed in the play *Madame le Diable* (Théâtre de la Renaissance, with Jeanne Granier).

[2413] Pretty Women p.71.

[2414] Could this have been at no. 4? In May 2004, this was adorned by a poster in which a lady dressed in a champagne coupe announced 'Les hôtesses en sein nu ont le plaisir de vous recevoir du lundi au vendredi de 15h à l'aube, le samedi à partir de 16h. Fermeture dimanche.'

[2415] Casselaer p.23; Julian Chevalier: *Inversion sexuelle* 1893. Van Casselaer calls this book 'the main source of relatively scientific information'. Chevalier took the line that there was an increase in 'saphism' caused by the masculinisation of women through sport, smoking, the use of slang and easy social relationships as students. This does not seem scientific sociology, even 'relatively'.

[2416] Musée de l'Art Modern et Contemporaine, Strasbourg.

[2417] Musée d'Orsay ref. RF 1937-8.

[2418] There is a photograph of her in Hartmann p.39. The sister of Armand duc de Guiche, she was known as the Red Duchess. She appears as the duchesse Clitoressa in Djuna Barnes: *Ladies Almanack*. Privately printed 1928.

[2419] This was Hélène, née Rothschild. The baronne became the lover of Renée Vivien, whom she compelled to live 'in a dark, suffocating, incense filled apartment whose windows were nailed shut'. Rachel Mesch: *The Hysteric's Revenge, French Women Writers at the Fin de Siècle*. Nashville: Vanderbilt University Press 2006 p.59. She married baron van Zuylen de Nyvelt in 1887, and was known variously as 'The Master' or 'La Brioche', depending upon where one stood with her. The baron was of Dutch descent, and had a property near Utrecht. He was known for his enthusiasm both for horses and for horsepower. The two did not live together.

[2420] Cossart pp.83-5.

[2421] Joan Schenkar: *Truly Wilde – The Unsettling Story of Dolly Wilde, Oscar Wilde's Unusual Niece*. London: Virago 2000 p.381. Hereafter cited as Schenkar.

[2422] Casselaer p.84.

[2423] Casselaer p.84.

[2424] Mirbeau p.92. Mirbeau's Célestine herself has a brief affaire out of curiosity with a fellow servant, Clémence (Cléclé), for whom 'it was a passion ever since she had been seduced by one of her mistresses, a General's wife' *ibid.* p.210.

[2425] Sorel pp.23,48.

[2426] Jill Davis: 'The New Woman and the new life' in Viv Gardner & Susan Rutherford (edd.): *The New Woman and Her Sisters, Feminism and Theatre 1850-1914*. Hemel Hempstead: Harvester Wheatsheaf 1992 p.25.

[2427] Orczy p.143. This taste for dubious company was persistent. 'Though [Anastasia] is the mother of the Crown Princess of Germany and related to all these people who are turning Europe upside down at the present moment, she lives only for gambling; she discusses systems with the tarts, and knows all the croupiers, those who spin well and those who spin badly.' Sermoneta, p.245.

[2428] Battersby p.155.

[2429] Casselaer p.47; Bashkirtseff p.464. Diary entry for 1st May 1881.

[2430] Fouquières pp.200-1. After her death (she was found gassed in her flat), the obsequies were led by Sacha Guitry.

[2431] In 1944, Colette had a quiet joke at Polaire's expense when in *Gigi* she gave her a 'dancing partner' called Sandomir, a skating instructor who forsakes her for the cocotte Liane d'Excelmans.

[2432] Boulestin pp.85,92. Conversely, when Colette confessed to Jean Lorrain a passion for a woman who was giving her piano lessons, Lorrain pointed out that 'she' was a man. Frank Richardson (1871-1917), playwright and novelist.

[2433] Crosland pp.96-7,141-2.

[2434] Whiteing p.156.

[2435] Nordau p.93. Bonheur's reputation has survived better as a cross-dresser than as a painter, but that is more than can be said for the other fashionable horse painter of the day, René Princeteau (1843-1914), now chiefly to be discovered in the biography of Toulouse-Lautrec, who studied under him, no easy task for Princeteau was deaf-mute.

[2436] Grenville-Murray p.73.

[2437] There is a photograph of Gallifet in Hartmann p.37.

[2438] Casselaer p.43. Gunderax is a mistake for Ganderax: Casselaer is cavalier with names, referring for example to Karl-Joris Huysmans instead the more usual Joris-Karl. There may be something about writing about inversion that causes such confusion.

[2439] Natalie Clifford Barney edited an in memoriam Volume called *In Memory of Dorothy Ierne Wilde: Oscaria*. Dijon: Darantière 1951.

[2440] Schenkar pp.31,144,190.

[2441] Lucie Delarue-Mardrus: *Les Amours d'Oscar Wilde*. Paris: Flammarion 1930. She was the wife of Joseph-Charles Mardrus, who was working on his translation (or 'perfumed travesty' according to the Arabist Geert Jan van Gelder, *TLS* 23/01/09, p.7) into French of the *Thousand and One Nights*. This suitably esoteric task was realised in sixteen Volumes between 1898 and 1904 by the Éditions de la Revue Blanche. The two separated. Mardrus is said to have been born in Egypt with the rank of emir, which must have helped him identify with his subject. Casselaer p.101. There is a photograph of Lucie Delarue-Mardrus in Hartmann p.87.

[2442] Reproduced in Conway opp. p.179. Chapter XVII is devoted to Whistler.

[2443] The Yellow Book writer Ella d'Arcy also lived in the rue Jacob in her last years in the 1930s. 'In the summer she liked to sit in the sun in front of the Café des Deux Magots, drinking bock and watching the young Bohemians stroll by. They reminded her of the happy days of her youth'. Mix p.236. Wilde would eat at Chez Béchet at number 42 rue Jacob in his last period.

[2444] Schenkar pp.160-1. Vivien (née Pauline Tarn) lived in Paris in a pension with Violet Shilleto from 1890 to 1893; and then after an American period, returned to Paris in 1898. Shilleto, who died in June 1901, was a lover of Marcelle Senard and Mabel Gunson Evans Dodge Luhan.

[2445] Schenkar pp.166,168. Alice Barney was of Jewish descent. The phrasing ran in the family, Oscar once addressing Reggie Turner as 'you dear little Jew'. Not many Jews would be happy under this form of philo-semitism.

[2446] George Wickes: *The Amazon of Letters, The Life and Loves of Natalie Barney.* New York: G.P. Putnam's Sons 1976 Chapters I-VIII; Miron Grindea: obituary of Natalie Clifford Barney, London: *The Times* 4th January 1972.

[2447] His real name was François Carcopino.

[2448] Mac-Orlan was no more Irish (or Scots) than either Philothée O'Neddy or Max O'Rell, his real name being Pierre Dumarchey. He arrived in Paris in 1898 with the ambition of becoming a painter. http://www.airlibre.com/MacOrlan.html

[2449] Aston p.115.

[2450] The transgressiveness of Bernhardt's Hamlet is reinforced by Mucha's poster, where the head was that of Bernhardt, but the body that of a model.

[2451] Whiteing p.180.

[2452] Whiteing p.63.

[2453] Paris: Chamuel n.d.

[2454] Rachel Mesch: *The Hysteric's Revenge, French Women Writers at the Fin de Siècle.* Nashville: Vanderbilt University Press 2006.

[2455] Johnson pp.393-4

[2456] Volume 48, issue 4 (August 1894).

[2457] Editor of *The Atlantic M*onthly.

[2458] Paris: 1885.

[2459] Paris: Hachette 1904.

[2460] For further information on Bentzon see Joan M. West: 'America and American Literature in the Essays of Th. Bentzon: Creating the Image of an Independent Cultural Identity' in *History of European Ideas* 1987 Volume 8 (4-5) pp.521-535. The quotation from Banville is in Steegmuller/Maupassant p.286.

[2461] Dearly (Lucien Paul Marie-Joseph Rolland 1874-1943) began with an English mime troupe known in France as 'Les Willi-Willi', substituting for an actor called Dealy and taking his name as well, later changing this to Dearly. Harding p.112.

[2462] Osgood p.65.

[2463] *Tartuffe, Hernani* and *Théodora*; as well *The Marriage of Figaro* (but he missed the music) and *Œdipus Rex* with Mounet-Sully. He also spent time in the Musée de Cluny and the Egyptian and Assyrian galleries of the Louvre.

[2464] Peter Gay: *Freud, A Life for Our Time.* London: J.M. Dent 1988 p.49. The statue by Falguière of Charcot (1825-1893) that formerly stood in front of the Salpetrière was melted down by the Germans in 1942.

[2465] Reade p.29.

[2466] Ambroise Vollard: *Recollections of a Picture Dealer.* London: Constable 1936 p.181.

[2467] This did not stop the great ball held at Versailles being characterised by 'deplorable mismanagement', or the outstanding beauty at it being the Countess of Dudley. Sir Horace Rumbold: *Further Recollections of a Diplomatist.* London: Edwin Arnold 1903 p.170.

[2468] James/Sketches p.6. Letter of 22nd November 1875.

[2469] Zola/L'Assommoir p.275.

[2470] Zola/Nana/Holden p.272. This can be discussed as a starting point for *Dr Jekyll and Mr Hyde*, six years later.

[2471] Mirbeau pp.15,36,94.

[2472] Hemmings 1977 p.137.

[2473] Emile Zola: *La Joie de Vivre*. 1884. Translated as *Zest for Life* by Jean Stewart. London: Elek 1955 p.118.

[2474] Richard Pine: *Oscar Wilde*. Dublin: Gill & Macmillan 1986 p.83; McCormack p.81; Knox p.22; Hichens 1999 p.46.

[2475] Tydeman/Price p.120; McKenna p.169. No sources given.

[2476] Langlade pp.54,67,148,163. Unfortunately, as he further adds that Wilde was with his mother and Frank Miles at the first night of *Patience* (23rd April 1881), this part of the story diminishes rather than increases in probability. In the well-known painting by Frith of the General Private View for the Royal Academy Summer Exhibition on 29th April 1881, a reproduction of which is on the cover of Langlade's book, Wilde is clearly wearing a lily. For Langlade himself, citing anonymous callers at Lady Wilde's house in 1884, Wilde always wore a carnation (though the colour is not specified). *Ibidem* p.110.

[2477] Osgood p.69.

[2478] Rupert Croft-Cooke: *Bosie, The Story of Lord Alfred Douglas, His Friends and Enemies*. London: W.H. Allen1963 p.58. It is curious that Bourget was greatly taken with Margaret, one of the daughters of the homosexual John Addington Symonds, whom he described as 'Belle à se mettre à genoux devant elle' – beautiful enough to make one go down on one's knees in front of her. Leaf p.192n.

[2479] Dennis Proctor (ed.): *The Autobiography of G. Lowes Dickinson, and Other Unpublished Writings*. London: Duckworth 1973 pp.140,150. Roger Fry's portrait of Dickinson, now in the Courtauld, dates to 1893.

[2480] Leslie p.64. It is possible to date this encounter to 1st September 1898. When Loti was received by Lord Curzon in India, the Viceroy thought that 'although he curled his hair and painted his cheeks' he 'seemed "otherwise to be a very clever and cultivated little man"' – a rare example of Curzon's prejudices wavering. David Gilmour: *Curzon, Imperial Statesman 1859–1925*. London: John Murray 1994 p.208.

[2481] Quoted in Whiteing 1900p.206. 'Engleesh! Aoh yays!' seems to have been a common taunt in the streets.

[2482] Maupassant/Fifi p.54. H.N.P. Sloman's translation is harsher:
In fact she was one of those fanatically obstinate Puritan spinsters, so common in England, who haunt the hotel dining rooms of Europe, spoil Italy, poison Switzerland and make the charming Mediterranean towns impossible, taking everywhere with them their strange crazes, the morals of a fossilized Vestal Virgin, their indescribable clothes and a kind of smell of india-rubber, as if they were put away at night in an indiarubber bag.
Maupassant/Harriet p.149.

[2483] Thomas Mann: *Buddenbrooks* (1902); translated by H.T. Lowe-Porter 1924. Harmondsworth: Penguin Books 1957p.68.

[2484] Laver p.255. Laver adds, 'Huysmans did not care for the English under any circumstances'.

[2485] Between consumer and consumed there appears to have been no great difference; this is Huysmans at his most Zola-esque. J.-K. Huysmans: *À Rebours*. London: The Fortune Press n.d. [1946] p.114.

[2486] Victoria Glendinning: *Vita, the Life of V. Sackville-West*. London: Weidenfeld & Nicolson 1983 pp.18,21.

[2487] Pretty Women p.142.

[2488] Ohnet p.123.

[2489] Quoted in Tint p.147. Tint adds 'One might fervently hope that he had his tongue in his cheek. Nothing is more unlikely.'

[2490] Locke p.65.

[2491] Locke, with his 'handsome, slightly ravaged face', is described by his publisher's historians as 'the quintessential Bodley Head novelist of the period'. Lambert/Ratcliffe pp.144, 145. Locke was born in Demerara, and educated in Trinidad and at Cambridge. He was 'a keen and active supporter of Zola' (*ibid.* p.192).

[2492] Elizabeth Robins: *Votes for Women!* first performed in 1907 and published in 1909. Jean Chothia (ed.): *The New Woman and Other Emancipated Woman Plays*. Oxford: Oxford University Press 1998 p.145.

[2493] Anon: *Teleny, or The Reverse of the Medal*. Edited with an introduction by John McRae. London: Gay Mens Press 1986, second impression 1989 p.52.

[2494] Marcel Proust: *A l'ombre des jeunes filles en fleurs*, tome I p.111 in the France Loisirs edition, Paris 1988; and p.83 in James Grieve's English translation, London: Penguin 2003.

[2495] Somerville/Ross pp.53-5. Written in January 1895. The insistence of a peculiarly English quality in the bonnet lends meaning to Wilde's references to Lady Chiltern in *An Ideal Husband*.

[2496] Dumas wrote of Marguerite that 'even her thinness became her', implying a different construction of what was ordinarily becoming. Dumas p. 170.

[2497] Polnay p.46. 'Girls' in its specific sense of streetwalkers, naturally.

[2498] Anthony Glyn: *Elinor Glyn, A Biography*. London: Hutchinson 1957 pp.72,56.

[2499] Low p.31.

[2500] Dietschy p.123.

[2501] Belloc 1943 p.242.

[2502] Maugham pp.134-5.

[2503] Zola/Pot-Bouille p.169.

[2504] Skinner p.208.

[2505] Sir George Arthur: *A Septuagenarian's Scrapbook*. London: Thornton Butterworth 1932 p.71. My translation.

[2506] c.23rd February 1893. Holland & Rupert Hart-Davis p.555. 'Frankie' Forbes-Robertson was the sister of Johnston, Norman, Eric and Ian. Wilde had been re-reading *Salomé*, and said he was sending Frances 'a copy in Tyrian purple and tired silver', a useful allegory of his idea of how *Salomé* should make an impact. Wilde had an especial *tendresse* for her, naming her as one of the only two people who should be sent a typescript copy of *De Profundis* (the other was Adela

Schuster), adding that she could show it to her brother Ian. He also asked Ross to send her a copy of *The Ballad of Reading Gaol* when it was published (adding mysteriously 'I suppose I would have no right to send Miss Schuster one?'). She and her husband Henry Dawes Harrod invited Wilde to stay with them in England in 1899, and he sent her a copy of the limited edition of *The Importance of being Earnest.* She deserves a larger place in the list of those who did not turn from Wilde than she has been accorded, an attitude she passed to her son, Sir Roy Harrod.

[2507] Jürgen Habermas: 'Modernity – An Incomplete Project'. Translated by Seyla Ben-Habib.   In Hal Forster (ed.): *The Anti-Æsthetic, Essays in Post-Modern Culture.* Port Townsend, Washington 1983 p.14.

[2508] Tydeman/Price p.14.

[2509] Tydeman/Price p.30. Puffett p.2, citing an article by Ellmann.

[2510] I have identified 13è articles, conference papers or chapters published between 2001 and 2015.

[2511] Ellmann p.324. Hyde, who does not name Rigo, calls him 'the leader of the Tziganer orchestra', a word apparently of Hyde's own invention.   Hyde 1976 p.131.

[2512] *Née* Clara Ward of Detroit, she had married Prince Joseph Caraman-Chimay in 1890. They were divorced in 1898. Déclassée, and therefore, no longer received in Society, Rigo seems to have used her as a courtesan, and at one time she appeared in 'tableaux vivants' at the Folies Bergère, her contract stipulating that she and Rigo got married, an assertion of the moral order in an unlikely context. She left Rigo for Giuseppe Ricciardi, who is said to have superintended the railway that took sightseers up Vesuvius. He divorced her after seven years, and she married a man reported to be Ricciardi's driver. She died in 1916 in Padua.

[2513]   Ralph Nevill: *Unconventional Memories.* London: Hutchinson 1923; Louÿs/Tinan p.300n.

[2514]   de Lara p.227; 'La belle époque des Tziganes', sleevenotes for the L.P. recording of 'La Veuve Joyeuse', Philips P 77.106 L, 1956; Symons p.14; Newnham-Davis p.13.

[2515] Healy p.337.

[2516] Du Maurier/Trilby p.302.

[2517] Painter I p.147; Hartmann p.29. There is a photograph of Prince and Princess de Caraman-Chimay *ibid.*; perhaps the very one that the Baron de Charlus treasured. Proust/Ombte p.345.

[2518] Baroness Orczy: *Links in the Chain of Life.* London: Hutchinson & Co. 1947 p.43.

[2519] Beerbohm/Tree p.51.

[2520] Nevill 1926 pp.225-6. 'Boldi's languorous eyes rolled in accompaniment to his violin at the Ritz.' Mott pp.76-7.

[2521] Ernest Dimnet: *My Old World.* London: Jonathan Cape 1935 p.60. Wilde was an admirer of Reni's picture of St Sebastian, which he went to see in Genoa in 1877. Lindsay Kemp linked two traditions when in the 1970s his production of *Salomé* featured Jokanaan being shot to death with arrows.

[2522] Healy p.330.

[2523] Merrill pp.10-12.

[2524] Richard Ellmann: 'Overtures to Wilde's Salomé', in Puffett p.34. The conflicts within the play as representing conflicts within Wilde are more convincingly treated in Knox, notably p.xvi.

[2525] Newnham-Davis p.39. Newnham-Davis goes on 'At one time it used to be very smart indeed, but its cuisine then was no better than it is now'.

[2526] Harris p.269.

[2527] Nevill p.15. In exile, Wilde dined twice at Maire's, with Frank Harris and with Lord Alfred Douglas, and lunched there once with the latter. Ellmann pp.756,801, 828.

[2528] Mistinguett p.28.

[2529] This was not her real name, which was Puenta Valga, Otero presumably suggesting ôter, to remove one's clothes.

[2530] My translation. Robert Sayre: 'De Huysmans à Oscar Wilde: néo-romantisme et "décadence" dans la littérature française et anglaise.' 'Quarante-huit/Quatorze' 1848-1914, Conférences du Musée d'Orsay 6. Paris: Réunion des Musées Nationaux 1994 p.27.

[2531] Gomez Carillo: 'Comment Oscar Wilde rêva de Salomé', La Plume 1902 pp.1147-52. Translated as 'How Oscar Wilde Dreamed of Salomé', Mikhail Volume II pp.192-5. Mikhail does not date the appearance of the article in La Plume beyond the year, and his usual meticulous footnoting falls away.

[2532] Quoted by Kerry Powell: Women and Victorian Theatre. Cambridge: Cambridge University Press 1997 p.167. Hereafter cited as Powell 1997.

[2533] Puffett p.175 n.10; Ellmann cited ibid. p.2. It is not clear whether n.10 (an endnote) is Ellmann's or Puffett's. Spanish speakers, and I am not one of them, may consult José Ismael Gutierrez: 'Dos aceramientos a un motivo literario de fin de siglio: la Salomé de Oscar Wilde y la de Enrique Gomez Carillo.' Hispanic Review Volume 63 no 3 Summer 1995.

[2534] Aquien/Salomé p.9.

[2535] Symons p.92. D'Auban appeared thus in, of all things, a pantomime of Robinson Crusoe; it apparently did her no harm, for in 1882 she played Nelly Bly in Sydney Grundy's The Vicar of Bray at the Globe Theatre.

[2536] Oscar Wilde to Leonard Smithers 2nd September 1900. Holland and Hart-Davis p.1196.

[2537] The possible Beardsley translation is mentioned by Pascal Aquien in Aquien/Salomé p.25, and by Caspar Wintermans in Caspar Wintermans: Alfred Douglas: A Poet's Life and His Finest Work. London: Peter Owen 2007 p.37. Hereafter cited as Wintermans. Holland's remark is in Oscar Wilde: Salomé. Introduction and translation by Vyvyan Holland. London: The Folio Society 1977 unnumbered page.

[2538] Wintermans pp.37-8.

[2539] Virginie Pouzet-Duzer: Les voiles de Salomé Labyrinthique errance, virevoltes et volutes http://lesvoilesdesalome.hautetfort.com/

[2540] Ably treated by divers hands in Dottin-Orsini.

2541 Aquien/Salomé p.9.

2542 The whole poem is printed in Puffett pp.16-18.

2543 This seems excessive, which is underemphasised in the Wilde accounts. Des Esseintes owns two versions of Moreau's 'Salomé', and they are described (together with the sensations they evoke) in great detail. Not surprisingly, Des Esseintes also collects Odilon Redon. Huysmans/Baldick pp.63-9,72-3. One may note that the Impressionists 'loathed' Moreau. Lazzaro p.26n.

2544 Now in the Musée d'Orsay, ref. RF 104, and I believe has hitherto escaped the attention of Wilde scholars.

2545 Now in the Metropolitan Museum of Art, New York. Wilde too thought Regnault's Salomé more gypsy than Judaean.

2546 Musée d'Orsay, ref. RF 1997-16.

2547 Laurent Croizier: Programme notes for Salomé. Nice: Opéra de Nice 2005 p.9.

2548 Bonnat's picture is in the Panthéon. St Denis is said to have picked up his head and walked off with it. His statue in the church of St-Denis in Varenne l'Arconce, Seine-et-Loire shows him holding his head with a hand under its chin. He looks rather surprised.

2549 Ref. INV.1758.

2550 Musée d'Orsay, ref. RF 22.

2551 Reproduced in J.L. Tancock: The Sculpture of Auguste Rodin. Philadelphia: Philadelphia Museum of Modern Art 1976 p.206. I am not clear if this refers to the 1878 bust, of which there is an example in Metropolitan Museum of Art, New York ref.93.11.

2552 Zola/Nana/Parmée p.136.

2553 Monique Dubar: 'Oscar Wilde et Strauss, ou le corps dansant' in Dottin-Orsini p.114.

2554 English Officer p.28.

2555 8 boulevard des Italiens.

2556 Frazier p.261. Moore published the piece as 'A Reaction' in The Speaker 13th July 1895, and reprinted it as 'After Parsifal' as a supplement to the same journal 30th November 1895. As Frazier points out, it was a dangerous time to be publishing homoerotic work, however covert, but Moore adds to the contemporary view of Wagner's music as decadent, and attracting the support of decadents.

2557 Steegmuller/Maupassant p.279.

2558 Dorian Gray owns a copy of Emaux et Camées, 'Charpentier's Japanese-paper edition, with the Jacquemart etching. The binding was of citron-green leather, with a design of gilt trellis-work and dotted pomegranates'.

2559 One of the Trois Contes, published by Charpentier in April 1877. Hérodias is an unusual version of the name usually rendered Hérodiade in French, though always Herodias in English and German. Mireille Dottin-Orsini has pointed out the loading of the French name with associations of 'hero', 'diadem' and 'diamond', associations that are attenuated in English, and the loading of Salomé with associations of 'Salomon', Mireille Dottin-Orsini: 'Le banquet d'Hérode' in Dottin-Orsini p.21. The other loading is with Goncourt's Jewish 'Manette Salomon'. These associations vanish with the English 'Solomon'. The Hebrew association is with 'shalom', peace, viâ the name usually transliterated as Shulamith ולמית. The English variant pronunciation of Salomé, *viz.* Salóme, is on the whole to be deplored.

[2560] I have used the editions *Hérodias*. Postface de Julien Cendres. n.p: Éditions Mille et Une Nuits 2000 and *Trois Contes*. Translated as *Three Tales* with an Introduction by Robert Baldick. London: Penguin Books 1961. Both 'Jokanaan' and 'Jochanaan' are to be found in the German translations of *Salomé*, and the programmes and libretto of the opera.

[2561] Roland Tenschert: 'Strauss as Librettist'. Puffett p.36.

[2562] There is an odd sequel to this. According to Derrick Puffett, 'Wilde admired Flaubert enormously. He copied shamelessly from *Hérodias* and affected not to understand when the older man failed to appreciate the compliment'. Puffett p.2. This is sourced from John Espey and Richard Ellmann: *Oscar Wilde, Two Approaches*. Los Angeles: William Andrews Clark Memorial Library 1977 p.21, a citation which reads 'But, tell me now, is Flaubert still read? I regret to say we no longer speak: he, most foolishly, objects to the use of those few details I borrowed from him in my *Salomé…*' Puffett does not source this further, and I have not seen Espey and Ellmann, but the problem is that Flaubert died in 1880, which makes nonsense of the passage. Could 'Flaubert' have been a slip for 'Mallarmé'? If so, this would radically alter our idea of the relations between the two. Be that as it may, .it is possibly Puffett who unwittingly misled Laurent Crozier into calling Strauss' *Salomé* 'après la pièce d'Oscar Wilde, elle-même écrite après *l'Hérodiade* de Flaubert'. Laurent Crozier: Programme notes for the Opéra de Nice production, directed by Jean-Louis Pichon and conducted by Marco Guidarini, Nice May/June 2005.

[2563] Pierre Cadars: 'La mère, la fille et l'opéra' in Dottin-Orsini p.132, hereafter cited as Cadars. Yet Saint-Saëns' *Samson et Dalila* belongs also to the realisation of biblical lust pieces, with its bacchanale as ecstatic dance.

[2564] Since December 1878 no longer in the Salle Ventadour, which had become a branch of the Banque de France. Pierre Dufay incorrectly gives Théâtre-Italien, and adds that Maurel, with the Corti brothers, was behind a short-lived attempt to resurrect it. Tailhade p.135. Eugène Lami's painting of the interior, which dates to 1843, is given as the cover illustration of Geneviève Latour and Florence Claval (edd.): *Les Théâtres de Paris*. Paris: Délégation de l'action artistique de la ville de Paris, Bibliothèque historique de la ville de Paris, Association de la Régie Théâtrale 1991.

[2565] Her real name was Tremel.

[2566] Oscar Wilde to Robert Ross, June 1898. Hart-Davis 1962 p.753. Wilde was given tickets by Georgette Leblanc. *Sapho* had opened at the Opéra-Comique the previous November.

[2567] I do not claim that this list is exhaustive.

[2568] Cadars p.125.

[2569] Holmes p.167.

[2570] Holmes pp.167-8.

2571 Blunt p.58. Montgomery Hyde says this breakfast took place in London. Hyde 1976 p.128.

2572 Holland and Hart-Davis p.491. My italics.

2573 Lady Emily Lutyens to the Revd. Whitwell Elwin 3rd November 1891 (my italics). Lady Emily Lutyens: A *Blessed Girl: Memoirs of a Victorian Girlhood, Chronicled in an Exchange of Letters 1887-1896.* London: Hart-Davis 1953 p.68, hereafter cited as Lutyens. This can hardly have been *Salomé*, written by Wilde in French.

2574 Oscar Wilde to Mrs W.H. Grenfell 12th November 1891. Hart-Davis 1985 p.100.

2575 Gide/Mason 1905 p.7n (by Mason). At other times Wilde 'showed an amusing disdain for his comedies'. Gide/Frechtman p.9. This suggests to me that in France Wilde took more care to appear *un homme sérieux* than in England. Again, the passage that Mason translates as 'My plays are not good, I know, and I don't trouble about that' (p.48) is given more weight by Bernard Frechtman: 'My plays are not at all good, and I don't set any store by them' (p.29).

2576 Elizabeth Marbury: *My Crystal Ball, Reminiscences.* New York: Boni & Liveright 1923 p.102. Hereafter cited as Marbury.

2577 Lutyens p.68. Lady Emily had been born in the Embassy on Boxing Day 1874, when Lytton was First Secretary, and married Edwin Lutyens. Their daughter Elizabeth set Wilde's 'Birthday of the Infanta' to music as a ballet in 1932.

2578 Lytton had been a supporter of the grant of the Civil List Pension to Lady Wilde in 1890.

2579 Newton Volume II. Appendix by Mrs Wilfrid Ward p.428. Mrs Wilfrid (née Hope-Scott) was the grand-daughter of Lyons' sister, the Duchess of Norfolk.

2580 Ainslie p.178.

2581 By 1900, Molière had been played there more often than the next four most popular dramatists put together.

2582 It is just possible that Wilde had the Odéon in mind, though I think this unlikely.

2583 Carlson p.5. A painting dating to this period, 'Le foyer de la Comédie Française' by Gaston Latouche is the collection of the Théâtre Français. This shows Réjane, Maurice Barrès and Henri de Régnier in the crowd.

2584 And is so referred to by Sorel p.29. Sorel tells how she took lessons from her, as well as from Favart, Charles Le Bargy and Maurice de Féraudy. *Ibidem* pp.20,29.

2585 Sherard/Maupassant p.196.

2586 This antedates the announcement in *La Bataille* of 9th February 1892 cited in Tydeman/Price 1996 p.20.

2587 *L'École décadent*e. Paris: Vanier 1887.

2588 Deak pp.22-3.

2589 Vyvyan Holland: Introduction to Oscar Wilde: *Salomé*. London: The Folio Society 1977 unnumbered page.

2590 Mireille Dottin-Orsini: 'Le banquet d'Hérode' and Monique Dubar: 'Oscar Wilde et Strauss, ou le corps dansant', both in Dottin-Orsini pp.56,195.

[2591] Melissa Knox: *Oscar Wilde, A Long and Lovely Suicide*. New Haven & London: Yale University Press 1994, after p.76.

[2592] 17th March 1896, with de Max as the Emperor and Nerey as the king of the barbarians. Sérusier designed the programme.

[2593] Pretty Women p.140.

[2594] From 'Les Horizontales' of 1883. Koning was presumably Victor Koning, sometime husband of Jane Hading and director of the Gymnase; Marais played Macbeth to Sarah Bernhardt's Lady Macbeth in 1884.

[2595] Aquien/Salomé p.29.

[2596] Langlade p.244.

[2597] Tydeman/Price p.29.

[2598] Beaumont p.91; Jacques Robichez: *Lugné-Poe*. Paris: L'Arche 1955 p.123.

[2599] Gide/Mason 1905 p.71.

[2600] Skinner p.xvii.

[2601] Lyceum Theatre June 1896, put on by Johnston Forbes Robertson, but the latter's attempt to produce Sudermann's *Johannis* was twice frustrated by the censor. Sudermann also wrote a play on the theme of John the Baptist.

[2602] Bernard Shaw: 'Duse and Bernhardt', *The Saturday Review* 15th June 1895, reprinted in Bernard Shaw: *Plays and Players*. Selected with an Introduction by A.C. Ward. London: Oxford University Press 1952 p.34.

[2603] Schom pp.79,147.

[2604] D. Forbes-Winslow: *Daly's, the Biography of a Theatre*. London: W.H. Allen 1944 p.15.

[2605] Maurice Baring chose a photograph of Bernhardt as Adrienne Lecouvreur for the frontispiece of his biography. Baring 1935.

[2606] Alice Comyns Carr, who translated the play for a production with Helen Modjeska and Johnston Forbes-Robertson, thought Aimée Desclées 'the first of the great Frou-Frous', and as such Desclées was admired by Banville. Carr p.23. Forbes-Robertson called the play 'remarkable and an epoch maker of its kind', and agreed that Desclées was superior to Modjeska. Forbes-Robertson p.56.

[2607] Max Beerbohm: *Around Theatres*. London: Rupert Hart-Davis 1953 p.5. Hereafter cited as Beerbohm 1953.

[2608] Baring 1935 p.18. The Odéon, 14th January 1868.

[2609] Baring 1935 p.122.

[2610] Baring 1935 p.121.

[2611] Théodora, Fédora, Tosca, Cléopâtre and Gismonda.

[2612] See Victorien Sardou: *Mes plagiats! réplique à Mario Uchard*. Paris: Imprimerie et librairie universelle 1882.

[2613] Gramont p.266. *La Tosca* was played in London in 1889 with Mrs Bernard Beere as Tosca and Johnston Forbes-Robertson as Scarpia; translation by Henry Hulton.

[2614] Belloc 1943 p.194.

[2615] The Irish actor Robert Mantell played Loris Ipanoff to Davenport's Fédora.

[2616] Puccini saw her as Tosca in Milan in 1890 and again in Florence in 1895.

[2617] Robert Burnand: *Le duc d'Aumale et son temps*. Paris: Librairie Hachette 1949 p.226.

[2618] Reade p.3. Bernhardt gave Mucha a six-year contract and subsequent posters include *La Dame aux Camélias* (Théâtre de la Renaissance, 30th November 1896), *Lorenzaccio* (Théâtre de la Renaissance, 3rd December 1896) and *Medée* (Théâtre de la Renaissance, 28th October 1898).
http://www.webcom.com/ajarts/mucha.html

[2619] Jones p.194.

[2620] Baring 1935 p.143. A recording survives from which one can distinguish a tremendous verve and attack, but little else. This was played on in the BBC Radio 4 Great Lives series, October 2003.

[2621] Hartrick p.87.

[2622] There is a photograph of her in this production in Hartmann p.79, and it was then that Toulouse-Lautrec depicted her in the rôle.

[2623] Forbes-Robertson p.233.

[2624] Rachel had played Phèdre in London in 1846, 1853 and 1855. Queen Victoria saw her in the two former years, and also her Adrienne Lecouvreur in 1853.

[2625] Sir George Arthur: *Sarah Bernhardt*. London: William Heinemann 1923 p.52.

[2626] Dubeux p.v. My translation.

[2627] Judith p.31.

[2628] Sir George Higginson to Sir George Arthur. Sir George Arthur: *Sarah Bernhardt*. London: William Heinemann 1923 p.123n.

[2629] Robertson p.198. Bernhardt had also to match the highly charged playing of Phèdre invented by Goncourt for 'La Faustin'.

[2630] Sardou's Cléopâtre, not Shakespeare's.

[2631] Jules Barbier's Joan of Arc, not Shaw's. This adaptation of Schiller's *Jungfrau von Orleans* was used by Auguste Mermet as a libretto for the opera *Jeanne d'Arc* staged in Paris in April 1876, this then being adapted by Tchaikowski for his opera, first performed at the Mariinsky on 13th January 1881.

[2632] Howard p.46. This was in 1881 at the Port Saint-Martin.

[2633] Max Beerbohm: *More Theatres*. London: Rupert Hart-Davis1969 p.42. Hereafter cited as Beerbohm 1969.

[2634] Baring 1935 p.73. Arthur too would gladly have foregone *Léna*. Sir George Arthur: *Sarah Bernhardt*. London: William Heinemann 1923 p.83.

[2635] Jullian 1969 pp.250-1.

[2636] George Taylor: 'Svengali: mesmerist and æsthete' in Richard Foulkes (ed.): *British Theatre in the 1890s*. Cambridge: Cambridge University Press 1992 p.94.

[2637] Oscar Wilde: *Salomé*. Introduction and translation by Vyvyan Holland. London: The Folio Society 1977 unnumbered page.

[2638] Neither Frantisek Deak nor John Henderson mention this: my source is Rudorff p.143. Tydeman and Price do mention Fort's interest, but suggest 1892, following an announcement in *La Bataille*. Tydeman/Price pp.6,20. The date of 1891 if Rudorff is correct, is strange, and suggests that this may not have been Wilde's *Salomé* at all.

[2639] Gerda Taranow: *Sarah Bernhardt, the Art within the Legend.* Princeton: Princeton University Press 1972 p.201.

[2640] Delbourg-Delphis p.153.

[2641] Skinner p.254. It is perhaps stretching a close reading too far but in Ohnet's *Lise Fleuron*, there is an actor called Demazure who like de Max wears pearl-grey gloves (p.224).

[2642] Edward Wagenknecht: *Seven Daughters of the Theater.* Norman: University of Oklahoma Press 1964 p.73.

[2643] Tellegen, half Greek, half Dutch, who seems to have been a body without a mind, was the nude model for Rodin's 'Eternal Springtime'. He acted, after a fashion, at the Odéon, having been befriended by Edouard de Max. In the new century he married Geraldine Farrar for five years (1916-1921) and committed suicide in 1934. His real name was Isidor van Dameler.

[2644] Bernhardt's granddaughter was in no doubt of this. Bernhardt pp.58-60. They met at a fancy dress ball where Ligne was Hamlet and Bernhardt Queen Elizabeth of England, one of which rôles was later reversed. The Prince died in 1918. 'Are you married?' Ligne's eighteenth century ancestor was once asked, gaining the reply 'Oui, mais si peu'. It was a detachment that seemed to run in the family.

[2645] Michael Harrison: *Clarence, The Life of H.R.H. the Duke of Clarence and Avondale.* London: W.H. Allen 1972. p.110. This was the unfortunate Prince Eddy, elder son of the Prince of Wales. The claim was indeed more than improbable: Eddy and Maurice were the same age. Bernhardt also suggested that Maurice might have been the son of either Gambetta or Boulanger. Skinner p.52.

[2646] Baring 1935 p.119.

[2647] Dumas p.11.

[2648] Formalised at one time as 'le Cercle des Escholiers'.

[2649] Gold/Fizdale 1991 p.293.

[2650] Abbéma was one of Bernhardt's permanent hangers-on, and there is a marble of her by Bernhardt in the Musée d'Orsay, ref. RF 3756. Abbéma also painted Gyp de Martel.

[2651] Musée d'Orsay ref.1585. Reproduced in Ackerman figure s.33. The dating is Ackerman's, the Orsay only saying 'vers 1895'.

[2652] Robertson pp.112,125,197. Clairin's portrait of Bernhardt, in the collection of the Comédie Française, has her in one of her famous spiral or 'corkscrew' poses.

[2653] Robertson p.241.

[2654] Not only his 'Salomé' of 1888, now in the Musée royale des Beaux Arts, Brussels, but also shown as a picture on the easel in his painting 'In the Studio', Metropolitan Museum of Art, New York ref. 1986.339.2.

[2655] This is the date given by Gold/Fizdale 1991 p. 263. Skinner p.256 and Ruth Brandon: *Being Divine, A Biography of Sarah Bernhardt.* London: Secker & Warburg 1991 p.362 (hereafter cited as Brandon) give 10th December; Jack Rennart and Alain Weill: *Alphonse Mucha, The Complete Posters and Panels.* Uppsala: Hjert & Hjert 1984 give 9th November. The menu by Mucha reproduced by Battersby p.156 makes it clear that the date was indeed the 9th December 1896. The menu itself is given by Skinner, *ibid.* p.257.

[2656] boulevard de Saint-Martin 18.

[2657] Lalique was a goldsmith before making his name as a glassmaker.

[2658] Surprisingly little is recorded about this painter, a friend and supporter of Whistler, and, like Helleu, a frequent visitor to Whistler's house in the rue du Bac. La Gandara painted Clara Caraman-Chimay; his portrait of Montesquiou's lover Gabriel Yturri is in the Musée d'Orsay.
See http://lagandara.fr/siteanglais/index2anglais.htm.

[2659] Deak p.236. http://www.gidiana.net/guidedesspectacles.htm.

[2660] Based in the rue Turgot, the Théâtre de l'Œuvre (a name reflecting that of Zola's novel) had grown out of the Théâtre d'Art of Paul Fort and Princess Metschcheskaia, with whom Lugné-Poë worked.

[2661] Charles Ricketts: *Pages on Art*. London: Constable 1913 p.243.

[2662] Tydeman/Price p.45.

[2663] Sir George Arthur: *Sarah Bernhardt*. London: William Heinemann 1923 p.67. The crossing had been rough, and Bernhardt had originally refused to take part. A photograph of Bernhardt in London in 1879 forms the frontispiece of Richardson/ Bernhardt. For this Season see Richard Foulkes: 'The French Play in London: The Comédie-Française at the Gaiety Theatre 1879', *Theatre Research* 56, 2002, pp.125-131.

[2664] Cornelia Otis Skinner: *Madame Sarah*. New York: Houghton Miflin. 1966. New edition New York: Paragon 1988 p.122.

[2665] Michel Peyramaure: *La Divine, le roman de Sarah Bernhardt*. Paris: Robert Laffont 2002 pp.194,200. Yet is Peyramaure more at fault than Emmanuel Haymann, who resites the episode to Dover? Emmanuel Haymann: 'Oscar Wilde ou la fatalité du génie', in Emmanuel Haymann (ed.): *Oscar Wilde, Les Pensées*. Paris: Le Cherche Midi 1990 p.21.

[2666] Henry W Nevinson: *Changes & Chances*. London Nisbet & Co 1923 p.38. The other actors were Gustave Worms and Mounet-Sully. Mr Gladstone saw this production in October 1879 and found Bernhardt 'incomparable'. H.G.C. Matthew: *The Gladstone Diaries, with Cabinet Minister and Prime Ministerial Correspondence* Volume IX January 1875-December 1880. Oxford: The Clarendon Press 1986 p.451.

[2667] Sarah Bernhardt: *My Double Life*. 1907. Photographic reprint London: Peter Owen 1977 p.297. Hereafter cited as Bernhardt.

[2668] Thénard Chapter VII. Quotation from p.138. Thénard played Œnone in *Phèdre*.

[2669] Suze Rueff: *I Knew Sarah Bernhardt*. London: Frederick Muller 1951. Hereafter cited as Rueff.

[2670] Aston.

[2671] London: Max Reinhardt 1959.

[2672] Richardson/Bernhardt p.71.

[2673] Maurice Willson Disher: *The Last Romantic, the Authorised Biography of Sir John Martin-Harvey*. With a foreword by D.L. Murray. London: Hutchinson n.d.

[2674] Brandon p.108. Norman Forbes had already begun his stage career in W.G. Wills' *Olivia* (adapted from *The Vicar of Wakefield)* at the Court Theatre in March 1878.

[2675] J.C. Trewin: 'Bernhardt on the London Stage' in Eric Salmon (ed.): *Bernhardt and the Theatre of her Time.* Westport, Conn. and London: Greenwood Press 1977 p113. Wilde later suggested to Richard D'Oyley Carte that Johnston Forbes-Robertson might be successfully cast as the Czarevitch in *Vera.*

[2676] But when she arrived at Le Havre in May 1881, there were fifty thousand 'Saradoteurs' (or 'Sarassins') to greet her.

[2677] Whiteing p.212. This was Alix-Marie Pasquier, or Alice Marie Angèle Pasquier, *dite* Madame Pasca, one of Flaubert's 'three angels'. Francis Steegmuller describing her as one of the mourners at Maupassant's funeral, only calls her 'an elderly actress who had been a friend of Flaubert's'. Steegmuller/Maupassant p.313. There is no elucidation in the reference to her in Stanley Jackson: *Guy de Maupassant.* London: Duckworth 1938 p.103. A picture of Alix-Marie Pasca is in English Officer 1908, facing p.130. Pierre Dufay gives Pasca's dates as 1835-1914. Tailhade p.74n. The label with the portrait 'Madame Pasca' by Bonnat, dated 1874, (Musée d'Orsay, ref. RF 2245) gives her dates as 1855-1914 but according to the website http://maupassant.free.fr/ these were 1836-1906.

[2678] *Zaïre* was also an opera by Marc de la Nux (Palais Garnier, 1890). De la Nux, a cousin of Leconte de Lisle and a student of Liszt, seems to have fallen out of history, save for his presence as M. La Pérouse in Gide's *Les faux-monnayeurs.* See Sheridan p.45.

[2679] A rôle first played by Bernhardt in 1876, with Coquelin as the duc de Septmonts, Sophie Croizette as his wife and Frédéric Febvre as 'un Yankee plus vrai que nature'. Dubeux p.97. In the 1884 Paris production, Julia Bartet played the duchess and Blanche Pierson Mrs Clarkson.

[2680] Gold/Fizdale 1991 p.151.

[2681] Jullian 1969 p.71.

[2682] Miller p.7.

[2683] For Guérard, Skinner p.15; for Claude, John Boon: *Victorians, Edwardians, and Georgians, The Impressions of a Veteran Journalist extending over Forty Years.* London: Hutchinson n.d. p.18. Hereafter cited as Boon. I cannot be certain that Claude was with her in 1879, as Boon only met her in 1884, when she was playing *Macbeth.*

[2684] Langlade p.57.

[2685] Sir George Arthur: *Sarah Bernhardt.* London: William Heinemann 1923 pp.68-9.

[2686] Thénard p.147. Bernhardt had recited at an earlier reception given by Lady Brassey, when she and Thénard gave the first scene of *Les Femmes savants,* Bernhardt had recited from de Musset, and she, Thénard, Reichenberg and Talbot gave *Le Printemps.* Other social occasions included the formal dinner given by the Lord Mayor of London and a reception given by Lady Borthwick.

[2687] Beerbohm 1953 p.115.

[2688] Volume IV number 20.

[2689] Called Phêdre by Stuart Mason: *Bibliography of Oscar Wilde*. London: T. Werner Laurie n.d. [1914] p.5. Bernhardt's other rôles in comparison seem to have made little impression on Wilde.

[2690] Jerome p.95.

[2691] Baring 1935 p.83.

[2692] Carr p.215.

[2693] Bernhardt p.114.

[2694] Bernhardt p.300.

[2695] This letter, forwarded to *The Standard* by Bernhardt's solicitors Brandon & Nicholson, is reproduced in James Agate (ed.): *Those Were the Nights, An Anthology of Criticism 1880-1896.* London: Hutchinson n.d. p.31.

[2696] Millward pp.261-2.

[2697] Matthews pp.91,99.

[2698] Waddington 1981 p.263. This sounds rather tenuous, but Professor Waddington is a Turgenev scholar of such eminence that it gives the piece a greater authority than one would otherwise credit. I am grateful to June Courage for drawing my attention to this reference.

[2699] This is not as easy to date as one might suppose, for it turns on the date that the news reached London. The Prince was killed on 1st June. Sir George Arthur, the source for this account, which implies that the reception was early in June, also says that the Prince and Princess of Wales had left for Paris on the same day that the Comédie Française company arrived in London. Lord Suffield, who was also there, confirms the presence of the Prince, and dates the event 'towards the end of June'. Queen Victoria was told on Thursday 19th June, and Eugénie on the 20th. We know from Marie Bashkirtseff that the news only reached Paris on 20th June. Sir George Arthur: *Sarah Bernhardt*. London: William Heinemann 1923 pp.67-8; Lord Suffield P.C., G.C.V.O., K.C.B., V.D.: *My Memories 1830-1913*. Edited by Alys Lowth. London: Herbert Jenkins 1913 pp.330-1; Kurtz pp.308-9; Bashkirtseff p.370. Diary entry for 21st June 1879. Bernhardt was back in Paris by the 26th, when she appeared in *Andromaque*; Wilde produced a facile poem on the event.

[2700] Henry James was less favourable: 'Of Madeleine Brohan there is little to say. She is a delightful person to listen to, and she is still delightful to look at, in spite of that redundancy of contour which time has contributed to her charms. But she has never been ambitious and her talent has had no particular original quality. It is a long time since she created an original part'. James 1878 p. 341.

[2701] Baring 1935 p.36.

[2702] According to Langlade, this was under the patronage of Gustave Doré. Langlade p.57.

[2703] Harry Marillier: Unpublished memoirs, quoted in Jonathan Fryer: 'Harry Marillier and the Love of the Impossible', *The Wildean* 28, January 2006 p.4.

[2704] Bentley p.30. Cresswell is Cresswell Augustus Cresswell, at Magdalen 1875-1879, who became a London stockbroker. Holland and Hart-Davis p.40. Langlade seems to have considered him as Florence Balcombe's rival for Wilde's attentions. Langlade p.40. Wilde was later to make cutting remarks about stockbrokers.

[2705] Although one quotation is referenced as 'as some one said'. Bentley p.40. Not are there only no notes but the bibliography is pitiful.

[2706] On the corner of rue de la Chaussée d'Antin and boulevard des Capucines, and it is so shown in a painting by Jean Béraud, although the photograph in Steven Adams: *The World of the Impressionists*. London: Thames & Hudson 1985 p.36 shows a street frontage, flanked by the other buildings. Hereafter cited as Adams 1985. Next to it in the photograph (S.L.) is the Café de Vaudeville.

[2707] It is not possible to consider this corner house in the avenue de Villiers / rue Fortuny, and Bernhardt's entourage of Georges Clairin, Richepin, Abbéma and the rest, without reflecting upon Nana's corner house in the avenue de Villiers and her entourage of Muffat, Satin, Philippe and Georges Hugon and the rest. Bernhardt's house (entrance at 35 rue Fortuny) has been replaced, although one may gain some idea of Escalier from no. 43, now the Musée Jean-Jacques Henner, which he also designed for the painter Guillaume Dubufe in the 1870s. As for Nana's house, on the corner of the avenue de Villiers and the rue Cardinet, one can choose between the Lycée Carnot, the bar-restaurant Abbaye de Leffe, the modern block over a bookshop or, most fittingly, a branch of the Banque Nationale de Paris-Paribas.

[2708] Sherard 1908 p.67. For Jonathan Fryer, this becomes 'Oscar [...] paid court to' Bernhardt. Fryer 1997 p.18.

[2709] 1843-1910. Escalier's wife deserted him to marry Alexandre Dumas *fils*. Even here we see the intricate web of Parisian relationships in the world of literature and the arts.

[2710] Should not be confused with Paul Margueritte's pantomime *Pierrot Assassin de sa Femme* at the Théâtre Libre.

[2711] Ellmann p.213. This is derived from Sherard 1908 p.68 and Sherard 1911 p.268. Ellmann also miscalls the rue Fortuny, the rue Fortune (it was named in 1877 after the Spanish painter José-Maria Fortuny). Langlade's version is that Richepin and Parodi, who was also there, were 'tous deux un peu agacés de cette presence insolite'. Langlade p.97.

[2712] He later married Cora Lapercerie, a member of Lugné-Poë's company. There is a photograph of her in Hartmann p.94.

[2713] Gold/Fizdale 1991 p.205. Beardsley's portrait of Réjane is said to have caused her to weep and scream. Mix p.113.

[2714] Symons p.87.

[2715] Skinner p.221.

[2716] We have the benefit of the website http://www.jeanrichepin.free.fr/sitejr.htm.

[2717] Siegel p.277.

[2718] Parker had been born in Calvados in 1852 – hence his names Louis Napoleon.

[2719] Sherard 1905 p.54.

[2720] Shercliff p.83. Ms Shercliff writes 'I have used little invention and much care' (p.9).

[2721] Fryer 1997 p.18.

[2722] One would like to think that this was Pauline in the place de la Madeleine, 'well-known for her caustic tongue and power of repartee'. Harry de Windt: *My Note Book at Home and Abroad*. London: Chapman & Hall 1923.

[2723] Rueff p.107.

[2724] She also appeared in *Phèdre*, as the boy king Edward V (one of 'the princes in the Tower') in Casimir Delavigne's *Les Enfants d'Edouard*, and as Gilberte in *Frou-frou*.

[2725] Bernhardt married Damala in London on the 4th April and played her usual rôles in *La Dame aux Camélias*, *Adrienne Lecouvreur*, *Frou-frou* and *Hernani* at the Gaiety Theatre in May / June.

[2726] This opened at the Gaiety Theatre on the 9th July.

[2727] Constance Wilde to Otho Lloyd 3rd June 1884. Hart-Davis 1962 p.156. Judic should not be confused with the actress Judith.

[2728] Boon p.18.

[2729] Bashkirtseff p.675. Diary entry for 16th June 1884.

[2730] Tailhade p.146.

[2731] Not mentioned by Ellmann, this is in Jullian 1969 p.152.

[2732] Boon p.19.

[2733] As had Richepin's *Nana Sahib*, and Bernhardt's 1901 *Phèdre*.

[2734] Baring 1935 p.120. This strangely pre-figures Bernhardt's Pelléas. *Théodora* opened on 26th December 1884.

[2735] And, more improbably as a Saint Theresa who adores the moon. This is quoted unsourced by Pascal Aquien in Aquien/Salomé p.25. I have not found the original. Aquien also discusses in detail the departures from the original of the Douglas text as published. *Ibidem* pp.26-8.

[2736] Langlade p.199.

[2737] Holland and Hart-Davis p.529 n.1. This presumably follows Tydeman/Price p.21. Tydeman and Price say that Darmont was 'likely'. There is no other reference to Darmont in the Wilde or Bernhardt literature known to me. His real name was Alphonse Petit.

[2738] Langlade p.167.

[2739] She was renting Alpha House in St John's Wood.

[2740] Lord Lytton to Lady Betty Balfour 24th October 1890.Balfour Volume II p.405.

[2741] Oscar Wilde to Leonard Smithers 2nd September 1900. Hart-Davis 1962 p.834.

[2742] Bernhardt's Cleopatra is analysed in Gerda Taranow: *Sarah Bernhardt, the Art within the Legend*. Princeton: Princeton University Press 1972 p.107.

[2743] Camma is the priestess in Tennyson's verse drama, *The Cup*, produced at the Lyceum on 3rd January 1881.

[2744] I extend considerably here the reference to the letter S made by Mireille Dottin-Orsini in her essay 'Le banquet d'Hérode' in Dottin-Orsini p.21 and by Monique Dubar in her essay 'Oscar Wilde et Strauss, ou le corps dansant', in the same collection p.105. The Clairin portrait is in the Petit Palais.

[2745] Karen Usborne: *'Elizabeth', The Author of Elizabeth and her German Garden*. London: The Bodley Head 1986 p.47.

[2746] Hudson p.22.

[2747] Bennett dedicated *Anna of the Five Towns* to Schwob 'my literary Godfather in France'.

[2748] Sherard 1906 p.180.

[2749] Jullian 1969 p.254. My italics.

[2750] Sherard 1908 p.135.

[2751] She had managed the Porte Saint-Martin 1883-1886, and was to manage the Théâtre de la Renaissance from November 1893 to January 1899, before taking over the Théâtre des Nations which she renamed the Théâtre Sarah Bernhardt and ran until her death in 1923.

[2752] In France until recently it had been staged only five times: the original 1896 productions, by Ida Rubinstein at the Théâtre de Châtelet in 1912, in a version by Maurice Bourgeois at the Comédie des Champs-Élysée in 1922, and by Pitoëff at the Théâtre des Arts in 1931, followed only in 1988 by Francis Sourbié at the Théâtre Mouffetard. There has been a resurgence of interest by young companies and productions have been staged by Christine Farenc at the Théâtre de Nesle and Charles Di Meglio at the Théâtre des Enfants Terribles 2006, and in 2010 by Anne Bisang at the Théâtre Artistic Athévains, by Olivier Bruaux at the Folie Théâtre, and by Jérémie Le Louët, Théâtre 13, (with many revivals).

[2753] Robert H. Sherard: *Oscar Wilde, the Story of an Unhappy Friendship*. London: Greening & Co. 1905 pp.135 *seqq.*

[2754] Sherard 1937 p.187.

[2755] Peter Raby (ed.): *The Cambridge Companion to Oscar Wilde*. Cambridge: Cambridge University Press 1997 p.xv.

[2756] Dorian Gray's picture is also the mirror of his soul.

[2757] Lisa A. Kazmier: '"More a Symbol Than a Woman": Ellen Terry, Mrs. Patrick Campbell, The Image of the Actress and the Performance of Self'. Paper given at the 1998 Warren I. Susman Memorial Conference, Rutgers University. http://intranet.rutgers.edu/~kazmier/SUSMAN.HTM

[2758] Baring 1935 p.8.

[2759] James 1878 p.344. This is taken from an essay James originally wrote in December 1877.

[2760] Bernhardt p.106. Holland only permitted himself one footnote, explaining why he did not translate a poem by Naudet.

[2761] Richardson/Bernhardt p.185.

[2762] Oscar Wilde to Robert Ross n.d. Hart-Davis 1962 p.775. No one has attempted to explain why after this, Wilde did not call on Bernhardt in Paris.

[2763] One must distinguish between the three men of that name. This Pierre Berton was the great-great grandson of the composer Pierre Berton (1727-1780), and 'Pierre Berton' is also the name of a character in *The Black Domino*, a play by George R. Sims, Robert Buchanan, and Henry Sprake, staged at the Adelphi Theatre in London in 1893, with George W Cockburn as Berton.

[2764] Mme van de Velde's play *Germaine* was less fortunate, not even becoming a failed matinée – Kerry Powell's trenchant phrase. Powell 1997 p.157.

[2765] Aston p.98.

[2766] Her name is sometimes given as Mrs Bernard-Beere. Kate Terry Gielgud, who was certainly in a position to know, refers to her as Mrs Bernard Beere when writing contemporanæously about her in *A Woman of No Importance*. Kate Terry Gielgud: *A Victorian Playgoer*. With forewords by John Gielgud, Val Gielgud and Elinor Gielgud. Edited by Muriel St Clair Byrne. London: Heinemann 1980 p.7. Hereafter cited as Gielgud. Jonathan Fryer inexplicably refers to her as 'the socialite and philanthropist Mrs Bernard Beere'. Fryer 2000 p.133.

[2767] Bernhardt pp.297-8.

[2768] Du Maurier/Martian p.172.

[2769] Quoted by Emmanuel Signoret as an epigraph to his poem 'Les Alcyons', dedicated to Camille Mauclair.

[2770] 31st May 1897, from Berneval. Holland & Hart-Davis p.869.

[2771] Langlade p.225.

[2772] H. Montgomery Hyde: *Lord Alfred Douglas, A Biography*. London: Methuen 1984 p.119.

[2773] Mikhail Volume II pp.466-8. This was the first English publication of the piece.

[2774] In 1889 Sturges had published a Volume of translations from Maupassant with an introduction by Henry James; and James put something of Sturges into the character of Little Bilham in *The Ambassadors*.

[2775] Merrill pp.10-12. Merrill's biographer only says of London that Merrill's friendship with Wilde dated to what was a brief visit in 1890. Henry 1927 p.64.

[2776] Sherard 1937 p.171.

[2777] Douglas/Wintermans pp.39,40.

[2778] Gide/Mason 1905 pp.21,82. Langlade agrees that La Jeunesse's account was a faithful one. Langlade p.302. The piece by La Jeunesse is presumably *Souvenirs d'Oscar Wilde*, which La Jeunesse published in the *Revue blanche* 15th December 1900. The passage is removed from Gide/Frechtman.

[2779] Gide/Mason 1905 p.10.

[2780] Sherard 1908 pp.254,255. Sherard later told André Maurois that 'Almost every book that has ever been written about this unhappy man has proceeded from my writings'. Robert Sherard to André Maurois 1st May 1928, quoted in Sherard 1937 p.33.

[2781] Hetherington p.10: 'This story must be regarded as one of her more ambitious melo-dramatizations [...] A greater realist than Melba never walked, but at times she was capable of seeing life in the most absurd operatic terms [...] Whatever Wilde's shortcomings, he was never a furtive beggar in a scene from grand opera. The costume would not have been fitted him'. The measure of Melba's view of Wilde may be understood in her statement that 'My memory of him is firstly the inimitable wit and brilliance of his conversation, and secondly a strange, almost macabre element in his character which made me feel always a little uneasy when he was in the room.' Melba p.49. Her charitable instincts were shown when she once withdrew from a charity concert because Yvette Guilbert was also to sing.

[2782] Marbury p.102.

[2783] Sherard 1906 p.282.

[2784] 'Saki' (H.H. Munro): *Reginald in Russia*. London: John Lane, The Bodley Head 1910. Reprinted in *The Complete Short Stories of 'Saki'*. London: The Bodley Head 1930.

[2785] Le Rouge p.462.

[2786] Ernest La Jeunesse, writing in *La Revue Blanche* 15th December 1900. Translated by Perceval Pollard. Reprinted in E.H. Mikhail: *Oscar Wilde, Interviews and Recollections*. London: Macmillan 1979 Volume II p.479.

[2787] Vance Thompson: *The Two Deaths of Oscar Wilde*. San Francisco: Helen Gentry 1930, *passim* through unnumbered pages, hereafter cited as Thompson; O'Sullivan 1934 pp.185-6; La Jeunesse p.479. Visiting the Hôtel d'Alsace in 1908, Vyvyan Holland found it not 'a mean and squalid place' but 'a small but very pleasant and comfortable hotel with a courtyard in the centre. In the middle of this courtyard grows a fig-tree, over-looked by my father's two bright, sunlit rooms'. Vyvyan Holland: *Son of Oscar Wilde*. London: Hart-Davis 1954 p.194; hereafter cited as Holland 1954. For all that, Baedeker drily commented that Left Bank hotels are not for the pleasure-seeker.

[2788] Louÿs/Tinan p.202n.

[2789] Huddleston p.51.

[2790] Julia Frey: *Toulouse-Lautrec, A Life*. London: Weidenfeld & Nicolson 1994 p.425.

[2791] Painter I p.213.

[2792] Douglas/Wintermans p.42. La Jeunesse had praised Douglas's poems when they were published by Mercure de France in 1896, always a sure way to Bosie's heart. More surprisingly, La Jeunesse also designed the programme for the Théâtre de l'Œuvre production of Ibsen's *A Comedy of Love*, 23rd May 1897. Wintermans adds 'Ernest La Jeunesse was the pseudonym of the journalist, caricaturist, novelist and playwright Ernest-Henri Cohen (1874-1917), who enthusiastically reviewed Bosie's *Poems* (1896) in *Le Journal* on 11 January 1897.' He had, according to Douglas, 'an impish sense of humour, a great deal of erudition, and a real gift of wit. He kept one laughing all the time' (*Without Apology* p278); His turgid novel *Le Boulevard* (Paris: Jean Bosc et Cie, 1906) features a character called Odin Howes who is clearly modelled on Wilde. See Jean-Paul Goujon: 'Ernest La Jeunesse', *L'Étoile-Absinthe*, 23è et 24è Tournées 1984, pp.49-52.

[2793] Robert Ross to Max Meyerfeld, Prefatory Dedication to *De Profundis* London: Methuen 1908 (thirteenth impression) p.xiv. Ross of course is referring to Sherard's *Oscar Wilde, the Story of an Unhappy Friendship*., which was published privately in 1902 and then in London by Greening & Co. in 1905 (new edition 1908), and dedicated to Ross; and to Sherard's *The Life of Oscar Wilde*. London: T. Werner Laurie 1906, in which there is also (p.148) a tribute to Ross that verges on the maudlin.

[2794] Boris Brasol: *Oscar Wilde, The Man, The Artist*. London: Williams & Norgate 1938 p.7. Brasol's further acknowledgment of help from Lord Alfred Douglas gives one a sense of foreboding, amply justified in the course of this book.

[2795] Sherard 1906 pp.12,339,181,355-6. 'On record' is a good example of Sherard's humbug.

[2796] Healy pp.131,137.

[2797] Healy pp.133, 138.

[2798] Sherard 1937 p.163.

[2799] Gide/Mason 1905 p.xii.

[2800] Sherard 1906 p.412.

[2801] Robert Ross to André Gide 21st March 1910. Gide/Frechtman p.70.

[2802] St John Ervine: *Oscar Wilde: A Present Time Appraisal*. London: Allen & Unwin 1951 pp.65-6.

[2803] Merrill pp.10-12.

[2804] Gide/O'Brien p.307. Diary entry for 18th June 1918.

[2805] Harris p.241.

[2806] Philippa Pullar: *Frank Harris*. London: Hamish Hamilton 1975 p.179. Hereafter cited as Pullar.

[2807] Sherard 1937 p.23.

[2808] Langlade p.280.

[2809] J. Joseph-Renaud: Preface to Oscar Wilde: *Intentions*. Paris: Stock 1905 p.xx.

[2810] Oscar Wilde to Reginald Turner 6th December 1898. Hart-Davis 1962 p.768; Holland & Hart-Davis p.1107.

[2811] Le Rouge p.461.

[2812] O'Sullivan 1934 p.180. See also Hyde 1976 pp.363-4.

[2813] 'J'ai rarement rencontré plus grande distinction, culture plus élégante et plus aimable urbaniste'. Langlade p.292. I take this to be Langlade's translation from Dario's Spanish. Wilde 'Levé tard dans l'après-midi, il rejoignait vers cinq heures à « Calisaya », un grand bar du boulevard des Italiens, quelques écrivains; le plus souvent, Jean de Mitty, Paul Adam, Henri de Régnier, Jean Moréas, Ernest La Jeunesse, Jean de Bonnefon, Gomez Carillo et moi-même, qui étais le benjamin de ce groupe notoire.' Jean Joseph-Renaud: Preface to Oscar Wilde, *Intentions*, P.-V. Stock, Bibliothèque cosmopolite N°14, 1905; reprinted in Mikhail vol. I pp.167-8.

[2814] Black, known as Laddie, was special correspondent of *The Morning Leader*. Brian Kennedy identifies him as a friend of Haweis's, rather than of Henry's. Kennedy 2000 p.23.

[2815] Henry p.15.

[2816] Jepson p.243. When in October 1898 Erik Satie, who was not all that fastidious himself, moved into Bibi's old room in the Maison de Quatre Cheminées, 22 rue de Cauchy, he had to have it disinfected. Robert Orledge (ed.): *Satie Remembered*. London: Faber & Faber 1995 p.61.

[2817] Belford p.293. This is also stated in Anon: *Paris et ses cafés*. Catalogue of the exhibition of the same name. Paris: Action artistique de la Ville de Paris. Paris 2004 p.11, at any rate for the Deux Magots ('Oscar Wilde y traîne sa viellesse et l'amertume de son exil'). The same source says that Léon Daudet and Rosny *aîné* went there for its peacefulness. It is a mistake to assume that cafés famous after 1918 were equally so before 1900.

[2818] http://www.ila-chateau.com/lipp/index.htm

[2819] or 1891 according to Anon: *Paris et ses cafés*. Catalogue of the exhibition of the same name. Paris: Action artistique de la Ville de Paris. Paris 2004 p.11.

[2820] Vanbrugh pp.34-5. If my surmise is right that 'French' is a slip for 'British', the Secretary in question sounds like Robert Vansittart.

[2821] Hansen p.45n.

[2822] 'I go to cafés like Pousset's where I meet writers and artists'. Oscar Wilde to Robert Ross 24th May 1898. Hart-Davis 1962 p.743. See also Hart-Davis 1962 pp.770-1, three letters dated 14th December 1898 and Rupert Hart-Davis (ed.): *More Letters of Oscar Wilde*. London: John Murray 1985 p.174, letter dated 26th November 1898. Pousset's is pictured in Adams 1985 p.50. Wilde frequently used the writing paper provided when asked for in such places, both in London and Paris. Thus on ?28th October 1891, he wrote to the Princess of Monaco from the Hôtel Normandie, rue de l'Echelle. Holland and Hart-Davis p.492.

[2823] Stanley Weintraub: *Reggie, A Portrait of Reginald Turner*. New York: George Braziller 1965 p.73. Hereafter cited as Weintraub.

[2824] Baedeker.

[2825] Langlade p.286. A complete documentation of Whistler's time in France in the late 1890s has not been attempted. He painted 'The Shore at Pourville' in the summer/autumn of 1899. Ashmolean Museum, Oxford, ref A985.

[2826] Christa Satzinger: *The French Influences on Oscar Wilde's 'The Picture of Dorian Gray' and 'Salomé'*. Lewiston, New York: Edwin Mellen Press 1995 pp.21,79. It was here that Douglas last saw Wilde, in the summer of 1900, 'perfectly well and in the highest spirits'. Douglas/Wintermans p.43.

[2827] The Grand Café de France in the boulevard de Bonne-Nouvelle was also a billiards centre, with nine tables. Polnay p.55.

[2828] Holland & Hart-Davis p.1097. He had had his quarterly allowance from Robert Ross shortly before.

[2829] My italics. In fact we get very little philosophy from Lord Goring, and if Wilde supposed that an Inverness cape in conjunction with a silk hat was one of the delicate fopperies of Fashion, then so much the worse for foppery.

[2830] Eltis p.162. One must also add that June and July 1899 were not marked by any particular incidents of Wilde's being shunned, and he was sufficiently in funds to visit Trouville, Le Havre and Chennevières-sur-Marne.

[2831] Sherard 1908 pp.129-31.

[2832] Sherard 1908 p.255.

[2833] Sherard 1908 p.253.

[2834] Sherard 1906 p.417.

[2835] Fox pp.95-6. There was also a pastrycook's in the rue Bonaparte and Philippe's wine shop in the rue des Beaux Arts.

[2836] If this was the Restaurant des Beaux-Arts at 11bis rue Bonaparte, by the 1920s it had improved enough to attract the gourmet A.J. Liebling, although it remained very cheap. Hansen p.54.

[2837] Sherard 1908p.256. My italics. Sherard also says that the translation of Barbey d'Aurevilley's *Ce qui ne meurt pas* that later appeared under the name of Sebastian Melmoth was indeed by Wilde.

[2838] This had been produced at the Criterion Theatre in 1895, then under the management of Charles Wyndham, when Wilde would have neither needed (before April) nor in a position (after April) to have written it. It was published by William Heinemann in 1900. The rumour was known to Chambers, who was exasperated by it (J.C. Trewin: *The Edwardian Theatre*. Oxford: Basil Blackwell 1976 p.58) and to Stuart Mason, who dismissed it (Gide/Mason 1905 p.87n).

[2839] Zweig p.8. Not all share this view: Anthony Hartley calls Verhaeren 'almost a great poet'. Hartley p. xxxvii.

[2840] 1867-1938. Eekhoud, who had the triple disadvantage of being anarchist, Belgian and gay, visited Paris in 1876 and 1892 and was associated with the *Mercure de France*. See Mirande Lucien and Patrick Cardon (edd.): *Un illustre Uraniste*. Textes de et sur Georges Eekhoud. Cahier Question de genre. Lille: GKC n.d. (in print); Mirande Lucien: *Eekhoud le rauque*. Septentrion n.d. (in print).

[2841] Georges Eekhoud: 'Saint Sebastien dans la peinture'. *Akdemos* 1 15th February 1909 pp.171-75. Eekhoud, dedicated his *Cycle patibulaire* 'A Monsieur Oscar Wilde/ Au Poète et au martyr païen / Torturé au nom de la / Justice et de la vertu protestantes' (1896). Langlade p.50. Unfortunately, his name is given as Elkhoud.

[2842] Chesson p.375-81.

[2843] Langlade p.287. Twenty years earlier Wilde had had a slight acquaintance with Lord Plunket's uncle David. This is a rather tenuous connection.

[2844] Bancroft 9 p.409.

[2845] Bashkirtseff p.329. Diary entry for 17th August 1878.

[2846] This elicited a startling confession from Arnold Bennett, about his review: 'For sufficiently weighty reasons I praised *Trilby* to the skies though privately I am convinced that is a damn silly worthless namby pamby piece of putrid rot.' Arnold Bennett to George Sturt 11th November 1895. James Hepburn (ed.): *Letters of Arnold Bennett* Volume II 1889-1915. London: Oxford University Press 1968 p.28. Hereafter cited as Hepburn.

[2847] First performed at the Teatro Regio, Turin 1st February; the first English production was by the Carl Rosa Opera Company in Manchester, 22nd April 1897.

[2848] The stage version was particularly associated with Jane Hading, but Bartet took it on for her 1901 London season and Bernhardt did the same in 1903. The novel was declined for American publication by Funk & Wagnalls as the Revd Dr Funk mistrusted its title. Johnson pp.492-4.

[2849] In April 1897, while still in prison, Wilde asked Ross to procure white ties for him, a clear indication that he saw himself returning to the beau monde. Holland and Hart-Davis p.793.

[2850] Charpentier's study is reconstructed in the Musée de Vieux Montmartre. Gustave Charpentier should not be confused with the publisher Georges Charpentier.

[2851] William Henry Bartlett's 'The Neighbours' shows a rather relaxed artist's garret, with a view of a similar one with resident grisette. Reproduced in McConkey p.22. This is not, evidently, the William Henry Bartlett (1809-1854) of the myriad topographical engravings.

[2852] Turnbull p.24.

[2853] *Louise* was revived at the Théâtre du Châtelet in June 2000. Charpentier has been more fortunate than those other successes of 1900 Lucien and Paul Hillemacher, now as forgotten as their musicals *Le Drac* and *Claudie Saint-Mégrin*. Paul Hillemacher (1852-1933); Lucien Hillemacher (1860-1909).

[2854] President 1899-1906, 'a small, not distinguished-looking man, who rolled his r's, but seemed, as they all do, very polite'. Coolidge p.155.

[2855] 'Saki' (H.H. Munro): *The Toys of Peace*. London: John Lane, The Bodley Head 1914. Reprinted in *The Complete Short Stories of 'Saki'*. London: The Bodley Head 1923 p.451.

[2856] Vechten p.46.

[2857] Maugham p.139.

[2858] In 'Evening over Sussex', *The Death of the Moth and Other Essays*. London: Hogarth Press 1942.

[2859] Pullar p.122.

[2860] Les Trois Frères Provençaux was described by the American Minister to Paris as 'one of the most recherché restaurants in the city'. Washburne p.195. As we have seen, du Maurier recommended it in *Trilby*, and Ouida, in her short story 'Slander and Sillery', clearly thought of it as incarnating high bohemia:
Wild and careless, high spirited, and lavish in his Opera suppers, his cabaret dinners, his Trois Frères banquets, his lansquenet parties, his bouquets for baronnes, and his bracelets for ballerinas, Ernest gained his reputation as a *Lion*, and – ruined himself, too, poor old fellow!
It remained open throughout the Commune and was much patronised by the Communard leader Raoul Rigault who was perhaps honouring Les Trois Frères for having been the first restaurant in Paris to serve tomatoes, for the Fête de la Fédération Nationale of 14th July 1790. Rigault's taste in food might also have been recherché if D.W Brogan's description of him is accurate, 'disciple more of the Marquis de Sade than of Robespierre or Condorcet'. Brogan p.156. For a contemporary English view of Rigault, see March p.26. March describes him as a man of multiple and contradictory opinions, 'Socialist, Jacobin, Hébertist [...] of a reckless and defiant disposition', but for all March's hostility to the Communards his view was that Rigault, while unscrupulous, was vigorous and able, and he does not allude to any sadistic aspects. Perhaps Brogan was confusing him with Rigaud in *Little Dorrit*. He was taken prisoner by the Government forces and shot out of hand in the rue Gay-Lussac on the 24th May 1871.

[2861] Pullar p.204.

[2862] McKenna p.452. Unsourced.

[2863] Villiers de l'Isle Adam also stayed at Nogent at the end of his life.

[2864] Constance Wilde to Carlos Blacker 4th March 1898. J. Robert Maguire: 'Oscar Wilde and the Dreyfus Case', *Victorian Studies* 41/1 Autumn 1997; hereafter cited as Maguire. Constance died on the 7th April.

[2865] Oscar Wilde to Robert Ross 27th June 1898. This is the passage omitted from Hart-Davis 1962 p.754.

[2866] Maguire; Hichens 1999 p.151.

[2867] M.Oxford p.121. 'Tex' owned a copy of the sixth impression of *Ballad of Reading Gaol*, but perhaps never read it. The copy with his bookplate offered in Jarndyce catalogue 126 (Summer 1998) for £50 had uncut pages.

[2868] O'Sullivan 1934 p.165.

[2869] Jonathan Fryer deprives him of his O'. Fryer 2000 p.148. He is not mentioned in Hansen; nor in Green.

[2870] The correspondence between Vielé-Griffin and Whistler in the Hunterian Museum in Glasgow is a possible source for further study.

[2871] Vincent O'Sullivan: *Opinions*. With an Introduction by Alan Anderson. London: Unicorn Press 1959 p.102. This neglected little book contains essays on Wilde (a long and critical review of *La Vie d'Oscar Wilde* by Léon Lemonnier), George Moore, 'Ouida', George Gissing, Gertrude Atherton, Baron Corvo, 'John Oliver Hobbes' and Frank Harris, and a review of Albert J. Farmer: *Le Mouvement Esthétique et Décadent en Angleterre*.

[2872] Rothenstein Volume I p.87.

[2873] Ford Madox Ford: *Return to Yesterday*. London: Victor Gollancz 1931 pp.40-5 as cited in E.H. (ed.): *Oscar Wilde, Interviews and Recollections*. London: Macmillan 1979 Volume II p.364-5. The mistake in Bibi's name by the grandson of Ford Madox Brown is particularly curious, given the place of Rose La Touche in the circle of the Pre-Raphaelites.

[2874] Rothenstein Volume I p.348

[2875] Michael Holroyd: *Augustus John, A Biography* Volume I: The Years of Innocence. London: Heinemann 1974 p.95; hereafter cited as Holroyd. The quotations are from Augustus John's autobiography, *Chiaroscuro*. Augustus John should have felt more at home in the Régence than Wilde: 'Usually a French *bon vivant* invited his lights of love to the Régence *before* the seduction, so the couples to be seen there were attentive, from the male angle, and coy or reserved on the part of the female.' Paul p.218.

[2876] Robert Speaight: *William Rothenstein, The Portrait of an Artist in His Time*. London: Eyre & Spottiswoode 1962 p.143. Of Alice Rothenstein, Speaight writes 'Even in extreme old age her prejudices were caustic; but she still professed a deep admiration for Oscar Wilde and the person she always disliked beyond anyone else was Alfred Douglas' – *ibid.* p.127. Alice Rothenstein was the daughter of the painter Walter Knewstub, a protégé of Constance Wilde's friend Lady Mount Temple

[2877] Ada Leverson: *Letters to the Sphinx from Oscar Wilde*. London: Duckworth 1930 p.47. Adrian Frazier argues that George Moore loomed larger in Ada Leverson's life than did Wilde. Frazier p.223. Leverson's sister Violet and her husband, Sidney Schiff, were friends of Marcel Proust's, and Schiff completed Scott-Moncrieff's translation of *À la recherche*. Leverson's Paris connections may have therefore have been deeper than appear through seeing her through the Wilde biography.

[2878] Harold Acton: *Memoirs of an Æsthete*. London: Methuen 1948. New edition 1970 p.381.

[2879] Daniel Farson: *The Man Who Wrote Dracula, A Biography of Bram Stoker*. London: Michael Joseph 1979 p.235.

[2880] Barbara Belford: *Bram Stoker, A Biography of the Author of Dracula*. London: Weidenfeld & Nicolson 1996 p.247.

[2881] George Gissing to Morley Roberts 6th February 1899, quoted in Jacob Korg: *George Gissing: A Critical Biography*. London: Methuen 1965 p.294.

[2882] Christopher Hussey: *The Life of Sir Edwin Lutyens*. London: Country Life 1950. New edition, Antique Collectors Club 1984 p.89. Hereafter cited as Lutyens.

[2883] Sir William Agnew, Professor Aitcheson, Sir Purdon Clarke, Lionel Earle (secretary), Sir Arthur Ellis, Colonel Herbert Jekyll, Sir Charles Rivers Wilson, Thompson Lyon.

[2884] Lutyens p.85.

[2885] Orczy p.114. *The Old Man in the Corner* is set in a London tearoom, and owes nothing to Paris.

[2886] Blunt p.370. Diary entry for 6th September 1900.

[2887] Merrill pp.10-12.

[2888] Henri Mazel: 'My Recollections of Oscar Wilde', *Everyman* Volume I:1 18th October 1912, reprinted in Mikhail Volume II p.446; Henry 1927 p.89.

[2889] Reproduced in the bilingual edition (French/English) of *The Portrait of Mr W.H.* Paris: Gallimard 2000 opp. p.143. I am grateful to Madame Danielle Guérin for drawing this to my attention.

[2890] One hundred and twenty-seven, making Paris a major academic centre. It is estimated that forty-eight million people visited the Exposition (the total population of France was fifty-eight million). Greenhalgh 2000. My contemporary note.

[2891] Bentley p.74.

[2892] Ernest Bowen-Rowlands: *In the Light of the Law*. London: Grant Richards 1931 pp.151-4. There is no mention of *de Brémont v Gilbert* in Clarke's memoirs.

[2893] Brémont p.178. The meeting should be capable of precise dating as Brémont records that there was a thunderstorm the same night. De Brémont described herself as 'Irish by right of blood'. *Ibidem* p.46. The Spanish Café was perhaps the one in the Spanish Pavilion at the Exposition Universelle. It was here that Henri de Régnier saw Wilde for the last time, watching the dancers. He did not see de Régnier and the two did not speak.

[2894] Brémont p.186.

[2895] Robert Ross to Adela Schuster, Christmas 1906, printed as a dedicatory preface to *The Duchess of Padua* London: Methuen 1908.

[2896] Brémont p.187.

[2897] Ellmann p.359.

[2898] Sherard 1905 p.416.

[2899] Oscar Wilde to Robert Ross c. 28th May 1898. Hart-Davis 1962 p.747.

[2900] Robert Sherard: *Emile Zola. A Biographical and Critical Study*. London: Chatto & Windus 1893.

[2901] From the Index of biographical notes to Zola's Correspondence, Centre for Studies in Naturalism, Centre d'Études sur le Naturalisme 1997. Republished with the permission of Les Presses de l'Université de Montréal.

[2902] Sherard 1906 p.208.

[2903] Sherard 1905 pp.438, 440-1,471-84.

[2904] Oscar Wilde to Robert Ross 16th August 1898; 3rd October 1898. Hart-Davis 1962 pp.759,762.

[2905] Mark Longaker: *Ernest Dowson*. Philadelphia: University of Pennsylvania Press 1945; 3rd edition 1967 p.256.

[2906] Maguire.

[2907] This was fairly widely known. John Butler Yeats told W.B. that Wilde 'is in debt and cannot live within his bounds', a state with which the elder Yeats was quite familiar. J.B. Yeats to W.B. Yeats 15th October 1898. Warwick Gould, John Kelly and Deirdre Toomey (edd.): *The Collected Letters of W.B. Yeats* Volume II 1896-1900. Oxford: The Clarendon Press 1997 p.282n.

[2908] Gramont p.224.

[2909] Robert Ross to Adela Schuster, Christmas 1906, printed as a dedicatory preface to *The Duchess of Padua* London: Methuen 1908.

[2910] Oscar Wilde to Clarisse Moore April or May 1883. Hart-Davis 1962 p.146.

[2911] Lutyens p.68. 'He thought still more highly of it than before, and that it was very true and wonderfully well done'. Lytton, a heavy smoker, had cancer, and Hyde's view that his death was sudden and unexpected is debatable. Hyde 1976 p.130.

[2912] Tucker's presence and practice in Paris awaits research, as does that of Dr Prendergast, who attended Beardsley in 1897.

[2913] Paderewski pp.151-2.

[2914] Richardson/Gautier p.205.

[2915] Albert Barry: *The Life of Count Moore*. Dublin: M.H. Gill & Son 1905 p.128, hereafter cited as Barry.

[2916] Barry p.199.

[2917] Douglas 1940 p.16. Whistler stayed at the parent Hôtel Chatham in the winter of 1899-1900. With what one is able to characterise as a want of delicacy, Bosie took his wife on their honeymoon to the rue Daunou, the Hôtel Rastadt at number 4, now the site of a rather louche bar.

[2918] 'Un gros homme à l'œil vague, aux joués flétries, ventru et sale'. Langlade p.303, but not sourced.

[2919] Callow p.92.

[2920] Oscar Wilde to Frances Forbes Robertson June 1899. Hart-Davis 1962 p.803.

[2921] Henry p.13.

[2922] Menpes p.90. There is a telling though anecdotal description of one of these scavengers in Macdonald pp.12-20, and Georges Ohnet has described them outside the theatres struggling to open the doors of carriages in the hope of finding butts, 'amid, shouts, disputes and oaths'. Ohnet p.6.

[2923] Maria Morris Hambourg, Françoise Heilbrun and Philippe Néagu (edd.): *Nadar*. New York: Metropolitan Museum of Art 1995 p.10. Zola borrowed Fauchery's name for that of the journalist in *Nana*.

[2924] In 1883, *Gil Blas* had paid Maupassant eight thousand francs for *Une Vie*.

[2925] Low p.290.

[2926] Healy p.93.

[2927] Oscar Wilde to Robert Ross July 1899. Hart-Davis 1985 p.183.

[2928] Maupassant/Bel Ami p.4.

[2929] Thurston p.292.

[2930] Oscar Wilde to Arthur Humphreys August 1899. Hart-Davis 1985 p.184.

[2931] Ambroise Vollard: *Recollections of a Picture Dealer*. London: Constable 1936 p.100.

[2932] Oscar Wilde to Reginald Turner 25th May 1898. Hart-Davis 1962 p.747. Manifestly this was before Jarry started turning himself into Ubu.

[2933] Ambroise Vollard: *Recollections of a Picture Dealer*. London: Constable 1936 p.45. One could also dine very well on lobster there. Richards p.269.

[2934] Maupassant/Bel Ami p.40.

[2935] Oscar Wilde to Robert Ross 24th May 1898.Hart-Davis 1962 p.743.

[2936] Jullian 1977p.94.

[2937] Mott p.76.

[2938] Viscountess Milner: *My Picture Gallery 1886-1901*. London: John Murray 1951 p.17.

[2939] Menpes p.148. Sixty years earlier Henri Murger had paid forty-five centimes at Mère Cadet's the rue Chaussé-de-Maine.

[2940] Conway p.166.

[2941] Sherard February 1893 p.323.

[2942] Huysmans 1891 pp.143-4.

[2943] Exposition 'Paris à Table', Musée d'Orsay winter 2001.

[2944] Somerville/Ross p.36. Written in November 1894.

[2945] Nevill 1913 p.111.

[2946] This was in 1903, though he did not actually write the book until 1908.

[2947] Symons 1925 p.24.

[2948] There is a painting of Catherine Booth by Baron Cederström, 'La Maréchale au café', details of which I have so far failed to find.

[2949] Aubrey Beardsley to Leonard Smithers c.9th March 1896. Maas/Duncan/Good p.117. This defies the claim that the Café Anglais 'disappeared with the second empire'. Sir Paul Harvey and J.E. Hesletine (edd.): *The Oxford Companion to French Literature*. London: Oxford University Press 1959 p.97, hereafter cited as Harvey and Hesletine. At the very least they should have remembered that Swann seeks Odette there.

[2950] Bernard Falk: *Five Years Dead, A Postscript to He Laughed in Fleet Street*. London: the Book Club 1938 p.106.

[2951] He died in 1920, outliving Cora Pearl by thirty-four years.

[2952] Do I need to explain this multiple play? Godefroy de Bouillon, a consummate gentleman, was a Crusader, but bouillon and consommé here of course refer to soup.

[2953] Berlanstein pp.107-8.

[2954] Berlanstein p.40.

[2955] Ernest Dowson and Lionel Johnson both dedicated poems to him, respectively 'To William Theodore Peters on His Renaissance Cloak' and 'Glories'.

[2956] Sherard 1908 p.90.

[2957] Stevenson/Osbourne p.66.

[2958] Lucy p.77.

[2959] Richards p.170. Felbermann p.37. Oswald Frewen: *Sailor's Soliloquy*. Edited by G.P. Griggs. London: Hutchinson 1961 p.125. The reference is to 1907, but this was an age of stable prices. One can of course read this as getting a 'Continental breakfast for *only* a franc'. Jepson p.166. Newnham-Davis p.28.

[2960] Newnham-Davis p.21.

[2961] Holland & Hart-Davis p.1175.

[2962] Sometime actor with the Théâtre de l'Œuvre, editor and anthologist.

[2963] 14 rue Monsieur-le-Prince, in 1891.

[2964] Harding 1971 p.45.

[2965] Maupassant/Bel Ami p.291.

[2966] In the rue de la Huchette, a street immortalised many years later by Elliot Paul in *The Narrow Street*, perhaps the best book on Paris of all those cited in these pages. Alas, the rue de la Huchette is to-day as much changed from what it was like in Paul's time as it has from what it was like in Prévost's, its tiny theatre perhaps the sole survivor from less commercial days. 'Behind the façades of its houses and shops were to be found the treasures and traditions and the fine or ignoble predicaments of living in the present. Love and hunger and hope and kindness and fear and humour and the struggle to survive on the rue de la Huchette, as elsewhere in France and the world were the components of the drama frequently called human and now and then divine.' Paul p.88. The German tank that smashed its way into the rue de la Huchette in 1940 was a harbinger.

[2967] Bayard pp.131, 88.

[2968] Holland 1966 pp.10-11. Hyde 1976 p.361. Hyde says rather sloppily 'When he was on his own [Wilde] would stroll along the quais, stopping at a little restaurant in the rue Jacob for a meal'. This is an odd stroll. Chez Bechet is now the pleasingly named Josephine Bakery.

[2969] 'Anarchists, more than any other group, put the café at the centre of their politics'. Haine p.230. Dr Haine, however, does not consider gay or lesbian cafés.

[2970] Holroyd p.90.

[2971] Weinberg.

[2972] Laura Beatty: *Lillie Langtry, Manners, Masks and Morals*. London: Chatto & Windus 1999 p.189.

[2973] Lapierre p.131.

[2974] Freud then moved into the Hôtel de Bresil, rue de Goff, for a hundred and fifty-five francs a month to include board.

[2975] If indeed that was its name. In September 1908, Arnold Bennett dated a letter from the Hôtel du Portugal et de l'Univers. Hepburn p.225. W.J. Locke's 'Hôtel du Soleil et de l'Écosse', 'a flourishing third rate hostelry in the neighbourhood of the Halles Centrales' is surely a private joke at this hotel's expense. Locke p.179.

[2976] It is a pity that Kelly arrived after the death of Wilde as he said that Wilde's essays were amongst his favourite reading. Bell p.154.

[2977] Spalding 1997 p.43. Grant was studying at the Académie Julian.

[2978] Norman Angell: *After All, the Autobiography of Norman Angell*. London: Hamish Hamilton 1951 p.92.

[2979] Conway p.239. Jose Shercliff refers to a café/restaurant called Le Père Laveur in the rue Serpente as 'the centre of the intellectual élite' – this is probably the same place. Shercliff p.90. Tante Marie is affectionately recalled by Macdonald pp.52-6.

[2980] Meriel Buchanan: *Ambassador's Daughter*. London: Cassell & Co 1958. Sir George Buchanan was British Diplomatic Agent to the Arbitration Commission.

[2981] Oscar Wilde to an unidentified correspondent 26th November 1898. Rupert Hart-Davis (ed.): *More Letters of Oscar Wilde*. London: John Murray 1985 p.174.

[2982] Jones p.200.

[2983] Lord Alfred Douglas: *Autobiography*. London: Martin Secker 1929 Appendix.

[2984] Angela V. John: *Elizabeth Robins, Staging a Life 1862-1932*. London: Routledge 1995 p.4.

[2985] Now in the Metropolitan Museum of Art, New York.

[2986] The label accompanying the picture at the Metropolitan says that it was given by Cornelius Vanderbilt. Perhaps he paid for it? This canvas should not be confused with 'The Horse Fair' by Rosa Bonheur and Nathalie Micas commissioned by Ernest Gambart and bequeathed by Jacob Bell to the National Gallery, London, ref NG 621.

[2987] It was this house, presumably, rather than that of Charles Ephrussi, of which the American Minister noted 'It is fitted up in the richest and most careful manner. The dining-room and the principal bedroom have nothing in them that is not Empire, from the paper on the wall to the brushes on the table'. Coolidge p.184. The Jewish newspaper magnate Walter in Maupassant's *Bel-Ami* buys a house in the rue de Faubourg-Saint-Honoré from the prince de Carlsbourg for three million francs. Maupassant/Bel Ami p.241. Maurice Ephrussi's house must now be sought in the avenue Foch, and it has become the Embassy of the Republic of Angola.

[2988] Moore had also stayed here. Wilde's room was on the second floor.

[2989] Newnham-Davis p.55. St Galmier might have been a Loire wine, but might also have been the mineral water Badoit, which comes from St Galmier.

[2990] Ellmann p.542.

[2991] This was the École Romane, encouraged by Frédéric Mistral. I have discovered no intersection between Mistral and Wilde, even putative.

[2992] Starkie p.99.

[2993] Harold Nicolson: *Some People*. Constable & Co 1927 p.59.

[2994] Pierné is referred to as Gabriel Pierre by Jill Edmonds: 'Princess Hamlet' in Viv Gardner & Susan Rutherford (edd.): *The New Woman and Her Sisters,*

Feminism and Theatre 1850-1914. Hemel Hempstead: Harvester Wheatsheaf 1992 p.700. Cornelia Otis Skinner says that the translation 'followed the original version with pedantic exactitude'. Skinner p.261. Pedantic exactitude is not a quality much manifested by Skinner herself. The Théâtre Sarah Bernhardt in the place du Châtelet was the former seventeen hundred seat Théâtre des Nations, and much larger than the previous theatre that Bernhardt had taken over, the nine hundred seat Théâtre de la Renaissance, which she had also renamed the Théâtre Sarah Bernhardt.

[2995] Bernhardt p.123.

[2996] Guedalla p.21. Was it deliberate policy not to have opened on the 16th, the 44th anniversary of the birth of Napoléon IV?

[2997] *Dit* comte Houssaye. Arnold Bennett wrote of him that 'He has written one or two Volumes which, without being unreadable, have achieved immense popularity', and adds that Stevenson consulted them for material. Bennett 1917 p.81

[2998] His play *Théroigne de Méricourt* of 1902 was written for Bernhardt.

[2999] Baring 1935 p.139. In his memoirs, Baring adds himself, Reginald Lister, comtesse Greffulhe and Arthur Strong. Baring 1922 p.199. He could also have added Zola.

[3000] Sorel p.57.

[3001] Sorel p.58.

[3002] *Saturday Review* 4th April 1896, reprinted in Shaw 1932 Volume II p.85.

[3003] An interior photograph dating to 1910 is in Hans Christian Adam (ed.): *Eugène Atget's Paris*. Cologne 2001 p.103.

[3004] Her assertion that in 1919 the British Ambassador, Lord Derby, wanted to marry her to enhance his diplomatic position in Paris attracts similar scepticism. It is not mentioned by Derby's biographer, Randolph S. Churchill: *Lord Derby "King of Lancashire", the Official Life of Edward, 17th Earl of Derby*. London: William Heinemann 1959.

[3005] Holland 1954 p.198.

[3006] Richard Ellmann: *Golden Codgers – Biographical Speculations*. London: Oxford University Press 1973 p.80.

[3007] Powell 1990 p.143.

[3008] Sherard 1908 p.83.

[3009] Housman p.33.

[3010] Quoted in Knox p.xvii.

[3011] Knox p.2. This is of course setting *De Profundis* on one side.

[3012] William Archer called Phillips 'the elder Dumas speaking with the voice of Milton', which falls short of enthusing one.

[3013] Worth, especially pp.5-6 and Chapter IV '*Salomé* and *A Full Moon in March*'.

[3014] Powell 1990 p.185.

[3015] Gielgud p.94.

[3016] Borsa pp.84-5.

[3017] Robertson p.230.

[3018] This is not a direct reference, as Daly's Thatre was not built until 1893, although Wilde may have known of Daly's reputation in New York.

[3019] Sherard 1937 p.305.

[3020] Oscar Wilde to Ada Rehan 8th June 1899. Rupert Hart-Davis (ed.): *More Letters of Oscar Wilde*. London: John Murray 1985 pp.182-3. Rehan's name is completely linked with Daly's as his leading lady, but although she never married, her partnership with him was a commercial one and Forbes-Winslow says 'she had no "affaires"; no stories of temperament trail after her; she was never involved in anything more serious than an occasional outbreak of the giggles on stage'. D. Forbes-Winslow: *Daly's, the Biography of a Theatre*. London: W.H. Allen 1944 p.22.

[3021] Robertson p.232. My italics.

[3022] Oscar Wilde to Robert Ross 16th August 1898. Hart-Davis 1962 p.760.

[3023] Bolitho p.133. They parted in 1914 when Cosmo joined a medical corps in France.

[3024] Bolitho pp.13, 42-3,250.

[3025] Bolitho p.13.

[3026] Bolitho pp.117,305.

[3027] Whittington-Egan p.182.

[3028] Whittington-Egan p.282.

[3029] Whittington-Egan p.363.

[3030] Whittington-Egan p.403.

[3031] Whittington-Egan p.403.

[3032] Robert Harborough Sherard: *Oscar Wilde, the Story of an Unhappy Friendship*. London: privately printed at the Hermes Press 1902.

[3033] Whittington-Egan p.403. Unfortunately Whittington-Egan and Smerdon provide no sources for any of their quotations so it is hard to identify which days 'those days' were. Le Gallienne spent much of the 1890s in the United States.

[3034] Richard Le Gallienne: *The Romantic '90s*. New edition. London: Putnam & Co 1951 pp.141,142.

[3035] Oscar Wilde to Richard Le Gallienne 1st December 1890. Holland & Hart-Davis p.457.

[3036] Healy pp.220,219.

[3037] Healy p.136.

[3038] Fouquières pp.87-8.

[3039] Rothenstein Volume I p.87.

[3040] Sherard 1906 p.178.

[3041] Leslie p.18. Ellmann, who took against Bodley, gives the substance of this story but does not quite see its nuances. Ellmann p.539. At the time Bodley was in high regard: his book France had been published by Macmillan in February of the previous year, reprinted in April and again reprinted in 1899.

[3042] Henri de Régnier: *Lettres à André Gide*. Préface et Notes par David J. Niederauer. Geneva: Librairie Droz and Paris: Librairie Minard 1972 p.133.

[3043] Robert Ross to Adela Schuster 23rd December 1900. Holland 2003 p.367. This is a rather sanitised view, but not one entirely favourable to Wilde.

[3044] Beatrix Whistler's first husband was E.W. Godwin who had designed Wilde's house in Tite Street. This probably occasioned Beatrix' hostility.

[3045] Weintraub p.100.

[3046] Joan Ungersma Halperin: *Félix Fénéon, Æsthete & Anarchist in fin-de-siècle Paris*. New Haven: Yale University Press. 1988 p.321: Donald Mead: *Oscar Wilde in Paris*. 2nd edition London: The Oscar Wilde Society 2005 p.17.

[3047] Émile Zola: *L'Assommoir*. Translated by Margaret Mauldon with an Introduction by Robert Lethbridge. World's Classics 1995; reissued as an Oxford World's Classics. Oxford: Oxford University Press 1998 p.424.

[3048] Emile Zola: *L'Œuvre*. 1886. Translated as 'The Masterpiece' by Thomas Walton; translation revised by Richard Pearson. World's Classics 1993; reissued as an Oxford World's Classics. Oxford: Oxford University Press 1999 p.398.

[3049] Robert H Sherard: *Oscar Wilde, the Story of an Unhappy Friendship*. London: Greening & Co. 1905. Popular edition 1908 p.50.

[3050] Ohnet pp.297-8.

[3051] Oscar Wilde to Robert Ross n.d. Holland and Hart-Davis p.1177. Even at this juncture, Wilde felt the need to Hellenise his pick-up.

[3052] Siegfried Sassoon: 'The destruction of Oscar Wilde', (review of Vyvyan Holland's edition of *De Profundis*), *The Observer* 30th October 1949.

[3053] Léon Lemonnier: *Oscar Wilde*. Paris: Henri Didier n.d. p.248.

[3054] Symons 1925 p.81.

[3055] *The Saturday Review* 5th November 1898, in Beerbohm 1969 p.76. This is an interesting conjunction, for we tend to see Jones through Wilde's jibes. A.E. Morgan in 1924 was rather dismissive of Wilde as passé, while regarding Jones's *Saints and Sinners* of 1884 a key text in the creation of the modern drama, and stating that 'in his belief in drama as a great art that Mr Jones was a revolutionist […] He wanted to restore it to its high place as a great form of art and criticism of life'. Morgan 1924 p.32.

[3056] A phrase which 'sounded ringingly' in the ear of Yeats. R.F. Foster: *W.B. Yeats: A Life* Volume I: *The Apprentice Mage 1865-1914*. Oxford: Oxford University Press 1997 p.80.

[3057] In the spirit with which Neil Sammells has offered us an analysis of Wilde and Quentin Tarantino (*Irish Studies Review*, Summer 1995), I would draw a parallel between Wilde and the eponymous character played by John Wayne in his final film, *The Shootist*.

[3058] Maud Wynne: *An Irishman and His Family, Lord Morris and Killanin*. London: John Murray 1937 p.187.

[3059] Judith p.14.

[3060] Francis Carco: *De Montmartre au Quartier Latin*. Paris: Albin Michel 1928. Translated by Madeleine Lloyd as *From Montmartre to the Latin Quarter*. London: Grant Richards 1929 p.104.

[3061] Barclay pp.334,335.

[3062] Henri de Régnier in *Les Annales Politiques et Littéraires* Volume LXXXV 29th November 1925 p.563. Mikhail Volume II p.465. E.H. Mikhail's translation.

[3063] Waddington 1903 p.401.

[3064] From Robert Ross' 'Oscar's last days', printed in Harris p.352. The mistakes are corrected by Ellmann pp.549-50.

[3065] Written in December 1901. Gide 1989 p.11.

[3066] His dates are given by Harvey and Hesletine as 1867-1938. Sir Rupert Hart Davis, however, gives Rictus' dates as 1867-1933 and adds de Saint-Arnaud to his surname. This perhaps suggests kinship with Marshal Saint-Arnaud, who died while commanding the French army in the Crimea. General Boulanger was known contemptuously as 'le Saint-Arnaud des cafés-concerts', which returns us to Rictus rather tidily. His *Soliloques du pauvre* was illustrated by Steinlen. Velter's dates agree with Hart Davis. Velter p.497.

[3067] Philippe Jullian: *Jean Lorrain, ou Le Satyricon 1900.* Paris: Fayard 1974 p.51.

[3068] Oscar Wilde to Robert Ross June 1899. Hart-Davis 1962 p.802; Holland and Hart-Davis p.1157.

[3069] Mix pp.79,139.

[3070] Thompson unnumbered page.

[3071] Henry p.20.

[3072] Ellmann p.550.

[3073] Hichens p.158. Hichens does not mention the incident of Robbie Ross adding the initials C.B. to the wreath and also implies that Blacker did see Wilde's body in the hotel room. *Ibidem* p.152.

[3074] Oscar Wilde to Robert Ross c. 28th May 1898. Hart-Davis 1962 p.1076 and footnote. Fabulet is miscalled Falulet in Delbourg-Delphis p.73.

[3075] Sherard 1937 p.307. Sherard dissents from this idea, but adds 'Harris basely defrauded Wilde over *Mr & Mrs Daventry*' and quotes a letter to himself from Alfred Douglas where the latter writes 'I have always believed Oscar's rage and indignation against Harris about this killed him. Harris completely ruined the play and never paid Oscar the royalties'. *Ibidem* p.305.

[3076] Quoted in Delbourg-Delphis p.58. D'Humières fell in the Great War at the head of his company of Zouaves.

[3077] Caspar Wintermans: Unpublished TS of the Author's translation of his *Bosie*, Chapter II p.1. Mauclair had originally met Wilde *chez* Pierre Louÿs when he was unfavourably impressed, thinking better of Wilde after a second encounter at Schwob's, where the Irishman was less full of himself. Langlade p.179.

[3078] The choreographer for Fuller was Nicolas Guerra. The ballet was also produced for a gala matinée at the Opéra in April 1919 with Ida Rubinstein in the name part and new choreography by Guerra. It was revived without Rubinstein in 1922. For a photograph of Rubinstein as Salomé, see Michael de Cossart: *Ida Rubinstein (1885-1960), A Theatrical Life.* Liverpool: Liverpool University Press 1987 p.113. Loïe Fuller was not only painted by Toulouse-Lautrec, but most surprisingly also by Jean Léon Gérôme, who was swept up in the enthusiasm and for once abandoned his vapid classicism and portrayed the dancer under her red and orange spotlights in a Whistler-esque swirl of draperies. Ackerman figures 413 and 414.

[3079] David Escott: 'Florent Schmitt' in Lionel Carley (ed.): *Frederick Delius, Music Art and Literature.* Aldershot: Ashgate 1998 p.115.

[3080] Green of course was the colour that Wilde had said 'in individuals is always the sign of a subtle artistic temperament, and in nations is said to denote a laxity, if not a decadence, of morals' – this last statement an odd one as coming from an Irishman.

[3081] Brémont pp.189-93.

[3082] Langlade p.280. Langlade says that Antoine invited Wilde to his production of Hauptmann's *The Weavers*, and joined Wilde's circle, but the production was in May 1893, not the spring of 1898 as Langlade implies. *Ibidem* p.289.

[3083] Langlade p.308.

[3084] Langlade pp.292,308.

[3085] Thompson unnumbered page; Le Rouge p.463; Callow p.81; Ernest La Jeunesse: *La Revue Blanche* 15th December 1900. Translated by Perceval Pollard. Reprinted in Mikhail Volume II p.480; Brémont p.195; Langlade p.308; Gide/Mason 1905 p.86. This passage does not appear in Bernard Frechtman's translation (Gide/Frechtman).

[3086] Beerbohm 1969 pp.310.

[3087] Quoted by Sir Charles Petrie: *Scenes of Edwardian Life*. London: Eyre & Spottiswoode 1965 p.33. His other asset for playing in *Mr and Mrs Daventry* was his affaire with Mrs Patrick Campbell who played Hilda Daventry. The play is passed over in silence in Daphne du Maurier: *Gerald, A Portrait*. London: Victor Gollancz 1934.

[3088] Antoine p.169.

[3089] Geoffrey Smith: *The Savoy Operas – A New Guide to Gilbert and Sullivan*. London: Robert Hale 1983 p.99.

[3090] Steegmuller/Flaubert p.241.

[3091] Laver p.48.

BIBLIOGRAPHY

'The most comprehensive bibliography will never drain the secrets of the Parisian society which bestraddled the end of the nineteenth and beginning of the twentieth centuries.'
— Franco Borsi & Ezio Godoli: *Paris 1900*.
London: Granada Publishing 1978 p.7.

[For supplementary bibliographies, please see http://oscholars-oscholars.com/bibliographies/]

À Beckett, Arthur W.: *London at the Turn of the Century, A Book of Gossip.* London: Hurst & Blackett 1900.

Abel, Richard: *The Cine Goes to Town, French Cinema 1896-1914.* Berkeley: University of California Press 1994.

Abels, Jules: *The Parnell Tragedy.* London: The Bodley Head 1966.

Ackerman, Gerald M.: *The Life and Work of Jean Léon Gérôme, with a catalogue raisonné.* London: Sotheby's 1986.

'A Cosmopolitan' [Madame v.d. Velde]: *Random Recollections of Courts & Society.* London: Ward & Downey 1888.

Acton, Harold: *Memoirs of an Æsthete.* London: Methuen 1948. New edition 1970.

Adam, Eve (ed.): *Mrs J. Comyns Carr's Reminiscences.* London: Hutchinson n.d.

Adam, Hans Christian (ed.): *Eugène Atget's Paris.* Cologne 2001.

Adams, Henry: *The Education of Henry Adams, an Autobiography.* London: Constable & Co. n.d.

Adams, Steven: *The World of the Impressionists.* London: Thames & Hudson 1985.

Adhémar, Jean and others: *Toulouse-Lautrec.* Paris: Hachette 1963.

Adler, Kathleen and Garb, Tamar: *Berthe Morisot.* Oxford: Phaidon 1987.

Adler, Kathleen: *Camille Pissarro, A Biography.* London: B.T. Batsford 1978.

Adolphus, F.: *Some Memories of Paris.* Edinburgh: William Blackwood & Sons 1895.

Agate, James (ed.): *Those Were the Nights, An Anthology of Criticism 1880-1896.* London: Hutchinson n.d..

Agulhon, Maurice: *The French Republic 1879-1992.* Translated by Antonia Nevill. Oxford: Blackwell 1993.

Ainslie, Douglas: *Adventures Literary and Social.* London: T. Fisher Unwin 1922.

'Alb' [Richard Whiteing]: *Living Paris and France, A Guide to the Manners, Monuments, Institutions and the Life of the People.* London: Ward & Downey; Paris: Galignani 1886.

Aldrich, Mrs Thomas Bailey: *Crowding Memories.* London: Constable 1921.

Allen, Tony: *An American in Paris.* London: Linkline Publications/Bison Books 1977.

'An English Officer' [George Greville Moore]: *Society Recollections in Paris and Vienna 1879-1904.* London: John Long 1907.

'An English Officer': *More Society Recollections.* London: John Long 1908.

Anderson de Novarro, Mary: *A Few More Memories.* London: Hutchinson 1936.

Anderson, Mary: *A Few Memories.* London: Osgood, McIlvaine & Co 1896.

André, Marie-Sophie and Beaufils, Christophe: *Papus, biographie, la belle époque d'occultisme.* Paris: Berg International 1995.

Andrieu, Pierre: *Souvenirs des frères Isola, cinquante ans de vie Parisienne.* Paris: Flammarion 1943.

Angell, Norman: *After All, the Autobiography of Norman Angell.* London: Hamish Hamilton 1951.

Anon [Constance E. Maud]: *An English Girl in Paris.* John Lane: The Bodley Head 1902.

Anon [Julian Osgood Field]: *More Uncensored Recollections.* London: Eveleigh Nash & Grayson. 1926.

Anon: *Kings, Courts & Society, Recollections of a V*eteran. London: Jarrolds n.d.

—. *Paris et ses cafés.* Catalogue of the exhibition of the same name. Paris: Action artistique de la Ville de Paris. Paris 2004.

—. *Teleny, or The Reverse of the Medal.* Edited with an introduction by John McRae. London: Gay Mens Press 1986, second impression 1989.

—. *The Pretty Women of Paris* 1883. New edition with an introduction by Robin de Beaumont. Ware, Herts: Wordsworth Classics 1996.

—. *Toulouse-Lautrec.* Bergamo: Istituto Italiano d'Arti Grafiche n.d.

Anstey, F. [Thomas Anstey Guthrie]: *A Long Retrospect.* London & New York: Oxford University Press 1936.

Antoine, André: *Mes Souvenirs sur le Théâtre Antoine et sur l'Odéon.* Paris: Bernard Grasset 1927.

Aquien, Pascal: *Oscar Wilde, Les mots et les songes.* Croissy-Beaubourg: Éditions Aden 2006.

Arkell, David: *Looking for Laforgue, An Informal Biography.* Manchester: Carcanet Press 1979.

Armstrong, Isobel: Unpublished lecture at the University of Exeter, 29th November 2004.

Arthur, Sir George: *A Septuagenarian's Scrapbook.* London: Thornton Butterworth 1932.

—. *Sarah Bernhardt.* London: William Heinemann 1923.

Aston, Elaine: *Sarah Bernhardt, A French Actress on the London Stage.* Oxford, New York, Munich: Berg Publishing 1989.

Atherton, Gertrude: *Adventures of a Novelist.* London: Jonathan Cape 1932.

Aubenas, Sylvie: 'Le petit monde de Disdéri. Un fonds d'atelier du Second Empire', *Études photographiques* n° 3, novembre 1997.

Baju, Anatole: *L'École décadente.* Paris: Vanier 1887.

Baldick, Robert: *The Siege of Paris.* London 1964.

Balfour, Lady Betty (ed.): *Personal and Literary Letters of Robert, First Earl of Lytton.* London: Longmans, Green & Co. 1906.

Balfour, Lady Frances: *Ne Obliviscaris – Dinna Forget.* London: Hodder and Stoughton n.d.

Bancroft, Marie & Squire: *Recollections of Sixty Years.* London: John Murray 1909.

Barbey d'Aurevilly, Jules: *Les Diaboliques.* Introduction by Peter Quennell (no translator named). London: Paul Elek 1947.

Barclay, Sir Thomas: *Thirty Years Anglo-French Reminiscences 1876-1906.* London: Constable & Co 1914.

Baring, Maurice: *French Literature.* London: Ernest Benn 1927.

—. *Sarah Bernhardt.* London: Peter Davies 1935.

—. *The Puppet Show of Memory.* London: William Heinemann 1922.

Barker, Paul R.: *Stanny, The Gilded Life of Stanford White.* New York: The Free Press and London: Collier Macmilllan 1989.

Barry, Albert: *The Life of Count Moore.* Dublin: M.H. Gill & Son 1905.

Bashkirtseff, Marie: *The Journal of Marie Bashkirtseff.* Translated by Mathilde Blind. London: Cassell & Co 1890. With a new Introduction by Rozsika Parker and Griselda Pollock. London: Virago 1985.

Battersby, Martin: *The World of Art Nouveau.* London: Arlington Books 1968.

Battersea, Constance Lady: *Reminiscences.* London: Macmillan & Co 1922.

Bayard, Jean-Emile: *The Latin Quarter, Past and Present.* Translated by Percy Mitchell. London: T. Fisher Unwin 1926.

Beach, Sylvia: *Shakespeare & Company.* London: Faber & Faber 1960.

Beatty, Laura: *Lillie Langtry, Manners, Masks and Morals.* London: Chatto & Windus 1999.

Beaumont, Keith: *Alfred Jarry – A Critical and Biographical Study.* Leicester: Leicester University Press 1984.

Beauvoy, Jacques, Marc Bertrand and Edward T. Gargan (edd.): *The Wolf and the Lamb, Popular Culture in France from the Old Regime to the Twentieth Century.* Stanford French and Italian Studies volume III. Saratoga, Cal.: Anima Libri 1977.

Beckson, Karl: *Henry Harland, His Life and Work.* London: The Eighteen Nineties Society 1978.

Beecham, Sir Thomas: *Frederick Delius.* London: Hutchinson 1959; new edition London: Severne Books 1975.

Beerbohm, Max (ed.): *Herbert Beerbohm Tree, Some Memories of Him and His Art.* London: Hutchinson n.d.

Beerbohm, Max: *Around Theatres.* London: Rupert Hart-Davis 1953.

—. *Letters to Reggie Turner.* Edited by Rupert Hart-Davis. London: Rupert Hart-Davis 1964.

—. *Mainly on the Air.* London: Heinemann. New enlarged edition 1957.

—. *More Theatres.* London: Rupert Hart-Davis 1969 pp.310.

—. *Zuleika Dobson.* London: The Bodley Head 1911. New edition London: The Folio Society 1966.

Belford, Barbara: *Bram Stoker, A Biography of the Author of Dracula.* London: Weidenfeld & Nicolson 1996.

—. *Oscar Wilde, A Certain Genius.* London: Bloomsbury 2000.

Bell, Clive: *Old Friends, Personal Recollections.* London: Chatto & Windus 1956.

Bell, Quentin: *Victorian Painters.* London: Routledge 1967.

Bellet, Guy de: *Gaby Deslys.* Paris: La Vie Amoureuse n.d.

Belloc Lowndes, Mrs: *"I, too, Have Lived in Arcadia", A Record of Love and Friendship.* London: Macmillan & Co. 1941.

—. *The Merry Wives of Westminster.* London: Macmillan 1946.

—. *Where Love and Friendship Dwelt.* London: Macmillan 1943.

Bennett, Arnold: *Books and Persons, being Comments on a Past Epoch.* London: Chatto & Windus 1917.

—. 'Henri Becque' in *Books and Persons, being Comments on a Past Epoch.* London: Chatto & Windus 1917.

—. *The Old Wives' Tale*. Introduced by Dudley Barker. London: Dent Everyman 1966.

Benois, Alexandre: *Memoirs*. Translated by Moura Budberg. London: Chatto & Windus 1964 pp.144-5.

Benson, E.F.: *Final Edition*. London: Longmans, Green & Co 1940.

Benstock, Sharon: *No Gifts from Chance, A Biography of Edith Wharton*. London: Hamish Hamilton 1994.

Bentley, E.C.: *Trent's Last Case*. London 1912. Harmondsworth: Penguin Books 1937.

Bentley, Joyce: *The Importance of being Constance*. London: Robert Hale 1983.

Bergner, Klaus: *Odilon Redon – Fantasy and Colour*. London: Weidenfeld & Nicolson 1964.

Berlanstein, Lenard R.: *The Working People of Paris 1871-1914*. Baltimore & London: Johns Hopkins University Press 1984.

Bernac, Pierre: *Poulenc, The Man and His Songs*. Translated by Winifred Radford. London: Victor Gollancz 1977.

Bernard, Jean-Pierre Arthur: *Le gout de Paris*. Paris: Mercure de France 2004.

Bernhardt, Lysiane: *Sarah Bernhardt, My Grandmother*. Translated by Vyvyan Holland. London: Hurst & Blackett 1949.

Bernhardt, Sarah: *My Double Life*. 1907. Photographic reprint London: Peter Owen 1977.

Berresford Ellis, Peter: *H. Rider Haggard, A Voice from the Infinite*. London: Routledge & Kegan Paul 1978.

Bertout, Jules *Henri Gervex Souvenirs receuillis*. Paris: Flammarion 1924 pp.50-1.

Bialek, Mireille: *Jacques-Emile Blanche à Offranville, peintre-écrivain*. Offranville: Musée Jacques-Emile Blanche 1997.

Bibliothèque Electronique de Lisieux.

Billy, André: *The Goncourt Brothers*. Translated by Margaret Shaw. London: André Deutsch 1960.

Binder, Polly: *The Truth about Cora Pearl*. London: Weidenfeld & Nicolson 1986.

Blackburn, Bonnie and Holford-Strevens, Leofranc: *The Oxford Companion to the Year*. Oxford: Oxford University Press 1999.

Blanchard, Mary Warner: *Oscar Wilde's America: Counter Culture in the Gilded Age*. Yale University Press: New Haven1998.

Blanche, Jacques-Emile: *La Pêche aux souvenirs*. Paris: Flammarion 1949 pp.18769.

—. *Portraits of a Lifetime – The Late Victorian Era, the Edwardian Pageant*. Translated and edited by Walter Clement. Introduction by Harley Granville Barker. London: J.M. Dent & Sons 1937.

Blumenfeld, R.D.: *R.D.B.'s Diary*. London: William Heinemann 1930.

Blunt, Wilfrid Scawen: *My Diaries, being a Personal Narrative of Events 1880-1914* volume I: 1880-1900. New York: Alfred A. Knopf 1921.

Bodley, John Edward Courtenay: *France*. London: Macmillan 1898; new edition revised 1899.

Bois, Albert du: *Julia Bartet*. Essai critique. Sansot 1920.

Bolitho, Hector: *Marie Tempest*. London: Cobden Sanderson 1936.

Boon, John: *Victorians, Edwardians, and Georgians, The Impressions of a Veteran Journalist extending over Forty Years*. London: Hutchinson n.d.

Booth, Bradford A. and Mehew Ernest (edd.): *The Letters of Robert Louis Stevenson*. New Haven and London: Yale University Press 1995 volume V: July 1884 to August 1887.

Bordwell, David E. and Thompson Kristin: 'The power of Mise-en-scene' in *Film Art, an Introduction*. McGraw Hill 1997.

Borland, Maureen: *D.S. MacColl, Painter, Poet, Art Critic*. Harpenden: Lennard Publishing 1995.

Borland, Maureen: *Wilde's Devoted Friend – A Life of Robert Ross 1869-1918*. Oxford: Lennard Publishing 1990.

Borsa, Mario: *The English Stage of To-day*. Translated from the original Italian and edited with a prefatory note by Selwyn Brinton M.A. London: John Lane The Bodley Head 1908.

Borsi, Franco and Godoli, Ezio: *Paris 1900*. London: Granada Publishing 1978.

Boudaille, Georges: *Gauguin*. Translated by Alise Jaffa. London: Thames & Hudson 1964.

Bouillon, Jean Paul: *Art Nouveau 1870-1914*. London: Weidenfeld & Nicolson 1985.

Boulestin, X.-M.: *Myself, My Two Countries*. London: Cassell & Co 1936.

Bourke, Marcus: *John O'Leary, A Study in Irish Separatism*. Athens: University of Georgia Press 1967 .

Bowen-Rowlands, Ernest: *In the Light of the Law*. London: Grant Richards 1931.

Bowra, C.M.: *The Heritage of Symbolism*. London: Macmillan 1963.

Brackenbury, General the Right Hon. Sir Henry,: *Some Memories of My Spare Time*. Edinburgh & London: William Blackwood & Sons 1909.

Bradbury, Malcolm: *The Modern World, Ten Great Writers*. London: Martin Secker & Warburg 1988.

Brandon, Ruth: *Being Divine, A Biography of Sarah Bernhardt*. London: Secker & Warburg 1991.

Brasol, Boris: *Oscar Wilde, The Man, The Artist*. London: Williams & Norgate 1938.

Brémont ,Anna, comtesse de: *Oscar Wilde and His Mother, A Memoir*. London: Everett & Co 1918.

Brettell, Richard R.: *French Impressionists*. Chicago: The Art Institute of Chicago 1987.

Brogan, D.W.: *The French Nation, from Napoléon to Pétain 1814-1940*. London: Hamish Hamilton 1957.

Broido, Lucy: *The Posters of Jules Chéret*, with a Catalogue Raisonné. New York: Dover Books 1980.

Brookfield, Charles H.E.: *Random Reminiscences*. London: Edwin Arnold. 2nd impression 1902.

Brooks, Van Wyck: *Howells, His Life and World*. London: J.M. Dent & Sons 1959 pp209, 210.

—. *The Confident Years 1885-1915*. New York: E.P. Dutton & Co.

Browning, Oscar: *Memories of Sixty Years, at Eton, Cambridge and Elsewhere*. London: John Lane: The Bodley Head 1910.

Browse, Lilian (ed.): *Constantin Guys*. London: Faber & Faber 1946.

Buchanan, Meriel: 'The Grand Duchess Vladimir' in *Victorian Gallery*. London: Cassell & Co 1956.

Buchanan, Meriel: *Ambassador's Daughter*. London: Cassell & Co 1958.

Buckle, Richard: *Diaghilev*. London: Weidenfeld & Nicolson 1979.

Burnand, Robert: *Le duc d'Aumale et son temps*. Paris: Librairie Hachette 1949.

Burnand, Sir Francis: *Records and Reminiscences, Personal and General*. London: Methuen 1904.

Burns, Niamh: 'The Imagery of Debussy', unpublished lecture given at the National Gallery of Ireland 29th June 1999.

Cadars, Pierre: 'La mère, la fille et l'opéra' in Dottin-Orsini.

Caird, Mona: *The Daughters of Danaus*. London: Bliss, Sands & Foster 1894.

Callow, Simon: *Oscar Wilde and His Circle*. London: National Portrait Gallery Publications 2000.

Callwell, Major-General Sir C.E.: *Stray Recollections*. London: Edwin Arnold 1923.

Carco, Francis: *De Montmartre au Quartier Latin*. Paris: Albin Michel 1928. Translated by Madeleine Lloyd as *From Montmartre to the Latin Quarter*. London: Grant Richards 1929.

Carley, Lionel (ed.): *Frederick Delius, Music Art and Literature*. Aldershot: Ashgate 1998.

Carlson, Marvin: *The French Stage in the Nineteenth Century*. Metuchen, New Jersey: The Scarecrow Press 1972.

Carr, John Dickson: *The Waxworks Murders*. London: Hamish Hamilton 1932.

Carroll, E. Malcolm: *French Public Opinion and Foreign Affairs 1870-1914*. London: Frank Cass & Co 1936.

Cars, Laurence des: 'Burne-Jones and France' in Stephen Wildman and John Christian: *Edward Burne Jones, Victorian Artist-Dreamer*. New York: Metropolitan Museum of Art 1998.

Casselaer, Catherine van: *Lot's Wife, Lesbian Paris 1890-1914*. Liverpool: Janus Press.

Castle, Charles: *The Folies Bergère*. London: Methuen 1982.

Cate, Phillip Dennis (ed.): *The Graphic Arts and French Society 1871-1914*. New Brunswick & London: Rutgers University Press with the Jane Voorheese Zimmerli Art Museum 1988.

Caws, Mary Ann: *Marcel Proust*. Woodstock, NY: The Overlook Press 2003.

Celebonovic, Aleksa: *Chefs d'Œuvres du réalisme bourgeois*. Adapted and edited by Sacha Tolstoî and translated by Peter Willis as *The Heyday of Salon Painting, Masterpieces of Bourgeois Realism*. London: Thames & Hudson 1974.

Cevasco, G.A.: *J-K Huysmans, A Reference Guide*. Boston: G.K. Hall 1980.

—. *Oscar Wilde, British Author, Poet & Wit*. Charlotteville, NY: Samhar Press 1972.

Chai, Leon: *Æstheticism, The Religion of Art in Post-Romantic Literature*. New York: Columbia University Press 1990.

Chamberlain The Rt. Hon. Sir Austen: *Down the Years*. London: Cassell & Co 1935.

Chartier, Monique: *Zola, Trois Etés à Royan*. Préface de Colette Becker. Royan: Editions Bonne Anse 2003.

Chesson, Wilfred: 'A Reminiscence of 1898'. New York: *The Bookman* volume 34 December 1911.

Child, Theodore: 'Dining in Paris', Chapter VIII of Whiteing, q.v .

Chothia, Jean (ed.): *The New Woman and Other Emancipated Woman Plays*. Oxford: Oxford University Press 1998.

Chothia Jean: *André Antoine*. Cambridge: Cambridge University Press 1991.

Churchill, Randolph S.: *Lord Derby "King of Lancashire", the Official Life of Edward, 17ᵗʰ Earl of Derby*. London: William Heinemann 1959.

Clark, Timothy J.: 'The Bar at the Folies Bergères' in Beauvoy Jacques; Bertrand, Marc and Gargan, Edward T. (edd.): *The Wolf and the Lamb, Popular Culture in France from the Old Regime to the Twentieth Century*. Stanford French and Italian Studies volume III. Saratoga, Cal.: Anima Libri 1977.

Clement, Russell T. and Houze Annick: *Neo-Impressionist Painters : A Sourcebook on Georges Seurat, Camille Pissarro, Paul Signac, Theo Van Rysselberghe, Henri Edmond Cross, Charles Angrand*. Greenwood Publishing Group 1999.

Cline, Catherine Anne: *E.D. Morel 1873-1924, The Strategies of Protest*. Belfast: Blackstaff Press 1980.

Clive, H.P.: *Pierre Louÿs (1870-1925), A Biography*. Oxford: Clarendon Press 1978.

Clunn, Harold: *The Face of Paris*. London: Spring Books n.d.

Cockburn, Claud: *Bestseller, The Books that Everyone Read 1900-1939*. London: Sidgwick & Jackson 1972.

Cogniat, Raymond: *Sisley*. Translated by Alice Sachs. Naefels: Bonfini Press 1978.

Coleman, Elizabeth Ann: *The Opulent Era – Fashions of Worth, Doucet and Pingat*. London & New York: Thames & Hudson and the Brooklyn Museum 1989.

Colette: *Chéri*. London: The Folio Society 1963.

—. *Gigi*. Lausanne: La Guild du Livre 1944. New edition, with a foreword by Alain Brunet. Paris: Hachette n.d.

—. *Gigi*. Translated by Roger Senhouse 1949. Harmondsworth: Penguin Books 1958.

Colin, Paul: 'Le créateur de l'affiche moderne', Chapter VI of Adhémar, q.v.

Colle, Robert: *L'Histoire de Royan et de la Côte de Beauté*. Royan: Jeune Chambre Economique 1988.

Collell, Carmen; Greenacre, Francis; Hedley, Gillian; and Mendes-Murao, Maria: *An Anthology of Victorian and Edwardian paintings from the collection of the City Art Gallery, Bristol*. Swansea: The Glynn Vivian Art Gallery, Bristol: The City Art Gallery 1975.

Colvin, Ian: *The Life of Jameson*. London: Edwin Arnold 1932.

Conway, John Joseph: *Footprints of Famous Americans in Paris.* With an Introduction by Mrs John Lane. London: John Lane The Bodley Head 1912.

Conway, Moncure Daniel: *Autobiography, Memories and Experiences.* London: Cassell & Co. 1904;.

Coolidge, T. Jefferson: *An Autobiography.* Boston: Massachusetts Historical Society 1923.

Cortissoz, Royal: *The Life of Whitelaw Reid.* London: Thornton Butterworth 1921.

Cossart, Michael de*: Ida Rubinstein (1885-1960), A Theatrical Life.* Liverpool: Liverpool University Press 1987.

Cossart, Michael de: *The Food of Love – Princesse de Polignac (1865-1943) and Her Salon.* London: Hamish Hamilton 1978.

Coustillas, Pierre: *Gissing's Writings on Dickens*. London: Enitharmon Press, 1969.

Coustillas, Pierre (ed.): *London & the Life of Literature in late Victorian England, The Diary of George Gissing, Novelist.* Hassocks: The Harvester Press 1978.

Craig, Edward Gordon: *Index to the Story of My Days 1872-1907.* London: Hulton Press 1957.

Crespelle, Jean-Paul: *La vie quotidienne à Montmartre à la Grande Epoque 1905-1930.* Paris : Hachette 1976.

Croft-Cooke, Rupert: *Bosie, The Story of Lord Alfred Douglas, His Friends and Enemies.* London: W.H. Allen 1963.

Crosland, Margaret: *Colette, The Difficulty of Loving.* London: Peter Owen 1973.

Crozier, Laurent: Programme notes for *Salomé,* the Opéra de Nice productionNice May/June 2005.

Cruysmans, Philippe: 'Vienne-Bruxelles et les origines du Jugendstil'. *L'Œil* no.387 October 1987.

Current, Richard Nelson and Current Marcia Ewing: *Loïe Fuller, Goddess of Light.* Boston: Northeastern University Press 1997.

Cust, Sir Lionel: *King Edward VII and His Court, Some Reminiscences.* London: John Murray 1930.

Daly, Joseph Francis: *The Life of Augustin Daly.* New York: The Macmillan Company 1917.

Dandois, Bernard: *Entre Marx et Bakounine: César de Paepe.* Paris: Maspéro 1974.

Daniel, Mary: *The French Drama of the Unspoken.* Edinburgh: Edinburgh University Press 1953.

Darcos, Xavier: *Oscar a toujours raison.* Paris: Plon 2013.

Dark, Sidney: *Mainly About Other People*. London: Hodder & Stoughton 1925.

Daudet, Alphonse: *Twenty Years of Paris and of My Literary Life*. Translated by Laura Ensor. London: George Routledge & Sons 1888.

Daudet, Lucien: *L'Impératrice Eugénie*. Paris: Fayard n.d.

Daulte, François: *Alfred Sisley, Catalogue Raisonné de l'Œuvre Peint*. Paris: Éditions Durand-Ruel 1959.

Daurelle, Jacques: *Echo de Paris* 6th December 1891, reprinted in Mikhail volume I.

Davis, Jill: 'The New Woman and the new life' in Gardner and Rutherford, q.v.

Davis, Peter G.: *The American Opera Singer, The Lives and Adventures of America's Great Singers in Opera and in Concert from 1825 to the Present*. New York: Doubleday 1997.

Davis, Richard Harding: *About Paris*. New York: Harper Brothers 1895.

Dawson, Brigadier General Sir Douglas: *A Soldier-Diplomat*. London: John Murray 1927.

Day, Helen: 'Female daredevils' in Viv Gardner & Susan Rutherford (edd.): *The New Woman and Her Sisters, Feminism and Theatre 1850-1914*. Hemel Hempstead: Harvester Wheatsheaf 1992.

Deak, Frantisek: *Symbolist Theater, The Formation of an Avant-garde*. Baltimore: Johns Hopkins University Press 1993.

Delafond, Marianne and Genet-Bondeville, Caroline: *Jean-François Raffaëlli*. Paris: Musée Marmotton-Monet 1999.

Delaney, J.G.P.: *Charles Ricketts – A Biography*. Oxford: Clarendon Press 1990.

Delarue-Mardrus, Lucie: *Les Amours d'Oscar Wilde*. Paris: Flammarion 1930.

Delbourg-Delphis, Marylène: *Masculin Singulier, le dandysme et son histoire*. Paris: Hachette 1985.

Delevoye, Robert, Lascault Gilbert; Verheggen, Jean-Pierre and Cuvalier, Guy: *Felicien Rops*. Lausanne & Paris: Comos Monographies / Bibliothèque des Arts 1985.

Dictionnaire des Peintres, Sculpteurs, Dessinateurs et Graveurs. Paris: Librairie Gründ 1976.

Diehl, Alice: *The True Story of My Life, An Autobiography*. London: John Lane The Bodley Head 1907.

Dietschy, Marcel: *La Passion de Claude Debussy*. Neuchâtel: Éditions de la Baconnière 1962. Translated and revised by William Ashbrook and Margaret G. Cobb as *A Portrait of Claude Debussy*. Oxford: Oxford University Press 1990.

Dimnet, Ernest: *France Herself Again*. London: Chatto & Windus 1913.
—. *My New World*. London: Jonathan Cape 1938.
—. *My Old World*. London: Jonathan Cape 1935.
Distel, Anne; Druick, Douglas W.; Groom, Gloria and Ropetti, Rodolphe: *Gustave Caillebotte, Urban Impressionist*. Paris: La Réunion des Musées Nationaux and the Musée d'Orsay; Chicago: The Art Institute 1995.
Donna, Maurice: *Autour du Chat Noir*. Paris: Bernard Grasset 1926.
Dorais, Lucie: *J.W. Morrice*. Toronto: National Gallery of Canada, Canadian Artists Series 1985.
Dottin-Orsini, Mireille (ed.): *Salomé*. Collection 'Figures Mythiques'. Paris: Éditions Autrement 1996.
Dottin-Orsini, Mireille: 'Le banquet d'Hérode' in Dottin-Orsini, q.v.
Douglas, Lord Alfred: *Autobiography*. London: Martin Secker 1929 Appendix.
—. *Oscar Wilde, A Plea and a Reminiscence*. Introduced and annotated by Caspar Wintermans. Woubrugge: Avalon Press 2002.
—. *Oscar Wilde, A Summing Up*. London: Richards Press 1940.
—. *Without Apology*, 278).
Doyle, Sir Arthur Conan: *Memories and Adventures*. London: Hodder & Stoughton n.d. [1924].
Drabble, Margaret: *Arnold Bennett, A Biography*. London: Weidenfeld & Nicholson 1974.
Dubar, Monique: 'Oscar Wilde et Strauss, ou le corps dansant' in Dottin-Orsini, q.v.
Duberman, Martin: *James Russell Lowell*. Boston, Mass.: Houghton Miflin Co 1966.
Dubeux, Albert: *Julia Bartet*. Préface de Maurice Donnay. Paris: Plon 1938.
Duff Gordon, Lucy Lady: *Discretions and Indiscretions*. London: Jarrolds 1932.
Dugdale, Edgar T.S.: *Maurice de Bunsen, Diplomat and Friend*. London: John Murray 1934.
Dumas, Alexandre *fils*: *La Dame aux Camélias*. 1848. Translated by David Coward. Oxford: Oxford University Press 2000.
Duncan, Barry: *The St James' Theatre, Its Strange and Complete History*. London: Barrie & Rockcliff 1964.
Duncan, Isadora: *My Life*. London: Victor Gollancz 1928.
Dunraven, The Earl of: *Past Times and Pastimes*. London: Hodder & Stoughton n.d. [1922].

Duret, Théodore: *Histoire de J. McN. Whistler, et de son Œuvre.* Paris: Floury 1904.

Dussert, Eric: 'La main dans le sac' in *Le Matricule des Anges* Numéro 22 janvier/mars 1998.

—. 'Les Egarés Les Oubliés', *Le Matricule des Anges*, no 20 juillet/août 1997.

Duval, E. L.: *Théodor de Wyzewa, Critic without a Country.* Geneva: Librairie Droz 1961.

Eckardt, Wolf von; Gilman, Sander L. and Chamberlin, J. Edward: *Oscar Wilde's London: A Scrapbook of Vices & Virtues 1880-1900.* New York Anchor Press / Doubleday.

Edel, Leon: *Henry James, A Life.* London: Collins 1987.

—. Introduction to Henry James: *Guy Domville.* London: Rupert Hart-Davis 1961.

Edmonds, Jill: 'Princess Hamlet' in Gardner and Rutherford, q.v.

Eekhoud, Georges: 'Saint Sebastien dans la peinture'. *Akdemos* 1 15th February 1909.

Ellmann, Richard: *Four Dubliners.* London: Hamish Hamilton 1987; New York: George Braziller 1988.

—. *Golden Codgers – Biographical Speculations.* London: Oxford University Press 1973.

—. 'The mark of the aristocrat', review of A.W. Raitt: *The Life of Villiers de Lisle Adam.* Oxford: Clarendon Press 1981. *Times Literary Supplement* 23rd October 1981.

—. *Oscar Wilde.* London: Hamish Hamilton 17.

—. 'Overtures to Wilde's Salomé', in Puffett, q.v.

Eltis, Sos: *Revising Wilde: Society and Subversion in the Plays of Oscar Wilde.* Oxford: Clarendon Press 1996.

Emanuel, Frank L.: *Illustrators of Montmartre.* London: A. Siegel 1904.

Escott, T.H.S.: *England, Its People, Polity and Pursuits.* London: Chapman & Hall 1884. New and revised edition 1890.

Evans, Henry Ridgely: 'A Day With Alexander the Great', *The Sphinx*, Kansas City, volume 4, Nos. 3 & 4, May and June 1905.

Falk, Bernard: *Five Years Dead, A Postcript to He Laughed in Fleet Street.* London: The Book Club 1938.

Farcy, Gérard-Denis: 'Shaw et la scène française', in Paul Brennan & Thierry Dubost (edd.): *G. B. Shaw : un dramaturge engagé.* Caen : Presses Universiaires de Caen 1998.

Farnham, Charles Haight: *A Life of Francis Parkman.* London: Macmillan 1900.

Farson, Daniel: *The Man Who Wrote Dracula, A Biography of Bram Stoker*. London: Michael Joseph 1979.

Felbermann, Renée (ed.): *The Memoirs of a Cosmopolitan*. By Heinrich Felbermann. London: Chapman & Hall 1936.

First, Ruth and Scott, Anne: *Olive Schreiner*. London: André Deutsch 1988.

Fisher, H.A.L.: *A History of Europe*. London: Eyre & Spottiswoode 1935. New and enlarged edition 1938, republished 1952. Volume II: From the Beginning of the Eighteenth Century to 1937.

—. *An Unfinished Biography*. London: Oxford University Press 1941.

Fitzgerald, Penelope: *The Knox Brothers*. London: Macmillan 1977.

Flaubert, Gustave: *Hérodias.* Postface de Julien Cendres: Éditions Mille et Une Nuits 2000.

—. *Trois Contes*. Paris: Charpentier 1877. Translated as *Three Tales* with an Introduction by Robert Baldick. London: Penguin Books 1961.

Fleming, G.H.: *Lady Colin Campbell, Victorian 'Sex Goddess'.* Adlestrop: Windrush Press 1989.

Fleming, John and Honour, Hugh: *The Penguin Dictionary of Decorative Arts*. London: 1977.

Flower, Newman (ed.): *The Journals of Arnold Bennett 1896-1910*. London: Cassell 1952.

Forbes-Robertson, Sir Johnston: *A Player under Three Reigns*. London: T. Fisher Unwin. 1925.

Forbes-Winslow, D.: *Daly's, the Biography of a Theatre*. London: W.H. Allen 1944.

Ford, Ford Madox: *Return to Yesterday*. London: Victor Gollancz 1931.

Foster, R.F.: *W.B. Yeats: A Life* volume I: *The Apprentice Mage 1865-1914*. Oxford: Oxford University Press 1997.

Foulkes, Richard: 'The French Play in London: The Comédie-Française at the Gaiety Theatre 1879', *Theatre Research* 56, 2002, pp.125-131.

Fouquières, André de: *Mon Paris et ses Parisiens*. Paris: Éditions Pierre Horay 1953.

Fox, Shirley: *An Artist's Reminiscences of Paris in the Eighties*. London: Mills & Boon 1909.

France, Anatole: *On Life and Letters*. First series. Translated by A.W. Evans. London: John Lane The Bodley Head 1910. New edition 1924.

Frantz, Henri: *A Forgotten Artist: Constantin Guys* (London: The Studio 1905.

Frazier, Adrian: *George Moore, 1852-1933*. New Haven & London: Yale University Press 2000.

Frèches, Claire and José: *Toulouse-Lautrec, Painter of the Night*. Translated by Alexandra Campbell. London: Thames & Hudson 1994.

Frederic, V.: *Rodin, A Biography*. London: Hutchinson 1987.

Freeman, William: *The Life of Lord Alfred Douglas, Spoilt Child of Genius*. London: Herbert Joseph 1948.

Frewen, Oswald: *Sailor's Soliloquy*. Edited by G.P. Griggs. London: Hutchinson 1961.

Frey, Julia: *Toulouse-Lautrec, A Life*. London: Weidenfeld & Nicolson 1994.

Fryer, Jonathan: *André and Oscar – Gide, Wilde and the Gay Art of Living*. London: Constable 1997.

Fryer, Jonathan: 'Harry Marillier and the Love of the Impossible', *The Wildean* 28, January 2006.

—. *Robbie Ross, Oscar Wilde's True Love*. London: Constable 2000.

Gallant, Mavis: 'Paul Léautaud, 1872-1956' in *Paris Notebooks*. London: Hamish Hamilton 1989.

Gardner, Viv & Rutherford, Susan (edd.): *The New Woman and Her Sisters, Feminism and Theatre 1850-1914*. Hemel Hempstead: Harvester Wheatsheaf 1992.

Gay, Peter: *Freud, A Life for Our Time*. London: J.M. Dent 1988.

Gaze, Delia (ed.): *Dictionary of Women Artists*. London & Chicago: Fitzroy Dearborn 1997.

Gide, André: *Correspondence avec Francis Vielé-Griffin 1891-1931*. Édition établie, presentée et annotée par Henry de Paysac. Lyon: Presses Universitaires 1986.

—. *Journals 1889-1949*. Translated, selected and edited by Justin O'Brien. London: Secker & Warburg 1947.

—. *Oscar Wilde, A Study from the French*. Translated by Stuart Mason. Oxford: Holywell Press 1905.

—. *Oscar Wilde*. Paris: Mercure de France 1989.

—. *Oscar Wilde*. Translated by Bernard Frechtman. London: William Kimber 19 51.

—. *Si le grain ne meurt*. Translated by Dorothy Bussy as *If It Die...An Autobiography*. 1935. New York: Vintage Books 2001.

Gielgud, Kate Terry: *A Victorian Playgoer*. With forewords by John Gielgud, Val Gielgud and Elinor Gielgud. Edited by Muriel St Clair Byrne. London: Heinemann 1980.

Gildea, Richard: *Marianne in Chains, in search of the German 0ccupation 1940-1945*. London: Macmillan 2002 pp.153-5.

Gillies, Midge: *Marie Lloyd, the One and Only*. London: Victor Gollancz 1999.

Gilmour David: *Curzon, Imperial Statesman 1859–1925*. London: John Murray 1994.

Gindertael, Roger van: *Ensor*. Translated from the French by Vivienne Menkes. London: Studio Vista 1975.

Glendinning, Victoria: *Vita, the Life of V. Sackville-West*. London: Weidenfeld & Nicolson 1983.

Glyn, Anthony: *Elinor Glyn, A Biography*. London: Hutchinson 1957.

Gold, Arthur & Fizdale, Robert: *Misia, The Life of Misia Sert*. London: Macmillan 1980.

Gold, Arthur & Robert, Fizdale: *The Divine Sarah, A Life of Sarah Bernhardt*. New York: Alfred A. Knopf 1991.

Gomez Carillo, Ernesto: 'Comment Oscar Wilde rêva de Salomé', *La Plume* 1902 pp.1147-52. Translated as 'How Oscar Wilde Dreamed of Salomé', in Mikhail, q.v..

Goncourt, Edmond et Jules de: *Journal – Mémoires de la Vie Littéraire*. Paris: Robert Laffont 1989.

Goncourt, Edmond and Jules de: *Pages from the Goncourt Journal*. Edited, Translated and Introduced by Robert Baldick. London: Oxford University Press 1962.

Gooch, G.P.: *Court and Cabinets*. London: Longmans, Green & Co 1944.

—. *Under Six Reigns*. London: Longmans, Green & Co 1958.

Gosling, Nigel: *Nadar*. Amsterdam: Meulenhoff: London: Secker & Warburg 1976.

Gosse, Edmund: 'Marcel Schwob'. *The Athenæum* 4th March 1905.

—. *Aspects & Impressions*. London: Cassell & Co 1922.

—. *Books on the Table*. London: William Heinemann 1923 dedication.

—. *Father & Son, A Study of Two Temperaments*. Edited by Peter Abbs. London: Penguin Books 1983, reprinted 1986.

—. *Leaves and Fruit*. London: William Heinemann 1927.

Got, Edmond: *Journal*. Publiée par son fils Médéric Got. Paris: Plon 1910.

Gottlieb, Marc J.: *The Plight of Emulation, Ernest Meissonier and French Salon Painting*. Princeton: Princeton University Press 1996.

Goujon, Jean-Paul: "Ernest La Jeunesse", *L'Étoile-Absinthe*, 23è et 24è Tournées, 1984..

Gould, Warwick, Kelly John and Toomey Deirdre (edd.): *The Collected Letters of W.B. Yeats* volume II 1896-1900. Oxford: The Clarendon Press 1997.

Gourmont, Remy de: 'La littérature anglaise en France', reprinted in Remy de Gourmont: *Promenades Littéraires*. Paris: Mercure de France. 17e édition 1919.

Gramont, Elizabeth de, ex-duchesse de Clermont-Tonnerre: *Au temps des Equipages*. Translated as *Pomp and Circumstance* by Brian W. Downs, with an Introduction by Louis Bromfield. London: Jonathan Cape 1929.

Green, Julian: *Memories of Happy Days*. London: J.M. Dent & Co. 1944. 3rd impression 1946.

Green, Nancy: *The Other Americans in Paris 1880-1941*. University of Chicago Press 2014.

Greenhalgh, Paul: 'The Paris Exposition Universelle 1900'. Unpublished lecture given at the Royal Academy, London 4th February 2000.

Grenville-Murray, Eustace: *High Life in France under the Republic, Social and Satirical Sketches in Paris and the Provinces*. London: Vizetelly & Co 1884.

Gribble, Francis: *The Tragedy of Isabella II*. London: Chapman & Hall 1913.

Grierson, Francis: *Parisian Portraits*. London: Stephen Swift 1911.

Griffin, Susan: *The Book of the Courtesans, A Catalogue of their Virtues*. New York: Broadway Books 2001.

Grindea, Miron: Obituary of Natalie Clifford Barney, London: *The Times* 4th January 1972.

Groom, Gloria: *Edouard Vuillard, Painter Decorator. Patrons and Projects 1892-1912*. New Haven: Yale University Press 1993.

Grunfeld, Frederic V.: *Rodin, A Biography*. London: Hutchinson 1987S.

Guedalla, Philip: *The Second Empire*. London: Hodder & Stoughton 1922. Uniform edition 1946.

Gury, Christian: *Bibi-la-Purée, Compagnon de Verlaine*. Paris: Editions Kimé 2004.

Gutierrez, José Ismael: 'Dos aceramientos a un motivo literario de fin de siglio: la *Salomé* de Oscar Wilde y la de Enrique Gomez Carillo.' *Hispanic Review* volume 63 no 3 Summer 1995.

Habermas, Jürgen: 'Modernity – An Incomplete Project'. Translated by Seyla Ben-Habib. In Hal Forster (ed.): *The Anti-Æsthetic, Essays in Post-Modern Culture*. Port Townsend, Washington 1983.

Haine, W. Scott: *The World of the Paris Café – Sociability among the French Working Class 1789-1914*. Baltimore: Johns Hopkins University Press.

Halperin, Joan Ungersma: *Félix Fénéon, Æsthete & Anarchist in fin-de-siècle Paris*. New Haven: Yale University Press 1988.

Hamburger, Michael: *The Truth of Poetry, Tensions in Modernist Poetry since Baudelaire.* London: Weidenfeld and Nicolson 1968. New edition London: Anvil Press1996.

Hamerton, Philip Gilbert: *An Autobiography 1834-1858*, and a Memoir by His Wife 1858-1894. London: Seely & Co 1897.

Hamilton, Lord Frederic: *Here, There and Everywhere.* London: Hodder & Stoughton n.d.

Hamilton, Lord Frederic: *The Days before Yesterday.* London: Hodder & Stoughton 1924, republished as *The Vanished World of Yesterday.* London: Hodder & Stoughton 1950.

Hansen, Arlen J.: *Expatriate Paris, A Cultural and Literary Guide to the Paris of the 1920s.* New York: Little, Brown & Co 1990.

Hanson, Ellis: *Decadence and Catholicism.* Cambridge, Mass: Harvard University Press 1997.

Harding, James: *Folies de Paris, The Rise and Fall of French Operetta.* London: Chappell & Co / Elm Tree Books 1979.

Harding, James: *Gounod.* London: George Allen & Unwin 197.

Harding, James: *Lost Illusions, Paul Léautaud and His World.* London: George Allen & Unwin 1971.

Harding, James: *Massenet.* London: J.M. Dent & Sons 1970.

Hardy Thomas: *Far From the Madding Crowd* (1874) Chapter XXII.

—. *The Return of the Native.* 1878. London: Macmillan Library edition 1949 pp. 358, 284.

—. *The Well-Beloved, A Sketch of a Temperament.* 1897. New Wessex Edition. Introduction by J. Hillis Miller and Notes by Edward Mendelson. London: Macmillan 1975.

—. *The Woodlanders.* 1887. Edited with an introduction and Notes by Patricia Ingham. London: Penguin 1997.

—. *Two on a Tower.* Edited by Sally Shuttleworth. London: Penguin 1999.

Harlan, Louis R.: *Booker T. Washington, The Making of a Black Leader.* New York Oxford University Press 1972.

Harris, Frank: *Oscar Wilde.* New edition, London: Robinson Publishing 1992.

—. *Oscar Wilde: His Life and Confessions.* New York: Crown Publishing Co 1930£.

Harris, Geraldine: 'Yvette Guilbert' in Gardner and Rutherford, q.v.

Harrison, Mrs. Burton: *Recollections Grave and Gay.* New York: Charles Scribner's Sons 1911.

Harrison, Frederic: *Autobiographic Memoirs.* London: 1911.

Harrison, Michael: *Clarence, The Life of H.R.H. the Duke of Clarence and Avondale*. London: W.H. Allen 1972.

Harriss, Joseph: *The Eiffel Tower, Symbol of an Age*. London: Paul Elek 1976.

Hart-Davis, Rupert (compiler): *A Catalogue of the Caricatures of Max Beerbohm*. London: Macmillan 1972.

Hart-Davis, Rupert (ed.): *Max Beerbohm, A Peep into the Past and other Prose Pieces*. London: Heinemann 1972.

—. *More Letters of Oscar Wilde*. London: John Murray.

Harte, Geoffrey Bret (ed.): *The Letters of Bret Harte*. London: Hodder & Stoughton.

Hartley, Anthony (ed.): *The Penguin Book of French Verse* volume III: The Nineteenth Century. Harmondsworth: Penguin 1957.

Hartrick, A.S., R.W.S.: *A Painter's Pilgrimage through Fifty Years*. Cambridge: Cambridge University Press 1939.

Harvey, David: *Consciousness and the Urban Experience*. Oxford: Basil Blackwell 1985.

Harvey, Sir Paul and Hesletine, J.E. (edd.): *The Oxford Companion to French Literature*. London: Oxford University Press 1959.

Hause, Stephen C.: *Hubertine Auclert, the French Suffragette*. New Haven & London: Yale University Press 1987.

Hawthorne, Melanie: 'Peripheral Publishing, or Is Tolla Dorian Totally boring?' in Timothy Raser (ed.): *Peripheral nineteenth-century French studies: view from the edge*. Cranbury NJ: Associated University Presses 2002.

Hay, John: *Letters of John Hay and Extracts from His Diary*. Washington, D.C.: Privately printed 1908.

Haymann, Emmanuel (ed.): *Oscar Wilde, Les Pensées*. Paris: Le Cherche Midi 1990.

Haymann, Emmanuel: *Pauline Metternich, la jolie laide du Second Empire*. Paris: Perrin 1991.

Healy, Chris: *Confessions of a Journalist*. London: Chatto & Windus 1904.

Hefting, Paul: Catalogue of the Kröller-Müller Museum, Otter.

Hemmings, F.W.J.: *Culture and Society in France 1848-1898 – Dissidents and Philistines*. London: Batsford 1971.

Hemmings, F.W.J.: *The Life and Times of Emile Zola*. London: Paul Elek 1977.

—. *The Theatre Industry in Nineteenth Century France*. Cambridge: Cambridge University Press 1993.

—. *Theatre and State in France 1760-1905.* Cambridge: Cambridge University Press 1994.

Henderson, John A.: *The First Avant-Garde 1887-1894.* Sources of Modern French Theatre. London: George G. Harrap & Co 1971.

Hendricks, Gordon: *Eadweard Muybridge, The Father of the Motion Picture.* London: Secker & Warburg 1975.

Henry, Marjorie Louise: *Stuart Merrill, la contribution d'un Américain au symbolisme français.* Paris: Honoré Champion 1927.

Henry, Paul: *An Irish Portrait, the Autobiography of Paul Henry R.H.A.* London: B.T. Batsford Ltd 1951.

Hepburn, James (ed.): *Letters of Arnold Bennett* volume II 1889-1915. London: Oxford University Press 1968.

Herbert, Robert L.: *Impressionism, Art, Leisure and Parisian Society.* New Haven & London: Yale University Press 1988.

Hetherington, John: *Melba, A Biography.* London: Faber & Faber London 1967.

Hibbert, Christopher: *King Edward VII, A Portrait.* London: Allen Lane 1976.

Hichens, Mark: *Oscar Wilde's Last Chance – The Dreyfus Connection.* Edinburgh: The Pentland Press 1999.

Higonnet, Anne: *Berthe Morisot, A Biography.* London: Collins 1990.

Hobson, Sir Harold: *French Theatre since 1830.* London: John Calder 1978.

Hohenlohe-Schillingsfürst, Prince Chlodwig von: *Memoirs.* Edited by Friedrich Curtius for Prince Alexander von Hohenlohe-Schillingsfürst, translated from the first German edition and supervised by George W. Chrystal, B.A. London: William Heinemann 1906.

Holden, W.H.: *The Pearl from Plymouth – Eliza Emma Crouch alias Cora Pearl.* With notes on some of her celebrated contemporaries. London: British General & Technical Press 1950.

Holland, Merlin & Hart-Davis Rupert: *The Complete Letters of Oscar Wilde.* London: Fourth Estate 2000.

Holland, Merlin (ed.): *Oscar Wilde, A Life in Letters.* Selected and edited by Merlin Holland. London: Fourth Estate 2003.

Holland, Vyvyan: Introduction to Oscar Wilde: *Salomé.* London: The Folio Society 1977.

—. *Son of Oscar Wilde.* London: Hart-Davis 1954.

—. *Time Remembered, After Père Lachaise.* London: Gollancz 1966.

Holmes C.J.: *Self & Partners (mostly Self).* London: Constable 1936.

Holmes, Diana: *Rachilde, – Decadence, Gender and the Woman Writer.* Oxford and New York: Berg 2001.

Holmes, Oliver Wendell: *The Autocrat of the Breakfast Table.* Volume I of the Collected Works. Boston: Houghton, Miflin & Co. 1892.

Holmes, Oliver Wendell: *Our Hundred Days in Europe.* Boston & New York: Houghton. Miflin & Co 1895.

Holmes, Oliver Wendell: *Over the Teacups*, volume IV of the Collected Works. Boston: Houghton, Miflin & Co. 1892.

Holroyd, Michael: *Augustus John, A Biography* volume I: The Years of Innocence. London: Heinemann 1974.

Holt, Edgar: *The Tiger, the Life of George Clemenceau 1841-1929.* London: Hamish Hamilton 1976.

Houfe, Simon: *Fin-de-siècle, the Illustrators of the Nineties.* London: Barrie & Jenkins.

House, John and Stevens, Mary-Anne (edd.): *Post-Impressionism, Cross-Currents in European Painting.* London: Royal Academy of Arts in association with Weidenfeld & Nicolson 1979.

Housman, Laurence: *Echo de Paris.* London: Jonathan Cape 1923.

Houssaye, Arsène: *Man About Paris. The Confessions of Arsène Houssaye.* Translated and edited by Henry Knepler. London: Victor Gollancz 1972.

Howard of Penrith, Lord: *Theatre of Life* volume I: Life seen from the Pit 1863-1905. London: Hodder & Stoughton 1935.

Huddleston, Sisley: *In and About Paris.* London: Methuen 1927.

—. *Poincaré, A Biographical Portrait.* London: T. Fisher Unwin 1924.

Hudson, Derek: *For Love of Painting, The Life of Sir Gerald Kelly K.C.V.O., P.R.A.* London: Peter Davis 1975.

Hughes, Spencer Leigh: *Press, Platform and Parliament.* London: Nisbet & Co 1918.

Hull, Jerusha Mac Cormack: *John Gray, Poet, Dandy and Priest.* Hanover NH: Brandeis University Press 1991.

Hunt, Violet: *The Flurried Years.* London: Hurst & Blackett n.d.

Huntington, Henry G.: *Memories, Personages, People, Places.* London: Constable 1911.

Hussey, Christopher: *The Life of Sir Edwin Lutyens.* London: Antique Collectors Club 1984.

Huysmans, J.K.: *À Rebours.* With an introduction by P.G. Lloyd. London: The Fortune Press n.d. [1946].

—. *Against Nature, A new translation of À Rebours.* Translated and introduced by Robert Baldick. Harmondsworth: Penguin 1959.

—. *La Bièvre et Saint Séverin.* On line at http://www.huysmans.org/betsseverin/severin.htm.

—. *La Cathédrale*. Translated as *The Cathedral* by Clara Bell. London: Kegan Paul, Trench, Trübner & Co 1898.

—. *Là-Bas*. 1891. Translated by Keene Wallace, Paris 1928. New edition: New York: Dover Publications 1972.

—. 'Instrumentum Diaboli', printed as an introduction to Lee Revens (ed.): *The Graphic Work of Felicien Rops*. New York: Léon Amiel 1975.

Hyde, H. Montgomery: *Famous Trials 7, Oscar Wilde*. New and enlarged edition. Harmondsworth: Penguin Books 1962.

—. Introduction to Richard Le Gallienne: *The Romantic '90s*. New edition. London: Putnam & Co 1951.

—. *Lord Alfred Douglas, A Biography*. London: Methuen 1984.

—. *Oscar Wilde, A Biography*. London: Eyre Methuen 1975.

Hynes, Samuel: *The Edwardian Turn of Mind*. Princeton & London: Princeton University Press 1968.

Ireland, G.W.: *André Gide, A study of his creative writings*. Oxford: Oxford University Press 1970.

Jackson, Stanley: *Guy de Maupassant*. London: Duckworth 1938.

Jacob, Wilbur R. (ed.): *Letters of Francis Parkman*. Norman: University of Oklahoma Press 1960.

James, Henry: *A Little Tour of France*. Boston: James R. Osgood 1884. Edited by Geoffrey Grigson. Oxford: Oxford University Press 1984.

—. *The Ambassadors*. London: Methuen 1903; Harmondsworth: Penguin Books 1973.

—. *French Poets and Novelists*. 1878. New edition London: Macmillan 1893.

—. *Parisian Sketches – Letters to the New York Tribune 1875-1876*. Edited with an Introduction by Leon Edel and Ilse Desoir Lind.

—. *Portraits of Places*. London: Macmillan 1883.

—. *Washington Square*. New York University Press 1957.

Jebb, Caroline: *The Life and Letters of Richard Claverhouse Jebb O.M., Litt.D*. Cambridge: Cambridge University Press 1907.

Jepson, Edgar: *Memories of a Victorian*. London: Victor Gollancz 1933.

Jerome, Jerome K.: *My Life and Times*. London: John Murray 1926. New edition 1983.

John, Angela V.: *Elizabeth Robins, Staging a Life 1862-1932*. London: Routledge 1995.

Johnson, Robert Underwood: *Remembered Yesterdays*. London: George Allen and Unwin 1923.

Jones, Ernest: *Sigmund Freud, Life and Work* volume I: The Young Freud 1856-1900. London: Hogarth Press 1953.

Jones, Henry Thaddeus: *Recollections of a Court Painter*. London: John Lane The Bodley Head 1912.

Joseph-Renaud, J.: Introduction to Oscar Wilde *Intentions*. Paris: Stock, Bibliothèque cosmopolite N°14, 1905.

Judith, Madame: *My Autobiography*. Edited by Paul G'Sell and translated from the French by Mrs Arthur Bell. London: Eveleigh Nash 1912.

Jullian, Philippe: *De Meyer*. Edited by Robert Brandau. London: Thames & Hudson.

Jullian, Philippe: *Edouard VII*. Paris: Hachette 1962. Translated as *Edward and the Edwardians* by Peter Dawnay. London: Sidgwick & Jackson 1967.

Jullian, Philippe: *Jean Lorrain, ou Le Satyricon 1900*. Paris: Fayard 1974.

—. *Montmartre*. Translated by Anne Carter. Oxford: Phaidon 1977.

—. *Oscar Wilde*. Translated by Violet Wyndham. London: Constable 1969 Chapter XVII.

Kaufmann, Martine (ed.): *Claude Debussy, Textes*. Paris: Radio France 1999.

Kazmier, Lisa A.: '"More a Symbol Than a Woman": Ellen Terry, Mrs. Patrick Campbell, The Image of the Actress and the Performance of Self'. Paper given at the 1998 Warren I. Susman Memorial Conference, Rutgers University.

Kennedy, Ambrose: *American Orator, Bourke Cockran, His Life and Politics*. Boston: Bruce Humphries Inc 1958.

Kennedy, S.B.: *Paul Henry*. New Haven & London: Yale University Press 2000.

Kington, Miles (ed.): *The World of Alphonse Allais*. London: Chatto & Windus 1977.

Kipling, Rudyard: *Something of Myself*. Edited by Robert Hampson with an introduction by Richard Holmes. London: Penguin Books 1977 reprinted 1992.

Knox, Melissa: *Oscar Wilde, A Long and Lovely Suicide*. New Haven & London: Yale University Press 1994.

Kohler, Stephan: 'Warum singt der Franzose anders als er spricht?': Richard Strauss und die französische Fassung seiner Oper *Salomé*. *Jahrbuch der Bayerischen Staatsoper*. Vol. 2 1978/9.

Korg, Jacob: *George Gissing: A Critical Biography*. London: Methuen 1965.

Kurtz, Harold: *The Empress Eugénie 1826-1920*. London: Hamish Hamilton 1964.

La Jeunesse, Ernest: *Le Boulevard*. Paris: Jean Bosc et Cie 1906.

—. *Souvenirs d'Oscar Wilde*. *Revue blanche* 15th December 1900. Reprinted in E.H. Mikhail (ed.): *Oscar Wilde – Interviews and Recollections*. volume II. London: Macmillan 1979.

Lachasse, Pierre (ed. établie, présentée et annotée par;): *Correspondance (1895-1921) / Edouard Ducoté, André Gide*. [ed. par l'association des amis d'André Gide]. Nantes: Centre d'études gidiennes 2002.

Lack, Léo: 'Avertissement' in Oscar Wilde: *Une Maison de Grenades*. Traduit de l'anglais par Léo Lack. Paris: Mercure de France 1948.

Lago, Mary M. and Beckson, Karl (edd.): *Max and Will, Max Beerbohm and William Rothenstein Their Friendship and Letters 1893-1945*. London: John Murray 1975.

Lambert, J.W. & Ratcliffe, Michael: *The Bodley Head 1887-1987*. London: The Bodley Head 1987.

Lambourne, Nigel: *Renoir, Paintings, drawings, lithographs and etchings*. London: The Folio Society 1965.

Langlade, Jacques de: *Oscar Wilde, ou la vérité des masques*. Préface de Robert Merle. Paris: Mazarine 1987.

Lapierre, Alexandra: *Fanny Stevenson, Muse, Adventuress and Romantic Enigma*. Translated from the French by Carol Cosman. London: Fourth Estate 1995.

Lara, Isidore de: *Many Tales of Many Cities*. London: Hutchinson & Co n.d. [1926].

Larisch, Countess Marie: *My Past*. London: Eveleigh Nash 1913.

Latour, Geneviève and Claval Florence (edd.): *Les Théâtres de Paris*. Paris: Délégation de l'action artistique de la ville de Paris, Bibliothèque historique de la ville de Paris, Association de la Régie Théâtrale 1991.

Laughton, Bruce: *Philip Wilson Steer 1860-1942*. Oxford: Clarendon Press 1971.

Laver, James: *The First Decadent, being the Strange Life of J.K. Huysmans*. London: Faber & Faber 1954.

Lazzaro, G. di San: *Painting in France 1895-1949*. Translated by Baptista Gilliatt-Smith and Bernard Wall. London: Harvill Press 1950.

Le Gallienne, Richard: *Robert Louis Stevenson, An Elegy, and Other Poems Mainly Personal*. London: John Lane 1895.

Le Gallienne, Richard: *The Romantic '90s*. London: John Lane 1925.

Le Rouge, Gustave in *Nouvelles Littéraires* 3rd and 10th November 1928, reprinted in Mikhail volume II.

Leaf, Charlotte (ed.): *Walter Leaf 1852-1927, Some Chapters of Autobiography*. London: John Murray 1932.

Léautaud, Paul: *Le Petit Ami*, with *In Memoriam* and *Amours*. Translated by Humphrey Hare as *The Child of Man*. London: The Bodley Head 1959.

Lebovics, Herman: *True France, The Wars over Cultural Identity*. Ithaca and London: Cornell University Press 1992.

Lee, Sir Sidney: *King Edward VII, A Biography* volume I: From Birth to Accession. London: Macmillan 1925 pp.359-60.

Lejeune, Dominique: *La France de la belle époque 1896-19*14. Paris: Armand Colin 1991.

Lemonnier, Léon: *Oscar Wilde*. Paris: Henri Didier n.d.

Lerner, Michael G.: *Maupassant*. London: George Allen & Unwin 1975.

Leslie, Anita: *Jennie, The Life of Lady Randolph Churchill*. London: Hutchinson & Co 1969.

Leslie, Shane: *Memoir of John Edward Courtenay Bodley*. London: Jonathan Cape 1930.

Leveque, Jean-Jacques: *Les années de la Belle Époque: 1890-1914*. Paris: ACR Edition 1991.

Leverson, Ada: *Letters to the Sphinx from Oscar Wilde*. London: Duckworth 1930.

Levin, Miriam R.: *Republican Art & Ideology in Nineteenth Century France*. Ann Arbor: University of Michigan Research Press 1986.

Lloyd, Christopher: *J.-K. Huysmans and the fin-de-siècle Novel*. Edinburgh: Edinburgh University Press 1990.

Locke, W.J.: *The Joyous Adventures of Aristide Pujol*. Illustrations by Alec Ball. London: John Lane The Bodley Head 1912.

Locke, William J.: *The Belovéd Vagabond*. London: John Lane The Bodley Head 1906.

Lockspeiser, Edward: *Debussy, His Life and Mind*. London: Cassell 1962 volume I 1862-1902.

Lodge, David: *Author, Author*. London: Secker & Warburg 2004.

Logue, William: *Léon Blum, The Formative Years 1872-1914*. DeKalb: Northern Illinois University Press 1973.

Lomax, Pamela: *The Golden Dream: A Biography of Thomas Cooper Gotch*. Sansom & Co. 2004.

Longaker, Mark: *Ernest Dowson*. Philadelphia: University of Pennsylvania Press 1945; 3rd edition 1967.

Lory, Marie-Joseph: *Léon Bloy et son époque*. Paris: Desclée de Brouwer 1944.

Louÿs, Pierre et Tinan Jean de: *Correspondance 1894-1898*. Présentée et annotée par Jean-Paul Goujon. Ouvrage publié avec le concours de Centre national du livre. Paris: Éditions du Limon 1995.

Low, Will H.: *A Chronicle of Friendships 1873-1900.* London: Hodder & Stoughton 1908.

Lowther, Lieut.-Colonel H.C., C.M.G., M.V.O., D.S.O.: *From Pillar to Post.* London: Edwin Arnold 1911.

Loyer, François: *Paris Nineteenth Century, Architecture and Urbanism.* Translated by Charles Lyon Clark. New York: Abbeville Press 1988.

Loyrette, Henri: *Entre le théâtre et l'histoire. La famille Halévy (1790-1960).* Paris: Coédition Réunion des musées nationaux, Fayard 1996.

Lucas, E.V.: *A Wanderer in Paris.* London: Methuen 1909.

Lucien, Mirande: *Eekhoud le rauque.* Septentrion n.d.

Lucien, Mirande et Cardon Patrick (edd.): *Un illustre Uraniste.* Textes de et sur Georges Eekhoud. Cahier Question de genre. Lille: GKC n.d.

Lucie-Smith, Edward: *Fantin-Latour.* Oxford: Phaidon 1977.

Lucy, Henry W.: *Sixty Years in the Wilderness, Some Passages By the Way.* London: Smith, Elder & Co 1909.

Ludovici, A.: *An Artist's Life in London and Paris 1870-1925.* London: T. Fisher Unwin 1926.

Lumière, Auguste and Louis: *Letters.* Edited and Annotated by Jacques Rittaud-Hutinet with the collaboration of Yvelise Dentzer, preface by Maurice Trarieux-Lumière. Translation by Pierre Hodgson. London: Faber & Faber 1995.

Lutyens, Lady Emily: A *Blessed Girl: Memoirs of a Victorian Girlhood, Chronicled in an Exchange of Letters 1887-1896.* London: Hart-Davis 1953.

Lyall, Sir Alfred: *The Life of the Marquess of Dufferin and Ava.* London: John Murray 1905.

Lycett Andrew: *Rudyard Kipling.* London: Weidenfeld & Nicolson 1999.

Lynch, Arthur: *Human Documents, Character Sketches of Representative Men and Women of the Time.* London: Bertram Dobell 1896.

Maas, Henry; Duncan, J.L. and Good, W.G. (edd.): *The Letters of Aubrey Beardsley.* London: Cassell 1970.

Mac Liammoír, Micheál: 'An Introduction to the Author' in *The Happy Prince and Other Stories.* Harmondsworth: Puffin Books 1962.

MacColl, D.S.: *Life, Work and Setting of Philip Wilson Steer*, with a full catalogue of paintings and list of watercolours in public collections by Alfred Yockney. London: Faber & Faber 1945.

Mc Cormack, W.J.: *Yeats's Politics since 1943, Approaches and Reproaches.* The Yearbook of English Studies volume 35 2005.

MacDonald, John F.: *The Amazing City.* London: Grant Richards 1918.

Mac-Orlan, Pierre: 'De Montmartre à Buffalo', in Adhémar, q.v.

Maguire, J. Robert: 'Oscar Wilde and the Dreyfus Case', *Victorian Studies* 41/1 Autumn 1997.

Mainardi, Patricia: *The End of the Salon – Art and State in the Early Third Republic*. Cambridge: Cambridge University Press 1993.

Mainwaring, Marion: *Mysteries of Paris, The Quest for Morton Fullerton*. Hanover & London: University Press of New England 2001.

Mäkinen, Helka Maria: 'Politics, Sexuality and Emancipated Women: The Reception of Oscar Wilde's Salomé in Finland 1905 and 1919', *Nordic Theatre Studies* 1999.

Malet, Sir Edward: *Shifting Scenes*. London: John Murray 1901.

Mallarmé, Stéphane: *Correspondence*. Receuillée, Classée et Annotée par Henri Mondor et Lloyd James Austin. Paris: Gallimard 1965.

Mallet, Donald: *The Great Collector, Lord Hertford and the Founding of the Wallace Collection*. London: Macmillan 1979.

Mann, Thomas: *Buddenbrooks* (1902); translated by H.T. Lowe-Porter 1924. Harmondsworth: Penguin Books 1957p.68.

Marbury, Elizabeth: *My Crystal Ball, Reminiscences*. New York: Boni & Liveright 1923.

March Thomas: *The History of the Paris Commune of 1871*. London: Swan Sonnenschein & Co 1896.

Marchesi, Mathilde: *Marchesi and Music, Passages from the Life of a famous Singing Teacher*. With an introduction by Massenet. London & New York: Harper & Brothers 1897.

Markham, Violet: *Return Passage, The Autobiography of Violet R. Markham, C.H.* London: Oxford University Press 1953.

Martel, Gyp de: *La Joyeuse Enfance de la Troisième République*. Paris: Calmann-Lévy 1931.

Martin, Ralph G.: *Jennie, The Life of Randolph Churchill* volume I: The Romantic Years 1854-1895. Englewood Cliffs: Prentice-Hall 1969.

Martin, Ralph G.: *Lady Randolph Churchill, A Biography* volume II The Dramatic Years 1895-1921. London: Cassell 1971.

Mason, Stuart: *Bibliography of Oscar Wilde*. London: T. Werner Laurie n.d. [1914].

Mathew, David: *Lord Acton and His Times*. London: Eyre & Spottiswood 1968.

Matthew, H.C.G. (ed.): *The Gladstone Diaries, with Cabinet Minister and Prime Ministerial Correspondence*. Volume IX January 1875-December 1880. Oxford: The Clarendon Press 1986; volume XIII. Oxford: The Clarendon Press. 1994.

Matthews, J. Brander: *The Theatres of Paris*. London: Sampson Low, Martston, Searle & Rivington 1880.

Maugham, W. Somerset (ed.): T*he Truth at Last, from Charles Hawtrey.* London: Thornton Butterworth 1924.

Maugham, W. Somerset: *Of Human Bondage.* London: William Heinemann 1915. Harmondsworth: Penguin Books 1963.

Maugham, W. Somerset: *The Moon and Sixpence.* London: William Heinemann 1919. Harmondsworth: Penguin Books 1944.

Maupassant, Guy de: 'The Mask' in *The Mountain Inn and Other Stories.* A New Translation by H.N.P. Sloman. Harmondsworth: Penguin Books 1955.

—. *A Life.* Translated with an Introduction and notes by Roger Pearson. Oxford: Oxford University Press 1999.

—. *A Parisian Affair and Other Stories.* Translated with an Introduction and Notes by Siân Miles. London: Penguin Books 2004.

—. *Bel-Ami.* Translated by Margaret Mauldon with an Introduction and Notes by Robert Lethbridge. Oxford: Oxford University Press 2001.

—. *Best Short Stories.* Ware, Herts: Wordsworth 1997.

—. *Miss Harriet and Other Stories.* A New Translation by H.N.P. Sloman. Harmondsworth: Penguin Books 1951.

—. *Mademoiselle Fifi and Other Stories.* Translated with an Introduction and notes by David Coward. Oxford: Oxford University Press 1993.

—. *The Mountain Inn and Other Stories.* A New Translation by H.N.P. Sloman. Harmondsworth: Penguin Books 1955.

—. *Selected Short Stories.* Translated with an Introduction by Roger Colet. London: Penguin Books 1971.

Maurier, Daphne du: *Gerald, A Portrait.* London: Victor Gollancz 1934.

Maurier, George du: *Peter Ibbetson.* London: James R. Osgood, McIlvaine & Co 1896.

—. *The Martian, A Novel.* London & New York: Harper Brothers 1898.

—. *Trilby, A Novel.* London: Osgood, McIlvaine & Co 1895.

Maurois, André: 'De Ruskin à Wilde', in *Études anglaises.* Paris: Bernard Grasset 1927.

McConkey, Kenneth: *Impressionism in Britain.* With an essay by Anita Gruetzner Robins. New Haven & London: Yale University Press 1995.

McGurrin, James: *Bourke Cockran, A Free Lance in American Politics.* New York: Charles Scribner's Sons 1948.

McKenna, Neil: *The Secret Life of Oscar Wilde.* London: Century/Random House 2003.

McLynn, Frank: *Robert Louis Stevenson, A Biography.* London: Hutchinson 199.

McMillan, James F.: *Housewife or Harlot, The Place of Women in French Society 1870-1940*. Brighton: Harvester Press 1981.

Meadmore, W.S.: *Lucien Pissarro, Un Cœur Simple*. London: Constable.

Melba, Nellie: *Melodies & Memories*. London: Hamish Hamilton. New edition 1980.

Melville, Joy: *Mother of Oscar, The Life of Jane Francesca Wilde*. London: John Murray 1994.

Menpes, Mortimer: *Paris*. With text by Dorothy Menpes. London: Adam & Charles Black 1909 pp.143-5.

Méral, Jean: *Paris dans le littérature américaine*. Translated as *Paris in American Literature* by Laurette Long. Chapel Hill & London: University of North Caroline Press 1989.

Merrick, Leonard: *A Chair on the Boulevard*. London: Hodder & Stoughton n.d.

—. *While Paris Laughed, being Pranks and Passions of the Poet Tricotin*. London: Hodder & Stoughton n.d.

Merrill, Stuart: 'Some Unpublished Recollections of Oscar Wilde', translated and partially edited by H. Montgomery Hyde. London: *Adam International Review* nos. 241-3 1954.

Mesch, Rachel: *The Hysteric's Revenge, French Women Writers at the Fin de Siècle*. Nashville: Vanderbilt University Press 2006.

Meyer, Michael: *Strindberg, A Biography*. London: Secker & Warburg 1985.

Mikhail, E.H. (ed.): *Oscar Wilde – Interviews and Recollections*. London: Macmillan 1979.

Miller, Robert Keith: *Oscar Wilde*. New York: Frederick Ungar 1982.

Millward, Jessie: *Myself and Others*. In Collaboration with J.B. Booth. London: Hutchinson & Co 1923.

Milner, John: *The Studios of Paris, the Capital of Art in the late Nineteenth Century*. New Haven & London: Yale University Press 1988.

Milner, Viscountess: *My Picture Gallery 1886-1901*. London: John Murray 1951.

Mirbeau Octave: *The Diary of a Chambermaid*. Translated by Douglas Jarman and with an Introduction by Richard Ings. Sawtry, Cambs: Dedalus 1991; new edition 2001.

Mistinguett: *Mistinguett, Queen of the Night*. Translated by Lucienne Hill. London: Elek Books 1954.

Mitford, Nancy: *The Blessing*. London: Hamish Hamilton 1951. Harmondsworth: Penguin Books 1957.

Mitchell, Lady: *Three Quarters of a Century.* London: Methuen 1940. *PAGE*.

Mitford, Nancy: *The Blessing.* London: Hamish Hamilton 1951. Harmondsworth: Penguin Books 1957.

Mix, Katherine Lyon: *A Study in Yellow, The Yellow Book and Its Contributors.* Lawrence: University of Kansas Press and London: Constable 1960.

Miyoshi, Masao: *The Divided Self, A Perspective on the Literature of the Victorians.* New York: New York University Press 1969.

Mockel, Albert: *Emile Verhaeren,* avec une note biographique par F. Vielé-Griffin. Paris: Mercure de France 1895.

Montgomery-Massingberd, Hugh (ed.): Burke's *Irish Family Records.* London: Burke's Peerage 1976.

Moore, George: *Ave.* London: William Heinemann 1911.

Moore, George: *Confessions of a Young Man.* London: Swann, Sonnenschein 1889. Ebury Edition, William Heinemann in 1937.

Moore, George: *Impressions and Memories.* London: T. Werner Laurie 1914.

Moore, George: *Memoirs of My Dead Life.* London: William Heinemann 1906. Revised edition 1928.

Moore, George: *Salve.* London: William Heinemann 1912.

Morgan, A.E.: *Tendencies of Modern English Drama.* London: Constable 1924.

Morgan, H. Wayne (ed.): *Making Peace with Spain, The Diary of Whitelaw Reid September - December 1898.* Austin: University of Texas Press 1965.

Morley, John Viscount: *Recollections.* London: Macmillan & Co. 1917.

Moscheles, Felix: *Fragments of an Autobiography.* London: James Nisbet & Co. 1899.

Mott, Colonel T. Bentley: *Twenty Years as a Military Attaché.* New York: Oxford University Press 1937.

Murger, Henri: *Vie de Bohème.* Translated by Norman Cameron. London: The Folio Society 1960.

Murray, Douglas: *Bosie, A Biography of Lord Alfred Douglas.* London: Hodder & Stoughton 2000.

Myers, Rollo: *Emmanuel Chabrier and His Circle.* London: J.M. Dent & Sons 1969 pp.5, 7. Roger Nichols (ed.) *Debussy Remembered.* London: Faber & Faber 1992.

Nectoux, Jean-Michel: *Gabriel Fauré, A Musical Life.* Translated by Roger Nichols. Cambridge: Cambridge University Press 2004.

Nelson, Walter W.: *Oscar Wilde's Allusions and References to Baudelaire, An Essay* (Lund: The Author 2001.

Nevill, Ralph: *Days and Nights in Montmartre and the Latin Quarter.* London: Herbert Jenkins 1927.

Nevill, Ralph: *Fancies, Fashions and Fads.* London Methuen 1913.

Nevill, Ralph: *Night Life, London and Paris Past and Present.* London: Cassell & Co 1926.

Nevill, Ralph: *The Gay Victorians.* London: Eveleigh Nash & Grayson 1930 pp.114-5.

Nevill, Ralph: *The Man of Pleasure.* London: Chatto & Windus 1912.

Nevill, Ralph: *Unconventional Memories.* London: Hutchinson 1923; Louÿs/Tinan.

Nevinson, Henry W.: *Changes & Chances.* London Nisbet & Co 1923.

Newnham-Davis, Lt.-Col. Nathaniel: *The Gourmet's Guide to Europe.* London: Grant Richards 1903. Third edition 1911.

Newton Lord P.C.: *Retrospection.* London: John Murray 1941.

Newton, Lord: *Lord Lyons, A Record of British Diplomacy.* London: Edwin Arnold 1913.

Nichols, Roger & Langham Smith, Richard: *Claude Debussy, Pelléas et Mélisande.* Cambridge: Cambridge University Press 1989.

Nichols, Roger (ed.): *Debussy Remembered.* London: Faber & Faber 1997.

Nicolson, Harold: *Helen's Tower.* London: Constable 1937.

—. *Some People.* Constable & Co 1927.

—. *Verlaine.* Constable n.d.

Nordau, Max: *On Art and Artists.* Translated by W.F. Harvey, M.A. London: T. Fisher Unwin 1907.

Norman, Geraldine: *Nineteenth Century Painters and Painting, A Dictionary.* London: Thames & Hudson 1977.

Novick, Sheldon M.: *Henry James, the Young Master.* New York: Random House 1996.

Novotny, F.: *Cézanne.* London: Phaidon 1961; 3rd edition 1972.

O'Connor, Ulick: T*he Ulick O'Connor Diaries 1970-1981.* London: John Murray, new edition 2003 pp.21-2.

O'Meara, Kathleen: *Madame Mohl, Her Salon and Her Friends, A Study of Social Life in Paris.* London: Richard Bentley & Son 1885.

O'Shea, John Augustus: *Roundabout Recollections.* London: Ward & Downey 1892.

O'Sullivan, Vincent: *Aspects of Wilde.* London: Constable 1934.

—. *Opinions.* With an Introduction by Alan Anderson. London: Unicorn Press 1959.

Offenstadt, Patrick: 'Le Paris Disparu de Jean Béraud'. *L'Œil* n° 380, March 1987.

Ogg, David: *Herbert Fisher 1865-1940, A Short Biography*. London: Edward Arnold 1947.

Ohnet, Georges: *The Rival Actresses*. Edited by G.F. Monkshood. London: Greening & Co 1909, originally published as *Lise Fleuron* in 1884.

Orczy, Baroness: *Links in the Chain of Life*. London: Hutchinson & Co 1947.

Orledge, Robert (ed.): *Satie Remembered*. London: Faber & Faber 1995.

Ormond, Leonée: *George du Maurier*. London: Routledge 1969.

Ory, Pascal: 'Paris, capitale culturelle de la *fin-de-siècle*.' *'Quarante-huit/Quatorze' 1848-1914*, Conférences du Musée d'Orsay 6. Paris: Réunion des Musées Nationaux 1994.

Osgood, Samuel M.: *French Royalism since 1870*. 2nd enlarged edition The Hague: Martinus Nijhoff 1970.

Ouida: 'Slander and Sillery', in *Beatrice Boville and Other Stories*. Philadelphia: J. B. Lippincott Company 1905.

Oxford, Margot: *More Memories*. London: Cassell & Co 1933.

Pacaud, Serge: *Chroniques mémorables de la Belle Epoque*. Paris: Éditions CPE 2004.

Paderewski, Ignace Jan & Lawton, Mary: *The Paderewski Memoirs*. London: Collins 1939.

Painter, George D.: *Marcel Proust, A Biography* volume I. London: Chatto & Windus 1959.

Paul, Elliot: *The Narrow Street* (also published as *The Last Time I Saw Paris*). New York: Random House and London: The Cresset Press 1942; Harmondsworth: Penguin 1947.

Pemberton, T. Edgar: *The Life of Bret Harte*. London: C. Arthur Pearson 1903.

Perot, Philippe: *Les Dessus et les Dessous de la bourgeoisie, une histoire du vêtement au XIXe siècle*. Paris: Librairie Athène Fayard 1891. Translated with an Introduction by Richard Bienvenu as *Fashioning the Bourgeoisie, A History of Clothing in the 19th Century*. Princeton: Princeton University Press 1994.

Perruchot, Henri: *Manet*. Translated by Humphrey Ware. London: Perpetua Books 1962.

Petrie, Sir Charles: *Scenes of Edwardian Life*. London: Eyre & Spottiswoode 1965

Peyramaure, Michel: *La Divine, le roman de Sarah Bernhardt*. Paris: Robert Laffont 2002.

Philippe, Charles-Louis: *Bubu de Montparnasse*. Paris: La Revue Blanche 1910; new edition Grasset 2005.

Phillips, Olga Somech: *Solomon J. Solomon, A Memoir of Peace and War*. London: Herbert Joseph n.d. [1933].

Pierce, David: *Yeats's Worlds, Ireland, England and the Poetic Imagination*. New Haven and London: Yale University Press 1995.

Pierre-Quint, Léon: *André Gide, L'homme, Sa Vie — Son Œuvre. Entretiens Avec Gide et Ses Contemporains*. Paris: Stock 1952.

Pine, Richard: *Oscar Wilde*. Dublin: Gill & Macmillan 1986.

Pingeot, Anne and Hoozee, Robert: *Paris-Bruxelles / Bruxelles-Paris, les relations artistiques entre la France et la Belgique 1848-1914*. Paris: Réunion des musées nationaux 1997.

Poiret, Paul: *My First Fifty Years*. Translated by Stephen Haden Guest. London: Victor Gollancz 1933.

Pollock, Sir Frederick: *For My Grandson, Remembrances of an Ancient Victorian*. London: John Murray 1933.

Polnay, Peter de: *Aspects of Paris*. London: W.H. Allen 1968.

Poulenc, Francis: *Emmanuel Chabrier*. Translated by Cynthia Jolly. London: Denis Dobson 1981.

Pouzet-Duzer, Virginie: *Les voiles de Salomé Labyrinthique errance, virevoltes et volutes* http://lesvoilesdesalome.hautetfort.com/.

Powell, Kerry: *Oscar Wilde & the Theatre of the 1890s*. Cambridge: Cambridge University Press 1990.

Powell Kerry: *Women and Victorian Theatre*. Cambridge: Cambridge University Press 1997.

Preston, Sir Harry: *Leaves from My Unwritten Diary*. London: Hutchinson & Co, n.d.

Proctor, Dennis (ed.): *The Autobiography of G. Lowes Dickinson, and Other Unpublished Writings*. London: Duckworth 1973.

Proust Marcel: *A la recherche de temps perdu : Du coté de chez Swann*. Translated by Lydia Davis as *In Search of Lost Time* vol. I: *The Way by Swann's*. London: Penguin 2003.

Proust, Marcel: *A la recherche de temps perdu : A l'ombre des jeunes filles en fleur*. 1919. Translated by James Grieve as *In Search of Lost Time* vol. II: *In the Shadow of Young Girls in Flower*. London: Penguin 2002.

—. *A la recherche du temps perdu: La Prisonnière*. 1923. Translated by Carol Clark as *In Search of Lost Time* vol. V: *The Prisoner*. London: Penguin 2002.

Proust, Marcel: *A la recherche du temps perdu: Albertine Disparue.* 1925. Translated by Peter Collier as *In Search of Lost Time* vol. V: *The Fugitive.* London: Penguin 2002.

Puffett, Derrick (ed.): *Richard Strauss, Salomé.* Cambridge: Cambridge University Press 1989.

Pullar, Philippa: *Frank Harris.* London: Hamish Hamilton 1975.

Raby, Peter (ed.): *The Cambridge Companion to Oscar Wilde.* Cambridge: Cambridge University Press 1997.

Racowitza, Princess Helena von: *An Autobiography.* Authorised Translation from the German by Cecil Mar. London: Constable & Co 1910.

Raczymow, Henri: *Le Paris littéraire et intime de Marcel Proust.* Paris: Parigramme 1997.

Radziwill, Princess Catherine: *These I Remember.* London: Cassell 1924 pp.101-2.

Ragghianti, Carlo L.: *L'Opera completa di Boldini.* Con apparati critici e filologici de Ettore Camesasca. Milano: Rizzoli 1970.

Rathcreedan, Lord: *Memories of a Long Life.* London: John Lane, The Bodley Head 1931 pp.110, 128.

Reade Brian: *Art Nouveau and Alphonse Mucha.* London: Her Majesty's Stationery Office 1963.

Rearick, Charles: *Pleasures of the Belle Époque, Entertainment and Festivity in Turn-of-the Century France.* New Haven & London: Yale University Press 1985.

Rebell, Hugues et. al.: *Pour Oscar Wilde, des Écrivains français au secours du condamné.* Rouen: Elisabeth Brunet 1994.

Recouly, Raymond*: The Third Republic.* 1928. New edition, translated by E.F. Buckley, New York: AMS Press 1967.

Redesdale, Lord: *Further Memories.* With an Introduction by Edmund Gosse C.B. London: Hutchinson 1917.

Reff, Theodore: *Manet and Modern Paris.* Washington DC: National Gallery of Art and Chicago & London: University of Chicago Press 1982.

Reid, Joyce M.H. (ed.): *The Concise Oxford Dictionary of French Literature.* Oxford: Oxford University Press 1976 *Nouveau Petit Larousse.* Paris: Librairie Larousse 1969.

Reinach, Joseph: *Récits et Portraits Contemporains.* Paris: Librairie Félix Alcan 1915.

Renard, Jules: *Journal.* Paris: Gallimard 30th edition 1935.

Renard, Jules: *The Journal of Jules Renard*. Edited and translated by Louise Bogan and Elizabeth Royat. New York: George Brazillier 1964.

Rennart, Jack and Weill, Alain: *Alphonse Mucha, The Complete Posters and Panels*. Uppsala: Hjert & Hjert 1984.

Repington, Mary: *Thanks for the Memory*. London: Constable n.d.

Retté, Adolphe: *Symbolisme, Anecdotes et Souvenirs* 1903.

Revens, Lee (ed.): *The Graphic Work of Felicien Rops*. New York: Léon Amiel 1975.

Rewald, John (ed.): *Paul Cézanne, Letters*. Oxford: Bruno Cassirer 1941. 4th edition revised and enlarged 1976.

Rewald, John: *Cézanne*. London: Thames & Hudson 1986.

Rhodes, Henry F.T.: *Alphonse Bertillon, Father of Scientific Detection*. George G. Harrap 1956.

Ribblesdale, Emma Lady: *Letters and Diaries*. Collected by her daughter Beatrix Lister. London: Private printed at the Chiswick Press 1930.

Ribblesdale, Lord: *Impressions and Memories*. With a preface by his daughter Lady Wilson. Cassell & Co. 1927.

Rice, Shelley: *Parisian Views*. Cambridge, Mass: MIT Press 1997.

Richards, Grant: *Memories of a Mis-Spent Youth*. London: William Heinemann 1932.

Richardson, Joanna: *Judith Gautier, A Biography*. London: Quartet Books 1986.

—. *Princess Mathilde*. London: Weidenfeld & Nicolson 1969.

—. *Sarah Bernhardt*. London: Max Reinhardt 1959.

—. *The Bohemians, La Vie Bohème in Paris 1830-1914*. London: Macmillan 1969.

Ricketts, Charles: *Pages on Art*. London: Constable 1913.

Ritz, Marie Louise: *César Ritz, Host to the World*. Paris: Hotel Ritz; London: Bodley Head 1981.

Rive, Richard (ed.) *Olive Schreiner Letters*. Oxford: Oxford University Press 1988.

Robertson, W. Graham: *Time Was, being Reminiscences*. London: Hamish Hamilton 1931.

Robichez, Jacques: *Lugné-Poe*. Paris: L'Arche 1955.

Robinat, Francis, Montgolfier Bernard and Debrandère-Descamps Béatrice: *Henri Gervex 1852-1929*. Paris: Paris-Musées 1992.

Roditi, Edouard: *Oscar Wilde*. New York: New Dimensions 1947. New & enlarged edition 1986.

Roittinger, Anita: *Oscar Wilde's Life as Reflected in his Correspondence and His Autobiography.* Salzburg: Institut für Anglistik und Amerikanistik, Universität Salzburg 1980.

Rothenstein, William: *Men and Memories, Recollections.* London: Faber and Faber 1931.

Rounding, Virginia: *Grandes Horizontales, The Lives and Legends of Four Nineteenth Century Courtesans.* London: Bloomsbury 2003.

Rudorff, Raymond: *Belle Époque – Paris in the 1890s.* London: Hamish Hamilton 1972.

Rueff, Suze: *I Knew Sarah Bernhardt.* London: Frederick Muller 1951.

Rumbold, Sir Horace: *Recollections of a Diplomatist.* London: Edwin Arnold 1902.

—. *Further Recollections of a Diplomatist.* London: Edwin Arnold 1903.

Russell, John: *Seurat.* London: Thames & Hudson 1965.

Saint-Gaudens, Augustus: *The Reminiscences of Augustus Saint-Gaudens.* Edited and amplified by Homer Saint-Gaudens. London: Andrew Melrose 1913.

Saix, Gilles de: *Souvenirs inédits sur Oscar Wilde.* Paris: L'Européen n.d.

'Saki' (H.H. Munro): 'The Boar Pig'. *Beasts and Superbeasts.* London: John Lane, The Bodley Head 1914. Reprinted in *The Complete Short Stories of 'Saki'.* London: The Bodley Head 1930.

—. *Reginald in Russia.* London: John Lane, The Bodley Head 1910. Reprinted in *The Complete Short Stories of 'Saki'.* London: The Bodley Head 1930.

'Saki' (H.H. Munro): *The Toys of Peace.* London: John Lane, The Bodley Head 1914. Reprinted in *The Complete Short Stories of 'Saki'.* London: The Bodley Head 1923.

Salmon, Eric (ed.): *Bernhardt and the Theatre of her Time.* Westport, Conn. and London: Greenwood Press 1977.

Saltus, Edgar: *Oscar Wilde, An Idler's Impression.* Chicago: Brothers of the Book 1917.

Samuels, Ernest: *Henry Adams: The Middle Years.* Cambridge, Mass: Harvard University Press 1958.

Sarawak, H.H. the Dayang Muda of: *Relations and Complications.* With a foreword by T.P. O'Connor P.C., M.P. John Lane: the Bodley Head 1929.

Sarcey, Francisque: *Quarante Ans de Théâtre.* Paris: Bibliothèque des Annales 1900-1902.

Sardou Victorien: *Mes plagiats! réplique à Mario Uchard.* Pari:, Imprimerie et librairie universelle 1882.

Sassoon Siegfried: 'The destruction of Oscar Wilde', *The Observer* 3th0 October 1949:

—. *Meredith*. London: Constable 1948.

Satzinger, Christa: *The French Influences on Oscar Wilde's 'The Picture of Dorian Gray' and 'Salomé'*. Lewiston, New York: Edwin Mellen Press 1995.

Sayre Robert: 'De Huysmans à Oscar Wilde: néo-romantisme et "décadence" dans la littérature française et anglaise.' *'Quarante-huit/Quatorze' 1848-1914*, Conférences du Musée d'Orsay 6. Paris: Réunion des Musées Nationaux.

Schenkar, Joan: *Truly Wilde – The Unsettling Story of Dolly Wilde, Oscar Wilde's Unusual Niece*. London: Virago 2000.

Schiff, Richard: 'Ascribing to Manet, Declaring the Author', in Radford R. Collins (ed.): *Twelve Views of Manet's Bar*. Princeton: Princeton University Press 1996.

Schom, Alan: *Emile Zola, A Biography*. New York: Henry Holt & Co 1987.

Schwab Arnold T.: *James Gibbons Huneker, Critic of the Seven Arts*. Stanford: Stanford University Press 1963.

Scobell Armstrong, His Honour Judge J.W.: *Yesterday*. London: Hutchinson 1955.

Scott, Clement: *From 'The Bells' to 'King Arthur', A Critical Record of the First Night Productions at the Lyceum Theatre from 1871 to 1895*. London: John MacQueen 1896.

Scott, Dixon: 'The Innocence of Bernard Shaw'. *The Bookman* 1913, reprinted in Dixon Scott: *Men of Letters*. London: Hodder & Stoughton 1916.

Scudder, Horace Elisha: *James Russell Lowell, A Biography* volume II. Boston: Houghton, Mifflin & Co 1901.

Segal, Harold B.: *Turn of the Century Cabaret – Paris, Barcelona, Berlin, Munich, Vienna, Cracow, Moscow, St Petersburg, Zürich*. New York: Columbia University Press 1987.

Sermoneta, Vittoria Colonna Duchess of: *Things Past*. With a foreword by Robert Hichens. London: Hutchinson n.d.

Service, Robert W.: *Ballads of a Bohemian*. London: T Fisher Unwin 1921.

Shattuck, Roger: *The Banquet Years – The Arts in France 1885-1918*. New York: Anchor Books 1961.

Shaw, George Bernard: 'Duse and Bernhardt', *The Saturday Review* 15th June 1895, reprinted in Bernard Shaw: *Plays and Players*. Selected with an Introduction by A.C. Ward. London: Oxford University Press 1952.

—. *Fanny's First Play*. 1911. London: Penguin Books 1987.

—. *Our Theatres in the Nineties*. London: Constable 1932.

Sheehy, Jeanne: *Walter Osborne*. Ballycotton, Co Cork: Gifford and Craven 1974.

Sherard, Robert H.: 'Notes from Paris' in *The Author* volume II/9 February 1892.

—. 'Notes from Paris' in *The Author* volume II/10 March 1892.

—. 'Notes from Paris' in *The Author* volume II/11 April 1892.

—. 'Notes from Paris' in *The Author* volume III/2 July 1892.

—. 'Notes from Paris', *The Author* volume III/5 October 1892.

—. 'Notes from Paris' in *The Author* volume III/7 December 1892.

—. 'Notes from Paris' in *The Author* volume III/10 January 1893.

—. 'Notes from Paris' in *The Author* volume III/9 February 1893.

—. 'Notes from Paris' in *The Author* volume III/10 March 1893.

—. 'Notes from Paris' in *The Author* volume III/11 April 1893.

—. *Bernard Shaw, Frank Harris and Oscar Wilde*. With a preface by Lord Alfred Douglas and an additional Chapter by Hugh Kingsmill. London: T. Werner Laurie 1937.

—. *Emile Zola. A Biographical and Critical Study*. London: Chatto & Windus 1893.

—. *Oscar Wilde, the Story of an Unhappy Friendship*. London: privately printed at the Hermes Press 1902.

—. *Oscar Wilde, the Story of an Unhappy Friendship*. London: Greening & Co. 1905.

—. *Oscar Wilde, Twice Defended (from André Gide's Wicked Lies and Frank Harris's Cruel Libels)*. Chicago: Argus 1934.

—. *The Life of Oscar Wilde*. London: T. Werner Laurie 1906.

—. *The Life, Work and Evil Fate of Guy de Maupassant (Gentilhomme de lettres)*. London: T. Werner Laurie 1926.

—. *The Real Oscar Wilde, to be used as a supplement to, and in illustration of 'The Life of Oscar Wilde'*. Philadelphia: David McKay 1911.

—. *Twenty Years in Paris, being Some Recollections of a Literary Life*. London: Hutchinson 1905.

—. *Oscar Wilde, the Story of an Unhappy Friendship*. London: Greening & Co. 1905. Popular edition 1908.

Shercliff, Jose: *Jane Avril of the Moulin Rouge*. London: Jarrolds 1952.

Sheridan, Alan: *André Gide, A Life in the Present*. London: Hamish Hamilton 1998.

Shipley, A.E.: *'J'. A Memoir of John Willis Clark*. London: Smith, Elder & Co 1913.

Siegel, Jerrold: *Bohemian Paris – Culture, Politics and the Boundaries of Bourgeois Life 1830-1930*. New York: Viking 1986.

Silverman, Debora L.: *Art Nouveau in fin-de-siècle France – Politics, Psychology and Style*. Berkeley: University of California Press 1989.

Silverman, Willa Z.: *Gyp, The Notorious Life of Gyp, Right Wing Anarchist in fin-de-siècle France*. Oxford: Oxford University Press 1983.

Sisley, Maurice: 'La Salomé de M. Oscar Wilde'. *Le Gaulois* 29th June 1892, reprinted in Mikhail, q.v.

Sitwell, Sir Osbert: *Left Hand, Right Hand! An Autobiography* volume I: The Cruel Month. London: Macmillan 1945.

Skinner, Cornelia Otis: *Madame Sarah*. New York: Houghton Miflin. 1966. New edition New York: Paragon 1988.

Slater, Maya (ed.): *Three Pre-Surrealist Plays*. Oxford: Oxford University Press 1997.

Smith, Geoffrey: *The Savoy Operas – A New Guide to Gilbert and Sullivan*. London: Robert Hale 1983.

Somerville, E.Œ. and Ross, Martin: *Stray-Aways, a volume of Studies and Sketches*. London: Longmans, Green & Co 1920.

Sorel, Cécile: *An Autobiography*. Translated by Philip John Stead. Foreword by M. Willson Disher. London: Staples 1953.

Spalding, Frances: *Duncan Grant*. London: Chatto & Windus 1997.

Spalding, Frances: *Roger Fry, Art and Life*. London: Paul Elek Granada Publishing 1980.

Speaight, Robert: *William Rothenstein, The Portrait of an Artist in His Time*. London: Eyre & Spottiswoode 1962.

Speedie, Julie: *Wonderful Sphinx, the Biography of Ada Leverson*. London: Virago 1993.

Spender, J.A.: *The Life of the Right Hon. Sir Henry Campbell-Bannerman G.C.B.* London: Hodder & Stoughton n.d. [1923?].

Spilett, Gedeon: 'An Interview with Oscar Wilde', *Gil Blas* 22nd November 1897, reprinted in Mikhail volume II, q.v.

St Aubyn, Giles: *Edward VII, Prince and King*. London: Collins 1979.

Stallman, R.W.: *Stephen Crane, A Biography*. New York: George Brazillier 1968 pp.316-7.

Stamper, C.W.: *What I Know. Reminiscences of Five Years Attendance upon his late Majesty King Edward the Seventh*. London: Mills & Boon 1913.

Stang, Ragna: *Edvard Munch, the Man and the Artist*. London: Gordon Fraser 1979.

Starkie, Enid: *From Gautier to Eliot – The Influence of France on English Literature 1851-1939*. London: Hutchinson 1960. New edition 1962.

Steedman, Carolyn: 'New Times, Mignon and Her Meanings', in John Stokes (ed.): *Fin-de-siècle / fin du Globe, Fears and Fantasies of the late Nineteenth Century*. Basingstoke: Macmillan 1992.

Steegmuller, Francis: *Maupassant*. London: Collins 1950.

Steinman, Michael: *Yeats's Heroic Figures: Wilde, Parnell, Swift, Casement*. London: Macmillan 1983.

Stevens, Mary Anne: *Emile Bernard 1868-1941, A Pioneer of Modern Art*. Zwolle: Waanders n.d.

—. 'Innovation and Consolidation in French Painting', in House/Stevens.

Stevenson, Robert Louis: *An Inland Voyage*. New Impression. London: Chatto & Windus 1908.

Stevenson, Robert Louis and Lloyd Osbourne: *The Wrecker*. London: Cassell & Co 1892.

Stoeckl, Baroness de: *Not All Vanity*. Edited by George Kinnaird. London: John Murray.

Stokes, John (ed.): *Fin-de-siècle / fin du Globe, Fears and Fantasies of the late Nineteenth Century*. Basingstoke: Macmillan 1992.

Strauss, Richard et Romain, Rolland: *Correspondence et Fragments de Journal*. Avant-propos de Gustave Samazueilh. Paris: Albin Michel 1961.

Suffield, Lord: *My Memories 1830-1913*. Edited by Alys Lowth. London: Herbert Jenkins 1913.

Sugana, G.M.: *The Complete Paintings of Toulouse-Lautrec*. London: Weidenfeld & Nicolson 1973.

Sutherland Gower, Lord Ronald: *Old Diaries 1881-1901*. London: John Murray 1902.

Sutton, Denys (ed.): *The Letters of Roger Fry*. London: Chatto & Windus 1972.

Symons, Arthur: *Dramatis Personæ*. London: Faber & Gwyer 1925.

—. *From Toulouse-Lautrec to Rodin, with Some Personal Recollections*. London: John Lane The Bodley Head.

Symons, Julian (ed.): *Essays and Biographies by A.J.A. Symons*. London: Cassell 1969.

Syrett, Netta: *The Flowering Tree*. London: Geoffrey Bles 1939.

Tailhade, Laurent: *Lettres à sa Mère 1874-1891*. Introduction, Notes et Index par Pierre Dufay. Paris: René van den Berg & Louis Enlart 1926.

Tancock, J.L.: *The Sculpture of Auguste Rodin*. Philadelphia: Philadelphia Museum of Modern Art 1976.

Taranow, Gerda: *Sarah Bernhardt, the Art within the Legend*. Princeton: Princeton University Press 1972.

Taylor, George: 'Svengali: mesmerist and æsthete' in Richard Foulkes (ed.): *British Theatre in the 1890s*. Cambridge: Cambridge University Press 1992.

Temple, A.G.: *Guildhall Memories*. London: John Murray 1918.

Tenschert, Roland: 'Strauss as Librettist' in Puffett, q.v.

Tharp, Louise Hall: *Mrs Jack, A Biography of Isabella Stewart Gardner*. Boston: Little, Brown & Co 1965.

Tharp, Louise Hall: *Saint-Gaudens and the Gilded Era*. Boston: Little, Brown & Co 1969.

Thayer, William Roscoe: *The Life & Letters of John Hay* volume II. London: Constable & Co.; Boston: Houghton Miflin Co. 1905.

Thénard, Jenny: *Ma Vie au Théâtre, (choses vues, choses vècues)*. Préface de Jules Clarétie. Paris: Librairie Ambert n.d.

Thompson, Vance: *The Two Deaths of Oscar Wilde*. San Francisco: Helen Gentry 1930,.

Thurston, Katherine Cecil: *Max*. London: Hutchinson 1910.

Thwaite, Ann: *Edmund Gosse, a Literary Landscape 1859-1928*. London: Secker & Warburg 1984.

Tint, Herbert: *The Decline of French Patriotism*. London: Weidenfeld & Nicolson 1964.

Toesca, Maurice: *Jules Renard*. Paris: Albin Michel 1977.

Tóibín, Colm: *The Master*. London: Picador 2004.

Tonks, Henry: 'The Vicissitudes of Art' in *Fifty Years, Memories and Contrasts. A Composite Picture of the Period 1882-1932*. By Twenty-Seven Contributors to *The Times*. London: Thornton Butterworth & Co 1932. Keystone Library Edition 1936.

Traubner, Richard: *Operetta, A Theatrical History*. London: Victor Gollancz 1984.

Trewin, J.C.: *The Edwardian Theatre*. Oxford: Basil Blackwell 1976.

Trottenberg, Arthur D. (ed.): *A Vision of Paris – The Photographs of Eugène Atget, the Words of Marcel Proust*. New York: Macmillan 1963.

Turnbull, Michael: *Mary Garden*. Aldershot: Scolar Press 1997.

Turner, Jane (ed.): *Grove Dictionary of Art*. London: Macmillan 1996.

Twombly, Robert: *Louis Sullivan*. Chicago: University of Chicago Press 1987.

Tydeman, William and Price Steven: *Wilde Salomé.* Cambridge: Cambridge University Press 1996.

Usborne, Karen: *'Elizabeth', The Author of Elizabeth and her German Garden.* London: The Bodley Head 1986.

Vanbrugh, Irene, D.B.E.: *To Tell My Story.* London: Hutchinson & Co 1948.

Vanderbilt, Cornelius Jr: *The Vanderbilt Feud, the Fabulous Story of Grace Wilson Vanderbilt.* London: Hutchinson 1957.

Vanderbilt II, Arthur: *Fortune's Children, the Fall of the House of Vanderbilt.* London: Michael Joseph n.d.

Varnedoe, Kirk: *Gustave Caillebotte.* New Haven & London: Yale University Press 1987.

Vechten, Carl van: *Sacred and Profane Memories.* London: Cassell and Co *DATE*.

Velter, André (ed.): *Les Poètes du Chat Noir.* Paris: Gallimard 1996.

Vickers, Jonathan & Copeland Peter: 'The Voice of Oscar Wilde: An Investigation'. *British Association of Sound Collections News* 2, 1987.

Vierney, Dina and others: *Félix Vallotton.* Paris: Réunion des Musées Nationaux 1997.

Volkonsky, Prince Serge: *My Reminiscences.* Translated by A.E. Chamot. London: Hutchinson & Co 1925.

Vollard, Ambroise: *Recollections of a Picture Dealer.* London: Constable 1936.

Waddington, Mary King: *Letters of a Diplomat's Wife 1883-1900.* London: Smith, Elder & Co 1903.

—. *My First Years as a Frenchwoman 1876-1879.* London: Smith, Elder & Co 1914.

Waddington, Patrick (ed.): *Ivan Turgenev and Britain.* Oxford: Berg Publishers, Anglo-Russian Affinities Series 1995.

—. *Turgenev and England.* New York: New York University Press 1981.

Wagenknecht, Edward: *Seven Daughters of the Theater.* Norman: University of Oklahoma Press 1964.

Warrack, John and Ewan: *The Oxford Dictionary of Opera.* Oxford: Oxford University Press. 1992.

Washburne, E.B.: *Recollections of a Minister to France.* London: Sampson Low, Marston, Searle & Rivington 1887.

Washington, Booker T.: 'On the Paris Boulevards', New York *Age* June 1899, reprinted in Louis R. Harlan & Raymond W. Smock (edd.): *The Booker T. Washington Papers* volume V: 1899-1900. Urbana: University of Illinois Press 1976.

Wearing, J.P. (ed.): *The Collected Letters of Sir Arthur Wing Pinero.* Minneapolis: University of Minnesota Press 1974.

Weinberg, H. Barbara: *The Lure of Paris – Nineteenth Century American Painters and their French Teachers.* New York: Abbeville Press 1991.

Weintraub, Stanley: *Reggie, A Portrait of Reginald Turner.* New York: George Braziller 1965.

Weisberg, Gabriel: *The Realist Tradition, French Painting and Drawing 1830-1900.* Cleveland, Ohio: Cleveland Museum of Art and Indiana University Press 1980.

Welldon D.D., J.E.C.: *Recollections and Reflections.* London: Cassell 1915.

Wertheim, Stanley & Sorento, Paul: *The Crane Log, a Documentary Life of Stephen Crane.* New York: G.K. Hall 1994.

West, Joan M.: 'America and American Literature in the Essays of Th. Bentzon: Creating the Image of an Independent Cultural Identity' in *History of European Ideas* 1987 volume 8 (4-5) pp.521-535.

West, W.J. (ed.): *Orwell, The War Broadcasts.* London: Duckworth / BBC 1985.

Whiteing, Richard: *The Life of Paris.* London: John Murray 1900.

Whiting, Steven Moore: *Satie the Bohemian, from Cabaret to Concert Hall.* Oxford: Oxford University Press 1999.

Whittington-Egan, Richard and Smerdon, Geoffrey: *The Quest of the Golden Boy, the Life and Letters of Richard Le Gallienne.* London: The Unicorn Press 1960.

Wickes, George: *The Amazon of Letters, The Life and Loves of Natalie Barney.* New York: G.P. Putnam's Sons 1976.

Wilde, Oscar: *De Profundis.*

—. Review of Eric Robertson: *Longfellow, The Pall Mall Gazette* 28th March 1887, reprinted in Wyse Jackson, q.v.

—. Review of William Rossetti's *Life of John Keats* in the *Pall Mall Gazette* 27th September 1887 reprinted in Wyse Jackson, q.v..

—. 'The American Invasion', *Court and Society Review* 23rd March 1887, reprinted in Wyse Jackson, q.v.

—. 'The Practical Application of the Principles of Æsthetic Theory to Exterior and Interior House Decoration', delivered in America on 11th May 1882, reprinted in Wyse Jackson, q.v.

—. Petition to the Home Secretary 2nd July 1896, printed in Holland & Hart Davis, q.v., p.657.

—. Review of Eric Robertson: *Longfellow, The Pall Mall Gazette* 28th March 1887, reprinted in Wyse Jackson, q.v.

—. *The Portrait of Mr W.H.* bilingual edition (French/English). Paris: Gallimard 2000.

—. *Salomé.* Présentation de Pascal Aquien. Paris: Flammarion 1993 pp.18-19.

—. *Salomé.* Introduction and translation by Vyvyan Holland. London: The Folio Society 1977.

Wildman, Stephen and Christian, John: *Edward Burne Jones, Victorian Artist-Dreamer.* New York: Metropolitan Museum of Art 1998.

Williamson, Audrey: *Gilbert and Sullivan Opera, An Assessment.* London: Marion Boyars 1982.

Willson Disher, Maurice: *The Last Romantic, the Authorised Biography of Sir John Martin-Harvey.* With a foreword by D.L. Murray. London: Hutchinson n.d.

Wilson, Barbara: *Dear Youth.* London: Macmillan & Co 1937.

Wilson, Edmund: *Axel's Castle, A Study in the Imaginative Culture of 1870-1930.* New York: Charles Scribner's Sons 1940;.

Wilson, Elizabeth: *Bohemians, the Glamorous Outcasts.* London & New York: I.B. Tauris 2000.

Wilson, Sir Charles Rivers.: *Chapters from My Official Life.* Edited by Everilda McAlister. London: Edwin Arnold 1916.

Windt, Harry de: *My Restless Life.* London: Grant Richards 1909.

Winock, Michel: *La Belle Époque.* Paris: Perrin 2002.

Wintermans, Caspar: Unpublished TS of the Author's translation of his *Bosie*, Chapter IX.

Winterton, Lord: *Pre-War.* London: Macmillan 1932.

Woolf, Virginia: 'Evening over Sussex', *The Death of the Moth and Other Essays.* London: Hogarth Press 1942.

Worth, Katharine: *The Irish Drama of Europe from Yeats to Beckett.* London: Athlone Press 1986.

Wrench, John Evelyn: *Uphill, The First Stage in a Strenuous Life.* London: Ivor Nicholson & Watson 1934.

Wykeham, Peter: *Santos-Dumont, A Study in Obsession.* London: Putnam 1962.

Wynne, Maud: *An Irishman and His Family, Lord Morris and Killanin.* London: John Murray 1937.

Wyse Jackson, John (ed.): *Aristotle at Afternoon Tea: the Rare Oscar Wilde.* London: Fourth Estate 1991.

'X': *Myself Not Least.* London: Thornton Butterworth 1925 (The London Library identifies the author as H. Vivian).

Xanrof: *Chansons à rire.* Paris: Flammarion 1891.

Yandell, Enid; Loughborough Jean, and Hayes Laura: *Three Girls in a Flat*. Chicago: Knight, Leonard & Co. 1892.

Yeats, W.B.: *Autobiographies*. London: Macmillan 1955.

Young, Filson: *The Sands of Pleasure*. London: Grant Richards 1905.

Zapolska, Gabriela: *Madame Zapolska et la scène parisienne*. Textes traduits du polonais par Lisbeth Virol et Arturo Nevill. Paris: Éditions de la Femme Presse 2004.

Zeldin, Theodore: *France 1848-1945* volume I: Ambition, Love and Politics. Oxford: The Clarendon Press 1973.

Zola, Emile: *Au Bonheur des Dames*. 1883. Translated as 'The Ladies' Paradise' with an Introduction and Notes by Brian Nelson. World's Classics 1995; reissued as an Oxford World's Classics. Oxford: Oxford University Press 1998.

—. *L'Assommoir*. Translated by Leonard Tancock. London: Penguin Books 1970.

—. *L'Œuvre*. 1886. Translated as 'The Masterpiece' by Thomas Walton; translation revised by Richard Pearson. World's Classics 1993; reissued as an Oxford World's Classic. Oxford: Oxford University Press 1999.

—. *La Joie de Vivre*. 1884. Translated as *Zest for Life* by Jean Stewart. London: Elek 1955.

—. *La Ventre de Paris*. Translated as *Savage Paris* by David Hughes & Marie-Jacqueline Mason. Preface by Hugh Shelley. London: Elek Books 1955.

—. *Le Débâcle*. Translated with an Introduction by Leonard Tancock. Harmondsworth: Penguin Books 1972.

—. *Le Rêve*. Translated as *The Dream* by Eliza E.Chase. With eight illustrations by Georges Jeannot. London: Chatto & Windus 1893.

—. *Madeleine Férat*. 1868. Translated by Alec Brown. London: Elek 1957.

—. *Nana*. 1880. Translated with an introduction by George Holden. Harmondsworth: Penguin Books 1972.

—. *Nana*. 1880. Translated with an introduction by Douglas Parmée. World's Classics 1992; reissued as an Oxford World's Classics. Oxford: Oxford University Press 1998.

—. *Paris*. Translated with a preface by Ernest Alfred Vizetelly. London: Chatto & Windus 1898.

—. *Pot-Bouille*. Translated as *Pot Luck* with an introduction and notes by Brian Nelson. Oxford: Oxford University Press 1999.

—. *Un Page d'Amour*. Translated as *A Love Affair* by Jean Stewart. London: Elek 1957.

Zweig, Stefan: *Emile Verhaeren*.   Translated by Jethro Bithell.   London: Constable & Co 1945.

http://abu.cnam.fr/cgi-bin/go?ren93982,5621.
http://diamond.boisestate.edu/GaS/whowaswho/R/RooseveltBlanche.htm.
http://docsouth.dsi.internet2.edu/harrison/harrison.html.
http://intranet.rutgers.edu/~kazmier/SUSMAN.HTM.
http://pinafore.www3.50megs.com/b-roosevelt.html.
http://rick.stanford.edu/opera/Bizet/main.html.
http://tfaoi.com/newsm1/n1m556.htm.
http://theses.mit.edu/Dienst/UI/2.0/Describe/0018.mit.theses/1982-128.
http://web.uvic.ca/lancenrd/french/topics/adj02/note01.htm.
http://www.airlibre.com/MacOrlan.html .
http://www.burtonartgallery.co.uk/painting3.htm.
http://www.chanson.udenap.org/fiches_bio/fragson/fragson.htm.
http://www.chapelle-humanite.fr/.
http://www.csufresno.edu/folklore/BalladIndex.html.
http://www.cuisineaz.com/tournedos_rossini.htm.
http://www.fencingroom.com/article.html.
http://www.gidiana.net/guidedesspectacles.htm.
http://www.gutenberg.org/files/995/995-h/995-h.htm#link2H_4_0002.
http://www.gutenberg.org/files/995/995-h/995-h.htm#link2H_4_0002.
http://www.ila-chateau.com/lipp/index.htm.
http://www.jeanrichepin.free.fr/sitejr.htm.
http://www.kiki.pp.se/kiki1.htm.
http://www.lang.nagoya-u.ac.jp/~matsuoka/GG-Coustillas-CD.html.
http://www.mle.asso.fr/banquet/97/n28/inedits5.htm.
http://www.moulinrouge.fr/hist/home_6.htm.
http://www.musee-rodin.fr/fr/collections/sculptures/la-duchesse-de-choiseul#sthash.70Z740YQ.dpuf.
http://www.musexpo.com/aage/ag9901/beraud/index.html.
http://www.npg.org.uk/search/Images/weblg/0/0/mw06900.jpg.
http://oscholars-oscholars.com.
http://www.poetes.com/merrill/index.php.
http://www.providenceproductions.com/ccros/ccros.html.
http://www.ritz.com/fr/R0100.asp.
http://societeoscarwilde.fr/
http://www.tc.columbia.edu/~academic/taylor/artonart/ManetMC.stm.
http://www.uelectric.com/pastimes/hermann.htm.
http://www.whistler.arts.gla.ac.uk/biog/Ford_S.htm.
http://www.whistler.arts.gla.ac.uk/biog/Stor_J.htm.

INDEX

Note: the placing of the *particule* d', de or du is fraught with difficulty. In this index I have followed French usage e.g. *Goncourt, Edmond de.* For consistency I have also applied this to, e.g. *Maurier, George du* although *Du Maurier, George* might have been expected; and also to names that include van or von. There are, however, anomalies in the main text where I have followed ordinary practice, e.g. de Nittis rather than Nittis.

Catlin, Edith, 266
Cavalieri, Lina, 144
Cave du Néant, 230
Cazals, F.-A., 148
Caze, Juliette, 49
Caze, Robert, 65, 258
Cazin, Jean-Charles, 38, 45, 66, 183, 243
Céard, Henri, 110, 145
Céard, Henri, 118, 138, 146, 197
Cent Milles Colonnes, 140
Cercle de l'Union, 139
Cercle de la Presse, 139
Cercle de Mirlitons, 138
Cercle de Paris, 148
Cercle des Echecs, 139
Cercle National des Armées de Terre et de Mer;, 138
Cercle St Simon, 139
Cézanne, Paul, 45, 63, 66, 69, 70, 76, 113, 132, 133, 146, 179, 180, 181, 285
Chabannes La Palice, comtesse de, 87
Chabrier, Emmanuel, 63, 68, 73, 128, 306
Chahine, Edgar, 200
Chambers, Robert W., 298
Champfleury, Jules François Félix Husson, *dit* 21, 69, 132
Chandon de Briailles, comtesse, 278
Chanvin, Charles, 188
Chaplin, Charles Joshua, 247
Charles, James, 38
Charnes, Xavier, 183
Charpentier, Alexandre, 67, 363
Charpentier, Georges, 67, 148, 149
Charpentier, Gustave, 388
Charvet, *191, 204, 326*
Chat Noir, 94, 95, 104, 114, 120, 121, 122, 220, 228, 231, 232, 257, 276, 304, 392
Château Rouge, 118, 232
Chatham Bar, 140, 399
Chausson, Ernest, 52

Cherbiliez, Victor, 81
Chéret, Jules, 67, 95, 115, 145, 202, 203, 251, 326, 363
chess, 6, 139
Chesson, Wilfred, 42, 387
Chevalier, Albert, 54
Chevassu, François, 168
Chiappe, Jean, 24
chiffoniers, 200
Child, Theodore, 55, 148, 171, 176, 404
Chirac, Théodore de, 120
Choiseul, Claire duchesse de, 278, 280
Christie, James Elder, 38
Christiné, madame (dancer), 54
Churchill, Lady Randolph, 273
Churchill, Winston, 16, 189
Cigale, 125
Cimiotti, Gustave, 269
Cirque d'Été, 126, 309
Cirque d'Hiver, 121, 125, 126, 271, 272, 285
Cirque Fernando, 126, 127
Cladel, Léon, 97, 182, 207
Clairin, Georges, 102, 237, 305, 362, 370, 374
Claretie, Jules, 9, 83, 224, 354
Clark, J.W., 106
Clark, James, 238
Clarke, Campbell, 134
Claudel, Camille, 182
Claudel, Paul, 20, 182, 333
Clay, Arthur Temple, 35
Clemenceau, Georges, 145, 259, 279, 301, 420
Clerc, madame, 29
Clermont-Tonnerre, duchesse de, 167, 181, 186, 191, 315, 330, 333, 358
Club de La Clay-Pipe, 218
Club des Rieuses, 331
Cockran, Bourke, 273, 274
Cocks, Arthur, 92
cocottes, 197, 311, 312, 318, 323, 340

Gallifet, Gaston marquis de, 146, 332

Galsworthy, John and Ada, 18

Gambetta, Léon, 58, 82, 147, 405

Gandara, Antonio de La, 363

Ganderax, Louis 107

Garden, Mary, 144, 149, 284, 286, 287, 388, 389

Gardner, Isabella Stewart, 289

Garrard, Florence, 31, 36

Gascoyne, George, 36

Gauguin, Paul, 37, 45, 66, 69, 70, 109, 135, 179

Gaumont, Léon, 123

Gautier, Judith, 6, 114, 117, 214, 226

Gautier, Théophile, 14, 68, 132, 149, 161, 359

Gautreau, Marcel, 341

Gavarni, Paul, 119, 207, 324

Gebhardt, Émile, 82

Geffroy, Gustave, 118,145

Gérard, Frédéric, 231

Germain, Louis, 92, 116

Germinie Lacerteux, 256

Germiny, comte de, 253

Gérôme, Jean-Léon, 32, 36, 39, 69, 124, 144, 237, 249, 250, 260, 266, 268, 270, 295, 301, 345, 347, 362

Gérôme, Raymond, 111

Gervex, Henri 69, 128, 129, 143, 156, 183, 214, 215, 237, 249, 252, 269, 279, 296, 318, 363

Ghéon, Henri, 188, 384

Ghil, René, 21, 71, 152, 257

Gibbon (art student), 37

Gide, André, 6, 20, 21, 23, 65, 115, 121, 135, 137, 141, 151, 153, 154, 157, 159, 163, 166, 171, 172, 174, 177, 179, 188, 191, 214, 333, 339, 356, 363, 379, 382, 395, 396, 408, 419, 421

Gigolette, 101

Gill, André, 92, 220, 231

Gissing, George, 394

Gladstone, William, 14, 34, 43, 79, 127, 242, 370

Glatigny, Albert, 92

Glehn, Wilfred De, 39

Gleyre, Charles, 26, 249, 250, 329

Glyn, Elinor, 341

Goblet, René, 254

Godebska, Misia, 92

Goethen, Marie van, 44

Gogh, Vincent van, 45, 70, 181, 243, 251, 406

Goncourt, Edmond de, 62, 67, 71, 72, 99, 118, 126, 145, 146, 148, 152, 160, 164, 171, 172, 210, 253, 254, 257, 316, 329

Gonne, Maud, 168

Gontaut-Biron comte Louis de, 265

Gooch, G.P., 82

Gordon Lennox, Cosmo, 87, 412

Gosse, Edmund, 16, 28, 42, 94, 170, 176, 216, 232, 303

Got, Edmond, 88, 354

Got, Frédéric 98

Gotch, Thomas, 39

Goudeau, Emile104, 147, 265

Gould, Anna, 280

Gounod, Charles, 34, 52, 66, 127, 249, 287, 329, 372

Gourmont, Remy de, 31, 83, 116, 135, 152, 178

Gower, Lord Ronald, 89

Gramont-Caderousse, duc de, 258

Grand Café, 87, 110, 123, 139, 203, 344, 385

Grand Hôtel de Russie, 201

Grand Hôtel, 139, 145, 146, 217, 218, 223, 263, 276, 279, 282, 291, 363, 414

Grandmougin, Charles, 116, 121

Granier, Jeanne, 87, 129, 357, 408

Grant, Duncan, 196

Granville, Lord, 144

Grave, Jean, 256

Graves, Abbot Fueller, 269

Gray, John, 33, 153

Gray, Mrs Griswold, 281